A Reference Publication in Black Studies

Dorothy Porter, *Editor*

James A. Page

Selected Black American Authors: An Illustrated Bio-Bibliography

compiled by
James A. Page

G. K. HALL & CO., 70 LINCOLN STREET, BOSTON, MASS.

LIBRARY OF CONGRESS CATALOGING IN PUBLICATION DATA

Page, James Allen, 1918–
   Selected Black American authors.

   (Reference publications in Black studies)
   Bibliography: p.
   Includes indexes.
   1. American literature--Afro-American authors--
Bio-bibliography. 2. Afro-American authors--Biography.
I. Title. II. Series.
PS153.N5P3   810'.9'896 [B]   77-16009
ISBN 0-8161-8065-2

This publication is printed on permanent/durable acid-free paper
MANUFACTURED IN THE UNITED STATES OF AMERICA

Contents

Preface

In my work as a librarian over the years, I have become increasingly interested in Afro-American writers and writing, and have sought more and more information on the subject. In seeking biographical information on these authors I soon discovered that it was practically non-existent--except for six or eight quite prolific and prominent Blacks. It was true that by culling anthologies, specialized handbooks and other references, I could find some information. But what was badly needed, especially in this time of Black awareness, was a compilation bringing together into one source information on all of these writers.

I began the task of compiling this work by sending questionnaires to both authors and publishers. More than 200 authors were sent questionnaires requesting full biographical information and photographs; the publishers of more than 200 living and many deceased authors were sent a similar questionnaire. This guide is a product, therefore, of information submitted by the authors themselves and/or their publishers, as well as of information already available in a wide variety of published sources. In a few instances, information was provided by children or other family members of deceased or very elderly authors.

Of course, this, like any other project of large proportions, required many, many hours, weeks and months of involvement, search, and research. In fact, it has taken over five years to compile. In the interim, others sensed the same need and made similar efforts. Therefore, two other dictionaries have already appeared: Living Black American Authors and Black American Writers Past and Present. However, mine is different, as I wished to make my compilation broader and more representative than any I had seen.

As a result, I have ranged widely--including novelists, poets, essayists, playwrights, historians, social scientists, theologians and others. I have included a representative sampling of Black American writers from the very earliest--Lucy Terry's "Bars Fight" in 1746, for example--to the present highly acclaimed Roots by Alex Haley. A few West Indians and Africans are also included, if they lived, wrote and were published in the continental United States. Because of the increase in the number of black authors in the last two decades, most authors included in this Guide are alive today.

The 453 authors listed in Selected Black American Authors have been chosen as a representative sample of the many Black American authors whose works have been published from colonial times to the present. My criteria of selection are as follows: (1) Authors must have had at least one book published, or two, depending on the prominence of the person or his subject matter. (2) Authors must have been included in other sources, i.e., anthologies, critical studies, handbooks, biographical references. (3) Poets must have had more than one book of poems published--unless the poet is outstanding in another field, i.e., teaching, lecturing, editing. (4) Playwrights are usually included if they have had one or more plays published other than in anthologies. (5) Essayists must have produced significant work in the arts, biography, criticism, history, sciences, social sciences, theology or other areas.

I have also included writers concerned with current events and civil rights; Black authors discussed by scholars and critics or listed in references cited in the "Bibliography of Sources"; and publishers or editors of newspapers and magazines that have an impact on writing (such as John Sengstacke, John H. Johnson and Ida Lewis).

Excluded from this selection are: (1) Authors who have published their own books; (2) Authors who have published only in anthologies or other compilations; (3) Authors who have published in journals; (4) Most Authors who have published "as told to" works; and (5) Sports and entertainment figures, except those of unusual prominence. My intention is that this work be not only a viable and significant tool for general reference and research, but that it also be readable and interesting in itself. For that reason I have included photographs of 285 authors.

The main body of Selected Black American Authors is arranged alphabetically by the author's last name. The text is followed by both a title index and a subject index to facilitate searching. A list of abbreviations used in the text follows the preface and a bibliography of sources appears at the end of the work.

Each entry contains biographical information including birth and death dates, family, education, address and career information. Also included in each entry is a bibliography of the author's works, selected sidelights on the author's career and a list of sources.

I plan to update this biographical dictionary periodically to keep the information current and to add new authors. In spite of the fact that I have made every effort to avoid errors and mistakes, there are undoubtedly omissions and oversights. Any additions or corrections from the reader will be most welcome.

Acknowledgments

I am indebted to numerous works and authors. Among the most important are: Living Black American Authors, compiled by Ann A. Shockley and Sue P. Chandler, and Black American Writers Past and Present, compiled by Theressa Rush, et al. Other important references are: Black World, Contemporary Authors, Directory of American Scholars, Historical Negro Biographies, Something About the Author, and Who's Who in America.

I also wish to acknowledge the valuable contribution of Agnes Moreland Jackson, Professor of English, Pitzer College (Claremont Colleges), who in the early stages of this compilation served as a collaborator. Another person who lent his indefatigable energy, loyal assistance and expertise to completing this compilation is Jae Min Roh, scholar, friend and former library staff member. And the late Paul Villiard, a prolific and wide-ranging non-fiction writer, inspired me greatly with his persistence and dedication.

In addition, I commend reference libararians Ruth Berry and William Osuga at the Research Library at UCLA (where the Black collection is the best I have encountered). I also wish to credit especially Oscar Sims, Afro-American Bibliographer at UCLA. Two other libraries I used rather extensively were the Doheny at the University of Southern California and the Los Angeles Public Library (where I was assited by Helene Mochedlover and M. J. Campbell in literature and Riva Bresler in the fiction department). In the East, I consulted Morgan State College; Peabody Collection, Hampton Institute; Schomburg Collection, The New York Public Library; Trevor Arnett Library, Atlanta University; and the Archives, Tuskegee Institute.

Many other people supported this project. Professor Jackson reports that John O. Killens "...gave generously of both his time and his incalculably helpful ideas on procedure, possible inclusions and references for a wide range of additional information. We cannot overstate our appreciation for Brother Killens's support.... Virginia Lacy Jones, Dean of the School of Library Service at Atlanta University, and Richard A. Long Director of the Center for African

Acknowledgments

and African American Studies at Atlanta University, graciously and enthusiastically shared many suggestions for content...."

I am indebted to the following friends: Alfred Benjamin, my professional photographer, for advising me on close-up photography; Nolan Davis, novelist, biographer and free-lancer, who has been my advisor and guide throughout the project; and Lorenz Graham, young adult author and teacher of Black literature, who also advised me. In addition, I would like to thank all the writers and publishers who supplied information, and to acknowledge the help of all persons, whether in libraries, bookstores or elsewhere, who have been of assistance on this project. And finally, I want to acknowledge the tremendous encouragement, moral support and help of my wife, Ethel S. Page, and my daughters, Ramona and Anita.

Abbreviations

Acad.--Academy; academic

ACRL--Associate of College & Research Librarians

ACTFL/SCOLT--American Council for Teaching of Foreign Languages/Southern Conference on Language Teaching

admin.--administration; administrator

advis.--advisory, advisor

Ala.--Alabama

ALA--American Library Association

A & M--Agricultural & Mechanical

AME--African Methodist Episcopal

Amer.--American

anthol(s).--anthology, anthologies

apptd.--appointed

Apr.--April

Ariz.--Arizona

Ark.--Arkansas

ASCAP--American Society of Composers, Authors and Publishers

ASNLH--Association for the Study of Negro Life and History

Assn.--Association

Assoc.--Associate; Associated

Asst.--Assistant

Aug.--August

autobiog.--autobiography

Ave.--Avenue

B.A.--Bachelor of Arts

Bap.--Baptist

B.F.A.--Bachelor of Fine Arts

B.Phil.--Bachelor of Philosophy

bd.--board

B.D.--Bachelor of Divinity

bk(s).--book(s)

bldg.--building

Brit.--Britain; British

B.S.--Bachelor of Science

bull.--bulletin

bus.--business

c.--circa

Cal.--California

Can.--Canada

CEA--College English Association

c/o--care of

chap.--chapter

Chgo.--Chicago

chrmn.--chairman

Cin.--Cincinnati

CLA--College Language Association

ABBREVIATIONS

Co.--Company

co-ed.--co-editor

Coll.--College

collec.--collection

Colo.--Colorado

Com.--Committee; Commission

comp.--compiler

conf.--conference

Conn.--Connecticut

cons.--consultant

contrib.--contributor; contributing; contribution

coop.--cooperative

coord.--coordinator; coordinating

CORE--Congress of Racial Equality

Corp.--Corporation

corresp.--correspondent; corresponding

counc.--council

CUNY--City University of New York

d.--daughter

D.C.--District of Columbia

D.C.L.--Doctor of Civil Law

D.D.--Doctor of Divinity (honorary)

dec.--deceased

Dec.--December

Del.--Delaware

dept.--department

develop.--development

Dir.--Director

dist.--district

div.--division; divorced

Dr.--Doctor; Drive

e.--east

econ.--economic

ed.--editor; edition; editorial

educ.--education; educational; educator

encycl.--encyclopedia

Eng.--English; England

Feb.--February

Fed.--Federal

fellow.--fellowship

fic.--fiction

Fla.--Florida

Found.--Foundation

Ga.--Georgia

gen.--general

govt.--government

grad.--graduate

HARYOU--Harlem Youth Opportunities Unlimited

Her.--Heritage

HEW--Health, Education and Welfare, Department of

H.H.D.--Doctor of Humanities

hist.--history; historical

hon.--honorary; honorable

Ill.--Illinois

ILO--International Labor Organization

Inc.--Incorporated

Ind.--Indiana

indust.--industry; industrial

inform.--information

Inst.--Institute; Institutional

instr.--instructor; instruction

internat.--international

Jan.--January

ABBREVIATIONS

J.D.--Doctor of Jurisprudence

Jl.--Journal

Jr.--Junior

Kan.--Kansas

Ky.--Kentucky

La.--Louisiana

L.A.--Los Angeles

lab.--laboratory

lang.--language

Lectr.--Lecturer

Legis.--Legislature

L.H.D.--Doctor of Humane Letters; Doctor of Humanities

lib.--library

librn.--librarian

lit.--literature

Litt.D.--Doctor of Letters

LL.B.--Bachelor of Laws

LL.D.--Doctor of Laws

LLM--Master of Laws

lt.--lieutenant

m.--married

M.A.--Master of Arts

mag(s).--magazine(s)

Mar.--March

Mass.--Massachusetts

Md.--Maryland

M.Ed.--Master of Education

mem.--member

M.F.A.--Master of Fine Arts

mgr.--manager

Mich.--Michigan

Minn.--Minnesota

Miss.--Mississippi

M.L.A.--Modern Language Association

M.L.S.--Master of Library Science

Mo.--Missouri

mod.--modern

M.S.--Master of Science

M.S.L.S.--Master of Science, Library Science

M.S.W.--Master of Social Work

Mt.--Mount

mus.--museum

Mus.B.--Bachelor of Music

n.--north, northern

NAACP--National Association for the Advancement of Colored People

nat'l.--national

N.C.--North Carolina

N.Dak.--North Dakota

NDEA--National Defense Education Act

NEA--National Endowment for the Arts

Neb.--Nebraska

NEH--National Endowment for the Humanities

NET--National Educational Television

Nev.--Nevada

N.H.--New Hampshire

N.J.--New Jersey

N.Mex.--New Mexico

no.--number

nonfic.--nonfiction

Nov.--November

N.Y.--New York

N.Y.C.--New York City

Abbreviations

N.Y.U.--New York University

OBAC--Organization of Black American Culture

Oct.--October

OEO--Office of Equal Opportunity

Okla.--Oklahoma

Ore.--Oregon

org.--organization

Pa.--Pennsylvania

pam.--pamphlet

P.E.N.--Poets, Playwrights, Editors, Essayists and Novelists

period.--periodical(s)

Ph.D.--Doctor of Philosophy

Phila.--Philadelphia

Pl.--Place

polit.--political

post grad.--post graduate

Pr.--Press

Pres.--President

Presby.--Presbyterian

prin.--princiapl

prod.--producer; produced

Prof.--Professor

prog.--program

PTA--Parent Teachers Association

pub.--published; publisher; publishing

public.--publication

quart.--quarterly

Rd.--Road

ref.--reference

relat.--relations

relig.--religion; religious

rep.--representative

repr.--reprinted

res.--research

Rev.--Reverend

rev.--revised

R.I.--Rhode Island

s.--south; southern

S.C.--South Carolina

sch.--school

sci.--science

S.Dak.--South Dakota

secy.--secretary

SEEK--Search for Education, Elevation and Knowledge

Sem.--Seminary

Sept.--September

ser.--series

serv.--service

Sgt.--Sergeant

SNCC--Student Nonviolent Coordinating Committee

Soc.--Society; social

sociol.--sociological; sociology

spec.--specialist; special

St.--Street; Saint

S.T.D.--Doctor of Sacred Theology

S.T.M.--Master of Sacred Theology

stud.--studies

SUNY--State University of New York

supt.--superintendent

supv.--supervisor; supervision

tchg.--teaching

tchr.--teacher

tech.--technical

Tenn.--Tennessee

ABBREVIATIONS

Tex.--Texas

Th.D.--Doctor of Theology

Theol.--Theologian; Theological

transl.--translated; translation

Trus.--Trustee

TV--television

U.--University

UCLA--University of California at Los Angeles

UN--United Nations

U.S.--United States

USIA--United States Information Agency

USIS--United States Information Service

U.S.S.R.--Union of Soviet Socialist Republics

v.--vice

Va.--Virginia

vis.--visiting

vol(s).--volume(s)

Vt.--Vermont

w.--west; western

Wash.--Washington

Wash., D.C.--Washington, D.C.

Wis.--Wisconsin

WPA--Works Progress Administration

W. Va.--West Virginia

Wyo.--Wyoming

YMCA--Young Men's Christian Association

YMHA--Young Men's Hebrew Association

YWCA--Young Women's Christian Association

yr(s).--year(s)

Selected Black American Authors

ABBOTT, ROBERT SENGSTACKE. 1870–1940. Publisher

Biographical-Personal. Born Nov. 24, 1870, on St. Simon's Island, off coast of Ga. Son of Rev. John H. H. Sengstacke (stepfather) and Flora Abbott Sengstacke. Educ.: Beach Inst., Savannah, Ga.; Claflin Inst., Orangeburg, S.C.; Hampton Inst., Va.; Kent Coll. of Law, Chgo. Family: 1st m. Helen Thornton Morrison in 1918 (div.); 2nd m. Edna Brown Dennison. Died 1940.

Career-Professional. Newspaper pub. Apprentice printer, Savannah News; Founder-pub., Chicago Defender, 1905- . Grew from weekly to daily; sells all over U.S.

HONORS AND AWARDS: Apptd. mem. Ill. Race Relat. Com., 1919; Pres., Hampton Alumni Assn.; Laurel Wreath for Distinguished Serv., Kappa Alpha Psi; Hon. degrees from Morris Brown U., Ga. & Wilberforce U., Ohio.

SIDELIGHTS: Abbott had no children, but was devoted to his nephew, John Sengstacke, to whom he left the Chicago Defender. The Black community of Chicago bought two million dollars worth of war bonds during World War II, at the Defender's urging. This led to the U.S. Maritime Commission's naming a liberty ship the USS Robert S. Abbott. In 1945 the Chicago Defender established the Robert S. Abbott Memorial Scholarship at Lincoln U. Sch. of Journalism (Famous American Negroes).

Sources. Famous American Negroes, Langston Hughes (Dodd, Mead, 1955); The Lonesome Road, Saunders Redding (Doubleday, 1958); They Showed the Way, Charlemae Rollins (Crowell, 1964).

ABDUL, RAOUL. 1929- . Opera Singer, Editor

Biographical-Personal. Born Nov. 7, 1929, in Cleveland, Ohio. Educ.: Karamu House; Cleveland Inst. of Music; Cleveland Music Sch. Settlement; New York Coll. of Music; New Sch. for Soc. Res.; Mannes Coll. of Music; (grad.) Acad. of Music & Dramatic Art, Vienna. Family: Single. Mailing address: 360 W. 22nd St., N.Y., N.Y. 10011

Alba, Nanina

Career-Professional. Public relat., Karamu House, Cleveland; Youth Ed., Cleveland Call & Post; Cultural ed., New York Age; Ed. Asst. to Langston Hughes; Syndicated columnist, "The Cultural Scene," Assoc. Negro Pr.; Organizer, Coffee Concerts (chamber music), Harlem, 1958-59.
WRITINGS: 3000 Years of Black Poetry, co-ed. with Alan Lomax (Dodd, Mead, 1970); Magic of Black Poetry, ed. (Dodd, Mead, 1972); Famous Black Entertainers of Today (Dodd, Mead, 1974). Anthol.: Anthology of the American Negro in the Theatre (Internat. Lib. of Negro Life & Hist., 1967); The Negro in Music and Art (Internat. Lib. of Negro Life & Hist., 1967).
SIDELIGHTS: Singer: Marlboro Music Festival, 1956; Vienna Music Festival, 1962; Christlische-Juedische Zusammenarbeit, Nuremberg (opened Brotherhood Week 1962); Schubert cycle, "Die Winterreise," Harvard Summer Sch. (1966); German Lieder recital (with John Wustman), Carnegie Hall (debut before SRO audience, 1967); Karl Orff's "Die Kluge"; Mozart's "Cosi Fan Tutte"; Menotti's "Amahl and the Night Visitors"; Darius Milhaud's "Les Malheures d'Orphée" (title role).
Sources. Pub. inform. (Dodd, Mead); 3000 Years of Black Poetry, E. Alan Lomax and Raoul Abdul (Fawcett, 1970).

ALBA, NANINA. 1917-1968. Poet, Teacher
Biographical-Personal. Born Nov. 21, 1917 in Montgomery, Ala.
Educ.: Haines Inst., Augusta, Ga.; B.A., Knoxville Coll., 1935; Grad. work, Indiana U. Died 1968.
Career-Professional. Tchr., Eng., French and music, Eng. Dept., Tuskegee Inst.
WRITINGS: The Parchments, poetry (1963); The Parchments II. Anthol.: For Malcolm; Poetry of the Negro (1949, 1970); Poetry of Black America. Period.: Phylon; Negro Digest; Peninsula Poets; Message Magazine; Commercial Appeal Yearbook; CEA Bulletin. HONORS AND AWARDS: Ester R. Beer Memorial Poetry Prize, Nat'l. Writers' Club (2nd pl.).
Sources. For Malcolm, Ed. by Dudley Randall & Margaret G. Burroughs (Broadside Pr., 1969); Poetry of Black America, Ed. by Arnold Adoff (Harper & Row, 1973).

ALLEN, SAMUEL W. [Paul Vesey]. 1917- . Poet, Lawyer, Translator
Biographical-Personal. Born Dec. 9, 1917 in Columbus, Ohio. Son of Alexander Joseph & Jewett [Washington] Allen. Educ.: B.A., Fisk U., 1938; J.D., Harvard Law Sch.; New Sch. for Soc. Res.; the Sor-

Amini, Johari M.

bonne. Family: div.; d. Marie-Christine.
Mailing Address: Eng. Dept., Boston U.,
Boston, Mass. 02215.
Career-Professional. U.S. Army, Office of Judge
Advocate Gen.; Deputy Asst., Dist. Attorney,
N.Y.C.; Ed., Eng. Lang. section, Présence
Africaine, 1950; U. of Cal. Pr., Proceedings
3rd annual conf., Amer. Soc. of African Cul-
ture (AMSAC), 1960; Prof., Texas S.U., Sch.
of Law, Houston; Avalon Prof. of Humanities,
Tuskegee Inst., 1968-70; Legal Counsel, Com-
munity Relat. Serv.; Asst. Gen. Counsel.
USIA; Prof., Eng., Boston U., 1971- .
WRITINGS: Elfenbein Zähne (Ivory Tusks), bi-
lingual vol. of poetry (Roethe, 1956); Pan
Africanism Reconsidered, Co-ed. (1962); Ivory
Tusks and Other Poems (Poets Pr., 1962); Poems from Africa, Ed.
(Crowell, 1973); Paul Vesey's Ledger (Broadside Pr., 1975);
Transl.: Jean-Paul Sartre's "Orphée Noir," (London, Présence
Africaine, 1960); Aimé Césaire's "Africa" (Voices in the Whirl-
wind, Hill & Wang, 1972); Léopold Senghor's "Elegy for Martin
Luther King" Benin Review. Essays: Présence Africaine, 1958;
Background to Black American Literature (Scranton, 1971); Negro
Digest, May 1967; What Black Educators Are Saying, Ed. by Nathan
Wright, Jr. (1970); Journal of Afro-American Studies (1971); Black
World (1971).
SIDELIGHTS: Delegate & panelist on African Lit., UNESCO Conf.,
Boston, 1961; Delegate, 2nd Internat. Conf. of Negro Writers &
Artists, Rome, 1959. Pub. in some 60 anthols. Recorded poetry
reading at Lib. of Congress, Nov. 1972.
Sources. Author inform.; Blackamerican Literature, Ed. by Ruth Mil-
ler (Glencoe Pr.); Negroes in Public Affairs & Government, Ed. by
Walter Christmas (Educ. Her., 1966); Poetry of Black America, Ed.
by Arnold Adoff (Harper & Row, 1973).

AMINI, JOHARI M. [Jewell Christine McLawler Latimore]. 1935- .
Poet, Teacher
Biographical-Personal. Born Feb. 13, 1935 in Philadelphia, Pa. D. of
William & Alma [Bazel] McLawler. Educ.: A.A., Chgo. City Coll.,
1968; U. of Chgo., 1968-69; B.A., Chgo. State Coll., 1970; M.A.,
U. of Chgo., 1972. Family: widowed; d. Marciana, son Kim Allan.
Mailing Address: 7848 Ellis Ave., Chgo., Ill. 60619 (c/o Third
World Pr.).
Career-Professional. Lectr., Black Stud., U. of Ill., Chgo. Circle
Campus, 1972- ; Instr., Psychology, Black Lit., Soc. Sci., Ken-•
nedy-King Coll., Mini Campus, Chgo., 1970-72; Co-instr., The Black
Aesthetic, Ind. U., Bloomington, Spring 1971.

3

Anderson, Marian

WRITINGS: <u>Images in Black</u> (Third World Pr., 1967); <u>Black Essence</u> (Third World Pr., 1968); "A Folk Fable," single poem issue (Third World Pr., 1969); <u>Let's Go Somewhere</u> (Third World Pr., 1970); "A Hip Tale in the Death Style" (Broadside Pr., 1972); <u>An African Frame of Reference</u> (Inst. of Positive Educ., 1972); <u>A Common Sense Approach to Eating</u> (Inst. of Positive Educ., 1973); <u>Re-Definition: Concept As Being</u> (Third World Pr., 1973). Anthol.: <u>Afro-American Literature</u>, Ed. by Darwin Turner; <u>Black Arts</u>, Ed. by Alamisi & Wangara; <u>Black Culture</u>, Gloria Simmons; <u>Black Expressions Anthol.</u>, Ed. by Eugene Perkins; <u>The Black Poets</u>, Ed. by Dudley Randall; <u>Black Spirits</u>, Ed. by Woodie King; <u>Jump Bad</u>, Ed. by Gwendolyn Brooks, etc. Period.: <u>Black Expression</u>; <u>Black Women's Committee News</u>; <u>Black World/Negro Digest</u>; <u>Journal of Black Poetry</u>; <u>Nommo</u>; <u>Pan African Journal</u>.
HONORS AND AWARDS: U. of Chgo. scholarship, 1968.
MEMBER: Phi Theta Kappa; OBAC; African Hist. Stud. Assn.; Congress of African Peoples.
SIDELIGHTS. Name legally changed to Johari M. Amini. Treasurer, OBAC, 1967- .
Sources. Author inform.; <u>Black Arts</u>, Ahmed Alhamisi & Kofi Wangara (Black Arts, 1969); <u>Broadside Authors & Artists</u>, Comp. by Leaonead P. Bailey (Broadside, 1974); <u>Contemporary Authors</u>, Vols. 41-44, Clare D. Kinsman (Gale Res., 1974); <u>Poetry of Black America</u>, Comp. by Arnold Adoff (Harper & Row, 1973).

ANDERSON, MARIAN. 1902- . Concert Singer
Biographical-Personal. Born 1902 in Phila., Pa.
<u>Educ.</u>: Phila. public schs.; Musical educ.: private study: Phila., N.Y., abroad; hon. degrees from 22 Amer. inst., 1 Korean.
<u>Family</u>: m. Orpheus H. Fisher, July 24, 1943.
<u>Mailing address</u>: Danbury, Conn.
Career-Professional. Career launched when she won 1st prize in competition with 300 others at N.Y. Lewisohn Stadium, 1925. Many concert tours of the U.S. and Europe. Retired as professional musician, 1965.
WRITINGS: <u>My Lord What a Morning</u>, autobiog. (Viking, 1956).
HONORS AND AWARDS: $10,000 Bok Award, 1940; Finnish decoration "probenignitate humana," 1940; decorations from Sweden, Philippines, Haiti, France, numerous cities and states in the U.S. Rosenwald scholarship for study

Angelou, Maya

in Germany. Request for command performance by Brit. crown;
Spingard Medal; Order of African Redemption of Republic of Liberia. First Black to sing at Metropolitan Opera; Nat. Conf. of
Christians and Jews Award, 1957 (for autobiog.); Named one of
world's 10 most admired women by Amer. Inst. of Public Opinion
poll, 1961.
MEMBER: Delegate to 13th Gen. Assembly, U.N.; Alpha Kappa Alpha.
SIDELIGHTS: One of the world's leading contraltos; has appeared
in all famous concert halls. Miss Anderson has established a
trust fund to aid talented American artists.
Sources. Historical Negro Biographies, Wilhelmena S. Robinson
   (ASNLH, 1967); Negro Handbook, Comp. by the eds. of Ebony (Johnson
   Pub., 1966); Negroes in Public Affairs & Government, Ed. by Walter
   Christmas (Educ. Her., Inc., 1966).

ANGELOU, MAYA [Marguerite Johnson]. 1928- .
Singer, Dancer, Author, Lecturer, Actress
Biographical-Personal. Born Apr. 4, 1928 in St.
   Louis, Mo. Educ.: George Wash. High Sch.,
   San Francisco, Cal.; studied music 7 yrs.;
   studied dance with Pearl Primus, Martha Gra-
   ham, Ann Halprin; Drama with Frank Silvera,
   Gene Frankel. Family: son, Guy Johnson.
   Mailing address: c/o Random House, 201 E.
   15th St., N.Y., N.Y. 12022.
Career-Professional. Toured Europe & Africa for
   State Dept. in Porgy and Bess (singer & danc-
   er); Taught dance in Rome & Tel Aviv; prod.,
   directed & starred in Cabaret for Freedom
   (with Godfrey Cambridge) at N.Y.'s Village
   Gate; Starred in Genet's The Blacks, St.
Mark's Playhouse; Northern Coord., S. Christian Leadership Conf.
(for Martin L. King, Jr.); Assoc. Ed., Arab Observer, Cairo,
Egypt; Free-lance writer, Ghanaian Times & Ghanaian Broadcasting
Corp., Accra; Asst. Admin., Sch. of Music & Dance, U. of Ghana;
Feature Ed., African Review (Ghana); Wrote & prod. 10-part TV series on African tradition in Amer. life; Wrote original screenplay
& musical score for film "Georgia, Georgia"; modern version adaptation of Sophocles's Ajax, premiered at Mark Taper Forum, L.A.
(1974).
WRITINGS: I Know Why the Caged Bird Sings, autobiog. (Random
House, 1970); Gather Together in My Name, autobiog. (Random House,
1974); Just Give Me a Cool Drink of Water 'Fore I Diiie, poetry
(Random House, 1971); The Least of These, one-act play; The Claw-
ing Within, play; All Day Long, short stories; The True Believers,
poetry with Abbey Lincoln.
SIDELIGHTS: Linguist; fluent in 6 languages. Received scholarship to dance with Pearl Primus in 1952. Has sung at the Blue

5

Atkins, Russell

Angel & The Village Vanguard (N.Y.C.) & at Mr. Kelly's in Chgo. Joined "The Theatre of Being" in Hollywood, where under direction of Frank Silvera, played major role in Jean Anouilh's Medea. Gave series of lectures on "The Negro Contribution to American Culture," UCLA, 1966.
Sources. The First Time, Karl & Anne T. Fleming (Simon & Schuster, 1975); Gather Together in My Name (Random House, 1974); Just Give Me a Cool Drink of Water 'Fore I Diiie (Random House, 1971); Pub. inform.

ATKINS, RUSSELL. 1926- . Author, Composer, Editor
Biographical-Personal. Born Feb. 25, 1926 in Cleveland, Ohio. Son of Perry Kelly and Mamie Atkins. Educ.: Cleveland Public Schs.; Cleveland Inst. of Art; Cleveland Inst. of Music. Family: Single. Mailing address: 6005 Grand Ave., Cleveland, Ohio 44104.
Career-Professional. Ed.-founder, Free Lance mag., 1950; Public. mgr. & asst. to Dir., Sutphen Sch. of Music, 1957-60; Cons., writers workshops: Opportunities Industrialization Center, Free Lance Poets, Muntu Poets, Karamu Poetry Workshop; Affiliated with Iowa Workshop & Cleveland State U. Poetry Forum; Advis. ed., Ju Ju mag.
WRITINGS: Phenomena (Wilberforce U. Pr., 1961); Objects (Hearse Pr., 1963); Objects 2 (Renegade Pr., 1963); Heretofore (Paul Breman, 1968); Presentations (Podium, 1968); Psychovisualism, pam. ser. (Free Lance, 1956-58); The Nail & Maleficium (Free Lance, 1971). Anthol.: Moderne Dichtung: Neue Sammlung (Carl Hanser Verlag, München, 1954-63); Voix Prismatique: Une Anthologie Internationale (Falcon's Pr.); Sixes & Sevens (Paul Breman, 1962); Olivant Festival Anthol. (Olivant Pr.); Silver Cesspool (Renegade, 1964); Four, Six, Five (Seven Flowers, 1966); Sounds and Silences (Dell Pub., 1969). Poetry mags.: View (1947); Experiment; Voices; Beloit Poetry Journal; Poetry Today; Four Winds; Western Review; Minnesota Quarterly; New York Times Book Review; American Weave; Botteghe Oscure; Writers Forum; Tribute to J L; Fine Arts.
HONORS AND AWARDS: Scholarships: Mus. of Art & Karamu; Cleveland Music Sch. Settlement; Free Lance awarded grant, NEA.
MEMBER: Poet Lectrs.' Alliance; Poetry Seminar, WCLV; Ohio Poets Assn.; Com. of Small Mags. & Ed. & Pub. (Cal., N.Y.); Coord. Counc. of Literary Mags., NEA; Amer. Biographical Inst., Nat'l. Soc. Directory.
SIDELIGHTS: Musician: works include pieces for piano, cello & piano, violin & piano.

SELECTED BLACK AMERICAN AUTHORS

Sources. Author inform.; Poetry of Black America, Ed. by Arnold
   Adoff (Harper & Row, 1973).

ATTAWAY, WILLIAM ALEXANDER. 1911- . Novelist, Composer
Biographical-Personal. Born 1911 in Greenville, Miss. Son of Wil-
   liam A. (doctor) and Florence [Parry] Attaway. (The father mi-
   grated with his family to Chgo., Ill.) Educ.: Chgo. public
   schs.; U. of Ill. Family: Lives with his wife and children in
   Barbados.
Career-Professional. Seaman; Salesman; Labor organizer; Actor
   (played in You Can't Take It With You).
   WRITINGS: Let Me Breathe Thunder, novel (Doubleday, 1939); Blood
   On the Forge, novel (Doubleday, 1941); Calypso Song Book (McGraw-
   Hill, 1957); The Man, film script.
   SIDELIGHTS: Considered an interpreter of the Great Migration of
   the Thirties. A composer as well as a writer, Attaway has ar-
   ranged songs for Harry Belafonte. He wrote the script for the
   screen version of Irving Wallace's The Man; as well as other TV
   and film scripts.
Sources. Cavalcade, Ed. by Arthur P. Davis & Saunders Redding
   (Houghton Mifflin, 1971); Current Biography, 1941, Ed. by Maxine
   Block (H. W. Wilson, 1941); A Native Sons Reader, Ed. by Edward
   Margolies (Lippincott, 1970); Negro Novel in America, Robert Bone
   (Yale U. Pr., 1958).

BAILEY, PEARL MAE. 1918- . Singer, Comedienne
Biographical-Personal. Born March 29, 1918 in
   Newport News, Va. D. of Rev. Joseph James
   and Mrs. Bailey. Family: 1st m. John R.
   Pinkett, Jr.; div., Mar. 20, 1952; 2nd m.
   Louis Bellson, Jr. (drummer) in London, Eng.,
   Nov. 19, 1952.
Career-Professional. Vocalist with Cootie Wil-
   liams Band and Count Basie Band. Made stage
   debut, March 30, 1946, when she shared top
   billing in Negro musical "St. Louis Woman" at
   Martin Beck Theatre. 1st film was "Variety
   Girl"; also in "Carmen Jones"; sang in thea-
   tre operetta "Arms and the Girl." Role of
   Madame Fleur in "House of Flowers" which
   opened at N.Y.'s Alvin Theatre on Dec. 30,
   1954.
   WRITINGS: Raw Pearl (1968); Talking to Myself (1971); Pearl's
   Kitchen (1973); Duey's Tale (Harcourt, 1975).
   HONORS AND AWARDS: Donaldson Award for most promising new per-
   former of 1946 for her work in musical show "St. Louis Woman."
Sources. Current Biography, 1955, Ed. by Margaret Dent Candee (H. W.
   Wilson, 1955).

Baker, Augusta.

BAKER, AUGUSTA. 1911- . Librarian, Juvenile Author

Biographical-Personal. Born April 1, 1911 in Baltimore, Md. D. of Winfort J. and Mabel [Gough] Braxston. Educ.: B.A., N.Y. State Coll., Albany, 1933, B.S. (Lib. Sci.), 1934. Family: 2nd m. Gordon Alexander, 1944; son (1st m.) James Baker III. Mailing address: 115-33 174th St., St. Albans, N.Y. 11434.

Career-Professional. Children's Libr., N.Y. Public Lib., 1937-53; Storytelling Spec., 1953-61; Coord. of Children's Serv., 1961- Organized children's lib. serv. for Trinidad Public Lib., Port of Spain, Trinidad, 1953; Tchr., Sch. of Lib. Sci., Columbia U., 1956- .

WRITINGS: Edited: Talking Tree (Lippincott, 1955); Golden Lynx (Lippincott, 1960); Young Years with Eugenia Gerson (Home Lib. Pr., 1960); Once Upon a Time (1964); Recordings for Children (1964); The Black Experience in Children's Books (N.Y. Public Lib., 1971; 1974). Comp. of numerous reading lists & pams. In progress: editing collection of stories by Valery Garrick. HONORS AND AWARDS: Dutton-Macrae Award of Amer. Lib. Assn. for advance study in field of lib. work with children, 1953; Parents Magazine Medal Award, 1966 for "outstanding service to the nation's children"; ALA Grolier Award, 1968 for "outstanding achievement in guiding and stimulating the reading of children and young people"; Women's Nat'l. Bks. Assn. Constance Lindsay Skinner Award, 1971. MEMBER: ALA (Bd. of Dir., Children's Serv., 1958-61; Executive Bd., 1968-72; Counc.); N.Y. Lib. Assn.; N.Y. Lib. Club; Women's Nat'l. Bk. Assn.; N.Y. Folklore Soc.; NAACP; Delta Sigma Theta. SIDELIGHTS: Founder, James Weldon Johnson Memorial Collec., a collec. of children's books about Negro life, located at Countee Cullen Regional Branch of N.Y. Public Lib. Began ser. of weekly broadcasts, "The World of Children's Literature," on WNYC-Radio on Nov. 1, 1971.

Sources. Something About the Author, Ed. by Anne Commire, Vol. 3 (Gale Res., 1973).

BAKER, HOUSTON A., JR. 1943- . English Professor, Scholar

Biographical-Personal. Born March 22, 1943 in Louisville, Ky. Son of Houston A., Sr., and Viola Elizabeth Baker. Educ.: B.A., Howard U., 1965, M.A., 1966, Ph.D., 1968, U. of Calif., L.A.; U. of Edinburgh, Scotland (1 yr. of doctoral work), 1967-68. Family: m. Charlotte Baker; son Mark Frederick. Mailing address: 204 Bennett Hall, U. of Pa., Phila., Pa. 19174.

Career-Professional. Instr., Eng., Howard U., 1968; Instr., Eng., Yale U., 1968-69; Asst. Prof., Eng. (apptd. for 4-yr. term) 1969;

BANKS, IRMA LOUISE. Teacher, Novelist
Biographical-Personal. Born in South Carolina. Educ.: B.A. (French
and Eng.), Allen U., Columbia, S.C.; grad. study, UCLA. Family:
m.; 2 children. Mailing address: Englewood, Cal.
Career-Professional. Tchr., Eng.
WRITINGS: Love in Black and White, novel.
Source. "Second Annual Authors Autograph Party" (brochure), Cal.
Librns. Black Caucus, July 1975.

BANNEKER, BENJAMIN. 1731-1806. Mathematician,
Astronomer, Surveyor
Biographical-Personal. Born Nov. 9, 1731, in
Baltimore, Md. Son of Robert (a freed African) and Mary Banneker (free woman, half
Eng.-half African). Fundamentally educated &
self taught. Family: Single. Died in Oct.,
1806.
Career-Professional. Inventor of first hour-
striking clock in America. In 1787 George
Ellicott, a neighbor, loaned Banneker Fer-
guson's Astronomy, Mayer's Tables, and
Leadbetter's Lunar Tables, with some astro-
nomical instruments. He thoroughly mastered
the books, so much so that in 1789 he was
commissioned for the surveying of the Federal
Territory (District of Columbia).
WRITINGS: In 1791 he began issuing the Almanac, and continued annually until 1802. (A remarkable scientific achievement for a
Black American in the 1790's.)
SIDELIGHTS: Thomas Jefferson, then Secretary of State, to whom
Banneker sent a letter along with a copy of his almanac, said in
reply, "Nobody wishes more than I do to seek such proofs as you
exhibit, that nature has given to our black brethren talents equal
to those of the other colors of men" (Early Negro American Writers).
"Benjamin Banneker was more than a self-taught mathematician,
astronomer, surveyor, poet, and mechanic. He was also a humanitarian. He cared intensely about the quality of life for, black
people in America. He spoke out boldly in his letters and conversations with the nation's leaders for the humane treatment of his
people. He showed to a slave-holding nation that Blacks are a
part of the human family. He used his own achievements as proof
that the idea of the inferiority of black people of African descent should be destroyed. His life was a search for independence,
just as it was for the American colonies during the 1700's and the
Revolutionary War" (Seven Black American Scientists).

Baraka, Imamu Amiri

Sources. Early Negro American Writers, Benjamin Brawley (U. of N.C.
  Pr., 1935); Seven Black American Scientists, Robert C. Hayden
  (Addison-Wesley, 1970).

BARAKA, IMAMU AMIRI [Everett LeRoi Jones]
1934- . Poet, Playwright, Activist
Biographical-Personal. Born Oct. 7, 1934, in
    Newark, N.J. Son of Coyt LeRoi (postal
    supt.) and Anna [Russ] Jones (soc. worker).
    Educ.: B.A., Howard U., 1954; New Sch. for
    Soc. Res.; M.A. (German Lit.), Columbia U.
    Family: 1st m. Hettie Cohen, Oct. 13, 1958;
    d. Kellie Elizabeth; d. Lisa V. Chapman; div.
    Aug. 1965; 2nd m. Amini Baraka [Sylvia Rob-
    inson], Aug. 1966; children: Obalaji Malik
    Ali, Ras Jua Al Aziz. Mailing address: 33
    Stirling St., Newark, N.J. 07103.
Career-Professional. Founder, Yugen (with 1st
    wife), 1958. Contrib. Evergreen Review,
    Poetry, Saturday Review, and The Nation.
Ed.: ("little mags."), Kulchur, The Floating Bear. Jazz critic:
Downbeat, Jazz, Jazz Review. Tchr.: (poetry), New Sch. for Soc.
Res.; (drama), Columbia U.; (lit.), U. of Buffalo; Vis. Prof.,
San Francisco State. Leader, Black Community Develop. & Defense,
Newark, 1968. Founder, Theaters: Spirit House (Newark); Black
Arts Repertory Theatre (Harlem). Pub.: Jihad Public. Polit.
organizer: United Brothers, Newark, 1967; Com. for Unified New-
ark; Chrm., Congress of African People; Co-Convenor Nat'l. Black
Polit. Convention; Secy.-Gen., Nat'l. Black Assembly, Nat'l.
Polit. Counc. of Black Polit. Convention; Polit. Prisoners Fund;
All African Games; African Liberation Day Com.; African Libera-
tion Day Support Com.; Pan African Federation Groups; 2nd Inter-
nat. World Festival of Black Arts; IFCO Internat. Task Force.
WRITINGS: Preface to a Twenty-Volume Suicide Note, poetry (Totem
Pr., 1961); Blues People, sociol. essay (Morrow, 1963); The Mod-
erns (Corinth Bks., 1963); The Dead Lecturer poetry (1964); Bap-
tism, Dutchman, The Slave & The Toilet (plays prod. 1964); The
System of Dante's Hell, novel (Grove, 1965); Home (Morrow, 1966,
1972); Black Music, essays (Morrow, 1967); Black Art (Jihad, 1967);
Tales, short fic. (Grove, 1967); Black Magic (Bobbs-Merrill, 1969);
Black Revolutionary Plays (1969); In Our Terribleness (1971);
Raise ---- (1971); A Black Value System (1969); It's Nationtime
(1971); Strategy and Tactics of a Pan African Nationalist Party
(1972); African Congress, Ed. (1972); Kawaida Studies (1972);
Spirit Reach (1972). Black Fire, Co-ed., anthol. (Morrow, 1971);
The Cricket, Black Music Journal (1968-).

Barrax, Gerald William

HONORS AND AWARDS: Fellow: John Hay Whitney Opportunity, 1961;
Guggenheim, 1965; Yoruba Acad., 1965; Doctorate of Humane Let-
ters, Malcolm X Coll., Chgo., 1972.
MEMBER: Black Acad. of Arts & Letters.
SIDELIGHTS: Yugen served as forum for Allen Ginsberg, William S.
Burroughs, Herbert Selby, Jr., Robert Creeley, A. B. Spellman,
Diane de Prima, Charles Alson & Edward Dahlberg. New Arabic name
means, "spiritual leader." Major theatrical production includes:
Dutchman (Off-Broadway award Best Amer. Play, 1964); The Slave
(2nd prize, Internat. Art Festival, Dakar, 1966); The Toilet, The
Baptism, Jello, A Black Mass; theatrical works prod. in major U.S.
cities, also Dakar, Paris, Berlin. Other plays prod.: Dante,
1962; Experimental Death Unit, 1965; Mad Heart, 1967; Slave Ship,
1967; Great Goodness of Life, 1968; Junkies, Bloodrite, 1970;
Columbia, The Gem of the Ocean, 1972.
Sources. Author inform.; Black Drama in America, Ed. by Darwin T.
Turner (Fawcett, 1971); Black Insights, Ed. by Nick A. Ford (Ginn,
1971); Black Voices, Ed. by Abraham Chapman (New Amer. Lib.,
1968); Cavalcade, Ed. by Arthur P. Davis & Saunders Redding
(Houghton Mifflin, 1971); Current Biography Yearbook, 1970 (H.W.
Wilson, 1970); Poetry of Black America, Ed. by Arnold Adoff (Harper & Row, 1973); Who's Who in America, 37th ed., 1972-73 (Mar-
quis, 1972).

BARRAX, GERALD WILLIAM. 1933- . Poet,
Teacher
Biographical-Personal. Born June 21, 1933, in
    Attala, Ala. Educ.: B.A., Duquesne U.,
    1963; M.A., U. of Pittsburgh, 1969.
Career-Professional. U.S. Air Force, 1953-57;
    Clerk & carrier, U.S. Post Office, 1958-67;
    Instr., Eng. Dept., N.C. Central U., 1969-70;
    Spec. Instr., N.C. State U., 1970- .
    WRITINGS: Another Kind of Rain, poetry
    (Pittsburgh U. Pr., 1970). Period.: Journal
    of Black Poetry. Anthol.: Kaleidoscope; The
    Young American Poets; Poetry of Black
    America.
    HONORS AND AWARDS: Bishop Carroll Scholar-
    ship for Creative Writing; Gold medal award,
    Catholic Poetry Soc. of America.
SIDELIGHTS: "He says that sometimes he speaks as 'a vulnerable
mortal and sometimes as a vulnerable Black American' and that
Blackness and death 'are implicit in all my responses to people
and the world I live in and in everything I write'" (New Black
Voices).
Sources. New Black Voices, Ed. by Abraham Chapman (New Amer. Lib.,
1972); Poetry of Black America, Ed. by Arnold Adoff (Harper & Row,
1973).

Bell, James Madison

BELL, JAMES MADISON. 1826-1902. Poet
Biographical-Personal. Born April 3, 1826, in
    Gallipolis, Ohio. Family: m. at age 22.
    Died 1902.
Career-Professional. Plasterer; Abolitionist;
    Delegate, Republican Convention, Ohio, 1868;
    Delegate, National Convention (nominated
    U. S. Grant).
    WRITINGS: The Progress of Liberty; The Day
    and the War; Poetical Works of James Madison
    Bell (Black Her. Lib. Collec. Ser.) Repr. of
    1901, Bks. for Lib.
    SIDELIGHTS: Was able speaker; read his poems
    with strong effect; appreciated as something
    of an actor. Some of best poems: "Emancipa-
    tion," "The Dawn of Freedom," "Lincoln," "The
Future of America in the Unity of the Races," "Song for the First
of August," "The Blackman's Wrongs," "The Progress of Liberty,"
and "The Triumph of the Free" (Historical Negro Biographies).
Personal friend of John Brown (Early Negro American Writers).
Sources. Early Black American Poets, Ed. by William H. Robinson, Jr.
    (William C. Brown, 1969); Early Negro American Writers, Ed. by
    Benjamin Brawley (U. of N.C., 1935); Historical Negro Biographies,
    Ed. by Wilhelmena S. Robinson (ASNLH, 1967).

BENNETT, HAL. 1930- . Novelist
Biographical-Personal. Born April 21, 1930, in
    Buckingham, Va.
    WRITINGS: A Wilderness of Vines (Doubleday,
    1966); The Black Wine (Doubleday, 1968); Lord
    of Dark Places (W. W. Norton, 1970); Wait
    Until the Evening (Doubleday, 1974); Spirit
    Guides: Access to Secret Worlds, with Mi-
    chael Samuels (Random House, 1974); Be Well,
    with Mike Samuels (Random House, 1975).
Source. Books in Print, Supplement, 1975-76
    (Bowker, 1976).

BENNETT, LERONE, JR. 1928- . Magazine Editor, Historian
Biographical-Personal. Born Oct. 17, 1928, in Clarksdale, Miss.
    Son of Lerone and Alma [Reed] Bennett. Educ.: B.A., Morehouse
    Coll., 1949, D. Letters (hon.) 1966. Family: m. Gloria Sylves-
    ter, July 21, 1956; d. Alma Joy, d. Constance, son, Courtney, son,
    Lerone III. Mailing address: 820 S. Mich. Ave., Chgo, Ill. 60605.

Billingsley, Andrew

Career-Professional. Reporter, Atlanta Daily
World, 1949-51, City Ed., 1952-53; Assoc.
Ed., Ebony mag., 1953-58, Senior Ed.,
1958- . Vis. Prof., Hist., Northwestern U.,
1969-71, Chmn., Dept. of African-Amer. Stud.,
1972- .
WRITINGS: Before the Mayflower: A History
of the Negro in America, 1619-1964 (Johnson
Pub., 1962, rev. 1964); The Negro Mood
(1964); What Manner of Man: A Biography of
Martin Luther King, Jr. (1964, Simon &
Schuster, 1968); Confrontation: Black and
White (1965); Black Power U.S.A. (1968);
Pioneers in Protest (1968); The Challenge of
Blackness (1972); Shaping of Black America
(Johnson Pub., 1975). Contrib.: New Negro
Poets: U.S.A. (1964); American Negro Short Stories (1966).
HONORS AND AWARDS: Patron Saints Award; Soc. of Midland Authors,
1965; Bk. of Yr. Award, Capital Pr. Club, 1963.
MEMBER: Black Acad. of Arts & Letters; Kappa Alpha Psi; Bd. of
Dir., Parkway Community House; Bd. of Dir. Race Relat., Inform.
Center; Inst. of Black World; Trus., Martin Luther King Memorial
Center; Senior Fellow, Inst. of the Black World, 1969.
SIDELIGHTS: Lerone Bennett is often referred to as the "resident
historian" of Johnson Pub. Co. "As a social historian, his candid
views on the present state of race relations and the resulting so-
cial change creates a great demand for him as a lecturer." (Con-
frontation: Black and White)
  "Bennett's style has the power and force of the historical writ-
ings of W. E. B. DuBois, and reveals the same passionate attack on
white racism and the same dedication to human dignity and freedom"
(Black Historians).
Sources. Black Historians, Ed. by Earl E. Thorpe (Morrow, 1969);
Confrontation: Black and White, Ed. by Lerone Bennett (Johnson
Pub., 1965); Negro Almanac, Comp. by Harry A. Ploski & Ernest
Kaiser (Bellwether, 1971).

BILLINGSLEY, ANDREW. 1926- . University Administrator,
Sociologist
Biographical-Personal. Born March 20, 1926, in Marion, Ala. Son of
Silas and Lucy Billingsley. Educ.: Hampton Inst., Va., 1947-49;
B.A. Grinnell Coll., Grinnell, Iowa, 1951; M.S., Boston U., 1956;
M.A., U. of Mich., 1960; Ph.D., Brandeis U., Waltham, Mass., 1964.
Family: m. Amy Loretta Tate; d. Angela Eleanor, d. Bonita Rebec-
ca. Mailing address Office of V.Pres. for Acad. Affairs, 2400
6th St., N.W., Howard U., Wash., D.C. 20001.
Career-Professional. V. Pres. for Acad. Affairs, Prof. of Sociol.,
Howard U., 1970- ; Asst. Chancellor for Acad. Affairs, U. of Cal.,

Boggs, James

Berkeley, 1968-70; Asst.-Assoc. Prof. of Soc. Welfare, U. of Cal., Berkeley, 1964-70; Fellow, Metropolitan Applied Res. Center & Prog. Cons., Nat'l. Urban League, N.Y.C. (on leave), 1968; Asst. Dean of Stud., U. of Cal., Berkeley, 1964-65; Soc. worker & Res. Asst., Mass. Soc. for Prevention of Cruelty to Children, 1960-63; Psychiatric Soc. Worker, Wis. Dept. of Pub. Welfare (Mendota State Hospital), 1956-58; Dir. of Youth Serv. Project, Amer. Friends Serv. Com. (Quakers), Chgo., Regional Office, 1951-54.
WRITINGS: Black Families in White America (Prentice-Hall, 1968); Children of the Storm with Jeanne Giovannoni (Harcourt, 1972); Contrib.: The Strengths of Black Families; Social Service in the Model Cities; Race, Reason and Research; What Black Educators Are Saying. Period.: Alumni Journal (1970); Child Welfare (1964); Social Service Review (1965); Public Welfare (1966); Social Work (1968); American Sociological Review (1969); Amer. Journal of Sociology (1969); Social Work Education Reporter (1969).
HONORS AND AWARDS: Michael Schwerner Memorial Award, N.Y.C., 1969; The Soc. Sci. Fellow., Metropolitan Applied Res. Center, N.Y.C., 1968.
MEMBER: Com. to Review the Afro-Amer. Stud. Dept., Howard U., 1972-73; Com. to Review Africana Stud. Center, Cornell U., 1972-73; Bd. of Dir., Joint Center for Polit. Stud., 1972-73; Ed. Bd., The Black Scholar; Amer. Sociol. Assn., Chmn., Family Section; Nat'l. Assn. of Soc. Workers.
SIDELIGHTS: Has spoken extensively in the U.S. Visited educ. inst. in Monrovia, Liberia; Accra, Ghana; Lagos, Nigeria; & Dar Es Salaam, Tanzania, Africa (1971). (Author).
Sources. Author inform.

BOGGS, JAMES. 1919- . Automobile Worker, Essayist
Biographical-Personal. Born May 28, 1919 in Marion Junction, Ala. Educ.: Dunbar High Sch., grad. 1937. Mailing address: 3061 Field St., Detroit, Mich. 48214.
Career-Professional. Auto worker, Detroit, 1941-68.
WRITINGS: The American Revolution: Pages from a Negro Worker's Notebook (Monthly Review Pr., 1963); Racism and the Class Struggle: Further Pages from a Black Worker's Notebook (Monthly Review Pr., 1970); Manifesto for a Black Revolutionary Party and Race and Class Struggle; Revolution and Evaluation in the Twentieth Century, with Grace Lee Boggs (Monthly Review Pr., 1974).

Bond, Horace Julian

SIDELIGHTS: <u>The American Revolution</u> has been translated in Latin America, France, and Japan, and articles on Black Power have been published in Italy and Argentina.

Sources. <u>Black Fire</u>, Ed. by LeRoi Jones & Larry Neal (Morrow, 1968); <u>The Black Seventies</u>, Ed. by Floyd Barbour (Porter Sargent, 1970).

BOGLE, DONALD. Editor, Essayist
Biographical-Personal. Born in N.Y.C. <u>Educ.</u>:
    Lincoln U. (grad. with honors); Ind. U.;
    Harvard U.; Columbia U.
Career-Professional. Movie Story Ed.; Staff
    Writer, Asst. Ed., <u>Ebony</u> mag.
    WRITINGS: <u>Toms, Coons, Mulattoes, Mammies,
    and Bucks</u> (Viking, 1973, Bantam, 1974).
Source. Pub. inform.

BOND, HORACE JULIAN. 1940- . State Legislator,
Civil Rights Leader
Biographical-Personal. Born Jan. 14, 1940, in
    Nashville, Tenn. Son of Horace Mann (educa-
    tor) and Julia Agnes [Washington] Bond.
    <u>Educ.</u>: George Sch. (Quaker preparatory
    sch.); B.A. Morehouse Coll., 1971. <u>Family</u>:
    m. Alice Clopton, July 28, 1961; d. Phyllis
    Jane, son, Horace Mann, son, Michael, son,
    Jeffrey, d. Julia.
Career-Professional. Founder, Com. on Appeal
    for Human Rights (COAHR), Atlanta U., 1960;
    Founder, and Communications Dir., SNCC; Man-
    aging Ed., <u>Atlanta Inquirer</u>; Elected to Ga.
    House of Reps., 1965 (Jan. 9, 1967, took
    seat).
WRITINGS: <u>A Time to Speak, a Time to Act; the movement in poli-
tics</u> (Simon & Schuster, 1972). Period.: <u>Negro Digest</u>; <u>Motive</u>;
<u>Rights and Reviews</u>; <u>Life</u>; <u>Freedomways</u>; <u>Ramparts</u>. Anthol.: <u>Beyond
the Blues</u>; <u>New Negro Poets</u>; <u>American Negro Poetry</u>; <u>Book of Negro
Humor</u>.
HONORS AND AWARDS: Hon. trus., Inst. of Applied Politics; Co-
chmn., Ga. Nat'l Democratic Delegate (insurgents) to 1968 Democratic Nat'l Convention (unseated regular Ga. delegation); nominated for Vice Pres. of U.S., but withdrew because of age. Hon.

Bond, Horace Mann

degrees: (LL.D.), Dalhousie U., 1969; U. Bridgeport, 1969; Wesleyan U., 1969; U. Ore., 1969; Syracuse U., 1970; Eastern Mich. U., 1971; Tuskegee Inst., 1971; Howard U., 1971; Morgan State U., 1971; Wilberforce U., 1971; (D.C.L.), Lincoln U., 1970.
MEMBER: Southern Corresp. Reporting Racial Equality Wars (SCREW); Bd. mem.: Delta Ministry Porject, Nat'l Counc. of Churches; Robert F. Kennedy Memorial Fund; Martin Luther King, Jr. Center for Social Change; Nat'l Sharecropper's Fund; S. Regional Counc.; New Democratic Coalition; Voter Educ. Project; S. Elections Fund (Chmn.); Vis. Fellow, Metropolitan Applied Res. Center, N.Y.C.
SIDELIGHTS: First elected to seat created by reapportionment in Ga. House of Rep., but prevented from taking office (legis. objected to his statements about Vietnam War). After winning 2nd election (Feb. 1966) to fill his vacant seat, again barred. Won 3rd election, Nov. 1966. U.S. Supreme Court unanimously ruled that Ga. House had erred in refusing him seat. Took oath of office on Jan. 9, 1967 (Author).
Sources. Author inform.; Black Politicians, Richard Brunner (McKay, 1971); Who's Who in America, 37th ed. 1972-73 (Marquis, 1972).

BOND, HORACE MANN. 1904-1972. Educator, Researcher, Social Scientist
Biographical-Personal. Born Nov. 8, 1904, in Nashville, Tenn. Son of James and Jane [Browne] Bond. Educ.: B.A., Lincoln U., Pa., 1923; M.A., 1926, Ph.D., 1936, U. of Chgo. Family: m. Julia Agnes Washington, 1929; d. Jane, son Horace Julian, son, James. Died 1972.
Career-Professional. Prof., Langston U., Langston, Okla., 1924-27; Prof., Ala. State Coll., Montgomery, 1927-28; Prof. & Researcher, Fisk U. & Rosenwald Fund, 1928-33, 1937-39; Dean, Dillard U., New Orleans, La., 1933-37; Pres., Fort Valley State Coll., Fort Valley, Ga., 1939-45; Pres., Lincoln U., Pa., 1945-57; Dean, Atlanta U., 1957- .
WRITINGS: Education of the Negro in the American Social Order (Prentice-Hall, 1934); Negro Education in Alabama, A Study in Cotton and Steel (Assoc. Pub., 1939); Education for Production (U. of Ga. Pr., 1944); The Search for Talent (Harvard U. Pr., 1959); A History of African Students in the United States; A History of Lincoln University. Contrib. to many professional & encycl. works.
AWARDS AND HONORS: LL.D.: Lincoln U. (Pa.), 1941; Temple U., 1955; Amer. Educ. Res. Assn. Award, 1939; Assn. for Study of Negro Hist. Award, 1943.
MEMBER: Amer. Tchrs. Assn. (life mem.); Amer. Assn. of Sch. Admin.; Nat'l. Soc. for Study of Educ.; African Stud. Assn.; Amer.

Bontemps, Arna Wendell

Educ. Res. Assn.; S. Sociol. Soc.; Amer. Soc. of African Culture
(Pres., 1958- .); Kappa Alpha Psi.
SIDELIGHTS: He made at least 14 trips to Africa for educational
surveys (Contemporary Authors).
Sources. Contemporary Authors, Vol. 1, Ed. by James M. Ethridge
  (Gale Res., 1962); Current Biography, 1954, Ed. by Margaret Dent
  Candee (H. W. Wilson, 1954); Negro Caravan, Ed. by Sterling A.
  Brown & Others (Arno Pr., & N.Y. Times, 1969).

BONTEMPS, ARNA WENDELL. 1902-1973. Librarian,
Juvenile Writer, Poet, Critic, Biographer,
Anthologist, Playwright, English Teacher
Biographical-Personal. Born Oct. 13, 1902, in
  Alexandria, La. Son of Paul Bismark and
  Maria [Pembrook] Bontemps. Educ.: B.A.,
  Pacific Union Coll., 1923; M.A., Sch. of
  Lib. Sci., U. of Chgo., 1943. Family: m.
  Alberta Johnson, 1926; d. Joan Marie Wil-
  liams, son, Paul Bismark, d. Poppy Alberta
  Cooke, d. Camille Ruby Graves, d. Constance
  Rebecca Thomas, son, Arna Alex. Died June 4,
  1973.
Career-Professional. High Sch. Tchr. & Princ.,
  1924-41; Free-lance writer, 1941-43; Head
  Librn., Fisk U., Nashville, Tenn., 1943-65;
Prof. Eng., U. of Ill., Chgo. Circle Campus, 1966-69; Curator,
James Weldon Johnson Collec., Yale U., 1969-73; Writer-in-Resi-
dence, Fisk U., 1973.
WRITINGS: God Sends Sunday (Harcourt, 1931); Popo and Fifina,
Children of Haiti (Macmillan, 1932); You Can't Pet a Possum (Mor-
row, 1934); Black Thunder (Macmillan, 1936); Sad Faced Boy (Hough-
ton Mifflin, 1937); Drums at Dusk (Macmillan, 1939); Golden Slip-
pers, anthol. (Harper & Row, 1941); The Fast Sooner Hound (Hough-
ton Mifflin, 1942); We Have Tomorrow (Houghton Mifflin, 1945);
Story of the Negro (Knopf, 1948, 3rd ed., 1958); The Poetry of the
Negro, Ed. with Langston Hughes (Doubleday, 1949); Chariot in the
Sky (Winston, 1941); The Story of George Washington Carver (Grosset, 1954); Lonesome Boy (Houghton Mifflin, 1955); The Book of
Negro Folklore, anthol. (1958); Frederick Douglass (Knopf, 1959);
100 Years of Negro Freedom (Dodd Mead, 1961); Father of the Blues,
Ed. (W. C. Handy's autobiog.); Anyplace But Here (1967); Famous
Negro Athletes; They Seek A City (1945); Great Slave Narratives
(1969). Plays: Saint Louis Woman (1946); Free and Easy (1949).
HONORS AND AWARDS: Guggenheim fellow. for creative writing, 1949-
50; Julius Rosenwald fellow, 1938-39, 1942-43; Jane Adams Children's Book Award for Story of the Negro; James L. Dow Award, Soc.
of Midland Authors for Anyplace But Here, 1967; various poetry &
short story prizes.

Booker, Simeon Saunders

MEMBER: P.E.N.; Author's League of America; Dramatists Guild;
ALA; Amer. Assn. of U. Prof.; Amer. Soc. for Aesthetics; Sigma Pi
Phi; Omega Psi Phi; Mu Alpha.
SIDELIGHTS: One of the writers of the Harlem Renaissance. "As
poet, novelist, author of short stories and juvenile literature,
critic, anthologist, playwright, librarian and educator, Arna Bontemps is a central figure in the creation, dissemination and
teaching of Negro American Literature" (Black Voices).
 "Arna Bontemps became the first historical novelist among Negroes. God Sends Sunday portrays the glamorous days of horse
racing during the 1890's. Black Thunder is a historical novel
dealing with a Virginia slave insurrection. Drums at Dusk is a
recreation of that phase of the San Domingo Revolution that pre-
ceded the leadership of Toussaint L'Ouverture" (Black Insights).
 He was writing his autobiog. at the time of his death (Library
Journal, July 1973).
Sources. Black American Literature--Poetry, Ed. by Darwin T. Turner
(Merrill, 1969); Black Insights, Ed. by Nick A. Ford (Ginn, 1971);
Black Voices, Ed. by Abraham Chapman (New Amer. Lib., 1968); Cavalcade, Ed. by Arthur P. Davis & Saunders Redding (Houghton Mifflin, 1971); Contemporary Authors, vol. 1, Ed. by James M. Ethridge (Gale Res., 1962); Jones, Virginia Lacy, "Arna Bontemps,
1902-1973," Library Journal, July 1973.

BOOKER, SIMEON SAUNDERS. 1918- . Journalist
Biographical-Personal. Born Aug. 27, 1918, in Baltimore, Md. Son of
Simeon Saunders (YMCA Secy.) and Roberta [Waring] Booker. Educ.:
B.A., Va. Union U., Richmond, 1942; further study: Cleveland
Coll.; Harvard U. (Nieman Fellow), 1950-51. Family: m. Thelma
Cunningham; d. Theresa, son, Simeon, Jr., son, James. Mailing
address: Johnson Pub. Co., 1750 Pa. Ave., N.W., Wash., D.C.
Career-Professional. Chief, Washington, D.C. Bureau, Johnson Pub.
Co., Inc.
WRITINGS: Black Man's America (Prentice-Hall, 1964).
Sources. Contemporary Authors, Vols. 11-12, Ed. by James M. Ethridge
& Barbara Kopala (Gale Res., 1965).

BRAITHWAITE, WILLIAM STANLEY. 1878-1962. Poet, Anthologist, Critic
Biographical-Personal. Born Dec. 6, 1878, in Boston, Mass. Son of
William Smith and Emma D. Braithwaite (W. Indian Blacks). Educ.:
Boston Latin Sch.; M.A. (hon.) Atlanta U., 1918; Litt. D. (hon.),
Talladega Coll., 1918. Family: m. Emma Kelly of Montrose, Va.,
1903. Died 1962.
Career-Professional. Literary Ed., Boston Transcript, annual "An-
thology of Magazine Verse," 1913-1929; Ed., anthol. of Restoration,
Georgian, and Victorian verse; Prof. of Creative Lit., Atlanta U.,
1944.

Branch, William Blackwell

WRITINGS: Lyrics of Life and Love, poetry (1904); The House of Falling Leaves, poetry (1908); The Poetic Year for 1916; The Story of the Great War (1919); The Five Wisdoms of Graine (1920); Going Over Tendal (1920); Our Essayists and Critics of Today (1920). Ed./ Comp.: The Book of Elizabethan Verse (1906); The Book of Georgian Verse (1908); The Book of Restoration Verse (1909); Anthology of Magazine Verse 1913-29; Golden Treasury of Magazine Verse (1918); Book of Modern British Verse (1918); Victory: Celebrated by 38 American Poets; Selected Poems (1948); Anthology of Magazine Verse for 1958 (Pentelic Pr., 1959). The House Under Arcturus: An Autobiography (1940); The Bewitched Parsonage, biography of the Brontës (1950); The William Stanley Braithwaite Reader (U. of Mich. Pr., 1972). Contrib. to Forum, Century, Lippincott's, Scribner's, Atlantic, etc.

HONORS AND AWARDS: NAACP Spingarn Medal, 1918.

SIDELIGHTS: His annual "Anthology of Magazine Verse," included early works of Edgar Lee Masters, Vachel Lindsay and Carl Sandburg, among others. "In the early part of his career, it was not generally known that he was a Negro" (Cavalcade). "Refusing to write as a 'Negro poet' or to use racial themes, he elected to fight for equality by competing with white writers on their terms" (Negro Almanac). "He was one of the pioneer forces in stimulating the 'revival' of poetry in America, which began about 1912" (Book of American Negro Poetry).

Sources. American Literature by Negro Authors, Herman Dreer (Macmillan, 1950); An Anthology of Verse by American Negroes, Ed. by Newman I. White & Walter C. Jackson (Moore Pub. Co., 1924); Black American Literature--Poetry, Ed. by Darwin T. Turner (Merrill, 1969); Book of American Negro Poetry, rev. ed., Ed. by James W. Johnson (Harcourt, 1959); Cavalcade, Ed. by Arthur P. Davis & Saunders Redding (Houghton Mifflin, 1971); Negro Almanac, Comp. by Harry A. Ploski & Roscoe C. Brown, Jr. (Bellwether, 1967).

BRANCH, WILLIAM BLACKWELL. 1927- . Writer, Producer, Director, Lecturer

Biographical-Personal. Born Sept. 11, 1927, in New Haven, Conn. Son of James Mathew (minister) and Iola [Douglas] Branch. Educ.: B.S. (Speech) Northwestern U., 1949; M.F.A. (Dramatic Arts), Columbia U., 1958, Postgraduate, 1958-59; Resident Fellow, Yale U. Drama Sch., 1965-66. Family: div., d. Rochelle Ellen. Mailing address: 53 Cortlandt Ave., New Rochelle, N.Y. 10801.

Career-Professional. Pres., William Branch Assoc. (TV & film prod.); Assoc. in Film, Columbia U. Sch. of the Arts, 1968-69; Vis. Play-

Brawley, Benjamin Griffith

wright: Smith Coll., Northampton, Mass., 1970; N.C. Central U., Durham, 1971; St. Lawrence U., 1973. Educ. Instr., U.S. Army, 1951-53; Actor: theater, films, radio & TV, 1946-55.
WRITINGS: Films: "Together for Days," 1971; "Still A Brother: Inside the Negro Middle Class," (NET) 1968; "Benefit Performance," movie for Universal Studios & NBC TV. TV: "Afro-American Perspectives" (30-prog. TV ser. on Black hist.); "Light in the Southern Sky," 1958; Prod., Spec. Unit, NBC News, N.Y.C., 1972-73. Plays: A Medal for Willie (off-Broadway), 1951-52; In Splendid Error (Greenwich News Theatre, N.Y.C.), 1954-55; A Wreath for Udomo (Lyric Hammersmith Theatre, London), 1961. Plays pub. in Black Theatre (Dodd, Mead, 1971); Black Scenes (Zenith, 1971); Black Drama Anthology (Columbia U. Pr., 1972); & Black Theater U.S.A. (Free Pr., 1974). Radio: "The Jackie Robinson Show," NBC Radio, 1959; "The Alma John Show" (Coca-Cola). Other: "The Jackie Robinson Column," N.Y. Post (writer & gen. partner), 1959-61; Ebony mag., Field Rep., 1949-50; Articles in N.Y. Times & N.Y. Amsterdam News & others.
HONORS AND AWARDS: Guggenheim Fellow (creative writing in the drama), 1959-60; Yale U. Amer. Broadcasting Co. Fellow (creative writing in TV drama), 1965-66; Amer. Film Festival Blue Ribbon Award for "Still A Brother," 1969; Robert E. Sherwood TV Award (NBC TV Drama, "Light in the Southern Sky"), 1958; Nat'l. Counc. of Christians & Jews Citation for "Light in the Southern Sky," 1958; Nat'l. Acad. of TV Arts & Sci. "Emmy" Award Nomination for "Still A Brother," 1969; Kirk Award; Northern Oratorical Prize; Sigmund Livingston Fellow; Hannah B. Del Vecchio Prize in Play-writing, 1958.
SIDELIGHTS: Guest Lectr.: Harvard, Columbia, UCLA, U. of Cal., Santa Barbara, San Jose State, Spelman, U. of Utah, U. of Ghana, Legon, Ghana (Summer, 1964). Counc. on Student Travel, trans-Atlantic sailing, June, 1962. Delegate to Internat. Conf. on the Arts, Lagos, Nigeria, Dec. 1961. Acted in "Anna Lucasta" (Author).
Sources. Author inform.

BRAWLEY, BENJAMIN GRIFFITH. 1882-1939. Literary and Social Historian
Biographical-Personal. Born 1882 in Columbia, S.C.; Son of Dr. Edward M. and Margaret D. Brawley. Educ.: B.A., Morehouse Coll., 1901; B.A., U. of Chgo., 1906; M.A., Harvard U., 1908. Family: m. Hilda Prowd of Kingston, Jamaica in 1912. Died in 1939.

Brewer, John Mason

Career-Professional. Prof. of Eng.: Morehouse
Coll., Shaw U. & Howard U.; Dean, Morehouse
Coll., 1912-?; Instr., Summer Sch., Hampton
Inst. (several yrs.); Pres., Assn. of Coll.
of Negro Youth; Lectr.
WRITINGS: A Short History of the American
Negro (1918); Women of Achievement (1919); A
Short History of English Drama (1921); A New
Survey of English Literature (1925); Doctor
Dillard of the Jeanes Fund (Bks. for Lib.,
Black Her. Ser., 1930); The Negro Genius
(1937; Apollo Eds., 1970); Negro Builders
and Heroes (1937). Also The Negro in Litera-
ture and Art (1910); A Social History of the
American Negro in 1921 (Basic Afro-Amer.
Repr. Lib., Johnson Pub., 1969); Richard Le
Gallienne: A Study of His Poetry; Africa and the War; History of
Morehouse College; Early Negro American Writers (Bks. for Lib.,
Essay Index Repr., 1968). Poetry: A Toast to Love and Death;
The Desire of the Moth for the Star; The Dawn and Other Poems;
The Problem and Other Poems; The Seven Sleepers of Ephesys.
SIDELIGHTS: Brawley's books were mainly concerned with literary
and social history. The Negro in Literature and Art went through
several editions. It was the first, and one of the most valuable,
comprehensive books on the subject.
   "Benjamin G. Brawley in The Negro Genius (1937) and Negro Builders and Heroes (1937) produced 2 volumes of sketches of Negro
notables. The first book deals largely with men and women whose
endeavors were in art and literature; the second, covering a wid-
er field, he described as 'an introduction to Negro biography'"
(Negro Caravan).
   Professor Brawley was the author of poems and short stories
which had not been collected at the time of his death (The Poetry
of the Negro, 1746-1949).
Sources. An Anthology of Verse by American Negroes, Ed. by Newman I.
White & Walter C. Jackson (Moore, 1924); Book of American Negro
Poetry, rev. ed., Ed. by James W. Johnson (Harcourt, 1959); Negro
Caravan, Ed. by Sterling Brown & Others (Arno Pr. & N.Y. Times,
1969); Poetry of the Negro, 1746-1949, Ed. by Langston Hughes &
Arna Bontemps (Doubleday, 1949).

BREWER, JOHN MASON. 1896- . Folklorist
Biographical-Personal. Born March 24, 1896, in Goliad, Tex. Son of
J. H. and Minnie T. Brewer. Educ.: B.A., Wiley Coll., Marshall,
Tex.; M.A., Ind. U., Bloomington; Lit. D. (hon), Paul Quinn Coll.,
Waco, Tex. Family: m. Ruth Helen Brewer; son. Mailing address:
2824 Laurel Lane, Commerce, Tex. 75428.

Brewer, John Mason

Career-Professional. Distinguished Vis. Prof.
of English, E. Tex. State U. (presently);
Distinguished Vis. Prof. of Anthropology,
N.C. Agricultural & Technical U., Greensboro,
1967-69; Gen. Ed., Negro Her. Ser., Pemberton
Pr., Austin, Tex.
WRITINGS: Negrito, A Volume of Negro Dialect
Poems (Naylor, 1933); Negro Legislators of
Texas (Mathis Van Nort, 1935); Little Dan
From Dixieland: A Story in Verse (Bookcraft,
1940); Negro Folktales from Texas (Webster,
1942); The Life of John Wesley Anderson: A
Story in Verse (pub. by Dr. Anderson, 1938);
An Historical Outline of the Negro in Travis
County (Samuel Houston Coll., 1940); Humorous
Folktales of the South-Carolina Negro (S.C.
Folklore Guild, vol. 1, 1945); The Word of the Brazos (U. of Tex.
Pr., 1953); Dog Ghosts and Other Texas Negro Folk Tales (U. of
Tex. Pr., 1958); North Carolina Negro Oral Narratives (N.C. Folk-
lore Soc., 1961); Worser Days and Better Times (Quadrangle, 1965);
American Negro Folklore (Quadrangle, 1968); American Negro Folk-
lore, Ed. (Quadrangle, 1968). Anthol.: The Illustrated Book of
American Folklore; Texas Folk and Texas Folklore: A Treasury of
American Anecdotes; The Book of Negro Folklore; Laughing on the
Outside; The Book of Negro Humor; African Animal Tales; Black Ex-
pression: Encyclopedia of Black Folklore and Humor; Mother Wit
from the Laughing Barrel; More of the Work on the Brazos. Period.:
The Negro American Magazine, 1934; Crisis, 1941; Journal of Ameri-
can Folklore, 1947; New Mexico Quarterly Review, 1946; Southern
Folklore Quarterly, 1948; Dallas Morning News, 1943; Ebony, 1948;
Interracial Review, 1959, 1962; Phylon, 1945.
HONORS AND AWARDS: Grant-in-aid, Gen. Educ. Bd.; Amer. Philos.
Soc.; Piedmont U. Center (for res. at Lib. of Congress, Nat'l.
Lib. Mexico, & Nat'l. U. of Mex.). The Word on the Brazos, called
by the New York Times, "the best book of Negro stories that has
made its appearance in this country in twenty-seven years." His
Worser Days and Better Times, which the Charlotte Observer called
"the most valuable volume of North Carolina Negro folklore that
has been printed since the time of Charles Chesnutt...." At 21st
Annual Writers Roundup, Austin, Tex., Nov. 27, 1969, American Ne-
gro Folklore was awarded "one of outstanding books written by a
Texan during the year"; and in May, 1968, was selected at the
Chicago Book Fair as one of the 60 best books published in the
United States in the year 1968" (Author).
MEMBER: Res. Com., Amer. Folklore Soc.; Texas Inst. of Letters;
Nat'l. Folk Festival Assn. (Bd. of Dir.); S. Central M.L.A.;
Louisiana Folklore Soc.

SIDELIGHTS: "...rated by American Folklore Scholars and literary critics as America's most distinguished Negro folklorist, and one of the four leading folktale authors writing in this country today, regardless of race, creed, or color" (Author).
Sources. Author inform.

BRIMMER, ANDREW FELTON. 1926- . Economist, Governmental Official

Biographical-Personal. Born Sept. 13, 1926, in Newellton, La. Son of Andrew and Vellar [Davis] Brimmer. Educ.: Tensas Parish Training Sch., St. Joseph, La.; B.A. (Econ.), M.A., 1951, U. of Wash.; Ph.D., Harvard, 1957. Family: m. Doris Millicent Scott July 18, 1953 (then grad. student at Radcliffe); d. Esther Diane.

Career-Professional. Economist, Fed. Reserve Bank, N.Y., 1955-58; Tchr.; Harvard, City Coll. of N.Y.; U. of Cal., Berkeley; Mich. State U.; Res. at M.I.T., Center for Internat. Stud. & Wharton Sch. of Finance, U. of Pa.; Apptd. Deputy Asst. Secy. for Econ. Affairs, U.S. Dept. of Commerce, 1963; Asst. Secy., 1965; Apptd. to Bd. of governors of Fed. Reserve Bd., 1966.

WRITINGS: Life Insurance Companies in the Capital Markets (Michigan State U. Pr., 1962); When the Marching Stopped, an analysis of Black Issues in the Seventies (Nat'l. Urban League, 1973). Period.: Banker, Journal of Finance, Review of Economics and Statistics.

HONORS AND AWARDS: Fulbright Fellow, Universities of Bombay & Delhi (India) 1951-52. Named Government Man of the Year by Nat'l. Bus. League, 1963. Arthur S. Fleming Award for outstanding contribution to public service, 1966. Russworm Award of Nat'l. Newspaper Pub. Assn. 1966. Pub. Serv. Award of Capital Pr. Club, 1966. Received Golden Plate Award of Amer. Acad. of Achievement in 1967.

SIDELIGHTS: Assisted in preparation of Dept. of Commerce testimony on discrimination in interstate commerce. Has been particularly interested in impact of desegregation on members of Black middle class (Current Biography, 1968).

Sources. Current Biography, 1968, Ed. by Charles Moritz (H. W. Wilson, 1968); Negro Handbook, Comp. by ed. of Ebony (Johnson Pub., 1966).

BROOKE, EDWARD WILLIAM. 1919- . United States Senator

Biographical-Personal. Born Oct. 26, 1919, in Wash., D.C. Son of Edward W. (lawyer) and Helen [Seldon] Brooke. Educ.: B.S., Howard U., 1941; LL.B., 1948, LL.M., 1949, Boston U. Law Sch.

Brooks, Gwendolyn Elizabeth

Family: m. Remigia Ferrari-Scacco, June 7, 1947; div. 1977; d. Remi Cynthia, d. Edwina Helene. Mailing address: Senate Office Bldg., Wash., D.C. 20510.

Career-Professional. Officer, World War II; Attorney, Boston; Attorney Gen. of Mass., 1963-67; U.S. Senator, Mass., 1967- .

WRITINGS: The Challenge of Change: Crisis in Our Two-Party System (Little, Brown, 1966). Ed., Boston U. Law Review.

HONORS AND AWARDS: He won the Bronze Star and Combat Infantryman's Badge in World War II. Jr. Chamber of Commerce named him One of the Ten Outstanding Young Men of Greater Boston in 1952; NAACP Spingarn Medal, 1967; Charles Evans Hughes award for "courageous leadership in governmental service," Nat'l. Conf. of Christians and Jews, 1967. Former: Pres., Boston Opera Co.; Fellow, Amer. Acad. of Arts & Sci.; Trus., Boston U.

MEMBER: Nat'l. Assn. of Attorneys Gen.; Nat'l. Assn. of Dist. Attorneys; Amer., Mass., & Boston bar assns.

SIDELIGHTS: "Given a crash course in Italian, was sent behind enemy lines to serve as liaison officer with Italian partisans. Became Republican when he cross-filed for state representative in both parties and lost Democratic nomination. First elective office was Attorney General of Massachusetts. He was sworn in as the 35th Attorney General of Massachusetts on January 16, 1963. In January 1967 Brooke became the first Negro to be seated in the U.S. Senate during the 20th Century. It was all the more impressive because although a Republican and a Protestant, he was elected to the Senate from Massachusetts, a state that has only 2% Negro population and whose voters are predominately Catholics of Irish descent and members of the Democratic Party" (Current Biography).

Sources. Current Biography, 1967, Ed. by Charles Moritz (H. W. Wilson, 1967).

BROOKS, GWENDOLYN ELIZABETH. 1917- . Poet

Biographical-Personal. Born June 7, 1917, in Topeka, Kan. D. of David Anderson and Keziah [Wims] Brooks. Educ.: Chgo. public schs.; Wilson Jr. Coll., 1936; L.H.D. (hon.), Columbia Coll., Chgo., 1964. Family: m. Henry L. Blakely, Sept. 17, 1939; son, Henry L., d. Nora. Mailing address: 7428 S. Evans Ave., Chgo., Ill. 60619.

Career-Professional. Tchr., Creative Writing & Poetry, Columbia Coll., Elmhurst Coll., & Northeastern Ill. State Coll. (all in Chgo.); City Coll. of N.Y.; U. of Wis.; Columbia U.

Brooks, Gwendolyn Elizabeth

WRITINGS: A Street in Bronzeville (Harper &
Row, 1945); Annie Allen, Pulitzer prize win-
ning poems (Harper & Row, 1949); Maud Martha,
novel (Harper & Row, 1953); Poetry: The Bean
Eaters (Harper & Row, 1960); Selected Poems
(Harper & Row, 1963); In the Mecca (Harper &
Row, 1968); The World of Gwendolyn Brooks
(Harper & Row, 1972); Report from Part One:
The Autobiography of Gwendolyn Brooks (Broad-
side Pr., 1972); The Tiger Who Wore White
Gloves (Third World Pr., 1974); Beckonings
(Broadside Pr., 1975); Bronzeville Boys and
Girls, for children (1956); Riot (Broadside
Pr., 1969); Family Pictures (1970); Alone-
ness (Broadside Pr., 1971); To Gwen With Love:
A Tribute to Gwendolyn Brooks (Johnson Pub.,
1971). Anthol.: For Malcolm; Black Voices; The Writing on the
Wall; Black Poetry; The Black Experience; A Native Sons Reader;
The Black Poets; Black Writers of America; Poetry of Black
America; Modern Black Poets; Understanding the New Black Poetry;
Jump Bad, Ed. (Broadside Pr., 1971); A Broadside Treasury, Ed.
(Broadside Pr., 1971). Period.: The Black Position, Ed. (No. 1,
1971; No. 2, 1972; No. 3, 1973, Broadside Pr.); Common Ground;
Ebony; Harper's; Negro Digest; The Negro Quarterly; Poetry.
HONORS AND AWARDS: Mademoiselle Merit Award (One of 10 Women of
the Year), 1945; Amer. Acad. of Arts & Letters (for creative writ-
ing), 1946; Guggenheim fellow, 1946, 1947; Poetry mag.'s Eunice
Tietjens Memorial Award, 1949; Pulitzer Prize for Poetry, 1950;
Anisfield-Wolf Award, 1969; Named Poet Laureate of State of Ill.;
Kuumba Award, 1969; Black Award, 1971; many hon. doctorates.
MEMBER: Inst. for Internat. Educ. (advis. bd.); Soc. for Midland
Authors; Ill. Art Counc.
SIDELIGHTS: First Black poet in the U.S. to win a Pulitzer Prize.
Miss Brooks has recently contributed to new Black self-image by
conducting writer's workshops for alienated youth, and by support-
ing the newer so-called revolutionary poets, as well as the new
Black Broadside Press.
Sources. Black American Literature-Poetry, Ed. by Darwin T. Turner
(Merrill, 1969); Black Voices, Ed. by Abraham Chapman (New Amer.
Lib., 1968); Broadside Authors and Artists, Comp. by Leoanead P.
Bailey (Broadside Pr., 1974); Cavalcade, Ed. by Arthur P. Davis &
Saunders Redding (Houghton Mifflin, 1971); Kaleidoscope, Ed. by
Robert Hayden (Harcourt, 1967); Poetry of Black America, Ed. by
Arnold Adoff (Harper & Row, 1973); Soon, One Morning, Ed. by Her-
bert Hill (Knopf, 1963); Who's Who in America, 37th ed. 1972-73
(Marquis, 1972); Books in Print Supplement, 1975-76 (Bowker,
1976).

Brown, Cecil

BROWN, CECIL. Novelist
Biographical-Personal. Mailing address: 2711 Virginia, Berkeley,
    Cal.
Career-Professional. Writer; Playwright; Prof., Univ. of Cal.,
    Berkeley.
    WRITINGS: The Life and Loves of Mr. Jiveass Nigger (Farrar,
    Straus & Giroux, 1969).
Sources. New Black Voices, Ed. by Abraham Chapman (New Amer. Lib.,
    1972).

BROWN, CLAUDE. 1937- . Writer
Biographical-Personal. Born Feb. 23, 1937, in
    N.Y.C. Son of Henry Lee and Ossie [Brock]
    Brown. Educ.: B.A., Howard U., 1965; Stan-
    ford U. Law Sch.; Rutgers U. Law Sch. Fam-
    ily: m. Helen Jones, Sept. 9, 1961. Mailing
    address: 2736 8th Ave., N.Y., N.Y. 10039.
Career-Professional. Wrote plays performed by
    Afro-Amer. Negro Theater Guild, 1960-61.
    Mem. of Harlem Improvement Project Group.
    WRITINGS: Manchild in the Promised Land
    (Macmillan, 1965); The Children of Ham
    (Stein & Day, 1976).
    SIDELIGHTS: "After being a juvenile delin-
    quent, dropping out of school, and being in-
    carcerated in several reform schools, he de-
cided to return to school. He attended and graduated from Washington Irving Evening High School (1957). He obtained a grant
from the Metropolitan Community Methodist Church and went to Howard University..." (Current Biography Yearbook, 1967).
Sources. Cavalcade, Ed. by Arthur P. Davis & Saunders Redding
    (Houghton Mifflin, 1971); Current Biography, Yearbook, 1967, Ed.
    by Charles Moritz (H. W. Wilson, 1968); Who's Who in America,
    37th ed., 1972-73 (Marquis, 1972); Books in Print, Supplement,
    1975-76 (Bowker, 1976).

BROWN, FRANK LONDON. 1927-1962. Novelist, Short Story Writer
Biographical-Personal. Born Oct. 17, 1927, in Kan. City, Mo. Educ.:
    Wilberforce U.; Kent Coll. of Law, Chgo.; B.A., Roosevelt U.,
    1951; further study, U. of Chgo. Family: m. Evelyn Marie Brown;
    d. Debra, d. Cheryl, d. Pamela. Died 1962.
Career-Professional. Machinist, Union Organizer, Govt. Employee,
    Jazz Singer, Journalist, and Ed. Appeared with Thelonius Monk at
    "Gate of Horn" in Chgo.; in the "Five Spot" in N.Y.; Assoc. ed.,
    Ebony.
    WRITINGS: Trumbull Park, novel (Regnery, 1959); Pub. articles &
    short stories in: Downbeat, Chicago Review, Ebony, Negro Digest,
    Chicago Tribune, Chicago Sun-Times, and Southwest Review.

Brown, Roscoe C., Jr.

HONORS AND AWARDS: John Hay Whitney Award for creative writing; U. of Chgo. Fellow. SIDELIGHTS: Was the first to read short stories, rather than poetry, to jazz accompaniment. At the time of his death, at 34, was working on revised draft of second novel; was director of Union Leadership Prog. at U. of Chgo.; and was completing doctorate in political science (<u>Black Voices</u>).
Sources. <u>American Negro Short Stories</u>, Ed. by John Henrik Clarke (Hill & Wang, 1966); <u>Black Voices</u>, Ed. by Abraham Chapman (New Amer. Lib., 1968); Pub. inform.

BROWN, MARGERY. Juvenile Author
Biographical-Personal. Born in Durham, N.C. D. of John Leonidas and Margaret [Hervey] Wheeler. <u>Educ.</u>: B.A., Spelman Coll.; Art stud., Ohio State U., 1932-34. <u>Family</u>: m. Richard E. Brown, Dec. 22, 1936 (dec.); d. Janice (Mrs. Jan E. Carden). <u>Mailing address</u>: 245 Reynolds Terrace, Orange, N.J. 07050.
Career-Professional. Art tchr., Newark, N.J., 1948- ; Currently tchg. at an inner city sch.
WRITINGS: (All books self-illustrated.) <u>That Ruby</u> (Reilly & Lee, 1969); <u>Animals Made by Me</u> (Putnam, 1970). Contrib.: <u>Life</u> and <u>School Arts</u>. Illustrator: G. Allred, <u>Old Crackfoot</u> (Obolensky, 1965); Elberta Stone, <u>I'm Glad I'm Me</u> (Putnam, 1971).
Sources. <u>Something About the Author</u>, Ed. by Anne Commire (Gale Res., 1973).

BROWN, ROSCOE C., JR. 1922- . Editor, Radio and Television Host
Biographical-Personal. Born Mar. 9, 1922, in Wash., D.C. <u>Educ.</u>: B.S., Springfield Coll. (Mass.); M.A., Ph.D., N.Y.U. <u>Family</u>: m. Josephine; d. Doris, d. Diane, son, Dennis, son, Donald. <u>Mailing address</u>: N.Y.U., Wash. Pl., N.Y., N.Y. 10003.
Career-Professional. Dir. Inst. of Afro-Amer. Affairs, N.Y.U.; Host: Weekly TV ser., "Black Arts"; Weekly radio ser., "Soul of Reason"; Co-host, Jersey City State Coll. TV prog., "Black Letters."
WRITINGS: Co-ed., <u>Negro Almanac</u> (Bellwether, 1967); co-author, <u>Classical Studies in Physical Activity</u> (1968); co-author, <u>New Perspectives of Man in Action</u> (1969). Contrib.: More than 50 articles on educ. & physical fitness for various publications.
Source. <u>1000 Successful Blacks</u>, Eds. of <u>Ebony</u> (Johnson Pub., 1973).

Brown, Sterling Allen

BROWN, STERLING ALLEN. 1901- . Poet, Critic, Scholar

Biographical-Personal. Born May 1, 1901, in Wash., D.C. Son of a Howard U. Prof. Educ.: Williams Coll., Phi Beta Kappa, 1921; M.A., Harvard U., 1923. Family: m. in 1919. Mailing address: 1222 Kearney, N.E., Wash., D.C.

Career-Professional. Lit. Ed., Opportunity; bk. reviewer; Ed., Negro Affairs for Fed. Writers' Project, 1936-39; Staff mem., Carnegie-Myrdal Study of the Negro, 1939; Prof. of Eng., Howard U.; Vis. Prof., N.Y.U., Atlanta U., & Vassar Coll.

WRITINGS: Southern Road, poems (Harcourt, 1932; Beacon Pr., 1974); Outline for the Study of the Poetry of American Negroes (Assoc. in Negro Folk Educ., 1931); The Negro in American Fiction, criticism (Assoc. in Negro Folk Educ., 1937); Negro Poetry and Drama, criticism (Assoc. in Negro Folk Educ., 1937); The Negro Caravan, Ed. with Arthur P. Davis & Ulysses Lee (Dryden, 1941); The Last Ride of Wild Bill (Broadside Pr., 1974). Anthol.: The Poetry of the Negro, 1746-1949, rev. ed., 1746-1970; Afro-American Poetry; Black Writers of America; Understanding the New Black Poetry; The Poetry of Black America; You Better Believe It.

HONORS AND AWARDS: Guggenheim Fellow., 1937-38.

SIDELIGHTS: "Sterling A. Brown has probably done more than any other one person to influence and direct the course of Negro American writing" (Cavalcade).

John H. Clarke describes him in American Negro Short Stories as "the dean of American Negro poets." To Leopold Senghor, Pres. of Senegal, Brown and Langston Hughes were the "the most Negro" poets in American literature (Black Voices).

Sources. Black American Literature-Poetry, Ed. by Darwin T. Turner (Merrill, 1969); Black Insights, Ed. by Nick A. Ford (Ginn, 1971); Black Poets of the United States, Jean Wagner (U. of Ill. Pr., 1973); Black Voices, Ed. by Abraham Chapman (New Amer. Lib., 1968); Broadside Authors and Artists, Comp. by Leaonead P. Bailey (Broadside Pr., 1974); Cavalcade, Ed. by Arthur P. Davis & Saunders Redding (Houghton Mifflin, 1971).

BROWN, WILLIAM WELLS. 1816-1884. Abolitionist, Writer

Biographical-Personal. Born in 1816, near Lexington, Ky. Son of a white father and a mulatto mother. Educ.: Self-educated; studied medicine in Europe. Died 1884.

Career-Professional. Served under several masters and performed unusual kinds of work. Hired out to Elijah P. Lovejoy's newspaper

Bryant, F. J., Jr.

office in St. Louis; traveled up & down Ohio
& Miss. Rivers with riverboat captain master;
worked on steamboats on Lake Erie (helped
fugitive slaves to freedom). Agent, W.N.Y.
Anti-Slavery Soc., 1844-?; Agent, Mass. Anti-
Slavery Soc. (replacing Frederick Douglass).
Delegate to Paris Peace Conf. (remained in
Europe for several years because of harsh
fugitive slave law). Practiced medicine; be-
came writer
WRITINGS: The Escape, or a Leap for Freedom,
1st play by an American Negro (1858); The
Anti-Slavery Harp, Ed., collec. of abolitionist songs and poems. Major works: Narrative
of William W. Brown, a Fugitive Slave (Johnson repr. of 1847 ed., 1970); Three Years in
Europe (1852); Clotel; or the President's Daughter (1853); The
Black Man (1863); Black Man, His Antecedents, His Genius, and His
Achievements (Black Her., repr. of 1865); The Negro in the American Rebellion, His Heroism and His Fidelity (Basic Afro-Amer.
repr. of 1880 ed., 1969); The Rising Son (Bks. for Lib. repr. of
1874 ed., 1970); My Southern Home, or the South and Its People
(1880); Sketches of Places and People Abroad (Black Her., Bks. for
Lib., 1854).
SIDELIGHTS: On his second attempt to escape from slavery, he was
successful. He was helped by a Quaker named Wells Brown on his
way North; and promptly adopted the man's name. Brown was "the
first American Negro to write a novel, the first to write a play,
the first to write a book of travels, and among the first to write
history..." (Cavalcade).
Sources. Black American Literature-Essays, Ed. by Darwin T. Turner
(Merrill, 1969); Blackamerican Literature, Ed. by Ruth Miller
(Glencoe Pr., 1971); Cavalcade, Ed. by Arthur P. Davis & Saunders
Redding (Houghton Mifflin, 1971); Early Negro American Writers,
Benjamin Brawley (U. of N.C. Pr., 1935).

BRYANT, F. J., JR. 1942- . Poet
Biographical-Personal. Born 1942 in Phila., Pa. Educ.: Lincoln U.
(Pa.)
Career-Professional. Caseworker, Montgomery Mental Health Center.
Has had plays produced at Lincoln U.
WRITINGS: While Silence Sleeps, poetry (Windfall Press). Anthol.:
Black Fire (1968); The New Black Poetry (1969); To Gwen With Love
(1971); New Black Voices (1972); The Poetry of Black America
(1973). Period.: Journal of Black Poetry, Nickel Review & Negro
Digest/Black World.
HONORS AND AWARDS: Awarded Eichelburger Prize for prose and was
Poet Laureate of the school (both at Lincoln U.).

Bullins, Ed

Sources. <u>New Black Voices</u>, Ed. by Abraham Chapman (New Amer. Lib., 1972); <u>Poetry of Black America</u>, Ed. by Arnold Adoff (Harper & Row, 1973).

BULLINS, ED. 1935- . Playwright, Editor, Teacher, Activist
Biographical-Personal. Born July 2, 1935, in Phila., Pa. Son of Edward and Bertha Marie Bullins. <u>Mailing address</u>: 932 E. 212th St., Bronx, N.Y. 10469
Career-Professional. Formerly, Minister of Culture, Black Panther Party; playwright-in-residence, New Lafayette Theatre, N.Y.C.; Assoc. Ed., <u>The Drama Review</u>; Cofounder & Dir., Black Arts/West (community experiment in theater); Ed. <u>The Drama Review</u> (Summer 1968); Ed., <u>Black Theater Magazine</u>; Tchr. of Writing & Eng.: Fordham U.; Columbia U.; U. of Mass. (Boston); Bronx Community Coll.; Manhattan Community Coll., etc.
WRITINGS: "Has written more than thirty plays--some have been seen at the New Lafayette Theatre, LaMama, New Federal Theatre, The Public Theatre, Workshop of the Players Art, Lincoln Center, The American Place Theatre, etc." (Author). Plays: "The Ed Bullins' Plays," presented at American Place Theatre, 1968 were: <u>Clara's Old Man</u> (one-act), <u>The Electronic Nigger</u> (one-act), and <u>A Son Come Home</u> (one-act). Also <u>In New England Winter</u>, <u>In the Wine Time</u>, <u>Going A Buffalo</u>, <u>The Pig Sty</u>, <u>The Duplex</u> and <u>The Fabulous Miss Marie</u>. Also an autobiog. and <u>The Reluctant Rapist</u>, novel (Harper & Row, 1973). Anthol.: <u>New Plays from the Black Theater</u>. Period.: <u>The New York Times</u>, <u>Black World</u>, <u>The Drama Review</u>, <u>Performance</u>, <u>Illumination</u>, and <u>Wild Dog</u>, etc. "He continues to work on his projected series of twenty full-length plays, which he calls his 'Twentieth-Century Cycle,' six of them having been completed" (Author).
HONORS AND AWARDS: Drama Desk-Vernon Rice Award; Obie Award for Distinuighed Playwright; Guggenheim Fellow; Rockefeller Found. Playwriting Grant; Creative Artists Prog. Serv. (CAPS) Grant for Playwriting; NEA Grant for Playwriting.
SIDELIGHTS: "Has the unique distinction of working full time in the Black community as a playwright." Served literary apprenticeship in San Francisco's Black House. Assoc. with LeRoi Jones both in Black Arts Sch. & in film-making. "Bullins is a leader in the Black Experience school of Afro-American writing, and does not concern himself with whites, their stereotypes, nor their values" (<u>New Black Playwrights</u>).
Sources. Author inform.; <u>Black Scenes</u>, Ed. by Alice Childress (Doubleday, 1971); <u>Forgotten Pages of American Literature</u>, Ed. by Gerald W. Haslam (Houghton Mifflin, 1970); <u>New Black Playwrights</u>, Ed. by William Couch, Jr. (Avon, 1970); <u>The New Black Poetry</u>, Ed. by Clarence Major (Internat., 1969).

BUNCHE, RALPH JOHNSON. 1904-1971. Diplomat, Educator, Scholar

Biographical-Personal. Born Aug. 7, 1904, in Detroit, Mich. Son of Fred (barber) and Olive Agnes [Johnson] Bunche, (reared by grandmother, Mrs. Lucy Johnson). Educ.: B.A., UCLA (Polit. Sci., summa cum laude, valedictorian, Phi Beta Kappa), 1927; M.A., 1928, Ph.D. (Govt. & Internat. Relat.), Harvard U., 1934; Northwestern U., 1936; London Sch. of Econ., 1937; Capetown U., S. Africa (2-yr. post-doctoral fellow, Anthropology & Colonial Policy), 1937. Family: m. Ruth Harris, June 23, 1930; son, Ralph, Jr., d. Joan, d. Jane (Mrs. Burton Pierce). Died Dec. 9, 1971.

Career-Professional. Head, Dept. of Polit. Sci., Howard U.; 1st Black Prof. at Harvard U.; Investigator, Imperialism, Africa (Soc. Sci. Res. Counc. Fellow); Staff mem., Carnegie-Myrdal Study of the Negro (led to Gunnar Myrdal's An American Dilemma); During World War II was Spec., Africa, OSS; Assoc., Chief of Dependent Areas, State Dept.; UN Trusteeship Div., selected to represent UN's Secy.-Gen. in Arab-Israeli crisis; Became Acting Mediator when Count Folke Bernadotte was assassinated in 1948; Apptd. UN Under Secy. for Sepc. Polit. Affairs, 1955 (America's highest-ranking mem. of UN Secretariat); Spec. peace envoy, Revolution in Congo, 1960.

WRITINGS: A World View of Race (1936), The Political Status of the Negro in the Age of FDR, Ed. by Dewey W. Grantham (U. of Chgo. Pr., 1975). Articles in scholarly mags.

HONORS AND AWARDS: Some 50 hon. degrees. Tappan Prize, Harvard U., for best doctoral dissertation in soc. sci., 1934 (title: "French Administration in Togoland and Dahomey"); Nobel Peace Prize; One World Award; Spingarn Medal; Four Freedoms Award; Pres. Freedom Medal; Ralph Bunche Hall (Soc. Sci. Bldg., UCLA).

MEMBER: Oberlin Coll. trus.; Roosevelt U. trus.; Harvard U. Bd. of Overseers; Pres., Amer. Polit. Sci. Assn.; Trus., Rockefeller Found.

SIDELIGHTS: "First American Negro to win the Nobel Peace Prize, Ralph Bunche is an internationally acclaimed statesman whose record of achievement places him among the most significant American diplomats of the 20th century. Bunche received the coveted award in 1950 for his role in effecting a cease-fire in the Arab-Israeli dispute which threatened to engulf the entire Middle East in armed conflict" (Negro Almanac).

"U Thant (UN Secy. Gen.) appraised Dr. Bunche as 'an international institution in his own right, transcending both nationality and race in a way that is achieved by very few'" (Los Angeles Times).

Burrell, Evelyn [Patterson]

   Bunche has said, "One must believe that man can be saved--or
salvaged--from his inevitable follies, that all problems of human
relations are solvable...that conflict situations, however deep-
seated, bitter and prolonged, can be resolved; that a world at
peace is, in fact, attainable.
   "Otherwise one's work, all diplomacy, the United Nations itself,
become a fateful travesty and all mankind would be doomed" (Los
Angeles Times).
Sources. Los Angeles Herald Examiner, Dec. 9, 1971; Historical Negro
   Biographies, Wilhelmena S. Robinson (ASNLH, 1967); L. A. Sentinel,
   Dec. 16, 1971; L. A. Times, Dec. 10, 1971; Negro Almanac, Comp. by
   Harry A. Ploski & Ernest Kaiser (Bellwether, 1971); Negro Caravan,
   Ed. by Sterling A. Brown & Others (Arno Pr. & N. Y. Times, 1971);
   Negroes in Public Affairs & Government, Ed. by Walter Christmas
   (Educational Heritage, 1966); Books in Print, Supplement, 1975-76
   (Bowker, 1976).

BURRELL, EVELYN [PATTERSON]. Poet, English
Teacher
Biographical-Personal. Born in Baltimore, Md.
   Educ.: B.A. (Eng., magna cum laude), Morgan
   State Coll., Baltimore, 1959; M.A. (Eng.),
   Howard U., 1966, further study Afro-Amer.
   Stud., 1970-73. Mailing address: 3721 Gwynn
   Oak Ave., Baltimore, Md. 21207.
Career-Professional. Asst. Prof., Eng., Coppin
   State Coll., Baltimore; Asst. Prof., Eng.,
   Bowie State Coll., Bowie, Md.; Lectr., Afro-
   Amer. Lit., Howard U.; Lectr., Afro-Amer.
   Lit., Hood Coll., Frederick, Md.; Poet-in-
   Residence, Baltimore Pub. Schs. (Md. Arts
   Counc.): Conductor, Poetry Workshop, Rich-
   mond, Va. Intercultural Center for the Hu-
   manities (Poet-in-Residence Ser.).
WRITINGS: Weep No More, poems (Burton-Johns, 1973); Son to Mother,
poems (Richmond Intercultural Center for Humanities, Individual
Reading Ser., 1974). Weep No More, enlarged ed. (Burton-Johns,
1975) & collec. of speeches & lectures (Burton-Johns). Anthol.:
The Soul and the Singer (Young Pub., 1969); Anthology of American
Poetry-Book X (Wright, 1971); Yearbook of Modern Poetry (Young
Pub., 1972). Period.: Negro History Bulletin, Mar. 1971; Au
Verso 8 (St. John's Coll., Santa Fe, N.M.).
HONORS AND AWARDS: Alpha Kappa Mu Honor Soc.; Lambda Iota Tau
Honor Soc.; Theta Xi Chap.; Kappa Delta Pi Honor Soc.; Grad. fel-
low., Howard U.; Ford Found. Travel & Study grant.
MEMBER: Nat'l. Assn. of Humanities Educ.; Coll. Lang. Assn.;
Assn. for Study of Afro-Amer. Life & Hist.

Burroughs, Margaret G.

Sources. Pub. inform.; <u>Weep No More</u>, Evelyn P. Burrell (Burton-Johns, 1973).

BURRELL, WALTER PRICE, JR. 1944- . Publicist, Journalist, Play-wright
Biographical-Personal. Born Nov. 4, 1944, in Portsmouth, Va. <u>Educ</u>.:
  A.A. (Eng. & Music), Compton Coll., Cal.; B.A. (Eng.), Hampton
  Inst.; M.A. (Creative Writing), UCLA. <u>Family</u>: m. Enola; chil-
  dren: Tracey, Mario. <u>Mailing address</u>: P.O. Box 900, Beverly
  Hills, Cal. 90213.
Career-Professional. Unit-publicist, 20th Century-Fox Studios, Hol-
  lywood, Cal.; Mag. writer & columnist; Producer-Moderator (own
  syndicated radio show), "The Record." Actor (own plays) <u>All For A</u>
  <u>Place</u>; <u>Free, Black and 21</u>.
  WRITINGS: <u>Whatever Turns You On</u>; <u>The Black Entertainer Speaks</u>
  <u>Out</u>; <u>Poems of a Triple Scorpio</u>. Plays: <u>All For a Place</u>; <u>Free,</u>
  <u>Black and 21</u>.
Source. <u>1000 Successful Blacks</u>, Eds. of Ebony (Johnson Pub., 1973).

BURROUGHS, MARGARET G. 1917- . Artist,
Teacher, Museum Director, Writer
Biographical-Personal. Born Nov. 1, 1917, in
  St. Rose, La. D. of Alexander and Octavia
  [Pierre] Taylor. <u>Educ</u>.: Chgo. Normal Coll.,
  1935-37 (Elementary Tchrs. Certificate), 1939
  (Upper Grade Art Certificate); B.A.E., Art
  Inst. of Chgo., 1946, M.A.E., 1948; Esmerelda
  Art Sch., Mexico City, 1953; Columbia U.,
  Tchrs. Coll. (Post grad., summers), 1958-60.
  <u>Family</u>: 1st m. Bernard Goss, 1939 (div.
  1947), d. Gayle Goss Toller; 2nd m. Charles G.
  Burroughs (Mus. curator), 1949; son, Paul Bur-
  roughs. <u>Mailing address</u>: 3806 S. Mich.
  Ave., Chgo., Ill. 60653.
      Career-Professional. Tchr., Chgo., 1940-46; Art
Tchr., 1946- ; Founder, Dir., Mus. of African-Amer. Hist., 1961- ;
Asst. Prof., African & African-Amer. Art Hist., Chgo. Art Inst.,
1968; Asst. Prof., Humanities, Kennedy-King Coll., Chgo. (Present).
WRITINGS: <u>Jasper The Drummin' Boy</u>, juvenile, self-illustrated
(Viking, 1947); Anthol.: <u>Did You Feed My Cow?</u>, self-illustrated
(Crowell, 1955); <u>Whip Me Whop Me Pudding</u> (Praga, 1966); <u>What Shall</u>
<u>I Tell My Children?</u> (Davidson, 1968). Ed.: <u>For Malcolm</u>, with
Dudley Randall (Broadside Pr., 1969); "Prints for Peace," <u>Souvenir</u>
<u>Journal of Emancipation Centennial</u>. Period.: <u>Chicago Schools</u>
<u>Journal</u>; <u>Elementary English Journal</u>; <u>School Arts Magazine</u>; <u>Freedom-</u>
<u>ways</u>; in Assoc. Negro Press.
HONORS AND AWARDS: Print, Hon. mention, Atlanta U., 1947; 1st
Watercolor Purchase Award, Atlanta U., 1955; Best in Show Hallmark

Butcher, Margaret Just

Award, Lincoln U., Mo., 1962; NEH Fellow, Intern in Mus. Prac-
tices, Field Mus., Chgo., 1967-68; Ph.D. (Dr. of Honoris Causis),
Lewis Coll., Lockport, Ill., 1972.
MEMBER: New Crusader Negro Hist. Hall of Fame (Res. Dir.),
1960-62; State of Ill. Centennial of Emancipation Com., 1963;
Founder, Coord., Annual Lake Meadows Outdoor Arts & Crafts Fair,
1957- ; Founder, Ebony Mus. of Negro Hist. and Art, Chgo., 1961;
Amer. Forum, Internat. Study, U. of Ghana, 1969, U. of W. Indies,
Jamaica, 1970; Urban Gateways Bd., 1972; Governor's Com. on Fi-
nancing the Arts, State of Ill., 1971; Bd. mem. South Side Art
Center, 1971-72; Hull House Assn. of Chgo., 1973.
SIDELIGHTS: Travel in Mexico, USSR, Poland, Czechoslovakia,
Ghana, Togo, Dahomey, Nigeria, Ivory Coast, Ethiopia, Kenya, Tan-
zania, Egypt, Tunisia, Algeria, Morocco, Jamaica, Haiti, Trinidad.
Sources. Author inform.; Ebony (March 1974, Johnson Pub.); For Mal-
colm, Ed. by Dudley Randall & Margaret G. Burroughs (Broadside
Pr., 1969); Contemporary Authors (Gale Res., 1965).

BUTCHER, MARGARET JUST. 1913- . English
Teacher
Biographical-Personal. Born Apr. 28, 1913 in
  Wash., D.C. D. of Ernest Everett Just (bi-
  ologist). Educ.: Ph.D., Boston U., 1947.
  Family: m. James W. Butcher; d. Sheryl
  Everett.
Career-Professional. Tchr., Va. Union U.,
  1935-36; Tchr., public schs., Wash., D.C.;
  Prof., Engl., Howard U., 1942- ; Fulbright
  Vis. Prof. in Amer. Lit., Universities of
  Grenoble, Lyon & Dijon, in France, 1949-50.
  WRITINGS: The Negro in American Culture
  (Knopf, 1956; New Amer. Lib., paper, 1971).
  Has contrib. many articles to periodicals.
  MEMBER: Wash., D.C. Bd. of Educ., 1953-56.
SIDELIGHTS: "The late Alain Leroy Locke was working on (The Ne-
gro in American Culture) at the time of his death, and Dr. Butcher
has completed it brilliantly along the lines he had laid down"
(Book jacket).
Source. The Negro in American Culture (Knopf, 1956).

BUTCHER, PHILIP. 1918- . English Professor
Biographical-Personal. Born Sept. 28, 1918, in Wash., D.C. Educ.:
  B.A., 1942, M.A., 1947, Howard U.; Ph.D., Columbia U., 1956.
  Family: m. Ruth, d. Wendy, d. Mrs. Laurel B. Miles. Mailing Ad-
  dress: Morgan State Coll., Baltimore, Md. 21239.
Career-Professional. Tchr., Eng., Morgan State Coll., 1947- .
  Dean, Grad. Sch. & Prof. of Eng., Morgan State.

Campbell, James Edwin

WRITINGS: George W. Cable: The Northampton Years (1959); George W. Cable (1962); The William Stanley Braithwaite Reader (1972). SIDELIGHTS: "He is a nationally recognized authority on the life of the writer, social critic and humanitarian, George Washington Cable, and is the author of more than 85 books, articles and reviews" (1000 Successful Blacks).
Source. 1000 Successful Blacks, Eds. of Ebony (Johnson Pub., 1973).

CAIN, GEORGE. 1943- . Novelist
Biographical-Personal. Born 1943, in Harlem, N.Y. Educ.: N.Y.C. schs.; Iona Coll. Family: m. Jo Lynne, 1968; d. Nataya. Lives in Bedford-Stuyvesant, Brooklyn, N.Y.
Career-Professional. Traveled to Cal., Mex. and Tex. Spent some time in prisons. Began writing in 1966.
WRITINGS: Blueschild Baby, novel (Dell, paper, 1970).
SIDELIGHTS: "The most important work of fiction by an Afro-American since Native Son" (New York Times Book Review. "It will be inevitably compared to Manchild in the Promised Land, perhaps to Soul On Ice. It can stand on its own, infused with pride and compassion and revolutionary fervor" (Publishers Weekly).
   "...in one sense, Blueschild Baby represents a synthesis of a number of black artistic and social concerns. As a fictional autobiography, it stands at the far end of a tradition that begins with the narrative of Briton Hammon, matures in the work of Frederick Douglass, expands with James Weldon Johnson's Autobiography of an Ex-Colored Man, and receives acknowledgement during the early sixties in the works of Claude Brown and Malcolm X..." (Singers of Daybreak).
Source. Blueschild Baby (Dell, 1970); Singers of Daybreak; Studies in Black American Literature, Houston A. Baker, Jr. (Howard U. Pr., 1974).

CAMPBELL, JAMES EDWIN. c.1860-c.1905. Poet
Biographical-Personal. Born c. 1860 in Pomeroy, Ohio. Educ.: Miami Coll. Died c. 1905.
Career-Professional. Engaged in newspaper work; one of a group that issued Four O'clock Magazine (lit. public.).
WRITINGS: Echoes from the Cabin and Elsewhere, poems.
SIDELIGHTS: "...it appears that he was the first Aframerican poet to work in the dialect.... He also attempted poetry in literary English..." (Book of American Negro Poetry).
Sources. Book of American Negro Poetry, Ed. by James W. Johnson, rev. ed. (Harcourt, 1959); Negro Caravan, Ed. by Sterling A. Brown & Others (Arno Pr. & New York Times, 1969).

Carmichael, Stokely

CARMICHAEL, STOKELY. 1941- . Black Power Advocate

Biographical-Personal. Born June 29, 1941, in Port-of-Spain, Trinidad, Brit. W. Indies. Son of Adolphus (carpenter) and Mabel F. Carmichael. Educ.: Bronx High Sch. of Sci. (N.Y.C.): B.A. (Philosophy), Howard U., 1964. Family: m. Miriam Makeba (S. African-born singer), April 1968. Mailing address: Conakry, Guinea, W. Africa.

Career-Professional. Organizer, SNCC; Field Organizer, Voter Registration, Lowndes Co., Miss.; Organized all-Black Lowndes Co. Freedom Org.; Dir., Civil Rights activities, Miss. Summer Project, 1964; Prime Minister, Black Panthers.

WRITINGS: Black Power, with Charles V. Hamilton (Random House, 1967); Stokely Speaks: Black Power to Pan-Africanism (Random House, 1971).

SIDELIGHTS: "The slogan 'Black Power,' most popular rallying cry of black liberation groups in the United States in the late 1960's, was coined, or at least popularized, by Stokely Carmichael when he was Chairman of the Student Nonviolent Coordinating Committee, in 1966. He served as prime minister of the guerilla-like, urban North-oriented Black Panthers until 1969. Since late 1968, Carmichael, a Pan-Africanist, has spent most of his time in self-imposed exile in Guinea, W. Africa" (Current Biography, 1970).

Sources. Black Power, Stokely Carmichael & Charles V. Hamilton (Random House, 1967); Current Biography, 1970, Ed. by Charles Moritz (H. W. Wilson, 1970).

CARTER, RUBIN (Hurricane). Biographer, Athlete, Boxer

Career-Professional.

WRITINGS: The Sixteenth Round, autobiog. (Viking, 1974).

SIDELIGHTS: "On May 26, 1967, the Spiraling career of Rubin 'Hurricane' Carter, then the top contender for the middleweight boxing title of the world, came to a shuddering and tragic halt: he was convicted of the murder of three white people in a Paterson, New Jersey, Bar.... For the last seven years Rubin Carter has been #45472 of Rahway State Prison, New Jersey. Though he maintained his innocence throughout his long, highly emotional trial--at which he says he was not given the full protection of his constitutional rights--he was sentenced to triple life imprisonment. In The Sixteenth Round, the Rube pulls no punches. Writing in a language and style all his own, he supplies electrifying descriptions of his fights both in and out of the ring; his stories of the hell that is life in prison are unmatched in contemporary literature.

His book is a scathing indictment of the prison system he grew up in and out of, a tingling, soul-stirring, and slyly humorous account of his remarkable life" (Pub. inform.).
Source. Pub. inform.

CARTER, WILMOTH ANNETTE. Educator
Biographical-Personal. Born in Reidsville, N.C. D. of Dr. W. Percy and Maggie Lee [Milner] Carter. Educ.: B.A. (Eng.), Shaw U.; M.A. (Sociol.), Atlanta U., 1942; Ph.D. (Sociol.), U. of Chgo., 1959. Family: Single. Mailing address: 1400 E. Davie St., Raleigh, N.C.
Career-Professional. Assoc. Prof., Sociol., 1950-57, Prof. Sociol. 1959-63, Chmn., Dept. of Sociol., Southern U., New Orleans, 1963-64; Res. Assoc., Race Relat., U. of Mich. & Tuskegee Inst., 1964-66; Prof. of Sociol. & Dir. Div. of Soc. Sci., Shaw U., 1966-69; Distinguished Prof. of Urban Sci. & Dir. of Inst. Res., 1969-   ; Educ. Develop. Officer & Prof. of Urban Sci., 1971-73; V. Pres. of Instruction, 1973-74; Sr. V. Pres. & V. Pres. of Res. & Evaluation, 1974-   .
WRITINGS: The Urban Negro in the South (Vantage Pr., 1961); The New Negro of the South (Exposition Pr., 1967); Shaw's Universe (National Pub., 1973). Period.: Phylon, 1944, 1960; AME Church Review, July-Sept., 1961; Shawensis, 1969, 1970.
HONORS AND AWARDS: Alpha Omicron Honor Soc., Alpha Kappa Delta; Rosenwald Fellow, 1947-48; Danforth Found. Fellow, 1957-59; Delta Kappa Gamma, 1972.
MEMBER: Amer. Sociol. Assn.; S. Sociol. Soc.; Amer. Assn. of U. Profs.; Amer. Assn. of U. Women; Nat'l. Counc. of Women; Voters League; N.Y. Acad. of Sci.
SIDELIGHTS: Travel in Germany, France, Spain, Italy, Switzerland, Egypt, Lebanon, Jordan, Israel (Author).
Sources. Author inform.

CAYTON, HORACE R. 1903-1970. Sociologist, Researcher
Biographical-Personal. Born Apr. 12, 1903, in Seattle, Wash. Son of Horace R. (newspaperman) and Susie [Revels] Cayton. Educ.: B.A. (sociol.), U. of Wash., 1931; Grad. study: U. of Chgo., 1931-34; N.Y.U., 1956; Inst. for Psychoanalysis. Family: Divorced. Died 1970.
Career-Professional. Instr., Econ., Fisk U., 1935-36; Res. Asst. & Instr., Dept. of Anthropology, U. of Chgo., 1936-37; Dir., Parkway Community House, Chgo., Ill., 1939-49; Study of the Jewish Family, Amer. Jewish Com., N.Y., 1950-51; Corresp. to UN, Pittsburgh Courier, Pittsburgh, Pa., 1952-54; Res. Assoc., Nat'l. Counc. of

Chandler, Sue P.

Churches, N.Y., 1954-58; Lectr. in Sociol., City Coll. of N.Y., 1957-58; Spec. Asst., N.Y. Com. of Welfare, 1958-59; Res. Asst. for Study in Geriatric Mental Illness, Langley Porter Clinic, San Francisco, 1959-60; Inst. for Study of Crime & Delinquency, Internat. Survey of Correction, Berkeley, Cal., 1960-61. WRITINGS: Black Workers and the New Unions, with George S. Mitchell (U. of N.C. Pr., 1935); Black Metropolis, with St. Clair Drake (Harcourt, 1945); Social Work and the Church, with S. M. Nishi (Nat'l. Counc. of Churches, 1956). Contrib. to various books. Regular columnist for Pittsburgh Courier for 20 years. Period.: New Republic, Nation, Holiday, American Journal of Sociology, New York Times, Chicago Tribune, Chicago Sun-Times, Opportunity. HONORS AND AWARDS: Anisfield-Wolf Award (shared with St. Clair Drake) for Black Metropolis, as best scholarly book on race relations (N.Y. Public Lib. named this book Outstanding Book on Race Relations for 1945); Julius Rosenwald Fund Fellow, 1937-39. MEMBER: Bd. of Dir., Chgo. Counc. of Soc. Agencies, 1939-49. SIDELIGHTS: "Mr. Cayton's essays on mental illness, race relations, and religion have been included in several important studies..." (Soon, One Morning).
Sources. Anger and Beyond, Herbert Hill (Harper & Row, 1966); Contemporary Authors, Vols. 13-14, Ed. by James M. Ethridge & Barbara Kopala (Gale Res., 1965); Current Biography, 1946, Ed. by Ann Rothe (H. W. Wilson, 1947); Soon, One Morning, Ed. by Herbert Hill (Knopf, 1968).

CHANDLER, SUE P. Writer
Biographical-Personal. Born Nashville, Tenn.
Career-Professional.
    WRITINGS: Living Black American Authors, Comp. with Ann Shockley (Bowker, 1973).
Source. Living Black American Authors, Comps. Ann A. Shockley & Sue P. Chandler (Bowker, 1973).

CHESNUTT, CHARLES WADDELL. 1858-1932. Novelist, Short Story Writer
Biographical-Personal. Born in 1858, in Cleveland, Ohio. Educ.: Largely self-educated; studied law and passed Ohio State Bar (with unusually high score), never practiced. Died in 1932.
Career-Professional. Stenographer, Dow Jones, N.Y.; Commercial & Legal Stenographer, Cleveland.
    WRITINGS: "The Goophered Grapevine," short story (Atlantic Monthly, 1887); The Conjure Woman, novel (1889); The Wife of His Youth,

Childress, Alice

and Other Stories of the Color Line, short
stories (1889); Frederick Douglass (Johnson
repr. of 1899 ed.); The House Behind the
Cedars, novel (1900); The Marrow of Tradition, novel (1901); The Colonel's Dream,
novel (1905); Conjure Tales, retold by Ray
Shepard (Dutton, 1973).
HONORS AND AWARDS: Received Spingarn Gold
Medal from NAACP in 1928 for "pioneer work as
a literary artist depicting the life and
struggle of Americans of African descent."
SIDELIGHTS: Chesnutt spent the years between
ages 8 and 25 in N.C., where he learned the
Negro folklore and folkways of the South, for
which he was to find literary expression.
"Commonly considered the first Negro writer
in the United States to master the short story form and the craft
of fiction" (Black Voices). "His most significant contribution to
American literature may be the tales of The Conjure Woman, based
on folklore which he heard in North Carolina" (Black American Lit-
erature-Fiction).
Sources. Black American Literature-Fiction, Ed. by Darwin T. Turner
(Merrill, 1969); Black Voices, Ed. by Abraham Chapman (New Amer.
Lib., 1968); Cavalcade, Ed. by Arthur P. Davis & Saunders Redding
(Houghton Mifflin, 1971); Forgotten Pages of American Literature,
Ed. by Gerald W. Haslam (Houghton Mifflin, 1970).

CHILDRESS, ALICE. 1920- . Playwright,
Actress, Director
Biographical-Personal. Born 1920, in Charles-
ton, S.C. Educ.: Studied acting at Amer.
Negro Theatre; Radcliffe Inst. Family: m.
Nathan Woodard; d. Jean Lee. Mailing ad-
dress: c/o Flora Roberts, Inc., 116 E. 59th
St., N.Y., N.Y.
Career-Professional. While acting and writing,
worked as apprentice machinist, photo-nega-
tive retoucher, governess, saleslady & in-
surance agent. Received Harvard U. appoint-
ment to Radcliffe Inst., 1966-68.
WRITINGS: Plays: Florence, one-act play;
Gold Through the Trees; Just a Little Simple
(adaption of Langston Hughes's Simple Speaks
His Mind); Trouble in Mind; Wedding Band; When the Rattlesnake
Sounds: A Play About Harriet Tubman, rev. ed. (Coward, 1975).
Others: Like One of the Family; Conversations from a Domestic's
Life, topical humour; Martin Luther King at Montgomery, Alabama;

Chisholm, Shirley Anita

Black Scenes (Zenith). Novel: A Hero Ain't Nothing But a Sandwich (C. McCann).
HONORS AND AWARDS: Obie Award for best original off-Broadway play, 1955-56 season; was produced twice by BBC in London.
SIDELIGHTS: Notable off-Broadway productions: Gold Through the Trees; Just a Little Simple & Trouble in Mind. Wedding Band presented as Professional Theatre Production of 1966 at U. of Mich. (Ruby Dee, Abbey Lincoln & Jack Harkins were in the cast). Lectured at Radcliffe, Spelman & Clark colleges. Travel: Mainland China, Africa, Soviet Union, London, France, Italy (Author).
Sources. Author inform.; The Best Short Stories by Negro Writers, Ed. by Langston Hughes (Little, Brown, 1967); Black Drama, Loften Mitchell (Hawthorn, 1967); Black Scenes, Ed. by Alice Childress (Doubleday, 1971); Black Joy, Ed. by Jay David (Cowles, 1971); America, 37th ed., Vol. 1, 1972-73, Chgo. (Marquis, 1972); Books in Print, Supplement, 1975-76 (Bowker, 1976).

CHISHOLM, SHIRLEY ANITA. 1924- . United States Congresswoman
Biographical-Personal. Born Nov. 30, 1924, in Brooklyn, N.Y. D. of Charles Christopher and Ruby [Seale] St. Hill (Barbadians). Educ.: B.A. (cum laude, Sociol.), Brooklyn Coll.; M.A. (Childhood Educ.), Columbia U., 1952. Family: m. Conrad Q. Chisholm. Mailing address: 1108 Longworth House Office Bldg., Wash., D.C. 20515.
Career-Professional. Dir., Friends Day Nursery, N.Y.C.; Dir., Hamilton-Madison Day Care Center, Manhattan (largest in N.Y.C.); Educ. Cons., Day Care Div., Bureau of Child Welfare, N.Y. State, 1959-64; Assemblywoman, N.Y. State Legis., 1964-68; Congresswoman, N.Y., 12th Congressional District, 1969- .
WRITINGS: Unbought and Unbossed, semi-autobiog. (Houghton Mifflin, 1970); The Good Fight (Harper & Row, 1973).
SIDELIGHTS: "In 1968 she defeated James Farmer, former director of CORE, to win election to Congress from New York's 12th Congressional District, an area that includes the Bedford-Stuyvesant Community, becoming the first black woman in the United States Congress" (Pub. brochure).
Sources. Black Politicians, Richard Bruner (McKay, 1971); Contemporary Authors, vols. 29-32, 1972, Ed. by Clare D. Kinsman & Mary A. Tennenhouse (Gale Res., 1972); Pub. inform.

Clark, Kenneth Bancroft

CHURCHWELL, CHARLES DARRETT. 1926- . Academic Provost, Library
Administrator
Biographical-Personal. Born Nov. 7, 1926, in Dunnellon, Fla. Educ.:
B.S. (Math.), Morehouse Coll., 1952; M.S. (Lib. Sci.), Atlanta U.,
1953; Ph.D. (Lib. Sci.), U. of Ill., 1966; N.Y.C. Coll.; Hunter
Coll.; N.Y.U. Family: m. Yvonne; d. Linda, d. Cynthia. Mailing
address: 106 Rondebush Hall, Miami U., Oxford, Ohio 45056.
Career-Professional. Lib. Sci. Instr., Prairie View A & M Coll.,
1953-58; Ref. Librn., Circulation Dept., N.Y. Public Lib., 1959-61;
Asst. Circulation Librn., U. of Ill., 1965-67; Asst. Dir., Lib.,
U. of Houston, 1967-69; Dir., Lib., Miami U., 1969-72; Assoc.
Provost for Academic Serv., Miami U.
WRITING: A History of Education for Librarianship, 1919-1939.
MEMBER: Great Books discussion leader at N.Y. Public Lib.,
1960-61; Chmn., Advis. Task Force on Academic Priorities, Miami
U., 1971-72; ALA & NAACP (life mem.); Amer. Assn. of Higher Educ.
SIDELIGHTS: "He is responsible for all academic support services,
interdisciplinary studies and international programs (in his pres-
ent position)" (1000 Successful Blacks).
Source. 1000 Successful Blacks, Eds. of Ebony (Johnson Pub., 1973).

CLARK, KENNETH BANCROFT. 1914- . Psycholo-
gist, Educator
Biographical-Personal. Born July 24, 1914, in
Panama Canal Zone. Son of Arthur Bancroft
and Miriam [Hanson] Clark. Educ.: N.Y. Public Schs.; B.S., Howard U., 1935, M.S., 1936;
Ph.D., Columbia U., 1940. Family: m. Mamie
Phipps, Apr. 14, 1938; d. Kate Miriam, son,
Hilton Bancroft. Mailing address: MARC,
60 E. 86th St., N.Y., N.Y. 10028.
Career-Professional. Staff, Psychology Dept.,
CCNY, 1942- , Prof., 1960- ; Pres., Metropolitan Applied Res. Center; Res. Dir.,
Northside Center; Res. Dir., Northside Center
for Child Develop. (which he and wife founded), 1946- ; Soc. Sci. cons., legal & educ.
div., NAACP, 1950- ; Advis. Com. on Foreign Affairs Personnel,
1961-62. Founder, Chmn. of Bd., Harlem Youth Opportunity Unlimited (HARYOU), war-on-poverty prog.; Vis. Prof.: Columbia U., U. of
Cal., Berkeley, Harvard U.
WRITINGS: Prejudice and Your Child (Beacon Pr., 1955); Dark Ghetto: Dilemmas of Social Power (Harper & Row, 1965); A Relevant War
Against Poverty, with Jeannette Hopkins (Harper & Row, 1968); The
Negro Protest (Beacon Pr., 1964); The American Revolution (Bicentennial Lec. Ser., Amer. Enterprise, 1974); Negro American, with
Talcott Parsons (Houghton Mifflin, 1966); Pathos of Power (Harper

Clarke, Austin Chesterfield

& Row, 1975); How Relevant Is Education in America Today?, with
Alex C. Sheriffs (1970); Racism and American Education, with
Harold Howe (Harper & Row, 1970). Period.: Journal of Social
Issues, Vol. 9, no. 53 (1953).
HONORS AND AWARDS: Spingarn Medal, NAACP, 1961; Kirt Lewin Me-
morial Award, 1966; Elected 1st recipient, Distinguished Scholar
Award, Center for Safety, N.Y., 1968; Elected N.Y. Bd. of Regents,
1966; Pres., Amer. Psychological Assn., 1970.
MEMBER: Former Pres., Soc. for Psychological Study of Soc. Is-
sues; Trus., Howard U., 1959- ; Soc. Sci. cons., NAACP; State
Dept. advis.; Cons., Rand Corp.; Temporary State Com. on Consti-
tutional Convention (N.Y. State Constitutional Convention); Com.
on Integration of N.Y.C. Bd. of Educ., 1954-58; N.Y. State Youth
Com., 1956- ; Adv. Com. Div. Intercultural Relat. in Educ., N.Y.
State Dept. Educ., 1957- ; Dir., Nat'l. Child Labor Com.; Nat'l.
Scholarship Serv. & Fund for Negro Stud.; Dir., New Lincoln Sch.
SIDELIGHTS: Was research psychologist on staff of Gunnar Myrdal
study which resulted in An American Dilemma; his work on effect of
segregation of children, cited by U.S. Supreme Court in 1954 decision on school desegregation.
Sources. Current Biography, 1964, Ed. by Charles Moritz (H. W. Wilson, 1964); Negro Handbook, Comp. by Eds. of Ebony (Johnson Pub.,
1966).

CLARKE, AUSTIN CHESTERFIELD. 1934- .
Novelist, Short Story Writer
Biographical-Personal. Born July 26, 1934, in
Barbados, W. Indies. Son of Kenneth Trothan
(artist) and Gladys Clarke. Educ.: Harrison
Coll., Barbados; Oxford & Cambridge Higher
Certificate, 1950; additional study, Trinity
Coll., U. of Toronto. Family: m. Betty
Joyce (registered nurse), Sept. 14, 1958; d.
Janice, d. Loretta, son, Mphahlele. Mailing
address: Agent: Ronald Hobbs, 211 E. 43rd
St., N.Y., N.Y. 10017.
Career-Professional. Can. Broadcasting Corp.,
Toronto, Ontario, prod. & free-lance broad-
caster, 1963- ; Vis. Prof., Afro-Amer. Lit.
& Creative Writing, Yale U., 1968- .
WRITINGS: The Survivors of the Crossing, novel (McClelland &
Stewart, 1964); Amongst Thistles and Thorns, novel (McClelland,
1965); The Meeting Point, novel (Macmillan, Canada, 1967); Black
Literature, 20th Century, critical essays (Prentice-Hall); Storm
of Fortune (Little, Brown, 1973); When He Was Free and Young and
He Used to Wear Silks; Stories (Little, Brown, 1973). Author of
"Myths and Memories," "African Literature," and other filmscripts

Clarke, John Henrik

for Educational TV, Toronto, 1968- . Son of Learning: A Play in
Three Acts (Dufour, 1964); Old Fashioned Pilgrimage Poems (Dufour,
1967); Two Interludes (Dufour, 1968); Flight to Africa (Dufour,
1969); The Celtic Twilight and the Nineties (Humanities, 1969);
Collected Poems, Miller, Liam, eds. (Oxford U. Pr., 1974).
HONORS AND AWARDS: Canada Counc. Sr. Arts Fellow.; U. of W. Ontario President's Medal for best story, 1965; Belmont Short Story
Award, for "Four Stations in His Circle."
MEMBER: Yale New Haven Club.
SIDELIGHTS: "...In his review of Clarke's third novel, James Dale
noted 'Mr. Clarke's first two novels...were tidily constructed,
capably written, and inevitably, marked by racial bitterness and
singularity of outlook... Now, Mr. Clarke has written himself out
of his Barbaidan childhood and youth [and] he has escaped from the
constrictions of fiction which is neatly labelled and categorized;
The Meeting Point is primarily about people, not about a racial or
social situation.... The great achievement of The Meeting Point
is this very avoidance of the simplistic, this awareness of the
oddity and variety in human nature which defies neat sociological
pigeonholing...(it) is of major importance...!" (Contemporary Authors).
Sources. Contemporary Authors, Vols. 25-28, Ed. by Carolyn Riley
(Gale Res., 1971); Books in Print, Supplement, 1975-76 (Bowker,
1976).

CLARKE, JOHN HENRIK. 1915- . Editor, Educator,
Writer
Biographical-Personal. Born Jan. 1, 1915, in
Union Springs, Ala. Son of John and Willella
[Mays] Clarke. Educ.: (High sch.) Columbus,
Ga. & N.Y.C.; N.Y.U., 1948-52; New Sch. for
Soc. Res., 1956-58; U. of Ibadan, Nigeria; U.
of Ghana, Accra. Family: m. Eugenia Evans;
d. Nzingha, son, Sonni Kojo. Mailing address:
223 W. 137th St., N.Y., N.Y. 10030.
Career-Professional. Co-founder & Assoc. Ed.,
Harlem Quarterly; Book Review Ed., Negro Hist.
Bull.; Feature writer: Pittsburgh Courier & ·
Ghana Evening News; Dir., 1st U.S. African
Her. Exposition; Ed., African Heritage, 1959;
Assoc. Ed., Freedomways, 1962- ; (column,
"African World Bookshelf," distributed in U.S. & abroad by Assoc.
Negro Pr. & World Mutual Exchange, Internat. Feature; Tchr., Afri-
can & Afro-Amer. Hist., Malverne High Sch., Long Island, N.Y.;
Dir., Her. Tchg. Prog., HARYOU-ACT, 1964-69; Tchr., African &
Afro-Amer. Hist., Headstart Training Prog., N.Y.U.; Special Cons.
& Coord., CBS TV Ser., "Black Heritage: The History of the Afro-

Clay, Willie

Americans"; Prof., Dept. of Black & Puerto Rican Stud., Hunter Coll., 1969.
WRITINGS: Rebellion in Rhyme, poetry (Dicker Pr., 1948); The Lives of Great African Chiefs (Pittsburgh Courier Pub., 1958); Harlem, A Community in Transition (Citadel Pr., 1964, 1970); Harlem, U.S.A. (Seven Seas, 1965; Macmillan, paper, 1971); American Negro Short Stories, anthol. (Hill & Wang, 1966); William Styron's Nat Turner: Ten Black Writers Respond, Ed. (Beacon, 1968); Malcolm X The Man and His Times (Macmillan, 1969); Slavery and the Slave Trade, Ed. with Vincent Harding (Holt, 1970); Black Titan: W. E. B. DuBois, Ed. with eds. of Freedomways (1971); Marcus Garvey and the Vision of Africa, Ed. with Amy Jacques Garvey (Random House, 1974); Black Families in the American Economy (Ed. Com. Counsel, 1974); The Prescriber (Brit. Bk. Center, 1975).
HONORS AND AWARDS: Carter G. Woodson Award for Creative Contrib. in Ed., 1968; Natra Citation for Meritorious Achievement in Educ. TV, 1969; Carter G. Woodson Award for Distinguished & Outstanding Work in Tchg. of Hist., 1971; Doctor of Humane Letters, U. of Denver, 1970.
MEMBER: Pres., African Her. Stud. Assn.; Found. mem., Black Acad. of Arts & Letters.
SIDELIGHTS: Helped develop African Study Center, New Sch. for Soc. Res. Traveled through 11 countries in W. Africa & lectured extensively on African Hist., 1958-59 (Author).
Sources. American Negro Short Stories, John H. Clarke (Hill & Wang, 1966); Author inform.; Best Short Stories, Ed. by Langston Hughes (Little, Brown, 1967); Black Joy, Ed. by Jay David (Cowles, 1971); Black Voices, Ed. by Abraham Chapman (New Amer. Lib., 1968); Poetry of Black America, Ed. by Arnold Adoff (Harper, 1973); Who's Who in America, 37th ed., 1972-73 (Marquis, 1972); Books in Print, Supplement, 1975-76 (Bowker, 1976).

CLAY, WILLIE. 1933- . Essayist
Biographical-Personal. Born July 30, 1933, in Docena, Ala. Educ.: B.F.A., U. of Cin. Mailing address: 1728 S. Oxford, L.A., Cal. 90006.
Career-Professional. Employed with Headstart; Teenpost; Chmn. of Bd., Headstart Agency; Aided former Councilman Tom Bradley in establishing L.A. City Bureau of Consumer Affairs; Soc. Serv. Investigator; Personnel management; Artist management; Advertising & promotions. WRITINGS: The Big Walk (Ebony Internat., 1974).
SIDELIGHTS: "...the first Black American to walk across the United States from New York to Los Angeles, California.... Mr. Clay made

Cleaver, Leroy Eldridge

the 'Big Walk' on promotion to survey Black Communities to search for the basic problems of Black people. (The book) is based on (his) experiences with other people in numerous cities, and their reactions to him while he walked across the United States" (Brochure).

Source. "Second Annual Authors Autograph Party" (brochure), Cal. Librns. Black Caucus, July 1975.

CLEAVER, LEROY ELDRIDGE. 1935- . Black Militant, Writer

Biographical-Personal. Born 1935, in Wabbaseka, Ark. Son of Leroy and Thelma Cleaver. Educ.: Self-educated. Family: m. Kathleen Neal, Dec. 27, 1967; son, Antonio Maceo. Mailing address: 301 Broadway, San Francisco, Cal. 94133.

Career-Professional. Asst. Ed., Ramparts; Spokesman for Black Panthers, Minister of Inform.; Lectr.

WRITINGS: Soul on Ice, essays (McGraw-Hill, 1968); Post Prison Writings and Speeches (Random House, 1969); War Within: Violence or Nonviolence in the Black Revolution, with Others (Sheed & Ward, 1971). Eldridge Cleaver (Random House, 1967).

SIDELIGHTS: Sentenced to prison at an early age. Obtained high sch. diploma, read omnivorously, converted to Black Muslim faith & became ardent follower of Malcolm X while in prison. Soul on Ice was written while in Folsom Prison (1957-66). Became candidate of Peace and Freedom Party after Governor Reagan tried to stop his lectures on racism at U. of Cal., Berkeley (1968). Lectureship became a major issue in Cal. U.S. Senatorial election. Was ordered to return to jail again after having been paroled, for an exchange of gunfire with police. Went underground and fled the country (Current Biography, 1970). Subsequently lived in several countries, including Cuba, Algeria and France. Returned to U.S. in Fall, 1976.

Sources. Cavalcade, Ed. by Arthur P. Davis & Saunders Redding (Houghton Mifflin, 1971); Current Biography, 1970, Ed. by Charles Moritz (H. W. Wilson, 1970); Negro Almanac, 2nd ed., Ed. by Harry A. Ploski & Ernest Kaiser (Bellwether, 1971); Who's Who in America, 37th ed., 1972-73 (Marquis, 1973); Books in Print, Supplement, 1975-76 (Bowker, 1976).

Clifton, Lucille T.

CLIFTON, LUCILLE T. 1936- . Poet, Children's Writer

Biographical-Personal. Born June 27, 1936, in Depew, N.Y. D. of Samuel, Sr. and Thelma [Moore] Sayles. Educ.: Howard U., Fredonia State Tchrs. Coll. Family: m. Fred J. Clifton (Author & Educator); son, Sidney, d. Fredrica, son, Channing, d. Gillian, son, Graham, d. Alexia. Mailing address: 2605 Talbot Rd., Baltimore, Md. 21216.

Career-Professional. Poetry readings at colleges; Children's book fairs.

WRITINGS: Juvenile: Some of the Days of Everett Anderson (Holt, 1969); The Black B.C.'s (Dutton, 1970); Everett Anderson's Christmas Coming (Holt, 1971); All Us Come Cross the Water (Holt, 1972); The Boy Who Didn't Believe in Spring (Dutton, 1973); Good, Says Jerome (Dutton, 1973); The Times They Used To Be (Holt, 1974); Everett Anderson's Year (Holt, 1975); Don't You Remember? (Dutton, 1973); Three Wishes (Viking, 1975); My Brother Fine With Me (Holt, Rinehart & Winston, 1975); El Niño Ave No Creia En La Primavera, Alma F. Ada, transl. (Dutton, 1976); Everett Anderson's Friend (Holt, Rinehart & Winston, 1976); Generations (Random House, 1976). Poetry: Good Times (Random House, 1969); Good News About the Earth (Random House, 1972); An Ordinary Woman (Random House, 1974). In progress: Three Wishes, juvenile (Viking, 1975). Period.: Negro Digest/ Black World; The Massachusetts Review.

HONORS AND AWARDS: Discovery Award, YMHA, 1969; NEA Awards, 1970, 1972.

Sources. Author inform.; Poetry of Black America, Ed. by Arnold Adoff (Harper, 1973); Books in Print, Supplement, 1975-76 (Bowker, 1976).

COBB, CHARLIE. 1944- . Poet

Biographical-Personal. Born 1944, in Wash., D.C. Educ.: Howard U.

Career-Professional. SNCC in Miss.; Center for Black Educ., Wash., D.C.; Drum and Spear Pr., Wash., D.C. and Tanzania, E. Africa.

WRITINGS: Poetry: Furrowe (1967); Everywhere Is Yours (Third World Pr., 1971). Anthol.: Black Fire (1968); Campfires of the Resistance: Poetry from the Movement (1971); Poetry of Black America (1973).

Sources. Poetry of Black America, Ed. by Arnold Adoff (Harper & Row, 1973).

Collier, Eugenia

COBBS, PRICE M. Psychiatrist
Biographical-Personal. Educ.: M.D., Meharry
    Medical Coll., Nashville, Tenn.; Langley
    Porter Neuropsychiatric Inst., San Francisco,
    Cal.
Career-Professional. Private practice, psychi-
    atry, San Francisco; Asst. Prof., Psychiatry,
    San Francisco Medical Center, U. of Cal.
    WRITINGS: Black Rage, with William H. Grier
    (Basic Bks., 1968, Bantam, paper, 1969); The
    Jesus Bag, with William H. Grier (McGraw-
    Hill, 1971).
Source. Pub. inform.

COLLIER, EUGENIA. 1928- . Teacher, Writer
Biographical-Personal. Born April 6, 1928, in
    Baltimore, Md. D. of Dr. H. Maceo and
    Eugenia J. Williams. Educ.: B.A. (magna cum
    laude, Eng.), Howard U., 1948; M.A. (Amer.
    Lit.), Columbia U., 1950; Doctoral stud.
    (Amer. Stud.) U. of Md. Family: div.; son,
    Charles Maceo, son, Robert Nelson, son, Phil-
    lip Gilles. Mailing address: 2608 Chelsea
    Terrace, Baltimore, Md. 21216.
Career-Professional. Case Worker, Baltimore
    Dept. of Public Welfare, 1950-55; Tchr., Eng.,
    Morgan State Coll., 1955-66; Prof., Eng.,
    Community Coll. of Baltimore, 1966- ; Vis.
    Prof. Eng., S. Ill. U., Carbondale, Summer,
    1970; Afro-Amer. Stud., Atlanta U., Summer,
    1973, 1974.
WRITINGS: Impressions in Asphalt: Images of Urban America, with
Ruthe T. Sheffey (Scribner's, 1969); A Bridge to Saying It Well,
with Edward I. Meyers & Others (Norvec Co., 1970); Afro-American
Writing: Poetry and Prose, with Richard A. Long (N.Y.U. Pr.,
1972). Essays: In Langston Hughes, Black Genius, Ed. by Therman
O'Daniel; Phylon (Winter 1960, Autumn 1964 & Winter 1972); CLA
Journal (Sept. 1967, Spring 1972); Black World (Oct. & Nov. 1971,
June 1972); N.Y. Times (June 17, 1973 & Apr. 21, 1974); TV Guide
(Jan. 1974). Stories: "Marigolds," "Sinbad the Cat," "Sweet Po-
tatoe Pie." Several poems.
HONORS AND AWARDS: Story "Marigolds" won Gwendolyn Brooks Award
for fic., 1969. Selected for Outstanding Educators of America,

Colter, Cyrus

1972, 1973, 1974; To be included in Fisk U. taped interviews of
contemporary authors.
SIDELIGHTS: Cons., Workshop, Center for African & Afro-Amer.
Stud., 1969; Cons., Call & Response Workshop, Karamu House, 1970;
Mem., Middle States Evaluation Team for Lehigh Community Coll.,
Schnechtsville, Pa., 1970; Cons.: Bond Humanities Fair, Atlanta,
Ga. 1973-74; Black Stud. Com., Coll. Lang. Assn.; Pine Manor Jr.
Coll., Mass. since 1970; Elected to Community Coll. of Baltimore
Senate Executive Com., 1970.
Sources. Author inform.

COLTER, CYRUS. 1910- . State Commissioner of
Commerce, Short Story Writer
Biographical-Personal. Born Jan. 8, 1910, in
Noblesville, Ind. Educ.: Youngstown U.,
Ohio; Ohio State U.; LL.B., Kent Coll. of
Law, Chgo., 1940. Family: m. Imogene Colter.
Mailing address: 601 E. 32nd St., Apt. PH-2,
Chgo., Ill. 60616.
Career-Professional. YMCA, Youngstown, Ohio,
1932-34; YMCA, Chgo., 1934-40; Deputy Col-
lector of Internal Revenue, 1940-42; Captain,
U.S. Army, 1942-46; Attorney, Chgo., 1946- ;
Asst. Commissioner, Ill. Commerce Com., (Pub-
lic Utilities), 1950, Commissioner, 1951- ;
Chmn., Ill. Emergency Transport Bd.
WRITINGS: "The Beach Umbrella"; The River of
Eros (1972; Curtis, 1973); The Hippodrome (1973). Stories ap-
peared in: The Best Short Stories by Negro Writers (1967);
Threshold; U. of Kansas City Review; Epoch; Chicago Review; North-
west Review & Prairie Schooner. Also in Best American Short Sto-
ries, Honor Roll (1962, 1967).
HONORS AND AWARDS: U. of Iowa, Sch. of Letters Award for Short
Fic., 1970; Friends of Lit. Prize, 1971; Patron Saints Award of
Soc. of Midland Authors, 1971.
MEMBER: Admin. Conf. of U.S.; Com. on Railroads of Nat'l. Assn.
of Regulatory Utility Commissioners; Kappa Alpha Psi; NAACP; Chgo.
Urban League; V. Chmn., Citizens Com., Chgo. Pub. Lib.; Chgo. Bar
Assn.; Cliff Dwellers Club; Bd. of Trus., Chgo. Symphony Orches-
tra; Commercial Club.
SIDELIGHTS: His most popular work is "The Beach Umbrella." He
began writing fiction only in 1960 as a weekend hobby. Novelist
Vance Bourjaily, one of the judges for the Iowa School of Letters
Award, described Colter as "what a writer is and always has been--
a man with stories to tell, a milieu to reveal and people he cares
about" (New Black Voices).

Cone, James H.

Sources. Afro-American Literature-Fiction, Ed. by William Adams &
Others (Houghton Mifflin, 1970); Best Short Stories by Negro
Writers, Ed. by Langston Hughes (Little, Brown, 1967); New Black
Voices, Ed. by Abraham Chapman (New Amer. Lib., 1972); Soon, One
Morning, Ed. by Herbert Hill (Knopf, 1963).

CONE, JAMES H. 1938- . Theologian, Educator
Biographical-Personal. Born Aug. 5, 1938.
    Educ.: Shorter Coll. (Ark.); B.A., Philander
    Smith Coll., Little Rock, Ark., 1958; B.D.,
    Garrett Theological Seminary, 1961; M.A.,
    Northwestern U., 1963, Ph.D., 1965. Family:
    m. Rose Hampton; son, Michael Lawrence, son,
    Charles Pierson. Mailing address: Union
    Theological Seminary, 3041 Broadway, N.Y.,
    N.Y.
Career-Professional. Asst. Prof., Philander
    Smith Coll., 1964-66; Asst. Prof., Adrian
    Coll., Mich., 1966-69; Vis. Assoc. Prof. of
    Religion, Barnard Coll., 1969-71; Vis. Prof.
    of Theology, Drew U., N.J., 1973; Lectr.,
    Systematic Theology, Woodstock Coll., 1971-73;
Union Theological Seminary, N.Y.C.: Asst. Prof., 1969-70, Assoc.
Prof., 1970-73, Prof., 1973- .
WRITINGS: Black Theology and Black Power (Seabury, 1969); A Black
Theology of Liberation (Lippincott, 1970); The Spirituals and the
Blues (Seabury, 1972); God of the Oppressed (Seabury, 1975); The
Social Context of Theology (Seabury, 1975). Anthol.: Is Anybody
Listening to Black America: The Challenge of Black Theology in
South Africa; "Negro Churches," in Encyclopaedia Britannica, 15th
ed. Period.: Ladies Home Journal (Dec. 1969); The Annals (Jan.
1970); Theological Education (Spring 1970); Christianity and
Crisis (June 1970, July 10, 1972, Jan. 22, 1973); Christian Cen-
tury (Sept. 16, 1970, Sept. 15, 1971); Ebony (Aug. 1970); Enquiry
(Mar.-May, 1971); Theology Today (Apr. 1971); Risk (Vol. 7, no. 2,
1971; Vol. 9, no. 2, 1973); Concern (Dec. 1971); Reforme (May
1972); Pro Veritate (Jan. 15, 1972); Dialogue (Spring 1973); Mis-
sion (Apr. 1973); Rocco (Vol. 32, no. 10, 1973); Evangelische
Theologie (Jan./Feb. 1974); Union Seminary Quarterly Review
(Vol. 29, no. 2, Winter 1974); The Other Side (May-June 1974,
Vol. 10, no. 3).
HONORS AND AWARDS: Rockefeller Found. res. grant, 1973-74;
Contrib. Ed., Christianity and Crisis; Ed. Advis. Bd., Renewal;
Cons., Scholastic's Black Culture Program.
MEMBER: Nat'l. Com. of Black Churchmen (Bd. of Dir. & Theological
Com.); Black Methodists for Church Renewal; Rockefeller Doctoral
Fellow. in Religion; Amer. Theological Soc., N.Y.; Biblical The-

Cook, Mercer

ology; Amer. Assn. of Theological Schls.; Com. on Black Religious
Experience; Soc. for Study of Black Religion.
SIDELIGHTS: Has lectured at many colleges and theological sem-
inaries all over the U.S. Has given papers and addresses before
many major conferences and learned societies, etc. Has lectured
abroad at: Dar es Salaam, and Chateau De Bossev, Tanzania; Geneva, Switzerland; Turin and Milan, Italy; Mainz and Tubingen, Germany (Author).
Sources. Author inform.; Black Theology and Black Power, James H.
Cone (Seabury, 1969).

COOK, MERCER. 1903-   . Language Professor,
United States Ambassador
Biographical-Personal. Born Mar. 30, 1903, in
    Wash., D.C. Son of Will Marion Cook (Vio-
    linist & Composer) and Abbie Mitchell (Ac-
    tress & Singer). Educ.: B.A., Amherst Coll.,
    1925, LL.D., 1965; Tchrs. Diploma, U. of
    Paris, 1926; M.A., Brown U., 1931, Ph.D.,
    1936, LL.D., 1970. Family: m. Vashti Smith,
    Aug. 31, 1929; son, Mercer, son, Jacques.
    Mailing address: 4811 Blagden Ave., N.W.,
    Wash., D.C. 20001.
Career-Professional. Asst. Prof., Romance
    Lang., Howard U., 1927-36, Prof., 1945-60;
    Prof., French, Atlanta U., 1936-43; Prof.,
    Eng., U. of Haiti, 1943-45; Foreign Rep.,
Amer. Soc. Afridan Culture, 1958-60; Dir., African prog., Congress
Cultural Freedom, 1960-61; U.S. Ambassador to Niger, 1961-64, to
Senegal & Gambia, 1965-66; Prof., Head, Dept. of Romance Lang.,
Howard U., 1970.
WRITINGS: Le Noir (Amer. Bk., 1934); Portraits Americains (D. C.
Heath, 1938); Five French Negro Authors (Assoc. Pub., 1943); Edu-
cation in Haiti (Fed. Security Agency, 1948); Haitian American
Anthology, Ed. (Haiti: Imprimerie de l'état, 1944); Introduction
to Haiti, Ed. (Pan Amer. Union, 1961); Militant Black Writer in
Africa and the United States, with Stephen E. Henderson (U. of
Wis. Pr., 1969). Transl.: Senghor's African Socialism (1959);
Mamadou Dia's African Nations and World Solidarity (1961); Ed. &
transl. from French, Cheikh A. Diop's The African Origin of Civ-
ilization: Myth or Reality (Lawrence Hill, n.d.).
HONORS AND AWARDS: Phi Beta Kappa; Decoration from Haitian Govt.,
1945, from Nigerian Govt., 1964, from Senegal, 1966: Palmer Aca-
démiques (France).
MEMBER: Amer. Soc. of African Culture; ASNLH; NAACP; Amer. Assn.
Tchrs.; French Acad. Polit. Sci.; ASCAP.

Cornish, Samuel E.

Sources. Negro Handbook, Comp. by Eds. of Ebony (Johnson Pub.,
1966); Negroes in Public Affairs and Government, Ed. by Walter
Christmas (Educ. Her., 1966); Books in Print, Supplement, 1975-76
(Bowker, 1976).

COOMBS, ORDE. Writer
Career-Professional.
WRITINGS: We Speak As Liberators: Young Black Poets, An Antholo-
gy, Ed. (Dodd, Mead, 1970); What We Must See: Young Black Story-
tellers, An Anthology, Ed. (Dodd, Mead, 1971); Do You See My Love
for You Growing? (Dodd, Mead, 1972); Eastern Religions in the
Electric Age, with John H. Garabedian (Grosset & Dunlap, 1972);
Is Massa Day Dead? Black Moods in the Caribbean (Doubleday, 1974).
Source. Books in Print, 1976 (Bowker, 1976).

COOPER, CLARENCE L., JR. Writer
Career-Professional.
WRITINGS: The Scene (Crown, 1960); The Dark Messenger (Regency,
1962); Black: Two Short Novels (Regency, 1963); The Farm, a
novel (Crown, 1967).
Source. The Farm, a novel, Clarence L. Cooper, Jr. (Crown Pub.,
1967).

CORNISH, SAMUEL E. 1790-1859. Anti-Slavery Editor
Biographical-Personal. Born free in Del. in 1790. Educ.: Migrated
to Phila., attended the Free African Sch. Settled in N.Y. in
1822. Died in 1859.
Career-Professional. Organized first Black Presbyterian congrega-
tion, N.Y. With John B. Russwurm founded first Negro newspaper,
Freedom's Journal, 1827. Also associated with the Weekly Advocate (later Colored American).
SIDELIGHTS: "Freedom Journal played a major role in shaping a social and economic philosophy for the Negro. Such gifted persons
as James McCune Smith, Alexander Crummell, Martin R. Delany and
David Ruggles used it to express their opinions. Cornish, as the
editor, fought relentlessly for full rights of citizenship and
equality for the Negro. Cornish, a trustee of the free schools
for Negroes in New York, energetically promoted higher education
for Negroes. Participating in many reform movements, he was an
active member of the American Anti-Slavery Society" (Historical
Negro Biographies).
"...Cornish was responsible, in part, for the Negro press becoming identified with the role of protest. Cornish called for a
fight to the finish in America. 'Let there be no compromise,' he
said, 'but as though born free and equal, let us contend for all
the rights guaranteed by the Constitution of our native country'"
(Negro Handbook).

Cornish, Samuel James

Sources. <u>Historical Negro Biographies</u>, Wilhelmena S. Robinson
(ASNLH, 1967); <u>Negro Handbook</u>, Comp. by Eds. of <u>Ebony</u> (Johnson
Pub., 1966).

CORNISH, SAMUEL JAMES. 1938- . Poet, Teacher
Biographical-Personal. Born Dec. 22, 1938, in
W. Baltimore, Md. <u>Educ.</u>: Northwestern U.
<u>Family</u>: m. Jean Faxon. <u>Mailing address</u>:
395 Broadway, Cambridge, Mass. 02138.
Career-Professional. Writing spec., Enoch Pratt
Free Lib., Baltimore, 1965-66, 1968-69;
Bookseller, 1966-67; Ed., Hist., Assoc. Pr.;
Tchr., Creative writing, Highland Schools,
Roxbury, Mass., 1969- . Ed., <u>Mimeo</u> (poetry
mag.).
WRITINGS: Poetry: <u>People Under the Window</u>;
<u>In This Corner</u>; <u>The Shabby Breath of Yellow
Teeth</u>. Others: <u>Angles</u> (Bean Bag Pr., 1971);
<u>Winters</u> (Sans Souci Pr., 1968); <u>Your Hand in
Mine</u>, juvenile (Harcourt, 1970); <u>Generations</u>
(Beacon Pr., 1971); <u>Chicory: Young Voices from the Black Ghetto</u>,
Ed. (Assoc. Pr., 1969); <u>Grandmother's Pictures</u> (Bradbury Pr.,
1976). Period.: <u>Journal of Black Poetry</u>; <u>Massachusetts Review</u>;
<u>New American Review</u>; <u>Poetry of Black America</u>.
HONORS AND AWARDS: Poetry Prize, Humanities Inst., Coppin State
Coll., 1968; Grant, NEA, 1968.
Sources. <u>Black Fire</u>, Ed. by Leroi Jones & Larry Neal (Morrow, 1968);
<u>New Black Poetry</u>, Ed. by Clarence Major (Internat., 1969); <u>Poetry
of Black America</u>, Ed. by Arnold Adoff (Harper, 1973); <u>Books in
Print</u>, Supplement, 1975-76 (Bowker, 1976).

CORTEZ, JAYNE. 1936- . Poet, Lecturer
Biographical-Personal. Born May 10, 1936, in
Ariz. Reared in Watts. <u>Family</u>: son,
Denardo Coleman. <u>Mailing address</u>: P.O. Box
249, Village Station, N.Y., N.Y. 10014.
Career-Professional. Guest lectr.: Queens Coll.,
N.Y.; Wesleyan Coll., Conn.; Claremont Coll.,
Cal.; Ohio U., Athens; U. of Conn., Storrs;
Creighton U., Omaha, Neb.; Texas S. U.,
Houston; Rutgers Coll., New Brunswick, N.J.;
Richmond Coll., Staten Is., N.Y.; Antioch U.,
Yellow Springs, Ohio; Sacramento State Coll.,
Cal.; Hunter Coll., N.Y.C.; Cape Coast U.,
Ghana; U. of Ibadan, Nigeria; Chgo. Art
Inst., Ill.; Brooklyn Coll., N.Y.; Princeton
Coll., N.J.; Howard U., Wash., D.C.; Amherst
Coll., Mass.; Sarah Lawrence Coll., Bronxville, N.Y.; & others.

Crouch, Stanley

WRITINGS: Poetry: Pisstained Stairs and the Monkey Man's Wares (Phrasetext, 1969); Festivals and Funerals (1971); Scarifications (1973). Anthol.: We Speak As Liberators; Black Aesthetic; New Black Voices; The Poetry of Black America; Rock Against the Wind; Mundus Artuim. Period.: Confrontation; Discourses on Poetry; Black Dialogue; Umbra; American Dialogue; Black World; Pan African Journal; Works; Essence.
HONORS AND AWARDS: Rockefeller Found. Grant for res. & travel, 1970; C.A.P.'s N.Y. State Counc. On the Arts for Poetry, 1973.
Sources. Author inform.; New Black Voices, Ed. by Abraham Chapman (New Amer. Lib., 1972); Poetry of Black America, Ed. by Arnold Adoff (Harper & Row, 1973).

COTTER, JOSEPH SEAMON, SR. 1861-?. Poet
Biographical-Personal. Born 1861 in Bardstown, Ky. Self-educated. Deceased.
Career-Professional. Sch. tchr., Louisville, Ky.; Prize fighter.
WRITINGS: A Rhyming (1895); "Tragedy of Pete"; Collected Poems (1938); Links of Friendship; Caleb; The Degenerative; A White Song and a Black One; and Negro Tales.
HONORS AND AWARDS: Won Opportunity prize contest for "Tragedy of Pete."
Sources. Anthology of American Negro Literature, Ed. by V. F. Calverton (Mod. Lib., 1929); Caroling Dusk, Ed. by Countee Cullen (Harper & Row, 1927); Negro Caravan, Ed. by Sterling A. Brown & Others (Arno Pr. & N.Y. Times, 1969).

CROUCH, STANLEY. 1945- . Poet, Music Critic
Biographical-Personal. Born 1945 in Los Angeles, Cal.
Career-Professional. Has been columnist for Los Angeles Free Press & The Cricket; Arts Coord. of Cultural Afternoons, Watts Happening Coffee House; Playwright/Actor, Watts Repertory Theatre Co.; Tchr., Lit., Black Drama, & Music Appreciation, Black Stud. Center, Claremont Coll., Cal.
WRITINGS: Ain't No Ambulances for No Niggahs Tonight, poetry (Baron, 1972). The Music, novel. Period.: Negro Digest/Black World; Liberator; Black Dialogue. Anthol.: Black Fire (1968); We Speak As Liberators: Young Black Poets (1970); Black Spirits (1972); Poetry of Black America (1973).
SIDELIGHTS: Musician and music critic as well as a poet (Poetry of Black America).
Sources. The New Black Poetry, Ed. by Clarence Major (Internat., 1969); The Poetry of Black America, Ed. by Arnold Adoff (Harper & Row, 1973).

Crummell, Alexander

CRUMMELL, ALEXANDER. 1819-1898. Minister, Missionary, Writer
Biographical-Personal. Born Mar. 3, 1819, in N.Y.C. Paternal grandfather was son of W. African chief; mother's people had been free for generations. Educ.: Oneida Inst. (seminary), Boston; Queens Coll., Cambridge (grad. 1853). Died 1898.
Career-Professional. Ordained 1844. Solicited funds in Eng. Lived in Liberia for 20 yrs. Rector, St. Luke's Protestant Episcopal Church, Wash., D.C., 1873-1894. Leader in founding Amer. Negro Acad., 1897.
WRITINGS: The Man: the Hero: the Christian: A Eulogy on the Life and Character of Thomas Clarkson: Delivered in the City of New York, December, 1846 (New York, 1847); The Relations and Duties of Free Colored Men in America to Africa (1861); The Future of Africa: Being Addresses, Sermons, etc., etc., Delivered in the Republic of Liberia (1862); The Greatness of Christ, and Other Sermons (1882); Africa and America: Addresses and Discourses (1891).
SIDELIGHTS: The very eloquent Alexander Crummell was an outstanding spokesman and missionary with a global vision. He went to England to solicit funds and stayed to attend Cambridge. Crummell went to Liberia because of ill health. When he returned to America to stay, he was placed in charge of St. Mary's Mission, Washington, D.C. Worked to erect St. Luke's (The Negro Author in America).
Sources. Early Negro American Writers, Benjamin Brawley (U. of N.C. Pr.); Great Negroes Past and Present, Russell Adams (Afro-Amer. Pub., 1969); Men of Mark, William Simmons (Johnson Pub., 1970); Negro Author in America, Vernon Loggins (Kennikat, 1959); Negro Genius, Benjamin Brawley (Dodd, Mead, 1937).

CRUSE, HAROLD. Director, Afro-American Studies
Biographical-Personal. Born Petersburg, Va.; reared N.Y.C.
Career-Professional. Free-lance Writer, 1940- ; Organizer & Activist, political work, Black community, N.Y.C.; Assisted LeRoi Jones in establishing Jones' Black Arts Theatre and Sch., 1965-66; Film & Drama Critic, N.Y. Labor Pr.; Vis. Prof. Hist., Afro-Amer. Stud. & Interim Dir., Center for Afro-Amer. & African Stud., U. of Mich., Ann Arbor, 1968- .
WRITINGS: The Crisis of the Negro Intellectual (Morrow, 1967); Rebellion or Revolution (Morrow, 1968). Contributed to: Studies on the Left; Le Temps Moderne; Liberator.

Cullen, Countee Porter

Sources. Black American Writer, Ed. by C. W. E. Bigsby (Penguin
Bks., 1969); Black Fire, Ed. by LeRoi Jones & Larry Neal (Morrow,
1968).

CRUZ, VICTOR HERNANDEZ. 1949- . Poet
Biographical-Personal. Born 1949, in Aguas Buenas, Puerto Rico.
Came to N.Y.C. at age 4; grew up in El Barrio (Spanish Harlem).
Educ.: Benjamin Franklin High Sch.
Career-Professional. Ed., Umbra; Tchr., U. of Cal., Berkeley, Eng.
Dept.; San Francisco Neighborhood Arts Prog.
WRITINGS: Snaps, poetry (Random House, 1969); Mainland (Random
House, 1973). Period.: Down Here; Evergreen Review; Ramparts;
Umbra; New York Review of Books. Anthol.: Black Fire; New Black
Voices; Poetry of Black America.
SIDELIGHTS: "He writes out of the Black and Puerto Rican expe-
riences in the United States in his own individual way" (New Black
Voices).
Sources. New Black Voices, Ed. by Abraham Chapman (New Amer. Lib.,
1972); Poetry of Black America, Ed. by Arnold Adoff (Harper & Row,
1973).

CULLEN, COUNTEE PORTER. 1903-1946. Poet,
Editor, Teacher
Biographical-Personal. Born May 30, 1903, in
N.Y.C. Adopted by Frederick Asbury (Method-
ist Minister) and Carolyn Belle [Mitchell]
Cullen. Educ.: B.A., N.Y.U. (Phi Beta
Kappa), 1925; M.A., Harvard U., 1926.
Family: 1st m. Yolande DuBois (d. of W. E. B.
DuBois), Apr. 1928; div. 1929; 2nd m. Ida M.
Cullen. Died Jan. 9, 1946.
Career-Professional. Asst. Ed., Opportunity;
Lit. Ed., Crisis; French Tchr., N.Y.C.,
1934-45.
WRITINGS: Color, poetry (Harper & Row, 1925);
Caroling Dusk, anthol. (Harper & Row, 1927,
1974); Copper Sun, poetry (1927); The Ballad
of the Brown Girl (Harper & Row, 1927); The Black Christ (Harper &
Row, 1929); Transl.: Medea, in Medea and Other Poems (Harper &
Row, 1935); The Lost Zoo (Harper & Row, 1940), My Lives and How I
Lost Them, by Christopher Cat (Harper & Row, 1942; Curtis, paper,
1973); One Way to Heaven, novel (Harper & Row, 1932); St. Louis
Woman, with Arna Bontemps (play based on Bontemps's novel, God
Sends Sunday; became popular Broadway musical, 1946); On These I
Stand (Harper & Row, 1947). Contrib. poems to: Bookman, Century,
Poetry, Harper's, etc.

Danner, Margaret Esse

HONORS AND AWARDS: Color received Harmon Gold Award; N.Y.U.
awarded the Writter Bynner Poetry Prize; Awarded Guggenheim Fellow.
to France, (where he edited Caroling Dusk and wrote The Black
Christ).
SIDELIGHTS. "Countee Cullen began writing as an emotional lyrical
poet much under the influence of Keats and Tennyson, and showing
his partiality towards Millay, Housman and E. A. Robinson as well.
He has said, 'Most things I write I do for the sheer love of the
music in them. Somehow I find my poetry of itself treating of the
Negro, of his joys and sorrows--mostly of the latter--and of the
heights and depths of emotion I feel as a Negro'" (Twentieth Cen-
tury Authors).
   "A classicist in poetic forms and inherently a romantic in his
thematic interests, acknowledging Keats as a central influence,
Countee Cullen was a central figure of the Negro Renaissance..."
(Black Voices).
Sources. Black Poets of the United States, Jean Wagner, transl. by
Kenneth Douglas (U. of Ill. Pr., 1973); Black Voices, Ed. by Abra-
ham Chapman (New Amer. Lib., 1968); Book of American Negro Poetry,
Ed. by James Weldon Johnson (Harcourt, 1959); Cavalcade, Ed. by
Arthur P. Davis & Saunders Redding (Houghton Mifflin, 1971); Negro
Almanac, Comp. by Harry A. Ploski & Roscoe C. Brown, Jr. (Bell-
wether, 1967); Twentieth Century Authors, Ed. by Stanley J. Kunitz
& Howard Haycraft (H. W. Wilson, 1942).

DANNER, MARGARET ESSE. 1915- . Poet
Biographical-Personal. Born Jan. 12, 1915, in
   Chgo., Ill. Educ.: YMCA Coll. & Roosevelt
   U., Chgo.; Loyola U., Chgo. Family: 1st m.
   Cordell Strickland; 2nd m. Otto Cunningham;
   d. Naomi (Ms. Sterling M. Washington). Mail-
   ing address: 626 E. 102nd Pl., Chgo., Ill.
   60628.
Career-Professional. Asst. Ed., Poetry mag.
   (Chgo.), 1951-55; Poet-in-Residence: Wayne
   State U.; Va. Union U. (1968-69); Le Moyne-
   Owen Coll., Memphis, Tenn. Founder, Boone
   House (Center for the Arts), Detroit; Founder,
   Nologonyu's, Chgo.
   WRITINGS: Poetry: Impressions of African
   Art Forms (Broadside Pr., 1962); To Flower
(Hemphill, 1962); The Iron Lace (Hemphill, 1968); Poem: Counter-
poem, with Dudley Randall (Broadside Pr., 1966); Brass Horses, Ed.
(Va. Union U. Pr., 1968); Regroup (Va. Union U. Pr., 1969); The
Down of a Thistle (Country Beautiful, 1976). Anthol.: Midwestern
Writers Prize Anthology; Beyond the Blues; American Negro Poetry;
New Negro Poets, U.S.A.; Poets of Today; Ik Ben de Nieuwe Neger:

Davis, Allison

La Poesie Negro-Americaine. Period.: Accent; Poetry; Chicago
Magazine; Chicago Review; Negro Digest; Negro History; Bulletin;
Quicksilver.
HONORS AND AWARDS: John Hay Whitney Fellow. for poetry (Senegal,
Paris, 1966); Poetry Workshop, Midwestern Writers Conf., 1945;
Women's Auxiliary, Afro-Amer. Interest grant, 1950; African Stud.
Assn., 1950; Harriet Tubman, 1965; Amer. Soc. of African Culture,
1960; African Stud. Assn., 1961; Poets in Concert.
MEMBER: Pres., Writer's Inc., Nologonya African Cultural Org.
SIDELIGHTS: Traveled to Dakar to participate in the First World
Festival of Negro Arts, 1966 (Afro-American Writing). In 1959
came to Detroit, and later founded Boone House, a center for the
arts, where a group of poets including Gloria Davis, Oliver La-
Grone, Edward Simpkins, Alma Parks, Harold Lawrence, Naomi Madgett,
Dudley Randall, Betty Ford & Joyce Whitsett met together and gave
poetry readings (For Malcolm).
Sources. Afro-American Writing, Ed. by Richard A. Long & Eugenia W.
Collier (N.Y.U. Pr., 1972); Ebony (March, 1974, Johnson Pub.);
For Malcolm, Ed. by Dudley Randall & Margaret Burroughs (Broad-
side Pr., 1969); Poetry of Black America, Ed. by Arnold Adoff
(Harper & Row, 1973); Books in Print, Supplement, 1975-76 (Bowker,
1976).

DAVIS, ALLISON. 1902- . Anthropologist, Psychologist
Biographical-Personal. Born in Wash., D.C. Educ.: Williams Coll.,
B.A., 1924; Harvard U., M.A., 1925; London Sch. of Econ.; U. of
Chgo., Ph.D., 1942.
Career-Professional.
WRITINGS: Children of Bondage, with John Dollard (Amer. Counc. on
Educ., 1940); Deep South, with Elizabeth Davis & Burleigh & Mary
Gardener (U. of Chgo. Pr., 1941); Father of the Man, with Robert
J. Havighurst (Houghton Mifflin, 1947); Social-Class Influences
Upon Learning (Howard U. Pr., 1948); Intelligence and Cultural
Differences, with Kenneth Eells & Others (U. of Chgo. Pr., 1951);
Davis-Eells Test of General Intelligence, with Kenneth Eells
(World Bk., 1953); Psychology of the Child in the Middle Class (U.
of Pittsburgh Pr., 1960); Relationships Between Achievement in
High School, College and Occupation: a Followup Study (U.S. Of-
fice of Educ., 1963). Contrib.: Political Arithmetic, Ed. by
Lancelot Hogben (1938); Race Relations and the Race Problem, Ed.
by Edgar T. Thompson (1939).
Sources. Negro Caravan, Ed. by Sterling A. Brown, et al. (Arno Pr.
& N. Y. Times, 1969).

Davis, Angela Yvonne

DAVIS, ANGELA YVONNE. 1944- . Political Activist

Biographical-Personal. Born Jan. 26, 1944, in Birmingham, Ala. D. of B. Frank and Sallye E. Davis (teachers). Educ.: Parker High Sch., Birmingham, Ala.; Elizabeth Irwin High Sch., N.Y.C.; B.A. (French Lit., magna cum laude), Brandeis U., 1965; Johann Wolfgang von Goethe U., Frankfort, Germany (Philosophy); M.A. (Philosophy), U. of Cal., San Diego, 1968; further study. Family: Single. Mailing address: c/o Communist Party, U.S.A., 23 West 26th St., N.Y., N.Y. 10001.

Career-Professional. Organizer, Black Student Counc., U. of Cal., San Diego; San Diego Black Conf.; SNCC, L.A.; Che-Lumumba Club, Black Panthers; Communist Party (all L.A.); Instr., Philosophy, Dept., UCLA; Soledad Brothers Defense Com.; Lectr.

WRITINGS: If They Come in the Morning, Ed. (Okpaku, 1971); Angela Davis, An Autobiography (Random House, 1974). Articles pub. in Ebony (July 1971) & other period.

SIDELIGHTS: (Some of George Jackson's letters to her may be read in his book Soledad Brother, 1970, and a documentary on Miss Davis, "Portrait of a Revolutionary," has been filmed by one of her students at UCLA).

"In June 1972...Miss Davis was acquitted of charges of kidnapping, murder, and conspiracy in connection with a 1970 shootout at the Marin County (Cal.) Courthouse....

"...On the intellectual level (her radicalization) moved forward under the tutelage of aging political philosopher Herbert Marcuse at Brandeis in 1964-65, Marcuse's last year on the faculty before his mandatory retirement.

"...after intense soul-searching, she formally joined the Communist party on June 22, 1968.

"To effect social and economic change, Miss Davis favors a black-white coalition, rather than black separatism, and a strategy that would 'take over, not destroy, the production apparatus'" (Current Biography, 1972).

Sources. Angela Davis, An Autobiography (Random House, 1974); Current Biography, 1972, Ed. (Charles Moritz, 1972).

DAVIS, ARTHUR P. 1904- . Journalist, Critic, Editor, Educator

Biographical-Personal. Born in Hampton, Va. Educ.: Howard U.; Columbia Coll., N.Y. (Phi Beta Kappa), 1927; Columbia U., M.A., 1929, Ph.D., 1942.

Career-Professional. Prof. Eng., N.C. Coll., Durham, 1927-28; Prof. Eng., Va. Union U., Richmond, 1929-44; Prof., Howard U., 1944-69;

Davis, Frank Marshall

Columnist, "With a Grain of Salt," Journal & Guide newspaper (Nor-
folk), 1933-50.
WRITINGS: Isaac Watts: His Life and Works (Dryden, 1943, London
& N.Y.); The Negro Caravan, Ed. with Sterling Brown & Ulysses Lee
(1941); Cavalcade: Negro American Writers from 1760 to the Pres-
ent, Ed. with Saunders Redding (1971); From the Dark Tower, Afro-
American Writers, 1900-1960 (Harvard U. Pr., 1974); The New Negro
Renaissance (Holt, Rinehart, Winston, 1975). Period.: Crisis;
Phylon; CLA Journal; Journal of Negro Education; Journal of Negro
History; etc.
SIDELIGHTS: His Isaac Watts was hailed by The Times Literary Sup-
plement (London) for its "careful scholarship" and style (Black
Voices).
Sources. Black Voices, Ed. by Abraham Chapman (New Amer. Lib.,
1968); Cavalcade, Ed. by Arthur P. Davis & Saunders Redding
(Houghton Mifflin, 1971); Books in Print, Supplement, 1975-76
(Bowker, 1976).

DAVIS, CHARLES T. English Professor, Critic
Biographical-Personal. Born at Hampton Inst., Va. Educ.: Degrees
from Dartmouth Coll.; U. of Chgo.; N.Y.U.
Career-Professional. Vis. Prof.: Harvard, Rutgers, Bryn Mawr;
Tchr.: N.Y.U. & Princeton; Prof. Eng., Pa. State U.
WRITINGS: Walt Whitman's Poems, with Gay Wilson Allen; (E. A.
Robinson's) Selected Early Poems and Letters; (Ed. of Lucy Lar-
com's) A New England Girlhood; On Being Black; writings by Afro-
Americans from Frederick Douglass to the Present, Ed. with Daniel
Walden (Fawcett, 1970). Section on modern poetry in 1963 American
Literary Scholarship.
Source. On Being Black, Ed. by Charles T. Davis & Daniel Walden
(Fawcett, 1970).

DAVIS, FRANK MARSHALL. 1905- . Poet
Biographical-Personal. Born 1905 in Ark.
City, Kan. Educ.: Kan. State Coll. (Jour-
nalism), 3 yrs.
Career-Professional. Helped start Atlanta Daily
World, 1931. Executive Ed., Assoc. Negro Pr.,
Chgo., Ill.
WRITINGS: Poetry: Black Man's Verse (1935);
I Am the American Negro (1937); 47th Street
(1948).
HONORS AND AWARDS: Awarded 1st Sigma Chi
Perpetual Scholarship ever granted at Kan.
State Coll.; Julius Rosenwald Fellow in
Poetry, 1937.
Source. Negro Caravan, Ed. by Sterling A. Brown
& Others (Arno Pr. & N.Y. Times, 1969).

Davis, Nolan

DAVIS, NOLAN. 1942- . Novelist, Screenwriter, Composer

Biographical-Personal. Born July 23, 1942, in Kan. City, Mo. Son of William and Frances Ann Davis. Educ.: Bishop Lillis High Sch.; U.S. Navy Journalist Sch., 1960; San Diego Evening Coll., 1964-65; Stanford U., 1968. Family: m. Carol Christian (Artist); son, Arian, d. Pelia. Mailing address: SHARC Productions Intern., 5410 Wilshire Blvd., L.A., Cal. 90036.

Career-Professional. Biochemist; Undertaker's apprentice; Sailor; Janitor; Staff writer, San Diego Evening Tribune, Newsweek; Writer and Prod., NBC, ABC, CBS.

WRITINGS: Six Black Horses, novel (Putnam, 1971); O'Grady, non-fict. (Tarcher/Hawthorn, 1974). Screenplays: "Six Black Horses" (1975); "The Fighting 99th" (1975). TV series & scripts: "Storyline," ABC, 1971; "Further than the Pulpit," NBC, 1972; "The Jazz Show with Billy Eckstine," NBC, 1972; "Ironside," Universal, 1974; "Sanford and Son," NBC, 1975. Music: "The Good News Blues," recording (Crossover Records, 1975). Articles: Newsweek, Readers Digest, Black Enterprise, National Catholic Reporter & West, etc.

HONORS AND AWARDS: Attended Stanford U. on communications fellow.

MEMBER: Author's League of Amer.; Screenwriters Guild (WGAW); Sigma Delta Chi (Prof. Journalistic Soc.); ASCAP; Nat'l. Honor Soc.

SIDELIGHTS: Spent 3 years at Ozanam Boys Home of Kansas City, where he began his writing career at age 15. Traveled throughout U. S. & Mexico in relation to his writing. Co-founder, SHARC International (comprises several subsidiaries dealing with film, records, music publishing and finance) (Author).

Sources. Author inform.; Six Black Horses (Putnam, 1971).

DAVIS, OSSIE. 1917- . Actor, Playwright, Director

Biographical-Personal. Born Dec. 18, 1917, in Cogdell, Ga. Son of Kince Charles (Railroad construction engineer) and Laura [Cooper] Davis. Educ.: Central High Sch., Waycross, Ga.; Howard U., 1935-38; Columbia U. Family: m. Ruby Dee (Actress), 1948; d. Nora, son, Guy, d. La Verne. Mailing address: 44 Cortlandt Ave., New Rochelle, N.Y. 10801.

Career-Professional. Began stage career as member of Rose McClendon Players, 1941. Broadway debut in title role of Jeb (1946). Other

De Coy, Robert H.

roles on Broadway include Gabriel in Green Pastures, Walter Lee
Younger in A Raisin in the Sun, and the title role in his own
Purlie Victorious. Film debut in No Way Out (1950). Directed
film Black Girl. Acted in: Anna Lucasta (1948); The Wisteria
Trees (1950); No Time for Sergeants (1956); Movies: The Joe Louis
Story (1953); The Cardinal (1963).
WRITINGS: Plays: Goldbrickers of 1944; Alice in Wonder (1953);
Purlie Victorious (1961); Curtain Call, Mr. Aldridge, Sir (1963).
Cotton Comes to Harlem, co-authored film play (1969); "School
Teacher," of East Side, West Side, TV ser. (1963); Last Dance for
Sybil; Purlie Victorious (adapted for filming).
SIDELIGHTS: "In 1961 he wrote and played the title role in Purlie
Victorious which opened at the Court Theatre on September 28, 1961,
and ran for 261 performances. Appearing opposite him was his wife,
Ruby Dee, in the role of Lutiebelle....
    "...Purlie Victorious is a deft comic 'put-down' and 'put-on' of
both black and white.... Davis has constructed a brilliant comedy
containing the most inventive humor of any modern American play..."
(Black Drama).
    "'What Martin Luther King is doing with love, I am trying to do
with laughter,' Ossie Davis once commented. In Purlie Victorious,
Davis uses the comic medium to present the serious truths about
the black man's plight in America" (Afro-American Literature-
Drama).
    Davis has performed feature roles on TV in The Defenders, The
Nurses & Emperor Jones (Current Biography Yearbook).
Sources. Afro-American Literature: Drama, Ed. by William Adams &
Others (Houghton Mifflin, 1970); Black Drama, Ed. by William Bras-
mer & Dominick Consolo (Merrill, 1970); Black Scenes, Ed. by Alice
Childress (Doubleday, 1971); Cavalcade, Ed. by Arthur P. Davis &
Saunders Redding (Houghton Mifflin, 1971); Current Biography Year-
book, 1969, Ed. by Charles Moritz (H. W. Wilson, 1970).

DE COY, ROBERT H. Actor, Media Commentator
Biographical-Personal. Educ.: M.F.A., Yale U., 1951.
Career-Professional. Actor-playwright-journalist, radio & TV per-
    sonality. Creator-writer-narrator of radio ser. "This is Prog-
    ress," daily documentary of Black contrib. News cons. and writer
    (CBS, ABC). Arranger, writer, narrator of record album, "Martin
    Luther King at Zion Hill." Created role of Luke in James Bald-
    win's The Amen Corner.
WRITINGS: Nigger Bible (1967); The Big Black Fire (1969); Cold
    Black Preach (1971).
HONORS AND AWARDS: First Black to serve as TV news dir.-announcer
    & prog. dir.
SIDELIGHTS: "As a television-radio-newspaper commentator, de Coy
    has been recognized as America's most committed black critic and

Delaney, Samuel R.

agitator for reforms in the Judeo-Christian religion or the immediate rejection of it by his people" (Nigger Bible).
Sources. Black Writers in Los Angeles, California, Hilda G. Finney
(Center for Extending Amer. Hist.); The Nigger Bible, Robert H.
deCoy (Holloway House, 1967).

DELANEY, SAMUEL R. Science Fiction Writer
Career-Professional.
WRITINGS: Captives of the Flame (Avon, 1963); The Towers of Taron
(Avon, 1964); The Ballad of Beta-2 (Ace, 1965); City of a Thousand
Suns (Ace, 1965); Babel-17 (Ace, 1966); Empire Star (Ace, 1966);
The Einstein Intersection (Ace, 1967); Nova (Doubleday, 1968); The
Fall of the Towers (Ace, 1972); The Jewels of Aptor (Ace, 1972);
Triton (Bantam, 1976).
Sources. Afro-American Writers, Darwin T. Turner (Appleton, 1970);
Black American Writers Past and Present, Theressa Rush, et al.,
eds. (Scarecrow, 1975); Books in Print, Supplement, 1975-76
(Bowker, 1976).

DELANY, MARTIN R. 1812-1885. Physician-
Soldier, Author-Publisher
Biographical-Personal. Born May 6, 1812, in
Charleston, W.Va. Son of free Blacks, Samuel
and Pati Delany. Educ.: Attended sch. in
Chambersburgh, Pa.,(and received training and
inspiration in the Thelan Lit. Soc. in Pitts-
burgh). Began study of medicine at Harvard
U. Medical Sch. in 1849. Family: m. Kath-
rine A. Richards in 1843. Died in Xenia,
Ohio, in 1885.
Career-Professional. Began public. of The
Mystery (newspaper) in 1843; Assoc. with
Fredrick Douglass on The North Star, 1847-49;
Serv. with cholera epidemic in Pittsburgh,
1854; Became interested in colonization of
Amer. slaves (visiting Africa & Eng.); As-
sisted in recruiting Negro soldiers for Civil War & served as ex-
amining physician in Chgo.; Received commission as major, Feb. 8,
1865; Served in Freedman's Bureau as custom-house inspector & as
trial justice. Nominated for lt. gov. of S.C. (defeated).
WRITINGS: The Condition, Elevation, Emigration, and Destiny of
the Colored People of the United States, Politically Considered
(1852); Official Report Of the Niger Valley Exploring Party
(1861); Principia of Ethnology: the Origin of Races and Color
(1879); Blake; or the Huts of America, novel in 7 installments
(Jan.-Aug. 1859, Anglo-African Magazine).

SIDELIGHTS: "A man of great physical and mental energy, he was proud of his blackness, tracing his lineage to African chieftains with probably more accuracy than many later Negroes have done."
"Had a deep interest in science and invention. In 1853, he was one of the prime movers for an industrial college to train Negro mechanics and artisans, anticipating Booker T. Washington. In 1859, because of his interest in colonization (he did not, how-ever, approve of the Liberian experiment), he led an investigation into the Niger Valley in Africa" (Negro Caravan).
Sources. Early Negro American Writers, Benjamin Brawley (U. of N.C. Pr., 1935); Historical Negro Biographies, Wilhelmena S. Robinson (ASNLH, 1967); History of the Negro in Medicine, Herbert Morais; Men of Mark, William Simmons (Johnson Pub., 1970); Negro Builders and Heroes, Benjamin Brawley (U. of N.C. Pr., 1937); Negro Cara-van, Ed. by Sterling A. Brown & Others (Arno Pr. & N.Y. Times, 1969); Negro Genius, Benjamin Brawley (Dodd, Mead, 1937).

DEMBY, WILLIAM. 1922- . Novelist, Artist, Screenwriter
Biographical-Personal. Born in 1922 in Pitts-burgh, Pa.; spent early youth in Clarksburg, W. Va. Educ.: W. Va. State Coll.; B.A., Fisk U., 1947; U. of Rome, Italy. Family: married; son. Mailing address: c/o Avon Books, 959 Eighth Ave., N.Y., N.Y. 10019.
Career-Professional. Wrote for Stars and Stripes in Italy (Army); Contrib. art and stories to Fisk U. Herald; Wrote screen plays for Roberto Rossellini (Rome); Advertising agent, N.Y.; Tchr., Staten Island Community Coll., N.Y.
WRITINGS: Bettlecreek, novel (Pantheon, 1965); The Catacombs, novel (1965).
SIDELIGHTS: Studied art at U. of Rome where he has lived; trav-eled in Europe, Ethiopia, Japan, and Thailand (Black American Literature).
Sources. Black American Literature, Ed. by Ruth Miller (Glencoe Pr., 1971); Cavalcade, Ed. by Arthur P. Davis & Saunders Redding (Houghton Mifflin, 1971); Dark Symphony, Ed. by James A. Emanuel & Theodore L. Gross (Free Pr., 1968); The Negro Novel in America, Robert A. Bone (Yale U. Pr., 1958); Soon, One Morning, Ed. by Herbert Hill (Knopf, 1963).

DODSON, OWEN VINCENT. 1914- . Drama Professor, Playwright, Novelist, Poet
Biographical-Personal. Born Brooklyn, N.Y., in 1914. Educ.: Bates Coll.; M.F.A., Yale U.

Douglass, Frederick

Career-Professional. Instr., Atlanta U., Summer 1938-39, full-time, 1939-43; Instr., Hampton Inst., 1942; Dir. Drama, Atlanta U., Hampton Inst., & Spelman Coll.; Lectr.: Iowa U., Vassar, Kenyon, Cornell; Conductor of seminars in theater and playwriting; Dir., summer theater, the Theatre Lobby (Wash., D.C.), Lincoln U. (Mo.), Howard U.; Prof. Drama, Howard U., 1936-69; Poet-in-residence, Ruth Stephan Poetry Center, U. of Ariz., Spring, 1969.
WRITINGS: Boy at the Window, novel (1951, repr. as When Trees Were Green); Powerful Long Ladder, poetry (Farrar, Straus, 1946, 1970); A Bent House, novel; Cages, poetry; Divine Comedy, play; The Confession Stone: Song Cycles (London, Paul Bremen, 1970). The Morning Duke Ellington Praised the Lord and Seven Little Davids Tap Danced Unto. Numerous poems, plays, fiction represented in over 30 anthol.
HONORS AND AWARDS: Rosenwald Fellow; Gen. Educ. Bd. Fellow; Guggenheim Fellow, 1953; Paris Review Prize for short story, "The Summer Fire"; named Poet Laureate by Her Majesty the Queen of Eng., 1968; Maxwell Anderson verse award.
MEMBER: Executive Secy., Com. for Mass Educ. on Race Relat. of Amer. Film Center, NYC.
SIDELIGHTS: "While on a Guggenheim Fellowship to Italy he completed a second novel, A Bent House, and a second book of poems, Cages" (Soon, One Morning).
"Owen Dodson has contributed significantly in Negro college theatre, a little-known but important training ground for black playwrights and performers. His best known play is Divine Comedy first produced at Yale University in 1938. Based on the story of Father Divine, it is probably the best verse drama by a black playwright" (Black American Literature-Poetry).
Sources. Black American Literature-Poetry, Ed. by Darwin T. Turner (Merrill, 1969); Black Voices, Ed. by Abraham Chapman (New Amer. Lib., 1968); Cavalcade, Ed. by Arthur P. Davis & Saunders Redding (Houghton Mifflin, 1971); Interviews with Black Writers, Ed. by John O'Brien (Liveright, 1973); Kaleidoscope, Ed. by Robert Hayden (Harcourt, 1967); Soon, One Morning, Ed. by Herbert Hill (Knopf, 1963).

DOUGLASS, FREDERICK. c.1817-1895. Abolitionist, Journalist, Diplomat
Biographical-Personal. Born c.1817, in Tuckahoe, Md. A slave of Captain Aaron Anthony. Son of unknown white father and Harriet Bailey. Educ.: Learned reading and writing from his master's

Drake, [John Gibbs] St. Clair

wife; thereafter, self-educated. Escaped
slavery in 1838. Family: 1st m. Anna Murray, Sept. 1838; 2nd m., Helen Pitts, 1884.
Died Feb. 20, 1895 in Wash., D.C.

Career-Professional. Employed as agent, Mass.
Anti-Slavery Soc., 1841; Became central figure in "One Hundred Conventions" of New Eng.
Anti-Slavery Soc.; Visited Great Britain &
Ireland to avoid possible re-enslavement as
result of his biography, Narrative of the
Life of Frederick Douglass, 1845-47; Returned
to America with money to buy his freedom, established newspaper North Star, 1847; It became known as Frederick Douglass's Paper,
lasted until 1860. From 1858 to 1863 he
brought out Douglass's Monthly, and from
1869-1872 he prod. weekly New National Era.

WRITINGS: Autobiog: The Narrative (1845; John Harvard Lib. Ser.,
Harvard U. Pr., 1960); My Bondage and My Freedom (1855); and Life
and Times of Frederick Douglass (1881). (From Slave to Statesman, abridged ed., Noble, 1972). Biography: Narrative of the
Life of Frederick Douglass, 1845-47.

SIDELIGHTS: Frederick Douglass, significant contributor to the
Blackman's freedom struggle, viewed freedom as "the foundation of
all manly virtue." In his opinion the Bill of Rights was, for
Black people, a "bill of wrongs." Thus efforts of a lifetime were
devoted to achieving equality of opportunity for his race.

He assisted in recruiting 54th and 55th Mass. colored regiments,
& served as Lincoln's advisor on the Blackman during the Civil
War. During Reconstruction, lectured in Britain. Served as President of Freedman's Bank; Chargé d'Affaires to Santo Domingo, 1871;
Marshall & Recorder of Deeds, 1877-86; U.S. Minister to Haiti,
1889-91; Vigorous supporter of woman's suffrage (Afro-American
Literature: Non Fiction).

Sources. Afro-American Literature: Non-Fiction, Ed. by William
Adams & Others (Houghton Mifflin, 1970); Black American Litera-
ture-Essays, Ed. by Darwin T. Turner (Merrill, 1969); Black
Voices, Ed. by Abraham Chapman (New Amer. Lib., 1968); Cavalcade,
Ed. by Arthur P. Davis & Saunders Redding (Houghton Mifflin,
1971); Who Was Who in America Hist. Vol., 1607-1896, rev. ed.
(Marquis, 1967); Books in Print, Supplement, 1975-76 (Bowker,
1976).

DRAKE, [John Gibbs] St. CLAIR. 1911- . Sociologist, Anthropologist
Biographical-Personal. Born Jan. 2, 1911, in Suffolk, Va. Son of
Mr. Drake (a Barbadian immigrant) and Bessie Lee [Bowles] Drake.
Educ.: B.S., Hampton Inst., Va. (with hon.), 1931; Ph.D., U. of

DuBois, David Graham

Chgo., 1948. Family: m. Elizabeth Dewey Johns, June 1942; d. Sandra, d. Kail. Mailing address: 245 Leland Ave., Palo Alto, Cal.

Career-Professional. Res. Assoc., Carnegie-Myrdal Study of the Negro in America, Sept. 1940-June 1942; Instr., Dillard U., New Orleans, Sept. 1935-June 1946, Asst. Prof., Sept. 1941-June 1942; Warrant Officer, U.S. Maritime Serv., Sept. 1943-Dec. 1945; Asst. Prof., Roosevelt U., Chgo., Sept. 1946-Jan. 1954; Vis. Prof., U. of Liberia, Jan.-June 1954; Prof., Roosevelt U., Sept. 1955-Oct. 1958; Head, Dept. of Sociol., U. of Ghana, W. Africa, Oct. 1958-Feb. 1961; Prof., Roosevelt U., Feb. 1961-Oct. 1969; Prof., Sociol. & Anthropology, & Chmn., African' & Afro-Amer. Stud. Prog., Stanford U., Oct. 1969- ; Training Staff, Peace Corps Tchrs., Ghana, 1961, 1962, 1964.

WRITINGS: Churches and Voluntary Associations Among Negroes in Chicago (WPA, 1940); Black Metropolis, with Horace Cayton (Harcourt, 1945, rev. & enl., 1962, 1970); Social Work in West Africa, with Dr. Peter Omari (1963); Race Relations in a Time of Rapid Social Change (1966); Negro Americans and the African Interest; The Redemption of Africa and Black Religion (Third World Pr., 1971); Contrib. numerous articles to books and journals.

HONORS AND AWARDS: Calliope Medal (Hampton Inst.) for highest average over 4 yrs.; Ford Found. Fellow. for study of Mass Media in W. Africa, 1954-55; for Black Metropolis: Shared Anisfield-Wolf award, 1946; "One of five best on race relations" (Negro Digest).

MEMBER: African Stud. Assn.; Amer. Anthropological Assn.

SIDELIGHTS: Black Metropolis was "Generally compared to such works as Middletown by Robert & Helen Lynd, and An American Dilemma by Gunnar Myrdal, it was called 'a landmark not only in race studies but in the broader field of social anthropology'" (Current Biography, 1946).

Sources. Current Biography, 1946, Ed. by Anna Rothe (H. W. Wilson, 1947); Soon, One Morning, Ed. by Herbert Hill (Knopf, 1963).

DU BOIS, DAVID GRAHAM. Activist, Editor, Lecturer, Novelist

Biographical-Personal. Born in Seattle, Wash. Son of W. E. B. DuBois (stepfather) and Shirley Graham DuBois (both writers). Educ.: Oberlin Conservatory of Music; B.A. (Sociol.) Hunter Coll.; N.Y. Sch. of Soc. Work, Columbia U.; M.A., N.Y.U.; Peking U., China.

Career-Professional. Lectr., Cairo U., Egypt; News Ed., The Egyptian Gazette; Reporter & Ed., Middle East News & Features Agency; An-

DuBois, William Edward Burghardt

nouncer, Prog. Writer, Radio Cairo; Public Relat., Ghanaian Govt.
(under Kwame Nkrumah); Lectr., Sch. of Criminology, U. of Cal.,
Berkeley; Ed.-in-Chief, Black Panther Intercommunal News Serv.,
·1973- .
WRITINGS: And Bid Him Sing, novel (Ramparts Pr., 1975). In
progress: Racism, War and Revolution.
SIDELIGHTS: Returned to U.S. from Cairo, and settled in the San
Francisco Bay area. He is now spokesman for the Black Panthers.
His new book will link the emergence of Black rule in Southern
Africa with the struggle for Black equality in the U.S. (And Bid
Him Sing).
Source. And Bid Him Sing, David G. DuBois (Ramparts Pr., 1975).

DU BOIS, WILLIAM EDWARD BURGHARDT. 1868-1963.
Editor, Author, Educator, Historian, Scholar,
Sociologist
Biographical-Personal. Born Feb. 23, 1868, in
    Great Barrington, Mass., of African, French
    Huguenot, and Dutch ancestry. Son of Alfred
    and Mary [Burghardt] DuBois. Educ.: B.A.
    (Fisk U., 1888; Harvard U., 1890); M.A.,
    1891, Ph.D., 1895, Harvard U.; U. of Berlin;
    Hon. L.L.D. Howard U., 1930, Atlanta U.,
    1938; (Litt.D.) Fisk U., 1938; (L.H.D.) Wil-
    berforce U., 1940, U. of Sofia, 1958; D.Sci.
    of Hist. Charles U., Prague, 1950, Lomo-
    novska U., Moscow, 1959; (Econ.D.) Humboldt
    U., Berlin, 1958. Family: 1st m. Nina
    Gomer, May 12, 1896 (dec. 1950); son, Burg-
hardt Gomer (dec.), d. Nina Yolande; 2nd m. Shirley Graham, 1951;
son, David Graham. Died Aug. 29, 1963.
Career-Professional. Prof. Greek & Latin, Wilberforce U., 1894-96;
Asst. Instr. Sociol., U. of Pa., 1896-97; Prof. Econ. & Hist.,
Atlanta U., 1897-1910; Dir. Public., NAACP & Ed., Crisis, 1910-32;
Head, Dept. of Sociol., Atlanta U., 1943-44; V. Chmn., Counc. on
African Affairs, 1949-54; Founder-Ed., Phylon (Atlanta U. Review
of Race & Culture), 1940-44; Ed.-in-Chief, Encyclopedia of the
Negro, 1933-45; Dir., Dept. of Spec. Res., NAACP, 1944-48; Head,
Preliminary Planning, Encyclopedia Africana, 1961- .
WRITINGS: (Partial list) The Suppression of the African Slave
Trade, Ph.D. dissertation (Harvard U. Hist. Stud. Ser., 1896);
Philadelphia Negro, pioneer sociol. study (U. of Pa. Pr., 1899);
The Negro Artisan (Atlanta U. Pr., 1902); The Souls of Black Folk,
essays (A. C. McClurg, 1903); Some Notes on Negro Crime Particu-
larly in Georgia (Atlanta U. Pr., 1904); A Select Bibliography of
the Negro American (Atlanta U. Pr., 1905); Economic Co-Operation
Among Negro Americans (Atlanta U. Pr., 1907); The Negro American

DuBois, William Edward Burghardt

Family (Atlanta U. Pr., 1908); John Brown (G. W. Jacobs, 1909);
Efforts for Social Betterment Among Negro Americans (Atlanta U.
Pr., 1909); The College-Bred Negro American (Atlanta U. Pr.,
1910); The Common School and the Negro American (Atlanta U. Pr.,
1911); Quest of the Silver Fleece, novel (A. C. McClurg, 1911);
Atlanta University Studies, Ed. (Atlanta U. Pr., 1897-1911); The
Negro American Artisan (Atlanta U. Pr., 1912); Morals and Manners
Among Negro Americans (Atlanta U. Pr., 1914); The Negro (Henry
Holt, 1915); Darkwater, autobiog. essays (Harcourt, 1920); The
Gift of Black Folk (Stratford, 1924); Dark Princess, novel (Har-
court, 1928); Black Reconstruction (Harcourt, 1935); Black Folk:
Then and Now (Henry Holt, 1939); Dusk of Dawn, autobiog. (Harcourt,
1942); Color and Democracy (Harcourt, 1945); The World and Africa
(Viking, 1947); In Battle for Peace (Masses & Mainstream, 1952);
The Black Flame, trilogy (Mainstream, 1957-61); Autobiography of
W. E. B. DuBois, posthumous (Internat., 1968); The Education of
Black People: Ten Critiques, 1906-1960, Ed. by Herbert Aptheker
(Mod. Reader Paperback Ser., Monthly Review Pr., 1975); The Cor-
respondence of W. E. B. DuBois: Selections, 1877-1934. Herbert
Aptheker, ed. (Correspondence of W. E. B. DuBois: Vol. 1) (U. of
Mass. Pr., 1973).
HONORS AND AWARDS: Recipient, Internat. Peace Prize, 1952; Lenin
Internat. Peace Prize, 1958; Fellow AAAS.
MEMBER: Nat'l. Inst. of Arts & Letters; Phi Beta Kappa; Knight
Commander of the Liberian Order of African Redemption.
SIDELIGHTS: Dr. DuBois "was the intellectual father of current
black scholarship, current black militancy and self-consciousness,
and current black cultural development" (Black Voices).
    He was founder of the Pan-African Congresses and one of the
founders of the Niagara Movement in 1909, which paved the way for
the NAACP. This giant of a man was praised for his prophetic
foresight, "The problem of the twentieth century is the problem of
the color line," he wrote in 1903. He was respected for his 'radical' thought even by his opponents. DuBois became a citizen of
Ghana, W. Africa at age 94, after joining the Communist Party and
being hounded out of the U.S.A. He died at age 95 (Who Was Who in
America).
Sources. The American Negro Reference Book, Ed. by John P. Davis
    (Prentice-Hall, 1966); Black Voices, Ed. by Abraham Chapman (New
    Amer. Lib., 1968); Cavalcade, Ed. by Arthur P. Davis & Saunders
    Redding (Houghton Mifflin, 1971); Current Biography, 1940, Ed. by
    Maxine Block (H. W. Wilson, 1940); The Negro Almanac, 2d ed.,
    Harry A. Ploski & Ernest Kaiser (Bellwether, 1971); The Seventh
    Son..., Ed. by Julius Lester (Random House, 1971); Who Was Who in
    America, Vol. IV, 1961-68 (Marquis, 1968); Books in Print, Supple-
    ment 1975-76 (Bowker, 1976).

DUCKETT, ALFRED A. 1918- . Journalist, Poet, Public Relations
Adviser, Editor
Biographical-Personal. Born 1918 in Brooklyn, N.Y. Educ.: Boys
High Sch. (N.Y.); Columbia U.
Career-Professional. Newspaperman: Amsterdam News, New York Age,
Pittsburgh Courier; Dir., Assoc. Negro Pr.; Ed., Equal Opportunity
mag.
WRITINGS: Juvenile: Changing of the Guard; the New Breed of
Black Politicians (Coward, McCann & Geoghegan, 1972); Raps (Nel-
son-Hall, 1973). Anthol.: The Poetry of the Negro (1949, 1970);
American Negro Poetry (1963); Poetry of Black America (1973).
SIDELIGHTS: He lectures and reads his poems on many college cam-
puses. He worked with Jackie Robinson on a juvenile book and on
his memoirs. "He...closely associated with the late Martin Luther
King on numerous speeches and on preparation of his book Why We
Can't Wait" (Changing of the Guard).
Sources. Changing of the Guard, Alfred A. Duckett (Coward, 1972);
Poetry of Black America, Ed. by Arnold Adoff (Harper & Row, 1973);
Raps (Nelson-Hall, 1973).

DUMAS, HENRY. 1935-1968. Poet, Short Story
Writer
Biographical-Personal. Born 1935, in Ark. Came
to Harlem at age 10. Educ.: Rutgers U.
Family: m. Loretta Dumas; 2 sons. Died
May 23, 1968.
Career-Professional. Tchr., Hiram Coll., Hiram,
Ohio; Dir., Lang. Workshops & Tchr.-Counse-
lor, S. Ill. U.
WRITINGS: Ark of Bones and Other Stories and
Poetry for My People, both Ed. by Hale Chat-
field & Eugene Redmond (S. Ill. U. Pr.,
1970); Play Ebony Play Ivory, Ed. by Eugene
Redmond (Random House, 1974); Jonoah and the
Green Stone (Random House, 1976). Brothers
and Sisters (1970); & Poetry of Black Amer-
ica (1973). He has also appeared in many periodicals.
SIDELIGHTS: "...was shot and killed by a white policeman on the
Harlem Station platform of the New York Central Railroad. Little
else is known about the circumstances surrounding his death"
(Poetry of Black America).
Sources. The Poetry of Black America, Ed. by Arnold Adoff (Harper &
Row, 1973); Books in Print, Supplement, 1975-76 (Bowker, 1976).

Dunbar, Ernest

DUNBAR, ERNEST. 1927- . Editor, Non-Fiction
Writer
Biographical-Personal. Born Feb. 14, 1927, in
Phila., Pa. Son of Frank Willis and Alice
[O'Neal] Dunbar. Educ.: B.S., Temple U.,
1954; Grad. student in African Stud., Northwestern U., 1957-58. Family: m. Dorothy
Marie Grabusic, Dec. 18, 1965; d. Adrienne,
d. Gail, son, Dean Eliot. Mailing address:
33-04 93rd St., Jackson Heights, N.Y.
Career-Professional. Look, N.Y.C., Ed. staff,
1954- , Asst. Ed., 1958-59, Senior Ed.,
1959- ; WNDT, New York, Moderator of "World
at Ten"; Lectr. on African affairs.
WRITINGS: The Black Expatriates, collection
of interviews (Dutton, 1968); Nigeria (Watts,
1974). Contrib. to Portuguese-Africa section to Book of Knowledge Annual, 1963, and bk. reviews to Progressive.
HONORS AND AWARDS: Fund for Adult Educ. Mass Media Fellow.,
1957-58.
MEMBER: U.N. Correspondents Assn.; Overseas Pr. Club; Deadline
Club; Sigma Delta Chi.
SIDELIGHTS: Dunbar interviewed American Negroes living in Africa
and Europe for his book on sixteen expatriates. Much of his
traveling has been in sub-Saharan Africa (Contemporary Authors).
Source. Contemporary Authors. Vols. 25-28, Ed. by Carolyn Riley
(Gale Res., 1971).

DUNBAR, PAUL LAURENCE. 1872-1906. Poet, Short
Story Writer, Novelist
Biographical-Personal. Born June 27, 1872, in
Dayton, Ohio. Son of former slaves, Joshua
and Matilda [Murphy] Dunbar. Educ.: Dayton
Public Schs.; Grad. from high sch., 1891.
Family: m. Alice Moore (writer), Mar. 6,
1898. Died Feb. 9, 1906.
Career-Professional. Elevator operator; Em-
ployee, Lib. of Congress; Writer.
WRITINGS: Oak and Ivey (1893); Majors and
Minors (1895); Lyrics of Lowly Life (Bks. for
Lib. ed., 1896); Lyrics of the Hearthside
(1899); Poems of Cabin and Field (Bks. for
Lib. ed., 1899); Candle-Lightin' Time (Bks.
for Lib. ed., 1901); Lyrics of Love and
Laughter (1903); When Malindy Sings (Bks. for Lib. ed., 1903);
Li'l'gal (Bks. for Lib., 1903); Lyrics of Sunshine and Shadow
(1905); Howdy Honey Howdy (Bks. for Lib. ed., 1905); Joggin'erlong

(Bks. for Lib. ed., 1906); Complete Poems (1913); Folks from
Dixie (Bks. for Lib. ed., 1922). Novels: The Uncalled (1898);
The Love of Landry (1900); The Fanatics (1901); The Sport of the
Gods (1902); In Old Plantation Days (1903); The Heart of Happy
Hollow (1904). Strength of Gideon and Other Stories (Bks. for
Lib. ed., 1901); The Paul Laurence Dunbar Reader, Ed. by Jay Martin and Gossie Hudson (Dodd, Mead, 1975).
SIDELIGHTS: "First American Negro poet of real literary distinction" (Book of American Negro Poetry). "...his chief talents--
rhythm, narrative skill, and satirical characterization--are best
revealed in his dialect poems, his major contribution to American
literature" (Black American Literature--Poetry).
  Brought to national attention by William Dean Howells. Unhappy
life: four-year marriage ended in separation, tuberculosis rav-
aged his body, leading in turn to alcoholism. Would like to have
been considered for poems in standard English (Black Insights).
Sources. Black American Literature--Poetry, Ed. by Darwin T. Turner
(Merrill, 1969); Black Insights, Ed. by Nick A. Ford (Ginn, 1971);
Black Poets of the U.S., Jean Wagner, Transl. by Keneth Douglas
(U. of Ill., 1973); Black Voices, Ed. by Abraham Chapman (New
Amer. Lib., 1968); Book of American Negro Poetry, Ed. by James W.
Johnson, rev. ed. (Harcourt, 1959); Cavalcade, Ed. by Arthur P.
Davis & Saunders Redding (Houghton Mifflin, 1971); Kaleidoscope,
Ed. by Robert Hayden (Harcourt, 1967); Negro Almanac, Comps.
Harry A. Ploski & Ernest Kaiser (Bellwether, 1971).

DUNHAM, KATHERINE. 1910- . Dancer, Choreog-
  rapher, Anthropologist
Biographical-Personal. Born 1910, in Glen
  Ellyn, Ill. Educ.: M.A., U. of Chgo.;
  Northwestern U.
Career-Professional. Formed Negro Sch. of the
  Dance; 1st public appearance, Negro Rhapsody,
  Chgo. Beaux Arts Ball, 1931; 1st major dance
  performance, Chgo. World's Fair, 1934; Chgo.
  Opera Co., 1935-36; Dance Dir., Labor Stage,
  N.Y.C., 1939-40; Movies include: "Cabin in
  the Sky," 1940-41; "Carnival of Rhythm,"
  1941; "Stormy Weather," 1943. Choreographer,
  "Pardon My Sarong," 1942. Formed Katherine
  Dunham Sch. Cultural Arts, Inc., N.Y.C.,
  1945; Prod.-Dir., Katherine Dunham Dance Co.;
Starred in own prod., "Bal Negro," 1946-47, which toured country,
Jan.-Apr. 1948.
WRITINGS: Journey to Accompong (1946); Dances of Haiti: An Analy-
sis of Their Form and Function (1946, 1948); A Touch of Innocence,
autobiog. (1959); Kasamance: A Fantasy (Third World Pr., 1974).
Contrib. articles to Mademoiselle, Esquire, etc.

Duster, Troy

HONORS AND AWARDS: Julius Rosenwald Travel Fellow to W. Indies,
1936-37.
Sources. A Biographical History of Blacks in America Since 1528, Ed.
by Edgar A. Toppin (McKay, 1969); Soon, One Morning, Ed. by Herbert Hill (Knopf, 1963).

DUSTER, TROY. 1936- . Research Sociologist, Editor
Biographical-Personal. Born July 11, 1936, in Chgo., Ill. Son of
Alfreda [Barnett] Duster.
Career-Professional. Res. sociol., U. of Cal., Berkeley, 1966- .
WRITINGS: The Legislation of Morality, Law, Drugs and Moral Judg-
ment (Free Pr., 1969).
Source. The Legislation of Morality, Troy Duster (Free Pr., 1969).

DYMALLY, MERVYN MALCOLM. 1926- . California
Lieutenant Governor
Biographical-Personal. Born May 12, 1926, in
Trinidad, Brit. W. Indies. Son of Hamid A.
and Andried S. [Richardson] Dymally. Educ.:
M.A., Cal. State U., Sacramento, 1970.
LL.D. (hon.), U. of W. Los Angeles. Family:
m. Alice M. Gueno, 1969; son, Mark, d. Lynn.
Mailing address: State Capitol, Room 2082,
Sacramento, Cal. 95814.
Career-Professional. Elementary sch. tchr.,
L.A., Cal., 1954-60; Assemblyman, Cal. State
Assembly, 1962-66; Chmn., Com. on Indust.
Relat., 1965-66; Senator, Cal. State Senate
(Representing L.A. & Watts), Sacramento,
1967-75; Chmn., Com of Soc. Welfare, 1968-69,
Military and Veterans Affairs, 1969-70; Chmn., Election & Reap-
portionment, 1971; Chmn., Subcom. on Medical Educ. & Health Needs,
1972- , Child Develop. & Child Care Prog., 1972; Chmn. of Majori-
ty Caucus, 1970; Lectr. in Govt. at Claremont Coll., U. of Cal.
(Davis & Irvine), and Whittier Coll.; Vis. Fellow, Metropolitan
Applied Res. Center, N.Y.C.; Elected Lt. Governor, Cal., 1975- .
WRITINGS: The Black Politician: His Struggle for Power (Doxbury,
1971). Contrib. to Urban West. Founder & Ed.-in-Chief, Black
Politician.
MEMBER: Bd. of Advis., Joint Center for Polit. Stud.; Founder &
Chmn., Bd. of. Dir., Job Educ. Training Center; Cal. Advis. Com.,
U.S. Civil Rights Com.; Bd. of Dir., S. Central Area Welfare
Planning Counc.; Amer. Polit. Sci. Assn.; Amer. Acad. of Polit. &
Soc. Sci.; Amer. Assn. U. Prof.; Nat'l. Conf. Black Elected Offi-
cials (Founder & Co-Chmn.); Phi Delta Phi.
SIDELIGHTS: U.S. Dept. of State, Goodwill Ambassador to East &
Central Africa, 1964, & Guyana & the Caribbean, 1965. Dymally

visited Israel as guest of the government, 1967; was guest of
Ditchey Foundation in England, 1970 (<u>Contemporary Authors</u>).
Source. <u>Contemporary Authors</u>, Vols. 41-44, Ed. by Clare D. Kinsman,
(Gale Res., 1974).

EDMONDS, RANDOLPH. 1900- . Drama Professor, Playwright
Biographical-Personal. Born 1900, in Lawrenceville, Va. <u>Educ</u>.: St.
Paul Normal & Indust. Sch., Lawrenceville; B.A., Oberlin Coll.,
1926; M.A., Columbia U., 1932; Further study: Dept. of Drama,
Yale U.; Dublin U.; London Sch. of Speech Training & Dramatic Art;
Hon. Litt.D., Bethune-Cookman Coll., 1947.
Career-Professional. Tchr. of drama, a dir. and an organizer of
dramatic assns. in predominately Negro colleges, for over 40 yrs.
While at Morgan Coll., he organized the Negro Inter-Collegiate
Drama Assn. (Mar. 7, 1930), which included colleges of Pa., Md.,
Va., N.C. and D.C. At Dillard U. in New Orleans, he established
nation's first drama dept. at a predominately Black coll. (1935),
and founded S. Assn. of Drama & Speech Arts. At Fla. A. & M. U.
he chaired Theatre Arts Dept. for 23 years during which time he
twice took the A. & M. Players on theatrical tour of foreign countries at invitation of U.S. Govt. In addition to working with
colls., Edmonds organized high sch. drama assns. in La. & Fla. and
served as chief consultant for such assns. in Ga. & S.C. (<u>Black</u>
<u>Drama in America</u>).
WRITINGS: Author of numerous articles about theater. He has
written more than 40 dramas and has pub. 3 collec. of plays.
Plays: <u>Earth and Stars</u> (1946, rev. 1961); <u>Shades and Shadows</u>,
<u>Six Plays for a Negro Theater</u>; <u>The Land of Cotton and Other Plays</u>.
Included in: <u>The Negro in the Western World Theatre: Plays in</u>
<u>Color; Anthology of Full-Length Plays by Negro Authors</u>.
SIDELIGHTS: "In 1970 the Nat'l. Assn. of Dramatic & Speech Arts
honored Randolph Edmonds as 'the Dean of Black Academic Theatre.'
The title is well-deserved, for it is doubtful that any other individual has contributed more to the development of dramatic interest and organization in the Afro-American colleges.
    "In the original version of <u>Earth and Stars</u>, produced in 1946,
Edmonds explored problems of Southern leadership during the re-
conversion following World War II. The revised version brought
the problem up to date by emphasizing the civil rights struggle of
the 1960's. In the years since its first production at Dillard,
<u>Earth and Stars</u> has been staged more widely in Afro-American edu-
cational and community theaters than any other play by an Afro-
American" (<u>Black Drama in America</u>).
Sources. <u>American Literature by Negro Authors</u>, Ed. by Herman Dreer
(Macmillan, 1950); <u>Black Drama in America</u>, Ed. by Darwin T. Turner (Fawcett, 1971); <u>Directory of American Scholars, Vol. II,</u>
<u>English, Speech & Drama</u>, Ed. by Jacques Cattell, 5th ed. (Bowker,
1969).

Edwards, Harry

EDWARDS, HARRY. Teacher of Sociology
Career-Professional. Has been lectr. and grad. fellow in Dept. of
Sociol., Cornell U.; Tchr., San Jose State Coll., Cal.; Subject of
articles in Ramparts, Life, True, and New York Times.
WRITINGS: Revolt of the Black Athlete (Free Pr., 1969); Black
Students (Free Pr., 1970); Healing Intelligence (Taplinger, 1971);
Sociology of Sport (Dorsey, 1973). Contrib. to New Black Poetry
by Clarence Major.
SIDELIGHTS: Was instrumental in organizing the United Black Stu-
dents for Action (Revolt of the Black Athlete).
Sources. Revolt of the Black Athlete, Harry Edwards (Free Pr.,
1969); Books in Print, Supplement, 1975-76 (Bowker, 1976).

EDWARDS, JUNIUS. Novelist
Biographical-Personal. Educ.: Chgo. Public Schs.; U. of Chgo.; U.
of Oslo.
Career-Professional.
WRITINGS: If We Must Die, novel. Contrib.: Transatlantic Re-
view, The Urbanite, etc.
HONORS AND AWARDS: Eugene Saxton Fellow, 1959; winner, Writer's
Digest, Short Story Award, 1958.
Source. Black Joy, Jay David (Chgo., Cowles, 1971).

ELDER, LONNE, III. Playwright
Biographical-Personal. Born Americus, Ga.
Educ.: Yale U. Sch. of Drama.
Career-Professional. Worked after-hours clubs;
wrote poems, short stories; Dir., Play-
wright's-Dirs. Div., Negro Ensemble Co. of
N.Y.
WRITINGS: Ceremonies in Dark Old Men, play;
Camera 3, documentary teleplay CBS; The Ter-
rible Veil, play for NBC's Kaleidoscope;
Charades on East Fourth St., performed at
Expo '67, Montreal; Sounder, screenplay;
Deadly Circle of Violence, TV play; Part Two,
Sounder, screenplay.
HONORS AND AWARDS: Stanley Drama Award; John
Hay Whitney Fellow in play-writing; Alternate
winner, ABC-TV; Writing Fellow. Award, Yale Sch. of Drama, 1965-66;
"Playwright in residence" for Fiddler on the Roof; Charades com-
missioned by Cultural Arts Dept., N.Y. Mobilization for Youth,
Inc.
SIDELIGHTS: Influenced by Douglas Turner Ward. Negro Ensemble
Co. produced 1st play, Ceremonies, which won Stanley Drama Award.
Hailed by Richard Watts of New York Post as "best American play of
the season" (Black American Writer).

76

Ellington, Edward Kennedy (Duke)

Sources. Black American Writer, Vol. II: Poetry and Drama, Ed. by
C. W. E. Bigsby (Penguin, 1969); New Black Playwrights, Ed. by
William Couch, Jr. (Avon, 1970).

ELLINGTON, EDWARD KENNEDY (Duke). 1899-1974.
Composer, Band Leader, Pianist
Biographical-Personal. Born Apr. 29, 1899, in
    Wash., D.C. Son of James Edward (blueprint
    maker) & Daisy [Kennedy] Ellington. Educ.:
    Public schs., Wash., D.C.; studied music
    with Henry Grant. Family: m. Edna Thompson,
    1918; son, Mercer. Died Apr. 1974.
Career-Professional. 1st professional appear-
    ance as jazz musician, 1916; 1st appearance
    in N.Y.C., 1922, Hollywood, 1923; Cotton
    Club, N.Y.C., 1927-32; toured Europe, 1933,
    1950; toured Eng. & France, 1948; Annual
    Carnegie Hall concerts, 1943-50, Metropoli-
    tan Opera House, 1951. Motion pictures:
    Check & Double Check, 1930; She Got Her Man,
1935; Murder at the Vanities, 1935; The Hit Parade, 1937; Cabin
in the Sky, 1943, etc. Records: "Mood Indigo," "Solitude,"
"Sophisticated Lady," "Daybreak Express," "Rude Interlude,"
"Stompy Jones," "Harlem Speaks," "Take the A Train," etc. Pioneer in wordless use of voice as musical instrument in orchestra-
tion, also use of miniature concerto form in building jazz ar-
rangements around a soloist.
WRITINGS: Music is My Mistress, autobiog. (Doubleday, 1973).
HONORS AND AWARDS: "Far East Suite" played by Ellington's or-
chestra at White House Festival of the Arts, June 1965; "The
Golden Broom & the Golden Apple" suite performed at Lincoln Cen-
ter, where he conducted the N.Y. Philharmonic, July 1965; "In the
Beginning God," his first sacred concert, at Grace Episcopal
Cathedral, San Francisco, Sept. 1965 (repeated at Fifth Avenue
Presby. Church, N.Y.C., Christmas 1965; taped by CBS-TV & tele-
cast Jan. 1966). A Billy Strayhorn memorial album, "And His
Mother Called Him Bill," were chosen the "best performance by a
large group" by the Nat'l. Acad. of Recroding Arts & Sci., 1968.
"For their recordings the Ellingtonians have also garnered numer-
ous Grammy awards, and Ellington has won first place or top rank
repeatedly in polls or selections made by the magazines Esquire,
Down Beat, and Playboy" (Current Biography, 1970). Other awards:
Bronze Medal of City of N.Y.; NAACP Spingarn Medal; Pres. Medal
of Honor (on his 70th birthday); Elected to Nat'l. Inst. of Arts
& Letters, 1970.
SIDELIGHTS: "The single most impressive body of composition in
American jazz is the lush, complexly harmonic repertoire that

Ellison, Ralph Waldo

band leader-pianist-composer Duke Ellington has produced over the
past half century.... Jazz critic Ralph Gleason has called Ellington 'the greatest single talent...in the history of jazz'...
composer Gunther Schuller, president of the New England Conservatory of Music, described him as 'certainly the greatest American
composer'" (Current Biography, 1970).
Sources. Current Biography, 1970, Ed. by Charles Moritz (H. W. Wilson, 1970); Negro Handbook, Comp. by Eds. of Ebony (Johnson Pub.,
1966).

ELLISON, RALPH WALDO. 1914- . Novelist,
Essayist, Lecturer
Biographical-Personal. Born March 1, 1914, in
Okla. City, Okla. Son of Lewis Alfred and
Ida [Milsap] Ellison. Educ.: Tuskegee Inst.,
Ala., 1933-36; Hon. Ph.D. in Humane Letters,
Tuskegee Inst., Ala; Hon. degrees: Litt.D.:
Rutgers U., 1966; U. of Mich., 1967; Williams
Coll., 1970; L.H.D.: Grinnell Coll., 1967;
Adelphi U., 1971. Family: m. Fanny McCon-
nell, July 1946. Mailing address: 730 Riv-
erside Drive, N.Y., N.Y. 10031.
Career-Professional. Participated in N.Y.C.
Writer's Project; Lectr., Amer. Negro cul-
ture, folklore, creative writing, N.Y.U.,
Columbia, Fisk, Antioch, Princeton, Benning-
ton, others; Lectr., Salzburg Seminar in Amer. Stud., Austria,
1954; USIA, Dept. of State, tour of Italian cities, 1956; Tchr.,
Russian & Amer. Lit., Bard Coll., 1958-61; Alexander White Vis.
Prof., U. of Chgo., 1961; Vis. Prof. Writing, Rutgers U., 1962-64;
Albert Schweitzer Prof. of Humanities, N.Y.U., 1970- .
WRITINGS: Invisible Man, novel (Random House, 1952); Shadow and
Act, essays (Random House, 1964). Contrib. short stories, arti-
cles, book reviews, to popular and professional mags., i.e.,
Partisan Review, The Nation, Harper's, etc.
HONORS AND AWARDS: All for Invisible Man: Nat'l. Bk. Award for
fiction; Russwurm Award (1953); Nat'l. Newspaper Pub. Award (1954);
Nat'l. Arts & Letters Fellow (Rome, 1955); New York Herald Trib-
une's Book Review Poll 1965 (for most distinguished novel written
between 1945 and 1965). Cons. in Amer. Letters, Lib. of Congress,
1966- ; Rosenwald Fellow, 1945; Medal of Freedom, 1969; decorated
Chevalier Ordre des Artes et Lettres (France); Vis. Fellow Amer.
Stud., Yale, 1966; Amer. Acad. of Arts & Sci.; Rockefeller Found.
Award, 1954.
MEMBER: Carnegie Com. Educ. TV, 1966-67; Trus., John F. Kennedy
Center for Performing Arts; P.E.N. (v. pres., executive bd.);
Nat'l. Counc. Arts; Amer. Acad. Arts & Sci. Inst. Jazz Stud., Inc.

Emanuel, James Andrew

(bd. advis.); Nat'l. Inst. Arts & Letters (Counc.; chmn. lit. grants com.) 1964; Trus. Educ. Broadcasting Corp.; Nat'l. Citizen Com. for Broadcasting; Bd., WNDT, Channel 13; Assoc. Counc. of the Arts; Trus., Bennington Coll.
SIDELIGHTS: In Shadow and Act...Ellison explains, "Good fiction is made of that which is real, and reality is difficult to come by. So much depends upon the individual's willingness to discover his true self, upon his defining himself...against his background." He implied that what enabled him to rise above racial bitterness was his dedication to his art: "When I say that the novelist is created by the novel, I mean to remind you that fictional techniques are not a mere set of objective tools, but something more intimate: a way of feeling, of seeing, and of expressing one's sense of life. And the process of acquiring techniques is a process of modifying one's responses, of learning to see and feel, to hear and observe, to evoke and evaluate...of learning to conceive of human values in the ways which have been established by the great writers who have developed and extended the art" (Current Biography, 1968).
Sources. Negro Novel in America, Robert A. Bone (Yale U. Pr., 1958); Cavalcade, Ed. by Arthur P. Davis & Saunders Redding (Houghton Mifflin, 1971); Current Biography, 1968, Ed. by Charles Moritz (H. W. Wilson, 1968); Negro Almanac, 2d. ed., Ed. by Harry A. Ploski & Ernest Kaiser (Bellwether, 1971); Who's Who in America, 37th ed., 1972-73 (Marquis, 1972).

EMANUEL, JAMES ANDREW. 1921- . Poet, Teacher, Editor
Biographical-Personal. Born June 15, 1921, in Alliance, Neb. Son of Alfred A. and Cora Ann [Mance] Emanuel. Educ.: B.A., Howard U., 1950, M.A., Northwestern U., 1953; Ph.D., Columbia U., 1962. Family: m. Mattie Etha Johnson (div.), son, James Andrew, Jr. Mailing address: Dept. of Eng., City Coll., Convent Ave. at 138th St., N.Y., N.Y. 10031.
Career-Professional. Confidential Secy. to Gen. B. O. Davis, 1942-44; Sgt., 93rd Inf. Div., 1945-46; Supv., sec., Main Army & Air Force Induction Station, Chgo., 1950-52; Tchr., Harlem YWCA, Bus. & Secretarial Sch., N.Y., 1954-56; Prof. Lit., City Coll., City U. of N.Y., 1957- ; Gen. Ed., Broadside Critics Ser.
WRITINGS: Langston Hughes (Twayne, 1967); The Tree House and Other Poems (Broadside Pr., 1968); Dark Symphony, with Theodore L. Gross (Free Pr., 1968); Panther Man (Broadside Pr., 1970); How I Write/2, with Others (Harcourt, 1972). Gen. Ed.: Dynamite

Evans, Mari

Voices 1: Black Poets of the 1960's, Don L. Lee (Broadside Pr.,
1971); Claude McKay: The Black Poet at War, Addison Gayle
(Broadside Pr., 1972); In progress: The Folk Roots of Afro-
American Poetry, Bernard W. Bell (Broadside Pr., 1974). Anthol.:
America Sings; Modern American Lyrics; American Negro Poetry; New
Negro Poets: USA; La Poesie Negro Americaine; Kaleidoscope; A
Tune Beyond Us; Adventures in Living; Black Poetry; Negri U.S.A.;
New York Times Book of Verse; Black Power in the Arts; Black Out
Loud; A Broadside Treasury; Black Poetry for All Occasions; In-
vitation to Poetry; I, Too, Sing America; New Black Voices; Magic
of Black Poetry; Contemporary Novelists; Poetry of Black America;
Understanding the New Black Poetry. Period.: American Speech;
Books Abroad; Freedomways; Midwest Quarterly; Negro American Lit-
erature Forum; Negro History Bulletin; N. Y. Times; Phylon.
HONORS AND AWARDS: Summa cum laude 4 yrs., Howard U.; Who's Who
Among Students in American Colleges & Universities, 1950; John
Hay Whitney Opportunity Fellow, 1952-54; Eugene F. Saxton Memorial
Trust Fellow, 1965; Fulbright Vis. Prof. Amer. Lit., U. of Gre-
noble, France, 1968-69 & U. of Toulouse, France, 1971-72.
MEMBER: NAACP; Amer. Assn. of U. Prof.
SIDELIGHTS: Langston Hughes was translated into French by Jacques
Eymesse (Paris: Nouveaux Horizons, 1970). "Both my volumes The
Treehouse and Other Poems and Panther Man, read by me, are avail-
able in the Broadside Voices series, Broadside Press, Detroit,
Michigan" (author).
Sources. Author inform.; Broadside Authors and Artists, Comp. by
Leaonead P. Bailey (Broadside Pr., 1974); Dark Symphony, Ed. by
James A. Emanuel & Theodore L. Gross (Free Pr., 1968); New Black
Voices, Ed. by Abraham Chapman (New Amer. Lib., 1972); Poetry of
Black America, Ed. by Arnold Adoff (Harper & Row, 1973).

EVANS, MARI. Poet, Teacher
Biographical-Personal. Born in Toledo, Ohio.
  Educ.: U. of Toledo. Mailing address:
  750 W. Tenth Street, B-1, Indianapolis, Ind.
  46202.
Career-Professional. Writer-in-Residence &
  Instr., Black Lit., Indiana U.-Purdue U.,
  Indianapolis; Vis. Asst. Prof., Northwestern
  U., Evanston, Ill.; Prod./dir./writer
  (1968-73) for weekly-half-hour TV presenta-
  tion, "The Black Experience (Bobbs-Merrill);
  Cons. in Ethnic Stud. (1970-73) for Bobbs-
  Merrill; Presently Writer-in-Residence &
  Asst. Prof., Indiana U., Bloomington.
WRITINGS: I Am A Black Woman (Morrow, 1970);
  J.D., juvenile (Doubleday, 1973; paper, Avon,

Fabio, Sarah Webster

1974); <u>I Look At Me</u>, pre-school reader (Third World Pr., 1974);
<u>Rap Stories</u>, juvenile (Third World Pr., 1974).
HONORS AND AWARDS: "Her book <u>I Am A Black Woman</u>...received the
Indiana University Writers' Conference Award for the most distin-
guished work of poetry published by an Indiana Author in 1970, and
received the Black Academy of Arts and Letters first annual Poetry
Award in September 1971.
"A John Hay Whitney Fellow, 1965-66, she received a Woodrow Wil-
son Foundation Grant in 1968, and served as Consultant in the
1969-70 Discovery Grant Program of the National Endowment of the
Arts..." (author).
MEMBER: Authors Guild, Inc.; Authors League of Amer.; Lit. Advis.
Panel, Ind. State Arts Com.; Chmn., Statewide Com. for Penal Re-
form; Bd. of Management, Fall Creek Parkway YMCA; Region I Bd.,
Nat'l. Counc. of YMCA; Bd. Dir., Girls Clubs of Amer., Indian-
apolis.
SIDELIGHTS: "Her poetry has been used on record albums, several
television specials, two off-Broadway productions, and in nearly
150 textbooks and anthologies" (Author).
Sources. Author inform.; <u>Afro-American Writing</u>, Ed. by Richard A.
Long & Eugenia W. Collier (N.Y.U. Pr., 1972); <u>Black Voices</u>, Ed.
by Abraham Chapman (New Amer. Lib., 1968); <u>Broadside Authors and
Artists</u>, Comp. by Leaonead P. Bailey (Broadside Pr., 1974); <u>Ebony</u>
(Mar. 1974, Johnson Pub.); <u>For Malcolm</u>, Ed. by Dudley Randall &
Margaret Burroughs (Broadside Pr., 1969); <u>Kaleidoscope</u>, Ed. by
Robert Hayden (Harcourt, 1967); <u>New Black Voices</u>, Ed. by Abraham
Chapman (New Amer. Lib., 1972); <u>Poetry of Black America</u>, Ed. by
Arnold Adoff (Harper & Row), 1973).

FABIO, SARAH WEBSTER. 1928- . Poet, Teacher
Biographical-Personal. Born Jan. 20, 1928, in
Nashville, Tenn. Educ.: B.A., Fisk U.,
1946; M.A., San Francisco State U. Mailing
address: c/o Phase II Public., 143 East
Coll. St., 318, Oberlin, Ohio 44074.
Career-Professional. Tchr., Merritt Jr. Coll.,
Oakland, Cal.; Afro-Amer. Stud. Dept., U. of
Cal., Berkeley; Assoc. Prof., African &
African-Amer. Lit., Oberlin Coll.; Ed.,
Phase II, Jl. of Black Arts Renaissance.
WRITINGS: Poetry: A Mirror: A Soul (1969);
Black is A Panther Caged (1972); Rainbow
Signs, 7-vol. ser. Contrib. essays and
poetry to: Negro Digest/Black World; Race
Results, U.S.A. (1966), etc.
SIDELIGHTS: Ms. Fabio participated in the First World Festival of
Negro Art, Dakar, Senegal, 1966. She published two LP albums in

Fair, Ronald

1973 and has read her poems with jazz and rock bands. She also
participated in the Third Annual Writers Conference, Fisk U.,
1968 (Poetry of Black America).
Sources. Author brochure; Ebony (March 1974, Johnson Pub.); Poetry
of Black America, Ed. by Arnold Adoff (Harper & Row, 1973).

FAIR, RONALD. 1932- . Novelist
Biographical-Personal. Born Oct. 27, 1932, in
Chgo., Ill. Son of Herbert and Beulah Fair.
Educ.: Chgo. Public Schs.; Stenotype Sch. of
Chgo.; U.S. Navy. Family: div.; son, Rod-
ney, son, Glen, d. Nile. Mailing address:
c/o Hope Leresche & Steele, Literary Agent,
11 Jubilee Place, London, Eng. S.W.3.
Career-Professional. Court reporter, 1955-56;
Tchr., Columbia Coll., Chgo., 1967; Vis.
Tchr., Northwestern U.; Vis. Prof., Eng.
Dept., Wesleyan U., 1970-71.
WRITINGS: Novels: Many Thousand Gone (Har-
court, 1965); Hog Butcher (Harcourt, 1966).
Reprinted as: Cornbread, Earl and Me (Ban-
tam, 1975). Novellas: World of Nothing
(Harcourt, 1970); We Can't Breathe (Harcourt, 1972). Stories have
appeared in a variety of anthols. Excerpts, poetry (London, Paul
Breman, 1975).
HONORS AND AWARDS: Arts & Letters award, 1971; Best Bks. of the
Yr., 1972 (ALA for We Can't Breathe); NEA Fellow., 1974.
SIDELIGHTS: Began writing somewhere between the ages of twelve
and sixteen because of "my anger with the life I knew and inabili-
ty of anyone I knew to explain why things were the way they were"
(New Black Voices).
Sources. Author inform.; Best Short Stories by Negro Writers, Ed.
by Langston Hughes (Little, Brown, 1967); New Black Voices, Ed.
by Abraham Chapman (New Amer. Lib., 1972); Publisher inform.;
Books in Print, Supplement, 1975-76 (Bowker, 1976).

FAUSET, ARTHUR HUFF. 1899- . Novelist, Anthropologist
Biographical-Personal. Born Jan. 20, 1899, N.J. Son of Redmond and
Bella Fauset. Educ.: B.A., M.A., Ph.D., U. of Pa. Mailing ad-
dress: Apt. 8-K, 333 E. 30th St., N.Y., N.Y. 10016.
Career-Professional. Writer; Tchr., Prin., Phila. Public Schs.,
1918-46; Volunteer, AUS, World War II.
WRITINGS: Sojourner Truth: God's Faithful Pilgrim (U. of N.C.
Pr., 1938); For Freedom: A Biographical Story of the American
Negro (Franklin Pub., 1927); Folklore of Nova Scotia (Kraus
Repr., 1931); Black Gods of the Metropolis: Negro Religious Cults
of the Urban North (Octagon, 1944, 1970); America, Red, White,

Fauset, Jessie Redmond

Black and Yellow, with Nella B. Bright
(Franklin Pub., 1969). Contrib. numerous
short stories, essays, articles and reviews
to Opportunity & Crisis. In progress: African Lament, historical novel of life of
Shaka; Schlemiel, novel; Murder in NAJCP,
novel.
HONORS AND AWARDS: Fellow, Amer. Anthropological Assn.; Amer. Folklore Soc., studied
folklore extant among Blacks in Phila., Brit.
W. Indies, Nova Scotia & in the South, 1931;
prize short story "Symphonesque," repr. in
various public., including O'Brien Best
Short Stories & O. Henry Best Short Stories.
MEMBER: Alpha Phi Alpha.
Source. Author inform.

FAUSET, JESSIE REDMOND. 1884-1961. Novelist,
Poet
Biographical-Personal. Born 1884, in Snow Hill,
    N.J. D. of a minister. Educ.: Phila. Pub-
    lic Schs.; B.A., Cornell U. (Phi Beta Kappa);
    M.A., U. of Pa.; Sorbonne, Paris, France.
    Family: Single. Died 1961.
Career-Professional. Tchr., Dunbar High Sch.,
    Wash., D.C.; Lit. Ed., The Crisis; Tchr.,
    French, N.Y. Public Schs.
    WRITINGS: Novels: There Is Confusion (1924;
    AMS Pr. repr., 1974); Plum Bun (1929); The
    Chinaberry Tree (1931) & Comedy American
    Style (1933).
    SIDELIGHTS: Born into upper-class family.
    Studied French at Sorbonne, and lived in
Paris for several years. Skillful transl. of some of Black poets
of French West Indies. Taught at Dunbar High School which was
exclusively geared to training college bound Negroes. Some of
her poetry, written in French, attracted attention of W. E. B.
DuBois, who invited her to join The Crisis. The most prolific of
the Renaissance writers of the genteel school (Cavalcade).
Sources. An Anthology of Verse by American Negroes, Ed. by Newman
    I. White & Walter C. Jackson (Moore, 1924); Book of American Ne-
    gro Poetry, rev. ed., Ed. by James Weldon Johnson (Harcourt,
    1959); Cavalcade, Ed. by Arthur P. Davis & Saunders Redding
    (Houghton Mifflin, 1971).

Feelings, Muriel

FEELINGS, MURIEL. Juvenile Writer, Teacher
Biographical-Personal. Educ.: B.A., Cal. State U., L.A. Family:
m. Tom Feelings; son.
Career-Professional. Tchr., U.S. and E. Africa.
  WRITINGS: Juveniles: Zamani Goes to Market (Seabury, 1970);
Moja Means One: The Swahili Counting Book (Dial, 1971); Jambo
Means Hello: Swahili Alphabet Book (all illustrated by Tom
Feelings).
  HONORS AND AWARDS: Moja Means One was a Caldecott runner-up
(A.L.A.); Jambo Means Hello was selected Caldecott Honor Book.
  SIDELIGHTS: "Zamani Goes to Market, her first book for children,
was inspired by a stay with a family in a small village of West-
ern Kenya.
  Her artist, husband, Tom Feelings, traveled to East Africa just
before completing the drawings for Zamani. Highly respected for
his sensitive portrayal of Black people, he has illustrated many
books of distinction, including To Be a Slave and A Quiet Place"
(Zamani Goes to Market).
Source. Zamani Goes to Market, Muriel Feelings (Seabury, 1970).

FEELINGS, TOM. Artist, Juvenile Writer
Biographical-Personal. Born in Brooklyn, N.Y.
  Educ.: Sch. for Visual Arts. Family: m.
  Muriel Feelings; son.
Career-Professional. Illustrator, Ghana Govt.
  Pub. House, 1964-66; Guyana.
  WRITINGS: Book: Black Pilgrimage (N.Y.,
  Lothrop, Lee & Shepard, 1972). Illustrator:
  Zamani Goes to Market (Seabury, 1970); Moja
  Means One: A Swahili Counting Book (Dial,
  1971); & Jambo Means Hello: Swahili Alphabet
  Book (all juveniles by Muriel Feelings).
  HONORS AND AWARDS: Jambo Means Hello was
  selected Caldecott Honor Book by the ALA.
  Moja Means One was a Caldecott runner-up.
  SIDELIGHTS: Feelings worked for three years
in Guyana, where he lived with his wife and young son. They plan
to return to Africa to live permanently. In Mr. Feelings's words,
"My heart is with the Black people of America, but my soul is in
Africa" (Black Pilgrimage).
Sources. Black World (Johnson Pub., June 1975); Black Pilgrimage,
  Tom Feelings (N.Y.: Lothrop, Lee & Shepard, 1972).

Ferguson, Lloyd N.

FERGUSON, LLOYD N. 1918- . Chemist, Profes-
sor of Chemistry
Biographical-Personal. Born Feb. 9, 1918, in
Oakland, Cal. Son of Noel S. and Gwendolyn
L. [Johnson] Ferguson. Educ.: B.S., 1940,
Ph.D., 1943, U. of Cal., Berkeley. Family:
m. Charlotte W. Ferguson; son, Lloyd, Jr.,
son, Steve, d. Lisa. Mailing address: Cal.
State U., L.A., Cal. 90032.
Career-Professional. Res. Asst., Nat'l. Defense
Project, U. of Cal., 1941-44; Asst. Prof.,
Agricultural & Technical Coll., Greensboro,
N.C., 1944-45; Faculty Mem., Howard U.,
1945-65, Head, Dept. of Chemistry, 1958-65;
Prof., Cal. State U., L.A., 1965- . Chmn.,
Chemistry Dept., 1968-71; Chemist, Nat'l.
Bureau of Standards, Wash., D.C., Summer 1950; Chemist, Naval
Ordnance Lab., White Oak, Md., Summer 1951; Chemist, Dept. of
Agriculture, Pasadena, Ca., Summer 1967; Vis. Prof., U. of Oregon,
Eugene, Summer 1958; Vis. Prof., U. of Nairobi, Kenya, 1971-72.
WRITINGS: Electron Structures of Organic Molecules (Prentice-
Hall, 1952); Textbook of Organic Chemistry (Van Nostrand, 1958;
2nd ed., 1965; Far East ed., Affiliate East West Pr., New Delhi,
India, 1966); The Modern Structural Theory of Organic Chemistry
(Prentice-Hall, 1963; Japanese transl., Kagaku Dojin Sha, Tokyo,
1965; Far East ed., Prentice-Hall of India, New Delhi, 1969); Or-
ganic Chemistry: A Science and an Art (Willard Grant Pr., 1972);
Highlights of Alicyclic Chemistry (Franklin Pub., Vol. 1, 1973).
Structural Organic Chemistry: Gateway to Advanced Organic Chemis-
try (Willard Grant Pr.). Has contrib. 50 articles to journals.
HONORS AND AWARDS: Manufacturing Chemists Tchg. Award, 1974;
Hon. D.Sci., Howard U., 1970; Guggenheim Fellow, Cytochemistry
Dept., Carlberg Laboratorium, Copenhagen, Denmark, 1953-54; Nat'l.
Sci. Found. Faculty Fellow, Swiss Fed. Inst. of Technology, Zu-
rich, Switzerland, 1961-62; Oakland Mus. Assn. "in recognition of
contributions to science and technology for humanity," 1973; Cal.
State U. Outstanding Prof. Award, 1974; Featured in Chemistry,
July-Aug., 1971.
MEMBER: U.S. Nat'l. Com. to Internat. Union of Pure & Applied
Chemistry, 1973-76; Member-at-Large, Nat'l. Acad. of Sci., Nat'l.
Res. Counc., Div. of Chemistry & Chemical Technology, 1970-73;
Nat'l. Cancer Inst. Chemotherapy Advis. Com., 1972-76; Medicinal
& Organic Chemistry Review Com., Nat'l. Inst. of Health, 1966-70;
Amer. Assn. of U. Prof.; Sigma Xi; Phi Kappa Phi, Nat'l. Honor
Soc.; Fellow, Amer. Assn. for Advancement of Sci.; Fellow, Chemi-
cal Soc. of London; Fellow, Amer. Inst. of Chemists.
SIDELIGHTS: Listed in "World's Who's Who in Science; Leaders in
American Science: American Men of Science; Negro in Science.

Fisher, Miles Mark

Three talks at international conference on teaching of university
chemistry, U. of Nairobi, 1971; Talk, Pacific Coast Conf. on
Chemistry & Spectroscopy, San Diego, 1973.
  "As a member of the National Cancer Institute Chemotherapy Ad-
visory Committee, was one of two members to accompany two NCI ad-
ministrators on a one-month tour of Russian Laboratories in 1973
(Moscow, Riga, Leningrad, Kiev, and Yerevan) to discuss the cancer
chemotherapy programs of the two countries and to initiate an exchange of information and drugs under the U.S.--U.S.S.R. Joint
Committee on Research on Oncologic Diseases" (Author).
  Prog. Dir. of 5-year $1.1 million grant to Cal. State U., L.A.
from U.S. Public Health Serv. to support biomedical res. for minority students. Apptd. mem. of Ed. Bd. Journal of College Science Teaching, Nat'l. Sci. Tchrs. Assn. Fellow. Fund, Atlanta,
Ga., for screening applicants for Ford Found. fellow. from Black
predoctoral candidates (Author).
Source. Author inform.

FISHER, MILES MARK. 1899-1970. Minister,
Professor of Church History
Biographical-Personal. Born Oct. 29, 1899, in
  Atlanta, Ga. Son of Elijah John (minister)
  and Florida Neely Fisher. Educ.: B.A.,
  Morehouse Coll., 1918; B.D., N. Bap. Theol.
  Sem., 1922; A.M., 1922, Ph.D., 1948, U. of
  Chgo. Divinity Sch. Family: m. Ada Virginia
  Foster; d. Mrs. Florida Parker, son, Miles
  Mark IV, son, Alfred Foster, son, Elijah John
  III, son, Christopher Tennant, d. Ada Markita
  Fisher. Died Dec. 14, 1970, in Richmond, Va.
Career-Professional. Minister, White Rock Bap.
  Church, Durham, N.C., 1933-1965, Minister-
  Emeritus, 1965-70; Prof. of Church Hist.,
  Shaw U., Raleigh, N.C., 1933-65.
WRITINGS: The Master's Slave--Elijah John Fisher (1922); Virginia
Union University and Some of Her Achievements (1924); A Short His-
tory of the Baptist Denomination (1933); Negro Slave Songs in the
United States (Cornell U. Pr., 1953; Fuller & Fuller, 1968; paper,
Citadel, 1963).
HONORS AND AWARDS: Negro Slave Songs in the United States won
Amer. Historical Assn.'s prize for outstanding hist. vol. of 1953.
Selected as one of nation's top 10 ministers of 1954; Recipient of
Golden Anniversary Award, Nat'l. Recreation Assn.; Hon. D.D., Shaw
U.; Hon. member, Internat. Mark Twain Society.
MEMBER: Amer. Hist. Assn.; Amer. Soc. of Church Hist.; ASNLH;
Miss. Valley Hist. Assn.

Ford, Annie L.

SIDELIGHTS: Ph.D. dissertation: "The Evolution of Negro Slave Songs in the United States" (Author).
Sources. Inform. (author's widow); Pub. inform.

FISHER, RUDOLPH. 1897-1934. Physician, Novelist
Biographical-Personal. Born in 1897, in Wash., D.C. Educ.: B.A. (honors), 1919, M.A., 1920, Brown U.; Howard U. Medical Sch.; Columbia U. Medical Sch. Died 1934.
Career-Professional. Tchr., Biology; Physician; Affiliate, X-ray Div., Dept. of Health, N.Y.C.; Writer.
WRITINGS: Novels: The Conjure Man Dies (1932); The Walls of Jericho (1928); Short Stories: "The City of Refuge," and "The Blades of Grass," in Atlantic Monthly; in Best Short Stories; American Mercury; Survey Graphic & Story.
HONORS AND AWARDS: Excelled in Eng. lit. and biology at Brown U. Member of: Phi Beta Kappa, Sigma Psi & Delta Sigma Rho.
SIDELIGHTS: "Prominently associated with the 'Negro Renaissance' ...(Fisher was) unembittered, and one of the wittiest of the Renaissance group...(He) was among the first to light up the dark realities of Negro life with humor" (Cavalcade). "Beneath the comedy and caricature of Fisher, there is a revelation of the truth of Harlem as it was in the late twenties" (Negro Caravan). He was talented in music. He arranged a number of songs for Paul Robeson (Historical Negro Biographies).
Sources. Cavalcade, Ed. by Arthur P. Davis & Saunders Redding (Houghton Mifflin, 1971); Dark Symphony, Ed. by James A. Emanuel & Theodore L. Gross (Free Pr., 1968); Historical Negro Biographies, Ed. Wilhelmena S. Robinson (ASNLH, 1967); Negro Caravan, Ed. by Sterling A. Brown & Others (Arno Pr. & N.Y. Times, 1969); Negro Genius, Benjamin Brawley (Dodd, Mead, 1937); Negro Voices in American Fiction, Hugh Gloster (Russell, 1965).

FORD, ANNIE L. 1938- . Poet
Biographical-Personal. Born Dec. 14, 1938, in Miami, Fla. D. of Emanuel Luckie, Sr. and Clara McRae Brooks. Educ.: B.A., Va. Union U.; M.A., Cal. State U., Long Beach. Family: m.; one daughter, two stepsons. Mailing address: 2011 Knoxville Ave., Long Beach, Cal. 90815.
Career-Professional. Lectr.: Grossmont Coll., San Diego, Cal.; San Diego City Coll.; Bakersfield Coll., Cal.; Carson, Cal.; Cerritos, Cal.; Long Beach, Cal.; Los Angeles.

Ford, Nick Aaron

WRITINGS: <u>My Soul Bone Aches</u>, poetry (Christian Pr., 1973). Book in progress.
SIDELIGHTS: Hobbies: writing, interior designing, sewing, swimming, golfing; Award, Black Hist. Week (Morningside High Sch., Inglewood, Cal.) (Author).
Source. Author inform.

FORD, NICK AARON. 1904- . Scholar, Editor, Consultant
Biographical-Personal. Born Aug. 4, 1904, in Ridgeway, S.C. Son of Nick H. and Carrie Ford. <u>Educ.</u>: B.A., Benedict Coll., Columbia, S.C.; M.A., 1934, Ph.D., 1945, U. of Iowa. <u>Family</u>: m. Ola M. Ford; son, Leonard Aaron. <u>Mailing address</u>: 919 E. 43rd St., Baltimore, Md. 21212.
Career-Professional. Tchr., Coll. & Univ. in: Fla., Tex., Okla., Mass., Md.; Chmn., Dept. of Eng., Morgan State Coll., Baltimore, 1947-70; Alain Locke Prof. of Black Stud., Morgan State (currently).
WRITINGS: <u>The Contemporary Negro Novel</u> (Meador, 1936); <u>Baltimore Afro-American:</u> <u>Best Short Stories by Afro-American Writers, 1925-1950</u> (Kraus Repr., 1950); <u>Basic Skills for Better Writing</u>, Co-ed. with Waters Turpin (Putnam, 1959); <u>American Culture in Literature</u> (Rand McNally, 1967); <u>Language in Uniform</u> (Odyssey, 1967); <u>Extending Horizons: A Freshman Reader for Cultural Enrichment</u>, Co-ed. with Waters Turpin (Random House, 1969); <u>Black Insights: Significant Literature by Black American--1760 to the Present</u> (Ginn, 1971); <u>Black Studies: Threat or Challenge?</u> (Kennikat, 1973). Journals: <u>College English</u>; <u>English Journal</u>; <u>College Composition and Communications, The Teachers College Record</u>; <u>The Journal of Higher Education</u>; <u>New England Quarterly</u>; <u>Phylon</u>; <u>New Republic</u>; <u>Christian Century</u>; <u>CLA Journal</u>; & <u>Black World</u>.
HONORS AND AWARDS: U.S. Office Educ., 3-yr. grant for res. on improvement of reading and writing skills of disadvantaged coll. freshmen, 1964 (resulted in <u>Extending Horizons</u>). NEH Grant, for evaluative study of Black Stud. in Amer. Coll. & U., 1970 (visited more than 100 campuses & wrote <u>Black Studies: Threat or Challenge?</u>). Outstanding Serv. Award, Md. Council of Teachers of English, "significant efforts toward improving the instruction in the Language Arts for the students in the schools of Maryland and toward raising the professional standards of teachers of English," 1971; Community Serv. Award, African Assn. of Black Stud., 1974.
MEMBER: Past pres., CLA: Mid Atlantic Region (1971-73) & of Coll. Lang. Assn.; former member Executive Com., Assn. of Depts. of Eng.

Fortune, Timothy Thomas

SIDELIGHTS: "In constant demand as consultant in the use of resources for integrating the study of Afro-American life and culture into courses in American literature and Freshman English and
guidance in the organization and effective teaching of courses in
Black (Afro-American) literature" (Author). Served as consultant
for U.S. Office of Education; The Ford Foundation, & the National
Endowment for Humanities in connection with the conduct of Summer
Institutes for improvement of skills in organizing & teaching
courses in Black Studies (Author).
Sources. Author inform.; Contemporary Authors, Vols. 25-28, Ed. by
Carolyn Riley (Gale Res., 1971).

FORTEN, CHARLOTTE L. 1838-1914. Writer, Teacher
Biographical-Personal. Born in 1838, in Phila., Pa. Her father
(sailmaker) and mother were free Blacks. Educ.: Salem, Mass.
Normal Sch., grad., 1856. Family: m. Francis J. Grimke (Minis-
ter, who became spokesman for Negro people), 1878. Died 1914.
Career-Professional. Volunteer tchr., during Civil War, St. Helena
Island (off coast of S.C.); 2 yrs. Tchr., Salem, Mass. & Phila.
WRITINGS: Charlotte Forten's Journal (sporadic, 1854-64), considered unusual record & important hist. document. Contrib. to
Atlantic Monthly; transl. Erckmann-Chartrians's Madame Therese;
or, the Volunteers of '92. Most recent: The Journal of Charlotte
Forten, Ed. by Ray Allen Billington (Dryden, 1953; paper, Collier,
1967).
SIDELIGHTS: "The Forten family had been actively involved in the
black man's cause for two generations, and their Philadelphia home
was described as a 'mecca for abolitionists.' Eventually Charlotte herself counted John Greenleaf Whittier, William Lloyd Garrison, and Wendell Phillips among her friends. She was extremely
sensitive to the plight of the black man. Her Journal frequently
alludes to racial prejudice, discrimination, and injustice; her
tone is often one of bitter irony, occasionally hinting at de-
spair. She read widely and insatiably, wrote 'occasional' poems,
and taught enthusiastically--first white pupils in Salem, and then
black students in her aunt's school in Philadelphia" (Cavalcade).
Sources. Cavalcade, Ed. by Arthur P. Davis & Saunders Redding
(Houghton Mifflin, 1971); Historical Negro Biographies, Wilhelmena
S. Robinson (ASNLH, 1967); Negro Poets and Their Poems, Robert T.
Kerlin, 3d. rev. (Assoc. Pub., 1935); Profiles of Negro Womanhood,
Sylvia G. Dannett (Educ. Her., 1964).

FORTUNE, TIMOTHY THOMAS. 1856-1928. Journalist
Biographical-Personal. Born 1856 in Fla. Son of a Reconstruction
politician (Fla. Legis.). Educ.: Stanton Sch., Jacksonville,
Fla.; Howard U. Died in 1928.
Career-Professional. Tchr., Fla.; Compositor, a N.Y. newspaper.
Collaborator in founding & ed. New York Globe, 1881; Founder, New

Franklin, John Hope

York Age (1880's-1890's); Ed. The Negro World (public. of Marcus Garvey's Universal Negro Improvement Assn.); Co-organizer (with Booker T. Washington) of Nat'l. Negro Bus. League, 1900; Ed. staff, New York Evening Sun (white newspaper).
WRITINGS: Essays: Black and White: Land, Labor, and Politics in the South (1884); The Negro in Politics (1885); Dream of Life (Bks. for Lib. Repr., 1905).
SIDELIGHTS: "Skilled stylist, and one of the most celebrated journalists of his time..." (Negro Author in America). "During the period that he had worked as editor of The Globe, Fortune had formulated a policy position for effective journalism: to be a power for good among the people a paper must be fearless in tone, its editor should not fail to speak his just convictions, he should hold himself aloof from parties and maintain his position untrammelled by parties and party bosses" (Negro Handbook).
Sources. Afro-American Writing, Ed. by Richard A. Long & Eugenia W. Collier (N.Y.U. Pr., 1972); Historical Negro Biographies, Wilhelmena S. Robinson (ASNLH, 1967); Men of Mark, William Simmons (Johnson Pub., 1970); Negro Author in America, Vernon Loggins (Kennikat, 1959); Negro Caravan, Ed. by Sterling A. Brown & Others (Arno Pr., & N.Y. Times, 1969); Negro Handbook, Comp. by eds. of Ebony (Johnson Pub., 1966); Negro Vanguard, Richard Bardolph (Random House, 1959); 100 Years of Negro Freedom, Arna Bontemps (Dodd, Mead, 1961).

FRANKLIN, JOHN HOPE. 1915- . History Professor, Historian, Scholar
Biographical-Personal. Born Jan. 2, 1915, in Rentiesville, Okla. Son of Buck Colbert (lawyer) and Mollie [Parker] Franklin. Educ.: B.A. (magna cum laude), Fisk U., 1935; M.A., 1936, Ph.D., 1941, Harvard U. Family: m. Aurelia Whittington (librn.), 1940; son, John Whittington. Mailing address: 5805 S. Blackstone Ave., Chgo., Ill. 60637.
Career-Professional. Mem. Hist. Faculty: Fisk U., 1936-37; St. Augustine's Coll., Raleigh, N.C., 1939-43; N.C. Coll. at Durham, 1943-47; Howard U., 1947-56; Chmn., Dept. of Hist., Brooklyn Coll., 1956-65; Prof. Amer. Hist., U. of Chgo., 1964- ; Chmn., Dept. of Hist., 1967-70, John Mathews Manly Distinguished Serv. Prof., 1969- ;

Franklin, John Hope

Wm. Pitt Prof. Amer. Hist. & Inst., Cambridge U., 1962-63; Vis. Prof.: Harvard, U. of Wis., Cornell U., Salzburg Seminar, U. of Cal., Cambridge U. (Chmn. Bd. of Foreign Scholarships, 1966-69). WRITINGS: The Free Negro in North Carolina, 1790-1860 (U. of N.C. Pr., 1943); From Slavery to Freedom (Knopf, 1947; rev. 1957, 1967, 1974); The Militant South, 1800-1860 (Belknap Pr. of Harvard U. Pr., 1956); Reconstruction After the Civil War (U. of Chgo. Pr., 1961); The Emancipation Proclamation (Doubleday, 1963; Edinburgh U. Pr., 1963); Land of the Free, with Others (Franklin Pub., Benziger Bros., 1965); Illustrated History of Black Americans, with Eds. of Time-Life Bks. (Time-Life Inc., 1970, 1973). Ed.: The Civil War Diary of James T. Ayers (Ill. State Hist. Soc., 1947); Albion Tourgee's A Fool's Errand (Belknap Pr. of Harvard U. Pr., 1961); T. W. Higginson's Army Life in a Black Regiment (Beacon Pr., 1962); Three Negro Classics (Avon, 1965); The Negro in the Twentieth Century, with Isadore Starr (Random House, 1967); Color and Race (Houghton Mifflin, 1968); W. E. B. DuBois's, The Suppression of the African Slave Trade (La. State Univ. Pr., 1969); Reminiscences of An Active Life: The Autobiography of John R. Lynch (U. of Chgo. Pr., 1970); A Southern Odyssey--Travelers in the Antebellum North (La. State U. Pr., 1976). Gen. Ed., U. of Chgo. Pr. Ser. of Negro Biogs. and Autobiogs. Contrib. to: Problems in American History; The New Negro Thirty Years Afterward; The Americans: Ways of Life and Thought; Issues in University Education; Lincoln for the Ages; The Southerner as American; Soon, One Morning; The Atlantic Future; The South in Continuity and Change; The American Negro Reference Book; New Frontiers of the American Reconstruction; American Primer; The Comparative Approach to American History; History of American Presidential Elections, 1789-1964. Period.: New England Quarterly; North Carolina Historical Review; Journal of Negro History; Journal of the Illinois State Historical Society; Journal of Negro Education; Annals of the American Academy of Political & Social Science. HONORS AND AWARDS: Edward Austin Fellow, Harvard; Julius Rosenwald Fellow; (Post-doctoral) President's Fund, Brown U.; Soc. Sci. Res. Counc.; John Simon Guggenheim Mem. Found.; Center for Advanced Study in Behavioral Sci.; Founding mem., Fisk U., Phi Beta Kappa; Mem. Senate, Phi Beta Kappa, Pres. United Chapter, Phi Beta Kappa; Rep., Amer. Counc. of Learned Soc., U. of Calcutta, Madras, & Bombay, 1957; Fulbright Prof., several Australian U., 1960: Lincoln Lectr., Bd. of Foreign Scholarships in South Amer., the S. Pacific & E. Asia, 1973; Hon. degrees from 35 coll. & U. MEMBER: Ed. Bd., Journal of Negro History (20 yrs.); Executive com. Org. of Amer. Hist., 1958-61, V. pres., 1973; Counc. of Learned Soc.; Nat'l. Educ. TV; Salzburg Seminar in Amer. Stud.; Chmn. Fisk U. Bd. Trus.; Bd. Chgo. Pub. Lib.; Bd. Mus. of Sci. & Indus.; So. Hist. Assn. (pres., 1970-71); ASNLH; Amer. Stud. Assn.

Frazier, Edward Franklin

(past pres.); Amer. Assn. State & Local Hist.; Assn. Soc. Sci.
Tchrs.
Sources. Author inform.; <u>Black Historians</u>, Earl E. Thorpe (Morrow,
1969); <u>Current Biography, 1963</u>, Ed. by Charles Moritz (H. W. Wilson, 1963); <u>From Slavery to Freedom</u>, 2d rev. ed., John H. Franklin (Knopf, 1956); <u>Negro Almanac</u>, Comp. by Harry A. Ploski &
Ernest Kaiser (Bellwether, 1971); <u>Who's Who in America</u>, 37th ed.
m. 1972-73 (Marquis, 1972); <u>Books in Print</u>, Supplement, 1975-76
(Bowker, 1976).

FRAZIER, EDWARD FRANKLIN. 1894-1962. Sociologist, Scholar
Biographical-Personal. Born Sept. 24, 1894, in
E. Shore, Md. Son of James Edward and Mary
[Clark] Franklin. <u>Educ.</u>: Baltimore public
schs.; B.A. (cum laude), Howard U., 1916;
M.A., Clark U., 1920; Ph.D., U. of Chgo.,
1931. <u>Family</u>: m. Marie E. Brown, Sept. 14,
1922. Died May 17, 1962.
Career-Professional. Res. Fellow, N.Y. Sch. of
Soc. Work, 1920-21; Fellow, Amer.-Scandina-
vian Found. to Denmark, 1921-22; Dir., Atlanta U. Sch. of Soc. Work, 1922-27; Prof.
of Sociol., Fisk U., 1929-34; Prof. & Head,
Dept. of Sociol. Howard U., 1934-59 (25
yrs.); Lectr., N.Y. Sch. of Soc. Work, Co-
lumbia U.; Chmn., Com., of Experts on Race, UNESCO, 1949; Chief,
Div. Applied Soc. Sci., Paris, 1951-53.
WRITINGS: <u>The Negro Family in the United States</u> (U. of Chgo. Pr.,
1939; rev, 1966); <u>Black Bourgeoisie</u> (Free Pr., 1957; Collier,
1962); <u>The Negro in the United States</u> (Macmillan, 1957); <u>The Negro Church in America</u> (1963); <u>Race and Culture Contacts in the
Modern World</u>. Contrib. to journals.
HONORS AND AWARDS: Anisfield Award for <u>The Negro Family in the
United States</u>, 1939; Fellow, Guggenheim Found., to Brazil & W.
Indies, 1940-41; McIver Lectureship Award, Amer. Sociol. Soc.,
1956.
MEMBER: Fellow, Amer. Assn. for Advancement of Sci.; Inter-Amer.
Soc. Anthropology & Geography; Founding mem., Inst. Internacional
de Estudios Afroamericanos; Amer. Sociol. Soc. (pres., 1948); E.
Sociol. Soc. (pres.); Pres., Internat. Scientific Study Race
Relat.; Fellow, Lib. of Congress.
SIDELIGHTS: "...best remembered for his controversial book <u>Black
Bourgeoisie</u> in which he expounded the theory that the Negro mid-
dle class was isolating itself from the problems of marginal or
poverty-stricken Negroes.... The MacIver Lectureship for 1956
has been awarded to E. Franklin Frazier for <u>Black Bourgeoisie</u>...
by the American Sociological Society...to the student of society

Fuller, Hoyt W.

'who in the opinion of the Selection Committee has contributed to
the progress of sociology by his published or unpublished work
during the past two years, and is qualified to inform the academic
community or the educated public concerning the current achievements and work in progress in sociology'" (Black Bourgeoisie).
Sources. Black Bourgeoisie, E. Franklin Frazier, rev. ed. (Free Pr.,
1957); Current Biography, 1940, Ed. by Maxine Black (H. W. Wilson,
1940); Negro Almanac, Comp. by Harry A. Ploski & Ernest Kaiser
(Bellwether, 1971); Negro Church in America, E. Franklin Frazier
(Schocken, 1963); Who Was Who in America, Vol. IV, 1961-68 (Marquis, 1968).

FULLER, HOYT W. 1927- . Editor, Teacher
Biographical-Personal. Born Sept. 10, 1927, in
    Atlanta, Ga. Son of Thomas Fuller. Educ.:
    B.A., Wayne State U., Detroit, Advanced
    study. Family: Single. Mailing address:
    3001 S. Martin Luther King Drive, Apt. 1902,
    Chgo., Ill. 60616.
Career-Professional. (Present) Executive Ed.,
    Black World; Asst. Ed., Collier's Encyclo-
    pedia; W. African Corresp., Haagse Post
    (Amsterdam, Holland); Assoc. Ed., Ebony;
    Feature ed., Michigan Chronicle; Reporter,
    Detroit Tribune. Tchr.: Fiction Writing
    Seminar, Columbia Coll., Chgo.; Afro-Amer.
    Lit., Northwestern U.; Afro-Amer. Lit., Ind.
    U., Bloomington; Afro-Amer. Lit., Wayne
    State U.
WRITINGS: Journey to Africa (Third World Pr., 1971). Anthol.:
Black Expression, Ed. by Addison Gayle; American Negro Short Sto-
ries, Ed. by John H. Clarke; Black Aesthetic, Ed. by Addison
Gayle; Black Literature in America, Ed. by Houston Baker; Points
of Departure, Ed. by Ernece Kelly; Beyond the Angry Black, Ed. by
John A. Williams; Collier's Encyclopedia Yearbook (special arti-
cles); Black American Writer, Ed. by C. W. E. Bigsby; Afro-Ameri-
can Writing, Ed. by Richard A. Dong & Eugenia Collier. Period.:
New Yorker; The Nation; New Leader; New Republic; Midstream;
Southwest Review; North American Review; Chicago Defender; Black
Position; Chicago Jewish Forum; Book Week (N.Y. Herald Tribune);
Book Week (Chgo. Sun-Times); Books Today (Chgo. Tribune); African
Forum; Detroit News; Christian Science Monitor; New York Times
Book Review; Arts in Society.
HONORS AND AWARDS: John Hay Whitney Opportunity Fellow, 1965-66
(travel, study in Africa).
SIDELIGHTS: From 1957 to 1960, a legal resident of Spain (based
on the island of Mallorca); traveled in Europe & to North & West
Africa, spending three months in newly independent Guinea. "Re-

Gaines, Ernest J.

sponding to the challenge of reviving the Johnson Publishing Co.'s
Negro Digest, he turned that magazine into a major forum of original black world opinion, an achievement duly commemorated by the
change of the name of the magazine to Black World in 1970." He
has also conducted the weekly OBAC writers workshop in Chicago
(Afro-American Writing).

Sources. Afro-American Writing...Vol. 1, Ed. by Richard A. Long &
Eugenia W. Collier (N.Y.U. Pr., 1972); Author inform.

GAINES, ERNEST J. 1933- . Novelist, Short
Story Writer

Biographical-Personal. Born Jan. 15, 1933, on
a plantation near Oscar, La. Moved with family to Vallejo, Cal., at age 15. Educ.:
2 yrs., San Francisco State Coll. (drafted
into Army, 1953-55); returned to San Francisco State, B.A., 1957; Post grad., Stanford
U., 1958-59. Mailing address: 998 Divisa-
dero St., San Francisco, Cal. 94115.

Career-Professional. Writing; odd jobs; military service.

WRITINGS: Barren Summer, completed 1963;
individual stories appeared in Negro Digest
& elsewhere, collected into Bloodline (Dial,
1968); first pub. novel, Catherine Carmier
(Atheneum, 1964); Of Love and Dust (Dial, 1967); Autobiography of
Miss Jane Pittman (Dial, 1970), produced for CBS TV, 1974, with
Cicely Tyson in title role; Long Day in November (Dial, 1971).
HONORS AND AWARDS: Wallace Stegner Fellow. in creative writing,
Stanford U.; Joseph Henry Jackson Lit. Award for creative writing,
1959.
SIDELIGHTS: "He...seems intent upon exhuming from his native
Louisiana soil--to which he hopes to return from San Francisco--
what Henry James might call the 'stuff of consciousness' for a
novel of magnitude. Gaines who thinks that the artist is the only
free man left in the world, has so far been concerned in his fiction (usually about rural Louisiana) with individuals determined
often heroically, either to maintain their codes of conduct among
debasing or confusing forces, or to ride out the storm of conse-
quences attending their decisions to change with the times" (Dark
Symphony).

Sources. The Best Short Stories by Negro Writers, Ed. by Langston
Hughes (Little, Brown, 1967); Cavalcade, Ed. by Arthur P. Davis &
Saunders Redding (Houghton Mifflin, 1971); Dark Symphony, Ed. by
James A. Emanuel & Theodore L. Cross (Free Pr., 1968); New Black
Voices, Ed. by Abraham Chapman (New Amer. Lib., 1972).

GARLAND, PHYLLIS T. 1935- . Editor, Feature Writer
Biographical-Personal. Born Oct. 27, 1935, in McKeesport, Pa.
Career-Professional. N.Y. Ed., Ebony mag.
    WRITINGS: The Sound of Soul (Regnery, 1969).
Source. The Sound of Soul, Phyl Garland (Regnery, 1969).

GARNET, HENRY HIGHLAND. 1815-1882. Scholar,
Lecturer/Abolitionist, Minister
Biographical-Personal. Born 1815, in slavery on
    the Eastern Shore of Md. Taken to N.Y. as a
    child in his parents' escape from slavery,
    where he attended school. Attended Oneida
    Inst., Whitesboro, N.Y., graduated 1840.
    Died 1882.
Career-Professional. Agent, Amer. Anti-Slavery
    Soc.; Pastor, Liberty St. Presby. Church,
    Troy, N.Y.; Missionary, Jamaica (for United
    Presby. Church of Scotland); Pastor, Shiloh
    Church, N.Y.; Pres., Avery Coll., Pittsburgh;
    Minister, Liberia (died in 2 months).
    WRITINGS: An Address to the Slaves of the
    United States of America (1843); The Memorial
Discourse (1865), first time a Black spoke to U.S. House of Rep.;
Past and Present Condition, and the Destiny of the Colored Race
(Black Her., Bks. for Lib., 1848).
SIDELIGHTS: "The spiritual successor to David Walker and one of
the foremost advocates of full enfranchisement for the Negro, was
Henry Highland Garnet, whose militant addresses caused him to be
regarded as one of the most extreme of radicals" (Negro Genius).
    Six years after the 1843 address: An Address to the Slaves...,
John Brown had it published at his own expense (Historical Negro
Biographies).
    "His Address to the Slaves was probably the strongest that Gar-
net ever delivered. It was felt that it tended to promote insurrection. Among other remarks, Garnet said: 'Brethren, arise,
arise! Strike for your lives and liberties. Now is the day and
the hour. Let every slave throughout the land do this and the
days of slavery are numbered. You can not be more oppressed than
you have been; you can not suffer greater cruelties than you have
already. Rather die freemen than live to be slaves'" (Negro
Genius).
Sources. Afro-American Writing, Ed. by Richard A. Long & Eugenia W.
    Collier (N.Y.U. Pr., 1972); Historical Negro Biographies, Wilhel-
    mena S. Robinson (ASNLH, 1967); Negro Genius, Benjamin Brawley
    (Dodd, Mead, 1937); Negroes in Public Affairs and Government, Ed.
    by Walter Christmas (Educ. Her., 1966).

Garrett, Beatrice

GARRETT, BEATRICE. Novelist
Biographical-Personal. Mailing address: 1322 W. 60th St., L.A.,
    Cal. 90044.
Career-Professional.
    WRITING: Welfare on Skid Row, novel (Exposition Pr., 1974).
Source. Books in Print, 1976 (Bowker, 1976).

GARVEY, MARCUS. 1887-1940. Founder, Universal
Negro Improvement Association
Biographical-Personal. Born Aug. 17, 1887, in
    St. Ann's Bay, Jamaica. Son of Marcus &
    Sarah Garvey. Educ.: Common Sch. and Pupil-
    Teachers' Course, Jamaica; U. of London, Eng.
    Family: m. Amy Jacques Garvey. Died in 1940.
Career-Professional. Ed., Garvey's Watchman,
    Kingston, Jamaica; Timekeeper (banana planta-
    tion), United Fruit Co., Costa Rica; Founder,
    United Negro Improvement Assn., Jamaica &
    U.S.; Established Negro World, organ of UNIA,
    N.Y.C. (weekly) 1918-34.
    WRITINGS: Garvey and Garveyism, Ed. by Amy
    Jacques Garvey (1963); Philosophy and Opin-
    ions of Marcus Garvey, or Africa for the Af-
ricans, Ed. by Amy Jacques Garvey (2nd ed., London: Cass, 1967);
Marcus Garvey and the Vision of Africa, Ed. by John H. Clarke &
Amy Jacques Garvey (Random House, 1974); Collected Papers and
Documents, Ed. by E. U. Essien-Udom (Africana Mod. Lib. Ser.,
Humanities, 1974).
    SIDELIGHTS: "...permanently important for: Black pride, the uni-
ty of African people in and out of Africa, the beauty of Blackness, cooperative Black economic activity, the rejection of white
religion, the understanding of white racism as a historical con-
stant, distrust of white radicalism--all of these concepts and attitudes so prevalent today were pioneered by Marcus Garvey" (Black
Writers of America).
Sources. Black Moses; the Story of Marcus Garvey, E. David Cronon
    (U. of Wis. Pr., 1969); Black Writers of America, Richard Barks-
    dale (Macmillan, 1972); Harlem: Negro Metropolis, Claude McKay
    (Dutton, 1940); World's Great Men of Color, vol. 2, J. A. Rogers
    (Macmillan, 1972).

GAYLE, ADDISON, JR. 1932- . Editor, Teacher, Critic
Biographical-Personal. Born June 2, 1932, in Newport News, Va. Son
    of Addison and Carrie Gayle. Educ.: B.A., City Coll. of N.Y.;
    M.A., U. of Cal., 1966. Family: separated from Rosalie Gayle.
    Mailing address: 345 E. 80th St., N.Y., N.Y.

Gillespie, Marcia Ann

Career-Professional. Prof. Lit., Bernard M.
Baruch Coll. of City U. of N.Y., 1969; Asst.
Prof., Creative Writing, Dept. of Eng., Livingston Coll., Rutgers U., 1971-72; Lectr.,
incl. "Black Heritage," Channel 2 TV, Oberlin
Coll., U. of Va., Yale U., Dunbar Centenary,
U. of Cal., Irvine; Consultant, Minority
Writers, Doubleday & Random House; Ed.
staffs, Amistad mag., Third World Pr., Black
Lines mag.; Sponsor of Richard Wright Award
for SEEK student with highest average for
semester.
WRITINGS: Black Expression (Weybright & Tal-
ley, 1969); The Black Situation, Ed. (Hori-
zon, 1970); The Black Aesthetic, Ed. (Double-
day, 1971); Bondage, Freedom and Beyond
(Doubleday, 1971); Oak and Ivy: A Biography of Paul Laurence
Dunbar (Doubleday, 1971); Claude McKay; The Black Poet at War
(Broadside Pr., 1972); The Way of the New World: The Black Novel
in America (Doubleday, 1975); Contrib. numerous articles & reviews
to anthols., jls., & mags.
MEMBER: Pres. Com. on Student Unrest, Spring 1970; Baruch Coll.
Affirmative Action Com.
SIDELIGHTS: Lectures extensively, including Atlanta U., Clark
Coll., U. of Paris. In his introduction to The Black Aesthetic
he writes: "The black artist in the American society who creates
without interjecting a note of anger is creating not as a black
man, but as an American...The serious black artist of today is at
war with the American society as few have been throughout American
history.... The problem of the de-Americanization of black people lies at the heart of the Black Aesthetic" (New Black Voices).
Sources. Author inform.; Black Expression, Addison Gayle (Weybright
& Talley, 1969); Black World (Johnson Pub., Dec. 1974); New Black
Voices, Ed. by Abraham Chapman (New Amer. Lib., 1972).

GILLESPIE, MARCIA ANN. 1944- . Magazine Editor
Biographical-Personal. Born July 10, 1944, in Rockville Centre,
N.Y. D. of Charles Marshall and Ethel [Young] Gillespie. Educ.:
Southside High Sch., Rockville Centre; B.A. (Amer. Stud., with
honors), Lake Forest Coll., Ill., 1966. Family: Single. Mailing
address: Essence Magazine, 300 E. 42nd St., N.Y., N.Y. 10017.
Career-Professional. Res. reporter, Time, Inc., Time-Life Bks.,
1966-70; Managing Ed., 1970-71; Ed.-in-Chief, Essence, 1971- .
WRITINGS: Assisted with Illustrated History of Black Americans,
Ed. by John Hope Franklin (Time-Life Books, 1970). Columnist,
"Getting Down," Essence mag., 1971- .

Gilmore, Al-Tony

HONORS AND AWARDS: Distinguished Alumni Award, Lake Forest Coll.;
Bus. Achievement Awards, Nat'l. Assn. Black Bus. & Professional
Women's Clubs, Nassau Chap., N.Y.
MEMBER: Amer. Soc. of Mag. Eds.; Advis. Bd., Community News
Serv., N.Y.C.; Bd., Malcolm King Coll., N.Y.C.
SIDELIGHTS: Made repeated trips to more than 25 states as lec-
turer, speaker, panel member (Author).
Source. Author inform.

GILMORE, AL-TONY. 1946- . History Professor
Biographical-Personal. Born June 29, 1946, in S.C. Son of Margaret
Gilmore. Educ.: B.A. (Amer. Hist.); M.A. (Amer. Hist.); Ph.D.
(Amer. Hist.-Afro-Amer. & Progressive Era). Mailing address:
History Dept., Howard U., Wash., D.C. 20001.
Career-Professional. Hist. Prof. Has read papers before numerous
scholarly organizations and colleges all over the United States.
WRITINGS: Bad Nigger!: The National Impact of Jack Johnson (Ken-
nikat, 1975). In progress: History of the Amos n' Andy radio &
TV shows. Articles in: Journal of Negro History; Negro History
Bulletin; Journal of Social & Behavioral Science; Journal of Popu-
lar Culture.
HONORS AND AWARDS: Outstanding Young Man in America, 1974; listed
in Directory of American Scholars; Gussie Hudson's Directory of
Black Historians; Rayford Logan's & Michael Winston's Directory of
American Negro Biography.
Source. Author inform.

GIOVANNI, NIKKI [Yolande Cornelis Giovanni, Jr.]
1943- . Poet, Activist, Lecturer
Biographical-Personal. Born June 7, 1943, in
Knoxville, Tenn. D. of Jones (probation of-
ficer) & Yolande [Watson] Giovanni (soc.
worker). Educ.: B.A. (hist., honors), Fisk
U., 1967; U. of Pa.; Columbia U. Family:
Single; son, Thomas Watson Giovanni. Mailing
address: c/o Encore Magazine, 515 Madison
Ave., N.Y., N.Y. 10022.
Career-Professional. Arranged Black Arts Fes-
tival, Cincinnati, 1967; Helped in growth of
Black Theatre; Dir. Black Hist. Workshop.
Founded pub. coop., TomNik Ltd., 1970; Taught
creative writing, Livingston Coll., Rutgers
U.; Lectr., Coll. campuses. Ed. cons.,
Encore Magazine.
WRITINGS: Poetry: Black Feeling Black Talk (Broadside Pr.,
1968); Black Judgment (Broadside Pr., 1969); Re: Creation (Broad-
side Pr., 1970); Black Feeling Black Talk/Black Judgment (Morrow,

Gloster, Hugh Morris

1970); Night Comes Softly, Ed. poetry anthol. (TomNik Ltd.,
1970); Gemini: An extended autobiographical statement on my
first twenty-five years of being a black poet (Bobbs-Merrill,
1971); Spin A Soft Black Song, Children's poetry (Hill & Wang,
1971); Poem of Angela Yvonne Davis (TomNik Ltd., 1970) poetry
(Morrow, 1972); A Dialogue: James Baldwin and Nikki Giovanni
(Lippincott, 1972); Ego Tripping and Other Poems for Young Readers
(Lawrence Hill Co., 1973); A Poetic Equation: Conversations Between Margaret Walker and Nikki Giovanni (Howard U. Pr., 1974);
The Women and the Men (Morrow, 1975). Book reviews & short stories: Negro Digest/Black World. Jls.: Black Dialogue & City in
all Directions.
HONORS AND AWARDS: Hon. Doctorate of Humanities, Wilberforce U.,
1972; Plaque from Cook Co. Jail, 1971; Life Membership & Scroll,
Nat'l. Counc. of Negro Women, 1972; Mademoiselle mag. award for
outstanding achievement, 1971; Sun Shower Award from Prince
Matchiabelli, 1972; Omega Psi Phi Fraternity award, outstanding
contrib. to Arts & Letters, 1971; Proclamation from Mayor of Lincoln Heights, Ohio, Nikki Giovanni Day; Key to City of Lincoln
Heights, Ohio, 1972; Resolution of Commendation, City Counc., Lincoln Heights, Ohio, 1972; Black Heroines for People United Save
Humanity, 1972; Key to City of Gary, Ind., 1972; Key to City of
Dallas, Tex., 1974; Hon. Doctorate of Lit., U. of Md., Princess
Anne Campus, 1974; Hon. Doctorate of Lit., Ripon Coll., Wis.,
1974; Woman of the Yr., Ladies Home Journal, 1973.
SIDELIGHTS: This young Black revolutionary writer has been hailed
by a reviewer for Variety, as "Probably the most prominent black
poetess in America." She became political activist at age 16 when
she entered Fisk. After expulsion and return to Fisk, was instru-
mental in having SNCC reinstated on campus: (Grants) Ford Found.;
Nat'l. Found. of the Arts; Harlem Council on the Arts. (Records)
"Truth Is On Its Way," Right on Records, 1971; "Like A Ripple On
A Pond," NikTom, Ltd., distributed by Atlantic, 1973 (Current
Biography, April 1973).
Sources. Blackamerican Literature, Ed. by Ruth Miller (Glencoe Pr.,
1971); Current Biography, April 1973 (H. W. Wilson, 1973); Pub.
inform.; Soulscript, Ed. by June Jordan (Doubleday, 1970); Today's
Negro Voices, Ed. by Beatrice M. Murphy (Julian Messner, 1970);
Books in Print, Supplement, 1975-76 (Bowker, 1976).

GLOSTER, HUGH MORRIS. 1911- . College President
Biographical-Personal. Born in 1911. Educ.: B.A., Morehouse Coll.;
Ph.D., N.Y.U. Mailing address: Morehouse Coll., Atlanta, Ga.
30314.
Career-Professional. Prof. Eng. & Chmn. Dept. of Lang. & Lit.,
Hampton Inst., Va., 1946-67; Pres., Morehouse Coll., 1967- .
WRITINGS: Negro Voices in American Fiction (U. of N.C. Pr.,
1948, 1965); My Life, My Country, My World: College Readings for

Gordon, Roland

> Modern Living (Prentice-Hall, 1952); The Brown Thrush: An Anthol-
> ogy of Verse by Negro College Students, Co-ed. (1935). Contrib.
> to journals.
Sources. The Negro Novel in America, Robert A. Bone (Yale U. Pr.,
> 1958); Pub. inform.

GORDON, ROLAND. 1944- . Writer, Actor, Model, Producer
Biographical-Personal. Born Feb. 13, 1944, in Greenwood, Miss.
> Educ.: Gary (Ind.) Roosevelt High Sch.; B.A., Baldwin-Wallace
> Coll., Berea, Ohio. Lives in L.A., Cal.
Career-Professional. Writer, actor, model & prod., 1972- ; Roland
> Gordon Creations (own business), L.A., Cal.
> WRITINGS: A Message to the World. In progress: The Winds of
> Change, poetic musical.
Source. "Second Annual Authors Autograph Party" (brochure), Cal.
> Librns. Black Caucus, July 1975.

GORDON/E, CHARLES EDWARD. 1927- . Playwright, Director, Actor
Biographical-Personal. Born Oct. 12, 1927, in Cleveland, Ohio. Son
> of William and Camille Gordon/e. Educ.: B.A., Los Angeles State
> Coll.; N.Y.U.; Columbia U. Family: div., nine children. Mailing
> address: c/o Howard Rosenstone, William Morris Agency, 1350 Ave.
> of the Americas, N.Y., N.Y. 10019.
Career-Professional. Playwright, dir., actor. Assoc. prod. of play,
> Nothing But a Man.
> WRITINGS: Plays: No Place to be Somebody (Bobbs-Merrill, 1969);
> A Black Comedy in Three Acts (1969). Contrib. to Esquire and New
> York Times. "Presently writing for screen and television and
> starring as an actor in three films. Also working on two stage
> plays" (Author).
> HONORS AND AWARDS: Drama Desk, N.Y.; Critics Circle Award, N.Y.
> & L.A.; Pulitzer Prize, 1970.
> SIDELIGHTS: Won award as Best Actor of the Year off-Broadway in
> Luther James' all-black production Of Mice and Men. His first
> successful play, No Place to be Somebody, was introduced at the
> Sheridan Square Playhouse in 1967, with his wife as producer.
> Later it won acclaim for performances at the N.Y. Shakespeare
> Festival's Public Theater & a two-week engagement at the NTA
> Theater on Broadway.
> "Gordone is the only black playwright that critics have favor-
> ably compared with Eugene O'Neill, William Saroyan, and Arthur
> Miller" (Black Insights).
Sources. Author inform.; Black Insights, Ed. by Nick A. Ford (Ginn,
> 1971).

GRAHAM, LORENZ BELL. 1902- . Writer, Lecturer, Probation Officer, Teacher

Biographical-Personal. Born Jan. 27, 1902, in New Orleans, La. Son of David Andrew (Methodist minister) and Etta [Bell] Graham. Educ.: High Sch., Seattle, Wash.; (Undergrad.) UCLA; Columbia U.; U. of Paris; B.A., Va. Union U., Richmond, 1936; (Grad. student) N.Y.U.; Columbia U.; UCLA. Family: m. Ruth Morris, Aug. 20, 1929; son, Lorenz, Jr., d. Mrs. Joyce G. Johnson; d. Mrs. Ruth G. May, son, Charles M. Graham. Mailing address: 1400 Niagara Ave., Claremont, Cal. 91711.

Career-Professional. Tchr. & Missionary, Monrovia Coll., Liberia, W. Africa, 1924-28; Lectr. & fund raiser in U.S. for Foreign Mission Bd., Nat'l. Bap. Convention, 1929-32; Tchr., Richmond, Va., 1933-35; Camp Educ. Advis., Civil Conservation Corps., Va. & Pa., 1936-42; Mgr., Pub. housing, Newport News, Va., 1943-45; Freelance writer, real estate salesman, & bldg. contractor, Long Island, N.Y., 1946-49; Soc. Worker, Queens Federation of Churches, N.Y., 1950-57; Probation Officer, L.A., Cal., 1958-66; Instr., Cal. State U., Pomona, 1970.

WRITINGS: Juveniles: How God Fix Jonah (Reynal, 1946); Tales of Momolu (Reynal, 1974); The Story of Jesus (Gilberton, 1955); The Ten Commandments (Gilberton, 1956); South Town (Follett, 1958); North Town (Crowell, 1965); Whose Town? (Crowell, 1969); Every Man Heart Lay Down (Crowell, 1970); A Road Down In the Sea (Crowell, 1971); God Wash the World and Start Again (Crowell, 1971); David He No Fear (Crowell, 1971). Novelettes: Carolina Cracker (Houghton-Mifflin); Detention Center (Houghton-Mifflin); Stolen Car (Houghton-Mifflin); Runaway (Houghton-Mifflin, 1972); John Brown's Raid (Firebird Ser., Scholastic, 1971); Return to South Town (In Progress).

HONORS AND AWARDS: Thomas Alva Edison Citation, 1956; Queens Federation of Churches, Citation 1957; Charles W. Follett, Award, 1958; Child Study Assn. of America Award, 1958; ASNLH, Citation, 1959; L.A. City Counc. Citation, 1966; Vassie D. Wright Award, 1967; Cal. Assn. of Tchrs. of Eng. Citation, 1973. Member: Authors League of America; McCarty Christian Church, L.A.; P.E.N. Internat., L.A.; S. Cal. Writers Guild; United Prof. of Cal.

SIDELIGHTS: Travel: "West Indies 1967, three months; Round the world, Asia, Africa, Europe 1969-70, six months; Europe 1972 with one month U.S.S.R.; People's Republic of China, one month, 1974. Wife, Ruth, is an invaluable associate in my work; she is also a writer of ability" (Author).

Sources. Author inform.; Something About the Author, Vol. 2, Ed. Anne Commire (Gale Res., 1973).

Graham, Shirley Lola

GRAHAM, SHIRLEY LOLA. 1906-1977. Biographer, Musician, Editor

Biographical-Personal. Born Nov. 11, 1906, in Indianapolis, Ind. D. of David Andrew (Methodist minister) and Etta [Bell] Graham. Educ.: Advanced musical training, Paris, 1926-28; French Certificate, Sorbonne, 1929; B.A., Oberlin Coll., 1934, M.A., 1935; Yale U. Drama Sch., 1938-40; L.H.D. (hon.), U. of Mass., 1973. Family: 1st m. Shadrach T. McCanns, son, Robert Graham McCanns; 2nd m., W. E. B. DuBois, son, David Graham. Died 1977.

Career-Professional. Head, Fine Arts Dept., Tenn. State Coll., 1935-36; Dir. Negro Unit, Chgo. Fed. Theater, 1936-38; United Serv. Org. Dir.; YWCA Dir., 1940-42; Field Secy., NAACP, 1942-44; Organizing Dir., Ghana TV, 1964-66; Founding Ed., Freedomways, 1960-63; Eng. ed., Afro-Asian Writers Bureau, Peking, China, 1968. WRITINGS: Tom Tom, composer, music-drama (1932). Biography Dr. George Washington Carver, Scientist, with George Lipscombe (Julian Messner, 1944); Paul Robeson, Citizen of the World (Julian Messner, 1946); There Was Once A Slave, biography of Frederick Douglass (Julian Messner, 1947); The Story of Phyllis Wheatley (Julian Messner, 1949); Your Most Humble Servant, biography of Benjamin Banneker (Julian Messner, 1949); Jean Baptiste Point de Sable, Founder of Chicago (Julian Messner, 1953); Booker T. Washington, Educator (Julian Messner, 1955); The Story of Pocahontas (Grosset & Dunlap, 1954); His Day Is Marching On: A Memoir of W. E. B. DuBois (Lippincott, 1971); Gamal Abdel Nasser: Son of the Nile (Third Pr., 1972); The Zulu Heart, novel (1974); Julius K. Nyerere: Teacher of Africa (Julian Messner, 1975); Pictorial History of W. E. B. DuBois (Johnson Pub., 1976). Contrib. to numerous jls. & newspapers.

HONORS AND AWARDS: Julius Rosenwald Fellow, Yale U. Drama Sch., 1938-40; Guggenheim Fellow. for hist. res., 1945-47; Julian Messner award, There Was Once A Slave, 1950; Anisfield-Wolf Award, Your Most Humble Servant, 1950; Nat'l. Inst. of Arts & Letters grant for "contributions to American Literature."

MEMBER: Kappa Delta Pi; Sigma Delta Theta; P.E.N.

SIDELIGHTS: Shirley Graham states that her father was a devout Methodist minister who traveled from place to place to 'mend broken fences.' This father, who was proud of his race and confident of its destiny, instilled in his daughter a keen appreciation for the background of the Negro in Africa and of his contribution to American life (Twentieth Century Authors, 1st Supplement).

Greene, Lorenzo Johnston

The Author and Dr. DuBois became citizens of Ghana, where he spent his final days. Mrs. DuBois subsequently moved to Cairo, Egypt. She died in Peking, China in the Spring of 1977 (Compiler). Sources. Negro Almanac, Comp. by Harry A. Ploski & Ernest Kaiser (Bellwether, 1971); Paul Robeson, Citizen of the World, Shirley Graham (Julian Messner, 1946); Twentieth Century Authors. 1st Supplement, Ed. by Stanley J. Kunitz & Vineta Colby (H. W. Wilson, 1955); Books in Print, Supplement, 1975-76 (Bowker, 1976).

GREENE, LORENZO JOHNSTON. 1899- . Professor of History, Historian

Biographical-Personal. Born Nov. 16, 1899, in Ansonia, Conn. Son of Willis Hamilton and Harriet [Coleman] Greene. Educ.: B.A., Howard U., 1924; M.A., Columbia U., 1926, Ph.D. (Hist.), 1942; L.H.D. (Hon.) U. of Mo., 1971. Family: m. Thomasina T. Greene, son, Lorenzo Thomas Greene. Mailing address: Lincoln U., Jefferson City, Mo. 65101.

Career-Professional. Res. Assoc. (to Carter G. Woodson, Dir., ASNLH, 1928-32; Mem., Contrib. staff, Social Science Abstracts, Columbia U., 1932; Asst. Prof. & Prof. of Hist., Lincoln U. (Mo.), 1933 to present; Vis. Prof., Hist.: Tenn. Agricultural and Industrial U., summer 1945, So. Ill. U., U. of Kansas, Spring, 1969, 1970; Former Ed., Midwest Journal, 1947-56; Lectr.: Yale; Dartmouth; City Coll., Brooklyn Coll. & Hunter Coll. (N.Y.C.); U. of Mo.; Baker U.; Central Mo. State Coll., etc. Dir., Consortium, Lincoln U.; Westminster Coll. & William Woods Coll. on Inst. for Coll. Tchrs. in Afro-Amer. Hist. & Culture, summer 1970.

WRITINGS: The Negro Wage Earner, with Carter G. Woodson (1930); Negro Employment in the District of Columbia, with Myra Colson Callis (1932); Negro Housing, with Charles Johnson, et al. (1933); The Negro in Colonial New England, 1620-1776 (1942); Desegregation of Missouri Schools, 1954-1959 (1959, 1961); Massacre at Fort Pillow, in Battles of the Civil War (1960); "The Negro in Missouri," (in Official Manual State of Missouri), with Holland & Kremer (1973-74); "New Introduction" to Daniels In Freedom's Birthplace (Arno Pr., 1970). In progress: Abolition of Slavery in New England, 1652-1784; Abolition of the New England Slave Trade, 1658-1788; Missouri Negro Soldiers in the Civil War, 1861-1866; The Negro as seen by a Research Associate of Dr. Carter G. Woodson, 1928-1933. Articles in: Social Science Abstracts; Journal of Negro History; Phylon; Journal of Negro Education; Midwest Journal; Negro History Bulletin, etc.

Greenfield, Eloise

HONORS AND AWARDS: Grants: ASNLH, 1931-32; Julius Rosenwald Fellow, summer 1934, 1940-41; Gen. Educ. Bd., 1935; 1945, 1947.
MEMBER: Amer. Hist. Assn.; Miss. Valley Hist. Soc.; S. Hist. Soc.; ASNLH; Mo. State Hist. Soc.; Mo. Assn. for Soc. Welfare; Mo. State Advis. Com. to U.S. Com. on Civil Rights (since 1957).
SIDELIGHTS: Consultant for Introducing Courses in Negro History in Public Schools and/or colleges. Also Black Studies Paperback Book Project Study of Negroes on Western Frontier, Taft TV & Radio Corp. (1971). "For more than thirty years, as member of the Missouri Association for Social Welfare he worked to improve the health and welfare of all Missouri citizens..." (Author).
Source. Author inform.

GREENFIELD, ELOISE. Writer
Biographical-Personal. Born May 17, 1929, in Parmele, N.C.
Career-Professional.
WRITINGS: Sister; Rosa Parks (Crowell); Bubbles (1972); She Come Bringing Me That Little Baby Girl (Lippincott, 1974); Paul Robeson (Crowell, Biographical Ser., 1975); Me and Nessie (Crowell, 1975).
Source. Books in Print, Supplement, 1975-76 (Bowker, 1976).

GREENLEE, SAM. 1930- . Novelist
Biographical-Personal. Born July 13, 1930, in Chgo., Ill. Educ.: B.S., U. of Wis., Madison, 1952; U. of Chgo., 1954-57; U. of Thessaloniki, Greece, 1963-64.
Career-Professional.
WRITINGS: The Spook Who Sat by the Door (London: Allison & Bushy, Ltd., 1969); Blues for an African Princess (Third World Pr., 1970). Contrib. articles & short stories to mags., jls., & newspapers.
SIDELIGHTS: "...I have recently returned from 4 years of writing in Greece. I am employed, with fat salary and fancy title, by an otherwise white civil rights organization in Chicago. My job is to sit by the door" (The Spook Who Sat By the Door).
Sources. Black American Writers Past and Present, Theressa G. Rush & Others (Scarecrow, 1975); The Sppok Who Sat By the Door (Bantam, 1969).

GREGORY, RICHARD CLAXTON. 1932- . Social Satirist, Civil Rights Leader, Pacifist
Biographical-Personal. Born Oct. 12, 1932, in St. Louis, Mo. Son of Pressley and Lucille Gregory. Educ.: S. Ill. U., Carbondale, Ill. Family: m. Lillian Gregory, 1959; d. Michele, d. Lynn, d.

Grier, William H.

Pamela & Paula (twins), d. Stephanie, son, Gregory, d. Miss, son, Christian, d. Ayanna, son, Yohance. Mailing address: Tower Hill Farm, Long Pond Road, Plymouth, Mass. 02360.
Career-Professional. Won Mo. State Mile Championship, 1951, 1952, while in high sch. Named outstanding athlete, S. Ill. U., 1953; U.S. Army, Spec. Serv.; Night club performer; Civil rights protestor; Lectr., coll. campuses.
WRITINGS: Nigger, autobiog., Ed. by Robert Lipsyte (Dutton, 1964); From the Back of the Bus (Dutton, 1964); What's Happening (Dutton, 1965); The Shadow That Scares Me (Doubleday, 1968); Write Me In! (Bantam, 1968); No More Lies: The Myth and Reality of American History, Ed. by James R. McGraw (Harper & Row, 1971); Dick Gregory's Political Primer (Harper & Row, 1972); Dick Gregory's Natural Diet for Folks Who Eat: Cookin' with Mother Nature, Ed. by James R. McGraw and Alvemia M. Fulton (Harper & Row, 1973); Dick Gregory's Bible Tales with Commentary, Ed. by James R. McGraw (Stein & Day, 1974).
HONORS AND AWARDS: Doctor of Humane Letters, Malcolm X U., Chgo.; Doctor of Laws, Lincoln U., Pa.
SIDELIGHTS: Candidate for President of the United States in 1968; Candidate for Mayor of Chicago in 1967. As a Pacifist, has staged fasts to protest the War in Vietnam. Over 300 lectures annually on college campuses; concert, stage, television performances as a social satirist; numerous appearances on behalf of human rights causes (Author).
Sources. Afro-American Literature: Non Fiction, Ed. by William Adams, et al. (Houghton-Mifflin, 1970); Author inform.; Black Joy, Ed. by Jay David (Cowles, 1971); Current Biography, 1962, Ed. by Charles Moritz (H. W. Wilson, 1962); Negro Handbook, Comp. by Eds. of Ebony (Johnson Pub., 1966).

GRIER, WILLIAM H. Psychiatrist
Biographical-Personal. Educ.: M.D., U. of Mich. Medical Sch.; Psychiatric residence, Menninger Clinic.
Career-Professional. Psychiatrist; Asst. Prof. of Psychiatry, San Francisco Medical Center, U. of Cal.
WRITINGS: Black Rage, with Price Cobbs (Basic Books, 1968); The Jesus Bag, with Price Cobbs (McGraw-Hill, 1971).
Source. Pub. inform.

Griggs, Sutton E.

GRIGGS, SUTTON E. 1872-1930. Minister, Religious Administrator,
Novelist
Biographical-Personal. Born 1872, in Chatfield, Tex. Educ.: Bishop
    Coll., Dallas, Tex.; Richmond Theological Sem., grad. 1893. Died
    1930.
Career-Professional. Minister, Bap. Church, Berkeley, Va., 2 yrs.
    Corres. Secy., Educ. Dept., Nat'l. Bap. Convention, Nashville,
    Tenn., 20 yrs.; Founder, Nat'l. Relig. & Civic Inst., Houston,
    Tex.
    WRITINGS: Novels: Imperium in Imperio (1899); Overshadowed
    (1901); Unfettered (1902); The Hindered Hand (1905); & Pointing
    the Way (1908); Wisdom's Call (Black Her., Bks. for Lib., 1911).
    (These are among 30 works altogether.)
Sources. Cavalcade, Ed. by Arthur P. Davis & Saunders Redding
    (Houghton-Mifflin, 1971); Negro Novel in America, Robert A. Bone
    (Yale U. Pr., 1958); Negro Voices in American Fiction, Hugh Glos-
    ter (Russell, 1965).

GRIMKÉ, ANGELINA WELD. 1880-1958. Playwright,
Poet
Biographical-Personal. Born 1880 in Boston,
    Mass. Educ.: Girls' Latin Sch.; Boston
    Latin Sch.; Boston Normal Sch. of Gymnastics.
Career-Professional. Tchr., Eng., Dunbar High
    Sch.; Tchr., Armstrong Manual Training Sch.
    (both Wash., D.C.).
    WRITINGS: Rachel, a "pardon" drama (pro-
    duced 1916; pub. 1971); Letters to Catherine
    E. Beecher (Black Her., repr. of 1938 ed.,
    Bks. for Lib.). Poetry in anthol.: The
    Poetry of the Negro (1949, 1970); American
    Negro Poetry (1963); Poetry of Black America
    (1973).
Sources. Negro Caravan, Ed. by Sterling A.
Brown & Others (Arno Pr. & N.Y. Times, 1969); Negro Vanguard,
Richard Bardolph (Random House, 1959); Poetry of Black America,
Ed. by Arnold Adoff (Harper & Row, 1973).

GRIMKÉ, ARCHIBALD H. 1849-1930. Attorney, Educator, Editor,
Biographer
Biographical-Personal. Born Aug. 17, 1849, in Charleston, S.C. Son
    of Henry Grimke (White) and Nancy Weston (slave). Educ.: B.A.,
    1870, M.A., 1872, Lincoln U. (Pa.), (then a white school); LL.B.,
    Harvard U., 1874. Family: m. Sarah E. Stanley in 1879. Died
    1930.
Career-Professional. Lawyer, Boston, Mass.; Assoc. of abolitionists:
    Summer & Garrison; U.S. Consul, Santo Domingo, 1894-98; Pres.,

Guy, Rosa Guthbert

Amer. Negro Acad., Wash., D.C., 1903-16;
NAACP: Pres., Boston Branch, V. Pres.,
Nat'l.; Ed., Hub newspaper; Freelance writer,
Boston Traveler, Boston Herald, Atlantic
Monthly.
WRITINGS: ("American Reformers" ser.) William Lloyd Garrison, the Abolitionist (1891);
and The Life of Charles Sumner, the Scholar
in Politics (1892).
HONORS AND AWARDS: NAACP Spingarn Medal,
1919.
MEMBER: Pres., Frederick Douglass Memorial
& Hist. Assn.; Amer. Soc. Sci. Assn.; Authors'
Club of London.
SIDELIGHTS: "Archibald H. Grimké was one of
two brothers well known for their public
spirit, the other being the Rev. Francis J. Grimké.... He with
his brother was encouraged even while in college by two sisters of
his father who found the South uncongenial" (Negro Genius).
Sources. Historical Negro Biographies, Wilhelmena S. Robinson (ASNLH,
1967); Negro Author in America, Vernon Loggins (Kennikat, 1959);
Negro Genius, Benjamin Brawley (Dodd, Mead, 1937); Negroes in Public Affairs and Government, Ed. by Walter Christmas (Educ. Her.,
1966); They Showed the Way, Charlemae Rollins (Crowell, 1964).

GROSVENOR, VERTA MAE. 1938- . Writer
Biographical-Personal. Born Apr. 4, 1938, in
Fairfax, Allendale Co., S.C.
Career-Professional.
WRITINGS: Vibration Cooking (Doubleday,
1970); Thursdays and Every Other Sunday Off,
A Domestic Rap (Doubleday, 1972).
Source. Vibration Cooking or The Travel Notes
of A Geechee Girl, Verta Mae Grosvenor (Doubleday, 1970).

GUY, ROSA GUTHBERT. 1925- . Novelist
Biographical-Personal. Born Sept. 1, 1925, in Trinidad. D. of
Henry and Audrey [Gonzales] Guthbert. Educ.: N.Y.U. (writing).
Family: m. Warner Guy (dec.); son, Warner. Mailing address:
Agent, Bill Berber Assoc., Inc., 538 E. 72nd St., N.Y., N.Y.
10021.

Gwaltney, John Langston

Career-Professional. Amer. Negro Theatre;
garment piece worker; helped found Harlem
Writers Guild.
WRITINGS: Bird at My Window, novel (Lippin-
cott, 1965); "Venetian Blinds," one-act play
(1954); Children of Longing (Holt, Rinehart
& Winston, 1971); The Friends (Holt, Rine-
hart & Winston, 1973); Ruby (Viking, 1976).
In progress: Benidine, novel; Research in
African languages. Contrib. to Cosmopolitan
and Freedomways.
Sources. Bird at My Window, Rosa Guy (Lippin-
cott, 1965); Contemporary Authors, Vol. 17-
18, Ed. by James M. Ethridge and Barbara
Kopala (Gale Res., 1967); Books in Print,
Supplement, 1975-76 (Bowker, 1976).

GWALTNEY, JOHN LANGSTON. 1928- . Anthropologist, Ethnographer
Biographical-Personal. Born Sept. 25, 1928, in Orange, N.J. Son of
John Stanley and Mabel [Harper] Gwaltney. Educ.: B.A., Upsala
Coll., E. Orange, N.J., 1952; M.A., New Sch. for Soc. Res., 1957;
Ph.D. (Anthropology) Columbia U., 1967. Mailing address: An-
thropology Dept., 500 University Pl., Syracuse U., Syracuse, N.Y.
13210.
Career-Professional. Assoc. Prof., Syracuse U., Dept. of Anthropolo-
gy, 1971-present; Assoc. & Asst. Prof., SUNY at Cortland, Dept. of
Sociology and Antrhopology, 1967-71; Ethnographer among the Shin-
necook & Poospatuck Indians of Suffolk Co., Long Island, N.Y.,
Summer, 1969; Ethnographer among the highland Chinantec of Oaxaca,
Mexico, 1963-64; Ethnographer, Allopsychic Res. Project, 1961;
Past Chmn., Presidential Advis. Com. on the Caste Disadvantaged,
Cortland Coll.; Past Faculty Advis. to Uhuru Assn. of Black Stu-
dents, Cortland Coll.
WRITINGS: The Thrice Shy: Cultural Accommodation to Blindness
and Other Disasters in a Mexican Community (Columbia U. Pr.,
1970); Anthol.: "Myth Charter in the Minority-Majority Context,"
in Morton Fried's Explorations in Anthropology (Crowell, 1973).
Period.: The American Scholar (Winter 1965-66); Renaissance 2,
vol. 1, no. 3 (1973). In progress: Jivin' On the Blood of the
Martyrs: The Devolution of Black Studies (Emerson Hall Pr.).
HONORS AND AWARDS: Ruth Benedict Memorial Award; John Hay Whitney
Found. Fellow; Nat'l. Inst. of Health Fellow; Ansley Dissertation
Award; Faculty Grant, N.Y. State Educ. Dept.; Faculty Res. Fellow.
& Grant-in-aid, State U. of N.Y.; Grant-in-aid, to Minority Schol-
ars, Soc. Sci. Res. Counc.; Grant-in-aid, Amer. Philosophical
Soc.; NEH Sr. Fellow.
SIDELIGHTS: Cons. to Presidential Com. on Black Stud., Harpur
Coll., State U. of N.Y. at Binghampton, Nov. 1969; Ethnographer

Halliburton, Warren J.

among highland Maroons of St. Elizabeth Parish, Jamaica, Summer, 1972; Ethnographer among Northeastern urban Afro-Americans, July 1973-present (Author).
Source. Author inform.

HALEY, ALEX. 1921- . Writer
Biographical-Personal. Born in Ithaca, N.Y. Aug. 11, 1921.
Career-Professional. Journalist, U.S. Coast Guard, 1939-59; Free-lance writer.
WRITINGS: The Autobiography of Malcolm X, collaborator (Grove Pr., 1965); Roots (Doubleday, 1976). Contrib. stories to Reader's Digest and other mags.
SIDELIGHTS: Roots is the extraordinary result of Haley's 12-year search for authentication of the story of his ancestor, "the African," told to him during his childhood (Roots).
Source. Roots, Alex Haley (Doubleday, 1976).

HALLIBURTON, WARREN J. 1924- . Teacher, Editor, Textbook Writer
Biographical-Personal. Born Aug. 2, 1924, in N.Y., N.Y. Son of Richard and Blanche Halliburton. Educ.: Euander Childs High Sch., Bronx, N.Y.; B.S., M.A., N.Y.U.; (candidate for Educ. Doctorate, Tchrs. Coll., Columbia U.) Family: m. Frances Halliburton; d. Cheryl, d. Stephanie, son, Warren, Jr. Mailing address: 19 Emery St., Hempstead, N.Y. 11550.
Career-Professional. Assoc., Inst. for Internat. Educ.; Assoc., N.Y. State Dept. of Educ.; Tchr.; Ed., McGraw Hill; Vis. Prof., Eng., Hamilton Coll.; (presently) Dir., Center for Ethnic Stud., Tchrs. Coll., Columbia U.
WRITINGS: New Worlds of Literature, anthol. (Harcourt); America's Color Caravan, essays (Singer-Graflex); America's Majorities and Minorities, syllabus with Wm. L. Katz (Arno Pr.); Urban Reader, short stories (D. C. Heath). Novellas: The Heist (McGraw-Hill, 1968); Cry Baby! (McGraw-Hill, 1968); Some Things That Glitter (McGraw-Hill, 1969). Adaptations, juveniles: Negro Doctor; The Year the Yankees Lost the Pennant, from Douglas Wallop (McGraw-Hill, 1968); Marty; Printer's Measure; Call of the Wild (McGraw-Hill, 1968); The Picture Life of Jesse Jackson (Watts, Picture Life Bks., 1972); English Writing Series (Cambridge Bks.); Language and Literature Series (Globe); Short Stories Anthology (Globe). New York Times tchr. manuals; N.Y. State Educ. Dept., Lesson plans; Educ. Develop. Lab. & Educ. Design, tapes. "... plus approximately 100 short stories and plays" (Author). Macmillan reading ser. Harlem: A History of Broken Dreams, with

Hamilton, Charles Vernon

Ernest Kaiser (Doubleday, 1974); Composing With Sentences, with
Agnes A. Pastva, Sr. (Cambridge Bks., Cambridge Writer's Prog.
Ser., 1974).
SIDELIGHTS: Cons. & Lectr.: Dade Co., Fla.; U. of Cal., Santa
Cruz; Princeton U.; Columbia U.; N.Y.C. Bd. of Educ. (Author).
Source. Author inform.; Books in Print, Supplement, 1975-76 (Bowker,
1976).

HAMILTON, CHARLES VERNON. 1929- . Political
Scientist, Lawyer
Biographical-Personal. Born Oct. 19, 1929, in
Muskogee, Okla. Son of Owen and Viola
[Haynes] Hamilton. Educ.: B.A., Roosevelt
U., Chgo., 1951; J.D., Loyola U. Sch. of Law,
Chgo., 1954; M.A., 1957, Ph.D., 1963, U. of
Chgo. Family: m. Dona Louise Hamilton; d.
Valli, d. Carol. Mailing address: Columbia
U., Dept. of Polit. Sci., N.Y., N.Y.
Career-Professional. Tchr., Tuskegee Inst.;
Albany State Coll., Ga.; Rutgers U., Newark;
Lincoln U.; Chmn., Dept. of Polit. Sci.,
Roosevelt U.; Prof., Dept. of Polit. Sci.,
Columbia U. (present).
WRITINGS: Black Power: The Politics of
Liberation in America, with Stokely Carmichael (Random House,
1967); The Black Preacher in America; The Black Experience in
American Politics (Putnam, 1973); The Bench and the Ballot, South-
ern Federal Judges and Black Voters (Oxford U. Pr., 1974).
Period.: Black World; The Black Scholar; Ebony; New York Times
Magazine; Harvard Educational Review; Wisconsin Law Review.
HONORS AND AWARDS: John Hay Whitney Fellow; U. of Chgo. Profes-
sional Alumni Award; Roosevelt Alumni Award.
SIDELIGHTS: Phi Beta Kappa Vis. Lecture Scholar, 1972-73 (Au-
thor).
Sources. Author inform.; Black Power, Stokely Carmichael & Charles
V. Hamilton (Random House, 1967).

HAMILTON, VIRGINIA ESTHER. 1937- . Juvenile Writer, Lecturer
Biographical-Personal. Born Mar. 12, 1937, in Yellow Springs, Ohio.
D. of Kenneth James and Etta Belle [Perry] Hamilton. Educ.:
Antioch Coll., 1953-56; Ohio State U., 1956-58; New Sch. for Soc.
Res., 1958-59. Family: m. Arnold Adoff (anthologist & writer);
d. Leigh Hamilton, son, Jaime Levi. Mailing address: Agent,
McIntosh & Otis, 18 E. 41st St., N.Y., N.Y. 10017.
Career-Professional. "Every source of occupation imaginable, from
singer to bookkeeper" (Somthing About the Author). Symposium on
Children's Lit., Marymount Coll., N.Y.; Symposium, U. of Cal.,
Berkeley.

WRITINGS: Novels: <u>Zeely</u> (Macmillan, 1967); <u>The House of Dies Drear</u> (Macmillan, 1968). Short Stories: <u>Time-Ago Tales of Jahdu</u> (Macmillan, 1969); <u>The Planet of Junior Brown</u> (Macmillan, 1971); <u>Time-Ago Lost: More Tales of Jahdu</u> (Macmillan, 1973); <u>M. C. Higgins, The Great</u> (Macmillan, 1974). Biog.: <u>W. E. B. Dubois: A Biography</u> (Crowell, 1972); <u>Paul Robeson: The Life and Times of a Free Black Man</u> (Harper & Row, 1974); <u>Writings of W. E. B. DuBois: An Anthology</u>, Ed. (Crowell, 1975). HONORS AND AWARDS: For <u>Zeely</u> (ALA Notable Bk. List; Nancy Block Memorial Award); for <u>The House of Dies Drear</u> (ALA Notable Bk. List; Edgar Allan Poe award for best juvenile mystery; Ohioana Lit. Award for 1968); for <u>Time-Ago Tales of Jahdu</u> (ALA Notable Bk. List); for <u>Planet of Junior Brown</u> (ALA Notable Bk. List; Newbery Honor Bk., Award, 1972); for <u>M. C. Higgins, the Great</u> (Newbery Award, 1975). Lewis Carroll, Shelf Award, Nat'l. Bk. Award nominee. Listed in <u>Thirty Mid-Century Children's Books Every Adult Should Know</u>, issued by the <u>Horn Book</u>; <u>More Books by More People</u> (Interviews with sixty-five authors of Bks. for Children by Lee Hopkins).
Sources. Author inform.; <u>Something About the Author</u>, vol. 4, Ed. by Anne Commire (Gale Res., 1973).

HAMMON, JUPITER. 1720?-1806?. Poet
Biographical-Personal. Born c. 1720, on Long Island, N.Y. Slave of Henry Lloyd and descendants; esteemed by family who assisted him in placing verses before the public; won his freedom. Died c. 1806.
Career-Professional.
WRITINGS: "An Evening Thought. Salvation by Christ, with Penetential Cries: Composed by Jupitor Hammon, a Negro belonging to Mr. Lloyd of Queens Village on Long Island, the 25th of December, 1760," (1st poetical composition by a Black pub. in this country); Other broadsides: "An Address to Miss Phyllis Wheatly (sic), etc.," (1778); "An Essay on Ten Virgins," (1799); "A Winter Piece," (Hartford, 1782); "A Poem for Children, with Thoughts on Death," and final poem, "An Evening's Improvement..." (of autobiog. interest). Presented to African Soc. of City of N.Y., "An Address to the Negroes of the State of New York," Sept. 24, 1786 (1787, went into 3rd ed.).
SIDELIGHTS: "Revealing as much about the White world in which he moved as anything else, Hammon's broadside verses have historical, sociological and some literary interest" (<u>Early Black American Poets</u>). "He was strongly influenced by the evangelical hymns of Charles Wesley, John Newton, and William Cowper. His 'An Address ...' shows the writer as feeling it his personal duty to bear

Hansberry, Lorraine

slavery with patience, but strongly opposed to the system and as urging that young Negroes be manumitted" (Early Negro American Writers).

Sources. Early Black American Poets, Ed. by William H. Robinson, Jr. (Wm. C. Brown, 1969); Early Negro American Writers, Benjamin Brawley (U. of N.C. Pr., 1935); Famous American Negro Poets, Charlemae Rollins (Dodd, Mead, 1955); Historical Negro Biographies, Wilhelmena S. Robinson (ASNLH, 1967); Negro Almanac, Comps. Harry A. Ploski & Roscoe C. Brown (Bellwether, 1967); Negro Poets and Their Poems, Robert T. Kerlin, 3rd rev. ed. (Assoc. Pub., 1935); Negro Vanguard, Richard Bardolph (Random House, 1959).

HANSBERRY, LORRAINE. 1930-1965. Playwright
Biographical-Personal. Born May 19, 1930, in Chicago, Ill. D. of Carl Augustus, Sr., (realtor) and Nannie [Perry] Hansberry. Educ.: Art Inst. of Chgo.; U. of Wis.; Guadalajara, Mexico. Family: m. Robert Nemiroff (music pub. & song writer) June 20, 1953. Died Jan. 2, 1965.
Career-Professional.
WRITINGS: Plays: Raisin in the Sun (Random House, 1959); The Sign in Sidney Brustein's Window (Random House, 1964); Les Blancs; To Be Young, Gifted and Black, adapted from her writings, by her husband, after her death (New Amer. Lib., 1965). Book: The Movement (1964).

SIDELIGHTS: Youngest American, fifth woman, and only black dramatist to win New York Drama Critics Circle Award for Best Play of the Year, 1959 (Raisin in the Sun). Film adaptation of Raisin received numerous awards. Produced and published in 30 countries. Recipient special award, Cannes Film Festival, 1961. Premature death from cancer; buried in Bethel Cemetery, Croton-on-Hudson, New York (Black Insights).

Sources. Afro-American Literature: Drama, Ed. by William Adams et al. (Houghton-Mifflin, 1970); Black American Writer. Vol. II: Poetry and Drama, Ed. by C. W. E. Bigsby (Penguin, 1969); Black Insights, Ed. by Nick A. Ford (Ginn, 1971); Black Scenes, Ed. by Alice Childress (Doubleday, 1971); Negro Almanac, Comp. by Harry A. Ploski & Ernest Kaiser (Bellwether, 1971); Who Was Who in America. Vol. IV, 1961-68 (Marquis, 1968).

HANSBERRY, WILLIAM LEO. 1894-1965. African Historian and Scholar
Biographical-Personal. Born in 1894. Died in Chgo., Ill., Nov. 3, 1965.
Career-Professional. Prof., Hist., Howard U. (40 yrs.); Prof., Inst. of African Stud., U. of Nigeria.

WRITINGS: Pillars in Ethiopian History: The William Leo Hansberry African History Notebook, vol. 1 Ed. by Joseph E. Harris
(Howard U. Pr., 1974).
HONORS AND AWARDS: $28,000 grant for res. in anthropology from
Haile Selassie of Ethiopia (1964); Inst. of African Stud. established in his honor by U. of Nigeria (1963).
SIDELIGHTS: "He was one of the early exponents of the idea of African genesis..." (Negro Handbook). "...the African-American Institute, founded originally by Dr. W. Leo Hansberry of Howard University, but destined to become a large-scale, foundation-support-
ed effort with a scholarship and teacher placement program and a
publication, Africa Report" (American Negro Reference Book).
Source. American Negro Reference Book, Ed. by John P. Davis (Englewood Cliffs, N.J.: Prentice-Hall, 1966); Negro Almanac, Ed. by
Harry A. Ploski & Roscoe C. Brown, N.Y. (Bellwether, 1966); Negro
Handbook, Comp. by Eds. of Ebony (Johnson Pub., 1966).

HARDING, VINCENT. 1931- . Historian, Civil
Rights Leader, Professor
Biographical-Personal. Born July 25, 1931, in
N.Y., N.Y. Educ.: B.A., City Coll. of N.Y.,
1952; M.S. (Journalism), Columbia U., 1953;
M.A. (Hist.), 1956, Ph.D., 1965, U. of Chgo.
Family: m. Rosemarie Freeney; d. Rachel So-
journer, son, Jonathan DuBois. Mailing ad-
dress: 87 Chestnut St., Atlanta, Ga. 30314.
Career-Professional. U.S. Army, 1953-55; Lay
Pastor (part time), Seventh Day Adventist
Mission Church, Chgo., 1955-57; Lay Pastor
(part time), Woodlawn Mennonite Church,
Chgo., 1957-61; S. Rep., Mennonite Serv.
Com., Atlanta, Ga.; Acting, Civil Rights
Negotiator, various "Movement" orgs.,
1961-65; Chmn., Dept. of Hist. & Sociol., Spelman Coll., 1965-69;
Dir., Martin Luther King Lib. Project, 1968-70; Dir., Inst. of the
Black World, 1969- ; Chmn., Advis. Coord. Com. for "Black Heri-
tage," (108 TV prog. on Afro-Amer. Hist.--CBS TV), 1968-69.
WRITINGS: Must Walls Divide? (Friendship Pr., 1965); Black Heri-
tage Books ser., Ed., with John H. Clarke (22 vols. 1970). In
progress: Documents of the Black Experience, Ed., with Wilfred
Carter & Hoyt Fuller (Multi-vol. ser.); Black Radicalism in Amer-
ica; Origins of Afro-Americans, with J. H. Clark (Holt, Black Her.
Ser., Vol. 1, n.d.).
HONORS AND AWARDS: Res. grants; Amer. Counc. of Learned Socs.; The
Atlanta U. Center Res. Com.; Atlanta U. Center Non-Western Stud.
Com.; Kent Fellow, Sociol. of Relig. in Higher Educ.
MEMBER: Ed. Bd., Concern; Christianity and Crisis; Christian Cen-
tury; others.

Hare, Nathan

Sources. <u>Books in Print</u>, Supplement, 1975-76 (Bowker, 1976); <u>Who's Who in America</u>, 37th ed., 1972-73 (Marquis, 1972).

HARE, NATHAN. 1934- . Publisher, Activist, Professor

Biographical-Personal. Born Apr. 9, 1934 in Slick, Okla. Son of Seddie Henry (farmer) and Tishia [Davis] Hare. <u>Educ</u>.: B.A., Langston U., 1954; M.A. (Sociol.), 1957, Ph.D., 1962, U. of Chgo.; Northwestern U. <u>Family</u>: m. Julie Reed (public relat. spec.), Dec. 27, 1956. <u>Mailing address</u>: <u>The Black Scholar</u>, Box 31245, San Francisco, Ca. 94131.

Career-Professional. Briefly, professional boxer; Instr., Sociol., Va. State Coll., Petersburg, 1957-58; Interviewer, Nat'l. Opinion Center, Chgo., 1959-61; Res. Asst., Population Res. Center, U. of Chgo., 1960-61; Instr., 1961-63, Asst. Prof. Sociol., 1964-67, Howard U.; Dir., Black Stud. Curriculum, 1968, Chmn., Dept. of Black Stud., 1968-69; Dir., Center for Educ. Innovation, Summer 1968, Cal. State U., San Francisco; Pub., <u>Black Scholar</u>, San Francisco, 1969- ; Part time Vis. Prof., Lone Mt. Coll., 1972- .

WRITINGS: <u>The Black Anglo-Saxons</u> (Collier, 1970); <u>Black Political Life in the United States</u>, Ed. (Chandler, 1972); <u>Guidelines for Black Studies</u> (Black World Found.); <u>Contemporary Black Thought</u>, Ed., with Robert Chrisman (Bobbs-Merrill). In progress: <u>Black Consciousness</u> (Macmillan); <u>Notes of a Black Professor</u> (Parnassus); <u>The White Psyche</u>, Ed. (Bantam); <u>From the Black Scholar</u> (Bobbs-Merrill). Contrib. many articles to jls. & period: <u>Newsweek</u>; <u>Ramparts</u>; <u>Saturday Review</u>; <u>U.S. News & World Report</u>. Contrib. Ed., <u>Journal of Black Studies</u>; <u>Journal of Black Education & Black Law Journal</u>.

HONORS AND AWARDS: Danforth Fellow, 1954-57; Tuition scholarship, U. of Chgo., 1960-61; "Black Is Beautiful" citation from United Black Artists, 1968; "Favorite Prof.," Howard U., 1965-66, 1966-67; Elected to N.Y. Acad. of Sci.; Bay Area Black Educ., Merritt Coll., Oakland, 1969.

MEMBER: Bd. of Dir., Point Found., San Francisco, 1973- ; Amer. Sociol. Assn.; Assn. of Behavioral & Soc. Sci.; Amer. Assn. of U. Prof.; E. Sociol. Assn.; Sigma Gamma Rho; Pres., Howard U. Chap., Amer. Assoc. U. Prof., 1967; Bd. of Dir., N. Amer. Zone, 2nd World Black & African Festival of Arts & Culture (Lagos, Nigeria, 1975).

SIDELIGHTS: Introducing an interview with Dr. Hare on Black Studies, in May 1970, <u>College and University Business</u> noted: "Dr. Nathan Hare was the first coordinator to be hired for a black studies program--and the first to be fired. He was appointed to the

post at San Francisco State College in the spring of 1968 'to appease' (his words) the Black Students Union. By fall, the black students and Dr. Hare were embarked on a five-month strike to press their demand for an autonomous black studies department. It was Mr. Hare who coined the phrases 'Third World Liberation Front' and 'ethnic studies'" (New Black Voices).
Sources. Author inform.; Contemporary Authors, vols. 41-44, Ed. by Clare D. Kinsman (Gale Res., 1974); New Black Voices, Ed. by Abraham Chapman (New Amer. Lib., 1972).

HARPER, FRANCES ELLEN WATKINS. 1825-1911.
Poet, Abolitionist
Biographical-Personal. Born 1825, in Baltimore, Md.; of free parents. Educ.: Baltimore. Family: m. Fenton Harper. Died 1911.
Career-Professional. Tchr., Union Sem., Columbus, Ohio; Underground railroad worker, Little York, Pa.; Lectr., Anti-Slavery Soc. of Maine. (Lectured in Boston, Phila. & New Bedford, Mass.; Lectr. in every s. state but Tex. & Ark.)
WRITINGS: Poetry: Autumn Leaves; Poems on Miscellaneous Subjects (1854); Moses, A Story of the Nile (1869); Poems (1871-1900); Sketches of Southern Life (1872); Atlanta Offering (Bks. for Lib., 1895); Poems of Frances E. W. Harper (Bks. for Lib., 1895). Iola Leroy, or the Shadows Uplifted, best known prose work. The Sparrow's Fall and Other Poems, final work; Idylls of the Bible (AMS Pr., repr., 1975). Frequent contrib. to Godey's Lady's Book.
SIDELIGHTS: Mrs. Harper wrote the first published short stories by a Negro author. Among her best individual poems were, "Eliza Harris," "The Slave Mother," "Bible Defense of Slavery," "The Freedom Bell," and "Bury Me In a Free Land." After the Civil War she traveled extensively as Women's Christian Temperance Union representative (An Anthology of Verse by American Negroes).
Sources. American Negro Reference Book, Ed. by John Davis (Prentice-Hall, 1966); An Anthology of Verse by American Negroes, Ed. by Newman I. White & Walter C. Jackson (Moore, 1924); Early Black American Poets, Ed. by William H. Robinson, Jr. (Brown, 1969); Poetry of the Negro, 1946-1949, Ed. by Langston Hughes & Arna Bontemps (Doubleday, 1949); Books in Print, Supplement, 1975-76 (Bowker, 1976).

Harper, Michael Steven

HARPER, MICHAEL STEVEN. 1938- . Poet, Teacher
Biographical-Personal. Born Mar. 18, 1938, in Brooklyn, N.Y. Son of Walter Warren and Katherine [Johnson] Harper. Educ.: B.A., 1961, M.A. (Eng.), 1963, UCLA; M.A. (MFA), Writer's Workshop, U. of Iowa. Family: m. Shirley Harper; son, Roland, son, Patrice, d. Rachel. Mailing address: 26 First St., Barrington, R.I. 02806.
Career-Professional. Prof., Dir., Writing prog., Brown U.; Center for Advanced Study, U. of Ill., Urbana; Cal. State U., Hayward; Lewis & Clark Coll. (Poet-in-Residence); Reed Coll., Ore.; Contra Costa Coll., Cal.; L.A. City Coll.

WRITINGS: Dear John, Dear Coltrane (U. of Pittsburgh Pr., 1970); History Is Your Own Heartbeat (U. of Ill. Pr., 1971); Photographs, Negatives: History as Apple Tree (Scarab Pr., 1973); Song: I Want a Witness (U. of Pittsburgh Pr., 1972); Debridement (Doubleday, 1973); Nightmare Begins Responsibility (U. of Ill. Pr., 1974); Heartblow: Black Veils (U. of Ill. Pr., 1974). Anthol.: Interviews with Black Writers; The Lyric Potential; Coltrane; To Gwen with Love; Natural Process. Period.: Carolina Quarterly; Southern Review; Black World; Black Scholar; & Poetry.
HONORS AND AWARDS: Postdoctoral fellow, U. of Ill., Center for Advanced Study, 1970-71; Award for creative writing, Amer. Acad./ Nat'l. Inst. of Arts & Letters, 1972; Best poetry bk., Black Acad. of Arts & Letters, 1972 (for History Is Your Own Heartbeat).
SIDELIGHTS: Frequent poetry cons. and reader; lectr. John Callahan, Lewis & Clark Coll., Portland, Ore.; is in the process of writing a book of criticism of Michael Harper's poetry (Author).
Sources. Author inform.; Contemporary Authors, Vol. 33-36, Ed. by Clare D. Kinsman & Mary A. Tennenhouse (Gale Res., 1973); New Black Voices, Ed. by Abraham Chapman (New Amer. Lib., 1972); Poetry of Black America, Ed. by Arnold Adoff (Harper & Row, 1973); Pub. inform.

HARRIS, ABRAM LINCOLN. 1899-1963. Economist, Professor of Economics
Biographical-Personal. Born 1899 in Richmond, Va. Son of butcher and normal sch. grad. Educ.: Armstrong High Sch., Richmond; Va. Union U., Richmond, grad., 1922; M.A., U. of Pittsburgh; Ph.D. (Econ.), Columbia U., 1931. Died 1963.
Career-Professional. Instr., Econ., W. Va. State Coll., 1924, Executive Secy., Minneapolis Urban League, 1925; Researcher, Columbia U., Dept. of Banking, 1926; Asst. Prof., 1927, Head, Dept. of Econ., 1930, Prof., 1936, Howard U.; Vis. Prof., Econ., U. of

Chgo., 1946-63; Vis. Prof., summers: City Coll. of N.Y., 1942; U. of Puerto Rico, 1957. WRITINGS: The Black Worker, with Sterling Spero (1931); The Negro as Capitalist (1936); Economics and Social Reform (1958). Pub. many articles, including "The Social Philosophy of Karl Marx." HONORS AND AWARDS: Social Sci. Res. Counc. Fellow, 1928-30; Simon Nelson Patten Res. Fellow, 1932-33; Guggenheim Fellow, 1935-36, 1943-44, 1953-54. SIDELIGHTS: "The most outstanding academic economist among American blacks was Abram Lincoln Harris. Author of several major studies, he divided his teaching career between a black school, Howard University (1927-1945), and a white school, the University of Chicago (1946-63). "His best known work was The Negro as Capitalist (1936), a definitive study of the black man in banking, insurance, and other enterprises" (A Biographical History of Blacks in America Since 1528).

Source. A Biographical History of Blacks in America Since 1528, Edgar A. Toppin (McKay, 1971).

HARRIS, MIDDLETON. 1908- . Writer
Biographical-Personal. Born Jan. 22, 1908, in Brooklyn, N.Y.
Career-Professional.
   WRITINGS: A Negro History Tour of Manhattan (Greenwood, 1968); Casebook #1: Uncle Spike, the Negro History Detective (Negro Hist. Assn., 1967); The Black Book, Ed. (Random House, 1974).
Source. Books in Print, 1976 (Bowker, 1976).

HASKETT, EDYTHE RANCE. 1915- . Teacher, Juvenile Writer
Biographical-Personal. Born Dec. 28, 1915, in Suffolk, Va. D. of E. L. H. (dentist) and Ivy [Miller] Rance. Educ.: St. Paul's High Sch., Lawrenceville, Va.; B.A., Shaw U., Raleigh, N.C.; M.A., N.Y.U.; Postgrad.: Rutgers U., New Brunswick, N.J., Columbia U. Family: div.; son, John O. Haskett. Mailing address: 2741 Woodland Ave., Norfolk, Va. 23504.
Career-Professional. Tchr., Norfolk, Va.; Tchr., Episcopal High Sch., Robertsport, Liberia, W. Africa.
   WRITINGS: Juvenile: Grains of Pepper; Folktales from Liberia (John Day, 1967); Some

Haskins, James

Gold, a Little Ivory: Country Tales from Ghana and the Ivory
Coast (John Day, 1971).
HONORS AND AWARDS: "Outstanding Citizen," Radio Station WRAP,
Norfolk, 1962; "Distinguished Community Service," Alpha Kappa
Alpha Sorority, 1967; Citation--"Building Bridges of Understand-
ing," Com. for Improvement of Educ., 1968; Certificate of Hon.,
St. Paul's Coll., Lawrenceville, Va., 1972.
SIDELIGHTS: Spent two years teaching in Liberia, where she col-
lected the stories told in her two books. Three subsequent trips
to Liberia, Ghana, Ivory Coast, Nigeria, Dahomey. Two trips to
Europe (Author).
Source. Author inform.

HASKINS, JAMES. 1941- . Writer, Biographer
Biographical-Personal. Born Sept. 19, 1941, in Ala. Son of Henry
and Julia Haskins. Educ.: B.A., Georgetown U., 1960; Ala. State
U., 1962; M.A., U. of N. Mex., 1963; Further study: New Sch. for
Soc. Res.; Queens Coll., Flushing, N.Y. Mailing address: 668
Riverside Dr., N.Y., N.Y. 10031.
Career-Professional. Stock trader, Smith Barney & Co., 1963-65;
Tchr., N.Y.C. Bd. of Educ., 1966-68; Instr. in Urban Educ., New
Sch. for Soc. Res., N.Y.C., 1970- ; Instr. in Psychology of Black
Lang., 1971; Instr. in Eng., Staten Island Community Coll., Staten
Island, N.Y., 1970- ; Mem., Bd. of Dir., Psi Systems; Faculty,
Grad. Sch. of Educ., Manhattanville Coll.
WRITINGS: Juveniles: Resistance: Profiles in Nonviolence (Dou-
bleday, 1971); The War and the Protest: Vietnam (Doublday, 1971);
Revolutionaries: Agents of Change (Lippincott, 1971); A Minority
of One: a Biography of Lew Alcindor (Lothrop); Beautiful Are the
Souls of My People: Biography of Langston Hughes (Holt); A Piece
of the Power: Four Black Mayors (Dial); Profiles in Black Power
(Doubleday); Babe Ruth and Hank Aaron: The Home-run Kings
(Lothrop, 1974); Creoles of Color of New Orleans (Crowell, 1975);
Fighting Shirley Chisholm (Dial, 1975); From Lew Alcindor to Ka-
reem Abdul Jabbar (Lothrop, 1974); Witchcraft, Mysticism and Magic
in the Black World (Doubleday, 1974); The Picture Life of Malcolm
X (Watts, 1975); Snow Sculpture and Ice Carving (Macmillan, 1974).
Doctor J: A Biography of Julius Erving (Doubleday, 1975); A Time
to Win: The Story of the Kennedy Foundation's Special Olympics
for the Mentally Retarded (Doubleday, 1976); Aging in America:
the Great Denial (Hastings, 1976); The Story of Stevie Wonder
(Lothrop, 1976). Adult books: Under name "Jim Haskins":
Diary of a Harlem School Teacher (Grove, 1970); The Educational
Politic, with Mario Fantini (Doubleday); On Black Education (Mor-
row); The Psychology of Black Language, with Hugh Butts, M.D.
(Barnes & Noble, 1973); Pinckney Benton Steward Pinchback: a

Hatch, James Vernon

Biography (Macmillan, 1973); Street Gangs; Yesterday and Today
(Hastings, 1974); Black Manifesto for Education (Morrow, 1974);
Children Have Rights, Too (Hawthorn, 1975); The Consumer Movement
(Watts, 1975); Your Rights, Past and Present (Hawthorn, 1975);
Pele: A Biography (Doublday, 1976); Teen-Age Alcoholism (Haw-
thorn, 1976).
Sources. Contemporary Authors, Vols. 33-36, Ed. by Clare D. Kinsman
& Mary A. Tennenhouse (Gale Res., 1973); Forthcoming Bks. (Bowker,
Sept. 1975); Books in Print, Supplement, 1975-76 (Bowker, 1976).

HATCH, JAMES VERNON. 1928- . Playwright, Film Writer
Biographical-Personal. Born Oct. 25, 1928, in Oelwein, Iowa. Son of
MacKenzie (boilermaker) & Eunice [Smith] Hatch. Educ.: B.A.,
State U. of N. Iowa, 1949; M.A., 1955, Ph.D., 1958, State U. of
Iowa. Family: 1st m. Evelyn Marcussen, 1949; children: Susan
(Mrs. Goeffry Simms), Dion. 2nd m. Camille Billops (artist),
1964. Mailing address: Dept. of English, City Coll. of City U.
of N.Y.
Career-Professional. High sch. Eng. & drama tchr., 1949-58; UCLA,
Asst. Prof. of Theatre Arts, 1958-62; High Cinema Inst., Cairo,
Egypt, Fullbright lectr., 1962-65; City Coll. of City U. of N.Y.,
Asst. Prof., 1965-72, Assoc. Prof. of Eng., 1973- . Resident
Playwright, Idylwild Arts Found., 1960, Huntington Hartford Found.,
1962. U.S. Dept. of State, theatre spec. in India, Pakistan &
Ceylon, 1968.
WRITINGS: (With Ibrahim Ibn Ismail) Poems for Niggers and Crack-
ers (Schindler Pr., 1965); The Black Image on the American Stage;
A Bibliography (Drama Bk. Specialist, 1970); Liar, Liar, a chil-
dren's musical play (1st prod. Nov. 1962, at ANTA children's
Theatre, L.A.--Gen. Music Corp., 1972); Ed. with Victoria Sul-
livan By and About Women (Random House, 1973); Ed., Black Theater,
U.S.A., 45 Plays by Black Americans, 1847-1974 (Free Pr., 1974).
Documentary films: "This is Worth Remembering" (1957); "Autumn"
(1957); "The Sole Survivor" (1960); "Modern Arabic Women" (1964);
"Three Days of Suez" (1964); "Paper Pulp from Sugar Cane" (1965);
"Denmark 43" (1972). Also writer of educ. films for State U. of
Iowa, 1956-58. Contrib. to Drama Review, Nation, Village Voice,
College English, & Changing Education.
HONORS AND AWARDS: Thomas Wood Stevens Award from Stanford U. &
Festival of Arts Award, Birmingham, Ala., both 1957 for "Easter
Song"; George Washington Honor Medal Award from Freedoms Found.,
1958, for "This is Worth Remembering"; Obie Award of Village Voice
for best off-Broadway musical in N.Y., 1961-62, for Fly Blackbird.
Unity Award of Better Race Relat. Bureau of Hollywood, 1962; 1st
prize at Atlanta Film Festival, & Golden Eagle Civic Award, both
1972 for "Denmark 43."
Source. Contemporary Authors, Vols. 41-44, Ed. by Clare D. Kinsman
(Gale Res., 1974).

Hawkins, Odie

HAWKINS, ODIE. 1937- . Screen Writer
Biographical-Personal. Born July 6, 1937, in Chgo., Ill. Son of
Odie Sr. and Lillian Hawkins. Educ.: High sch. "After high
school, most of my education has been what a friend calls 'attend-
ance at S.W.U....side walk university.'" Family: div.; d. Erika.
Mailing address: 5159 Clinton St., L.A., Cal. 90004.
Career-Professional.
WRITINGS: Screenplays: The Harlem Jet Set (Independent); P. K.
Harris (Warner Brothers); Elis Crames (Universal Studios); Sister
Woman (Universal Studios); Eagle in the Air, adaptation from book
of same name (MGM).
SIDELIGHTS: "UCLA, September '74, lecture on the esoteric aspects
of Black humor. Like why "motherfucker", the word, has a different
emotional quality for most blacks than whites. A lecture-teaching
series at Dorsey High School, Nov.-Jan. '74" (Author).
Source. Author inform.

HAYDEN, ROBERT C. Science Teacher, Science News Writer
Biographical-Personal. Educ.: M.S., Boston U.; Harvard U. (grad.
study).
Career-Professional. Sci. tchr.; Sci. news writer; Sci. ed. Execu-
tive Dir., Metropolitan Counc. for Educ. Opportunity (METCO),
Boston, Mass.
WRITINGS: Seven Black American Scientists (Addison-Wesley, 1970);
Eight Black American Inventors (Addison-Wesley, 1972).
MEMBER: Nat'l. Assn. of Sci. Writers; Nat'l. Sci. Teachers Assn.;
Amer. Assn. for the Advancement of Sci.
SIDELIGHTS: "In his research for many writing assignments, Mr.
Hayden often had thrilling experiences. In 1967, he flew in an
Air Force plane to experience the sensation of weightlessness for
an article he was preparing on the subject of zero-gravity. The
feature article he developed afterward won an award from The Edu-
cational Press Association of America" (Seven Black American Sci-
entists).
Source. Seven Black American Scientists, Robert C. Hayden (Addison-
Wesley, 1970).

HAYDEN, ROBERT E. 1913- . Poet, Teacher
Biographical-Personal. Born Aug. 4, 1913 in Detroit, Mich. Educ.:
B.A., Wayne State U.; M.A., U. of Mich. Family: Married; one d.
Mailing address: Dept. of Eng., U. of Mich., Ann Arbor, Mich.
48104.
Career-Professional. Tchr., Eng., U. of Mich., 1944-46; Prof., Eng.,
Fisk U., Nashville, 1946-69; Writer-in-Residence & Prof. of Eng.,
U. of Mich., 1969- .
WRITINGS: Heart-Shape in the Dust (1940); The Lion and the Archer,
with Myron O'Higgins (Hemphill, 1948); Figure of Time (1955);

Heard, Nathan Cliff

Selected Poems (October House, 1960); A Ballad for Remembrance (London: Paul Bremen);
Kaleidoscope, Ed. (Harcourt, 1967); Words in
the Mourning Time (1971); Night Blooming Ce-
reus (Paul Bremen, 1972). Afro-American Lit-
erature, An Introduction, Ed., with Others
(Harcourt, 1972); Mastering American English:
A Handbook-Workbook of Essentials, with Oth-
ers (Prentice-Hall, 1956); Angle of Ascent:
New and Selected Poems (Liveright, 1975).
Has ed. and pub. the Counterpoise Ser.; Ed.
Ba-ha'i mag. World Order. Music & drama
criticism to Michigan Chronicle; Poems to
Poetry; Atlantic Monthly; Phylon; & Midwest
Journal.
HONORS AND AWARDS: Awarded Grand Prize for
Poetry, 1st World Festival of Negro Arts, Dakar, Senegal, for A
Ballad for Remembrance, 1965; Hopwood Award from U. of Mich.,
1938 & 1942; Rosenwald Fellow, 1947; Ford Found. grant for travel
& writing in Mexico, 1954.
SIDELIGHTS: "Very much in demand as lecturer, reader-of-his-own-
works and visiting professor" (Cavalcade). Words in the Mourning
Time was nominated for National Book Award, 1972 (Poetry of Black
America).
Sources. Black Voices, Ed. by Abraham Chapman (New Amer. Lib.,
1968); Cavalcade, Ed. by Arthur P. Davis & Saunders Redding
(Houghton Mifflin, 1971); Dark Symphony, Ed. by James A. Emanuel
& Theodore L. Gross (Free Pr., 1968); For Malcolm, Ed. by Dudley
Randall & Margaret Burroughs (Broadside Pr., 1969); Interviews
With Black Writers, Ed. by John O'Brien (Liverright, 1973);
Kaleidoscope, Ed. by Robert Hayden (Harcourt, 1967); Poetry of
Black America, Ed. by Arnold Adoff (Harper & Row, 1973); Books in
Print, Supplement, 1975-76 (Bowker, 1976).

HEARD, NATHAN CLIFF. 1936- . Novelist
Biographical-Personal. Born Nov. 7, 1936 in Newark, N.J. Son of
Nathan E. and Gladys Heard. Educ.: Elementary sch. Family:
son, Melvin, son, Cliff, d. Natalie. Mailing address: 60 Parkway
Dr. E., E. Orange, N.J. 07017.
Career-Professional. Laborer, factory worker, musician; Lectr.,
Fresno State Coll.; Asst. Prof., Eng., Livingston Coll, Rugers U.
WRITINGS: Novels: Howard Street (Dial, 1968); To Reach A Dream
(Dial, 1971); A Cold Fire Burning (Simon & Schuster, 1974); The
House of Slammers; When Shadows Fall (Playboy, 1976).
HONORS AND AWARDS: Author Award, N.J. Assn. of Tchrs. of Eng.;
Award, Newark Coll. of Engineering.
SIDELIGHTS: "The Chicago Sun-Times Book Week called [Howard
Street] 'The stunningly rich story of the very bottom of the black

Hedgeman, Anna Arnold

ghetto, of the men whose idea of success is persuading their
sweethearts to turn prostitute, of the women who give in because
they need a strong pimp...Howard Street tells everything...tells
it like it is;' and To Reach A Dream, hailed by the New York Times
as a 'raw, brutal portrayal of street life in a Newark ghetto.
The setting is vividly drawn, the bars, after hours joints and
predawn haunts of living predators...overwhelming.'"
  "Nathan Heard's checkered past includes 12 years in Trenton
Prison for armed robbery and several movie roles, including one
in the recently released Gordon's War. He also sings regularly
in New York and Newark nightclubs" (A Cold Fire Burning).
Sources. Author inform.; A Cold Fire Burning, Nathan C. Heard (Simon
  & Schuster, 1974); Books in Print, Supplement, 1975-76 (Bowker,
  1976).

HEDGEMAN, ANNA ARNOLD. Social Worker, Federal
Official, Civil Rights Leader
Biographical-Personal. Born in Marshalltown,
    Iowa. Educ.: B.A., L.H.D. (hon.), 1948,
    Hamline U., St. Paul, Minn.; further study:
    N.Y. Sch. of Soc. Work; U. of Minn. Family:
    m. Merritt A. Hedgeman (concert artist &
    Dir., Hedgman Cons. Serv.), 1933. Mailing
    address: 10 West 135th St., Suite 15P, N.Y.,
    N.Y. 10037.
Career-Professional. Cons. on Urban Affairs &
    African Amer. Stud.; Tchr., Rust Coll., Holly
    Springs, Miss., 1922-24; Executive Secy.,
    YWCA: Springfield, Ohio, Jersey City, N.J.,
    N.Y.C., 1924-34, Brooklyn, 1938-41; Executive
    Dir., Nat'l. Counc. for a permanent FEPC,
1943-45; Staff, Dean of Women, Howard U., Wash., D.C., 1946; Asst.
Oscar R. Ewing, Administrator, Fed. Security Agency, 1949-53;
Asst., Mayor Wagner, N.Y.C., 1954-58; Ed. & Columnist, New York
Age, 1958-61; Cons., Div. of Higher Educ., United Church Bd. for
Homeland Ministries, 1961- ; Served variously as Assoc. Dir.,
Dept. of Soc. Justice & Dir., Ecumenical Action, Nat'l. Counc. of
Churches, 1963-68. Was a major architect of 1963, March On Wash-
ington. Exchange leader (Dept. of State), India, 1953. Discus-
sion, internat. problems, Middle East & Israel, 1956; Inspector,
United Seamen's Serv. Centers, Europe & Middle East; Participated,
internat. conf. (soc. work), Munich, Germany, 1956, Tokyo, Japan,
1958; Keynote speaker, 1st Conf. of Women of Africa & African
Descent, Accra, Ghana, 1960; N.Y.C. official rep. 10th Anniversary
Observation, UN, San Francisco, 1955.
WRITINGS: The Trumpet Sounds, autobiog. (Holt, Rinehart & Winston,
1965--now in 3rd print.); The Gift of Chaos: Decades of American

Discontent (Oxford U. Pr., 1977). Has written extensively for
orgs., public., newspapers, & jls. N.Y. radio prog., "One Woman's
Opinion" (1962-63). Weekly prog. WRVR, Riverside Church, "There
Are Things To Do," 1964.
HONORS AND AWARDS: NAACP; AFL-CIO; United Church Women's Award
for Christian Citizenship; U.S. Dept. of Health, Educ. & Welfare;
Nat'l. Human Relat. Award--State Fair Bd. of Texas; The Guardians
Assn. of the Police Dept., N.Y.C.; Montana Farmers Union; S.
Christian Leadership Conf.; Harmon Found. Exhibited portrait in
art galleries as "Distinguished American Negroes"; Listed, Who's
Who of Amer. Women; Leadership for Freedom Award, Women's Scholar-
ship Assn., Roosevelt U., Chgo., 1965; LL.D. (hon.), Upsala Coll.,
East Orange, N.J., 1970; Urban League's "Frederick Douglass Award"
for "Distinguished Leadership Toward Equal Opportunity," 1974;
10th Anniversary Award, Delta Ministry of Miss., 1974; Spec.
Achievement Award, Nat'l. Conf. of Christians & Jews.
MEMBER: Community Counc., N.Y.; Child Study Assn.; Nat'l. Conf.
of Christians & Jews (Bd.); United Seamen's Serv. (Bd.); Nat'l.
Urban League; NAACP; Speakers Res. Com., UN; Dept. of HEW; Nat'l.
Advis. Counc. on Vocational Rehabilitation; Mayor's Advis. Com.
for Bd. of Higher Educ. in N.Y.C.; Conf. on Faculty Mem., City
Coll. Sch. of Educ., Dir. of Sch. of Educ., Amer. Acad. of Pol. &
Soc. Sci.; Authors Guild; The African-Amer. Hist. Assn.
Sources. Author inform.; Negro Almanac, Comp. by Harry A. Ploski &
Ernest Kaiser (Bellwether, 1971); Negro Handbook, Comp. by Eds. of
Ebony (Johnson Pub., 1966); Kirkus Reviews, March 1, 1977, p. 260.

HENDERSON, DAVID. 1942- . Poet, Teacher
Biographical-Personal. Born 1942 in Harlem, N.Y. Educ.: Bronx Com-
    munity Coll.; Hunter Coll.; New Sch. for Soc. Res.; E.-W. Inst.,
    Cambridge, Mass.
Career-Professional. Tchr., Columbia U.; Tchr., City Coll. of N.Y.;
    with Free S. Theatre, New Orleans. Active in org. of Umbra mag. &
    East Village Other; Poet-in-Residence, City Coll. of N.Y., 1969-70;
    Tchr., Berkeley, Cal. & ed. Umbra/Black Works.
    WRITINGS: Felix of the Silent Forest (1967); De-Mayor of Harlem
    (Dutton, 1971); Joe Overstreet (Interbook, 1972). Poetry included
    in: Evergreen Review, New American Review, Negro Digest/Black
    World, Freedomways, Journal of Black Poetry, Paris Review & Es-
    sence. Anthol.: Black Fire, New Black Poetry, Black Out Loud &
    Black Spirits.
    SIDELIGHTS: As member of "Umbra Poets" group, has participated in
    more than a hundred poetry readings: Vassar, Princeton, Carnegie
    Hall, San Francisco State Coll. Poetry has been translated into
    French, Italian, Spanish & Chinese.
Sources. Black Fire, Ed. by LeRoi Jones & Larry Neal (Morrow, 1968);
    Contemporary Authors, Vols. 25-28, Ed. by Carolyn Riley (Gale Res.,

Henderson, George Wylie

1971); For Malcolm, Ed. by Dudley Randall & Margaret G. Burroughs
(Broadside Pr., 1969); Poetry of Black America, Ed. by Arnold
Adoff (Harper & Row, 1973).

HENDERSON, GEORGE WYLIE. 1904- . Novelist, Short Story Writer,
Printer
Biographical-Personal. Born 1904 in Warriors Stand, Ala. Son of an
A.M.E. minister. Educ.: (Printing) Tuskegee Inst.
Career-Professional. Printer.
  WRITINGS: Novels: Ollie Miss (1935); Jule (1946). Contrib.
  short stories to N.Y. Daily News, Redbook.
Sources. Negro Caravan, Ed. by Sterling A. Brown & Others (Arno Pr.,
  & N.Y. Times, 1969); Negro Novel in America, Robert A. Bone (Yale
  U. Pr., 1958).

HERCULES, FRANK. Novelist, Essayist
Biographical-Personal. Born in Port-of-Spain, Trinidad, W. Indies.
  Educ.: Hon. Soc. of the Middle Temple, London (for the English
  Bar). Came to U.S. Family: m. Amer.; became an Amer. citizen.
Career-Professional. Lectr.; Tchr.; Essayist.
  WRITINGS: Novels: Where the Hummingbird Flies (Harcourt, 1961);
  I Want A Black Doll (Simon & Schuster, 1967). American Society
  and Black Revolution, essay (Harcourt, 1972).
Source. Pub. inform.

HERNTON, CALVIN C. 1932- . Sociologist, Teacher
Biographical-Personal. Born Apr. 28, 1932, in Chattanooga, Tenn.
  Son of Magnolia Jackson. Educ.: B.A., Talladega Coll., 1954;
  M.A. (Sociol.), Fisk U., 1956; Columbia U., 1961. Family: m.,
  son, Anton. Mailing address: 160 N. Main St., Oberlin, Ohio
  44074.
Career-Professional. Soc. worker, Leake & Watts Home for Children,
  Yonkers, N.Y. Summer, 1954; Youth House for Boys, Welfare Island,
  N.Y., 1956-57; Soc. Investigator, N.Y. Dept. of Welfare, 1961-62;
  Instr., Sociol. & Hist., Southern U., Baton Rouge, La.; Edward
  Waters Coll., Jacksonville, Fla.; Ala. A. & M. Coll., Normal,
  Ala., 1957-61; Tech. Typist, Chemical Bank N.Y. Trust Co.; Coding
  & Res. Technician, Richard Manville Market Res., N.Y.; Writer-in-
  Residence, Central State U., Wilberforce, Ohio, Jan.-June, 1970;
  Assoc. Prof., Afro-Amer. Stud., Oberlin Coll.; Lectr.: W. Indian
  Writers' Conf. of Kent, Eng., 1967; Columbia U., 1964; Clarte
  Soc., Stockholm, Sweden, 1967; New Sch. for Soc. Res., 1964 &
  others. Co-founder, Umbra mag.
  WRITINGS: Sex and Racism in America (Doubleday, 1964); White Pa-
  pers for White Americans (Doubleday, 1966); Coming Together, White
  Hate, Black Power and Sexual Hangups (Random House, 1971). Poetry:
  The Coming of Chronos to the House of Nightsong (Interim Bks.,

1963); Social Struggle and Sexual Crisis (1970); The Cannabis Experience: An Interpretive Study of the Effects of Marijuana and Hashish, with Joseph Berke (Humanities, 1975).
HONORS AND AWARDS: Fellow, Inst. of Phenomenological Stud., London, 1965, 1968-69.
Sources. Amistad 1, Ed. by John A. Williams & Charles Harris (Vintage Bks., 1970); Black Fire, Ed. by LeRoi Jones & Larry Neal (Morrow, 1968); Contemporary Authors, Vols. 11-12, Ed. by James M. Ethridge & Barbara Kopala (Gale Res., 1965); New Black Poetry, Ed. by Clarence Major (Internat. Pub., 1969); Poetry of Black America, Ed. by Arnold Adoff (Harper & Row, 1973).

HILL, LESLIE PINCKNEY. 1880-1960. College President
Biographical-Personal. Born May 14, 1880, in Lynchburg, Va. Educ.: B.A., 1903, M.A., 1904, Harvard U.; Hon. Degrees: Lincoln U., Morgan State Coll., Haverford Coll., & Rhode Island Coll. of Educ. Died Feb. 16, 1960 in Phila., Pa.
Career-Professional. Tchr., Eng. Educ., Tuskegee Inst.; Prin., Manassas (Va.) Indust. Sch.; Pres., Cheyney State Tchrs. Coll. (Pa.). WRITINGS: The Wings of Oppression, poetry (Black Her. repr. of 1921 ed., Bks. for Lib., 1921); Toussaint L'Ouverture--A Dramatic History, blank-verse drama in 5 acts (1928). MEMBER: Founder and Pres. of Bd. of W. Chester Community Center; Founder & Past Pres. of Pa. State Negro Counc.; Del. Co. Bd. of Assistance.
Sources. Amsterdam News, Jan. 15, 1928; Book of American Negro Poetry, Ed. by James W. Johnson (Harcourt, 1959); Negro Caravan, Ed. by Sterling A. Brown & Others (Arno Pr. & N.Y. Times, 1969); Negro Poets and Their Poems, Ed. by Robert T. Kerlin (Assoc. Pub., 1935); New York Times, Feb. 16, 1960.

HIMES, CHESTER BOMAR. 1909- . Detective Story Writer
Biographical-Personal. Born July 29, 1909, in Jefferson City, Mo. Son of Joseph Sandy and Estelle [Bomar] Himes. Educ.: Ohio State U., 1926-29. Family: 1st m. Jean Lucinda Johnson; 2nd m. Lesley Himes. Mailing address: c/o Doubleday, Inc., 277 Park Ave., N.Y., N.Y. 10013.
Career-Professional. Bellhop, Cleveland, Ohio; Sentenced at 19 to 20 yrs. for armed robbery, served 7 yrs. in Ohio State Penitentiary

Hinton, William Augustus

where he began to write & contribute stories to mags.; Released
1935; Employed in various capacities as writer, WPA; Worked on
Louis Bromfield's farm, Malabar; Shipyard & aircraft employee,
World War II, L.A. & San Francisco; Traveled abroad, 1953.
WRITINGS: If He Hollers Let Him Go (New Amer. Lib., 1945); Cast
the First Stone (New Amer. Lib., 1953); Lonely Crusade U.S.A.
(Knopf, 1954); The Third Generation (World, 1954); The Primitive
(New Amer. Lib., 1956); Pinktoes (Dell, 1965); Cotton Comes to
Harlem, since made into a film (Dell, 1968); The Heat's On (1968);
Run Man Run (1968); Blind Man With a Pistol (Morrow, 1969); Hot
Day, Hot Night (Doubleday); Quality of Hurt, Vol. I (Doubleday,
1972); For Love of Inabelle (New Amer. Lib., Chester Himes Ser.,
1974); The Crazy Kill (New Amer. Lib., 1975); The Real Cool Kil-
lers (New Amer. Lib., 1975); All Shot Up (New Amer. Lib., 1975);
The Big Gold Dream (New Amer. Lib., 1975). Has also written numerous articles for Abbott's Monthly, The Crisis, Opportunity, Coro-
net & Commentary.
HONORS AND AWARDS: "Grand Prix Policier" for mystery writing,
1958; Rosenwald Fellow, Creative Writing, 1944-45.
SIDELIGHTS: An expatriate living in France, his novels have been
published in France, Norway, Sweden, Denmark and England; have
been translated into several languages. He has become renowned as
a detective story writer (Cavalcade).
Sources. Blackamerican Literature, Ed. by Ruth Miller (Glencoe Pr.,
1971); Cavalcade, Ed. by Arthur P. Davis & Saunders Redding (Houghton Mifflin, 1971); Soon, One Morning, Ed. by Herbert Hill (Knopf,
1963); Who's Who in America, 37th ed., 1972-73 (Marquis, 1972);
Books in Print, Supplement, 1975-76 (Bowker, 1976).

HINTON, WILLIAM AUGUSTUS. 1883-1959. Physi-
cian, Serologist, Bacteriologist
Biographical-Personal. Born Dec. 15, 1883, in
    Chicago, Ill. Educ.: B.S., 1905, M.D. (hon.),
    1912 Harvard U. Died Aug. 8, 1959.
Career-Professional. Dir., Lab. Dept. Boston
    Dispensary, 1915; Chief, Wasserman Lab.,
    Mass. Dept. of Public Health; Harvard U.:
    Instr., Preventive Medicine & Hygiene; Instr.,
    Bacteriology & Immunology, 1921-46; Clinical
    Prof., 1946-50; Prof. Emeritus, 1950-59.
    Spec. cons., U.S. Public Health Serv.; Cons.,
    Mass. Sch. for Crippled Children; Lectr.,
    Simmons Coll., Boston.
    WRITINGS: Syphillis and Its Treatment, uni-
    versally used professional ref. (1936).
Contrib. many articles to nationally recognized jls.
HONORS AND AWARDS: 1st Black granted a professorship at Harvard,
1949.

126

Hoagland, Everett H., III

MEMBER: Amer. Med. Assn.; Amer. Soc. of Clinical Pathology; Soc.
of Amer. Bacteriology; Amer. Assn. for Advancement of Sci.
SIDELIGHTS: "William A. Hinton (was a) bacteriologist in the area
of diseases of the blood.... As a serologist he originated the
Hinton test, an authoritative test for syphillis, and the serum
used to fight the disease" (Historical Negro Biographies).
  "Long one of the world's authorities on venereal disease...he
collaborated with Dr. J. A. V. Davies in what is now called the
'Davies-Hinton test' for the detection of syphillis" (Negro Al-
manac).
Sources. Historical Negro Biographies, Wilhelmena S. Robinson
  (ASNLH, 1967); Negro Almanac, Comp. by Harry A. Ploski & Ernest
  Kaiser (Bellwether, 1971).

HOAGLAND, EVERETT H., III. 1942- . Poet, Teacher
Biographical-Personal. Born Dec. 18, 1942, in Phila., Pa. Son of
  Everett, Jr. and Estelle Hoagland. Educ.: B.A., Lincoln U., Pa.,
  1964; M.A., Brown U., 1973. Mailing address: 8370 Chelwynde
  Ave., Phila., Pa. 19153.
Career-Professional. Tchr., Harding Jr. High Sch., Phila., 1964-67;
  Tchr., Eng., Adult Evening Sch., Phila., 1965-66; Asst. Dir. of
  Admissions, Lincoln U., Pa., 1967-69; Asst. to Dir., Black Stud.
  Center, Claremont Coll., Cal., 1969-70; Instr., African-Amer.
  Poetry, 1969-71, & Poet-in-Residence, Black Stud. Center, Clare-
  mont Coll., 1970-71; Coord. of & Tchr. in Afro-Culture & Soc.,
  Chino Inst. for Men (Cal.), evenings, 1970; Instr. of Amer. &
  Black Lit., Mt. San Antonio Coll., 1970-71; Instr. Eng.,'Upward
  Bound Prog., Claremont Coll., 1971; U. Fellow. in Creative Writing,
  Brown U., 1971-73; Instr. of Humanities Re-Enrollment Prog.,
  Swarthmore Coll., Summer, 1972.
  WRITINGS: Black Velvet (Broadside Pr., 1970). Anthol.: The New
  Black Poetry; Patterns; A Broadside Treasury; The Black Poets; New
  Black Voices; An Anthology of New Earth Writings. Period.: Black
  World; Essence; Evergreen; Journal of Black Poetry; Nickel Review;
  Ra.
  HONORS AND AWARDS: Silvera Award for Creative Writing, Lincoln U.,
  Pa., 1964; Outstanding Young Men of America, 1968-69; U. Fellow.
  for Creative Writing, Brown U., 1971-73.
  SIDELIGHTS: Mr. Hoagland has given poetry readings and presenta-
  tions all over the U.S. and in France, Spain and Mexico (Broad-
  side Authors and Artists).
Sources. Broadside Authors and Artists, Comp. by Leaonead P. Bailey
  (Broadside Pr., 1974); New Black Voices, Ed. by Abraham Chapman
  (New Amer. Lib., 1972).

Holland, Jerome Heartwell

HOLLAND, JEROME HEARTWELL. 1916- . College President, U.S. Ambassador to Sweden, Corporation Board Member

Biographical-Personal. Born 1916. Educ.: B.A., Cornell U.; Ph.D., U. of Pa.

Career-Professional. Pres., Del. State Coll.; Pres., Hampton Inst., Va.; Ambassador to Sweden; Corp. directorships: Amer. Telephone & Telegraph, Chrysler Corp., Continental Corp., Federated Dept. Stores, Gen. Cigars, Gen. Foods, Manufacturers Hanover Trust, N.Y. Stock Exchange, Union Carbide.

WRITING: Black Opportunity (N.Y.: Weybright & Talley, 1969).

HONORS AND AWARDS: "He received many honorary degrees and numerous awards from religious, civic and fraternal organizations...elected chairman of Planned Parenthood and the World Population Council" (Black Opportunity).

SIDELIGHTS: At Cornell "was All-American football player--the famous 'Brud' Holland of the sports pages and the campus" (Black Opportunity).

Sources. Black Enterprise (Sept. 1973); Black Opportunity (Weybright & Talley, 1969); In Black and White: Afro-Americans in Print, Ed. by Mary M. Spradling (Kalamazoo Lib. System, 1971).

HORNE, FRANK S. 1899-1974. Ophthalmologist, College President, Agency Administrator

Biographical-Personal. Born 1899, in N.Y., N.Y. Educ.: City Coll. of N.Y.; Columbia U.; U. of S. Cal.; N. Ill. Coll. of Ophthalmology (grad.). Died in N.Y.C., Sept. 7, 1974.

Career-Professional. Ophthalmologist; Pres., Fort Valley State Coll., Ga.; Dir. of Negro Affairs, Nat'l. Youth Admin.; Off. of Race Relat., U.S. Housing Authority, Housing & Home Finance Agency; Dir., N.Y.C. Com. on Intergroup Relat.; N.Y.C. Housing Redevelopment Bd.

WRITINGS: Poetry ser.: Letters Found Near a Suicide (won a Crisis mag. award in 1925); Haverstraw, poetry (pub. in London, 1963). Contrib. to numerous period. & anthols.

Sources. Black World (Johnson Pub., Nov. 1974); Poetry of Black America, Ed. by Arnold Adoff (Harper & Row, 1973).

HORTON, GEORGE MOSES. 1797-c.1883. Poet
Biographical-Personal. Born 1797 in Northampton County, N.C. Slave
of William Horton. The young man had an alert mind, & was almost
entirely self-taught. Married a slave belonging to Franklin
Snipes; became father of two children. Died in Phila. c.1883.
Career-Professional. Permitted to go to Chapel Hill and hire himself
out. In 1829 a booklet, The Hope of Liberty, was published. How-
ever, Horton's hope of obtaining his freedom from the sale of this
did not materialize. He settled down at the U. of North Carolina
at Chapel Hill for the next 30 years, working as a janitor and ex-
ecuting little commissions in verse from the students (Early Negro
American Writers).
WRITINGS: The Hope of Liberty repr. in Phila., 1837, as Poems by
a Slave. At Harvard U. is a copy of Poetical Works, 1845, and at
the Athenaeum in Boston one of Naked Genius, 1865. Another edition was printed in 1854, The Poetical Works of George M. Horton,
the Colored Bard of North Carolina.
Sources. Cavalcade, Ed. by Arthur P. Davis & Saunders Redding
(Houghton Mifflin, 1971); Early Black American Poets, Ed. by William H. Robinson (Wm. C. Brown, 1969); Early Negro American Writers, Benjamin Brawley (U. of N.C. Pr., 1935); Negro Caravan, Ed.
by Sterling A. Brown & Others (Arno Pr. & N.Y. Times, 1969).

HUGHES, JAMES LANGSTON. 1902-1967. Poet,
Novelist, Short Story Writer, Biographer, Playwright, Lecturer, Editor
Biographical-Personal. Born Feb. 1, 1902, in
Joplin, Mo. Son of James Nathaniel (engi-
neer & lawyer) and Carrie Mercer [Langston]
Hughes. Educ.: Columbia U., 1921-22; Lin-
coln U., Pa. (grad.), 1929, Litt.D. (hon.),
1943. Family: Single. Died May 22, 1967.
Career-Professional. Worked as seaman on voy-
ages to Europe & Africa; Cross-country tours
reading poems, 1946-48; Poet-in-Residence,
U. of Chgo. Lab. Sch., 1949; Lyricist & radio
writer; Columnist; Chicago Defender, New York
Post; Madrid Corresp. for Baltimore Afro-
American (Spanish Civil War, 1937).
WRITINGS: Weary Blues, poems (1926); Fine Clothes to the Jew,
poems (1927); Not Without Laughter, novel (Knopf, 1930); The Negro
Mother (1931); Popo and Fifina, with Arna Bontemps, children's
story (Watts, 1932); The Dream Keeper, poetry collec. (Knopf,
1932); The Ways of White Folks, novel (Knopf, 1934); The Big Sea
(Hill & Wang, 1940) & I Wonder As I Wander (Holt, Rinehart & Winston, 1956)--both autobiog.; Shakespeare in Harlem, poems; Fields
of Wonder, poems (1947); One Way Ticket, poems (1949); Simple

Hughes, James Langston

Speaks His Mind, humor (Simon & Schuster, 1950); Montage of a
Dream Deferred, poems (1951); Laughing to Keep From Crying (Holt,
1952); The First Book of Negroes (Watts, 1952); Simple Takes a
Wife, humor (Simon & Schuster, 1953); Biography: Famous American
Negroes (Dodd, 1954; Apollo Eds., 1969); First Book of Rhythms
(Watts, 1954); First Book of Jazz (Watts, 1954); First Book of the
West Indies (Watts, 1955). Libretto of opera The Barrier (1950).
Lyricist for Just Around the Corner. Transl.: Cuba Libre, poems
by Nicolas Guillen (Ward, 1948); Gypsy Ballads, poems by Garcia
Lorca (1951). Co-ed.: Poetry of the Negro, anthol. with Arna
Bontemps (Doubleday, 1949); Book of Negro Folklore, with Arna Bon-
temps (Dodd, 1958). Famous Negro Music Makers (Dodd, 1955); The
Langston Hughes Reader (Braziller, 1958); Selected Poems (Knopf,
1959); Tambourines to Glory, play (Day, 1959); The Best of Simple
(Hill & Wang, 1961); Five Plays by Langston Hughes (Ind. U. Pr.,
1963); Simple's Uncle Sam (Hill & Wang, 1965); The Best Short Sto-
ries By Negro Writers, Ed. (Little, 1967); Black Magic: A Picto-
rial History of the Negro in American Entertainment (Prentice-
Hall, 1967); The Panther and the Lash, posthumous poems (1967).
Libretto of Troubled Island, music by William Grant Still, prod.
at N.Y.C. Center. Ed., African Treasury (Crown, 1959); First
Book of Africa (Watts, 1960). Lyricist, Elmer Rice-Kurt Weill
musical Street Scene (1946); Don't You Turn Back, Ed. by Lee B.
Hopkins (Knopf, 1969); Good Morning, Revolution: Uncollected
Writings of Social Protest, Ed. by Faith Berry (Lawrence Hill,
1973). Contrib. verse and prose to mags.
HONORS AND AWARDS: Winner, 1st prize in poetry, Opportunity mag.
(offered to Negro writers), 1925; 1st prize, Witter Bynner Undergrad. Poetry Contest, 1926; Harmon Gold Award for Lit., 1930; Gug-
genheim Fellow, 1941; $1000 grant from Nat'l. Inst. of Arts & Let-
ters, 1946; Ainsfield-Wolf Award, Best Book on Race Relat., 1954;
Spingarn Medal, NAACP, 1960.
MEMBER: Nat'l. Inst. of Arts & Letters, ASCAP; Omega Psi Phi.
SIDELIGHTS: "The most prolific and perhaps best-known of modern
Negro American writers, Langston Hughes was the only Negro poet
who lived entirely on the professional earnings of his literary
activities in a long and diverse literary career..." (Black
Voices).
     Poems were set to music. Play "Mulatto," at Vanderbilt Theater,
N.Y.C., 1935. Has lived in Mexico, Paris and Italy. Spent year
in Soviet Union, 1932-33.
Sources. Black American Literature--Poetry, Ed. by Darwin T. Turner
(Merrill, 1969); Black Drama in America, Ed. by Darwin T. Turner
(Fawcett, 1971); Black Insights, Ed. by Nick A. Ford (Ginn, 1971);
Black Poets of the United States, Jean Wagner, Transl. by Kenneth
Douglas (U. of Ill. Pr., 1973); Black Voices, Ed. by Abraham Chap-
man (New Amer. Lib., 1968); Cavalcade, Ed. by Arthur P. Davis &

Saunders Redding (Houghton Mifflin, 1971); Kaleidoscope, Ed. by
Robert Hayden (Harcourt, 1967); Poetry of the Negro, 1746-1949,
Ed. by Langston Hughes & Arna Bontemps (Doubleday, 1949); Twenti-
eth Century Authors, Ed. by Stanley J. Kunitz & Howard Haycraft
(H. W. Wilson, 1942); Who Was Who in America, Vol. IV, 1961-1968
(Marquis, 1968); Books in Print, Supplement, 1975-76 (Bowker,
1976).

HUMPHREY, MYRTLE MOSS. Medical Records Librarian, Poet
Biographical-Personal. Born in West Point, Miss. Grew up in Baton
 Rouge, La. Educ.: M.S.L.S. (Lib. Sci.), U. of S. Cal., L.A.
 Family: married; 3 children.
Career-Professional. Medical Librn., Charles R. Drew Post Grad.
 Medical Sch., L.A., Cal.
 WRITINGS: Be a Man--'Boy' and Other Poems (Capricorn House W.,
 1973); & Others.
 SIDELIGHTS: "Mrs. Humphrey has read her poetry in the public high
 schools and branch libraries, and most recently at the annual con-
 vention in San Francisco of California State Council of Black
 Nurses" (Some Ground to Fall on).
Source. Some Ground to Fall on, Vermont Square Writers Workshop,
 L.A. Public Lib., 1971.

HUNTER, KRISTIN EGGLESTON. 1931- . Novelist,
 Juvenile Writer
Biographical-Personal. Born Sept. 12, 1931, in
 Phila., Pa. D. of George L. and Mabel L.
 [Manigault] Eggleston (sch. tchrs.). Educ.:
 B.S., U. of Pa., 1951. Family: m. John I.
 Lattany; son, Andrew Lattany. Mailing ad-
 dress: P.O. Box 8371, Phila., Pa. 19101.
Career-Professional. Columnist and Feature
 writer, Pittsburgh Courier, Phila., Ed.,
 1946-52; copywriter, Lavenson Bureau of Ad-
 vertising, Phila., 1952-59; Wermen & Schoor,
 Inc., Phila., 1962-63; Inform. Officer, City
 of Phila., 1963-64; free-lance writer, 1964- .
 Lectr. creative writing, U. of Pa., 1972.
 WRITINGS: God Bless the Child, novel (Scrib-
ners, 1964); The Landlord, novel (Scribners, 1966); The Soul
Brothers and Sister Lou, novel for teenagers (Scribners, 1968);
Boss Cat, juvenile (Scribners, 1971); Guests in the Promised Land,
short stories for older children (Scribners, 1973); The Survivors
(Scribners, 1975). TV documentary, "Minority of One," CBS, 1955.
HONORS AND AWARDS: Fund for the Republic Prize, best TV docu-
mentary script, 1955; John Hay Whitney Fellow., 1959-60; Phila.
Athenaeum Literary Award, 1964; Bread Loaf Writers' Conf. Fellow,

Hurston, Zora Neale

1965. For <u>The Soul Brothers and Sister Lou</u>, 1968: Nat'l. Conf. of Christians & Jews Mass Media Award; Counc. on Interracial Books for Children Award; Lewis Carroll Shelf Award; Red Fist Award (Holland); Silver Slate-Pencil Award (Holland). Sigma Delta Chi Best Mag. Reporting of the Year Award, 1968 (for an article on unwed mothers in <u>Philadelphia Magazine</u>). For <u>Guests in the Promised Land</u>, 1973: <u>Chicago Tribune</u> Book World Award for the best bk. for older children, 1973; Christopher Award; Nomination for Nat'l. Book Award.
SIDELIGHTS: Keynote speaker, ALA, Atlantic City, N.J., 1970; Delegate, Conf. to Assess State of Black Arts and Letters, U. of Chgo., 1972 (Black Acad. of Arts and Letters, Inc.); Lectr., Post Grad. Weekend, U. of Pa., Oct. 1973; Keynote speaker, Black Hist. Week, Albany, N.Y., Feb. 1974 (Author).
Sources. Author inform.; <u>The Best Short Stories by Negro Authors</u>, Ed. by Langston Hughes (Little, Brown, 1967); <u>Black American Literature--Fiction</u>, Ed. by Darwin T. Turner (Merrill, 1969); <u>Boss Cat</u>, Kristin Hunter (Scribners, 1971); <u>Contemporary Authors</u>, Vols. 13-14, Ed. by James M. Ethridge & Barbara Kopala (Gale Res., 1965).

HURSTON, ZORA NEALE. 1903-1960. Novelist, Folklorist
Biographical-Personal. Born 1903 in Eatonville, Fla. D. of John (minister) and Lucy Ann [Potts] Hurston. <u>Educ.</u>: High sch., Morgan Coll., grad. 1921; Howard U., 1921-24; B.A., Barnard Coll., 1928; Litt.D. (hon.), Morgan Coll., 1939. Died Jan. 28, 1960.
Career-Professional. Res. (with Dr. Franz Boas) and writing on folklore, Columbia U. (Private grant from Mrs. R. Osgood Mason & Fellow, Rosenwald Found.), 1928-32; Haiti & Brit. W. Indies (Guggenheim Fellow), 1936-38; Script writer, Paramount Pictures; Head, Drama Dept., N.C. Coll. for Negroes (Durham).
WRITINGS: <u>Jonah's Gourd Vine</u> (1934); <u>Mules and Men</u> (1935); <u>Their Eyes Were Watching God</u>, also pub. in Eng. & Italy (Lippincott, 1937); <u>Tell My Horse</u>, pub. London, 1939, as <u>Voodoo Gods</u> (1938); <u>Moses, Man of the Mountain</u> (1939, Chatham repr. of 1939 ed., 1975); <u>Dust Tracks on a Road</u>, autobiog. (Lippencott, 1942); <u>The Voice of the Land</u> (1945); & <u>Seraph On the Suwanee</u> (Scribners, 1948). Compiled <u>Collection of Bahamian Folk Songs</u>, with composer William Grant Still. Contrib. short stories & articles to <u>American Mercury</u>, <u>Saturday Evening Post</u>, <u>Opportunity</u>, <u>Story</u>, <u>New Negro</u>, <u>New Republic</u>, & <u>Negro Digest</u>.
HONORS AND AWARDS: Received $1000 Anisfield Award for <u>Dust Tracks on a Road</u>, 1943; Howard U. Alumni Award, Distinguished post-grad work in Lit., 1943.

MEMBER: Amer. Folklore Soc.; Amer. Anthropology Soc.; Amer. Ethnology Soc.;
SIDELIGHTS: Miss Hurston has been placed "in the front rank, not
only of Negro writers, but all American writers" (Black Joy).
She "became the first black writer since Charles Chesnutt to con-
centrate on the literary and cultural importance of folk material"
(Black American Literature--Fiction). "During the Renaissance...
she...joined such writers as Langston Hughes and Wallace Thurman
on the editorial staff of the avant-garde magazine Fire" (Cavalcade).
Sources. American Negro Short Stories, Ed. by John H. Clarke (Hill &
Wang, 1960); Black American Literature--Fiction, Ed. by Darwin T.
Turner (Merrill, 1969); Black Joy, Ed. by Jay David (Cowles,
1971); Cavalcade, Ed. by Arthur P. Davis and Saunders Redding
(Houghton Mifflin, 1971); Who Was Who in America, Vol. III,
1951-60 (Marquis, 1960).

Ida B. Wells Barnett. See Wells, (Barnett), Ida B.

Imamu Etheridge Knight Soa. See Knight, Etheridge.

JACKMON, MARVIN [Nazzam Al Fitnah]. Playwright, Poet
Career-Professional. San Francisco playwright and poet. His plays
have been performed in the San Francisco Bay Area and Southern
California. One of the founders of Black Arts West.
WRITINGS: Plays: Come Next Summer; Flowers for the Trashman.
His plays, poems, and essays have appeared in Black Dialogue,
Journal of Black Poetry and Soulbook. Contrib. Ed. to Journal of
Black Poetry.
Source. Black Fire, Ed. by LeRoi Jones & Larry Neal (Morrow, 1968).

JACKSON, CLYDE OWEN. 1928- . Author, Com-
poser
Biographical-Personal. Born April 7, 1928, in
Galveston, Tex. Son of Earl and Sarah
[Chatman] Jackson. Educ.: Central High
Sch., Galveston, 1945; B.S., Tuskegee Inst.,
1949; Music Educ., Texas S. U., 1960, M. Mu-
sic Educ., 1964. Family: Single. Mailing
address: 10863 Fairland Dr., Houston, Tex.
77051.
Career-Professional. Ed., Informer Group of
Newspapers, Tex., 1969-72; Gen. News Ed. &
Inform. Officer, Tex. S.U., 1968-71; Music
Dept., Tex. S.U. (Organizer, conductor, Men's
Glee Club); U.S. Army, Infantry.
WRITINGS: The Songs of Our Years, Afro-Amer.

Jackson, George

folk music (Exposition Pr., 1968). <u>Before the Darkness Covers Us</u>, essays, speeches, Ed. (Exposition Pr., 1969). In progress: <u>The Case for Music Literacy</u>; <u>Here, In This Quiet House</u>, autobiog.
HONORS AND AWARDS: Nat'l. Newspaper Pub. Assn. Merit Award for study on sch. desegregation, 1955; Nat'l. Counc. of Negro Women (Houston Chap.) Award for community serv., 1974; U.S. Army Commendation Award for news writing, 1954.
SIDELIGHTS: "Commenting on 'The Songs of Our Years,' internationally acclaimed composer William Grant Still called the book, 'thoughtful and carefully researched.' Popular folk singer, Leon Bibb, declared '...historians and collectors of Negro music will welcome this book...' and <u>Freedomways</u> magazine (Spring, 1969) declared: 'The Songs of Our Years'...is a useful companion to music history texts in the schools which may have omitted so much of the contributions of Black Americans'" (Program notes).
 Jackson holds lectures and workshops on Negro spirituals (Author).
Sources. Author inform. and brochure.

JACKSON, GEORGE. 1941-1971. Writer, Revolutionary
Biographical-Personal. Born Sept. 23, 1941, in Chgo., Ill. <u>Educ.</u>: Self-educated. Died Aug. 21, 1971.
Career-Professional. "Arrested at the age of eighteen for allegedly taking part in the robbery of a gas station netting $70, George Jackson was sentenced to one year to life in prison. At the time of his death he had served eleven years behind prison walls, seven of those years in solitary confinement. Long before the world had heard of him, George Jackson had already become a legendary figure inside the California prison system. When <u>Soledad Brother</u>...was published, he was hailed at home and abroad." (Pub. brochure)
WRITINGS: <u>Soledad Brother: The Prison letters of George Jackson</u> (Coward McCann, Bantam, 1970); <u>Blood in my Eye</u> (Random House, Bantam, 1972).
SIDELIGHTS: <u>Soledad Brother</u> is "The most important single book from a black since <u>The Autobiography of Malcolm X</u>" (Julius Lester, <u>New York Times Book Review</u>); <u>New York Times</u> described <u>Blood in my Eye</u>, as '...the last will and testament of George Jackson...'"
<u>Library Journal</u> described it as "a powerful and disturbing manifesto...both simplistic and complex...." <u>The Louisville Times</u> viewed <u>Blood in my Eye</u> as "an important and significant contribution" (Pub. information).
Sources. Pub. inform.; <u>Soledad Brother</u>, George Jackson (Bantam, 1970).

JACKSON, JESSE. 1908- . Juvenile Author
Biographical-Personal. Born Jan. 1, 1908, in
Columbus, Ohio. Son of Jesse (trucker) and
Mable [Rogers] Jackson. Educ.: Ohio State
U., 1927-29; Breadloaf Writers Conf., Bread-
loaf, Vt. Family: m. Ann Newman (social
worker), Sept. 19, 1938; d. Judith Ann.
Mailing address: Agent, Anita Diamant,
Writers' Workshop, Inc., 51 E. 42nd St.,
N.Y., N.Y. 10017.
Career-Professional. Sewer inspector; Laborer;
Postal worker; Journalist; Ed. Dept., Nat'l.
Bur. of Econ. Res.
WRITINGS: Juvenile: Call Me Charley (Harper
& Row, 1945); Anchor Man (Harper & Row, 1947);
Room for Randy (Friendship Pr., 1957); Charley
Starts from Scratch (Harper & Row, 1957); Tessie (Harper & Row,
1968); The Sickest Don't Always Die the Quickest (Doubleday, 1970);
I Sing Because I'm Happy, biography of Mahalia Jackson (Rutledge
Bks., 1970); Tessie Keeps Her Cool (Harper & Row, 1970); The
Fourteenth Cadillac (Doubleday, 1972); Black in America: A Fight
for Freedom, with Elaine Landau (Julian Messner, 1973); Make a
Joyful Noise to the Lord: The Life of Mahalia Jackson (Dell,
Women of America Ser., 1974). Contrib. articles & reviews to
Crisis & other periods.
SIDELIGHTS: "As a boy, Jackson lived much the same as his hero,
Charles Moss in Call Me Charley, and Charley Starts from Scratch.
While in college, he ran on the track team, entered the Olympic
trials, and learned to box. He spent the summers 'jerking sodas
in Atlantic City, boxing in a carnival, working for passage on a
Great Lakes' steamer, and hitchhiking—all of which made these
times memorable to me.' Call Me Charley was written with the hope
that it would be 'a small tribute to the good people who somehow
or other succeed in making bad things better'" (Something About
the Author).
Sources. Something About the Author, Ed. by Anne Commire (Gale Res.,
1973); Books in Print, Supplement, 1975-76 (Bowker, 1976).

JACKSON, JOSEPH H. President, National Baptist Convention, U.S.A.,
Inc.
Biographical-Personal. Born in Rudyard, Miss. Educ.: B.A., Jackson
Coll, Miss.; B.D., Rochester Divinity Sch.; M.A., Creighton U.,
Omaha, Neb.; Post grad. work at Nebraska U.; Pa. U.; U. of Chgo.
(Hon. D.D.); Jackson Coll., Coll. of Monrovia, Liberia; Central
State Coll., Wilberforce, Ohio; Bishop Coll., Dallas, Tex.
Family: m. Maude T. Alexander; d. Kenny [Jackson] Williams.
Mailing address: 4937 S. Kimbark Ave., Chgo., Ill.

Jackson, Mae

Career-Professional. Pastor, Rural District
Churches, Miss.; Bethel Bap. Church, Omaha,
Neb.; Monumental Bap. Church, Phila., Pa.;
Secy., Foreign Mission Bd., Nat'l. Bap. Con-
vention, U.S.A., Inc.; Pastor, Olivet Bap.
Church, Chgo. & Pres., Nat'l. Bap. Conven-
tion, Inc., since 1953.
WRITINGS: Stars in the Night (1950); The
Eternal Flame (1956); Many But One: The Ecu-
menic of Charity (1964).
HONORS AND AWARDS: Created Royal Knight of
the Republic of Liberia; Has taped messages
for The Voice of America; Preached in Russia;
Wrote campaign literature for John F. Ken-
nedy; Attended the 1962 Vatican Council in
Rome.
MEMBER: Amer. Philosophical Soc.; NAACP; Executive Comm., Bap.
World Alliance; Central Com., World Counc. of Churches; 32nd
degree Mason.
SIDELIGHTS: He has visited Asia, Africa, Europe & the Middle
West.
"Dr. Joseph H. Jackson has been the leader of some 5 million
U.S. Negro Baptists since 1953, the year he was elected to presi-
dency of the National Baptist Convention, U.S.A., Inc. Dr. Jackson has steered the organization into new spheres of influence,
notably into a more activist role in the civil rights struggle.
One of the most ambitious ventures initiated under Dr. Jackson
has been the Liberian land investment program whereby Baptists
hope to develop extensive farms on some 100,000 acres of Liberian
land, and thus raise additional funds to help sponsor their missionary labors in Africa. The convention has also purchased 400
acres in Fayette County, Tenn., and owns a Nashville publishing
house with sales of close to one million dollars annually" (Negro
Almanac).
Sources. Negro Almanac, Comp. by Harry A. Ploski & Ernest Kaiser
(Bellwether, 1971); Negro Handbook, Comp. by Eds. of Ebony (Johnson Pub., 1966).

JACKSON, MAE. 1946- . Teacher, Poet.
Biographical-Personal. Born Jan. 3, 1946, in
Earl, Ark. D. of Melissia Jackson. Educ.:
New Sch. of Soc. Res. (Human Relat.). Family:
Single; d. Nseri Ayoka Cruse. Mailing ad-
dress: 165 Clinton Ave., Apt. 2G, Brooklyn,
N.Y. 11205.
Career-Professional. Tchr., Creative writing,
Brooklyn. Active with SNCC & The H. Rap
Brown Anti-Dope Movement.

Jeffers, Lance

WRITINGS: Can I Poet With You, poetry (1969). Anthol.: Black out Loud (1970); Night Comes Softly (1970); Black Spirits (1972) & Poetry of Black America (1973). Period.: Negro Digest/Black World; Journal of Black Poetry; Black Creation & Essence.
HONORS AND AWARDS: Conrad Kent Rivers Third Memorial Award for Can I Poet With You.
Sources. Author inform.; Poetry of Black America, Ed. by Arnold Adoff (Harper & Row, 1973).

JAMES, CHARLES LYMAN. 1934- . Editor, Teacher

Biographical-Personal. Born April 12, 1934, in Poughkeepsie, N.Y. Son of Stanley and E. Romaine James. Educ.: B.S., State U. Coll., New Paltz, N.Y.; M.S., State U. of N.Y., Albany; Yale U. (1-yr. fellow.). Family: m. Jane Fisher; d. Sheila Ellen, d. Terri Lynn. Mailing address: 402 Laurel Lane, Wallingford, Pa. 19086.

Career-Professional. Assoc. Prof., Eng., Swarthmore Coll., Swarthmore, Pa.
WRITINGS: The Black Writer in America, Ed. (Albany, SUNY, 1969); From the Roots: Short Stories by Black Americans, Ed. (Dodd, Mead, 1970). Anthol.: Contemporary Poets (London: St. James Pr., 1974). Jls.: "Bigger Thomas in the Seventies: A Twentieth-Century Search for Significance," The English Record, Vol. XXII, no. 1 (Fall, 1971); "Batouala: Rene Maran and the Art of Objectivity," Studies in Black Literature, vol. 4, no. 3 (Autumn, 1973).
HONORS AND AWARDS: Danforth Found. Fellow., Yale U., 1972.
Source. Author inform.

JEFFERS, LANCE. 1919- . Poet, Fiction Writer, Teacher
Biographical-Personal. Born Nov. 28, 1919, in Fremont, Neb. Educ.: B.A. (cum laude), 1951, M.A., Columbia U.; U. of Toronto, Can. Family: m. Trellie Lee James (tchr.); son, Lance, d. Valjeanne, d. Sidonie Colette, d. Honoree. Mailing address: Dept. of Eng., Bowie State Coll., Bowie, Md.
Career-Professional. Prof. Eng., Fla. A&M, 1964-65; Tchg. Fellow, Eng., U. of Toronto, 1965-66; Lectr. Eng., Ind. U., 1966-68; Prof., Creative Writing & Black Lit., Cal. State Coll., Long Beach, 1968-71; Chmn., Dept. of Eng., Bowie State Coll., Bowie, Md.
WRITINGS: Poetry: My Blackness is the Beauty of This Land (Broadside Pr., 1970); Witherspoon; When I Know the Power of My Black Hand (Broadside Pr., 1975). Short stories in: The Best American Short Stories--1948; Quarto; A Galaxy of Black Writing.

137

Joans, Ted

Poetry pub. in: <u>Tamarack Review</u>, <u>Phylon</u>, <u>Burning Spear</u>, <u>Freedom-ways</u>, <u>Black Fire</u>, <u>Nine Black Poets</u>, <u>Beyond the Blues</u>, <u>Survive</u>, <u>Afroamerican Literature</u>, <u>Anthology of Negro American Literature</u>.
HONORS AND AWARDS: Franklin T. Baker Citation, Tchrs. Coll., Columbia U.
SIDELIGHTS: Jeffers has taught the writing of poetry and the novel at Cal. State Coll., Long Beach (<u>Poetry of Black America</u>).
Sources. <u>Black Voices</u>, Ed. by Abraham Chapman (New Amer. Lib., 1968); <u>Cavalcade</u>, Ed. by Arthur P. Davis & Saunders Redding (Houghton Mifflin, 1971); <u>New Black Poetry</u>, Ed. by Clarence Major (Internat. Pub., 1969); <u>New Black Voices</u>, Ed. by Abraham Chapman (New Amer. Lib., 1972); <u>Nine Black Poets</u>, Ed. by Baird, Shuman (Moore, 1968); <u>Poetry of Black America</u>, Ed. by Arnold Adoff (Harper & Row, 1973).

JOANS, TED. 1928- . Poet, Jazz Musician, Surrealist Painter
Biographical-Personal. Born July 4, 1928, in Cairo, Ill. Son of a riverboat entertainer. <u>Educ.</u>: B.A. (Fine Arts-Painting), Ind. U., 1950. <u>Family</u>: m. a Norwegian; son, Patrice Lumumba.
Career-Professional. Trumpeter; Jazz Poet; Surrealistic Painter.
WRITINGS: Poetry: <u>Beat</u>; <u>All of Ted Joans</u>; <u>Black Pow-Wow</u> (Hill & Wang, 1969); <u>Afrodisia</u> (Hill & Wang, 1970). <u>The Hipsters</u>, humorous pictorial. Pub. in: <u>Presence Africaine Nouvelle Somme de Poesie du Monde Noir</u> (1966); <u>La Poesie Negro Americaine</u> (Ed. Seghers 66); <u>Ik Bende Nieuwe Neger</u> (Holland, 1965); <u>Poetry Is for People</u> (Boston, 1965); <u>Black Poets, USA</u> (N.Y.C., 1964); <u>New Negro Poets</u> (Indiana, 1964); <u>City Lights Journal</u> (San Francisco, 1963); <u>Negro Verse</u> (London, 1963); & <u>Beyond the Blues</u> (England, 1962).
SIDELIGHTS: Was for a while one of the "Beats" of Greenwich Village. In an autobiographical note for <u>Beyond the Blues</u> he wrote: "Jazz is my religion...I have traveled to twenty-eight countries and dug the foreign scene and that's for me...I want to be free now...Free as the white American that is involved in the arts..." Joans lives in Morocco where he writes and paints (<u>Kaleidoscope</u>).
Sources. <u>For Malcolm</u>, Ed. by Dudley Randall & Margaret G. Burroughs (Broadside Pr., 1969); <u>Kaleidoscope</u>, Ed. by Robert Hayden (Harcourt, 1967); <u>New Negro Poets, USA</u>, Ed. by Langston Hughes (Ind. U. Pr., 1964).

JOHNSON, CHARLES RICHARD. 1948- . Editorial
Cartoonist, Teacher
Biographical-Personal. Born April 23, 1948, in
Evanston, Ill. Son of Benjamin Lee and Ruby
Elizabeth Johnson. Educ.: B.S. (Journal-
ism), M.A. (Philosophy), S. Ill. U., 1973;
Candidate for Ph.D. (Philosophy), SUNY, Stony
Brook. Family: m. Joan New. Mailing ad-
dress: Gen. Delivery, Port Jefferson, N.Y.
11777.
Career-Professional. Creator, Host & Co-prod.,
educ. TV ser., "Charlie's Pad," distributed
nationally, prod. by WSIU TV; S. Ill. U.,
1969, Tchg. Asst., Dept. of Black Amer.
Stud., 1969-70; Tutor, Marxist & Oriental
Philosophy, SUNY, Stony Brook, 1973-74,
Instr., Philosophy, 1974-75; Ed. & comic strip artist, Daily
Egyptian, So. Ill. U., 1966-71, Ed. cartoonist, Southern Illinois-
an, 1969-73; Cartoonist reporter, Chicago Tribune, 1969-70; Art
staff, St. Louis Proud mag., 1971-72.
WRITINGS: Black Humor, drawings (Johnson Pub., 1970); Faith and
the Good Thing, novel (Viking, 1974). Contrib., freelance car-
toons: Ebony, Jet, Black World, Players International, etc.
Anthol.: (drawings) Illus. Anatomy of Campus Humor (U. of Minn.
Pr., 1971); Making of a Journalist (U. of Minn. Pr., 1973).
Source. Author inform.; Pub. inform.

JOHNSON, CHARLES SPURGEON. 1893-1956. Sociolo-
gist, Race Relations Researcher, College Presi-
dent
Biographical-Personal. Born 1893 in Bristol,
Va. Educ.: B.A. (hon.) Va. Union U., Rich-
mond; Ph.D., U. of Chgo.; (Hon. doctorate)
Howard U., Columbia U., Harvard U., U. of
Glasgow, Scotland; Va. Union U. Died Oct.
1956.
Career-Professional. Assoc. Executive Secy.,
Chgo. Race Relat. Com.; Dir., Res. & Public.,
Nat'l. Urban League; Ed., Opportunity mag.;
Head, Dept. of Soc. Sci., Fisk U., 1928-46;
Pres., Fisk U., Nashville, 1946- .
WRITINGS: The Negro in American Civilization
(Holt, 1930); The Economic Status of the Ne-
gro (1933); The Shadow of the Plantation (1934); Race Relations,
with W. D. Weatherford (1934); The Collapse of Cotton Tenancy,
with Edwin R. Embree & W. W. Alexander (1935); A Preface to Racial
Understanding (1936); The Negro College Graduate (1938); Growing

Johnson, E. Richard

>Up in the Black Belt (1940). Contrib. to Survey, Modern Quarter-
>ly, World Tomorrow, Journal of Negro Education, Journal of Negro
>History.
>HONORS AND AWARDS: On President's commissions under: Hoover,
>Roosevelt, Truman and Eisenhower. Second Distinguished American
>named to Ebony Hall of Fame. The Negro College Graduate won Anis-
>field Award.
>MEMBER: Dir., Julius Rosenwald Fund; Pres., S. Sociol. Soc.;
>Executive Com., Amer. Sociol. Soc.
>SIDELIGHTS: While Associate Secretary of Chicago Race Relations
>Com., contrib. to their report The Negro in Chicago. "The obser-
>vations he made about mankind and its institutions and problems
>now fill 18 books. One of them, The Negro in Chicago, is consid-
>ered to be a 'landmark' in social research."
>   In 1923, while serving as director of research and investigation
>for the Chicago and National Urban Leagues, Dr. Johnson founded
>the magazine Opportunity: Journal of Negro Life, a League publi-
>cation which provided an avenue of expression for Negroes in lit-
>erature, art and music" (Ebony).

Sources. Anthology of American Negro Literature, Ed. by V. F. Cal-
verton (Mod. Lib., 1929); Current Biography, 1946, Ed. by Anna
Rothe (H. W. Wilson, 1947); Ebony (Johnson Pub., Feb. 1957);
Great Negroes Past and Present, Russell Adams, 3rd ed. (Afro-Amer.
Pub. Co., 1969); Historical Negro Biographies, Wilhelmena S. Rob-
inson (ASNLH, 1967); Negro Caravan, Ed. by Sterling A. Brown &
Others (Arno Pr. & N.Y. Times, 1969); 100 Years of Negro Freedom,
Arna Bontemps (Dodd, Mead, 1961); 13 Against the Odds, Edwin
Embree (Viking, 1944).

JOHNSON, E. RICHARD. Novelist
Career-Professional.
   WRITINGS: Novels: The Inside Man (1969); Mong's Back in Town
   (1969); Cage Five Is Going to Break (1970); Case Load–Maximum
   (1971); Cardinalli Contract (Pyramid, 1975).
Sources. L.A. Pub. Lib.; Cardinalli Contract, E. Richard Johnson
   (Pyramid, 1975).

JOHNSON, FENTON. 1888–1958. Poet
Biographical-Personal. Born 1888 in Chgo., Ill. Educ.: Chgo. pub-
   lic schs.; U. of Chgo. Died 1958.
Career-Professional. Magazine ed.; Writer.
   WRITINGS: Poetry: A Little Dreaming (1914); Visions of the Dusk
   (1915); Songs of the Soil (1916; AMS repr. 1975). Tales of Dark-
   est Africa, short stories (1920). For the Highest Good, essays.
   WPA Poems, posthumous. Contrib. to: New Poetry, Victory, Chicago
   Anthology, Anthology of Magazine Verse, Poetry of American Negroes,
   Negro Poets and Their Poems, Book of American Negro Poetry, To-
   day's Poetry & others.

Johnson, Georgia Douglas

SIDELIGHTS: Johnson "was one of the first black revolutionary poets" (Book of American Negro Poetry). He had some plays produced on the stage of the Old Pekin Theatre in Chicago when he was 19 years old.

"In 1918 and 1919 he published poems in Poetry magazine and Alfred Kreymborg's Others, where he appeared along with William Carlos Williams, Wallace Stevens, and Marianne Moore. He never became a major figure, but he cultivated his own distinctive voice and a fatalistic, nihilistic vision of life which was very rare in Negro American Literature" (Black Voices).

Sources. Black Voices, Ed. by Abraham Chapman (New Amer. Lib., 1968); Book of American Negro Poetry, Ed. by James W. Johnson (Harcourt, 1959); Caroling Dusk, Ed. by Countee Cullen (Harper & Row, 1927); Kaleidoscope, Ed. by Robert Hayden (Harcourt, 1967); Negro Almanac, Comp. by Harry A. Ploski & Ernest Kaiser (Bellwether, 1971); Negro Caravan, Ed. by Sterling A. Brown, & others (Arno Pr. & N.Y. Times, 1969); Negro Poets and Their Poems, Robert T. Kerlin, 3rd ed. rev. (Assoc. Pub., 1935); Negro Voices in American Fiction, Hugh Gloster (Russell, 1965).

JOHNSON, GEORGIA DOUGLAS. 1886-1966. Poet

Biographical-Personal. Born 1886 in Atlanta, Ga. Educ.: Atlanta U.; Oberlin Coll., Conservatory of Music. Family: m. Henry L. Johnson (Recorder of Deeds under William Howard Taft). Died 1966.

Career-Professional. Commissioner of Conciliation, Dept. of Labor; with other govt. agencies; writer.

WRITINGS: Poetry: The Heart of a Woman (1918, AMS Pr. repr., 1975); Bronze (1922, AMS Pr. repr., 1975); An Autumn Love Cycle (1928); and Share My World (1952).

SIDELIGHTS: Had two poems published in Crisis by W. E. B. DuBois. "She has helped to gather material for Heart of a Woman by Jessie Fauset. W. S. Braithwaite, a person she had admired since a little girl, wrote the introduction. Bronze had an introduction by DuBois, An Autumn Love Cycle had an introduction by Alain Locke" (Caroling Dusk).

"...First Negro woman after Frances Harper to gain recognition as a poet. Mrs. Johnson was purely a lyrist; she sang the emotions. Her song was not novel, nor did it display a wide range; it was based on age-old themes, and the treatment was conventional. It is not difficult to find in her work an obviousness in technique and a triteness of philosophy, but it also contains the sincere simplicity that carries conviction" (Book of American Negro Poetry).

Johnson, James Weldon

Sources. American Negro Poetry, Ed. by Arna Bontemps (Hill & Wang, 1963); Book of American Negro Poetry, Ed. by James W. Johnson (Harcourt, 1959); Caroling Dusk, Ed. by Countee Cullen (Harper & Row, 1927); Kaleidoscope, Ed. by Robert Hayden (Harcourt, 1967); Negro Caravan, Ed. by Sterling A. Brown & Others (Arno Pr. & N.Y. Times, 1969); Negro Genius, Benjamin Brawley (Dodd, Mead, 1937); Negro Poets and Their Poems, Ed. by Robert T. Kerlin, 3rd ed., rev. (Assoc. Pub., 1935).

JOHNSON, JAMES WELDON. 1871-1938. Poet, Essayist, Critic, Civil Rights Executive, Teacher

Biographical-Personal. Born June 17, 1871, in Jacksonville, Fla. Son of James (born free) and Helen Louise [Dillette] Johnson (from Nassau, Bahamas). Educ.: B.A., 1894, M.A. 1904, Atlanta U.; Columbia U. (Post grad. 3 yrs.); (Hon.) Litt D., Talledega Coll., Ala., 1917; Litt. D., Howard U., 1923. Family: m. Grace Nail, Feb. 3, 1910. Killed in automobile accident, June 26, 1938.

Career-Professional. Prin., high sch., Jacksonville (several yrs.); Admitted to Fla. bar, 1897, practiced law, Jacksonville; Moved to N.Y.C., 1901, to collaborate with brother, J. Rosamond Johnson (musician), in writing for light opera stage; Apptd. U.S. Consul to Puerto Cabello, Venezuela, 1906; Consul at Corinto, Nicaragua, 1909-12 (served during revolution which overthrew Zelaya, & through abortive revolution against Diaz); Secy., NAACP, 1916-30; Prof., Creative Lit., Fisk U., 1930-38; Vis. Prof., Creative Lit., N.Y.U., 1934-38; Dir., Amer. Fund for Public Serv. WRITINGS: The Autobiography of an Ex-Coloured Man, novel (Hill & Wang, 1912, 1927); Fifty Years and Other Poems (1917; AMS Pr. repr., 1975); Self Determining Haiti (1920); The Book of American Negro Poetry (Harcourt, 1921); The Book of American Negro Spirituals (Viking, 1925); and Second Book of American Negro Spirituals (1926) both with brother J. R. Johnson; God's Trombones: Seven Negro Sermons in Verse (Viking, 1927); Black Manhattan (1930; Arno Pr., 1968); St. Peter Relates   Incident of the Resurrection Day, satirical narrative poem (1930); Along This Way, autobiog. (Viking, 1933; 1968); Negro Americans, What Now? (1934); Utopian Literature: A Selection (Random House, 1968). Also wrote a number of songs. Made several transl. from the French. Contrib. ed., New York Age. Included in: Century, Independent, Crisis, and others. Wrote Eng. version of libretto of grand opera, Granados's "Goyescas," prod. Metropolitan Opera House, N.Y., 1915.

Johnson, John Harold

HONORS AND AWARDS: Trus., Atlanta U.; Spingarn Medal, NAACP, 1925; God's Trombones won Harmon Gold Award for Lit.; Rosenwald grant, 1929.
SIDELIGHTS: "A major figure in the creation and development of Negro American Literature and culture. He contributed in many ways: as a poet and songwriter, novelist, essayist and critic, collector of spirituals, pioneer anthologist and interpreter of black poetry, pioneer student of the history of the Negro in the drama, educator, and active participant in the early development of the civil rights movement" (Black Voices).
Sources. An Anthology of Verse by American Negroes, Ed. by Newman I. White & Walter C. Jackson (Moore, 1924); Black American Literature--Poetry, Ed. by Darwin T. Turner (Merrill, 1969); Black Insights, Ed. by Nick A. Ford (Ginn, 1971); Black Voices, Ed. by Abraham Chapman (New Amer. Lib., 1968); Book of American Negro Poetry, rev. ed., Ed. by James W. Johnson (Harcourt, 1959); Cavalcade, Ed. by Arthur P. Davis & Saunders Redding (Houghton Mifflin, 1971); Who Was Who in America, Vol. 1, 1897-1942 (Marquis, 1942); Books in Print, Supplement, 1975-76 (Bowker, 1976).

JOHNSON, JOHN HAROLD. 1918- . Editor, Publisher
Biographical-Personal. Born Jan. 19, 1918 in Ark. City, Ark. Son of Leroy (sawmill worker) and Gertrude [Jenkins] Johnson. Educ.: DuSable High Sch., Chgo.; U. of Chgo. (2 yrs.); Northwestern U., Sch. of Commerce; (Hon. LL.D.) Central State Coll., Shaw U.
Family: m. Eunice Walker, 1941; son, John, Jr., d. Linda. Mailing address: Johnson Pub. Co., 820 S. Mich. Ave., Chgo., Ill. 60605.
Career-Professional. Asst. to Ed., Supreme Life Insurance Co., house organ, 1936, later managing ed.; Pub., 1st issue: Negro Digest/ Black World, 1942; Ebony, 1945, Tan, 1950 (monthlies); Jet, 1951 (news weekly) all dealing with Black topics and aimed at the Black market.
HONORS AND AWARDS: Selected 1 of 10 outstanding men of the year by U.S. Jr. Chamber of Commerce, 1951; Accompanied V. Pres. Richard Nixon on goodwill trips to 9 African countries, 1957; to Russia and Poland, 1959; Spec. Ambassador, rep. U.S. at Independence Ceremonies, Ivory Coast, 1961 and Kenya, 1963; NAACP 1958 Freedom Fund Award (shared with Rudolph Bing); 1966 Horatio Alger Award; 1966 Lincoln Acad. of Ill. Order of Lincoln Award; Russwurm Award.
MEMBER: Chmn., Executive Com., & Chmn., Bd., Supreme Life Insurance Co.; Dir., Marina City Bank, Chgo; Serv. Fed. Savings & Loan Assn.; Mag. Pub. Assn.; Chgo. Assn. of Commerce & Industry; Nat'l. Advis. Counc., President's Com. on Econ. Opportunity; Trus.: Howard U., Tuskegee Inst., & Fisk U.; V. Pres., Nat'l. Urban League.
SIDELIGHTS: The most prosperous and influential publisher in American Negro history. Publishes four magazines in addition to

143

Jones, Aurilda Jackson

books, most popular is Ebony, founded in 1945, which passed
1,000,000 mark in circulation in 1967.

"In civil rights [Ebony] has geared its pace to that of the Negro community as a whole, so that it has now reached a point of
restrained militancy, particularly in its editorials.

Dr. Kenneth B. Clark, the noted Negro psychologist, has said of
Ebony: 'It is almost impossible to measure the morale-lifting
value of such a magazine. The mere fact of its existence and success has been an inspiration to the Negro masses'" (Current Biography).
Sources. Current Biography, 1968, Ed. by Charles Moritz (H. W. Wilson, 1968); Historical Negro Biographies, Wilhelmena S. Robinson
(ASNLH, 1967); Negro Handbook, Comp. by Eds. of Ebony (Johnson
Pub., 1966).

Marguerite Johnson. See Angelou, Maya.

JONES, AURILDA JACKSON. Poet, Librarian
Biographical-Personal. Born in Geneva, N.Y.
    Educ.: B.A. (Educ.) Wayne State U.; M.A.
    (Lib. Sci.) Syracuse U. Family: m. Al Jones
    (writer). Lives in L.A., Cal.
Career-Professional. Cataloger; Hospital
    Librn. (L.A. County Lib.). Children's
    Librn.; Senior Young Adult Spec.; Branch
    Librn. (L.A. City Lib.). Columnist, L.A.
    County Employees' mag.
    WRITINGS: Poetry: Untangled (1956); Earthly
    Poems; Love Touches the Earth.
Source. "Second Annual Authors Autograph Par-
    ty" (brochure), Cal. Librns. Black Caucus,
    July 1975.

JONES, CLARENCE B. 1931- . Publisher, Editor
Biographical-Personal. Born Jan. 8, 1931, in Phila., Pa. Educ.:
    Columbia U.; Boston U. Law Sch. Family: m. Charlotte; d. Chris-
    tine, son, Clarence, Jr., son, Dana, d. Alexia. Mailing address:
    2340 Eighth Ave., N.Y., N.Y. 10027.
Career-Professional. Attorney, entertainment & copyright law, cor-
    porate finance & org., state & fed. civil rights litigation.
    Firm: Lubell, Lubell & Jones. Spec. counsel to Dr. Martin L.
    King, Jr. & S. Christian Leadership Conf. Ed. & pub., Amsterdam
    News, N.Y.
    MEMBER: Bd. Chmn.: AmNews Corp.; Inner City Broadcasting Corp.
    (radio station WLIB); N.Y. Stock Exchange; Dir. & V. Pres., Hay-
    den, Stone, Inc.; N.Y. Delegate, 1968 Democratic Nat'l. Conven-
    tion; Delegate-at-Large 1972 Convention; Observer's Com., Attica
    prison massacre, 1971.
Source. 1000 Successful Blacks, Eds. of Ebony (Johnson Pub., 1973).

JONES, GAYL AMANDA. 1949- . Novelist, Poet,
Playwright
Biographical-Personal. Born Nov. 23, 1949, in
Lexington, Ky. D. of Franklin and Lucille
Jones. Educ.: B.A. (Eng.), Connecticut
Coll., New London, Conn., 1971; M.A. (crea-
tive writing), 1973, Candidate, Dr. of Arts
in Creative Writing, Brown U., June 1975.
Family: Single. Mailing address: Box 7126
Grad. Center, Brown U., Providence, R.I.
02912.
Career-Professional.
WRITINGS: Corregidora, novel (Random House,
Jan. 1975). Chile Woman, play (Hellcoal Pr.,
Brown U., 1974); Eva's Man (Random House,
1976). Anthol.: Soulscript, Ed. by June
Jordan; Amistad 2, Ed. by John A. Williams and Charles F. Harris;
Panache, Ed. by R. B. Frank; Keeping the Faith, Ed. by Pat Exum.
Period.: Silo 16 (Winter); Laureate (Amer. Coll. Poetry); Essence
(Sept. 1970, Oct. 1970, Aug. 1973, Nov. 1973, May 1974); "The
Ancestor: A Street Play," Greenfield Review; Oyez (Oct. 1974).
In progress: Heartblow: Black Veils, Ed. by Michael Harper;
Third World Voices, Ed. by Quincy Troupe; Panache (Poetry ed.),
Ed. by David Lenson; Period.: American Poetry Review, Ed. by
Leonard Adame.
HONORS AND AWARDS: One of 4 undergrad. poets to tour Conn. Poetry
Circuit, 1970; Conn. Coll. Award, best original poem, 1969, 1970;
Frances Steloff Award for Fict., 1970, for "The Roundhouse,"
Scholarship to Breadloaf Writer's Conf.; Acad. of Amer. Poets
Charles & Fanny Fay Wood Poetry Prize (Brown U.), 1973; Shubert
Found. Grant for Playwriting, 1973-74; Grant in Writing, R.I.
Counc. on the Arts, 1974-75; Fellow, Yaddo Artist's Colony, Sum-
mer 1974.
Source. Author Inform.; Books in Print, Supplement, 1975-76 (Bowker,
1976).

Le Roi Jones. See Baraka, Imamu Amiri.

JORDAN, JUNE [June Meyer]. 1936- . Poet, Journalist, Novelist
Biographical-Personal.. Born July 9, 1936, in Harlem, N.Y. D. of
Gravville and Mildred Jordan (Jamaicans). Educ.: Barnard Coll.,
N.Y.; U. of Chgo. Family: m. Michael Meyer, 1955 (div., 1965);
son, Christopher David. Mailing address: 285 Old Stone Highway,
E. Hampton, N.Y. 11937.
Career-Professional. Vis. Lectr., Depts. of Eng. & Afro-Amer. Lit.,
Yale U., 1974-75; Regular Columnist, Amer. Poetry Review, 1974- ;
Writing Faculty, Sarah Lawrence Coll., 1973-74; Eng. Faculty, City
Coll., City U. of N.Y.; Eng. Faculty, Conn. Coll., New London,

Jordan, June

Conn.; Eng. Faculty, SEEK Prog., City Coll., City U. of N.Y.; Eng. Faculty, Upward Bound Prog., Conn. Coll.; Co-founder & Dir., the Voice of the Children, Inc.; Res. Assoc. & Writer in Tech. Housing Dept., Mobilization for Youth; Asst. to the Prod., Frederick Wiseman, for motion picture, The Cool World. WRITINGS: Young adult: Who Look At Me (Crowell, 1969); Soulscript (Doubleday, 1970); Some Changes (Dutton, 1971); The Voice of the Children (Holt, 1971); His Own Where (Crowell, 1971); Dry Victories (Hold, 1972; Avon, 1975); Fannie Lou Hamer (Crowell, 1972; 1975); New Days: Poems of Exile and Return (Emerson Hall, 1974); I Love You (Emerson Hall, 1974); New Life: New Room (Crowell, 1975). Okay Now (Simon & Schuster, 1975). Anthol.: New Black Poetry; In the Times of Revolution; Dues: New Earth Writing, No More Masks, No More Mythologies; The Black Poets; Woman: The New Voice; Rising Tides; In the Modern Idiom; Poetry of Black America; Rock Against the Wind: Black Love Poems; To See the World Afresh. Period.: New York Times; Essence; Encore; Black World; Black Creation; Village Voice; Partisan Review; Chelsea; Ms.; Mademoiselle; Nation; Evergreen Review; Newsday; Washington Post; Blackstage; Broadside No. 78; American Report; Vista; New Republic; School Library Journal; Wilson Library Bulletin; American Poetry Review; Yardbird; Mosaic No. 5.
HONORS AND AWARDS: U.S. Lib. of Congress, 1-hr. recording of her poems, June 14, 1973; Rockefeller Grant in Creative Writing, 1969-70; Prix de Rome in Environmental Design, 1970-71; 1st novel, His Own Where selected as one of The Most Outstanding Bks. of 1971, by New York Times, and as one of the A.L.A. Best Bks., 1972 and nominated, 1972, for the National Bk. Award; Nancy Bloch Award, as co-ed., The Voice of the Children, 1971.
SIDELIGHTS: "Poetry readings at schools and institutions around the country, including poetry readings at the Guggenheim Museum and the Donnell Library, sponsored by the Academy of American Poets.
"Lectures to various groups and organizations and colleges on a variety of subjects, including the need to protect Black children from public school punishment of Black English, and the need to create against the cult of negative realism" (Author).
Sources. Author inform.; Contemporary Authors, Vols. 33-36, Ed. by Clare D. Kinsman & Mary A. Tennenhouse (Gale Res., 1973); His Own Where, June Jordan (Crowell, 1971); Soulscript, June Jordan (Doubleday, 1970).

JORDAN, NORMAN. 1938- . Poet, Playwright
Biographical-Personal. Born July 30, 1938 in Ansted, W. Va.
Career-Professional. Writer-in-Residence, Karamu House, Cleveland,
Ohio, 1970-71.
WRITINGS: Poetry: Destination: Ashes (Vibration Pr., 1969);
Above Maya (1971). Contrib. to Period.: Free Lance, Vibrations,
Cricket, Journal of Black Poetry, Negro Digest/Black World, Con-
frontation. Anthol.: Black Fire (1968), The New Black Poetry
(1969), Black Out Loud (1970), Poetry of the Negro (1970), Black
Spirits (1972), Poetry of Black America (1973).
SIDELIGHTS: Karamu House is a metropolitan center for the arts
and multiracial communication. No one is excluded from its programs because of race. Has been located in Cleveland's inner city
for 56 years. Jordan's plays have been staged in New York, San
Diego and Cleveland (Poetry of Black America).
Sources. New Black Voices, Ed. by Abraham Chapman (New Amer. Lib.,
1972); Poetry of Black America, Ed. by Arnold Adoff (Harper & Row,
1973).

JOSEY, ELONNIE JUNIUS. 1924- . State Library
Administrator, Social Critic
Biographical-Personal. Born Jan. 20, 1924 in
Norfolk, Va. Son of Willie and Frances
[Bailey] Josey. Educ.: B.A., Howard U.,
1949; M.A. (Hist.), Columbia U., 1950;
M.S.L.S., State U. of N.Y., 1953; L.H.D.
(Honoris Causa), Shaw U., Raleigh, N.C.,
1973. Family: m. Dorothy Johnson, Sept. 11,
1954 (div.); d. Elaine Jacqueline. Mailing
address: 120 Old Hickory Dr., Apt. 1A,
Albany, N.Y. 12204.
Career-Professional. Chief, Bureau of Acad. &
Res. Lib., Div. of Lib. Develop., N.Y. State
Educ. Dept., Albany, 1968- ; Assoc. in Acad.
& Res. Lib., N.Y. State Educ. Dept., 1966-68;
Librn. & Asst. Prof., Savannah State Coll, 1959-66; Librn. & Asst.
Prof., Del. State Coll., 1955-59; Instr., Soc. Sci., Savannah
State Coll., 1954-55; Librn. 1, Free Lib. of Phila., 1953-55.
WRITINGS: A Directory of College and University Libraries in New
York State, 1967; A Directory of Reference and Research Library
Resources in New York State (1967, 1972); A Survey of Texas South-
ern University Library, Houston, Texas (1967); The Black Librarian
in America (Scarecrow, 1970); What Black Librarians Are Saying
(Scarecrow, 1972); New Dimensions in Academic Library Service
(Scarecrow, 1975). Essays in Honor of Libraries and Librarianship
in North America, 1876-1976 (to be co-ed. with Sidney L. Jackson &
Eleanor B. Herling, Sch. of Lib. Sci., Kent State U., by ALA for

Just, Ernest Everett

1976 Centennial). Professional jls. (contrib. more than 80 articles & reviews including: Wilson Library Bulletin; Library Journal; Negro History Bulletin; Quarterly Review of Higher Education
Among Negroes; Savannah Tribune; Negro Education Review; College
& Research Libraries; School Activities; Journal of Negro Education; The Bookmark.
HONORS AND AWARDS: Savannah Branch, NAACP Certificate of Appre-
ciation Award, 1963; ALA John Cotton Dana Award, 1962, 1964; Savan-
nah State Coll. Chap., NAACP Award, 1964; Savannah State Coll. De-
bating Soc. Award, 1965; NAACP Nat'l. Office Award, 1965; Ga. State
Conf., NAACP Award, Youth work, 1966; Savannah Chatham Co. Merit
Award for Work on Econ. Opportunity Task Force, 1966; Savannah
State Coll. Lib. Award for Distinguished Serv. to Librarianship,
1967; Jl. of Lib. Hist. Award, 1970.
MEMBER: ALA (Counc.; nominating com.). ACRL: Chmn., Nom. Com.,
Coll. Lib. Section, 1972; Com. on Acad. Status 1969- ; Chmn.,
Com. on Community Use of Acad. Lib., 1964-69. ALA Ad Hoc Com. on
Equal Employment Opportunity; Assn. for Study of Afro-Amer. Life &
Hist.; Amer. Assn. of U. Prof.; Amer. Acad. of Polit. & Soc. Sci.;
N.Y. Lib. Assn.; Freedom to Read Found.; Founder, ALA Black Caucus
& 1st chmn., etc.
Sources. Author inform.; Contemporary Authors, Vols. 29-32; Ed. by
Clare D. Kinsman (Gale Res., 1972).

JUST, ERNEST EVERETT. 1883-1941. Biologist,
Zoologist
Biographical-Personal. Born 1883 in Charleston,
S.C. Son of a builder of wharves and a
school teacher. Educ.: B.A. (magna cum
laude, Phi Beta Kappa) Dartmouth Coll.; Ph.D.,
U. of Chgo., 1916. Family: m., d. Margaret
Just Butcher (Eng. Prof., Howard U.). Died
1941.
Career-Professional. Head, Dept. of Zoology,
Howard U., 1912-41; Head, Dept. of Physiolo-
gy & Prof., Howard U. Medical Sch.; Research-
er, Marine Biological Lab., Woods Hole, Cape
Cod, Mass. (summers), 1909-1930. Assoc. ed.:
Physiological Zoology (Chgo.), The Biological
Bulletin (Woods Hole, Mass.), & The Journal
of Morphology (Phila.).
WRITINGS: Basic Methods for Experiments in Eggs of Marine Animals;
The Biology of the Cell Surface. Pub. over 60 papers describing
his experiments.
HONORS AND AWARDS: 1st recipient of NAACP Spingarn Medal, 1914;
V. Pres., Amer. Soc. of Zoologists; name starred in American Men
of Science, when other distinguished biologists voted him a leader
in the field.

Kaiser, Ernest Daniel

SIDELIGHTS: "He brought a keen and highly trained mind to bear upon the problem of life, conducting research in fertilization, artificial parthenogenesis, and cell division" (Negro Builders and Heroes).
Sources. Historical Negro Biographies, Wilhelmena S. Robinson (ASNLH, 1967); Negro Almanac, Comp. by Harry A. Ploski & Ernest Kaiser (Bellwether, 1971); Negro Builders and Heroes, Benjamin Brawley (U. of N.C. Pr., 1937); Seven Black American Scientists, Robert C. Hayden (Addison-Wesley, 1970).

KAISER, ERNEST DANIEL. 1915- . Reviewer, Consultant, Editor
Biographical-Personal. Born Dec. 5, 1915, in Petersburg, Va. Son of Ernest Bascom and Elnora Blanche [Ellis] Kaiser. Educ.: City Coll. of City U. of N.Y.; Decades of further study. Family: m. Mary Orford; son, Eric, d. Joan. Mailing address: 31-37 95th St., E. Elmhurst, N.Y. 11369.
Career-Professional. Staff, Schomburg Center for Res. in Black Culture, Harlem (25 yrs.); Advis., Arno Pr. ser., "The American Negro: His History and Literature" (wrote introduction for 10 vols.); Co-found. & Assoc. Ed., Freedomways, 1961- ; Reviewer, Cons., Ed.: McGraw-Hill; R. R. Bowker; W. E. B. DuBois papers, U. of Mass. Pr. (with Herbert Aptheker & Sidney Kaplan).
WRITINGS: In Defense of the People's Black and White History and Culture (Freedomways, 1970); Harlem: A History of Broken Dreams, with Warren J. Halliburton (Doubleday, 1974). The Negro Almanac, co-ed., also pub. as Afro USA: A Reference Work on the Black Experience (Bellwether, 1971). Essays, etc.: William Styron's Nat Turner: Ten Black Writers Respond (Beacon Pr., 1968); Harlem: A Community in Transition (1964); In Black America 1968: The Year of Awakening (Vol. II in The International Library of Negro Life and History Encyclopedia, 1969); Black Titan: W. E. B. DuBois (1970); Black Expression: Essays by and about Black Americans in the Creative Arts (1969); The Black Seventies (1970); Twentieth Century Interpretations of Invisible Man (1970); A Galaxy of Black Writing (1970); Backgrounds to Black-American Literature (1971); A Bibliographic Guide to Afro-American Studies (1972); The American Negro Reference Book (1974); Paul Robeson: The Great Forerunner (1974); The Black New Yorkers (1974); Voices of Black Theatre (1974); No Crystal Stair: A Bibliography of Black Literature. Period.: Freedomways, Science & Society, Black World, Journal of Negro Education, Phylon, New York Amsterdam News, & others.
SIDELIGHTS: "Has also done some work with L. D. Reddick of Temple University, Philadelphia, on the documentation phase of Alex Haley's Kinte genealogical library project funded by the Carnegie Corporation...Herbert Aptheker has stated in the American Institute for Marxist Studies Newsletter (Jan.-Feb. 1972) that Kaiser

Kaufman, Bob Garnell

'has the most vast bibliographical knowledge in the area of Black
life and history of any person now living'" (Author).
Source. Author inform.

KAUFMAN, BOB GARNELL. 1925- . Poet
Biographical-Personal. Born Apr. 18, 1925, in
New Orleans, La. Son of Mr. and Mrs. Kaufman (1st names unknown; father, German,
mother from Martinique). Educ.: 6th grade;
self-taught. Family: m. Eileen Kaufman;
son, Parker. Mailing address: 143 Willow
Ave., Fairfax, Cal. 94930.
Career-Professional. Merchant Marine; Poet;
acted in "The Flower Thief," Spoleto, Italy
Film Award for 1960. NET TV "Soul" show (na-
tionwide), "Coming from Bob Kaufman, Poet,"
1972-73 (in which Ruby Dee & Ossie Davis
acted).
WRITINGS: First published in Beatitude Magazine in San Francisco in late 1950's. His
broadsides, "The Abomunist Manifesto," "Second April," and "Does
the Secret Mind Whisper," were first published separately by City
Lights and then included in his book, Solitudes Crowded with Lone-
liness (New Directions, 1964); The Golden Sardine (City Lights,
1966); Watch My Tracks (Knopf, 1971). Included in 27 anthols.
since 1970.
HONORS AND AWARDS: Nominated for Guiness Poetry Award for "Bagel
Shop Jazz," 1960-61.
SIDELIGHTS: "Was a leading poet during the 1950's...'renaissance.'
He was influential in the development of white 'beat' poets such
as Allen Ginsberg, Gregory Corso, and Lawrence Ferlinghetti. Bob
Kaufman had earned great respect for his work in England and
France before it became well known in this country..." (Poetry of
Black America).
Sources. Author inform.; New Black Voices, Ed. by Abraham Chapman
(New Amer. Lib., 1972); Poetry of Black America, Ed. by Arnold
Adoff (Harper & Row, 1973); Books in Print, Supplement, 1975-76
(Bowker, 1976).

KELLEY, WILLIAM MELVIN. 1937- . Novelist, Short Story Writer
Biographical-Personal. Born N.Y.C., 1937. Educ.: Fieldston Sch.;
Harvard Coll. Family: m. Karen Gibson; d. Jessica Gibson. Mail-
ing address: c/o Doubleday & Co., Inc., 277 Park Ave., N.Y., N.Y.
10017.
Career-Professional. Has taught at the New Sch.; Served as author-
in-residence at State U. Coll., Genesee, N.Y.
WRITINGS: A Different Drummer (Doubleday, 1962); Dancers on the
Shore, short stories (Doubleday, 1964); A Drop of Patience (Dou-

Kelsey, George Dennis

bleday, 1965); <u>dem</u> (Doubleday, 1967); <u>Dun-fords- Travels Everywheres</u> (Doubleday, 1970); Contrib. short stories to: <u>Mademoiselle</u>, <u>Saturday Evening Post</u>, <u>Black World</u>, <u>Cavalier</u>.
HONORS AND AWARDS: Recipient of Dana Reed Prize, 1960 for Harvard writing; Breadloaf Writers Conf. Fellow. (Vt.); N.Y. Writers Conf. Fellow.; John Hay Whitney Found. grant; for <u>A Different Drummer</u>, the Richard & Hinda Rosenthal Found. Award of Nat'l. Inst. of Arts & Letters.
SIDELIGHTS: At present living in Jamaica (<u>Dark Symphony</u>).
Sources. <u>Black American Literature--Fiction</u>, Ed. by Darwin T. Turner (Merrill, 1969);
<u>Black Insights</u>, Ed. by Nick A. Ford (Ginn, 1971); <u>Cavalcade</u>, Ed. by Arthur P. Davis & Saunders Redding (Houghton Mifflin, 1971); <u>Dark Symphony</u>, Ed. by James A. Emanuel & Theodore L. Gross (Free Pr., 1968); <u>Who's Who in America</u>, 37th ed., 1972-73, Chgo. (Marquis, 1973).

KELSEY, GEORGE DENNIS. 1910- . Professor of Religion
Biographical-Personal. Born July 24, 1910 in Columbus, Ga. Son of Andrew Z. and Marie H. [Jones] Kelsey. <u>Educ.</u>: B.A., Morehouse Coll., Atlanta, 1934; B.D., Andover Newton Theol. Sch., 1937; Ph.D., Yale U., 1946; Harvard U.; London Sch. of Econ.; Morehouse Coll., D.D., 1970. <u>Family</u>: m. Leola Brunnette [Hanks]; son, George D., Jr., son, Everett N. Kelsey (dec.). <u>Mailing address</u>: 5 Cedar St., Madison, N.J. 07940.
Career-Professional. Prof. of Relig. (Amer. Bap.) Drew U., Madison, N.J., Henry Anson Buttz Prof. of Christian Ethics, 1972- , Prof. of Christian Ethics, 1956-72, Assoc.
Prof., 1952-56, Guest Lectr., 1950-51; Assoc. Dir., Field Dept., Nat'l. Counc. of Churches, 1948-52; Dir., Sch. of Relig., Morehouse Coll., 1945-48, Prof. of Relig. & Philosophy, 1938-48.
WRITINGS: <u>Racism and the Christian Understanding of Man</u> (Scribners, 1965); <u>Social Ethics Among Southern Baptists, 1917-1969</u> (Scarecrow, 1973). Anthol.: <u>The Christian Way in Race Relations</u>; <u>Twentieth Century Encyclopedia of Religious Knowledge</u>; <u>Well-Springs of Life</u>; <u>City Churches and The Culture Crisis</u>. Jls.: <u>Journal of Religious Thought</u>; <u>Quarterly Review</u>; <u>Theology Today</u>; <u>Social Progress</u>; <u>The Drew Gateway</u>; <u>Andover Newton Quarterly</u>.

151

Kennedy, Adrienne

MEMBER: Assn. of Prof. of Christian Ethics; Soc. of Relig. in Higher Educ.; Amer. Acad. of Relig.; Amer. Acad. of Pol. & Soc. Sci.; Soc. for Study of Black Relig.
SIDELIGHTS: Traveled to Europe several times. Addressed World Baptist Alliance in Rio de Janeiro, Brazil, 1960; Visited Cuba (Author).
Source. Author inform.

KENNEDY, ADRIENNE. 1931- . Playwright
Biographical-Personal. Born 1931 in Pittsburgh, Pa. (Father--soc. worker, mother--tchr.) Educ.: Ohio State U.; Edward Albee's Workshop, 1962. Family: married.
Career-Professional. Instr., Lectr. Playwriting, Yale U., 1972-73.
WRITINGS: Plays: Funnyhouse of a Negro (1962); The Owl Answers (1963); A Lesson in Dead Language (1964); A Rat's Mass (1965); A Beast's Story (1966); In His Own Write, adapted from book by John Lennon. Has written stories and poems, as well as two novels.
SIDELIGHTS: Miss Kennedy acknowledges Edward Albee as a major influence; was member of his Playwright Workshop. Funnyhouse of a Negro received a Village Voice Obie Distinguished Play Award. First production of The Owl Answers, at White Barn Theater, Westport, Conn., sponsored by Eva Le Gallienne, Ralph Alswang, & Lucille Lortel; directed by Michael Kahn. The Theater Co. of Boston performed A Rat's Mass, April, 1966. In His Own Write, presented by National Theatre in London. New York Shakespeare Festival Public Theatre produced The Owl Answers, 1968 (Black Drama).
Sources. Black Drama, Ed. by William Brasmer & Dominick Consolo (Merrill, 1970); New Black Playwrights, Ed. by William Couch, Jr. (Avon, 1970).

KENT, GEORGE E. English Professor
Biographical-Personal. Born in Columbus, Ga. Son of a blacksmith and a sch. tchr. Educ.: B.A. (Eng.), Savannah State Coll.; M.A., Ph.D., Boston U. Family: m.; 2 children.
Career-Professional. Prof. of Eng., U. of Chgo.
WRITINGS: Blackness and the Adventure of Western Culture (Third World Pr., 1972). In progress: Faulkner and White Racial Consciousness (Emerson-Hall). Contrib. to CLA Journal.
SIDELIGHTS: He "has contributed substantial renown as a scholar of Richard Wright" (Blackness and the Adventure of Western Culture).
Source. Blackness and the Adventure of Western Culture, George E. Kent (Third World Pr., 1972).

KGOSITSILE, KEOROPETSE. 1938- . Poet, Essayist, Critic
Biographical-Personal. Born Sept. 19, 1938, in Johannesburg, S.
  Africa. Self-exiled in U.S. since 1961. Educ.: Lincoln U.; U.
  of N.H.; Columbia U.; New Sch. for Soc. Research.
Career-Professional. Vis. Prof.: Sarah Lawrence Coll., Queens Coll.,
  Bennett Coll. (N.C.), N.C. Central U. Currently Vis. Prof., U.
  of Denver.
  WRITINGS: Poetry: Spirits Unchained (Broadside Pr., 1969); For
  Melba (Third World Pr., 1970); My Name is Afrika (Doubleday, 1971);
  The Present is a Dangerous Place to Live (Third World Pr.); The
  World is Here, Ed., contemporary poems from Africa (Doubleday).
  Anthol.: For Malcolm (1969); Black Fire (1968); Black Arts (1969);
  Black Spirits (1972); Poetry of Black America (1973). Period.:
  Journal of Black Poetry, Negro Digest/Black World, The New Afri-
  can, Urban Review, Pan African Journal.
  HONORS AND AWARDS: Conrad Kent Rivers Memorial Award & others.
Sources. For Malcolm, Ed. by Dudley Randall & Margaret G. Burroughs
  (Broadside Pr., 1969); Pittsburgh Courier, Dec. 7, 1974 (Seng-
  stacke Public.); Poetry of Black America, Ed. by Arnold Adoff
  (Harper & Row, 1973).

KILLENS, JOHN OLIVER. 1916- . Novelist,
  Essayist, Teacher
Biographical-Personal. Born Jan. 14, 1916, in
  Macon, Ga. Son of Charles Myles, Sr. and
  Willie Lee [Coleman] Killens. Educ.: Edward
  Waters Coll.; Morris Brown Coll.; Howard U.;
  Terrell Law Sch.; Columbia U.; N.Y.U. Family:
  m. Grace Killens; son, Jon C., d. Barbara E.
  Wynn. Mailing address: 1392 Union St.,
  Brooklyn, N.Y. 11212.
Career-Professional. Writer-in-Residence, How-
  ard U.; Founder, Chmn., Harlem Writers' Guild
  Workshop; Writer-in-Residence, Fisk U.;
  Tchr., Creative Writing, New Sch. for Soc.
  Res.; Adjunct Prof., Columbia U.; Head, Crea-
  tive Writer's Workshop, Black Culture Seminar,
Formerly Nat'l. Labor Relat. Bd. staff. Served with armed forces,
World War II, PTO.
WRITINGS: Novels: Youngblood (Trident, 1954, 1966); And Then We
Heard the Thunder (Knopf, 1961, Pocket Bks., 1971). Black Man's
Burden, essays (Trident, 1966); 'sippi, novel (Trident, 1967);
Odds Against Tomorrow, screenplay (1960); The Trial Record of Den-
mark Vesey, Ed. (1970); The Cotillion, novel (Trident, 1971);
Great Gittin' Up Morning, biography of Denmark Vesey (Doubleday,
1972); Slaves (Pyramid Bks., 1969); A Man Ain't Nothing But a Man
(Little, 1970). John Henry (Little, Brown, 1975). Dramas: Lower

Than the Angels (staged by Amer. Pl. Theatre, 1965); Cotillion
(musical to be prod. by Woodie King Assoc. & Berry Gordy); Slaves
(prod. by Theatre Guild, 1969). Anthol.: Ten Black Writers Re-
spond; Black Short Story Anthology; American Negro Short Stories
Best Short Stories by Negro Writers; etc. Articles & essays in:
Ebony; Negro Digest; New York Times Magazine; Holiday; Redbook;
New York Herald Tribune; Nation; Black Scholar; Presence Afri-
caine; etc.
HONORS AND AWARDS: Afro-Arts Theatre Cultural Award, 1955; NAACP
Literary Arts Award, 1957; Culture, Human Relat. Award, Climbers
Bus. Club; Citation, Empire State Federation of Women; Cultural
Award, N.Y. State Elks; Charles Chesnutt Award, N.Y. Branch,
ASNLH; Award, N.Y. Chap. of Links; others.
MEMBER: Founding Mem. & V. Pres., Black Acad. of Arts & Letters;
Authors League; Dramatists Guild; P.E.N.; Executive Bd., Nat'l.
Center of Afro-Amer. Artists; Former Chmn., Writers Com., Amer.
Soc. of African Culture.
SIDELIGHTS: "Killens insists that the black writer has the re-
sponsibility to search for his subject matter within the expe-
riences of his race and to present those experiences with full
consciousness of his racial identity. In other words, a black
writer is not merely a writer who is black; instead, he is a black
man who is a writer" (Black American Literature--Essays).
   He has traveled in Japan, Korea, Africa, USSR, England, Germany,
China (Author).
Sources. Afro-American Literature: Non Fiction, Ed. by William
   Adams et al.(Houghton Mifflin, 1970); American Negro Short Stories, Ed. by John H. Clarke (Hill & Wang, 1966); Author inform.;
   Black American Literature--Essays, Ed. by Darwin T. Turner (Mer-
   rill, 1969); Black Insights, Ed. by Nick A. Ford (Ginn, 1971);
   To Gwen With Love, Ed. by Patricia L. Brown & Others (Johnson
   Pub., 1971); Who's Who in America, 37th ed., 1972-73 (Marquis,
   1972).

KING, CORETTA SCOTT. 1927- . Lecturer,
Author, Concert Singer
Biographical-Personal. Born April 27, 1927, in
   Marion, Ala. D. of Obie (pulpwood dealer)
   and Bernice [McMurry] Scott. Educ.: B.A.,
   Antioch Coll., 1951; Mus.B., New Eng. Con-
   servatory of Music, 1954; L.H.D. (hon.):
   Boston U., 1969, Marymount Manhattan Coll.,
   1969, Brandeis U., 1969, Wilberforce U.,
   1970, Bethune-Cookman Coll., 1970, Morehouse
   Coll., 1970, Princeton U., 1970, Keuka Coll.,
   1970; LL.D. (hon.): U. of Bridgeport, 1970;
   Morgan State Coll., 1970. Family: m. Martin

King, Helen H.

Luther King, Jr. (civil rights leader), June 18, 1953; d. Yolanda
Denise, son, Martin Luther III, son, Dexter Scott, d. Bernice
Albertine. Mailing address: 234 Sunset Ave., N.W., Atlanta, Ga.
30314.

Career-Professional. Concert singer debut, Springfield, Ohio, 1948;
concerts throughout U.S.; Instr. Voice, Morris Brown Coll., Atlanta, 1962; Lectr., 1st woman to deliver Class Day address, Harvard U., 1968; 1st woman to preach, Statutory Serv., St. Paul's
Cathedral, London, Eng., 1969; Pres., Martin Luther King, Jr.
Memorial Center.

WRITINGS: Martin Luther King, Jr., Where Do We Go From Here:
Chaos or Community?, author of foreword, memorial ed. (Bantam,
1968); Martin Luther King, Jr., Trumpet of Conscience, author of
foreword (Harper & Row, 1968); My Life With Martin Luther King,
Jr. (Holt, 1969). Contrib.: bk. about Robert Kennedy, Good
Housekeeping, New Lady, McCall's, Theology Today, others.

HONORS AND AWARDS: Annual Brotherhood Award, Nat'l. Counc. of
Negro Women, 1957; Louise Waterman Wise Award, Amer. Jewish Con-
gress of Women's Auxiliary, 1963; Woman of Conscience Award,
Nat'l. Counc. of Women, 1968; Acad. Nazionale Del Lincei, Human
Relat. Award, Italy; Gallup Poll, Fifth Most Admired Woman in the
World, 1968; & others.

MEMBER: Nat'l. Counc. of Negro Women; YWCA chmn., Com. on Econ.
Justice for Women; Women's Internat. League for Peace & Freedom;
Bd. of Dir., S. Christian Leadership Conf.; Martin L. King, Jr.,
Found. of Eng.; Links, Inc.; Alpha Kappa Alpha Sorority (hon.).

SIDELIGHTS: "Her particular contribution to the civil rights
movement is the freedom concert, inaugurated at Town Hall in New
York, November, 1964; since then has presented more than thirty
freedom concerts in which she sings, recites poetry, and lectures,
with benefits going to the Southern Christian Leadership Conference, its affiliates, and (more recently) the Martin Luther King,
Jr. Memorial Center, Atlanta" (Contemporary Authors).

Sources. Contemporary Authors, Vols. 29-32, Ed. by Clare D. Kinsman
& Mary A. Tennenhouse (Gale Res., 1972).

KING, HELEN H. 1931- . Teacher, Editor,
Publisher

Biographical-Personal. Born Oct. 15, 1931, in
Clarksdale, Miss. D. of Emmit and Mary
[Gage] Hayes. Educ.: DuSable High Sch.,
Chgo.; Wilson Jr. Coll.; DePaul U., Chgo.;
B.A. (Educ. & Eng. Lit.), U. of Mich., Ann
Arbor. Family: div.; son, Chad., d. Fenote.
Mailing address: P.O. 20747, Chgo., Ill.
60620.

Career-Professional. Tchr.: Pontiac, Mich.;
Chgo., Ill.; (Roeper City & County Sch. for

King, Martin Luther, Jr.

Gifted) Birmingham, Mich.; Assoc. Ed., _Jet_ Mag.; Assoc. Ed.,
Ebony mag.; Assoc. Ed. & free-lance writer, The Chicago Courier
& Ed., "Wee Black World," (children's page). Currently: Pres.,
Let's Save The Children, Inc. (Chgo. textbook pub. co.).
WRITINGS: Juvenile: _Willy_ (Doubleday, 1971); The Soul of Christ-
mas (Johnson, 1972). In progress: _Uncle Oscar_, juvenile; _A Place
for Hating_, novel & movie script; The Chicago Courier, ser., "The
Black Man, The Black Woman, and The Black Child."
SIDELIGHTS: Participant (Via "Willy") in Chgo. Children's Bk.
Festival, Chgo. Pub. Lib., Nov. 1971; Speaker, Jackson, Mich.,
Children's Bk. Festival, Nov. 1971; Guest Moderator: Merri Dee
Show (twice); Speaker, Howard U., Oct. 1971 (Author).
Source. Author inform.

KING, MARTIN LUTHER, JR. 1929-1968. Clergyman, Civil Rights Leader,
Nobel Peace Prize Winner
Biographical-Personal. Born Jan. 15, 1929, in Atlanta, Ga. Son of
Martin Luther, Sr. (minister) and Alberta [Williams] King (d. of
minister). _Educ._: B.A., 1948, L.H.D., 1957, Morehouse Coll.,
Atlanta; B.D., Crozier Theol. Sem., 1951; Ph.D., Boston U., 1955.
Family: m. Coretta Scott, June 17, 1953; d. Yolanda Denise, son,
Martin Luther III, son, Dexter Scott, d. Bernice Albertine. As-
sasinated April 4, 1968, in Memphis, Tenn.
Career-Professional. Began career as Pastor, Dexter Avenue Baptist
Church, Montgomery, Ala. Organized & directed boycott of city's
buslines, resulting in U.S. Supreme Court's declaring Alabama's
bus segregation laws unconstitutional (1956). Organized Southern
Christian Leadership Conference (1957), became first president and
remained its leader until his death.
WRITINGS: Essays: Stride Toward Freedom (Harper & Row, 1958);
Strength to Love (Harper & Row, 1963); Why We Can't Wait (Harper &
Row, 1964); Where Do We Go From Here: Chaos or Community? (1967).
HONORS AND AWARDS: Pearl Plafkner Award for Scholarship, Crozier
Theol. Sem., Chester, Pa., 1951; Selected one of 10 outstanding
personalities of 1956, _Time_ mag., 1957; Numerous awards for lead-
ership, Montgomery Movement; Nobel Peace Prize, Oslo, Norway,
1964.
SIDELIGHTS: "In April and May, 1963, King led a series of massive
demonstrations against racial segregation in Birmingham, Alabama
.... (His) classic 'Letter from a Birmingham Jail' became a new
document in the history of human freedom. Later that year King
reached new heights as a national leader with his 'I Have a
Dream' speech at the historic March on Washington" (Black Insights). Dr. King won national acclaim for the Black voter registration campaign in Selma, Ala. "Increasingly in 1966 and 1967 he
criticized the American war effort (in Vietnam) and became actively involved in antiwar demonstrations" (Black Insights). He was

assassinated in Memphis, Tenn., April 4, 1968, while leading a
garbage collector's strike (Compiler).
Sources. <u>Afro-American Literature--Non Fiction</u>, Ed. by William Adams
et al. (Houghton Mifflin, 1970); <u>Afro-American Writing</u>, Vol. I,
Ed. by Richard A. Long & Eugenia W. Collier (N.Y.U. Pr., 1972);
<u>Black Insights</u>, Ed. by Nick A. Ford (Ginn, 1971); <u>Who Was Who in
America</u>, Vol. IV, 1961-1968 (Marquis, 1968).

KING, WOODIE. 1937- . Director, Producer,
Free-Lance Writer, Editor
Biographical-Personal. Born July 27, 1937 in
Ala. Son of Woodie and Ruby King. <u>Educ</u>.:
Will-o-way Sch. of Theatre, Bloomfield Hills,
Mich., (Theatre Arts) 1958-62; Wayne State
U., Detroit (Theatre), 1961. <u>Family</u>: m.
Willie Mae King; d. Michelle, son, W. Geof-
fry, son, Michael. <u>Mailing address</u>: Woodie
King Assoc., Inc., 417 Covent Ave., N.Y.,
N.Y. 10031.
Career-Professional. Drama Critic, <u>Detroit
Tribune</u> (Free-lance writer), 1959-62; Founder-
Mgr., Concept-E. Theatre, Detroit, 1960-63;
Cultural Arts Dir., Mobilization for Youth,
N.Y.C., 1965-70; Cons., Arts & Humanities,
Rockefeller Found., 1968-70; Artistic Dir., Henry St. Settlement,
N.Y.C., 1970; Theatrical prod.
WRITINGS: Ed.: <u>A Black Quartet; four one-act plays</u> (New Amer.
Lib.); <u>Black Drama Anthology</u>, with Ron Milner (Columbia U. Pr.,
1972); <u>Black Poets and Prophets</u>, with Earl Anthony (New Amer.
Lib., 1972); <u>Black Short Story Anthology</u> (Columbia U. Pr., 1972);
<u>Black Spirits: New Black Poets in America</u> (Random House, 1972);
<u>The Forerunners, Black Poets in America</u> (Howard U. Pr., 1975).
Anthol.: <u>Best Short Stories by Negro Writers</u>; <u>Black Theatre
Anthology</u>; <u>City Street</u>. Period.: <u>Liberator</u>; <u>Black World</u>; <u>Drama
Review</u>; <u>Black Theatre Magazine</u>; <u>New York Times</u>; <u>Rockefeller
Foundation Quarterly</u>; <u>ASNLH</u>.
HONORS AND AWARDS: John Hay Whitney Fellow. for Dir., 1965-66;
Mobilization for Youth films won Venice Festival Award, Oberhausen
Award, Internat. Film Critics Award, & A. Phillip Randolph Award.
SIDELIGHTS: Mobilization for Youth program was the first training
program in the arts for young blacks & Puerto Ricans. It also was
the first to let the young participants produce their own art under
professional supervision--it took young people to Expo '67 in Canada, Hemisphere '68 in Texas, & to Rome, Italy in 1969." King produced the following in Black Theatre: LeRoi Jones, Ed Bullins,
Ronald Milner, & Ben Caldwell in <u>A Black Quartet</u>; LeRoi Jones's

Knight, Etheridge

Slaveship; William Mackey's Behold! Cometh the Vankerkellans;
Ed Bullins's In New England Winters; J. E. Franklin's Black Girl
New Black Poets in America: A three-day fesitval; & The Last
Poets in motion picture, Right On! Other motion pictures are:
The Game; Ghetto; Where We Live; You Did It? & Epitaph. Produced
record albums, "The New Black Poets in America" (Motown) & "Nation
Time" by LeRoi Jones (Motown). Plays directed at Concept-East
Theatre, Detroit: Study in Color; God's Trombones; The Toilet &
The Slave; Who's Got His Own, The Connections; Zoo Story; & Death
of Bessie Smith (Author).
Source. Author inform.

KNIGHT, ETHERIDGE [Imamu Etheridge Knight Soa]. 1931- . Poet,
Short Story Writer
Biographical-Personal. Born April 19, 1931, in Corinth, Miss. Son
of Bushie and Belzora [Cozart] Knight Taylor. Educ.: 9th grade;
self-educated. Family: 1st m. Sonia Sanchez (poet); 2nd m. Mary
Ellen McAnally; children, 2nd m., d. Mary Tandiwe, son, Etheridge
Bambata. Mailing address: 3323 W. 33rd Pl., Apt. 4, Indianapolis, Ind. 46222.
Career-Professional. Punch press operator; Poetry Ed., Motive mag.,
1969-71; Instr., U. of Pittsburgh, 1969-70; Instr., U. of Hartford, 1970-71; Poet-in-Residence, Lincoln U., Mo., Dec. 1971-72;
Contrib. Ed., Newsletters, 1973-74; Dir., "Self-Development
through the Arts" project in 1973 in Indianapolis on a $2500 grant
from United Presby. Church (community workshops, etc.).
WRITINGS: Poems from Prison (Broadside Pr., 1968); Black Voices
in Prison (Pathfinder Pr., 1970); Belly Song and Other Poems
(Broadside Pr., 1972). Poems appear in: Negro Digest, The Go-
liards; short stories in: Prison mag., Negro Digest & Jaguar.
Anthols.: City in all Directions (1969); The New Black Poetry
(1969); Dices or Black Bones (1970); Black Out Loud (1970) &
Poetry of Black America (1973).
HONORS AND AWARDS: $5000 grant NEA 1971; Guggenheim Found.
Fellow, 1974 ($12,000).
SIDELIGHTS: "In 1960 I was given a 20-year prison sentence for
robbery. After serving 18 months in jail awaiting trial, I was
sent to the Indiana State Prison in Michigan City where I spent
over six years, not emerging until 1968. It was during those
years in prison that, after overcoming my initial period of bitterness and hostility, I began to write poetry. Years of reading
and absorbing the poetry and creative writing of such greats as
Walt Whitman, Gwendolyn Brooks, and Langston Hughes helped me see
possibilities for myself and the person of Gwendolyn Brooks and
other black writers outside the walls encouraged me. After many,
many rejects, I finally began to have an occasional poem published
in an occasional magazine or journal, such as the Negro Digest/

Lacy, Leslie Alexander

<u>Black World</u>, etc. Finally I slipped out an entire manuscript which made its way to an Italian publisher, and was first published in Italy in the Italian language. That manuscript was published in 1970 by Pathfinder Press in New York City as <u>Black Voices from Prison</u>....

I am currently working on a manuscript of collected folk poems, ballads and toasts on a grant I have received from the Guggenheim Foundation in New York" (Author).

Sources. Author inform.; <u>Contemporary Authors</u>, Vols. 23-24, Ed. by Barbara Harte & Carolyn Riley (Gale Res., 1970); <u>For Malcolm</u>, Ed. by Dudley Randall & Margaret Burroughs (Broadside Pr., 1969); <u>New Black Voices</u>, Ed. by Abraham Chapman (New Amer. Lib., 1972); <u>Poetry of Black America</u>, Ed. by Arnold Adoff (Harper & Row, 1973).

KOINER, RICHARD B. 1929- . Novelist

Biographical-Personal. Born Jan. 28, 1929, in Atlantic City, N.J. Son of Mr. Koiner and Mrs. Elizabeth Jamison. <u>Educ.</u>: High Sch. of Music & Art (4 yrs.); Sch. of Visual Arts (4 yrs.); New Sch. of Soc. Sci. (1 yr.). Family: m. Jacqueline Maria Koiner; d. Kimberly Beth, d. Jacqueline Maria. <u>Mailing address</u>: 1365 St. Nicholas Ave., N.Y. N.Y. 10033.

Career-Professional. Lectr., City Coll. of N.Y., "The Novel as an Art Form;" Interviewed on Morristown, N.J. radio station, on <u>Jack Be Quick</u>.

WRITINGS: <u>Jack Be Quick</u>, novel (Lyle Stuart, 1966). "Another Silent American," featured article, <u>True</u> mag., June '70. Libretto for a musical, for 1975.

HONORS AND AWARDS: Breadloaf Literary Fellow., Middlebury Coll., Vt., 1966.

Source. Author inform.

LACY, LESLIE ALEXANDER. 1937- . Essayist, Teacher

Biographical-Personal. Born Aug. 8, 1937 in Franklin, La. Son of Nathaniel Lenard (physician) and Lillie Lacy. <u>Educ.</u>: Private sch.; coll. (New Eng.); M.A., U. of Cal., Berkeley; M.A., U. of Ghana, 1964. <u>Mailing address</u>: 3200 16th St., Apt. 508, N.W., Wash., D.C. 20010.

Career-Professional. Tutor, Dept. of Polit. Sci., U. of Ghana, 1964-66; Lectr., N.Y.U., 1968-70; Lectr., Howard U., 1968-70; Lectr., New Sch. for Soc. Res., 1969-70; Tchr., Creative Writing, Fed. City Coll., Wash., D.C.; Operator, Free Sch., Wash., D.C.

WRITINGS: <u>Cheer the Lonesome Traveler: The Life of W. E. B. DuBois</u>, Young adult (Dial, 1970); <u>The Rise and Fall of the Proper</u>

La Grone, Clarence Oliver

Negro, autobiog. (Macmillan, 1970); Black Africa on the Move, juvenile (Watts, 1969); Contemporary African Literature; Native Daughter (Macmillan, 1974); The Soil Soldiers: The Civilian Conservation Corps in the Great Depression (Chilton, 1975). Contrib. Gwendolyn Carter, Ed., Politics in Africa (Harcourt, 1966). Anthol.: Black Fire, Ed. by LeRoi Jones & Larry Neal (Morrow, 1968); Malcolm X, Ed. by John H. Clarke (Macmillan, 1969). SIDELIGHTS: "Active with political groups embracing 'explicit socialist alternatives to capitalism' while a law student in California, where he eventually joined the Afro-American Association; went to Africa in 1962 and spent four years studying and teaching at University of Ghana, Legon; returned to United States after Ghana's President, Kwame Nkrumah was deposed in 1966" (Contemporary Authors).
Sources. Black Fire, Ed. by LeRoi Jones & Larry Neal (Morrow, 1968); Contemporary African Literature, Leslie A. Lacy and Edris Makward (Random House, 1972); Contemporary Authors, Vols. 33-36, Ed. by Clare D. Kinsman & Mary A. Tennenhouse (Gale Res., 1973); Native Daughter, Leslie A. Lacy (Macmillan, 1974).

LA GRONE, CLARENCE OLIVER. Poet, Sculptor, Teacher, Lecturer
Biographical-Personal. Born in McAlester, Okla. Son of a minister. Educ.: Howard U.; B.A., U. of N.M.; Cranbrook Art Acad.; Wayne State U.
Career-Professional. Free-lance sculptor, artist, poet, 1940; Internat. rep., United Auto Workers & Congress of Indust. Org., 1946-54; Tchr., Spec. Educ., public schs., Detroit; Lectr., Afro-Amer. Hist., Northwestern High Sch.; Art exhibits, Wayne State U.; Cons., Black Stud. Dept., Wayne State U.; Public schs., Detroit; Vis. Lectr., Art & Afro-Amer. Hist. & Culture, Pa. State U., Middletown, 1970-71.
WRITINGS: Poetry: Footfalls (Darel Pr., 1950); They Speak of Downs (Brinkley-Leatherman, 1963). Anthol.: Beyond the Blues; New Negro Poets; La Poesie Negro-Americaine. Period.: Saturday Review; Correspondence; Negro History Bulletin; New York Times; Manchester Guardian; Negro Digest; Peninsula Poets.
HONORS AND AWARDS: 1st prize for poem "The Limited," Mich. Poetry Soc., 1966.
SIDELIGHTS: "La Grone's interest in Negro history and art has created a demand for his services as lecturer and consultant in the area of Afro-American culture. As a teacher in Detroit's public schools he has been an active advocate of curriculum changes that would bring a more historically honest picture of the Negro into school texts" (For Malcolm).
Sources. For Malcolm, Ed. by Dudley Randall & Margaret Burroughs (Broadside Pr., 1969); New Black Voices, Ed. by Abraham Chapman (New Amer. Lib., 1972).

LANE, PINKIE GORDON. 1923- . English Pro-
fessor, Poet
Biographical-Personal. Born Jan. 13, 1923, in
Phila., Pa. D. of William and Inez [West]
Gordon. Educ.: B.A., Spelman Coll., Atlan-
ta, 1949; M.A., Atlanta U., 1956; Ph.D.,
Louisiana State U., 1967. Family: Widow;
son, Gordon Edward Lane. Mailing address:
2738 77th Ave., Baton Rouge, La. 70807.
Career-Professional. Tchr.; Prof. of Eng.,
Southern U., Baton Rouge, La.; Poetry Read-
ings: Ill., Okla., Utah, N.Y., La., Miss.,
Tenn. & Ark.
WRITINGS: Wind Thoughts, poetry (South &
West, 1972). Discourses on Poetry, Ed.
(South & West, 1972). Poems by Blacks,
Vol. III, Ed., Anthol. (South & West, 1975).
HONORS AND AWARDS: Certificates of Merit: Nat'l. Writers' Club;
The Tulsa Poets; South & West, Inc.; Southern U. Lib. Staff; Re-
cognized in 1972 as one of "Louisiana Women in the Seventies;"
Works appear: The Beinecke Rare Bk. and Manuscript Lib., Yale U.,
James Weldon Johnson Memorial Collec. of Negro Arts & Letters.
MEMBER: Poetry Soc. of America; Nat'l. Org. for Women; Unitarian
Universalist Assn.; Delta Sigma Theta Sorority.
Source. Author inform.

LANGSTON, JOHN MERCER. 1829-1897. Lawyer,
Public Official, Educator
Biographical-Personal. Born Dec. 14, 1829, in
Louisa County, Va. Son of Ralph Quarles,
slave owner, and Lucy Langston, slave (of
African & Indian descent). Both parents died
when John was 5 yrs. old. He passed to
guardianship of Colonel William D. Gooch of
Chillicothe, Ohio. The Colonel moved to Missouri, left John in care of Richard Long,
abolitionist from New Eng. Educ.: Oberlin
Coll., (grad. from the coll. & the theol.
sch.); studied in law office of Philemon
Bliss. Family: m. Caroline M. Wall (Oberlin
grad.). Died 1897.
Career-Professional. Admitted to Ohio bar,
1855 (1st black to practice in West); Tried both civil & criminal
cases (mostly whites), but some fugitive slave cases; With brother
Charles, dominant figure in antebellum Negro conventions; Elected
several times to township offices, twice to Oberlin counc., served
11 yrs. on Oberlin bd. of educ.; Supv. schooling of Negro youth in

Lanusse, Armand

   Ohio; Helped recruit black troops in the Civil War; Inspector Gen.,
   freedman's schs. Dean of Law Dept. & Acting Pres., (newly established) Howard U.; Apptd. Minister-Resident & Consul-Gen. to
   Haiti, 1877. Pres., Virginia Normal & Collegiate Inst.; Elected
   to Congress from Va., 1888.
   WRITINGS: From the Virginia Plantation to the National Capitol,
   autobiog. (Amer. Pub. Co., 1894).
   SIDELIGHTS: Langston's father, Ralph Quarles "was a man of en-
   lightened social outlook, and believed that slaves should be
   emancipated as rapidly as possible by the voluntary act of owners.
   Accordingly he manumitted his children. The father was legally
   estopped from giving his four children by Lucy Langston his name,
   but he showed solicitude for their welfare, made provision for
   each of the sons, and was especially interested in John" (Negro
   Builders and Heroes).
Sources. Negro Author in America, Vernon Loggins (Kennikat, 1959);
   Negro Builders and Heroes, Benjamin Brawley (U. of N.C. Pr., 1937);
   Negro Caravan, Ed. by Sterling A. Brown, et al. (Arno Pr. & N.Y.
   Times, 1969).

LANUSSE, ARMAND. 1812-1867. Creole Poet
Biographical-Personal. Born 1812 in New Orleans, La. of French
   Creole ancestry. "He received an excellent education, but it is
   not clear at this date whether he studied in France, as did so
   many of the talented colored youth of his group at the time"
   (Poetry of the Negro). Died 1867.
Career-Professional. Served as conscripted Confederate soldier.
   Leader of group of young poets (in New Orleans) writing in French;
   Prin., Catholic Sch. for Indigent Orphans of Color, 1852-66.
   WRITINGS: Les Cenelles, poetry anthol. (1845). Contrib.: L'Union
   and La Tribune (newspapers).
   SIDELIGHTS: Lanusse was one of the most distinguished members of
   a social group in New Orleans known as free men of color. Les
   Cenelles was the first anthology of American Negro poetry.
Sources. Early Black American Poets, Ed. by William H. Robinson,
   Jr. (Wm. C. Brown, 1969); American Negro Reference Book, Ed. by
   John P. Davis (Prentice-Hall, 1966); Poetry of the Negro, Langston
   Hughes & Arna Bontemps (Doubleday, 1949).

LARSEN, NELLA. c.1893-? Novelist
Biographical-Personal. Born c.1893 in the Virgin Islands. Her
   father was black; her mother Danish. Educ.: Nursing Sch., Lin-
   coln Hospital, N.Y.C. (grad. 1915); N.Y. Public Lib. Training
   Sch.
Career-Professional. Apptd. Asst. Supt. of Nurses, Tuskegee (Ala.)
   Hospital (2 yrs.); City Health Dept., N.Y.C., 1918-22; Asst. &
   Children's Librn., N.Y. Public Lib., until 1926.

Lee, Don Luther

WRITINGS: Novels: <u>Quicksand</u> (Knopf, 1928); <u>Passing</u> (Knopf, 1929).
SIDELIGHTS: "Her novel, <u>Passing</u>...is probably the best treatment of the subject in Negro fiction...<u>Quicksand</u>...is tightly written ...is developed...with great power.
...There are those who are ahead of their time, and those who lag behind. Among the latter, during the Negro Renaissance of the 1920's was a group of novelists who sought a middle ground between the established traditions of the Negro novel and the radical innovations of the Harlem school...Nella Larsen, the only successful novelist among them.... Her first novel, <u>Quicksand</u>...is, perhaps the best of the period, with the exception of Jean Toomer's Cane" (<u>Negro Novel in America</u>).
Sources. <u>From the Dark Tower</u>, Arthur P. Davis (Howard U. Pr., 1974); <u>Negro Novel in America</u>, Robert A. Bone (Yale U. Pr., 1958); <u>Afro-American Writers</u>, Darwin T. Turner (Appleton, 1970).

Jewell Latimore. <u>See</u> Amini, Johari M.

LEE, DON LUTHER [Haki R. Madhubuti]. 1942- .
Poet, Black Nationalist, Editor, Publisher
Biographical-Personal. Born Feb. 23, 1942, in Little Rock, Ark. Son of James and Maxine [Graves] Lee. <u>Educ.</u>: A.A., Chgo. City Coll., Wilson Branch, 1963; DuSable Mus. of African Amer. Hist. Curator Apprenticeship 1963-67; Roosevelt U., 1966-67. <u>Family</u>: div.; son, Don. <u>Mailing address</u>: 7948 S. Ellis Ave., Chgo., Ill. 60619.
Career-Professional. Tchr.: Columbia Coll., Chgo., 1968; Northeastern Ill. State Coll., 1969-70; Tchr., Afro-Amer. Lit., Roosevelt U.; Poet-in-Residence, Cornell U., 1968-69; Instr., Black Lit., U. of Ill., 1969-71; Writer-in-Residence, Howard U., 1971; Morgan State Coll., 1972-73; Founder.-Dir., Third World Pr., Chgo. (1968); Ed., <u>Black Books Bulletin</u>; Founder, Inst. of Positive Educ.; Ed., <u>Black Pages Series</u>; Ed., Spec. Pan African Issue, <u>Journal of Black Poetry</u>.
WRITINGS: <u>Think Black</u> (Broadside Pr., 1967); <u>Black Pride</u> (Broadside Pr., 1968); <u>Don't Cry, Scream</u> (Broadside Pr., 1969); <u>We Walk the Way of the New World</u> (Broadside Pr., 1970); <u>Directionscore: Selected and New Poems</u> (Broadside Pr., 1971); <u>Dynamite Voices: Black Poets of the 1960's</u> (Broadside Pr., 1971). <u>To Gwen with Love</u>, Ed. with Patricia L. Brown & Francis Ward (Johnson Pub., 1971); <u>Book of Life</u> (Broadside Pr., 1973); <u>Minds and Institutions</u> (Broadside Pr., 1973); <u>From Plan to Planet; Life Studies: The</u>

Lee, Ulysses

Need for Afrikan Minds and Institutions, essays. In progress:
From the Beginning: Essays 1965-1974; Black Nationalist Poetry:
An Interpretation; Book of Ancestors, poetry; Son of Sundiata,
juvenile; Eight Weeks from Life, novel; Enemy: The Clash of
Races, essays. Anthol.: Potere Negro; For Malcolm; Black Arts;
The New Black Poetry; Black Poetry; A City in all Directions;
Black American Literature--Poetry; Today's Poets; Soulscript;
Grooving the Symbol; Doors into Poetry; etc. Period.: African
World; American Libraries; American Notes & Queries; Black Colle-
gian; Black Expressions; Black News; The Black Position; Black
Scholar; Black Talk; Black World; Change Magazine; Chicago Daily
Defender; Drum; Ebony; Evergreen; Freedomways; Journal of Black
Poetry; Liberator; Muhammed Speaks; Negro Digest; New York Times;
Pan-African; Roxbury Rebellion News; Scholastic Magazine; Washing-
ton Post.
HONORS AND AWARDS: Annual Poetry Award, Ellis's Bk. Stores, 1969;
Nat'l. Found. of the Arts (a working & recognition grant), 1970;
Black Recognition Award, Howard U. Student Govt., 1973.
SIDELIGHTS: Lee's new name means: Justice, Awakening, Strong.
His fields of interest include: criticism, publishing, editing
and farming (Broadside Authors and Artists).
  "Gwendolyn Brooks has written (in the introduction to Don't Cry,
Scream) 'Don Lee has no patience with black writers who do not di-
rect their blackness toward black audiences.' He has written,
'The black writer learns from his people...Black artists are cul-
ture stabilizers, bring back old values, and introducing new
ones'" (New Black Voices).
Sources. Black American Literature: Poetry, Ed. by Darwin T. Turner (Merrill, 1969); Black Insights, Ed. by Nick A. Ford (Ginn,
1971); Black World (Oct., 1974, Johnson Pub.); Broadside Authors
and Artists, Comp. by Leonead P. Bailey (Broadside Pr., 1974);
Cavalcade, Ed. by Arthur P. Davis & Saunders Redding (Houghton
Mifflin, 1971); Jump Bad, Ed. by Gwendolyn Brooks (Broadside Pr.,
1971); New Black Voices, Ed. by Abraham Chapman (New Amer. Lib.,
1972); To Gwen with Love, Ed. by Patricia L. Brown and Francis
Ward (Johnson Pub., 1971); Who's Who in America, 37th ed., 1972-73
(Marquis, 1972).

LEE, ULYSSES. 1914-1969. Lecturer, Historian
Biographical-Personal. Born 1914 in Wash., D.C. Educ.: Dunbar High
Sch., Wash., D.C.; B.A., (summa cum laude) Howard U.; Ph.D. (with
honors), U. of Chgo. Died 1969.
Career-Professional. Tchr.: Lincoln U. (Pa.), Virginia Union U.,
Lincoln U. (Mo.), Morgan State Coll., & U. of Pa.; Major, U.S.
Army (World War II).
WRITINGS: U.S. Army in World War II, the Employment of Negro
Troops, Spec. Stud. Ser. (Office of Chief of Military Hist.,

1966). The Negro Caravan, Ed. with Sterling A. Brown & Arthur P. Davis (1941). Contrib. to The Negro in Virginia (1940); and many nat'l. period. in fields of Eng. hist. and Amer. culture.
HONORS AND AWARDS: Phi Beta Kappa; Rosenwald Fellow, Rockefeller Post-War Fellow.
SIDELIGHTS: "In great demand as a lecturer, Lee appeared on many American campuses. Under the sponsorship of the American Society of African Culture, he lectured in 1965 in Nigeria, in Sierra Leone, and in the Cameroons....
    ...At the time of his death, Ulysses Lee was editor-designate of The Journal of Negro History" (Cavalcade).
Source. Cavalcade, Ed. by Arthur P. Davis & Saunders Redding (Houghton Mifflin, 1971).

LESTER, JULIUS. 1939- . Activist, Essayist, Juvenile Writer
Biographical-Personal. Born Jan. 27, 1939, in St. Louis, Mo. Educ.: B.A. (music & lit.) Fisk U., 1960. Family: m. Joan Steinau; d. Jody Simone, son, Malcolm Coltrane. Mailing address: Chilmark, Mass. 02535.
Career-Professional. Field Secy., SNCC; Columnist, The Guardian; Conducted weekly radio prog., WBAI, N.Y., "The Great Proletarian Cultural Revolution," 1968; Tchr., New Sch. for Soc. Res., "The History of Black Resistance," 1968-70; Traveled in Deep South collecting folk material; Folk singer; Has released two albums.
WRITINGS: Look Out Whitey! Black Power's Gon' Get Your Mama! (Dial, 1968); Revolutionary Notes (Baron, 1969); Black Folktales (Baron, 1969); Search for the New Land (Dial, 1969); To Be A Slave, juvenile (Dial, 1968; Dell, 1975); Seventh Son: The Thoughts and Writings of W. E. B. DuBois (Random House, 1971); The Knee-High Man and Other Tales (Dial, 1972); Long Journey Home: Stories from Black History (Dial, 1972; Dell, 1975); Two Love Stories (Dial, 1972); Who I Am (Dial, 1974). The Twelve String Guitar as played by Leadbelly, with Pete Seeger; All Is Well (Morrow, 1976). Contrib.: New York Times Sunday Book Review, Evergreen Review, Liberation, Nickle Review, Ebony.
HONORS AND AWARDS: Nancy Block Award; Runner-up, Newbery Award (both for To Be A Slave).
SIDELIGHTS. "...Lester is interested in black culture and in human rights, as is evident from his many political activities... attended the Bertrand Russell War Crimes Tribunal in Stockholm, and traveled to Vietnam to photograph the bombing there" (American Literature--Non Fiction).

Lewis, David Levering

Sources. <u>Afro-American Literature: Non Fiction</u>, Ed. by William
Adams (Houghton Mifflin, 1970); <u>Kaleidoscope</u>, Ed. by Robert Hayden (Harcourt, 1967); <u>Soulscript</u>, Ed. by June Jordan (Doubleday,
1970); <u>Books in Print</u>, Supplement, 1975-76 (Bowker, 1976).

LEWIS, DAVID LEVERING. 1936- . Teacher
Biographical-Personal. Born May 25, 1936, in Little Rock, Ark. Son
of John H. (educator) & Urnestine [Bell] Lewis. <u>Educ.</u>: B.A.,
Fisk U., 1956; M.A., Columbia U., 1958; Ph.D., London Sch. of
Econ. & Polit. Sci., U. of London, 1962. <u>Family</u>: m. Sharon Sis-
kind (book clerk), Apr. 15, 1966; son, Eric Levering, d. Allison
Lillian. <u>Mailing address</u>: 134 D St., S.E., Wash., D.C. 20003.
Career-Professional. Lectr., Mod. French Hist., U. of Ghana, Accra,
1963-64; Lectr., Mod. French Hist., Howard U., 1964-65; Asst.
Prof., Mod. French Hist., U. of Notre Dame, 1965-66; Assoc. Prof.,
Mod. French Hist., Morgan State Coll., 1966-70; Assoc. Prof., Mod.
French Hist., Fed. City Coll., Wash., D.C., 1970- . Fellow, Drug
Abuse Counc. of Ford Found., 1972-73.
WRITINGS: <u>Martin Luther King, A Critical Biography</u> (Praeger,
1971); <u>Prisoners of Honor: The Dreyfus Affair</u> (Morrow, 1973); <u>The
Public Image of Henry Ford: An American Folk Hero and His Company</u>
(Wayne State U. Pr., 1975).
HONORS AND AWARDS: Grants from Amer. Philosophical Soc., 1967, &
Social Sci. Res. Counc., 1971.
MEMBER: Amer. Hist. Assn.; Soc. for French Hist. Stud.; Amer.
Assn. of U. Profs.; Authors Guild; Phi Beta Kappa.
SIDELIGHTS: Bruce Douglas notes in <u>Christian Century</u>, "...a young
black intellectual [who] has written one of the best biographies
of Martin Luther King, Jr., to have appeared.... It is a crafts-
man's piece of work, carefully researched...well organized, felic-
itously written and sober and reflective in its judgments..."
(<u>Contemporary Authors</u>).
Sources. <u>Contemporary Authors</u>, Vols. 45-48, Ed. by Clare D. Kinsman
(Gale Res., 1974); <u>Books in Print</u>, Supplement, 1975-76 (Bowker,
1976).

LEWIS, EDWARD. 1940- . Publisher.
Biographical-Personal. Born May 15, 1940, in N.Y.C. <u>Educ.</u>: B.A.
(Polit. Sci.), 1963, M.A. (Internat. Relat.), 1965, U. of N. Mex.;
Public Admin.: Georgetown U., 1965-66; N.Y.U., 1967-69. <u>Family</u>:
Single. <u>Mailing address</u>: 300 E. 42nd St., N.Y., N.Y. 10017.
Career-Professional. Admin. Asst., City Mgr., Albuquerque, N. Mex.,
1964; Tchr., Internat. Relat. (Peace Corps Volunteers), U. of
N. Mex., 1964-65; Financial Analyst, 1st Nat'l. City Bank of N.Y.,
1964-65. Founder, Pub., <u>Essence</u> mag., 1970- .
Source. <u>1000 Successful Blacks</u>, Eds. of <u>Ebony</u> (Johnson Pub., 1973).

LEWIS, IDA ELIZABETH. 1935- . Publisher, Editor, Publishing Company Executive
Biographical-Personal. Born Sept. 22, 1935, in Malverne, Pa. D. of
Walter and Grace Mae [Walker] Lewis. Educ.: B.S., Sch. Public
Communications, Boston U., 1956. Mailing address: (Office) 515
Madison Ave., N.Y., N.Y. 10022.
Career-Professional. Financial & bus. writer, Amsterdam News, 1956-
59; Financial Ed., New York Age, 1960-63; Writer, Life mag.,
1964-65; Writer-broadcaster, BBC, 1967; Corresp., Jeune Afrique
mag., 1968-71; Ed.-in-Chief, Essence mag., 1970-71; Pres., Tanner
Public. Co., Inc., N.Y.C., 1972- ; Pub.-Ed., Encore American &
Worldwide News mag.; Pres., Teil House, Inc.
HONORS AND AWARDS: Recipient, Scarlet Key, Boston U., 1956; Jour-
nalism award, Assn. Study of Afro-Amer. Life & Hist., award, 1974;
Citizen of Yr. Award, Omega Psi Phi, 1975; Internat. Benin Award
for contrib. to Black people throughout world, 1975; Media execu-
tive Award, Nat'l. Youth Movement, 1975; Bicentennial Award,
Crisis mag., 1975.
MEMBER: Communication Inquiry into High Sch. Journalism; Bd. of
Dirs., Amer. Com. on Africa; Trus., Tougaloo Coll.; Nat'l. Counc.
of Negro Women; Amer. Management Assn.; Alpha Kappa Alpha.
Source. Who's Who in America, 39th ed., 1976-77 (Marquis, 1976).

LEWIS, SAMELLA SANDERS. 1924- . Art Historian,
Art Education
Biographical-Personal. Born Feb. 27, 1924, in
New Orleans, La. D. of Samuel and Rachel
[Taylor] Sanders. Educ.: Dillard U.,
1941-43; B.S., Hampton Inst., Va., 1945; Penn.
State U., 1947; M.A., 1948, Ph.D., 1951, Ohio
State U.; Tung-Hai U., Taiwan, 1962; N.Y.U.,
(summer) 1965; U. of S. Cal., 1964-66.
Family: m. Paul G. Lewis; son, Alan, son,
Claude. Mailing address: 1237 Masselin Ave.,
L.A., Cal. 90019.
Career-Professional. Assoc. Prof. of Art,
Scripps Coll. (Claremont Colls.), 1970- ;
Coord. of Educ., L.A. Co. Mus. of Art; Cal.
State Coll. at Dominguez Hills; Cal. State U.
at Long Beach; U. of State of New York; Fla. A. & M. U.; Morgan
State Coll.; Hampton Inst.
WRITINGS: Black Artists on Art, Vol. 1 (Ward Ritchie Pr., 1969);
Dimensions of Black, epilogue (1970); Black Artists on Art,
Vol. II (Ward Ritchie Pr., 1971); Portfolios on Contemporary Amer-
ican Artists: Raymond Saunders, Floyd Coleman, Elizabeth Catlett
(Contemp. Crafts, 1972). Art: African American (Harcourt, Brace
1975). Period.: "Significant Art," Informat, 1968; "Street Art

Lightfoot, Claude M.

of Black America," <u>Exxon Mag.</u>, 3rd quarter, 1973. Featured in:
"The Black Artist" (Film, Afro-Graphic, 1968); "<u>The Black Artist</u>,"
KNBC-TV, Los Angeles, 1968; feature article, <u>L.A. Times</u>, 1970;
<u>Essence Magazine</u>, 1973. Participation in other media: Prod. of
30 min. 16 mm color sound educ. films: "John Outterbridge/BLACK
ARTIST," 1969; "Bernie Casey/BLACK ARTIST," 1970; "Elizabeth Cat-
lett/BLACK ARTIST," 1972.
HONORS AND AWARDS: Delta Sigma Theta Scholarship, Dillard U.;
Hampton Inst. Art Scholarship; Amer. U. Fellow., Ohio State; Ful-
bright-1st Inst. of Chinese Civilization (Taiwan), Travel and
Study Grant to Far East--Chinese Art Hist., Lang. and Gen. Civili-
zation; NDEA Post-Doctorate Fellow. for study of Chinese Lang. &
Asian Civilization; N.Y. State-Ford Found. Grant, for study of
Chinese Art Hist.; Seminars: N.Y.U.; Metropolitan Mus. of Art;
Boston Mus. of Art; Harvard U.
MEMBER: Coll. Art Assn. of Amer.; Amer. Soc. for Aesthetics;
Nat'l. Conf. of Artists.
SIDELIGHTS: Lang. proficiency: Chinese, French, Spanish; Educ.
Specialties: Art Hist., Asian African, African-Amer. & European
Humanities, Studio-Painting, Graphics and Sculpture, Art Educ.
Rep. in Permanent Collec.: Atlanta U. Mus. of Contemporary Art;
Baltimore Mus. of Art; High Mus., Atlanta; Va. Mus. of Fine Arts;
Viktor Lowenfeld Memorial Collec., Penn State U.; U. of State of
N.Y.; Hampton Inst. Art collec.; Ohio Union Gallery, Columbus,
Ohio; Denison U. Art Gallery; Oakland Mus.; Palm Springs Mus.,
Joseph Hirshhorn Collec. Recent Exhibitions: Brockman Gallery,
Los Angeles, 1969; Occidental Coll., 1969; San Diego Art Mus.,
1969; Palm Springs Mus., 1969; Dimensions of Black, La Jolla Mus.
of Art, 1970; Cal. State Coll. at L.A., 1970; Lang Art Gallery,
1970 (Author).
Source. Author inform.

LIGHTFOOT, CLAUDE M. 1910- . Marxist Historian and Analyst
Biographical-Personal. Born 1910 in Lake Village, Ark. Moved with
family to Chgo. <u>Educ.</u>: Virginia Union U., Richmond.
Career-Professional. In 1930 became active spokesman for the Democratic Party, and was founder of 1st Young Men's Democratic Org.
in Chgo. Becoming active in unemployed struggles, joined Communist Party; headed Chgo.-area campaign to free Scottsboro Boys and
Angelo Herndon. Became Secy., League of Struggle for Negro
Rights; Bus. agent for Consolidated Trade Counc. of Negro Skilled
Workers; Elected to Communist Nat'l. Com. Since functioned on
both nat'l. & local levels.
WRITINGS: <u>Black Power and Liberation: A Communist View</u> (New Outlook, 1967); <u>Ghetto Rebellion to Black Liberation</u> (Internat.,
1968); <u>Black American and the World Revolution</u> (New Outlook,
1970); <u>Racism and Human Survival: The Lessons of Nazi Germany</u>

(Internat., 1972); The Effect of Education on Racism: The Two
German States and the USA (New Outlook, 1973).
SIDELIGHTS: In Chicago... "in 1919 he witnessed the race riots.
From an aunt, a follower of Marcus Garvey, he received his first
lessons in Black Nationalism.... Banned from membership in the
AFL, he was arrested and beaten by police as a result of numerous
picket lines and demonstrations. Under the Smith Act, he was
sentenced to five years in jail and a $10,000 fine and later re-
versed by the U.S. Supreme Court" (Ghetto Rebellion to Black Liberation).
Source. Ghetto Rebellion to Black Liberation, Claude M. Lightfoot,
(Internat. Pub., 1968); Books in Print, Supplement, 1975-76 (Bowker, 1976).

LINCOLN, CHARLES ERIC. 1924- . Professor of
Religion and Sociology, Lecturer, Consultant
Biographical-Personal. Born June 23, 1924, in
Athens, Ala. Son of Less and Mattie [Sowell]
Lincoln. Educ.: B.A., LeMoyne Coll., 1947;
M.A., Fisk U., 1954; B.D., U. of Chgo., 1956;
M.Ed., 1960, Ph.D., 1960, Boston U.; U. of
Chgo. Law Sch. (Post Baccalaureate), 1948-49;
Brown U. (Post Doctorate), 1964-65. Family:
1st m. Lucy Cook, 1961; son, Cecil Eric, d.
Joyce Elaine; from 2nd m.: d. Hilary Anne,
son, Less Charles II. Mailing address:
Dept. of Relig. & Philosophical Stud., Fisk
U., Nashville, Tenn. 37203.
Career-Professional. LeMoyne Coll., 1950-51;
Fisk U., 1953-54; Clark Coll.: Asst. Per-
sonnel Dean; Asst. & Assoc. Prof., Relig. & Phil.; Admin. Asst. to
Pres.; Prof. of Soc. Phil.; Prof. of Soc. Relat.; Dir. Inst. of
Soc. Relat., 1954-64. Boston U.: Dir., The Panel of Amer.,
Human Relat. Center, 1958-60; Adjunct Prof., Human Relat. Center,
1963-65. Dartmouth Coll., 1962-63; Brown U., Post-doctoral in-
tern, Coll. Admin., 1964-65; Portland State Coll., Prof. of
Sociol., 1965-67; Spelman Coll., 1966; San Francisco Theol. Sem.,
1966-67; Union Theol. Sem., Prof. of Sociol. & Relig., 1967-73;
Vassar Coll., Adjunct Prof. of Sociol., 1969-70; State U. of N.Y.
at Albany, Vis. Prof., 1970-72; Fordham U., Lincoln Center, Dir.,
African Stud. Prog., U. of Ghana at Fordham, (summer) 1970; U. of
Ghana, Dir. of Africa '70 Prog. of African Stud., Accra, Ghana,
1968-70; Queens Coll., Vis. Prof., Philosophy & Sociol., 1972;
(present) Prof. of Relig. & Sociol. & Chmn., Dept. of Relig. &
Philosophy Stud., Fisk U. and Adjunct Prof. of Ethics & Soc.,
Sch. of Divinity, Vanderbilt U.
WRITINGS: The Black Muslims in America (Beacon Pr., 1961, 1972);
My Face Is Black (Beacon Pr., 1964); Sounds of the Struggle (Mor-

Little, Malcolm

row, 1967); The Negro Pilgrimage in America (Bantam, 1967); Is
Anybody Listening? (Seabury, 1968); A Profile of Martin Luther
King, Jr. (Hill & Wang, 1969); The Blackamericans (Bantam, 1969);
The Black Church Since Frazier (Schocken, 1974); The Black Expe-
rience in Religion (Doubleday, 1974); Readings in Black Religion
(Doubleday, 1974); A Pictorial History of the Negro in America,
with Langston Hughes and Milton Meltzer (Crown, 1968, 1973). Ed.,
the C. Eric Lincoln Ser. in Black Religion, six titles, 1970-73.
Anthol.: Chronicles of Negro Protest, introd.; A Social History
of the American Negro; Great Documents in Black American History;
Bittersweet Encounter; and others. Pub. in ref. works: Encyclo-
pedia Americana; World Book; Encyclopaedia Britannica; American
Negro Reference Book; Encyclopedia of World Biography. Jls.:
Phylon; Central Christian Advocate; Reporter; Negro Digest; New
Englander; Progressive; New South; Perspective; New Leader; Jour-
nal of Social Issues; Concern; Christian Century; New York Times
Magazine; Church & Home; Ebony; Midstream; Pageant; Presbyterian
Survey; Daedalus; Current South African Outlook; Christianity &
Crisis; Union Seminary Quarterly Review; Psychiatry & Social Sci-
ence Review; Journal of Negro Education; Journal of Black Studies;
Evangelische Theologie; Black Collegian; & A.D.
HONORS AND AWARDS: Degrees: Carleton Coll., Northfield, Minn.,
LL.D., 1968; St. Michael's Coll., Winooski, Vt., L.H.D., 1972.
John Hay Whitney Fellow, 1957-58; Crusade Fellow, 1958-59; Human
Relat. Fellow, Boston U., 1958-60; Eli Lilly Fellow, 1959; Res.
Grant, Taconic Found., 1960; Post-Doctoral, Fund for Advancement
of Educ., 1964; Lectr., Amer. Spec. Abroad Prog. (State Dept.),
W. Europe, 1965; Art Inst. of Boston: Creative Communications
Award for "Distinctive Achievement in Lit.," 1970; Ford Found.
Res. Grant, 1970.
MEMBER: Bd. of Dirs.: Boston U.; Martin L. King, Jr. Memorial;
Black Acad. of Arts and Letters; Inst. for Relig. & Soc. Stud.;
Marquis Who's Who, Inc.
SIDELIGHTS: Toured Ethiopia as guest of His Holiness Abuna The-
ophilos, Patriarch of Ethiopian Orthodox Church. Guest lecturer,
97 colleges and universities; five distinguished university lec-
tures; consultant to 35 organizations and institutions, etc.
(Author).
Sources. Author inform.; Contemporary Authors, Vols. 1-4, Ed. by
James M. Ethridge and Barbara Kopala (Gale Res., 1967); Something
About the Author, Ed. by Anne Commire (Gale Res., 1973).

LITTLE, MALCOLM [Malcolm X]. 1925-1965. Black Nationalist
Biographical-Personal. Born May 19, 1925, in Omaha, Neb. Son of
Earl (minister) & Louise Little. Educ.: 8th grade; self-educated.
Family: m. Betty Shabazz; 6 daughters. Died Feb. 21, 1965.

Locke, Alain Leroy

Career-Professional. Sentenced to 10 yrs. in Charlestown (Mass.) State Prison for burglary; Black Muslim minister, Detroit; Founder, Black Muslim Temples throughout U.S.; Founder, Org. of Afro-Amer. Unity.
WRITINGS: The Autobiography of Malcolm X., in collaboration with Alex Haley (Grove, 1966); Malcolm X Speaks (1966); For Malcolm, Ed. by Dudley Randall & Margaret G. Burroughs (Broadside Pr., 1967).
SIDELIGHTS: "The Autobiography of Malcolm X ...is one of the greatest American success stories and most important social documents ever written" (Black Insights).

"In the society to which I was exposed as a black youth in America," he once commented, "for me to wind up in prison was just about inevitable." He also once remarked: "I believe that it would be almost impossible to find anywhere in America a black man who has lived further down in the mud of human society than I have been; or a black man who has been any more ignorant than I have been; or a black man who has suffered more anguish during his life than I have. But it is only after the deepest darkness that the greatest joy can come; it is only after slavery and prison that the sweetest appreciation of freedom can come" (Afro-American Literature--Non Fiction).

Sources. Afro-American Literature--Non Fiction, Ed. by William Adams, et al. (Houghton Mifflin, 1970); Black Insights, Ed. by Nick A. Ford (Ginn, 1971); Black Voices, Ed. by Abraham Chapman (New Amer. Lib., 1968); Forgotten Pages of American Literature, Ed. by Gerald W. Haslam (Houghton Mifflin, 1970).

LOCKE, ALAIN LEROY. 1886-1954. Philosopher, Writer, Critic, Scholar, Editor
Biographical-Personal. Born Sept. 13, 1886, in Phila., Pa. Son of Pliny Ishmael and Mary [Hawkins] Locke. Educ.: Phila. Sch. of Pedagogy, grad. 1904; B.A., Harvard U., 1907; Bachelor Litt. (Rhodes Scholar from Pa.), Oxford U., 1907-1910; U. of Berlin, 1910-11; Ph.D., Harvard U., 1918. Family: Single. Died June 1954.
Career-Professional. Asst. Prof., Philosophy & Educ., Howard U., 1912-16, Prof. and Head of Dept. of Philosophy for 40 yrs.; Exchange Prof., Fisk U.; Inter-Amer. Exchange Prof. New Sch. for Soc. Res., 1947; Coll. of City of N.Y., 1948.
WRITINGS: Race Contacts and Interracial Relations (1916); The New Negro (Boni, 1925); The Negro in America

171

Loftin, Elouise

(Amer. Literary Assn., 1933); Frederick Douglass, A Biography of
Anti-Slavery (1935); The Negro and His Music (1936); Negro Art--
Past and Present (1937); The Negro in Art (Assoc. in Negro Folk
Educ., 1941); When Peoples Meet, with Bernhard Stern (Hinds, Hay-
den & Eldredge, 1941). Ed.: Plays of Negro Life, with Montgomery
Gregory (1927); Four Negro Poets (1927); Associates in Negro Folk
Education, Bronze Booklet Ser. (1937). Contrib. ed., Survey
Graphic.
MEMBER: Phi Beta Kappa; Sigma Psi Phi; Theta Sigma; Phi Beta
Sigma; Amer. Ethnological Soc.; Amer. Negro Acad.; Negro Soc. for
Hist. Res.; Corresp. member, Academie des Sciences Coloniales
(Paris).
SIDELIGHTS: "As a philosopher, writer, critic, scholar in the so-
cial sciences, cultural mentor, and editor of The New Negro--the
Landmark collection of writing which registered the arrival of the
'Negro Renaissance' Alain Locke was a major force and figure in
the development of modern Negro American literature and culture"
(Black Voices).
  Toward the end of his life, Locke was preparing a study of the
Negro's place in American culture, which would have represented
his final views. Although he never lived to write the book, his
friend and colleague, Margaret Just Butcher, completed the study,
The Negro in American Culture (Knopf, 1956)" (Dark Symphony).
Sources. Blackamerican Literature, Ed. by Ruth Miller (Glencoe Pr.,
1971); Black Voices, Ed. by Abraham Chapman (New Amer. Lib.,
1968); Cavalcade, Ed. by Arthur P. Davis & Saunders Redding
(Houghton Mifflin, 1971); Dark Symphony, Ed. by James A. Emanuel
& Theodore L. Cross (Free Pr., 1968); Who Was Who in America,
Vol. III, 1951-60 (Marquis, 1960).

LOFTIN, ELOUISE. 1950- . Poet, Editor
Biographical-Personal. Born 1950 in Brooklyn, N.Y. Educ.: N.Y.U.
Career-Professional. Poetry Ed., Black Creation mag.
  WRITINGS: Jumbish, poetry (1972). Anthol.: Poetry of Black
America (1973). Period.: Essence, Présence Africaine, Confronta-
tion.
Source. Poetry of Black America, Ed. by Arnold Adoff (Harper & Row,
1973).

LOGAN, RAYFORD WHITTINGHAM. 1897- . Historian, Professor of
History
Biographical-Personal. Born Jan. 7, 1897, in Wash., D.C. Son of
Arthur C. and Martha [Whittingham] Logan. Educ.: B.A., 1917,
M.A., 1929, Williams Coll.; M.A., 1932, Ph.D., 1936, Harvard U.
Family: m. Ruth Robinson, 1927. Mailing address: 3001 Veazey
Terrace, N.W., Apt. 326, Wash., D.C. 20008.

Logan, Rayford Whittingham

Career-Professional. Head, Dept. of Hist., Va. Union U., 1925-30; Head, Dept. of Hist., Atlanta U., 1933-38; Prof., Howard U., 1938- , Head, Hist. Dept., 1942-64.
WRITINGS: The Diplomatic Relations of the United States with Haiti, 1776-1891 (U. of N.C. Pr., 1941; Kraus repr., 1969); The Senate and the Versailles Mandate System (Greenwood, repr. of 1945 ed., 1975); The Negro in American Life and Thought: The Nadir, 1877-1901 (Dial, 1954); The Negro in the United States, A Brief History (Van Nostrand, 1957); The African Mandates in World Politics (Public Affairs Pr., 1958); The Betrayal of the Negro: From Rutherford B. Hayes to Woodrow Wilson (Collier-MacMillan, 1965); The American Negro: Old World Background and New World Experience, with Irving S. Cohen (Houghton Mifflin, 1967, 1970); Haiti and the Dominican Republic (Oxford U. Pr., 1968); Howard University: The First Hundred Years, 1867-1967 (N.Y.U., auspices of Howard U., 1969). Ed.: What the Negro Wants (U. of N.C. Pr., 1944, Agathon Pr., repr., 1969); Memoirs of a Monticello Slave (U. of Va. Pr., 1951) & The Attitude of the Southern White Press Toward Negro Suffrage, 1932-1940 (1940); Four Took Freedom: The Lives of Harriet Tubman, Frederick Douglass, Robert Smalls and Blanche K. Bruce (Doubleday, n.d.). Jls.: Hispanic American History Review; Annals of Political & Social Science; Journal of Negro History; Journal of Negro Education; Negro History Bulletin; Crisis; Opportunity; Southern Workman; World Tomorrow; Inter-American Affairs; Current History; Phylon; Nation; New Republic; Current.
HONORS AND AWARDS: Phi Beta Kappa; Commander of Nat'l. Order of Honor & Merit, Republic of Haiti.
MEMBER: Amer. Hist. Assn.; Amer. Soc. of Internat. Law; Soc. for French Hist. Stud.; African Stud. Assn.; Latin Amer. Stud. Assn.; Alpha Phi Alpha; Sigma Pi Phi.
SIDELIGHTS: Lt., 372nd Inf., 93rd Div., World War I; Asst. to Carter G. Woodson, ASNLH (AFRO USA).
Sources. AFRO USA, Comp. by Harry A. Ploski & Ernest Kaiser (Bellwether, 1971); author inform.; Contemporary Authors, Vols. 1-4, rev., Ed. by James M. Ethridge & Barbara Kopala (Gale Res., 1967); Negro Caravan, Ed. by Sterling A. Brown, et al. (Arno Pr. & N.Y. Times, 1969); Books in Print, Supplement, 1975-76 (Bowker, 1976).

Lomax, Louis Emanuel

LOMAX, LOUIS EMANUEL. 1922-1970. Writer, News
Analyst
Biographical-Personal. Born Aug. 16, 1922, in
Valdosta, Ga. Son of James (teacher & cler-
gyman) and Fannie [Hardon] Lomax. Educ.:
B.A., Paine Coll., Augusta, Ga., 1942; Grad.
study: American U.; Yale U. Family: 4th m.
Robinette Kirk, Mar. 1, 1968; stepchildren:
William Kirk, Robinette Kirk. Killed in
automobile accident, 1970.
Career-Professional. Asst. Prof. of Philosophy,
Ga. State Coll., Savannah; Newspaperman;
Newscaster, WNTA-TV, N.Y., 1958-60; News
writer, "Mike Wallace Show"; Host on TV
prog., "Louis Lomax," L.A., Cal.; News ana-
lyst, KTTV, L.A.; Syndicated columnist, N.
Amer. Newspaper Alliance.
WRITINGS: The Reluctant African (Harper & Row, 1960); The Negro
Revolt (Harper & Row, 1962); When the Word Is Given (World, 1964);
Thailand: The War That Is, The War That Will Be (Random House,
1966). Contrib.: Life; Look; Saturday Evening Post; Harper's;
Pageant; Nation; New Leader.
HONORS AND AWARDS: Annisfield-Wolf Award for best book concerned
with racial problems, 1960, for The Reluctant African; Two honor-
ary doctorates.
SIDELIGHTS: Editor of college newspaper, The Paineite. First
member of his race to appear on TV as a newsman; later became Di-
rector of News for WNEW-TV, in New York (The Reluctant African).
Sources. Contemporary Authors, Vols. 25-28, Ed. by Carolyn Riley
(Gale Res., 1970); Negro Handbook, Comp. by Eds. of Ebony (Johnson
Pub., 1966); The Reluctant African, Louis Lomax (Harper & Row,
1960).

LOMAX, PEARL CLEAGE. 1948- . Playwright, Poet
Biographical-Personal. Born Dec. 7, 1948, in Springfield, Mass.
D. of Albert (minister) and Doris [Graham] Cleage. Educ.: Howard
U., 1966-69; Yale U., 1969; U. of W. Indies, 1971; B.A., Spelman
Coll., 1972; Atlanta U. (grad. study), 1972- . Family: m.
Michael L. Lomax (grad. student & tchr.) Oct. 31, 1969. Mailing
address: 1331 Sharon St., N.W., Atlanta, Ga. 30314.
Career-Professional. Martin Luther King, Jr. Archival Lib., Atlanta
(mem. of field staff), 1969-70; Asst. Dir., S. Educ. Prog., Inc.,
1970- ; Writer & Assoc. Prod., WQXI, Atlanta, 1972- ; Hostess/
Interviewer, "Black Viewpoints," prod. by Clark Coll., WETV,
Atlanta, 1972; Staff Writer, Ebony Beat Journal, WQXI, Atlanta,
1972.

Long, Charles Houston

WRITINGS: Hymn for the Rebels, one-act play (Howard U., 1968) and
Duet for Three Voices, one-act play (Howard U.); The Sale, one-act
play (Spelman Coll., Atlanta, 1972). We Don't Need No Music,
poetry (Broadside Pr., 1972). In progress: "Rap's Song," a play
& a second book of poems. Anthol.: The Insistent Present, Ed. by
John Mahoney & John Schmittroth; We Speak As Liberators, Ed. by
Orde Coombs; A Rock Against the Wind, Ed. by Lindsay Patterson.
Period.: Readers & Writers, Promethean, Afro-American Review,
Journal of Black Poetry, Dues, Essence, Pride, Black World, Ms.
SIDELIGHTS: "I am a Black woman. My writing of necessity re-
flects my blackness and my womanhood. I see myself as having a
responsibility to remain aware of, and a part of, Black people. I
think my work should be about changing Black people, informing
Black people, unifying Black people, and contributing to the
struggle for nationhood" (Contemporary Authors).
Sources. Contemporary Authors, Vols. 41-44, Ed. by Clare D. Kinsman
(Gale Res., 1974); Poetry of Black America, Ed. by Arnold Adoff
(Harper & Row, 1973).

LONG, CHARLES HOUSTON. 1926- . Professor, History of Religions
Biographical-Personal. Born Aug. 23, 1926, in Little Rock, Ark.
Son of Samuel Preston and Diamond Geneva [Thompson] Long. Educ.:
B.D., 1953, Ph.D., 1961, U. of Chgo. Family: m. Alice Freeman;
son, John, d. Carolyn, son, Christopher, son, David. Mailing ad-
dress: Murphey Hall, U. of N.C., Chapel Hill, N.C. 27514.
Career-Professional. U. of Chgo.: Dean of Students, Divinity Sch.
& Instr., Hist. of Relig., 1956-60; Asst. Prof., Hist. of Relig.,
1960-62; Assoc. Prof., Hist. of Relig., 1963-71; Prof., Hist. of
Relig., 1971-74. Cons., Encyclopaedia Britannica. Present:
William Rand Kenan, Jr., Prof., Hist. of Relig., U. of N.C. at
Chapel Hill & Prof., Hist. of Relig., Duke U., Durham, N.C.
WRITINGS: Ph.D. dissertation, Myth, Culture, and History in West
Africa (U. of Chgo., 1960); Alpha, the Myths of Creation (Brazil-
ler, 1963); Ed. with Joseph Kitagawa, The History of Religions:
Essays in Understanding (U. of Chgo., 1967); Ed. with Joseph Kita-
gawa, Myths and Symbols: Essays in Honor of Mircea Eliade (U. of
Chgo., 1969). Jls.: History of Religions, Criterion, Anglican
Theological Review, Journal of American Academy of Religion.
Articles in Encyclopaedia Britannica: "Hell in Other Religions,"
"Primitive Religion," "Celibacy," (all in 14th ed.); "Creation,
Myths and Doctrines," 15th ed. Also book reviews.
HONORS AND AWARDS: U. fellow, U. of Chgo., 1955; Guggenheim Fel-
low, 1971-72; Doctor of Humane Letters, Dickinson Coll., 1971.
MEMBER: Soc. for Relig. & Higher Educ.; Internat. Assn. of His-
torians of Relig.; Amer. Soc. for the Study of Relig.; Soc. for
Study of Black Relig.; Amer. Acad. of Relig.--Past Pres.

Long, Doughty

SIDELIGHTS: While at U. of Chgo., served as: Chmn., Hist. of
Relig. Field; Chmn., Hist. of Philosophy Prog., Coll. of U. of
Chgo.; Chmn. African Stud. Com. He was one of the founders, with
Mircea Eliade and Joseph Kitagawa, of journal, History of Reli-
gions and served as one of editors from 1961 through 1974 (Author).
Source. Author inform.

LONG, DOUGHTY. 1942- . Poet
Biographical-Personal. Born 1942 in Atlanta, Ga.
Career-Professional.
   WRITINGS: Poetry: Black Love, Black Hope (Broadside Pr., 1971);
Song for Nia (Broadside Pr., 1971). Contrib. to various periodi-
cals and anthologies.
   SIDELIGHTS: He has spent two years in Africa, and has traveled
extensively throughout the U.S. and the Caribbean (Poetry of Black
America).
Source. Poetry of Black America, Ed. by Arnold Adoff (Harper & Row,
   1973).

LONG, RICHARD ALEXANDER. 1927- . Scholar,
Teacher
Biographical-Personal. Born Feb. 2, 1927, in
   Phila., Pa. Son of Thaddeus and Leila [Wash-
   ington] Long. Educ.: B.A., M.A., Temple U.;
   Docteur ès Lettres, U. of Poitiers. Family:
   Single. Mailing address: Atlanta U., 223
   Chestnut St., S.W., Atlanta, Ga. 30314.
Career-Professional. Dir., Center for African
   and African-Amer. Stud., Atlanta U.; Vis.
   Prof., Afro-Amer. Stud. Dept., Harvard U.
   WRITINGS: Negritude: Essays and Studies,
   co-ed., with Albert H. Berrian (Hampton Inst.
   Pr., 1967); Afro-American Writing: Prose and
   Poetry, co-ed., with Eugenia Collier (N.Y.U.
   Pr., 1972); An Outline of African Art (1974).
Has also written poems, plays, and scenarios. Frequent contrib. to
CLA Journal & others.
HONORS AND AWARDS: Fulbright Scholar, France, 1957-58.
SIDELIGHTS: The theme of Long's presidential address to the 1970
convention of the College Language Association was that "the con-
temporary Black Arts and Black Studies movements are devoting at-
tention to the African roots of Black cultures....A student of
art and other branches of the humanities, in addition to litera-
ture, Professor Long has made more than ten trips to Europe...and
has traveled extensively in North and West Africa, the West Indies,
South America, and Mexico" (New Black Voices).
Sources. Author inform.; Afro-American Writing, Ed. by Richard A.
   Long & Eugenia Collier (N.Y.U. Pr., 1972); New Black Voices, Ed. by
   Abraham Chapman (New Amer. Lib., 1972).

176

LORDE, AUDRE. 1934- . Poet, Librarian
Biographical-Personal. Born Feb. 18, 1934, in N.Y.C. Educ.: U. of
Mexico, 1954-55; B.A., Hunter Coll., 1959; M.L.S., Columbia U.,
1961. Family: m. Edwin A. Rollins; d. Elizabeth, son, Jonno.
Mailing address: 626 Riverside Dr., N.Y., N.Y. 10031.
Career-Professional. Lib. clerk, N.Y. Public Lib., 1955-58; Arts &
Crafts supv., Police Athletic League, 1958-59; Soc. Investigator,
Bureau of Child Welfare, 1959-60; Young Adult Librn., Mt. Vernon
Public Lib., 1960-62; Self-employed, 1962-65; Head Librn., Town
Sch., 1965-68; Poet-in-Residence, Tougaloo Coll., Summer 1968;
Lectr., City Coll. N.Y., 1968-69; Lectr., Lehman Coll., City Coll.
N.Y., 1968-70; Lectr., John Jay Coll., City Coll. N.Y., 1970- .
WRITINGS: Poetry: The First Cities (Poets Pr., 1968); Cables To
Rage (London: Paul Bremen, 1970); From a Land Where Other People
Live. Anthol.: Beyond the Blues (1962); Sixes and Sevens (1962);
New Negro Poets: U.S.A. (1964); The New Black Poets (1969); The
Black Woman (1971); Poetry of Black America (1973). Period.:
Journal of Black Poetry; Negro Digest/Black World; Transatlantic
Review; Freedomways; Women: A Liberation Journal.
HONORS AND AWARDS: NEA grant, Poet-in-Residence, Tougaloo Coll.
Sources. Ebony (Johnson Pub., March 1974); New Black Voices, Ed. by
Abraham Chapman (New Amer. Lib., 1972); Poetry of Black America,
Ed. by Arnold Adoff (Harper & Row, 1973).

LUCAS, WILMER FRANCIS, JR. 1927- . Short
Story Writer, Playwright-Producer, Editor, Teacher
Biographical-Personal. Born Sept. 1, 1927, in
Brooklyn, N.Y. Son of Wilmer Francis, Sr. and
Inez [Williams] Lucas. Educ.: N.Y.U. (Eng.
Lit.), 1948. Family: m. Cleo Melissa Martin;
son, Alain Francis. Mailing address: 1936
Prospect Place, Knoxville, Tenn. 37015.
Career-Professional. Founder, Artistic & Execu-
tive Dir., The Carpetbag Theatre, Inc., Knox-
ville, 1971- ; Instr., Humanities, Div. of
Continuing Ed., U. of Tenn., Knoxville,
1972-73; Co.-Dir., Humanities Summer Prog.,
U. of Tenn., 1972; Spec. Humanities Cons. &
Lectr., Educ. Opportunities, Plan Center, U.
of Tenn., 1971-72; Dir., Black Experience
Inst. & Related Spec. Prog., U. of Tenn., 1970-71; Writer-in-
Residence, Knoxville Coll., 1968-70; Vis. Lectr., Eng. Lincoln U.,
Pa., 1966-67; Faculty, New Sch. for Soc. Res., N.Y.C., 1962-68;
Ed. at Large & Columnist, Knoxville News-Spectrum, 1974- ;
Contrib. Ed., Our Voice Magazine, Knoxville, 1970-72; Bk. Review
Ed., East Village Other, N.Y.C., 1968-69; Prod.-Dir., "The Carpet-
bag Theatre Presents," Radio Station WUOT-FM, Knoxville, 1972 to
present.

McCluskey, John A.

WRITINGS: Bottom Fishing; a novella and other stories (Carpetbag Pr., 1974); Patent Leather Sunday; and S'more One Act Plays, collec. of 10 one-act plays (Carpetbag Pr., 1975). In progress: Tropical Philadelphia, Bk. I of trilogy; Two collec. of short stories, untitled; Monkey See--Monkey Do: or The Hothouse Black, novel; The Hunchbacks of Knoxville, non-fic. dime novel; First Dominion, essays & criticisms; Uncle Willy's Laws, humorous & serious essays; Bagpipes, essays & criticism.
HONORS AND AWARDS: Day Found. Grant (for Writer-in-Residency, Knoxville Coll.), 1968-70; NEA Award & Grant (for perpetuation of Carpetbag Theatre, Inc.), 1973 to present; Spec. Proclamation for Carpetbag Theatre from City of Knoxville & Mayor Kyle Testerman, as "Carpetbag Theatre Week" (Oct. 8-13, 1973).
MEMBER: Authors Guild of Amer.; Duke Ellington Soc. (N.Y.); Amer. Comparative Lit. Assn.; Popular Culture Assn. (Coord. for State of Tenn.); Amer. Film Inst.; Theatre-Art Advis. Counc., Tenn. Arts Com.; Greater Knoxville Com. for the Arts; Black Merit Acad.; Chmn., Duke Ellington Cancer Center Fund, Knoxville Chap.
SIDELIGHTS: The following are affiliated with the Carpetbag Theatre, Inc.: Dance Theatre, Writers Workshop, Artists Workshop, Press, Drum & Bugle Ensemble, Children's Theatre, Film Associates, Lecture Bureau, & Summer St. Theatre (Author).
Source. Author inform.

McCLUSKEY, JOHN A. 1944- . Novelist, Teacher
Biographical-Personal. Born 1944 in Middletown, Ohio. Educ.: B.A., Harvard U., 1966; M.A. (Eng. & Creative Writing), Stanford U., 1972. Family: wife & son.
Career-Professional. Tchr. in Ala. and Ind. Tchr., Afro-Amer. Lit., Humanities Div., Case-Western Reserve U., Cleveland.
WRITINGS: Look What They Done to My Song, a novel (Random House, 1974). Stories from Black History: Nine Stories, 5 vols., Ed. (New Day Pr., 1975). Contrib. to Black World.
Source. Look What They Done to My Song, John A. McCluskey (Random House, 1974).

McGAUGH, LAWRENCE WALTER, JR. 1940- . Art Teacher, Poet
Biographical-Personal. Born Oct. 11, 1940, in Newton, Kan. Son of Lawrence and Mrs. McGaugh, Sr. Educ: B.F.A., San Francisco Art Inst., 1971. Family: m. Marcy McGaugh, d. Jhana, d. Genesse. Mailing address: 2419 Prince St., Berkeley, Cal. 94705.
Career-Professional. Art tchr., Berkeley Pub. Schs.
WRITINGS: A Fifth Sunday and Other Poems (Oyez, 1965); Vacuum Cantos and Other Poems

McKay, Claude

(Oyez, 1969). In progress: currently working on a novel and more poems. Anthol.: Black Out Loud: The Poetry of Black America.
SIDELIGHTS: He has had his artwork exhibited in San Francisco, in the Oakland Museum show "New Perspectives in Black Art," and was included in Black Artists on Art (1969) (Author).
Sources. Author inform.; The Poetry of Black America, Ed. by Arnold Adoff (Harper & Row, 1973).

McKAY, CLAUDE. 1889-1948. Poet, Novelist
Biographical-Personal. Born Sept. 15, 1889, in Sunny Ville, Jamaica, Brit. W. Indies. Son of Thomas Francis and Ann Elizabeth [Edwards] McKay. Educ.: Tuskegee Inst., 1912; Kan. State Coll., 1912-14. Family: m. and div. Died in Chicago, May 22, 1948.
Career-Professional. Apprentice to cabinet maker & wheelwright in Jamaica; Reporter, Workers' Dreadnaught, London; Assoc. Ed., The Liberator (under Max Eastman), 1919-22; Researcher, Nat'l. Catholic Org.
WRITINGS: Poems: Songs of Jamaica (1911); Constabulary Ballads (1912); Spring in New Hampshire (1920); Harlem Shadows (Harcourt, 1922). Novels: Home to Harlem (Harper & Row, 1928); Banjo (Harper & Row, 1929); Banana Bottom (Harper & Row, 1933); Gingertown, short stories (Harper & Row, 1932); A Long Way from Home, travel autobiog. (Furman, 1937); Harlem: Negro Metropolis (Dutton, 1940); Selected Poems of Claude McKay (Twayne, 1971); Selected Poems, posthumous (Bookman, 1953); My Green Hills of Jamaica (Howard U. Pr., 1975). Anthol.: This Singing World for Younger Children; Caroling Dusk; Twentieth Century Poetry; Lyric America, 1630-1930; The Book of American Negro Poetry; Modern American Poetry; Anthology for the Enjoyment of Poetry; Golden Slippers; Poetry of Freedom; Poetry of the Negro, 1746-1949; The Black Poets.
HONORS AND AWARDS: 1st Black awarded medal of Inst. of Arts & Sci. (Jamaica); Winner, Harmon Gold Medal Award for Lit. (for Home to Harlem).
SIDELIGHTS: Greatly influenced by an elder brother, a teacher and possessor of a good library, who contributed to his early education. Considered "l'enfant terrible" of Harlem Renaissance (Negro Novel in America); led revolt against middle class and identified with the masses. Travelled widely, living in England, France, Russia, and North Africa (Broadside Authors and Artists).
Sources. Black Insights, Ed. by Nick A. Ford (Ginn, 1971); Black Poets of the United States, Jean Wagner, Transl. by Kenneth Douglas (U. of Ill., 1973); Black Voices, Ed. by Abraham Chapman (New

McKissick, Floyd Bixler

Amer. Lib., 1968); <u>Book of American Negro Poetry</u>, Ed. by James W.
Johnson (Harcourt, 1959); <u>Broadside Authors and Artists</u>, Ed. by
Leaonead P. Bailey (Broadside Pr., 1974); <u>Negro Novel in America</u>,
Robert A. Bone (Yale U. Pr., 1958); <u>Who Was Who in America</u>,
Vol. 2, 1943-50 (Marquis, 1950); <u>Books in Print</u>, Supplement,
1975-76 (Bowker, 1976).

McKISSICK, FLOYD BIXLER. 1922- . Activist,
Lawyer, Organization Executive
Biographical-Personal. Born Mar. 9, 1922, in
Asheville, N.C. Son of Ernest Boyce and Mag-
nolia Ester [Thompson] McKissick. <u>Educ.</u>:
Morehouse Coll., Atlanta; B.A., N.C. Coll.,
Durham; LL.B., U. of N.C., Chapel Hill, 1952.
<u>Family</u>: m. Evelyn Williams, Sept. 1, 1942;
d. Jocelyn D., d. Andree Y., son, Floyd Bix-
ler, d. Stephanie Charmaine. <u>Mailing ad-
dress</u>: 414 W. 149th St., N.Y., N.Y. 10031.
Career-Professional. Attorney, 1952- ; Counsel, CORE & Nat'l. Dir., 1960-68.
WRITINGS: <u>Three-fifths of a Man</u> (Macmillan,
1968); <u>Black Power and the World Revolution</u>,
with W. W. Worthy (Harper & Row, 1972).
SIDELIGHTS: "...he applied for admission to the University of
North Carolina Law School at Chapel Hill and, with the legal
counsel of Thurgood Marshall, succeeded in breaking the racial
barrier at that institution and becoming the first Negro to take
an LL.B. degree there.
...during the James Meredith March Against Fear in Mississippi,
McKissick joined Stokely Carmichael in his rallying cry of 'Black
Power...'...'The black masses have not been elevated by the (anti-
poverty) program.' McKissick explained in a speech at the [1966
CORE] convention. 'As long as the white man has all the power and
money, nothing will happen. The only way to achieve meaningful
change is to take power.'"
...'Black power...means putting power in black people's hands.
We don't have any, and we want some. That is simply what it
means'" (<u>Current Biography</u>).
Source. <u>Current Biography, 1968</u>, Ed. by Charles Moritz (H. W. Wilson,
1968).

MCLLELAN, GEORGE MARION. 1860-1934. Poet, Minister, Teacher
Biographical-Personal. Born 1860 in Belfast, Tenn. <u>Educ.</u>: B.A.,
1885, M.A., 1890, Fisk U.; B.D., Hartford (Conn.) Theol. Sem.,
1886. <u>Family</u>: m. 1888. Died 1934.
Career-Professional. Tchr. & Chaplain, State Normal Sch., Normal,
Ala.; Pastor, Congregational Church, Memphis, 1897-99; Tchr., Eng.
& Latin, Central High Sch., Louisville, 1911-1917.

McNeil, Albert J.

WRITINGS: Poetry: <u>Poems</u> (Nashville, 1895); <u>Book of Poems and
Short Stories</u> (Nashville, 1895); <u>Old Greenbottom Inn</u> (1896); <u>Songs
of a Southerner</u> (Boston, 1896); <u>Path of Dreams</u> (Louisville, 1916).
SIDELIGHTS: "...Although, or perhaps because, he was well educated, he was kept on the go, serving as financial agent for Fisk
University seeking funds up and down the eastern seaboard, but
especially in New England" (<u>Early Black American Poets</u>).
   "He is a gentle poet of nature, of the seasons, of birds and
flowers and woodland scenes. His work is after the long-accepted
patterns, but possesses a distinct charm. His best poems are collected in <u>The Path of Dreams</u>.... He is exceptional in that writing when and where he did, this collection contains no dialect
poetry" (<u>Book of American Negro Poetry</u>).
Sources. <u>Book of American Negro Poetry</u>, Ed. by James W. Johnson
   (Harcourt, 1959); <u>Early Black American Poets</u>, Ed. by William H.
   Robinson, Jr. (Wm. C. Brown, 1969).

McNEIL, ALBERT J. 1920- . Professor of Music, Choir Director
Biographical-Personal. Born Feb. 14, 1920, in L.A., Cal. Son of
   John and Rhodier [Robertson] McNeil. <u>Educ.</u>: Polytechnic High
   Sch.; B.A., UCLA; M.A., Doctoral candidate, U. of S. Cal. <u>Family</u>:
   m. Helen; son, Richard. <u>Mailing address</u>: 3940 Cloverdale, L.A.,
   Cal. 90008.
Career-Professional. Tchr., music in L.A.: Hamil St. Elem. Sch.; Car-
   ver, Sun Valley & Audubon Jr. High; Dorsey High Sch.; Prof. of Mu-
   sic, U. of Cal., Davis. Choir director: Peoples Independent Church
   of Christ,L.A. & (Congregational) Church of Christian Fellowship,L.A.
   WRITINGS: Books: <u>Silver Burdette Music</u>, ser., grades Kinder-
   garten through 8, with Bennett Reimer & Mary Hoffman (Silver
   Burdette, 1975-76). Record: "Music of the Black Man in America,"
   with Roberta McLaughlin, performed by The Los Angeles Jubilee
   Singers. "Music of the Black Man in America," sound filmstrip
   sets, with Roberta McLaughlin--includes <u>Teaching Guides</u> for grades
   5 through 8 (Glendale, Cal., Bowmar Pub. Co., 1974).
   MEMBER: 1st V. Pres., Nat'l. Assn. of Negro Musicians; Chmn.,
   Ethnic Music, 1974 Nat'l. Convention of Music Educators Nat'l.
   Conf.
   SIDELIGHTS: "The Los Angeles Jubilee Singers toured Europe and
   the Middle East for six months during 1972, drawing ovations and
   rave reviews.... In 1971, they toured the Far East, and, in addition, represented the United States at the Festival Mundial del
   Folklore in Guadalajara, receiving the Mexican Government's medal
   of honor. They participated in the first performance of Margaret
   Bonds' "Credo" with the Los Angeles Philharmonic Orchestra under
   Zubin Mehta. Albert McNeil created this superb group and has attracted to its ranks some of the finest Black talent in the Western United States" (Brochure, Bowmar World Cultural Series).

McPherson, James Alan

Sources. Author inform.; <u>Silver Burdette Music</u>, Bennett Reimer, Mary
    Hoffman & Albert McNeil, Morristown N.J. (Silver Burdette, 1975-
    76); Wrodl Culture Series Brochure, "Music of the Black Man in
    America" (Bowmar Pub., 1974).

McPHERSON, JAMES ALAN. 1943- . Short Story
Writer, Contributing Editor, Teacher
Biographical-Personal. Born Sept. 16, 1943, in
    Savannah, Ga. Son of James Allen and Mabel
    [Smalls] McPherson. <u>Educ.</u>: Morris Brown
    Coll., Atlanta, 1961-63, 1964-65 (B.A.,
    1965); Morgan State Coll., Baltimore, 1963-
    64; LL.B. Harvard U., 1968; M.F.A., U. of
    Iowa, 1969. <u>Family</u>: m. Sarah C. McPherson.
    <u>Mailing address</u>: c/o Atlantic Monthly Pr.,
    8 Arlington St., Boston, Mass. 02116.
Career-Professional. Instr., Writing, Law Sch.,
    U. of Iowa, Iowa City, 1968-69, U. Instr. in
    Afro-Amer. Lit., 1969; Tchr., Fic. & Critical
    Writing, U. of Cal., Santa Cruz, 1969-70;
    Tchr., Fic. Writing, Harvard U., Summer 1972;
Contrib. Ed., <u>Atlantic Monthly</u>, 1969- .
WRITINGS: <u>Hue and Cry</u>, short stories (Atlantic-Little, Brown,
1969). Short stories, etc. in <u>Atlantic</u>, <u>Playboy</u>, <u>Reader's Digest</u>
and "little" magazines. In progress: a novel and a second collection of short stories.
HONORS AND AWARDS: Combined <u>Reader's Digest</u>-United Negro Coll.
Fund Prize for Lit., 1965; <u>Atlantic</u> Award for best new story of
1968; Award from <u>Atlantic</u> to write vol. of short stories which was
to be entitled <u>Hue and Cry</u>; Guggenheim Fellow, 1972-73.
SIDELIGHTS: Ralph Ellison has hailed McPherson as a "writer of
insight, sympathy, and humor and one of the most gifted young
Americans I've had the privilege to read" (<u>New Black Voices</u>).
Sources. Author inform.; <u>Black Insights,</u> Ed. by Nick A. Ford (Ginn,
    1971); <u>Contemporary Authors</u>, Vol. 25-28, Ed. by Carolyn Riley
    (Gale Res., 1971); <u>New Black Voices</u>, Ed. by Abraham Chapman (New
    Amer. Lib., 1972).

MADGETT, NAOMI LONG. 1923- . Poet, Teacher
Biographical-Personal. Born July 5, 1923, in Norfolk, Va. D. of
    Clarence Marcellus, Sr. (minister) and Maude Selena [Hilton] Long.
    <u>Educ.</u>: B.A. (hon.) Va. State Coll., 1945; M.A., Wayne State U.,
    1956; (Grad. study): U. of Detroit & Wayne State U. <u>Family</u>: m.
    Leonard P. Andrews, Sr.; d. Jill (Witherspoon) Boyer. <u>Mailing ad-
    dress</u>: 16886 Inverness Ave., Detroit, Mich. 48221.
Career-Professional. Tchr., Eng., Northwestern High Sch., Detroit,
    1955-68; Assoc. Prof. of Eng., E. Mich. U., 1968-73, Prof.,

Major, Clarence

1973-   ; Assoc. Ed., Lotus Press, 1974-   ;
Staff, Writers' Workshop (annual), Oakland
U.; Participant, Poetry Readings in the
Classroom (Mich. Counc. for the Arts).
WRITINGS: Poetry: Songs to a Phantom Night-
ingale (Fortuny's, 1941; U. of Mich. Micro-
film, 1970); One and the Many (Exposition
Pr., 1956, U. Microfilm, 1970); Star By Star
(Harlo, 1965; Evenill, 1970); Pink Ladies in
the Afternoon (Lotus, 1972). Success in Lan-
guage and Literature, textbook, with Ethel
Tincher & Henry B. Maloney (Follett, 1967).
Anthol. (included in more than 50): Poetry
of the Negro, 1746-1949; American Literature
By Negro Authors; Beyond the Blues; Afro-
Amerikaanze Poezie; New Negro Poets; Ik Ben
De Nieuwe Neger; Les Noirs Americains; Kaleidoscope; L'Idea Deglie
Antenati; Harlem Renaissance and Beyond; Right On!; Soulscript; A
Broadside Treasury; Afro-American Writing. Period.: Phylon;
Michigan Challenge; Freedomways; Journal of Black Poetry; The Free
Lance; Poetry News-Letter; Missouri School Journal; The Detroit
News; Michigan Chronicle; English Journal.
HONORS AND AWARDS: 1st recipient of $10,000 Mott Fellow. in Eng.
at Oakland U., 1965-66; Named Distinguished Tchr. of Yr., by Met-
ropolitan Detroit Eng. Club, 1967; 5th place Poetry Award, Nat'l.
Writers Club, 1957; 1 of 2 Soror of the Yr. Awards, Alpha Kappa
Alpha Sorority, 1969; Papers being collec. at Fisk U., Spec.
Collec.
MEMBER: Coll. Lang. Assn.; Nat'l. Counc. of Tchrs. of Eng.; Mod.
Lang. Assn.; Amer. Assn. of U. Prof.; Detroit Women Writers;
Nat'l. Writers Club; NAACP.
SIDELIGHTS: Traveled in Europe, Africa and the Middle East (Au-
thor).
Sources. Author inform.; Black Voices, Ed. by Abraham Chapman (New
Amer. Lib., 1968); Broadside Authors and Artists, Ed. by Leanonead
P. Bailey (Broadside Pr., 1974); Ebony (Johnson Pub., March 1974);
Kaleidoscope, Ed. by Robert Hayden (Harcourt, 1967); Poetry of
Black America, Ed. by Arnold Adoff (Harper & Row, 1973); Right On!,
Ed. by Bradford Chambers (New Amer. Lib., 1970).

Haki R. Madhubuti. See Lee, Don L.

MAJOR, CLARENCE. 1936- . Novelist, Poet, Short Story Writer, Essayist, Teacher, Editor
Biographical-Personal. Born Dec. 31, 1936, in Atlanta, Ga. Educ.:
Art Inst. of Chgo., 1952-54; Armed Forces Inst., 1955-56; New Sch.
for Soc. Res., N.Y.C., 1972. Mailing address: c/o Miss Marcia

Major, Clarence

Higgins, William Morris Agency, Inc., 1350 Ave. of the Americas, N.Y., N.Y. 10019. Career-Professional. Ed.: Coercion Review, 1958-60. Assoc. Ed.: Anagogic & Paideumic Review, 1961-63; Proof, Journal of Black Poetry, 1967-70; Caw!, 1967-70; Dues, 1972- . Guest Ed.: Works, 1972-73. Lectr., creative writing & lit., Harlem Educ. Prog., 1967; Brooklyn Coll., 1968; Cazenovia Coll., 1969; Brooklyn Coll., 1972; Sarah Lawrence Coll., 1972; Queen's Coll., 1972. Vis. Writer-coll. Goucher; Skidmore; Bowdoin; Aurora; New Sch.; Old Westbury; Orange Co. Community; Bernard; Marist; Conn. Vis. Writer-U.: Columbia; Nebraska; Rhode Island; Wesleyan; Wis. State; N.Y. State, Stony Brook; N.Y. State, Plattsburgh, 1967-74.

WRITINGS: All-Night Visitors, novel (Grove, 1969). Poetry: The New Black Poetry (Internat., 1970); Swallow the Lake (Wesleyan U. Pr., 1970); Private Line (1971); Symptoms & Madness (Corinth, 1971); The Cotton Club (Broadside Pr., 1972); Syncopated Cake-Walk (1973); The Dark (1974); Feeling (1974). Dictionary of Afro-American Slang (Internat., 1970); No, novel (1973); Reflex and Bone Structure (Fiction Collective, 1975). In progress: Scat; Slaveship and Relationship; Selected Poems. Anthol.: In a Time of Revolution; The Writing on the Wall; Open Poetry; Poems of War Resistance; Starting with Poetry; The Modern Age; Speech and Language Development of the Preschool Child--A Survey; American Negro Poetry; For Malcolm; New Black Voices; Where Is Vietnam; Black Poetry Supplement; The New Black Poetry; 19 Necromancers from Now. Period.: American Review; Essence; Trace; El carno emplumado; Chelsea; Works; Red Clay Reader; New York Quarterly; Negro Digest/ Black World; The Literary Review; Motive; Poetry Review; Letras da Provincia (Brazil); East & West (India); The Fiddlehead (Can.); American Poetry Review; Nickel Review; National Guardian; New Left Notes.

HONORS AND AWARDS: James Nelson Raymond Scholarship, Art Inst. of Chgo., 1951; Nat'l. Counc. on the Arts Award, 1970; N.Y. Cultural Found. Grant, 1971.

SIDELIGHTS: Vis. Writer, 1967-74: (N.Y.) Polytechnic Inst.; Guggenheim Mus.; Apollo Theatre; Soc. for Ethical Culture. Radio: Nat'l. Public.; Pacific. TV: CBS; ABC. Columnist, The American Poetry Review, 1973- . Travels: U.S., Mexico, Canada, Italy, England, France, Spain, the Bahamas, Jamaica, Haiti, Dominican Republic (Author).

Sources. Author inform.; Black Voices, Ed. by Abraham Chapman (New Amer. Lib., 1968); Broadside Authors and Artists, Comp. by Leaonead

Mandel, Bernard

P. Bailey (Broadside Pr., 1974); For Malcolm, Ed. by Dudley Randall & Margaret G. Burroughs (Broadside Pr., 1969); The New Black
Poetry, Ed. by Clarence Major (Internat., 1969); Soulscript, Ed.
by June Jordan (Doubleday, 1970).

MAJOR, REGINALD W. 1926- . Journalist
Biographical-Personal. Born Feb. 8, 1926, in
N.Y.C. Son of Wilford Reginald and Ethel
[Allman] Major. Educ.: U. of Chgo., 1946-
50. Family: m. Helen Ruth Gabriel, Aug. 3,
1949; son, David Robert, d. Deborah Ann.
Mailing address: c/o Sun Reporter, 1366 Turk
St., San Francisco, Cal. 94117.
Career-Professional. State of Cal., Dept. of
Motor Vehicles, Sacramento (driver improve-
ment analyst), 1963-68; 1st Dir., Educational
Opportunity Prog., San Francisco State Coll.,
1968-70; Part-time Journalist, San Francisco
Sun-Reporter, 1964- .
WRITINGS: A Panther Is a Black Cat (Morrow,
1971); Justice in the Round; The Trial of
Angela Davis (Third World Pr., 1973). Contributed to The Nation
& others.
MEMBER: NAACP (Educ. Chmn., San Francisco Chap., 1963-65).
Sources. Author inform.; Contemporary Authors, Vols. 29-32, Ed. by
Clare D. Kinsman & Mary A. Tennenhouse (Gale Res., 1972); Justice
in the Round, Reginald Major (Third World Pr., 1973).

Malcolm X. See Little, Malcolm.

MANDEL, BERNARD. 1920- . Teacher, Historian
Biographical-Personal. Born Jan. 4, 1920, in
Cleveland, Ohio. Son of Max and Jean Mandel.
Educ.: Ph.D., Case-Western Reserve U.,
Cleveland, 1952. Family: m. H. Althea War-
ner; d. Ann, d. Carla, d. Anita. Mailing ad-
dress: 1575 E. Blvd., Cleveland, Ohio.
Career-Professional. Tchr.; Lectr.; Historian.
WRITINGS: Labor, Free and Slave: Workingmen
and the Anti-slavery Movement in the United
States (Assoc. Authors, 1955); Samuel Gompers
(Kent State U. Pr., 1963); Young People's
History of the United States (Rawlings, 1968).
"Max Hayes," in Dictionary of American Biog-
raphy. Articles on Black history, Black lib-
eration, Black education, and Africa.
MEMBER: Black Caucus, Amer. Fed. of Tchrs.

185

Mapp, Edward

SIDELIGHTS: Extensive traveling in Africa. Lectures on the Black
experience (Author).
Source. Author inform.

MAPP, EDWARD. Library Administrator
Biographical-Personal. Born in N.Y.C. Educ.:
B.A., City Coll. of N.Y., 1953; M.S., Colum-
bia U., 1956; Ph.D., N.Y.U., 1970. Family:
son, Andrew. Mailing address: 950 E. 14th
St., Brooklyn, NY. 11230.
Career-Professional. Lib. Asst., Ref. Dept.,
N.Y. Public Lib., 1948-55; Asst. Librn.,
N.Y.C. Community Coll., 1956-57; Tchr. Librn.,
Bd. of Educ., N.Y.C., 1957-64; Chief Librn.,
N.Y.C. Community Coll., 1964- ; Reviewer,
Library Journal, Served on Middle States Assn.
Evaluation Teams.
WRITINGS: Books for Occupational Education
Programs: A List for Community Colleges,
Technical Institutes, and Vocational Schools
(Bowker, 1971); Blacks in American Films (Scarecrow, 1972); Puerto
Rican Perspectives (Scarecrow, 1974). Contrib. to professional
jls. & anthol.
HONORS AND AWARDS: Founders Day Award for Outstanding Scholarship,
N.Y.U., 1970.
MEMBER: ALA; Amer. Assn. U. Profs.; N.Y.C. Lib. Assn.; N.Y., Lib.
Club; Subcom. on Written Materials, Advis. Com. Nat'l. Project
Center for Film and the Humanities.
SIDELIGHTS: Appearance on WPIX-TV, "The Puerto Rican New Yorker,"
Feb., 1974 (Author).
Source. Author inform.

MARSH, CLIFTON ERNEST. 1946- . Poet, Teacher
Biographical-Personal. Born Aug. 10, 1946, in
L.A., Cal. Son of Clifton H. and Margaret
Marsh. Educ.: B.A., M.A., Cal. State U. at
Long Beach; (Ph.D. candidate) Syracuse U.,
Syracuse, N.Y. Family: Single. Mailing ad-
dress: 734 S. Beech St., Syracuse, N.Y.
13210.
Career-Professional. Tchg. Asst., 1973-74.
Tchr., Sociol. Dept., State U. of N.Y. at
Cortland, 1974.
WRITINGS: Journey to Shanara (Shanara
Public.). Pub. in Black Folk Journal, Black
History Museum, Third World Anthology, Black
Voice.

186

Martin, Herbert Woodward

HONORS AND AWARDS: Minority Faculty Fellow., 1969-70. L.A.
Weightlifting Champion, 5th in National Collegiate Weightlifting,
1970-71.
SIDELIGHTS: Active in Attica Brothers Defense Committee; Poetry
reading for Auburn prisoners at Folk Art Gallery; Active in writers' workshops in Syracuse area. Dissertation is to be on the influence of Black Nationalism on poetry (Author).
Source. Author inform.

MARSHALL, PAULE. 1929- . Novelist, Short
Story Writer
Biographical-Personal. Born Apr. 9, 1929 in
Brooklyn, N.Y. D. of Barbadian parents.
Educ.: B.A., (Phi Beta Kappa), Brooklyn
Coll., 1953; Hunter Coll., 1955. Family:
son, Evan. Mailing address: 407 Central
Park W., N.Y., N.Y. 10025.
Career-Professional. Staff Writer, Our World
mag., 1953-56; Lectr., Black Lit., numerous
coll. & universities, including Cercle Cul-
tural de Royaumont (Paris), Oxford U. (Eng.),
Columbia U., Cornell U., Mich. State, Fisk
U., Wesleyan, Lake Forest. Lectr., Creative
writing, Yale U. Present: Adjunct Prof. of
Writing, Columbia U. & Vis. Scholar to Nat'l.
Humanities Faculty, Concord, Mass.
WRITINGS: Brown Girl, Brownstones (Random House, 1959); Soul Clap
Hands and Sing, four novellas (Atheneum, 1961); The Chosen Place,
the Timeless People (Harcourt, 1969); Ceremonies at the Guest
House. Has contrib. short stories to mags. and anthol.
HONORS AND AWARDS: Guggenheim Fellow, 1960; Rosenthal Award,
Amer. Acad. of Arts and Sci., 1961; Ford Found. Grant for Poets
and Fiction Writers, 1964-65; Nat'l. Endowment on Arts and Hu-
manities, 1967-68.
Sources. Black Insights, Ed. by Nick A. Ford (Ginn, 1971); Cavalcade,
Ed. by Arthur P. Davis and Saunders Redding (Houghton Mifflin,
1971); Dark Symphony, Ed. by James A. Emanuel and Theodore L.
Gross (Free Pr., 1968); "National Conf. of Afro-Amer. Writers,"
(Program), Howard U., Inst. for Arts and Humanities, Nov. 1974.

MARTIN, HERBERT WOODWARD. 1933- . Poet, Playwright
Biographical-Personal. Born Oct. 4, 1933 in Birmingham, Ala. Reared
in Toledo, Ohio. Educ.: B.A., U. of Toledo. Mailing address:
1834 Glenwood Ave., Toledo, Ohio 43620.
Career-Professional. Tchg. Asst., State U. of N.Y., Buffalo, 1964-67;
Instr., Asst. Prof., and Poet-in-Residence, Aquinas Coll., 1967-70;
Asst. Prof. of Eng., U. of Dayton, 1970. Poetry reading, coll. &

Martin, Louis E.

universities, including Breadloaf; Mich. State Apple Blossom Fes-
tival; The Enjoyment of Poetry, WEVD radio.
WRITINGS: New York the Nine Million and Other Poems (1969); Three
Garbage Cans, a play (1969). Anthol.: The Urban Reader (1971);
Afro-American Literature (1969); Poetry of Black America (1973).
Period.: The Activists, Trace, Mainstream, Confrontation, Sumac,
& Rap.
HONORS AND AWARDS: Scholarships in poetry: Antioch Coll., U. of
Colorado, Breadloaf of Middlebury Coll.; Fellow. in Drama, Wagner
Coll.; Fellow. in Eng.: SUNY, Breadloaf Sch. of English.
MEMBER: Amer. Assn. of U. Prof.
Source. Poetry of Black America, Ed. by Arnold Adoff (Harper & Row,
1973).

MARTIN, LOUIS E. 1912- . Publisher, Editor
Biographical-Personal. Born Nov. 18, 1912, in Shelbyville, Tenn.
Son of Dr. L. E. and Willa [Hill] Martin. Educ.: B.A., 1934,
M.S., U. of Mich.; D.Litt., Wilberforce U., 1951. Family: m.
Gertrude Scott, Jan. 2, 1937; d. Gertrude, d. Anita, d. Toni, d.
Linda, d. Lisa.
Career-Professional. Ed., Pub., Michigan Chronicle, Detroit, 1936- ;
Ed.-in-Chief, Chicago Defender, 1947- ; Dir., Fed. Savings & Loan
Assn. of Chgo., 1950- ; Secy.-Treasurer, New York Age Pub. Corp.,
1952-60; V. Pres., Defender Pub.; V. Pres., Dir., Guaranty Life
Ins. Co. Ga.
MEMBER: Bd. of Supv., Wayne Co., Mich. (2 terms); V. Pres., Nat'l.
Urban League; former Asst. Pub. Dir., Democratic Nat'l. Com. &
Deputy Chmn. Clubs: Nat'l. Press (Wash., D.C.); Overseas Pr.
(N.Y.C.); Chicago Pr.
Sources. Negro Handbook, Comp. by Editors of Ebony (Johnson Pub.,
1966); Who's Who in the American Negro Press, Roy L. Hill (Royal
Pub., 1960).

Marvin X. See El Muhajir.

MATHEUS, JOHN FREDERICK. 1887- . Professor of Romance Languages,
Author, Playwright
Biographical-Personal. Born Sept. 10, 1887 in Keyser, W. Va. Son of
John William and Mary Susan Matheus. Educ.: B.A. (cum laude),
Western Reserve U., Cleveland, 1910; M.A. (Romance Lang. & Educ.,
with diploma as tchr. of French), Columbia U., 1921; La Sorbonne,
Paris, 1925; U. of Chgo., 1927. Family: 1st. m. Maude Roberts,
Sept. 1, 1906 (dec. 1965); 2nd, Mrs. Ellen Turner Gordon (Dayton,
Ohio), July 31, 1973. Mailing address: P.O. Box 1163, Charleston,
W. Va. 25324.
Career-Professional. Prof., Latin & Mod. Foreign Lang., Fla. A. & M.
Coll., Tallahassee, 1911-22; Prof. & Head, Dept. of Romance Lang.,
W. Va. State Coll., Inst., W. Va., 1922-53.

Mathis, Sharon Bell

WRITINGS: A Collection of Short Stories (Harlem Renaissance, 1974); Georges, by Alexandre Dumas, père, Ed. with W. Napoleon Rivers (intermediate French reader, Assoc. Pub., 1936); Ouanga: A Drama and a Libretto (music by Clarence Cameron White); Tambour (Haitian folk play, incidental music--Clarence C. White, staged, 1929); Voice (Pageant of the Negro, for 25th anniversary of Charleston NAACP, 1934). Anthol.: The New Negro; Plays of Negro Life; Plays and Pageants from the Life of the Negro; Caroling Dusk; Ebony and Topaz; Readings from Negro Authors; Negro; 365 Days, A Book of Short Stories; The Negro Caravan; The Haitian American Anthology; Anthology of American Negro Literature; Ebony Rhythm; Poetry of the Negro, 1746-1949. Period.: Opportunity; Crisis; Carolina Magazine; Poet Lore; Quarterly Review of Higher Education Among Negroes; Chronicle; Journal of Negro History; Arts Quarterly; Modern Language Journal; Journal of Negro Education; Bulletin of Association of American Colleges; Negro History Bulletin; W. Va. Digest; Color; The Race; The Americans; College Language Association Bulletin; Negro Education Review.
HONORS AND AWARDS: Sigma Delta Pi, Nat'l. Honor Soc. for Stud. of Spanish; Coll. Lang. Assn. Award as Treasurer, 1974; Cons., Black Lit. of French Expression, ACTFL/SCOLT, 1972; Haitian govt.: "Officier de l'Ordre Nationale d' 'Honneur et Merite'"
MEMBER: Treasurer, Coll. Lang. Assn., since 1942; Chmn., Mod., Foreign Lang. Section, W. Va. State Tchrs. Assn., since 1932; Pres., W. Va. Chapter, Mod. Lang. Tchrs. Assn., 1952-53.
SIDELIGHTS: Travel: Cuba, France, Switzerland, Italy, Haiti, England, Holland, Germany, Sierra Leone, Liberia, Canary Is., Mexico, Canada, Portugal, Spain, Brazil, Argentina. In 1930 spent 6 months in Liberia as Secretary to Dr. Charles S. Johnson, American member of International Com. of Inquiry to Liberia to investigate charges of Forced Labor, sponsored by President Hoover, American Department of State and League of Nations. In 1945-46, director of teaching of English in national schools of Haiti (Inter-American Educational Foundation). Ouanga had world premiere in 1949, South Bend, Ind. (also presented at Academy of Music, Philadelphia, 1950). Has had a festival of his plays given in Cleveland. Broadcast progressive lessons in English over radio, twice weekly while in Port-au-Prince, Haiti (Author).
Source. Author inform.

MATHIS, SHARON BELL. 1937- . Teacher, Juvenile Writer, Columnist
Biographical-Personal. Born Feb. 16, 1937, in Atlantic City, N.J.
    D. of John Willie and Alice [Frazier] Bell. Educ.: B.A., Morgan
    State Coll., Baltimore, 1958; M.S.L.S., Catholic U., 1974.
    Family: m. Leroy F. Mathis; d. Sherie, d. Stacy, d. Stephanie.
    Mailing address: 131 Elmira St., S.W., Wash., D.C. 20032.
Career-Professional. Spec. Educ. Tchr., Stuart Jr. High; Writer-in-
    Residence, Howard U., 1972-74; Columnist, "Ebony Jrs.! Speak,"

Mayfield, Julian

Ebony Jr.! mag.; Former Head, Children's
Div., D.C. Black Writers' Workshop.
WRITINGS: Juveniles: Brooklyn Story (Hill
& Wang, 1970); Sidewalk Story (Viking, 1971);
Teacup Full of Roses (Viking, 1972); Ray
Charles (Crowell, 1973); Listen for the Fig
Tree (Viking, 1974; Avon, 1975); The Hundred
Penny Box (Viking, 1975).
HONORS AND AWARDS: Counc. on Interracial
Bks. for Children Award, for Sidewalk Story;
The Coretta Scott King Award for Ray Charles:
A Biography; ALA Notable Bk. of 1972 for Tea-
cup Full of Roses.
MEMBER: Bd. of Advis., Lawyers Com., D.C.
Commission on the Arts.
Sources. Author inform.; Pub. inform.

MAYFIELD, JULIAN. 1928- . Novelist, Essayist,
Editor
Biographical-Personal. Born June 6, 1928, in
Greer, S.C. Son of Hudson and Annie Mae
[Prince] Mayfield. Educ.: Dunbar High Sch.,
Wash., D.C.; Lincoln U., Pa. Family: m. Ana
Livia Cordero (physician); son, Rafael Ariel,
son, Emiliano Kwesi. Mailing address: c/o
Vanguard Pr., 424 Madison Ave., N.Y., N.Y.
10017.

Career-Professional. Actor, Broadway play,
Lost in the Stars; Ed. & Theater Reviewer,
Puerto Rico World Journal; Ed. African Review, Accra, Ghana; Pub., Living Ghana, in
collaboration with Leslie Lacy (1966); Tchg.
fellow, Cornell U.; Currently works for
Guyana govt., (S. America), edits a newspaper and works in inform.
arm of country's admin.
WRITINGS: Novels: The Hit (Vanguard, 1957); The Long Night (Van-
guard, 1958); The Grand Parade (Vanguard, 1961); The World Without
the Bomb: The Papers of the Accra Assembly, Ed. (1963); Ten Times
Black: Stories from the Black Experience (Bantam, 1972). Period.:
Puerto Rico World Journal; The African Review (Accra); Commentary;
New Republic; The Nation.
MEMBER: Actors' Equity Assn.; Writers Guild of America, E.;
Ghanian Assn. of Journalists and Writers.
SIDELIGHTS: Has spent many years in both Africa and Europe. His
works have been translated into French, Japanese, Czech, and Ger-
man. His theatrical work has conisted of reviewing, writing, pro-
ducing and directing plays for presentation in Harlem and off-
Broadway; as well as acting (AFRO USA).

190

Mays, Benjamin Elijah

Sources. AFRO USA, Comp. by Harry A. Ploski and Ernest Kaiser (Bellwether, 1971); Contemporary Authors, Vols. 13-44, Ed. by James M.
Ethridge and Barbara Kopala (Gale Res., 1965); Dark Symphony, Ed.
by James A. Emanuel and Theodore L. Gross (Free Pr., 1968); From
the Dark Tower, Ed. by Arthur P. Davis (Howard U. Pr., 1974);
Pub. inform.; Books in Print, Supplement, 1975-76 (Bowker, 1976).

MAYS, BENJAMIN ELIJAH. 1894- . College
President, Theologian, Scholar
Biographical-Personal. Born Aug. 1, 1894, in
Epworth, S.C. Son of Hezekiah and Louvenia
Mays. Educ.: High Sch. Dept., S.C. State
Coll. (valedictorian), 1916; B.A. (with hon-
ors), Bates Coll., Lewiston, Me., 1920; M.A.,
1925, Ph.D., 1935, U. of Chgo.; 37 hon. doc-
torates. Family: Widower (Sadie G. Mays).
Mailing address: 3316 Pamilco Dr., S.W.,
Atlanta, Ga. 30311.
Career-Professional. Tchr., Higher mathematics,
Morehouse Coll., Pastor, Shiloh Bap., 1921-24;
Eng. Instr., State Coll., Orangeburg, S.C.,
1925-28; Nat'l. Student Secy., YMCA, 1928-30;
Study Dir., Negro churches, U.S.A. (Inst. of
Soc. & Religious Res.) 1930-32; Dean, Sch. of Relig., Howard U.,
1934-40; Pres., Morehouse Coll., Atlanta, 1940-67; Pres. Emeritus,
1967- .
WRITINGS: The Negro's Church, co-author (Inst. of Soc. & Religious
Res., 1933); The Negro's God (Atheneum, 1938; 1968); Seeking to be
Christian in Race Relations (Friendship Pr., 1957); A Gospel for
the Social Awakening (Assn. Pr., 1950); The Christian in Race Relations (pamphlet); Disturbed About Man (John Knox Pr., 1969); Born
to Rebel, autobiog. (Scribners, 1971). Contrib. to books: Ed.,
Race in Christus Victor (World Com. of YMCA, 1939); Encyclopedia
of Religion (1945); "Christian Light on Human Relationships,"
(Bap. World Alliance, 8th Cong., 1950); "Race: The Negro Perspective," Search for America (1959); "The Challenge to Religion as it
Ponders Science," Religion Ponders Science (1964); "The Moral Aspects of Segregation," Black, White and Gray; "Why I believe There
is a God," Why I Believe there is a God. Articles: Crisis;
Christian Century; Journal of Negro Education; Missions; Negro Di-
gest; Pittsburgh Courier, Weekly column since 1946; etc.
HONORS AND AWARDS: V. Pres., Fed. Counc. of Churches of Christ in
America, 1944-46; Alumnus of the Yr., Divinity Sch., U. of Chgo.,
1949; Pres., United Negro Coll. Fund, 1958-61; Appt., Advis.
Counc., U.S. Com. for the UN, 1959; Appt., Nat'l. Advis. Counc.,
Peace Corps, 1961; Recipient Christian Culture Award, Assumption
U., Windsor, Ont., Can., 1961; U.S. Rep., State Funeral, Pope

Mays, James

John XXIII, Rome, 1963; Peace Corps Rep., All-African conf. on
Educ., Addis Ababa, Ethiopia, 1961; Man of the Yr. Award, Soc. for
Advancement of Management, Greenville, S.C., 1968; Award of
Achievement, Black Educ. Serv., Chgo., 1970; Relig. Leaders Award,
Nat'l. Conf. of Christians and Jews, 1970; etc.
MEMBER: Chmn., Benedict Coll. Bd. of Trus.; Chmn. Bd., Nat'l.
Sharecropper Fund; Inst. of Internat. Educ., Southeastern Region;
Bd. Butler St. YWCA, Atlanta; United Negro Coll. Fund; U. of Chgo.
Alumni Assn.; Paine Coll. Bd.; Relig. Her. of Amer. Bd.; Martin L.
King, Jr. Center for Soc. Change; Cons., United Bd. for Coll.
Develop.
SIDELIGHTS: Vis. Prof. & Advis. to Pres., Mich. State U., East
Lansing, 1968-69; Cons., Office of Educ., HEW, 1969; Elected to
Atlanta Bd. of Educ., 1969 (elected Pres., 1970, reelected Pres.,
1971-74, reelected to Bd. 1974-78); Cons., Ford Found., 1970.
(Rep.) World Conf. of YMCAs, Mysore, India, 1937; YMCA of America,
Plenary Session World Com., Stockholm, Sweden, 1938; Oxford Conf.
on Church, Community & State, Oxford U., Eng., 1937; Former mem.,
Bd. of S. Educ. Found.; Mem. Delta Sigma Rho, Delta Theta Chi;
Omega Psi Phi,; Phi Beta Kappa Soc.; V. Pres., World Student Serv.
Fund; Delegate, World Counc. of Churches, Amsterdam, Holland,
1948; Mem. Central Com., World Counc. of Churches, 1949-53; Dele-
gate, Bap. World Alliance Assembly, Cleveland, Ohio 1950; Rep.,
Com. on the Church Amidst Racial and Ethnic Tensions, Geneva,
Switzerland, 1953; Co-Chmn., Citizens Crusade Against Poverty;
etc. (Author).
Sources. Author inform.; Negro Handbook, Comp. by Eds. of Ebony
(Johnson Pub., 1966); Pub. inform.

MAYS, JAMES. Cardiologist, Novelist
Biographical-Personal. Family: m. Lovella Mays
(tchr.); 4 children. Mailing address: 12021
S. Wilmington, L.A., Cal.
Career-Professional. Medical Dir., United High
Blood Pressure Found.; Chief of Cardiology,
L.A., Martin Luther King, Jr. Gen. Hosp.
WRITINGS: Mercy Is King, novel.
MEMBER: Bd. of Dir., Amer. Heart Assn. (L.A.
affiliate).
SIDELIGHTS: A nationally recognized authority
on the subject of high blood pressure (Cal.
Librns. Black Caucus, Brochure).
Source. "Second Annual Authors Autograph Party"
(brochure), Cal. Librns. Black Caucus, July
1975.

Millender, Dharathula (Dolly)

MERIWETHER, LOUISE. 1923- . Free-Lance Writer, Juvenile Writer
Biographical-Personal. Born May 8, 1923, in Haverstraw, N.Y. Educ.:
B.A., N.Y.U.; UCLA (Journalism). Family: Divorced. Mailing ad-
dress: c/o Jenkins, 1691 E. 174th St., Bronx, N.Y. 10472.
Career-Professional. Reporter, Los Angeles Sentinel; Story Analyst,
Universal Studios; Staff member, Watts Writers' Workshop; Legal
Secy.; An organizer and member, Black Concern (against accomoda-
tion with Republic of S. Africa).
WRITINGS: Daddy Was a Number Runner, novel (Prentice-Hall, 1970);
The Freedom Ship of Robert Smalls (Prentice-Hall, 1971); The Heart
Man; Story of Daniel Hale Williams (1972); Don't Ride the Bus on
Monday: The Rosa Parks Story (Prentice-Hall, 1973). Short sto-
ries: "A Happening in Barbados" Antioch Review (Spring, 1968);
"The Thick End is For Whipping," Negro Digest (Nov. 1968). Book
Reviews: Los Angeles Times (Apr. 1965 to 1967); "For Us the Liv-
ing," Freedomways (Spring, 1968). Articles: Sepia (Mar., Jan.,
Jul., 1962; Apr., Jun., 1963); Negro Digest (Aug. 1963; Jan. 1965,
Oct. 1965); Bronze America (Jun., Aug., 1964); Frontier (Oct.,
Nov., 1965); L.A. Committee for Protection of Bill of Rights (1966
Year Bk.). "Do Your Own Thing in School," pamphlet, U.S. HEW,
1969, Wash., D.C.
Sources. Author inform.; Daddy Was a Number Runner, Louise Meri-
wether (Prentice-Hall, 1970); 1000 Successful Blacks, Vol. 1,
Ebony Success Lib. (Johnson Pub., 1973).

June Meyer. See June Jordan.

MICHEAUX, OSCAR. Novelist
Career-Professional.
WRITINGS: Novels: The Wind from Nowhere (1943); The Case of Mrs.
Wingate (1945; AMS Pr. repr., 1975); Story of Dorothy Stanfield
(1946); Homesteader: a Novel (McGrath, 1969--originally pub.
1917); The Masquerade: an Historical Novel (AMS Pr. repr. of 1947
ed., 1975).
Source. The Case of Mrs. Wingate, Oscar Micheaux (AMS Pr. repr.,
1975).

MILLENDER, DHARATHULA (DOLLY). 1920- . Librarian, Children's
Writer
Biographical-Personal. Born Feb. 4, 1920, in Terre Haute, Ind. D.
of Orestes (electrical technician) and Daisy Eslick Hood (teacher).
Educ.: B.S., Ind. State U., 1941, grad. work in Lib. Sci.; other
grad. work in Lib. Sci., Ind. U., Catholic U. of Amer., & Purdue
U. Family: div.; d. Naomi Estelle, d. Justine Faye. Mailing ad-
dress: Pulaski Sch., 1867 Georgia St., Gary, Ind.
Career-Professional. Tchr. & sch. librn., Trenton, S.C., 1941-42 &
La Plata, Md., 1942-43; Lib. of Congress, ref. asst., 1943; Indi-

Miller, Adam David

antown Gap, Pa. Military Reservation, Libr., 1943-44; Jr. high
sch. librn., Baltimore, Md., 1952-60; Pulaski Jr. High Sch., Gary,
Ind., Librn., 1960- ; Chmn., Negro Hist. Week Observance, Gary,
1962-64, 1966, 1967.
WRITINGS: Crispus Attucks: Boy of Valor, juvenile (Bobbs-Merrill, 1965); Yesterday in Gary: History of the Negro in Gary
(1967). Writer of weekly column, "Yesterday in Gary," appearing
in local newspaper. Contrib. and former ed., Gary Crusader.
Contrib. to Education and Changing Education.
Source. Contemporary Authors, Vols. 19-20, Ed. by James M. Ethridge
and Others (Gale Res., 1968).

MILLER, ADAM DAVID. 1922- . Teacher, Editor, Theater Director
Biographical-Personal. Born Oct. 8, 1922, in Orangeburg, S.C.
Educ.: M.A. (Eng.), U. of Cal., Berkeley. Family: m. Lois
Grene; d. Carmen, d. Robin, d. Pemba. Mailing address: Box 162,
Berkeley, Cal. 94701.
Career-Professional. Tchr., Afro Lit. & Composition & Head, Tutoring
Serv. Laney Community Coll., Oakland, Cal.; Founder, theater dir.,
actor, Aldridge Players W., 1964- ; TV prod.; Radio prog. of
poetry, "The Imaged Word," KPFA-FM; Corresp. for Black Theatre;
Founding Ed., The Graduate Student Journal, U. of Cal., Berkeley.
WRITINGS: Dices or Black Bones: Black Voices of the Seventies,
Ed. (Houghton Mifflin, 1970). Contrib. articles on Black poetry,
drama, lit. film & esthetics to Drama Review, San Francisco Chron-
icle & others.
HONORS AND AWARDS: Award of merit for film, "Dices or Black
Bones," Cal. Assn. of Teachers of Eng., 1973.
Sources. New Black Voices, Ed. by Abraham Chapman (New Amer. Lib.,
1972); Poetry of Black America, Ed. by Arnold Adoff (Harper & Row,
1973).

MILLER, KELLY. 1863-1939. Educator, Writer
Biographical-Personal. Born 1863 in Winnsboro,
S.C. Educ.: B.A., Howard U.; M.A., Johns
Hopkins U. Family: d. May Miller (writer).
Died 1939.
Career-Professional. Howard U. for 44 yrs., as:
Prof. of Mathematics, Prof. of Sociol., Dean,
Coll. of Arts & Sci., & Dean, Jr. Coll.
WRITINGS: Race Adjustment (1908); Out of the
House of Bondage (Neal Pub., 1914); An Appeal
to Conscience (1918); History of the World
War and the Important Part Taken by the Ne-
groes (1919); and The Everlasting Stain
(1924).
SIDELIGHTS: "Helped W. E. B. DuBois edit
Crisis magazine and became first Negro acad-
imician to write a weekly column for the Negro Press.

194

Miller was called the father of the Sanhedrin, a 1924 movement
which attempted to unite all Negro organizations into one front.
    One of the major spokesmen, writers, and teachers of his race
in the early 20th Century, Kelly Miller has been referred to as a
'marginal man,' racially separated from the white world, and in-
tellectually distinct from his own group" (Historical Negro Biographies).
Sources. Afro-American Writing, Ed. by Richard A. Long & Eugenia W.
    Collier (N.Y.U. Pr., 1972); Anthology of American Negro Litera-
    ture, Ed. by V. F. Calverton (Mod. Lib., 1929); Historical Negro
    Biographies, Wilhelmena S. Robinson (ASNLH, 1967); Negro Caravan,
    Ed. by Sterling A. Brown & Others (Arno Pr. & N.Y. Times, 1969);
    Negro Poets and Their Poems, Robert T. Kerlin, 3rd ed. rev.
    (Assoc. Pub., 1935).

MILLER, LOREN. 1903-?. Lawyer, Judge, Editor
Biographical-Personal. Born Jan. 29, 1903, in Pender, Neb. Educ.:
    U. of Kan., 1920-23; Howard U., 1926-27; LL.B., Washburn School
    of Law, Topeka, Kan., 1929. Family: m. Juanita Ellsworth, 1930;
    son, Loren, Jr., son, Edward E. Dec.
Career-Professional. Admitted to Kan. bar, 1929, Cal. bar, 1934;
    Fed. Dist. Court, U.S. Court of Appeals, 9th Circuit, & U.S.
    Supreme Court, 1947. Ed., California Eagle, California News, Los
    Angeles Sentinel, 1930-34. European corresp., Assoc. Negro Pr.
    for 6 months, 1931-32. Apptd. Judge of Municipal Court of L.A.,
    1964.
    WRITINGS: The Petitioners (Random House, 1966).
    MEMBER: V. Pres., NAACP; Cal. Advis. Com., U.S. Com. on Civil
    Rights; V. Pres., Nat'l. Com. Against Discrimination in Housing;
    Bd., W. Coast Region of Nat'l. Urban League.
    SIDELIGHTS: Private practice of law in Los Angeles from 1934,
    argued many civil rights cases, especially housing discrimination
    suits (Negro Handbook).
Sources. Black Writers in Los Angeles, California, Hilda G. Finney
    (Center for Extending Amer. Hist.); Negro Handbook, Comp. by Eds.
    of Ebony (Johnson Pub., 1966); Pub. inform.

MILLER, MAY. Poet, Playwright
Biographical-Personal. Born in Wash., D.C. D. of Kelly Miller
    (writer). Educ.: Howard U. grad.; Advanced work at Amer. U. &
    Columbia U. Family: m. John Sullivan.
Career-Professional. Tchr., Speech & Dramatics, Frederick Douglass
    High Sch., Baltimore; Reader, panelist, lectr., & Poet-in-Resi-
    dence, Monmouth Coll., Monmouth, Ill.; Coord. for performing
    poets, Friends of the Arts, Dist. of Columbia Public Sch.; Mem.,
    Commission of the Arts, Wash., D.C.
    WRITINGS: Plays and Pageants from the Life of the Negro and Negro
    History in Thirteen Plays, collaborator, 2 vols. of 1-act plays;

Milner, Ronald

<u>Into the Clearing</u>, poetry (1959); <u>Poems</u> (1962). Represented as
one of three poets in <u>Lyrics of Three Women</u> (1964); <u>Dust of Un-
certain Journey</u> (Lotus, 1975). Has contrib. to <u>Antioch Review</u>;
<u>Common Ground</u>; <u>Crisis</u>; <u>The Nation</u>; <u>New York Times</u>; <u>Phylon</u>; <u>Poetry</u>;
<u>Alan Swallow's P.S.</u> & <u>Cafe Solo</u>.
Sources. Cavalcade, Ed. by Arthur P. Davis & Saunders Redding
  (Houghton Mifflin, 1971); <u>Books in Print</u>, Supplement, 1975-76
  (Bowker, 1976).

MILNER, RONALD. 1938- . Playwright
Biographical-Personal. Born May 29, 1938, in
  Detroit, Mich. <u>Educ.</u>: Attended various
  colls. in Detroit; Harvey Swados's writing
  workshop, Columbia U.
Career-Professional. Writer-in-Residence, Lin-
  coln U. (Pa.), 1966-67; Conductor, Cultural
  Workshop, Mich. State U.; Dir., Spirit of
  Shango Theater Co., Detroit.
  WRITINGS: Plays: <u>Who's Got His Own</u>; <u>The
  Warning: A Theme for Linda</u>; <u>The Monster</u>;
  <u>These Three</u>; <u>What the Wine Sellers Buy</u>.
  <u>Black Drama Anthology</u>, Ed. with Woodie King
  (New Amer. Lib., 1971).
  HONORS AND AWARDS: Rockefeller fellow; John
  Hay Whitney fellow.
SIDELIGHTS: "<u>Who's Got His Own</u> was first presented at the Ameri-
can Place Theater in New York City; it then toured through New
York state colleges under the auspices of the New York State
Council of the Arts. It was also the premiere show at Harlem's
New Lafayette Theatre. Milner's other New York productions in-
clude, most recently, <u>The Warning: A Theme for Linda</u>, which was
presented as a part of <u>A Black Quartet</u>, four one-act plays pro-
duced by Woodie King Associates, Inc." (<u>Black Drama Anthology</u>).
Sources. <u>Black Drama Anthology</u>, Ed. by Woodie King & Ron Milner (New
  Amer. Lib., 1971); "Nat'l. Conf. of Afro-Amer. Writers," (Program),
  Howard U. Inst. for Arts & Humanities, Nov. 1974.

MITCHELL, LOFTEN. 1919- . Playwright, Essayist
Biographical-Personal. Born 1919 in N.Y.C. <u>Educ.</u>: De Witt Clinton
  High Sch., the Bronx; City Coll. of N.Y.; B.A. (honors), Talladega
  Coll., 1943; Columbia U. (Playwriting). <u>Mailing address</u>: c/o
  Hawthorn Books, Inc., 70 Fifth Ave., N.Y., N.Y. 10011.
Career-Professional. Soc. investigator; has written stage plays,
  radio scripts, TV documentaries, & screenplays. Ed., <u>Freedom
  Journal</u> (NAACP).
  WRITINGS: Plays: <u>Tell Pharaoh</u>; <u>Land Beyond the River</u>; <u>No Separa-
  tion</u>. Collaborations: <u>Ballad of the Winter Soldiers</u>, with John O.

196

Molette, Barbara Jean

Killens; Ballad for Bimshire, with Irving
Burgie. (Creator) Star of the Morning & The
Cellar. Voices of the Black Theatre (J. T.
White, 1976). Films: Integration, Report
One, & I'm Sorry. Has written & co-authored:
The American Negro Writer and His Roots, The
First Book of Gypsies, & Black Drama: The
Story of the American Negro in the Theatre.
HONORS AND AWARDS: Guggenheim Award for
Creative Writing in the Drama, 1958-59;
Rockefeller Grant (New Dramatists Com.),
1961.
SIDELIGHTS: Studied playwriting with John
Gassner. Recently completed play: The Final
Solution to the Black Problem in the United
States of America or the Fall of the American
Empire (Black Scenes).
Sources. Afro-American Literature: Drama, Ed. by William Adams et
al. (Houghton Mifflin, 1970); Black American Writer, Vol. II:
Poetry and Drama, Ed. by C. W. E. Bigsby (Penguin, 1969); Black
Scenes, Ed. by Alice Childress (Doubleday, 1971); Negro Almanac,
Comp. by Harry A. Ploski & Roscoe C. Brown, Jr. (Bellwether,
1967).

Molefi Kete Asante. See Smith, Arthur L.

MOLETTE, BARBARA JEAN. 1940- . Costumer, Drama Instructor, Play-
wright
Biographical-Personal. Born Jan. 31, 1940, in L.A., Cal. D. of
Baxter R. and Nora L. [Johnson] Roseburr. Educ.: B.A. (with
highest honors), Fla. A. & M. U., 1966; M.F.A., Fla. State U.,
1969. Family: m. Carlton W. Molette II (drama prof.), June 15,
1960; d. Carla Evelyn, d. Andrea Rose. Mailing address: 3171
Mangum Lane, S.W., Atlanta, Ga. 30311.
Career-Professional. Makeup artist & designer, Costume designer,
Tech. theatre worker, Tuskegee Inst., 1960-61; U. of Iowa, 1961;
Iowa City Community Theatre, 1962; Des Moines Community Playhouse,
1962-63; & Howard U., 1964. Asolo Theatre Festival, Sarasota,
Fla., mem. of costume construction crew, Designer, & Wardrobe
mistress, summer 1968. Drama Coord. for Upward Bound Prog., Fla.
A. & M. U., Tallahassee, summer 1969. Costumer, Morehouse-Spelman
Players, Atlanta, 1969- . Instr. in Fine Arts, Spelman Coll.,
Atlanta, 1969-72, Instr. in Drama, 1972- . Costumer for motion
picture, "Together for Days," 1971. Book review ed., Encore,
1970-72.
WRITINGS: Rosalee Pritchett, with Carlton W. Molette, play (1st
prod. in Atlanta by Morehouse-Spelman Players, Mar. 20, 1970;

Molette, Carlton Woodard II

prod. Off-Broadway at St. Marks Playhouse, Jan. 12, 1971; Drama-
tists Play Serv., 1972); included in Black Writers of America, Ed.
by Richard Barksdale & Kenneth Kinnamon (Macmillan, 1972); Booji
Wooji, with Charles Mann (1st prod. at Atlanta U. Summer Theatre,
July 8, 1971); Doctor B. S. Black, musical, (1st prod. at Atlanta
U. Summer Theatre, July 20, 1972). Also author with husband of
screenplay of Booji Wooji. In progress: "Noah's Ark," play.
Contrib. to period.
HONORS AND AWARDS: Fla. Upward Bound Prog. Play Festival, 1st
place award, 1969.
MEMBER: Dramatists Guild of Authors League; Amer. Theatre Assn.;
Nat'l. Assn. of Dramatic & Speech Arts.
Sources. Black Writers of America, Ed. by Richard Barksdale & Ken-
neth Kinnamon (Macmillan, 1972); Contemporary Authors, Vols. 45-
48, Ed. by Clare D. Kinsman (Gale Res., 1974).

MOLETTE, CARLTON WOODARD II. 1939- . Drama Professor, Playwright,
Theatre Consultant
Biographical-Personal. Born Aug. 23, 1939, in Pine Bluff, Ark. Son
of Carlton William (coll. prof.) and Evelyn Adelle [Richardson]
(coll. dean of women) Molette. Educ.: B.A., Morehouse Coll.,
1959; M.A., U. of Iowa, 1962; Ph.D., Fla. State U., 1968. Family:
m. Barbara Jean Roseburr (coll. instr. & costumer), June 15, 1960;
d. Carla Evelyn, d. Andrea Rose. Mailing address: 3171 Mangum
Lane, S.W., Atlanta, Ga. 30311.
Career-Professional. Asst. Dir., Little Theatre, Tuskegee Inst.,
Ala., 1960-61; Tech. Dir., Des Moines Community Playhouse, Des
Moines, Ia., 1962-63; Asst. Prof. of Drama, Howard U., 1963-64;
Asst. Prof., 1964-66, Assoc. Prof., Speech & Drama, 1967-69, Fla.
A. & M. U., Tallahassee; Assoc. Prof. of Drama, Spelman Coll.,
Atlanta, 1969- , Chmn. of Dept., 1971- . Theatre cons. to coll.
festivals & org. Ed., Encore, 1965-71; Ed. Cons., Southern Speech
Journal, 1966-68; Mem., Advis. Bd., Journal of Black Studies,
1970-73.
WRITINGS: Plays: Doctor B. S. Black (Encore, Vol. 13, 1970);
musical version (with wife, Barbara Molette, & Charles Mann);
Rosalee Pritchett, with Barbara Molette (produced Off-Broadway at
St. Marks Playhouse, Jan. 12, 1971); included in Black Writers of
America, Ed. by Richard Barksdale & Kenneth Kinnamon (Macmillan,
1972); Booji Wooji, with Barbara Molette (1st prod. at Atlanta U.
Summer Theatre, July 8, 1971). Also author with wife of screen-
play of Booji Wooji. In progress: "Noah's Ark," play.
HONORS AND AWARDS: Carnegie Found. grant, 1966-68; Atlanta U.
Center Faculty Res. grant, 1970-71.
MEMBER: Dramatists Guild, Amer. Theatre Assn.; Nat'l. Assn. of
Dramatic Speech Arts; U.S. Inst. for Theatre Tech.; Alpha Phi
Alpha.

Morrow, Everett Frederic

Sources. Black Writers of America, Ed. by Richard Barksdale & Kenneth Kinnamon (Macmillan, 1972); Contemporary Authors, Vols. 45-48,
Ed. by Clare D. Kinsman (Gale Res., 1974).

MOODY, ANNE. 1941- . Writer
Biographical-Personal. Born 1941, in Wilkerson
    Co., Miss. D. of a sharecropper; spent early
    years in extreme poverty. Educ.: Natchez
    Jr. Coll.; Tougaloo Coll., Miss.
Career-Professional. Civil rights worker for
    SNCC.
    WRITINGS: Coming of Age in Mississippi,
    autobiog. (Dial, 1968); Mr. Death: Four Sto-
    ries (Harper & Row, 1975).
    HONORS AND AWARDS: Natchez Jr. Coll. Schol-
    arship.
Source. Afro-American Literature--Nonfiction,
    Ed. by William Adams & Others (Houghton
    Mifflin, 1970).

MORRISON, TONI [Chloe Anthony Wofford]. 1931- .
Novelist, Editor
Biographical-Personal. Born Feb. 18, 1931, in
    Lorain, Ohio. D. of George (laborer) and
    Ramah [Willie] Wofford. Educ.: B.A., Howard
    U., 1953; M.A., Cornell U., 1955. Family:
    son, Harold Ford, son, Slade Kevin. Mailing
    address: Random House, Inc., 201 E. 50th St.,
    N.Y., N.Y. 10022.
Career-Professional. Instr., Eng., Tex. S. U.,
    Houston, 1955-57; Instr., Eng., Howard U.,
    1957-64; Sr. Ed., Random House, N.Y., 1965- ;
    Assoc. Prof., SUNY at Purchase, 1971-72.
    WRITINGS: Novels: The Bluest Eye (Holt,
    1969); Sula, a Novel (Bantam, 1975). Contrib.
    numerous articles and bk. reviews to period.
    MEMBER: Authors Guild Counc.; Nat'l. Counc. Endowment of the Arts.
Source. Contemporary Authors, Vols. 29-32, Ed. by Clare D. Kinsman &
    Mary A. Tennenhouse (Gale Res., 1972).

MORROW, EVERETT FREDERIC. 1909- . Administrator, Businessman
Biographical-Personal. Born April 20, 1909, in Hackensack, N.J. Son
    of John Eugene Morrow and Mary Ann Hayes. Educ.: Bowdoin Coll.;
    LL.B., LL.D., Dr. Juris, Rutgers U. Sch. of Law. Family: m.
    Catherine Gordon of Chgo. Mailing address: 1270 Fifth Ave.,
    N.Y., N.Y. 10029.

Motley, Willard

Career-Professional. Bus. Mgr., Opportunity
mag. (Nat'l. Urban League), 1935; Coord. of
Branches, NAACP, 1937-49; Major, U.S. Army
Artillery; With CBS, 1949- ; Cons.-Advis.,
Eisenhower campaign train, 1952; Advis., Bus.
Affairs, Secy. of Commerce; Admin. Asst. to
Pres. Eisenhower, 1955; Asst. V. Pres., Bank
of America, Internat.
WRITINGS: Black Man in the White House
(Coward-McCann, 1963); Way Down South Up
North (1973).
HONORS AND AWARDS: Bowdoin Coll., LL.D.,
1971.
SIDELIGHTS: "Has chalked up many firsts.
Perhaps most significant was appointment as
Administrative Assistant to President Eisen-
hower in 1955. First time a Negro held an executive position on
the President's staff. Also first in an executive position with
CBS in 1949. He became Assistant Vice President of Bank of Ameri-
ca International" (Negroes in Public Affairs and Government).
Sources. Author inform.; Negroes in Public Affairs and Government,
Ed. by Walter Christmas (Educ. Her., 1966).

MOTLEY, WILLARD. 1912-1965. Novelist
Biographical-Personal. Born 1912 in Chgo., Ill.
Son of middle-class parents. Died Mexico
City, Mexico (where he had lived for 12 years).
Career-Professional. Farm worker, waiter, ship-
ping clerk, cook, and "coal hiker." Wrote
articles for Commonweal; Worked for Fed.
Writers Project (studying living conditions
in Chgo. Black community).
WRITINGS: Novels: Knock On Any Door (Apple-
ton, 1947); We Fished All Night (Appleton,
1951); Let No Man Write My Epitaph (Random
House, 1958); Let Noon Be Fair (Putnam, 1966).
SIDELIGHTS: Even though a product of a middle class home, he chose to live on Chicago's
Skid Row in order to write about its dere-
licts. Knock On Any Door became an immediate best seller, later
made into a successful motion picture. This work caused The New
York Times to comment: "An extraordinary and powerful new natur-
alistic talent herewith makes its debut in American letters."
"In his second and third novels...Mr. Motley continued to write
in the 'environmentalist' tradition of Richard Wright, although
his characters were not Negroes but Italian immigrants living and

El Muhajir

dying in the slums of Chicago. In these works there is protest but without considerations of race and racial conflict" (Soon, One Morning).
Sources. The Best Short Stories by Negro Writers, Ed. by Langston Hughes (Little, Brown, 1967); The Negro Almanac, Comp. by Harry A. Ploski & Ernest Kaiser (Bellwether, 1971); Soon, One Morning, Ed. by Herbert Hill (Knopf, 1963).

MOTON, ROBERT RUSSA. 1867-1940. Principal, Tuskegee Institute
Biographical-Personal. Born Aug. 26, 1867, in Amelia Co., Va. Son of Booker and Emily Moton. Educ.: Hampton Inst., Va. Family: 1st m. Elizabeth Hunt Harris, 1905 (dec. 1906); 2nd m. Jennie D. Booth; 5 children. Died 1940.
Career-Professional. Commandant, Hampton Inst., 1890-1914. Prin., Tuskegee Inst., 1915-1935. WRITINGS: Racial Good Will (1916); Finding a Way Out (1920); What the Negro Thinks (1929). HONORS AND AWARDS: Recipient, Harmon Award, 1930; Spingarn Medal, 1932. Several degrees conferred, including: M.A., Harvard; LL.D., Va. Union U., Oberlin, Williams, & Howard U.
MEMBER: Pres., Nat'l. Negro Bus. League, 1919- . Trus. & dir. in about 20 educ. or soc. agencies.
SIDELIGHTS: "Robert R. Moton was the successor to Booker T. Washington as principal of Tuskegee Institute; as such he inherited his predecessor's position as spokesman for industrial education" (Negro Caravan).
"...When the Commission on Interracial Cooperation was organized in Atlanta in 1918, Dr. Moton became one of the leading spirits.
"Moton stood his ground against bigotry when a hospital for Negro veterans was proposed at Tuskegee. He persisted until finally all black doctors and staff was appointed" (Negro Builders and Heroes).
Sources. Negro Builders and Heroes, Benjamin G. Brawley (U. of N.C., 1937); Negro Caravan, Sterling A. Brown, et al. (Arno Pr. & N.Y. Times, 1969).

EL MUHAJIR [Marvin X]. 1944- . Poet, Playwright-Director, Lecturer
Biographical-Personal. Born May 29, 1944, in Fowler, Cal. Educ.: Edison High Sch., Fresno, Cal.; Oakland City Coll., 1962-64; B.A. (Eng.), San Francisco State U., 1964-66, (grad. study), 1974. Family: m.; 5 children.

Muhammad, Elijah

Career-Professional. Founder (with Ed Bullins), Black Arts/W.
  Theatre/Sch., San Francisco, 1966; Founder, Al Kitab Sudan Pub.
  Co., San Francisco, 1967; Fict. Ed., Black Dialogue mag., 1965- ;
  Contrib. Ed., Journal of Black Poetry, 1965- ; Assoc. Ed., Black
  Theatre, 1968; Foreign Ed., Muhammad Speaks, 1970. Founder, Dir.,
  Your Black Educ. Theatre, Inc., San Francisco, 1971. Tchr., Black
  Stud.: Fresno State U.; 1969; U. of Cal., Berkeley, 1972; Mills
  Coll., 1973.
  WRITINGS: Sudan Rajul Samia, poems (Al Kitab Sudan, 1967); Black
  Dialectics, proverbs (Al Kitab Sudan, 1967); Fly to Allah, poems
  (Al Kitab Sudan, 1969); Son of Man, proverbs (Al Kitab Sudan,
  1969); Black Bird, parable (Al Kitab Sudan, 1972); Woman--Man's
  Best Friend, collected poems, proverbs, parables, songs (Al Kitab
  Sudan, 1973); Black Man Listen, poems and proverbs (Broadside
  Pr., 1970). Plays: Flowers for the Trashman, one-act; Come Next
  Summer; The Trial; Take Care of Business; Resurrection of the
  Dead; Woman--Man's Best Friend. Anthol.: Black Fire; New Plays
  from the Black Theatre; Vietnam and Black America; You Better Be-
  lieve It. Contrib. articles, interviews and poems to: Soulbook,
  Encore, Black World, Black Scholar, et al.
  HONORS AND AWARDS: Life member, Cal. Scholarship Federation;
  Dean's List, San Francisco State U.; Writing grants totaling
  $8,000 from Columbia U., 1969; NEA, 1972.
  SIDELIGHTS: Flowers for the Trashman, 1st prod. in San Francisco
  by drama dept., San Francisco State Coll., 1965; Come Next Summer,
  prod. by Black Arts W., 1966; The Trial, 1st prod. in Harlem,
  1970; Take Care of Business, musical version of Flowers for the
  Trashman, prod. San Francisco by Black Educ. Theatre, 1971; Resurrection of the Dead (ritual dance drama) 1st prod. San Francisco
  by Your Black Educ. Theatre, 1972; Woman--Man's Best Friend (musical dance drama), 1st prod. in Oakland at Mills Coll., 1973. Has
  given lecture/readings at more than 20 colleges & universities,
  including Stanford, Cornell, Loyola of Chgo., U. of Toronto, U. of
  Cal. Berkeley, U. of Cal. Davis, UCLA, U. of Cal. San Diego, U.
  of Okla. and Manhattan Community Coll., N.Y.C. (Author).
Source. Author inform.

MUHAMMAD, ELIJAH. 1897-1975. Religious Leader
Biographical-Personal. Born Elijah Poole, Oct. 10, 1897, in Sanders-
  ville, Ga. Son of former slaves, Wali (sharecropper & Bap. minister) & Marie Poole; 1 of 13 children. Self-educated. Family:
  m. Clara Evans, March 7, 1919; 6 sons, 2 daughters. Died Feb. 27,
  1975.
Career-Professional. Field hand, railroad laborer; Chevrolet Co.,
  Detroit, 1923-29; On relief, 1929-31. In 1930 met the founder of
  the Nation of Islam (Black Muslims), Wallace D. Fard, changed his
  name to Muhammad and took over leadership on disappearance of Fard
  in 1934.

Murphy, Beatrice Campbell

WRITINGS: Message to the Black Man (Muhammad's Mosque No. 2, 1964); How to Eat to Live. Muslim's weekly tabloid, Muhammad Speaks. SIDELIGHTS: "Like Marcus Garvey before him, Elijah Muhammad preaches that the only salvation for the black man in the United States is withdrawal into his own autonomous nation, away from a white social and economic system that is--in Muhammad's view--rigged against him. Tough-minded Muhammad claims to be the divinely appointed 'Messenger' of Allah, and thousands of poor, alienated blacks have accepted his message, changing their lives to join the Nation of Islam, with its stern morality, strict authoritarianism, pacifism (except in self-defense), racial dignity, and program of economic self-improvement..." (Current Biography, 1971).

Sources. Current Biography, 1971, Ed. by Charles Moritz (H. W. Wilson, 1971); Negro Almanac, Comp. by Harry A. Ploski & Ernest Kaiser (Bellwether, 1971); Negro Handbook, Comp. by Eds. of Ebony (Johnson Pub., 1966).

MURPHY, BEATRICE CAMPBELL. 1908- . Editor, Poet

Biographical-Personal. Born June 25, 1908, in Monessen, Pa. D. of Benjamin and Maude Campbell. Educ.: High Sch. and spec. courses. Family: div.; son, Alvin H. Murphy. Mailing address: 117 R. Street, N.E., Wash., D.C. 20002.

Career-Professional. Managing Ed.-Dir., Minority Res. Center, Inc., presently. Dir., The Negro Bibliographic & Res. Center, Inc.; Managing Ed., Bibliographic Survey: The Negro in Print.

WRITINGS: Poetry: The Rocks Cry Out, with Dr. Nancy Arnez (Broadside Pr., 1969); Love is a Terrible Thing (Hobson, 1945). Catching the Editor's Eye, how-to pam. for writers (1947). Ed.: Negro Voices (Harrison, 1938); Ebony Rhythm (Exposition Pr., 1948); Today's Negro Voices; an Anthology by Young Negro Poets (Messner, 1970).

Sources. Author inform.; Today's Negro Voices, Ed. by Beatrice M. Murphy (Julian Messner, 1970).

Murphy, Carl

MURPHY, CARL. 1889-1967. Publisher
Biographical-Personal. Born Jan. 17, 1889, in Baltimore, Md. Educ.:
B.A. (cum laude) Howard U., 1911; M.A., Harvard U., 1913, U. of
Jena (E. Germany); LL.D., Lincoln U. (Pa.), 1948; L.H.D., Central
State Coll., 1960. Family: 1st m. Vashti Turley, 1916 (dec.
1960); d. Martha Elizabeth, son, Phillips, d. Ida Ann Smith, d.
Carlita Jones, d. Vashti Turley Matthews, d. Frances L. Wood; 2nd
m. Lillian Matthews Prescott, 1961. Died 1967.
Career-Professional. Instr., Asst. Prof., German, Howard U., 1913-18;
Ed., Afro-American newspapers, 1918-44, Pub. & Chmn., Bd. of Dir.,
1922- .
HONORS AND AWARDS: Amer. Teamwork Award, Nat'l. Urban League,
1956; 30th Spingarn Medalist, NAACP, 1955.
MEMBER: V. Pres., Amalgamated Pub. Inc.; Advis. Bd., Post Off.
Dept., 1961- ; Chmn., Bd. Trus., Morgan State Coll.; Trus., Dow-
ington (Pa.) Indust. Sch.; Commander, Order of Star of Africa,
Liberia, 1952; NAACP, Nat'l. Bd. of Dir., 1931- .
Sources. Negro Handbook, Comp. by Eds. of Ebony (Johnson Pub.,
1966); In Black and White, Mary M. Spradling (Kalamazoo Lib.
System, 1971).

MURRAY, ALBERT L. 1916- . Air Force Officer,
Teacher, Consultant
Biographical-Personal. Born May 12, 1916, in
Nokomis, Ala. Son of Hugh and Mattie Murray.
Educ.: B.S., Tuskegee Inst.; M.A., N.Y.U.
Family: m. Mozelle Menefee; d. Michele.
Mailing address: 45 W. 132nd St., N.Y., N.Y.
10037.
Career-Professional. U.S. Air Force major, re-
tired. Tchr., Lit., Tuskegee Inst. Cons.:
(Cultural hist.) Nat'l. Educ. TV; U.S. Inform.
Agency.
WRITINGS: The Omni-Americans (Avon, 1970);
South to a Very Old Place (1972); The Hero
and the Blues (1973); Train Whistle Guitar
(McGraw, 1975). Essays, criticism, short
stories: New World Writing, Life, The New Leader, Book World,
Harper's, others.
SIDELIGHTS: Has also studied at the U. of Mich., the U. of Chgo.,
the U. of Paris, and Northwestern U. Book World says: "Murray
has set up an identifying mirror for Negroes, and for all of us,
more inviting, more durable and truer to our history than the
separatist-nihilist ones now so voguish" (Omni-Americans).
Sources. Author inform.; The Omni-Americans, Albert Murray (Avon,
1970).

MURRAY, PAULI. 1910- . Lawyer, Author, Priest
Biographical-Personal. Born 1910 in Baltimore,
Md. Her grandfather on the maternal side
fought with the Union armies in Civil War;
later helped to establish 1st sch. system
for free Blacks of Va. & N.C. (for Freedmen's
Bureau); maternal grandmother a slave. Educ.:
B.A., Hunter Coll.; LL.B. (cum laude), Har-
vard U. Sch. of Law; LL.M., Sch. of Juris-
prudence, U. of Cal., 1945.
Career-Professional. Member: Cal. & N.Y. State
Bars; Deputy Attorney Gen., Cal.; Staff, Com.
on Law & Soc. Action, Amer. Jewish Congress;
Tchr., Ghana Sch. of Law & Brandeis U.
(Mass.); Episcopal Priest.
WRITINGS: States' Laws on Race and Color, Comp. & Ed.; Proud
Shoes, the Story of an American Family (1956); Dark Testament,
poetry (1969). Articles and poems have appeared in Common Ground,
South Today, Saturday Review.
HONORS AND AWARDS: Eugene F. Saxton Fellow.; Resident fellow,
MacDowell Colony in Peterboro, N.H.; Mademoiselle mag. award for
distinguished achievement in practice of law.
SIDELIGHTS: Of Proud Shoes (the story of her own family) it has
been said: "This extraordinary memoir is important both as lit-
erature and as social history, and is based upon a record of fact"
(Soon, One Morning).
  She has been a pioneer in the areas of civil rights; she was a
"freedom rider" in the 1940's to protest segregated seating on
interstate buses, and she has brought action against various universities to admit women to their graduate schools (Poetry of
Black America). Recently became first Black woman priest in the
U.S. (Compiler).
Sources. American Negro Poetry, Ed. by Arna Bontemps (Hill & Wang,
1963); Poetry of Black America, Ed. by Arnold Adoff (Harper & Row,
1973); Soon, One Morning, Ed. by Herbert Hill (Knopf, 1963).

MYERS, WALTER DEAN. 1937- . Juvenile Author
Biographical-Personal. Born Aug. 12, 1937, in
Martinsburg, W. Va. Son of Herbert and
Florence Dean. Educ.: City U. Family:
son, Michael, d. Karen. Mailing address:
150 West 225th St., Sec. 10, Bronx, N.Y.
10463.
Career-Professional. Juvenile author.
  WRITINGS: Juveniles: Where Does The Day Go?
  (Parents Mag. Pr., 1969); The Dancers (Par-
  ents Mag. Pr., 1972); The Dragon Takes a Wife
  (Bobbs-Merrill, 1972); Fly, Jimmy, Fly (Put-

Neal, Lawrence P.

nam, 1974); <u>Fast Sam, Cool Clyde & Stuff</u> (Viking, 1975). In
progress: <u>World of Work</u> (Bobbs-Merrill). Anthol.: <u>We Be Word
Sorcerors</u> (Bantam); <u>What We Must See</u> (Dodd-Mead). Period.: <u>Black
World</u>, <u>Black Creation</u>, <u>Cavalier</u>, <u>The Swinger</u>, <u>Phoenix</u>, <u>Ebony, Jr.</u>,
<u>Scholastic</u>, others.
HONORS AND AWARDS: Interracial Counc. for Children's Bks. Award,
1968.
Source. Author inform.

Nazzam Al Fitnah. <u>See</u> Jackmon, Marvin.

NEAL, LAWRENCE P. 1937- . Poet, Editor,
Activist
Biographical-Personal. Born Sept. 5, 1937, in
    Atlanta, Ga. Educ.: B.A., Lincoln U., 1961;
    M.A., U. of Pa., 1963. Family: m. Evelyn
    Rodgers of Birmingham, Ala. Mailing address:
    12 Jumel Ter., N.Y., N.Y. 10032.
Career-Professional. Has acted as Arts Ed.,
    Liberator; Ed., The Cricket & Journal of
    Black Poetry, 1964-66; Tchr., City Coll. of
    N.Y., 1968-69; Writer-in-Residence, Wesleyan
    U., 1969-70; Fellow, Yale U., 1970-75.
    WRITINGS: Black Boogaloo, notes on Black
    Liberation (Journal of Black Poetry Pr.,
    1969); Hoodoo Hollerin' Bebop Ghosts (Random
    House, 1971); Analytical Study of Afro-Ameri-
can Culture (Random House, 1972). Black Fire, Co-ed. with LeRoi
Jones (Morrow, 1971); For Malcolm, anthol. Pub. in: Soulbook,
Black Dialogue, Negro Digest, Liberator and Cheyney Review.
HONORS AND AWARDS: Won lit. prizes in 1960 from Lincoln U.; was
awarded Guggenheim Fellow., 1971-72, for stud. in contemporary
Afro-Amer. culture; Yale fellow.
SIDELIGHTS: Was associated with LeRoi Jones and Black Arts move-
ment for several years. Was educational director for New York
Black Panther Party. "I see my work as the spiritual, cultural,
and political voice of my people, and I place it at their service.
I feel that Black America is the final arbiter of the works of her
artists" (For Malcolm).
Sources. Blackamerican Literature, Ed. by Ruth Miller (Glencoe Pr.,
    1971); Black American Writer, Vol. II: Poetry and Drama, Ed. by
    C. W. E. Bigsby (Penquin, 1967); Black Fire, Ed. by LeRoi Jones
    and Larry Neal (Morrow, 1968); For Malcolm, Ed. by Dudley Randall
    & Margaret Burroughs (Broadside Pr., 1969); New Black Voices, Ed.
    by Abraham Chapman (New Amer. Lib., 1972); Soulscript, Ed. by June
    Jordan (Doubleday, 1970).

NELL, WILLIAM COWPER. 1816–1874. Historian
Biographical-Personal. Born 1816 in Boston, Mass. Schooling was
  elementary, but he struggled for self-improvement.
Career-Professional. He was closely associated with William Lloyd
  Garrison in the publication of the Liberator, (as copyist, ac-
  countant and collector), and for a time with Frederick Douglass
  in publication of the North Star in Rochester, N.Y.
  WRITINGS: "Upon the suggestion of Whittier, Nell gathered the
  facts for a pamphlet, Services of Colored Americans in the Wars of
  1776 and 1812 (1851), which he enlarged into The Colored Patriots
  of the American Revolution (1855). Wendell Phillips and Harriet
  Beecher Stowe prepared introductions to this work, one of the best
  examples of early historical writing by American Negroes" (Negro
  Caravan).
Sources. Negro Author, Vernon Loggins (Kennikat, 1959); Negro Caravan, Ed. by Sterling A. Brown & Others (Arno Pr. & N.Y. Times,
  1969); Historical Negro Biographies, Wilhelmena S. Robinson
  (ASNLH, 1967).

NELSON, ALICE DUNBAR. 1875–1935. Journalist,
  Lecturer, Writer
Biographical-Personal. Born Alice Ruth Moore in
  1875, in New Orleans, La. Educ.: Straight
  Coll., New Orleans; U. of Pa.; Cornell U.;
  Sch. of Indust. Art. Family: 1st m. Paul
  Laurence Dunbar, 1898 (poet); 2nd m. Robert
  John Nelson, 1916. Died 1935.
Career-Professional. Tchr., New Orleans and
  Brooklyn, N.Y.; Journalist; Lectr. One of
  founders of White Rose Indust. Home, N.Y. &
  Indust. Sch. for Colored Girls, Del.
  WRITINGS: Violets and Other Tales (1894);
  The Goodness of St. Tocque (1899; AMS Pr.,
  repr.,1975); Masterpieces of Negro Eloquence,
  Ed. (1913); The Dunbar Speaker, Ed. (1920);
The Negro in Louisiana. People and Music, New ed. (Allyn, 1973).
Contrib. to mag. and newspapers, as short story writer and colum-
nist.
Sources. Caroling Dusk, Ed. by Countee Cullen (Harper & Row, 1927);
Negro Poets and Their Poems, Ed. by Robert T. Kerlin (Assoc. Pub.,
1935); Poetry of Black America, Ed. by Arnold Adoff (Harper & Row,
1973); Books in Print, Supplement, 1975-76 (Bowker, 1976).

NEWSOME, MARY EFFIE. 1885- . Librarian, Children's Poet
Biographical-Personal. Born Jan. 19, 1885, in Phila., Pa. D. of
  Benjamin Franklin (AME minister) and Mary Elizabeth [Ashe] Lee.
  Educ.: Wilberforce U.; Oberlin Coll.; U. of Pa. Family: m. Rev.
  Henry N. Newsome, 1920 (dec.). Mailing address: 954 Olive Rd.,
  Dayton, Ohio.

Newton, Huey P.

Career-Professional. Head, Children's Lib., Dept. of Educ., Central
State Coll., Wilberforce, Ohio.
WRITINGS: Children's poetry: Gladiola Garden (ASNLH, 1940); Come
Ye Apart (Inter-racial Missionary Assn.). Anthol.: The Poetry of
the Negro (1949, 1970); American Negro Poetry (1963); and six
others. Period.: Negro History Bulletin.
HONORS AND AWARDS: Chestnut Honorarium, NAPA.
SIDELIGHTS: Retired in 1963. Began writing verse at age 5; a
novel at age 11. Spent much of life at Wilberforce (Famous Ameri-
can Negro Poets).
Sources. Author inform.; Famous American Negro Poets, Charlemae Rol-
lins (Dodd, Mead, 1955); Poetry of Black America, Ed. by Arnold
Adoff (New Amer. Lib., 1973).

NEWTON, HUEY P. Revolutionary
Career-Professional. Black Panther leader.
    WRITINGS: Revolutionary Suicide, with as-
    sistance of J. Herman Blake (Harcourt, 1973);
    To Die for the People; the writings of Huey
    P. Newton (Random House, 1972); Insights and
    Poems, with Ericka Huggins (City Lights,
    1975); In Search of Common Ground, with E.
    Erikson (Dell, 1974).
Sources. Forthcoming Books, Sept. 1975 (Bowker,
    1975).

NICHOLS, CHARLES HAROLD. 1919- . English
Professor, Scholar
Biographical-Personal. Born July 6, 1919, in
    Brooklyn, N.Y. Son of Charles F. and Julia
    [King] Nichols. Educ.: B.A., Brooklyn Coll.,
    1942; Ph.D., Brown U., 1948. Family: m.
    Mildred Thompson; son, David, son, Keith, son,
    Brian. Mailing address: Box 1852, Brown U.,
    Providence, R.I. 02912.
Career-Professional. Prof. Eng., Hampton Inst.,
    1949-59; Prof. of N. Amer. Lit., Free U. of
    Berlin, 1959-69; Prof. of Eng. & Chmn., Afro-
    Amer. Stud. Prog., Brown U. (Presently).
    WRITINGS: Many Thousand Gone, The Ex-Slaves
    Account of Their Bondage and Freedom (E. J.
    Brill, 1963; Indiana U., 1969); Instructor's
Guide to Accompany Cavalcade: Negro American Writing (Houghton
Mifflin, 1970). Ed.: African Nights: Black Erotic Folk Tales
(Herden, 1971); Black Men in Chains: An Anthology of Slave Nar-
ratives (Lawrence Hill, 1972). In progress: Biography of Theo-
dore Parker. Articles: Phylon, William & Mary Quarterly, School

O'Daniel, Therman Benjamin

& Society, Fulbright Monitor (Copenhagen), College English, Det
Danske Magasin, The American-Scandinavian Review, Virginia Educa-
tion Bulletin, Modern Language Journal, Sonnenberg-Briefe, Uni-
versitätstage, Nation, Jahrbuch für Amerikastudien, America in
the 20th Century, Der Monat, Neusprachliche Mitteilungen aus Wis-
senschaft und Praxis, Praxis des Neusprachlichen Unterrichts.
Reviews: Commentary, Virginia Teachers Bulletin, Dayton Daily
News, Phylon, Studies on the Left.
HONORS AND AWARDS: Rachel Herstein Scholarship, 1938-42; N.Y.
State Regents Scholar; Rosenwald Fellow; Fulbright Grants; Sr.
Fellow, NEH, 1973-74. Guest Prof. of Amer. Lit., Aarhus U.,
1954-55; Guest Lectr., Oxford, Stockholm, Oslo, Rome, etc.
Source. Author inform.

O'DANIEL, THERMAN BENJAMIN. 1908- . Editor, English Professor
Biographical-Personal. Born July 9, 1908, in Wilson, N.C. Son of
John W. and Ernestine [Williams] O'Daniel. Educ.: B.A., Lincoln
U. (Pa.), 1930; M.A., U. of Pa., 1932; Ph.D., U. of Ottawa (Can.),
1956; further study: Harvard U., U. of Chgo. & Penn. State U.
Family: m. Lillian Davis. Mailing address: Morgan State Coll.,
Baltimore, Md. 21239.
Career-Professional. One of founders, CLA Journal, & Ed., 1957- .
Eng. tchr. (41 yrs.): Allen U., Columbia, S.C. (Head, Eng. Dept.,
Dean, Liberal Arts Coll., Acting Pres.); Fort Valley State Coll.,
Ga. (Head, Eng. Dept., Acting Registrar, Acting Dean, Registrar,
Dir., Summer Sch.); Morgan State Coll., Baltimore (Dir., Summer
Sch., 2 yrs.); Dillard U., New Orleans.
WRITINGS: Langston Hughes, Black Genius: A Critical Evaluation,
Ed. (Morrow, 1971); Introduction to The Blacker the Berry, by Wal-
lace Thurman (Collier, 1970); James Baldwin: A Critical Evalua-
tion (Howard U. Pr., 1976). Many scholarly articles.
HONORS AND AWARDS: Gen. Educ. Fellow, U. of Chgo.; Ford Found.
Fellow, U. of Ottawa. Recipient, Spec. Alice E. Johnson Memorial
Fund Award (from Black Acad. of Arts & Letters) for CLA Journal,
1972.
MEMBER: MLA; Nat'l. Counc. of Tchrs. of Eng.; CLA; The Melville
Soc.; Coll. Eng. Assn.; Nat'l. Educ. Assn.; Md. Counc. of Eng.
Tchrs.; Soc. for the Study of S. Lit.; ASNLH; African Her. Stud.
Assn.; NAACP (life mem.).
SIDELIGHTS: The CLA Journal, scholarly quarterly publication in
language & literature, is official publication of College Language
Association. O'Daniel served as Consultant & lecturer in Summer
Institutes in North Carolina & Louisiana. Traveled in England &
Europe, & rather extensively in the Caribbean & the U.S. and
Canada (Author).
Sources. Author inform.; Books in Print, Supplement, 1975-76 (Bow-
ker, 1976).

Oden, Gloria Catherine

ODEN, GLORIA CATHERINE. 1923- . Editor, Poet, Teacher

Biographical-Personal. Born Oct. 30, 1923, in Yonkers, N.Y. D. of Redmond Stanley and Ethel [Kincaid] Oden. Educ.: B.A. (Eng., Hist.), Howard U., 1944, J.D., 1948; Amer. Stud., N.Y.U. Family: divorced. Mailing address: U. of Md., Baltimore Co., 5401 Wilkens Ave., Baltimore, Md. 21228.

Career-Professional. Asst. Prof., Eng., U. of Md., Baltimore Co., 1971- ; Vis. Lectr., Black Poetry, State U. of N.Y., Stony Brook; Project Dir., Lang. Arts Bks., Holt, Rinehart & Winston, also Sr. Ed., Coll. Dept., Math. & Sci. Bks. (spec.: physics, engineering & calculus), 1968-71; Supv., all math & sci. bks., Appleton-Century-Crofts, 1967-68; Sr. Ed., Inst. of Electric & Electronic Engineers, 1966-67; Ed., The Amer. Inst. of Physics (sole responsibility: The American Journal of Physics), 1961-66.

WRITINGS: Poetry-period. contrib.: Quicksilver (Winter, 1958; Spring, 1960); Hawkeye Poetry Magazine (Sept.-Oct., 1959); Canadian Forum (Dec. 1959); Writer's Voice (Sept. 1959); Poetry Digest (Jan., Oct., 1959); The Muse (Autumn 1959); Voices (Sept.-Dec., 1959); Oak Leaves (June 1959); Jan.-Feb. 1960); The Blue River Poetry Magazine (Spring 1959); Targets (Sept. 1960); Half Moon (Summer 1960); Impetus (Winter, 1960-61); The Wormwood Review (1961, 1962); The Outsider (Fall, 1961, 1962); Epos (Spring 1961); Mutiny (Spring 1961); Poetry Northwest (Autumn 1963); Lynx (July 1963); Damascus Road (1972). Anthols. to: American Negro Poetry; New Negro Poets: USA; Schwarzer Orpheus; Kaleidoscope.

HONORS AND AWARDS: Creative Writing Fellow, John Hay Whitney Found., 1955-56; Fellow, Yaddo, Saratoga Springs, N.Y., 1956; Breadloaf Writers Scholar, Middlebury Coll., 1960; Summer Stipend, NEH, 1974; Interviewed for Black Oral Hist. Prog. at Fisk U. Lib., 1973.

Sources. Author inform.; Ebony (March 1974); Poetry of Black America, Ed. by Arnold Adoff (Harper & Row, 1973).

OLOGLONI, TEJUMOLA [Rockie D. Taylor]. 1945- . Artist, Poet

Biographical-Personal. Born 1945 in Salina, Kan. Educ.: B.A. & Art Educ. degrees, U. of Wis., Milwaukee; Further study: (Fine Arts & African Cultural Stud.), Ind. U.

Career-Professional. Lectr. & Black poet-in-residence, Afro-Amer. Stud. Dept., U. of Wis., Milwaukee.

WRITINGS: Drum Song, poetry (1969).

SIDELIGHTS: "He is a member of the Black Poetic Messengers, which provides a center for analysis and criticism of Black creative

writing in Milwaukee; he was one of the founders of the Gallery
Toward the Black Aesthetic in Milwaukee, a community-based organization 'working toward the establishment of the Black Aesthetic
that will cover all forms of expression'" (New Black Voices).
Source. New Black Voices, Ed. by Abraham Chapman (New Amer. Lib.,
1972).

OTTLEY, ROI VINCENT. 1906-1960. Social Historian
Biographical-Personal. Born Aug. 2, 1906, in N.Y.C. Son of Jerome
P. and Beatrice [Brisbane] Ottley. Educ.: St. Bonaventure Coll.,
1926-27; U. of Mich. (2 yrs.); Columbia U., 1934-35; N.Y.U.,
1935-36; St. John's U. Sch. of Law. Family: m. Gladys Tarr,
April 1941. Died 1960.
Career-Professional. Reporter, Columnist, Ed., Amsterdam Star News,
1930-37; Publicity Dir., Nat'l. CIO War Relief Com., 1943; War
Corresp., Liberty mag.
WRITINGS: New World A-Coming: Inside Black America (Houghton
Mifflin, 1943); Black Odyssey (Scribners, 1948); No Green Pastures
(Scribners, 1951); Lonely Warrior: Life and Times of Robert S.
Abbott (Regnery, 1955); White Marble Lady, novel (Farrar, Straus,
1965); Negro in New York: An Informal Social History, with Wil-
liam J. Weatherby, eds. (N.Y. Public Lib., 1967).
SIDELIGHTS: John Chamberlain comments in the New York Times, "He
writes a vigorous prose, mingling history, humor, irony, drama,
and sober reflection in a work that explains the current status
and the wholly reasonable demands of the Negroes as no other does."
Lewis Gannett describes (New World A-Coming) as "a shrewd, lively,
and often surprising interpretation of the present state of mind
of Negro America." Sam Halper of the New York Post wrote, "The
way to start in to learn about the Negroes is to read Ottley's
fine book" (Current Biography).
Sources. Afro-American Writers, Darwin T. Turner (Appleton, 1970);
Current Biography, 1943, Ed. by Maxine Block (H. W. Wilson, 1944);
Lonesome Road, Saunders Redding (Doubleday, 1958); Negro Almanac,
Comp. by Harry A. Ploski & Roscoe C. Brown (Bellwether, 1967);
Books in Print, Supplement, 1975-76 (Bowker, 1976).

OWENS, JESSE. 1913- . Track and Field Star
Biographical-Personal. Born Sept. 12, 1913, in Danville, Ala. Son
of Henry and Emma Owens. Educ.: E. Tech. High Sch., Cleveland,
Ohio; B.A., Ohio State U., 1937. Family: m. Ruth Solomon, 1935;
d. Gloria Hemphill, d. Beverly Prather, d. Marlene Runkin. Mail-
ing address: 3007 E. Ocotilla Lane, Phoenix, Ariz. 85028.
Career-Professional. Athlete, Org. official, Sales Executive, Pub-
lic Speaker, Cons.
WRITINGS: Black Think (Morrow, 1970); I Have Changed, with Paul
G. Neimark (Morrow, 1972).
HONORS AND AWARDS: Black Hall of Fame; E. Tech. Hall of Fame;
U.S., Track & Field Hall of Fame; State of Ala., Hall of Fame;

Parks, Gordon Alexander

Ambassador of "Good Will" to Far East (Eisenhower Admin.); Hon. doctorates: Otterbein Coll. (Public Serv.); Nevada U. (Law); Ohio State U. (Athletic Arts).

SIDELIGHTS: "The track and field records which Jesse Owens once set have all been eclipsed in the more than quarter century since he established them, but his reputation as one of the first great athletes with the combined talents of sprinter, low hurdler, and broad jumper has hardly diminished with the passing of time."

"In 1936, at the Berlin Olympics, Owens won four gold medals, at that time the most universally acclaimed feat in the history of the games. When Adolf Hitler refused to present him medals he had won in the various competitions, Owens's fame became even more widespread as a result of the publicity" (Negro Almanac).

Sources. Author inform.; Current Biography, 1956, Ed. by Margaret D. Candee (H. W. Wilson, 1956); Famous Negro Athletes, Arna Bontemps (Dodd, Mead, 1964); Negro Almanac, Comp. by Harry A. Ploski & Ernest Kaiser (Bellwether, 1971).

PARKS, GORDON ALEXANDER. 1912- . Photographer, Editorial Director, Film Producer, Director

Biographical-Personal. Born Nov. 30, 1912, in Fort Scott, Kan. Son of Andrew Jackson and Sarah [Ross] Parks. Educ.: High sch., St. Paul, Minn.; self-educated. Family: 1st m. Sally Alvis, 1933 (div. 1961); son, Gordon, Jr., d. Toni (Mrs. Jean-Luc Brouillard), son, David; 2nd m. Elizabeth Campbell, Dec. 1962 (div. 1973); d. Leslie. Mailing address: 15 Adams Pl., White Plains, N.Y. 10603.

Career-Professional. Wartime serv.: Office of War Inform., photographer & corresp., 1942-45. Photographer, Life mag., 1948-72; Ed. dir., Essence, 1970- ; Prod. & Dir., Warner Bros., 1968; Dir., Metro-Goldwyn-Mayer, 1970-72. Winger Corp., Pres.

WRITINGS: Autobiog.: The Learning Tree (Harper & Row, 1963); A Choice of Weapons (Harper & Row, 1966). A Poet and His Camera, with own photos (Viking, 1968); Whispers of Intimate Things, with own photos (Viking, 1971); Born Black (Lippincott, 1971); In Love (Lippincott, 1971); Moments Without Proper Names (Viking, 1975). HONORS AND AWARDS: Hon. degrees from educ. inst.; Photographer of Yr., Assn. of Mag. Photographers; Mass Media Award, Nat'l. Conf.

Patterson, Raymond Richard

of Christians & Jews, for outstanding contrib. to better human relat.; Carr Van Adna Award, 1970; Spingarn Medal, NAACP, 1972. MEMBER: Authors Guild (Counc.); Black Acad. of Arts & Letters (fellow); Dir. Guild of Amer. (Nat'l. counc.); ASCAP; Amer. Fed. of TV & Radio Artists; NAACP; Players Club; Dir. Guild of N.Y. (Counc.).
SIDELIGHTS: Beginning in 1954 served as consultant in filming of several Hollywood productions. In 1960's filmed 3 documentaries on Black ghetto life for National Educational TV, and The Weapons of Gordon Parks, a TV adaptation of his autobiography, narrated by Parks, was presented over CBS network in April 1968. The Learning Tree was filmed by Warner Bros.-Seven Arts--for which Parks wrote the score. His previous musical compositions include a piano concerto (1953) & three piano sonatas (1955). Second wife, Elizabeth Campbell, high fashion model, was the daughter of late cartoonist E. Simms Campbell (Current Biography, 1968).
Sources. Contemporary Authors, Vols. 41-44, Ed. by Clare D. Kinsman (Gale Res., 1974); Current Biography, 1968, Ed. by Charles Moritz (H. W. Wilson, 1969); Pub. inform.; Books in Print, Supplement, 1975-76 (Bowker, 1976).

PATTERSON, LINDSAY. Editor, Short Story Writer
Biographical-Personal. Born in Bastrop, La. Family: Single. Mailing address: 42 Perry St., N.Y., N.Y. 10014.
Career-Professional.
WRITINGS: Black Theater: A Twentieth-Century Collection of Its Best Playwrights, Ed. (Dodd, Mead, 1971); Anthology of the American Negro in the Theatre; a Critical Approach, Ed. (Pub. Co., 1968); A Rock Against the Wind: Black Love Poems. Black Films and Film-Makers (Dodd, Mead, 1975). Short story: "Red Bonnet." Contrib. to period.: The New York Times, Saturday Review, Freedomways, Essence.
HONORS AND AWARDS: National Found. on the Arts & the Humanities; MacDowell Colony; Edward Albee Found.
SIDELIGHTS: Writer and co-host of "Celebrity Hour," on WRVR-FM Radio.
Source. Author inform.

PATTERSON, RAYMOND RICHARD. 1929- . Teacher, Newsletter Editor, Poetry Reader
Biographical-Personal. Born Dec. 14, 1929, in N.Y.C. Son of John T. and Mildred Lena [Clemens] Patterson. Educ.: B.A., Lincoln U. (Pa.), 1951; M.A., N.Y.U., 1956. Family: m. Boydie Alice Cooke; d. Ama. Mailing address: 2 Lee Court, Merrick, N.Y. 11566.

Payne, Daniel A.

Career-Professional. Tchr.; Poetry newsletter ed.; Dir., Black Poets Reading, Inc.; Participated, N.Y. State Counc. on the Arts, poetry reading project.
WRITINGS: 26 Ways of Looking at a Black Man, poetry (Award Bks., 1969). In progress: African Words in the English Language. Anthol.: Sixes and Sevens (1962); Beyond the Blues (1962); For Malcolm (1967); I Am the Darker Brother (1968); Black Out Loud (1970); Poetry of the Negro (1949, 1970) & Poetry of Black America (1973).
HONORS AND AWARDS: Borestone Mt. Poetry Awards, 1950; NEA Award, 1970; Lib. of Congress poetry reading, 1971.
SIDELIGHTS: His poetry-reading project takes him throughout New York State to schools and libraries, reading and lecturing on his work (Author).
Sources. Author inform.; New Black Voices, Ed. by Abraham Chapman (New Amer. Lib., 1972); Poetry of Black America, Ed. by Arnold Adoff (Harper & Row, 1973).

PAYNE, DANIEL A. 1811-1893. Minister, Bishop, Teacher
Biographical-Personal. Born Feb. 24, 1811, in Charleston, S.C. Son of free parents, London & Martha Payne. "Learned shoemaking and carpentry and tailoring as a youth. At eighteen he was converted and received great inspiration from the Self-Interpreting Bible of John Brown of Scotland.... Went North and entered Lutheran Seminary at Gettysburg, Pa." (Early Black American Poets). Died Nov. 20, 1893.
Career-Professional. "Ordained as Lutheran clergyman in 1839.... He joined the AME church. Was appointed a bishop in 1852. He traveled far and wide and organized historical and literary societies. He led in the purchase by his church of Wilberforce University. He later served as president for 16 years." (First Negro college president) (Early Black American Poets).
WRITINGS: Pleasures and Other Miscellaneous Poems (Baltimore, 1850); Recollections of Seventy Years (1888); The Semi-Centenary and the Retrospection of the African Methodist Episcopal Church (Baltimore, 1866).
SIDELIGHTS: "...His life was one ceaseless round of activity.... He was an advocate of a trained ministry, and fought for this cause. Payne also introduced choral singing into worship.... He traveled far and wide, from New Orleans to Canada, consulting as to welfare of congregations, visiting homes of fugitive Negroes, and organized historical and literary societies and mother's clubs. He and Carl Schurz urged upon President Lincoln the sign-

ing of the emancipation in the District of Columbia..." (Early Negro American Writers).
Sources. Early Black American Poets, Ed. by William H. Robinson, Jr. (Wm. C. Brown, 1969); Early Negro American Writers, Benjamin Braw- ley (U. of N.C. Pr., 1935); Negro Caravan, Ed. by Sterling A. Brown & Others (Arno Pr. & N.Y. Times, 1969).

PERKINS, EUGENE. 1932- . Poet, Playwright, Editor
Biographical-Personal. Born Sept. 13, 1932, in Chgo., Ill. Educ.: B.S. (Group Work), M.S. (Group Work Admin.), George Williams Coll., Chgo.
Career-Professional. Founder, public. co., Free Black Pr. (will publish works of new Black writers).
WRITINGS: Poetry: An Apology To My African Brother; Black is Beautiful; Home Is a Dirty Street: The Social Oppression of Black Chil- dren (Third World Pr.); Black Expression, A Journal of Literature and Art, Ed. Plays: The Image Makers; Professor J. B. Contrib. Negro Digest, Liberator, Freedomways & others.
SIDELIGHTS: The Image Makers had a successful run at the Kuumba Workshop in Chicago. Professor J. B. has been performed by Chi- cago's X-Bag ("Nat'l. Conf. of Afro-Amer. Writers," Program).
Sources. New Black Voices, Ed. by Abraham Chapman (New Amer. Lib., 1972); "Nat'l. Conf. of Afro-Amer. Writers" (Program), Howard U., Inst. for Arts & Humanities, Nov. 1974.

PERRY, RICHARD H. Teacher, Writer
Career-Professional. Tchr., Lit. & Creative writing, Pratt Inst., Brooklyn; Mem., Tchrs. & Writers Collaborator (works part time with Harlem elementary sch. children).
WRITINGS: Changes, novel (Bobbs-Merrill, 1974). Has contributed short stories to Black Creation & Snakeroots mags.
Source. Black World (Johnson Pub., June 1974).

PETERS, GENE RAYMOND. 1933- . Airline Executive, Editor, Pub- lisher
Biographical-Personal. Born Aug. 24, 1933, in New Haven, Conn.
Educ.: San Diego City Coll.; U. of Chgo. Family: m. Mabel; son, Christopher, son, James, d. Patricia. Mailing address: Suite 207, 953 8th Ave., San Diego, Cal. 92101.

Petry, Ann Lane

Career-Professional. Co-founder & Pres., New World Airways, Inc.;
Exec. dir. & founder, New World Aviation Acad., Inc.
WRITINGS: Five Minutes to Freedom (1963); Prime Thoughts for
Black Folks (1969); Ed. & pub., Profiles of Black American History.
In progress: "Eagles Don't Cry," motion picture.
MEMBER: 1st V. Pres., S. Cal. Chap., Negro Airmen, Internat.; Co-
founder & Pres., Nat'l. Afro-Amer. Hist. Soc.; Org. Cal.'s 1st OEO
War on Poverty Agency.
SIDELIGHTS: "One of only five blacks who own an aviation trans-
portation firm in the United States.... The non-scheduled cargo
airline operates throughout California" (1000 Successful Blacks).
Source. 1000 Successful Blacks, Eds. of Ebony (Johnson Pub., 1973).

PETRY, ANN LANE. 1908- . Novelist, Short
Story Writer
Biographical-Personal. Born Oct. 12, 1908, in
Old Saybrook, Conn. D. of Peter Clarke
(druggist) and Bertha [James] Lane. Educ.:
U. of Conn., Coll. of Pharmacy, grad. 1931;
Columbia U. (Creative writing). Family:
m. George D. Petry, Feb. 22, 1938; d. Eliza-
beth Ann. Mailing address: 113 Old Boston
Post Road, Old Saybrook, Conn. 06475.
Career-Professional. Pharmacist, 1934-48; News-
paperwoman, Amsterdam News & The Peoples
Voice (Women's Ed.); With soc. agencies; Vis.
Prof. of Eng., U. of Hawaii, 1974-75.
WRITINGS: Novels: The Street (Houghton
Mifflin, 1946); Country Place (Houghton
Mifflin, 1947); The Narrows (Houghton Mifflin, 1953). Juveniles:
The Drug Store Cat (Crowell, 1949); Harriet Tubman: Conductor on
the Underground Railroad (Crowell, 1955); Tituba of Salem Village,
ALA Notable Book (Crowell, 1964). In Dark Confusion, novella.
Also Legends of the Saints (Crowell, 1970); Miss Muriel and Other
Stories (Houghton Mifflin, 1971).
HONORS AND AWARDS: Completed The Street on a Houghton-Mifflin
Literary Fellowship. Martha Foley dedicated annual volume The
Best American Short Stories in 1946 to Miss Petry.
SIDELIGHTS: "Convinced...that the most dramatic material avail-
able to a writer in this country is that which deals with the Ne-
gro, and his history in the United States" (Afro-American Litera-
ture--Fiction).
Sources. Afro-American Literature--Fiction, Ed. by William Adams et
al. (Houghton Mifflin, 1970); Author inform.; Black Voices, Ed. by
Abraham Chapman (New Amer. Lib., 1968); Cavalcade, Ed. by Arthur
P. Davis & Saunders Redding (Houghton Mifflin, 1971); Negro Almanac, Comp. by Harry A. Ploski & Ernest Kaiser (Bellwether,

1971); <u>Something About the Author</u>, Ed. by Anne Commire (Gale Res.,
1973); <u>Soon, One Morning</u>, Ed. by Herbert Hill (Knopf, 1963).

PHARR, ROBERT DEANE. 1916- . Novelist
Biographical-Personal. Born July 5, 1916, in
Richmond, Va. Son of Bap. minister and sch.
tchr. Raised in New Haven, Conn. <u>Educ.</u>:
New Haven High Sch.; B.A., Virginia Union U.,
Richmond.
Career-Professional.
WRITINGS: Novels: <u>Book of Numbers</u> (Double-
day, 1969); <u>S.R.O.</u> (Doubleday, 1971); <u>The
Welfare Bitch</u> (Doubleday, 1973); <u>The Soul
Murder Case: A Confession of the Victim</u>
(Avon, 1975).
SIDELIGHTS: "A man in his fifites when his
first novel, <u>The Book of Numbers</u>, was pub-
lished in 1969, Robert Deane Pharr exempli-
fies the difficulties Black Americans with
literary talent have so frequently found in attaining publication
and conditions to devote time to writing..." (<u>New Black Voices</u>).
Source. <u>New Black Voices</u>, Ed. by Abraham Chapman (New Amer. Lib.,
1972).

PHILLIPS, BILLIE ANN. 1925- . Early Childhood
Education Specialist, Art Teacher
Biographical-Personal. Born July 1, 1925, in
St. Louis, Mo. D. of William and Anne
McKindra. <u>Educ.</u>: B.A., Stowe Teachers
Coll., 1947; M.A., Webster Coll., (Aesthetic
Educ.); Further stud.: Harris Teachers
Coll., Indianapolis U.; Washington U.
<u>Family</u>: div.; son, Lamonte Hamilton Mays.
<u>Mailing address</u>: 8827 Torii Dr.-C, St.
Louis, Mo. 63121.
Career-Professional. Spec. Tchr., Chmn., Art
Dept., Sumner High Sch., St. Louis; Rep.,
<u>Early Years</u> mag., Darien, Conn.; Instr.,
Learning Center Workshops, Early Childhood
Educ.; Milton Bradley Rep., conducting work-
shops for educators; Dir., Little Theater Group, Learning Center,
St. Louis, Mo.
WRITINGS: <u>Early Childhood Education Guide</u>, co-author (<u>Grade
Teacher</u> Mag.); <u>Skyline Series</u>, co-author: <u>Out Jumped Abraham</u>
(McGraw-Hill, 1967); <u>Watch Out for C</u> (McGraw-Hill, 1965); <u>The Hid-
den Lookout</u>, 1965; <u>Who Cares</u>, 1965. <u>Early Years Magazine</u> "Green
Pages" (Raymond). Contrib. author, <u>Spectrum Magazine</u>, Dept. of
Art, St. Louis, Mo.

Pickens, William

HONORS AND AWARDS: "Lit. Achievement," Skyline Ser., St. Louis, 1967; Ed. Pr. Award for Excellence in Journalism, 1973.
MEMBER: St. Louis State Tchrs. Assn.; Nat'l. Educ. Assn.; Mo. Art Educ. Assn.; Mo. State Tchrs. Assn.
Source. Author inform.

PICKENS, WILLIAM. 1881-1954. Educator, NAACP Field Secretary
Biographical-Personal. Born Jan. 15, 1881, in Anderson Co., S.C.
Son of former slaves. Educ.: B.A., Talladega Coll., 1902; B.A. (Phi Beta Kappa), Yale U., 1904; M.A., Fisk U.; Diploma, Brit. Esperanto Assn., 1906. Died 1954.
Career-Professional. Prof. of Latin, Greek & German, Talladega Coll., Ala., 1904-14; Prof., Greek & Sociol., Wiley Coll., Marshall, Tex., 1914-15; Dean, Morgan State Coll., Baltimore, 1915-20; Field Secy., NAACP, 1920-41; Official, Treasury Dept.
WRITINGS: The Heir of Slaves, autobiog. (1910). Biography: Abraham Lincoln, Man and Statesman (1909); Frederick Douglass and the Spirit of Freedom (1912). Essays: Fifty Years of Emancipation (1913); The Ultimate Effects of Segregation and Discrimination; The New Negro (1916). Bursting Bonds, rev. autobiog. (1923). The Vengeance of the Gods and Three Other Stories of Real American Color Line Life (1922); and American Aesop: The Humor of the Negro, the Jew, the Irishman and Others (1926). Articles: The Crisis; The Nation; others.
HONORS AND AWARDS: Hon. degrees from: Fisk U.; Selma U.; Wiley Coll.
Sources. Afro-American Writing, Ed. by Richard A. Long & Eugenia W. Collier (N.Y.U. Pr., 1972); Historical Negro Biographies, Ed. by Wilhelmena S. Robinson (ASNLH, 1967); Negro Caravan, Ed. by Sterling A. Brown & Others (Arno Pr., & N. Y. Times, 1969); Negroes in Public Affairs & Government, Ed. by Walter Christmas (Educ. Her., 1966).

PITCHER, OLIVER. 1924- . Poet, Playwright
Biographical-Personal. Born 1924 in Mass.
Career-Professional. Taught Black Theatre at Vassar Coll.; Poet-in-Residence, Atlanta U. Center (presently); Ed., Atlanta University Center Sampler (presently).
WRITINGS: Poetry: Dust of Silence (Cal., 1958); Prose Poems, Cal. Plays: The One. Poetry pub. in period.: The Tiger's Eye, Totem, Points of Light, Umbra & Negro Digest/Black World. Included in anthol.: Schwarzer Orpheus (1954, 1963); Beyond the Blues (1962); & Kaleidoscope (1967).
SIDELIGHTS: The Negro Ensemble Co. has presented The One, which is included in Black Drama Anthology (1971) (Poetry of Black America).
Source. The Poetry of Black America, Ed. by Arnold Adoff (Harper & Row, 1973).

PLATO, ANN. Poet
Biographical-Personal. "There is factually nothing known of Miss
Plato except that she was a Negro member of the Colored Congregational Church in Hartford, Conn. in 1841, so identified in the
preface by her pastor, the Rev. J. W. C. Pennington, about whom
much is known. Certainly Hartford of the 1840's was one of New
England's busiest centers for anti-slavery agitation and senti-
ment. Frederick Douglass spoke there during this time, as did
other abolitionist lecturers..." (Early Black American Poets).
WRITINGS: Essays;/Including/Biographies and Miscellaneous Pieces
in/Prose and Poetry (Hartford, 1841).
SIDELIGHTS: "Important historically as the author of the second
volume of poetry by an American Negro woman published in the
United States" (Early Black American Poets).
Source. Early Black American Poets, Ed. by William H. Robinson (Wm.
C. Brown, 1969).

PLUMPP, STERLING DOMINIC. 1940- . Editor, Teacher
Biographical-Personal. Born Jan. 30, 1940, in Clinton, Miss. Son of
Cyrus Hampton (laborer) and Mary [Emmanuel] Plumpp. Educ.: St.
Benedict's Coll., 1960-62; B.A., Roosevelt U., 1968, Grad. Study,
1968-71. Family: m. Falvia Delgrazia Jackson (registered nurse),
Dec. 21, 1968. Mailing address: 1401 E. 55th, Apt. 816-N, Chgo.
Ill. 60615.
Career-Professional. Clerk, U.S. Post Office, 1962-69; Counselor,
N. Park Coll., 1969-71; Instr., Black Stud., U. of Ill., Chgo.
Circle, 1970- ; Managing Ed., Black Books Bulletin (Inst. of
Positive Education); Dir., Young Writer's Workshop for Urban
Gateways; Ed., Third World Pr.
WRITINGS: Portable Soul (Third World Pr., 1969); Half Black, Half
Blacker (Third World Pr., 1970); Black Rituals (Third World Pr.,
1972); Muslim Men (Broadside Pr., 1972); Steps to Break the Circle
(Third World Pr., 1974). In progress: Superbad and the Hip
Jesus; Res. on black critics & on work of Ernest Gaines & Henry
Dumas. Contrib. to: Black World & Journal of Black Poetry.
Sources. Contemporary Authors, Vols. 45-48, Ed. by Clare D. Kinsman
(Gale Res., 1974); Poetry of Black America, Ed. by Arnold Adoff
(Harper & Row, 1973).

POINSETT, ALEX. 1926- . Editor
Biographical-Personal. Born Jan. 27, 1926, in Chgo., Ill. Son of
Alexander Abraham and Adele Leola Poinsett. Educ.: B.S. (Journalism), M.A. (Philosophy), U. of Ill., 1953; Further study (Lib.
Sci.), U. of Chgo. Family: m. Norma R. Poinsett; d. Pierrette,
son, Pierre. Mailing address: 8532 S. Wabash Ave., Chgo., Ill.
60619.

Polite, Carlene Hatcher

Career-Professional. Yeoman 3/c, U.S. Navy,
1944-47; Asst. Ed., Assoc. Ed., Sr. Ed.,
Ebony mag.
WRITINGS: Black Power: Gary Style (Johnson
Pub., 1970); Common Folk in an Uncommon Cause
(Liberty Bap. Church, Chgo., 1972). In
progress: The Watergate Challenge to Black
Politics. Contrib. to: Ebony Pictorial His-
tory & The Ebony Success Library.
HONORS AND AWARDS: J. C. Penny, U. of Mo.
Journalism Award, 1968, ($1,000) for Aug.
1967 Ebony story, "Ghetto Schools: An Educa-
tional Wasteland."
MEMBER: Inst. of the Black World, Atlanta,
Ga.
SIDELIGHTS: "Lectured at nearly 50 universi-
ties on black politics, the black press, etc., under contract to
American Program Bureau in Boston, Mass.; traveled to the Soviet
Union, Kenya, Haiti, Jamaica, Canada, Mexico. For 20 years, trav-
eled more than one million miles as Johnson Publishing Co. editor;
broke 1958 story which led to commutation of death sentence of
Jimmy Wilson, an Alabama black man slated to die for $1.95 rob-
bery" (Author).
Source. Author inform.

POLITE, CARLENE HATCHER. 1932- . Novelist,
Teacher, Dancer, Elected Official
Biographical-Personal. Born Aug. 28, 1932, in
Detroit, Mich. D. of John and Lillian Hatch-
er. Educ.: Detroit Public schs.; Martha
Graham Sch. of Contemporary Dance. Family:
div. from Allen Polite; d. Glynda Bennett, d.
Lila Polite. Mailing address: Farrar,
Straus, & Giroux, 19 Union Sq. W., N.Y., N.Y.
10003.
Career-Professional. Dancer, Concert Dance
Theatre, N.Y.C., 1956-59; Actress & Dancer
Equity Theatre, Detroit, 1960-62; Guest
Instr., YWCA, 1960-62; Organizer, Girl Friday,
Mich. Democratic Party, 1962; Elected Mich.
Democratic State Central Com., 1962-63;
Co-ord., Detroit Counc. for Human Rights, 1963; Participated,
"Walk to Freedom" with Martin L. King, Jr., June 23, 1963; Assoc.
Prof., Dept. of Eng., SUNY, Buffalo, 1971- .
WRITINGS: The Flagellants, novel (Farrar, Straus, 1966). Sister
X and The Victims of Foul Play (Farrar, Straus, 1975). Anthol.:
To Be A Black Woman.

Porter, Dorothy Burnett

HONORS AND AWARDS: Nat'l. Found. of Arts & Humanities, 1965;
Rockefeller, 1969; Nominated, Pulitzer Prize, 1967.
SIDELIGHTS: The Flagellants published in 5 languages and 6 coun-
tries; film option, Aug. 1974 (Author).
Source. Author inform.

PORTER, DOROTHY BURNETT. 1905- . Librarian,
Bibliographer
Biographical-Personal. Born May 25, 1905, in
Warrenton, VA. Educ.: B.A., Howard U., 1928;
B.S., Columbia U., 1931- ; M.S. (Lib. Sci.),
Columbia U., 1932; American U. Cert., Preser-
vation and Admin. of Archives, 1957; D.Litt.
(hon.), Susquehanna Univ., 1971. Family:
m. James A. Porter; Widow, d. Constance
Uzelac. Mailing address: 7632 17th St.,
N.W., Wash., D.C. 20012.
Career-Professional. Librarian, The Moorland-
Spingarn Collection, Howard U., 1930-73;
cons.: Ford Found. Nat'l. Libs., Lagos, Ni-
geria; Kraus Pub.; Arno Press Negro History
Project. Advis. Ed., Black Studies, G. K.
Hall & Co.; Bd. of Advis., The Booker T. Washington Papers.
WRITINGS: Catalogue of Books in the Moorland Foundation Collec-
tion, Ed. (Howard U. Lib., 1939); North American Negro Poets: A
Bibliographical Checklist of Their Writings, 1760-1944 (The Book
Farm, 1945); Catalogue of the African Collection at Howard Univer-
sity (Howard U. Pr., 1958); Index to The Journal of Negro Educa-
tion, 1932-1962 (Howard U. Pr., 1963); The Negro in American Cities;
A Selected and Annotated Bibliography (Howard U. Pr., 1967); A
Working Bibliography on the Negro in the United States (Xerox, U.
Microfilms, 1969); The Negro in the United States, A Selected Bib-
liography (Lib. of Congress, 1970); Early Negro Writing 1760-1837
(Beacon Pr., 1971); Negro Protest Pamphlets (Arno, 1969); Afro-
Braziliana: A Working Bibliography and Union List (G. K. Hall,
forthcoming). Contrib. numerous articles & book reviews to jnls.
HONORS AND AWARDS: Julius Rosenwald scholarship, 1931-32; Julius
Rosenwald Fellow., 1944-45; Distinguished Achieve. Award, Nat.
Barristers Wives, Inc., for outstanding service, human relations,
1968; Distinguished Service to Howard U., 1970; Inst. of Arts and
Humanities Award, Howard U., 1973.
MEMBER: Exec. Council, ASNLH; Biblio. Soc. of Am.; Soc. of Am.
Archivists; African Studies Assn.; Nigerian Historical Soc.; Am.
Soc. of African Culture; Phi Beta Kappa; Black Academy of Arts and
Letters; Am. Antiquarian Soc., etc.
Sources. Author inform.; Books in Print, Supplement 1975-76 (Bowker,
1976); Pub. inform.

Powell, Adam Clayton, Jr.

POWELL, ADAM CLAYTON, Jr. 1908-1972. Congressman, Clergyman

Biographical-Personal. Born Nov. 29, 1908, in New Haven, Conn. Son of Adam Clayton, Sr. (minister) & Mrs. Powell. Educ.: B.A., Colgate U., 1930; M.A., Columbia U., 1932; D.D., Shaw U., 1935; LL.D., Va. Union U., 1947. Family: 1st m. Isabel G. Washington, March 8, 1933 (separated Nov. 1944); 2nd m. Hazel Scott (Aug. 1955 div.); son, Adam Clayton III; 3rd m. Yvette Diago; son, Adam Diago. Died April 1972.

Career-Professional. Minister, Abyssinian Bap. Church, 1937- ; Elected to N.Y.C. Counc., 1941; Founder, People's Voice, Ed. in Chief, co-pub., 1942; Elected to Congress, Nov. 1945; Mem. 79th to 87th Congresses from N.Y.'s 16th Dist., Chmn., Com. on Educ. & Labor; Mem. 88th to 89th Congresses, N.Y., 18th Dist.; Delegate, Parliamentary World Govt., Conf., London, 1951-52; ILO Conf. Geneva, 1961.

WRITINGS: Is This a White Man's War? (1942); Stage Door Canteen (1944); Marching Blacks (Dial, 1945); Adam Clayton Powell (1960); Adam by Adam.

HONORS AND AWARDS: Decorated Knight of the Golden Cross, Ethiopia, 1954.

SIDELIGHTS: "He went from the street corners of Harlem (where he preached black nationalism and passive resistance in the thirties) to the New York City Council (where he was the first Negro member in 1941) and to Congress (where he was the first Negro member from the East in 1945). In the process he acquired three wives (in lawful succession), two sons named Adam, a string of winter and summer homes stretching from Westhampton, L.I., to Cerro Gordo, Puerto Rico, a block of real estate, a directorship of an international insurance company, a Jaguar, a Nash-Healy and a host of passionate enemies. Now [1963] chairman of the House Education & Labor committee, the 55 year old congressman is one of the most powerful men in Congress" (Ebony).

Sources. Ebony (Johnson Pub., June 1963); Los Angeles Times (April 5, 1972); Negro Handbook, Comp. by eds. of Ebony (Johnson Pub., 1966).

PRITCHARD, NORMAN HENRY, II. 1939- . Poet-in-Residence, Poetry Instructor

Biographical-Personal. Born Oct. 22, 1939, in Manhattan Island, N.Y. Son of Dr. Norman Henry and Winnie Ursula [Ramsey] Pritchard. Educ.: B.A. (Art hist., honors), Washington Square Coll., N.Y.U., 1961; Grad. stud.: (Art hist.) Inst. of Fine Arts, N.Y.U. & Co-

Quarles, Benjamin Arthur

lumbia U. <u>Family</u>: div. from Sarah Dickin-
son. <u>Mailing address</u>: 131 E. 70th, N.Y.,
N.Y. 10021.
Career-Professional. Co-Chmn., Nat'l. Standing
Com. on Poetry, Amer. Festival of Negro Arts,
1963-64; Poet-in-Residence, Friends Sem.,
N.Y., 1968-74; Instr., Poetry Workshop, New
Sch. for Soc. Res., 1969- .
WRITINGS: Poetry: <u>The Matrix: Poems 1960-
1970</u> (Doubleday, 1970); <u>Eecchhooeess</u> (N.Y.U.
Pr., 1971). In progress: <u>The Mundus</u>, novel;
<u>Spheres: Poems 1970-1975</u>. Contrib. to
period.: <u>Umbra</u>, <u>Liberator</u>, <u>East Village
Other</u>, <u>Poetry Northwest</u> & <u>Eye</u>.
HONORS AND AWARDS: Abraham Woursell Found.
Award.
MEMBER: The Asia Soc.; St. George's Soc. of N.Y.; The Nat'l.
Trust for Hist. Preservation.
SIDELIGHTS: (Lectures, etc.) Sri Aurobindo Found.; Poetry Soc. of
Amer.; St. Paul's Chapel (Columbia U.); Channel 7, ABC TV; Internat.
House, N.Y.C., etc. Poetry recordings: "Destinations: Four Con-
temporary Poets" & "New Jazz Poets."
  "An experimental and original poet, frequently employing the
concretist style which appeals to the eye as well as to the ear,
N. H. Pritchard is highly regarded by critics and readers of the
new poetry.... At (Washington Square College) he was a contribu-
tor to the literary magazine and president of the Fine Arts So-
ciety" (<u>New Black Voices</u>).
Sources. Author inform.; <u>New Black Voices</u>, Ed. by Abraham Chapman
(New Amer. Lib., 1972); <u>Poetry of Black America</u>, Ed. by Arnold
Adoff (Harper & Row, 1973).

QUARLES, BENJAMIN ARTHUR. 1904- . Professor
of History, Historian
Biographical-Personal. Born Jan. 23, 1904, in
Boston, Mass. Son of Arthur Benedict and
Margaret [O'Brien] Quarles. <u>Educ.</u>: B. A.
(Hist.) Shaw U., Raleigh, N.C., 1931; M.A.,
1937, Ph.D., 1940, U. of Wis. <u>Family</u>: 1st
m. Vera Bullock (dec.); 2nd m. <u>Ruth Brett</u>;
d. Mrs. Roberta Allain Knowles, d. Pamela
Anne Quarles. <u>Mailing address</u>: Morgan State
Coll., Baltimore, Md. 21214.
Career-Professional. Instr., Hist., Shaw U.,
1934-36; Assoc. Prof., Dillard U., 1939-42,
Prof., 1942-53 (Dean of Instr., 1945-53);
Prof. of Hist., & Head of Dept., Morgan State
Coll., 1953- .

Randall, Dudley Felker

WRITINGS: Frederick Douglass (Assoc. Pub., 1948); The Negro in the Civil War (Little, Brown, 1953); The Negro in the American Revolution (U. of N.C. Pr., 1961); Lincoln and the Negro (Oxford U. Pr., 1962); The Negro in the Making of America (Collier, 1964); Black Abolitionists (Oxford U. Pr., 1969); Allies for Freedom: Blacks and John Brown (1974). Co-author: The Black American, with Leslie H. Fishel, Jr. (Morrow, 1970). Collaborated: Dorothy Sterling, Lift Every Voice (1965). Ed.: Narrative of the Life of Frederick Douglass (1962) and Frederick Douglass (Great Lives Observed Ser., 1968); Blacks on John Brown (1972). Other: Original chaps. in bks., 5; articles, 27; Shorter pieces, 48; Introduction to bks., 16.

HONORS AND AWARDS: Hon. doctorates: Shaw U., Towson State Coll., Kenyon Coll., U. of Md., Howard U., Morgan State Coll. Hon. cons. in U.S. Hist. to Lib. of Congress, 1970-74. Recipient: Rosenwald Fellow., 1938, 1945; U. of Wis., Pres. Adams Fellow. in Mod. Hist.; Social Sci. Res. Counc. Grants, 1941, 1955; Carnegie Corp., Advancement Tchg. Fellow., 1948, 1950; Guggenheim Grant, 1958; & the Amer. Counc. of Learned Soc. Grant-in-Aid, 1967.

MEMBER: V. Pres., ASNLH Bd. of ed. advis. Booker T. Washington Papers; Ed. Bd., Journal of Negro History; Com. on Public., Md. Hist. Soc.; Advis. Bd., Frederick Douglass Inst. of Negro Arts & Hist.; Hon. Fellow, Atlanta U. Center for African & Afro-Amer. Stud.; Ed. Bd., Frederick Douglass Papers Project; Advis. Com., Amer. Historians of Md. Bicentennial Com.; Bd. of Dir., Howard U. Pr.

SIDELIGHTS: "Dr. Benjamin Quarles has written what is perhaps a definitive study of Frederick Douglass. Frederick Douglass, praised for its very readable style, as well as organization, thoroughness of research, and accurate interpretation--represents years of study...." Quarles's The Negro in the American Revolution "is considered excellent and scholarly, and will stand for a long time." Black Abolitionists "will probably rank for years as an excellent study" (Black Historians).

Sources. Author inform.; Black Historians, Earl E. Thorpe (Morrow, 1969); Directory of American Scholars, Vol. I, Hist., 5th ed., Ed. by Jaques Cattel (Bowker, 1969); Negro Almanac, Comp. by Harry A. Ploski & Ernest Kaiser (Bellwether, 1971); Pub. inform.; Who's Who in America, 37th ed., 1972-73, Vol. 2 (Marquis, 1972).

RANDALL, DUDLEY FELKER. 1914- . Publisher, Poet, Librarian
Biographical-Personal. Born Jan. 14, 1914, in Wash., D.C. Son of Arthur George Clyde and Ada Viola [Bradley] Randall. Educ.: B.A. (Eng.), Wayne State U., 1949; M.A.L.S., U. of Mich., 1951; Post grad.: Wayne State (Humanities); U. of Ghana (African Arts). Family: m. Vivian Barnett Spencer, 1957; d. Mrs. Phyllis Ada Sherron III (from previous m.). Mailing address: 12651 Old Mill Place, Detroit, Mich. 48348.

224

Randall, Dudley Felker

Career-Professional. Ford Motor Co., Dearborn,
Mich., 1932-37; U.S. Post Office, Detroit,
1937-51; Librn., Lincoln U., Jefferson City,
Mo., 1951-54; Librn., Morgan State Coll.,
Baltimore, 1954-56; Librn., Wayne Co. Fed.
Lib. System, Detroit, 1956-69; Poet-in-Resi-
dence & Lbrn., U. of Detroit, 1969- . Pub.,
Broadside Pr., 1965- .
WRITINGS: Poem Counterpoem, with Margaret
Danner (Broadside Pr., 1966); For Malcolm,
Ed. with Margaret G. Burroughs (Broadside
Pr., 1967); Cities Burning (Broadside Pr.,
1968); Black Poetry, Ed. (Broadside Pr.,
1969); Love You (Paul Bremen, 1970); More to
Remember (Third World Pr., 1971); The Black
Poets, Ed. (Bantam, 1971); After the Killing
(Third World Pr., 1973). Broadsides: #1, 1965; #3, 1965; #8,
1966; #62, 1972. A Capsule Course in Black Poetry Writing, with
Gwendolyn Brooks & Keorapetse W. Kgositsile (Broadside Pr., 1975);
Broadside Memories: Poets I Have Known (Broadside Pr., 1975).
Anthol.: Beyond the Blues, American Negro Poetry, Ik Ben de
Nieuwe Neger, New Negro Poets: U.S.A., Potere Negro, La Poesie
Negro Americaine, Black Voices, Ten: A Detroit Anthology, Black
Arts, Poetry of the Negro, The Black Seventies, To Gwen With Love,
The Black Aesthetic, You Better Believe It. Period.: American
Libraries, Beloit Poetry Journal, Black World, Change (Paris),
Chicago Tribune, Detroit News, Essence, Journal of Black Poetry,
Michigan Chronicle, Midwest Journal, Negro History Bulletin, Novy
Mir (Moscow), Robotnitza (Moscow), Wayne Review.
HONORS AND AWARDS: Wayne State U.'s Tompkins Award (Poetry &
Fic.), 1962; Tompkins Award (Poetry), 1966; Kuumba Liberation
Award, 1973; Detroit Metropolitan Eng. Club, Citation, 1972.
MEMBER: ALA, Com. of Small Mag. Ed. & Pub.; Mich. Counc. for the
Arts, Advis. Panel on Lit.; New Detroit, Ind., Com. for the Arts.
SIDELIGHTS: "Perhaps (Randall's) greatest contribution to the
black revolution in poetry is his establishment and active direc-
torship of the Broadside Press, which was started in 1965 with the
publication of its first Broadside, 'Ballad of Birmingham'...at
first it reprinted favorite poems of well-known black poets, but
the Broadside Series widened its scope to publish previously unpublished poems by new writers" (Black Insights).
   In 1966 Randall "visited Paris, Prague, and the Soviet Union
with a delegation of black artists. In 1970 he studied African
Arts at the University of Ghana, and visited Togo and Dahomey. In
1973 he participated in the East-West Culture Learning Institute's
Seminar in Socioliterature, held in Honolulu, Hawaii" (Broadside
Authors & Artists).

Randolph, Asa Philip

Randall's "Cities Burning (1968), consists of 12 poems in the
mood of the new black poets, except that his quiet, reflective
manner and his concern for formal structure indicate a determina-
tion not to be engulfed completely by the new wave of black consciousness" (Kaleidoscope).
Sources. Author inform.; Black Insights, Ed. by Nick A. Ford (Ginn,
1971); Black Voices, Ed. by Abraham Chapman (New Amer. Lib.,
1968); Broadside Authors and Artists, Comp. by Leanonead P. Bailey
(Broadside Pr., 1974); Dark Symphony, Ed. by James A. Emanuel and
Theodore L. Gross (Free Pr., 1968); Kaleidoscope, Ed. by Robert
Hayden (Harcourt, 1967).

RANDOLPH, ASA PHILIP. 1889- . Labor Leader
Biographical-Personal. Born April 15, 1889, in
Crescent City, Fla. Son of traveling Methodist preacher. Educ.: Cookman Inst., Jacksonville, Fla.; City Coll. of N.Y.
Career-Professional. Organized Brotherhood of
Sleeping Car Porters, 1925; The Messenger became official organ of union; Amer. Fed. of
Labor granted union a charter (the 1st granted an all-Negro union in America); Randolph
was 1st Pres. Organized protest demonstra-
tion, March-on-Washington Movement, 1941, to
get Blacks into defense industry & unions
generally. Pres. Roosevelt issued Executive
Order #8802 against discrimination in employment by firms holding defense contracts
(brought about with threats of march). Regarded as "elder statesman" among civil rights leaders. President of Negro American
Labor Council; First Black v. pres. of AFL-CIO.
SIDELIGHTS: "Early imbued with intense dislike of racial discrimination. In 1917 he helped launch a magazine in New York, The
Messenger, to crusade for full democratic rights of Negroes. Sub-
title was, "The only radical Negro magazine in America." Editorials were bitterly critical of the Status quo. Randolph made
fiery speeches, was called "the most dangerous Negro in America"
(1918). He contended that he was simply agitating for fulfillment
of Constitutional guarantees for all citizens and the protection
of law for everybody" (Famous American Negroes).
Rand lph was associated with Chandler Owen in founding The Messenger. Owen was brilliant, an intellectual dragonfly...who
came later to be called the 'Negro Mencken.' "The magazine was
fearlessly forthright...It preached socialism."
Randolph publicized the union's cause in Opportunity and Survey
Graphic. He toured the country, explaining, protesting, defending (in attempting to organize the union) (Lonesome Road).

Sources. Famous American Negroes, Langston Hughes (Dodd, Mead,
1954); The Lonesome Road, Saunders Redding (Doubleday, 1958);
Negro Almanac, Comp. by Harry A. Ploski & Ernest Kaiser (Bellwether, 1971).

RAY, HENRIETTA CORDELIA. 1850-1916. Poet, Teacher
Biographical-Personal. "A descendant of an old Cape Cod, New England
family, Henrietta Ray was one of two daughters born to the dis-
tinguished minister and eloquent abolitionist, Rev. Charles B.
Ray of Falmouth, Mass. She was carefully reared in New York, re-
ceiving an excellent traditional education which helped her to
graduate from both New York University in Pedagogy and from the
Sauveveur School of Languages, where she became proficient in
Greek, Latin, French and German in addition to developing into an
English scholar" (Early Black American Poets).
Career-Professional. Tchr., Grammar Sch. No. 80 (while poet Charles
L. Reason was prin.). Writer.
WRITINGS: Commemoration Ode on Lincoln/written for the occasion
of the/unveiling of the Freedman's Monument (in Memory of Abraham
Lincoln)/Apr. 14, 1876 (New York, 1893); Sonnets (N.Y., 1893);
Poems (N.Y., 1887); and with her sister, Sketch of the Life of the
Rev. Charles B. Ray (N.Y., 1887).
Source. Early Black American Poets, Ed. by William H. Robinson, Jr.
(Wm. C. Brown, 1969).

REDDING, JAY SAUNDERS. 1906- . English Professor, Essayist,
Critic, Scholar
Biographical-Personal. Born Oct. 13, 1906, in Wilmington, Del. Son
of (Howard U. grads.) Lewis Alfred (Postal serv.) and Mary Ann
[Holmes] Redding (sch. tchr.). Educ.: Lincoln U. (Pa.), 1923-24;
Ph.B. (Eng.), 1928, M.A. (Eng. & Amer. Lit.), 1933, D.Litt., 1963,
Brown U.; H.H.D. (hon.): Hobart Coll., 1964; Dickenson Coll., U.
of Del., U. of Portland, 1970. Family: m. Esther Elizabeth
James, July 19, 1929; son, Conway Holmes, son, Lewis Alfred.
Mailing address: 310 Winthrop Dr., Ithaca, N.Y. 14850.
Career-Professional. Instr., Morehouse Coll., 1928-31; Instr.,
Louisville Municipal Coll., 1933-35; Eng. Prof. & Chmn., Southern
U., 1936-38; Eng. Prof. & Chmn., tchrs. Coll., Elizabeth City,
N.C.; Prof. Eng., Hampton Inst., 1943-66 (Johnson Prof. of Crea-
tive Lit.); Dir., Div. of Res. & Public., NEH, Wash., D.C.,
1966-70; Ernest I. White Prof. of Amer. Stud. & Humane Letters,
Cornell U., 1970- .
WRITINGS: To Make a Poet Black (U. of N.C. Pr., 1939); No Day of
Triumph (Harcourt, 1942); Stranger and Alone (Harcourt, 1950);
They Came in Chains (Lippincott, 1951); The Lonesome Road (Double-
day, 1958, Mainstream of Amer. Ser.); The Negro (Potomac, 1967);
& Cavalcade, with Arthur P. Davis (Houghton, 1971), etc. Contrib.
to jls.

Redmond, Eugene Benjamin

HONORS AND AWARDS: Phi Beta Kappa; Rockefeller Found. Fellow, 1940-41; Guggenheim Fellow, 1944-45; 1959-60; Vis. Prof. Eng., Brown U., 1949-50; Fellow in Humanities, Duke U., 1964-65; May-flower Award, N.C. Hist. Soc., (1st Black), 1944; Cited by N.Y. Amsterdam News "for distinction," 1944; By N.Y. Public Lib. "for outstanding contribution to interracial understanding," 1945, 1946; by Nat'l. Urban League "for outstanding achievement," 1949.
MEMBER: Fic. award com., Nat'l. Bk. Awards, 1955; ASNLH; Amer. Folklore Soc.; Eng. Assn.; Amer. Soc. of African Culture (executive bd.); Ed. Bd., American Scholar, 1954-62.
SIDELIGHTS: Redding "established a national reputation with his essays, literary criticism, fiction, and educational activities as Professor of English at Hampton Institute" (Black Voices).
   "Saunders Redding is a worthy disciple of W. E. B. DuBois, a scholar and a writer who is dedicated to the abolition of narrow provincialism in scholarship and in life" (Black Insights).
   "As a frequent contributor to periodicals, Redding has earned a reputation as a perceptive and knowledgeable historian of literature by Afro-Americans" (Black American Literature--Essays).
Sources. Black American Literature--Essays, Ed. by Darwin T. Turner (Merrill, 1969); Black Insights, Ed. by Nick A. Ford (Ginn, 1971); Black Voices, Ed. by Abraham Chapman (New Amer. Lib., 1968); Cavalcade, Ed. by Arthur P. Davis & Saunders Redding (Houghton Mifflin, 1971); Current Biography, 1969, Ed. by Charles Moritz (H. W. Wilson, 1970); Negro Almanac, Comp. by Harry A. Ploski & Ernest Kaiser (Bellwether, 1971); Who's Who in America, 37th ed., 1972-73 (Marquis, 1972).

REDMOND, EUGENE BENJAMIN. 1937- . Poet, Editor, Teacher
Biographical-Personal. Born Dec. 1, 1937, in St. Louis, Mo. Son of John Henry and Emma Jean Redmond. Educ.: B.A. (Eng. Lit.), S. Ill. U., 1964; M.A. (Eng. Lit.), Wash. U., St. Louis, 1966. Family: Single. Mailing address: 3700 Kings Way #2, Sacramento, Cal. 95821.
Career-Professional. Sr. Cons., Katherine Dunham's Performing Arts Training Center, S. Ill. U.; Dir., Lang. workshops and Poet-in-Residence, S. Ill. U. (Experiment in Higher Educ.); Writer-in-Residence (Ethnic Stud.), Cal. State U., Sacramento; Ed. Dir., Black Anthol. Project (Campus-prison-residential coop.).
WRITINGS: Poetry: A Tale of Two Toms (Black River Writers, 1968); A Tale of Time & Toilet Tissues (Black River Writers, 1969); Sentry of the Four Golden Pillars (Black River Writers,

Reed, Ishmael S.

1970); <u>River of Bones and Flesh and Blood</u> (Black River Writers,
1971); <u>Songs From an Afro/Phone</u> (Black River Writers, 1972); & <u>In</u>
<u>a Time of Rain and Desire</u> (Black River Writers, 1973). <u>Consider</u>
<u>Loneliness As These Things</u> (pub. in Italy, 1973 by the late Henry
Dumas). <u>'Ark of Bones' and Other Stories</u>, Ed. with Hale Chatfield
(1970, 1974); <u>Poetry for My People</u>, with Hale Chatfield (1970);
<u>Play Ebony Play Ivory</u>, Ed. (Random House, 1974). Adaptations &
scenarios: <u>9 Poets with the Blues</u> (1971, 1972); <u>Face of the Deep</u>;
<u>a Black Ritual</u> (1971); <u>River of Bones: A Poetic Ritual</u> (1971);
<u>The Night John Henry was Born</u> (1972, 1974); <u>Will I still Be Here</u>
<u>Tomorrow?</u> (1972, 1973); <u>There's a Wiretap in My Soup; or Quit Bug-</u>
<u>ging Me!</u> (1974). <u>Drumvoices The Mission of Black Poetry</u>, hand-
book (Doubleday, 1976). Anthol.: <u>The New Black Poetry</u> (1969); <u>A</u>
<u>Galaxy of Black Writing</u> (1971); <u>New Voices</u> (1972); <u>Poetry of Black</u>
<u>America</u> (1973). Period.: <u>Black Scholar</u>; <u>Negro Digest/Black</u>
<u>World</u>; <u>Free Lance</u>; <u>American Dialogue</u>; <u>Confrontation</u>; & <u>Journal of</u>
<u>Black Poetry</u>.
HONORS AND AWARDS: 1st Prize, Annual Festival of the Arts Poetry
Contest, Wash. U., 1965; 1st Prize, Annual Freelance Poetry Con-
test, 1966; Hon. Mention, Annual Wednesday Club, Sr. Original
Verse Contest, 1968; Award for Community Develop. & Creative Ex-
cellence, Community Sch. of E. St. Louis, Ill., 1972; Resolutions
citing "Community Work & Literary Excellence" from Governor, of
La. & Cal. State Assembly, 1974; Award for Lit. Achievement,
Sacramento Regional Arts Counc., 1974.
Sources. Author inform.; <u>New Black Voices</u>, Ed. by Abraham Chapman
(New Amer. Lib., 1972); <u>Poetry of Black America</u>, Ed. by Arnold
Adoff (Harper & Row, 1973); Pub. inform.

REED, ISHMAEL S. 1938- . Novelist, Poet,
Editor
Biographical-Personal. Born Feb. 22, 1938, in
Chattanooga, Tenn. Son of Bennie S. and
Thelma V. Reed. <u>Educ.</u>: U. of Buffalo.
<u>Mailing address</u>: 1633 Edith St., Berkeley,
Cal. 94703.
Career-Professional. Co-Founder: <u>The East Vil-</u>
<u>lage Other</u>, 1965; <u>Advance</u>, Newark Community
newspaper, 1965; Yardbird Pub. Co. Inc., Ed.
Dir., 1971; Reed, Cannon & Johnson Communica-
tions Co., Dir., 1973. Tchr.: Saint Mark's
in the Bowrie Prose Workshop, 1966; Amer.
Fic., Dept. of Eng., U. of Cal., Berkeley,
1968-69; Amer. Fic., Dept. of Eng., U. of
Wash., Seattle, 1969-70.
WRITINGS: Novels: <u>The Free-Lance Pallbearers</u> (Doubleday & Ban-
tam, 1967); <u>Yellow Back Radio Broke-Down</u> (Doubleday & Bantam,

SELECTED BLACK AMERICAN AUTHORS

Reid, Ira de Augustine

1969; <u>Mumbo Jumbo</u> (Doubleday & Bantam, 1972); <u>The Last Days of
Louisiana Red</u> (Random House, 1974); <u>Flight to Canada</u> (Random
House, 1976). Poetry: <u>Conjure</u> (U. of Mass. Pr., 1972); <u>Chatta-
nooga</u> (Random House, 1973). Anthol.: Ed., <u>19 Necromancers From
Now</u> (Doubleday, 1970); <u>Yardbird Reader, Vol. 1</u> (Yardbird Pub. Co.,
1972); Assoc. Ed., <u>Yardbird Reader, Vol. II</u> (Yardbird, 1974).
Period.: <u>New York Times</u>, <u>Washington Post</u>, <u>San Francisco Chroni-
cle</u>, <u>Black World</u>, <u>Ramparts</u>, <u>Essence</u>, <u>Encore</u>, <u>East Village Other</u>,
<u>Los Angeles Free Press</u>, <u>Arts Magazine</u>, <u>The Writer</u>.
HONORS AND AWARDS: Nominated for 1973 National Book Awards in
fiction and poetry, and 1973 Pulitzer in poetry. Was awarded the
1972 Cal. Association of English Teachers' Certificate of Merit
for <u>19 Necromancers From Now</u>.
SIDELIGHTS: Has been a resource authority for Summer Institute on
Resources on the Negro in American Literature held at Cazenovia
College (Author).
Sources. Author inform.; <u>New Black Poetry</u>, Ed. by Clarence Major
(Internat., 1969); <u>New Black Voices</u>, Ed. by Abraham Chapman (New
Amer. Lib., 1972); <u>Poetry of Black America</u>, Ed. by Arnold Adoff
(Harper & Row, 1973); <u>Soulscript</u>, Ed. by June Jordan (Doubleday,
1970); <u>Flight to Canada</u>, Ishmael Reed (Random House, 1976).

REID, IRA DE AUGUSTINE. 1901-1968. Sociolo-
gist, Educator, Writer
Biographical-Personal. Born July 2, 1901, in
Clifton Forge, Va. Son of D. Augustine (min-
ister) and Willie Robertha [James] Reid.
<u>Educ</u>.: B.A., Morehouse Coll., 1922; M.A., U.
of Pittsburgh, 1925; Ph.D., Columbia U.,
1939; London Sch. of Econ. <u>Family</u>: m.
Gladys Russell Scott in Oct. 1925. Died in
1968.
Career-Professional. Instr., Soc. Sci., Tex.
Coll., Tyler, 1922-23; Instr., Douglass High
Sch., Huntington, W. Va., 1923-24; Indust. &
Res. Secy., N.Y. Urban League, 1925-28; Dir.
of Res., Nat'l. Urban League, 1928-41; Dir.,
People's Coll., Atlanta U. & Chmn., Sociol.
Dept., 1942- ; Lectr., Negro Culture & Educ., N.Y.U. Sch. of
Educ., 1946-47; Vis. Prof. of Sociol., Haverford Coll., 1946- ;
Ed., <u>Phylon</u>.
WRITINGS: <u>In a Minor Key</u> (1940); <u>Sharecroppers All</u> (1941). <u>The
Negro Population of Denver, Colorado</u> (1929); <u>Social Conditions of
the Negro in the Hill District of Pittsburgh, Pennsylvania</u> (1930);
<u>Negro Membership in American Labor Unions</u> (1930); <u>The Negro's
Relation to Work and Law Observance</u> (1931); <u>The Problem of Child
Dependency Among Negroes</u> (1933); <u>The Urban Negro Worker in the</u>

Richardson, Nola M.

United States: 1925-1936 (1938). Contrib.: Social Forces, The
Virginia Quarterly, Opportunity, Nation & Survey Graphic.
HONORS AND AWARDS: Fellow, Julius Rosenwald Fund; 1st Black to be
named to full-time professorship at N.Y.U.
MEMBER: Assoc. Dir., Div. of Race Relat., Amer. Missionary Assn.;
Executive Dir., S. Regional Counc.; Amer. Sociol. Soc.; Acad. of
Polit. & Soc. Sci.; Bds.: S. Sociol. Soc.; S. Conf. for Human
Welfare; Com. on Mass Educ. in Race Relat.; Nat'l. Sharecroppers
Fund.
SIDELIGHTS: "His books and monographs on interracial problems...
are highly regarded by sociologists, and at least two, Sharecrop-
pers All, which he wrote with A. F. Raper, and In a Minor Key,
have been considered by reviewers to be worth the attention of
everyone concerned with the future of our civilization" (Current
Biography).
TRAVEL: W. Indies and W. Africa.
Sources. Current Biography, 1946, Ed. by Anna Rothe (H. W. Wilson,
1947); Jet mag. (Johnson Pub., July 9, 1970); Negro Caravan, Ed.
by Sterling A. Brown, et al. (Arno Pr. & N.Y. Times, 1969).

REYNOLDS, BARBARA A. Journalist, Journalism Teacher, Editorial
Director
Career-Professional. Police Reporter, Cleveland, Ohio; Public Relat.
Dir., Columbus, Ohio; Asst. Ed., Ebony; Urban Affairs writer,
Chicago Today; Gen. Assignment reporter, Chicago Tribune; Commen-
tator, WBBM radio; Regular panelist, WGN TV, "Issues Unlimited,";
Ed. Dir., Dollars and Cents & the Black Book Minority Business and
Reference Guide; Corresp., National Observer; Instr., Journalism,
Columbia Coll., Chgo.
WRITING: Jesse Jackson: the Man, the Movement, the Myth (Nelson-
Hall, 1975).
HONORS AND AWARDS: Journalist of the Year Award, Black Business
Awards Dinner, Chgo., 1974 (annual affair which honors achieve-
ments of outstanding Black professionals).
Source. Jesse Jackson: the Man, the Movement, the Myth, Barbara A.
Reynolds (Nelson-Hall, 1975).

RICHARDSON, NOLA M. 1936- . Poet
Biographical-Personal. Born Nov. 12, 1936, in
L.A., Cal. D. of Oscar and Jessie Mae [An-
derson] Smith. Educ.: Certificate in Management; Compton Jr. Coll. (Bus. & Eng.
major); Sawyer Bus. Coll. Family: div.;
son, Nolan, son, Virgil, son, Anthony, d.
Julie, d. Dawn. Mailing address: 10426
Crenshaw Blvd., #1, Inglewood, Cal. 90303.
Career-Professional. Has appeared at colleges,
libraries, conventions, etc., reciting poetry.

Richardson, Willis

Lectured at colleges and book clubs. Recently completed program
"Poetry in the Schools." Instructor, creative writing students,
Wash. High Sch.
WRITINGS: Poetry: <u>When One Loves</u> (Celestial Arts, 1974); "Medi-
cal Poems," "Hypertension/Apprehension," "Lead Poisoning," other
single poems. <u>Just a Teardrop</u>; Skit for a "One Woman Show" (Nar-
rative love story in poetry). <u>Even in a Maze</u> (Crescent, 1975).
SIDELIGHTS: A member of Watts Writer's Workshop for two years.
Works with young adults in poetry workshops, recitals, developing
special projects in the writing field, such as medical poems.
Source. Author inform.

RICHARDSON, WILLIS. 1897- . Playwright
Career-Professional. Postal clerk, Wash., D.C.; Playwright; Drama
anthologist.
WRITINGS: <u>The Broken Banjo</u>, play (1925). <u>Plays and Pageants from
the Life of the Negro</u>, Ed. (Assoc. Pub., 1930); <u>Negro History in
Thirteen Plays</u>, with co-ed., May Miller (Assoc. Pub., 1935). <u>The
King's Dilemma</u>, juvenile plays (1955).
SIDELIGHTS: The high point of his career as a dramatist occurred
at its beginning, when he received the <u>Crisis</u> prize for his play
"The Broken Banjo," in 1925 (<u>Black Writers in America</u>).
Source. <u>Black Writers in America</u>, Richard Barksdale (Macmillan,
1972).

RIVERS, CONRAD KENT. 1933-1968. Poet, Teacher
Biographical-Personal. Born Oct. 15, 1933, in
Atlantic City, N.J. <u>Educ.</u>: B.A., Wilber-
force U.; Chgo. Tchrs. Coll.; Ind. U. Died
(suddenly) 1968.
Career-Professional. Served in U.S. Army;
Taught high sch. Eng., Gary, Ind. (lived in
Chgo.). One of founders, with Ronald Fair
and others, of OBAC.
WRITINGS: Poetry: <u>Perchance to Dream,
Othello</u> (Free Lance, 1959); <u>These Black Bodies
and This Sunburnt Face</u> (Free Lance, 1962);
<u>Dusk At Selma</u> (Free Lance, 1965); <u>The Still
Voice of Harlem</u>. <u>To Make a Poet Black</u>, play.
Anthol.: <u>Beyond the Blues</u>; <u>American Negro
Poetry</u>; & <u>New Negro Poets: USA</u>. Period.:
<u>Kenyon Review</u>; <u>Antioch Review</u>; <u>Free Lance</u> & others. Stories and
dramatic work, including a play on life of Paul Laurence Dunbar,
unpublished.
HONORS AND AWARDS: While in high sch. won Savannah State Poetry
Prize for 1951; 3 times included in "America Sings," coll. verse
annuals.

Roberts, James Deotis, Sr.

SIDELIGHTS: Commenting in Sixes and Sevens on his aims and ideals
as a poet, Rivers said, "I write about the Negro because I am a
Negro, and I am not at peace with myself or my world. I cannot
separate my consciousness from the absolute injustice of hate"
(Kaleidoscope).
   Since his death Negro Digest/Black World has established an an-
nual Conrad Kent Rivers Poetry Award for the best poem published
in that magazine during the year (Poetry of Black America).
Sources. For Malcolm, Ed. by Dudley Randall & Margaret G. Burroughs
   (Broadside Pr., 1969); Kaleidoscope, Ed. by Robert Hayden (Har-
   court, 1967); The New Black Poetry, Ed. by Clarence Major
   (Internat., 1969); The Poetry of Black America, Ed. by Arnold
   Adoff (Harper & Row, 1973).

ROBERTS, JAMES DEOTIS, SR. 1927- . Dean,
School of Theology, Theologian
Biographical-Personal. Born July 12, 1927, in
   Spindale, N.C. Son of J. C. and Edith
   [Goode] Roberts. Educ.: B.A. (magna cum
   laude), Johnson C. Smith U., Charlotte, N.C.,
   1947; B.D., Shaw U., Raleigh, N.C., 1950;
   S.T.M., Hartford Sem., 1952; Ph.D., U. of
   Edinburgh, 1957. Family: m. Elizabeth Cald-
   well; d. Edin Charmaine, son, James Deotis,
   Jr., d. Carlita Rose, d. Kristina LaFerne.
   Mailing address: 1428 Whittier Pl., N.W.,
   Wash., D.C. 20011.
Career-Professional. Pastor, Union Bap. Church,
   Tarbora, N.C., 1948-50; Minister to Migrants
   (summer) Conn., 1951-52; Del. & N.Y. State,
1960-61; Asst. Pastor, Union Bap. Church, Hartford, Conn., 1950-52;
Dean of Relig., Ga. Bap. Coll., Macon, Ga., 1952-53; Asst. & Assoc.
Prof. of Philosophy & Relig. & Dir. of Relig. Life & Activities,
Shaw U., 1953-55, 1957-58; Pastor-ad-interim, Radnor Park Congre-
gational Church, Clyde Bank, Glasgow, Scotland, 1956-57; Instr. to
Prof. of Hist. & Philosophy of Relig. & Christian Theol., Sch. of
Relig., Howard U., 1958-73; Dean, Sch. of Theol., Virginia Union
U., 1973 to present.
WRITINGS: Faith and Reason in Pascal, Bergson and James (Christo-
pher, 1962); From Puritanism to Platonism in Seventeenth Century
England (Martinus Nijhoff, 1968); Liberation and Reconciliation:
A Black Theology (Westminister, 1971). Quest for a Black Theology,
co-ed. with Father James Gardiner (Pilgrim, 1971); Extending Re-
demption and Reconciliation (Christian Bd. of Public., 1973).
"The American Negro's Contributions to Religious Thought," in The
Negro Impact on Western Civilization. Articles: Journal of Religious Thought, Journal of Church & State, South East Asia Jour-

Robeson, Eslanda Cardozo

nal of Theology, The Upper Room Disciplines, 1973, Toward Whole-
ness, Professional Identity of the Black Campus Minister, Review
& Expositor, Journal of the Interdenominational Theological Center, Christian Century, etc.
MEMBER: Amer. Acad. of Relig.; Biblical Theol.; Hon. regent &
life fellow of Internat. Sociol. Res. Inst.; Continuing Com. of
World Relig.; Temple of Understanding Theolog. Com.; Nat'l. Com.
of Black Churchmen.
SIDELIGHTS: Further Study: Cambridge U.; Duke U.; U. of Wis.; U.
of Chgo.; U. of Cal., Berkeley; Harvard Divinity Sch. & World
Relig. Center; U. of Mich.; Mich. State U.; Study-Travel Fellow
(Japan, Korea, Formosa, Hong Kong, Thailand, Burma, India, Paki-
stan, Lebanon, Jordan, Egypt, Greece, Turkey, Italy, Switzerland,
France & United Kingdom). Travel-study: Sierra Leone, Liberia,
Ghana, Nigeria, Kenya, Ethiopia, Egypt, Denmark, W. Germany, etc.
Lectr. or Vis. Prof.: Catholic U. of Amer.; Swarthmore Coll.;
Wesley Theol. Sem.; U. of Va. (Author).
Source. Author inform.

ROBESON, ESLANDA CARDOZO. 1896-1965. Anthropologist, Writer,
Lecturer
Biographical-Personal. Born Dec. 15, 1896, in Wash., D.C. D. of
John I. & Eslanda [Cardozo] Goode. Educ.: U. of Chgo.; B.S.
(Chemistry), Columbia U., 1923; London U. & London Sch. of Econ.
(Anthropology), 1935-37; Ph.D., Hartford Sem. Found. (African
Stud.), 1945. Family: m. Paul Robeson (internationally-known
concert singer & actor), Aug. 17, 1921; son, Paul Robeson, Jr.
Died Dec. 13, 1965.
Career-Professional. Surgical Technician & Chemist, Presby. Hosp.,
N.Y., (in charge of Surgical Pathological Lab.), 1918-24; Bus.
mgr. (for husband); Counc. on African Affairs; UN corresp. for
New World Review; Lectr.: Africa & Race Relat.
WRITINGS: Paul Robeson, Negro (1930); African Journey (1945);
American Argument, with Pearl S. Buck (John Day, 1949). Articles:
New World Review; Asia and the Americas; Jewish Life.
SIDELIGHTS: Francis Lewis Cardozo, her maternal grandfather, was
elected South Carolina Secretary of State for a term and Secretary
of the Treasury for a term during Reconstruction. Mrs. Robeson's
father was a clerk in the War Department.
    "Mrs. Robeson has written many articles and lectured on the Ne-
gro Question, Africa, Race Relations, the United Nations, Peace
and International Relations. She attended, and covered as a correspondent, the founding of the United Nations in San Francisco,
in May 1945, the Federation celebrations of the West Indies in
Trinidad in April 1958, the All-African Peoples Conference in
Accra, in December, 1958, and the first All-Asian Women's Conference in Peking, China, in December 1949, as well as the Anti-

Robinson, William H., Jr.

Fascist Women's Conference in November 1949 in Moscow, USSR" (The Worker).
  African Journey was called "an excellent tourist account as well as a treatise on the color line" (Ernestine Evan).
  Mrs. Robeson was convinced "that racial inequality all over the world is part of one and the same problem, 'not a black problem, but a white problem, created by the behavior and attitudes of white people toward the darker races'" (Current Biography, 1945).
Sources. Current Biography, 1945, Ed. by Anna Roethe (H. W. Wilson, 1946); National Guardian (Dec. 18, 1965); Negro Caravan, Ed. by Sterling A. Brown, et al. (Arno Pr. & N.Y. Times, 1969); Negro Digest (Oct. 1945); New York Herald Tribune (Dec. 14, 1965); New York Times (Dec. 14, 1965); The Worker (Dec. 19, 1965).

ROBINSON, JAMES H. 1907-? Clergyman, Executive Director (Operation Crossroads)
Biographical-Personal. Born Jan. 24, 1907, in Knoxville, Tenn. Educ.: U. of Pa., grad. 1935; Union Theol. Sem., N.Y.C., 1938. Dec.
Career-Professional. Ordained 1938, Presby. Church; Founder & Dir., Church of the Master & Morningside Community Center, Harlem, 1938-61. 1958- , 1st Operation Crossroads Project. Apptd. Cons. on African Affairs for United Presby. Church, 1961; Cons. to Africa Desk, State Dept., 1962; Also served as Advis. Chmn. to Peace Corps; Apptd. Chmn., Youth Activities Com. of Internat. Cooperation Year, 1965.
  WRITING: Road Without Turning (1950); Tomorrow is Today (1954); Adventurous Preaching (1955 Lyman Beecher Lectures, Yale Divinity Sch.) (1955); Love of This Land, Ed. (1955); Africa at the Crossroads (1963).
SIDELIGHTS: Several missions to Africa and Europe; Fostered many internat. student programs; Took student seminar and work camp project to 5 W. African countries (Negro Handbook).
Sources. Negro Handbook, Comp. by Eds. of Ebony (Johnson Pub., 1966).

ROBINSON, WILLIAM H., JR. Writer
Biographical-Personal. Born in Newport, R.I.
Career-Professional.
  WRITINGS: Early Black American Poets (Wm. C. Brown, 1969); Early Black American Prose, 1734-1930 (Wm. C. Brown, 1970); Nommo: A Modern Anthology of Black African and Black American Literature (Macmillan, 1971); Phillis Wheatley (Broadside Pr., 1975).
Source. Early Black American Poets, Ed. by William H. Robinson, Jr., (Wm. C. Brown, 1969).

Rodgers, Carolyn Marie

RODGERS, CAROLYN MARIE. Poet, Teacher
Biographical-Personal. Born in Chgo., Ill. D.
of Clarence and Bazella Rodgers. Educ.:
U. of Ill.; B.A., Roosevelt U., 1965. Mailing address: 5230 S. Blackstone #203, Chgo.,
Ill. 60636.
Career-Professional. YMCA Soc. Worker, 1963-66;
Columbia Coll., Writer & Lectr., 1968-69; U.
of Wash., Writer-in-Residence, Summer, 1970;
Poet-in-Residence, Malcolm X. Community Coll.,
1972; Vis. Writer-in-Residence, Nat'l. Found.
of Humanities & Arts, Albany State Coll.,
1972; Ind. U., Summer, 1973; Columnist, Milwaukee Courier; Bk. reviewer, Chicago Daily
News.

WRITINGS: Poetry: Paper Soul (Third World
Pr., 1968); 2 Love Raps (Third World Pr., 1969); Songs of a Black-
bird (Third World Pr., 1969); How I Got Ovah: New and Selected
Poems (Doubleday, 1975). Anthol.: New Negro Poets: USA; Black
Arts; Brothers and Sisters; We Speak as Liberators; Natural Proc-
ess; To Gwen with Love; The Black Poets; Open Poetry; Exploring
Life Through Literature; Poetry of Black America; Understanding
the New Black Poetry. Period.: Black World; Chicago Daily News;
Colloquy Magazine; Ebony; Essence; Focus on Youth; Journal of
Black Poetry; Milwaukee Courier; Nation; Negro Digest.
HONORS AND AWARDS: The 1st Conrad Kent Rivers Writing Award,
1969; NEA Award, 1970; Soc. of Midland Authors, Poet Laureate
Award, 1970.
MEMBER: OBAC; Gwendolyn Brooks's Writers Workshop; Delta Sigma
Theta.
SIDELIGHTS: "She is one of the founders in 1968 with Don L. Lee
and Johari Amini, of Third World Press..." (Broadside Authors and
Artists).
Source. Broadside Authors and Artists, Comp. by Leaonead P. Bailey
(Broadside Pr., 1974).

ROGERS, JOEL AUGUSTUS. 1883-1966. Historian,
Journalist, Newspaper Columnist
Biographical-Personal. Born 1883 in Jamaica,
Brit. W. Indies. Son of Samuel and Emily
Rogers. Came to U.S. 1906; naturalized 1917.
Self-educated. Died in N.Y.C., Jan. 1966.
Career-Professional. Originally a journalist
traveling in Europe, Asia and Africa in
search of material on the Black Man. Served
with Brit. Army for 4 yrs.; Covered Haile
Selassie's coronation, Addis Ababa, Ethiopia,
1930; War Corresp. to Italo-Ethiopian con-

Rollins, Charlemae Hill

flict, 1935-36, for <u>Pittsburgh Courier</u> (thus became 1st Negro war
corresp. in U.S. hist.). Wrote an illustrated feature, "Your History," for <u>Pittsburgh Courier</u>.
WRITINGS: <u>From Superman to Man</u> (1917, 1971); <u>As Nature Leads</u>
(1919); <u>Maroons of the West Indies and South America</u> (1921); <u>The
Ku Klux Klan Spirit</u> (Messenger, 1923); <u>World's Greatest Men of African Descent</u> (1931); <u>Real Facts About Ethiopia</u> (1935); <u>Sex and
Race</u>, 3 vols. (1940-44); <u>World's Great Men of Color</u>, 2 vols. (Hel-
ga M. Rogers, 1946; Macmillan, 1972); <u>Nature Knows No Color-Line</u>
(1952); <u>Facts About the Negro</u> (Lincoln Park Studios, 1960); <u>Af-
rica's Gift To America</u> (Sportshelf, 1961); <u>She Walks in Beauty</u>,
novel (Western, 1963); <u>100 Amazing Facts About the Negro</u> (1963).
Contrib. to: <u>Survey Graphic</u>, <u>American Mercury</u>, <u>Crisis</u>, <u>Journal of
Negro History</u>.
MEMBER: Amer. Geographical Soc.; Acad. of Polit. Sci.
SIDELIGHTS: "For more than 50 years, Joel A. Rogers was one of
the foremost Negro historians in the United States.
   Although the work of Joel Rogers has at times been challenged
for the accuracy of its documentation and interpretation, it is
nonetheless impressive when one considers that Rogers was conduct-
ing much of his research at a time when Negro historians were
virtually non-existent in the U.S." (<u>Negro Almanac</u>).
   Rogers generally published his own works.
Sources. <u>Negro Almanac</u>, Comp. by Harry A. Ploski & Ernest Kaiser
   (Bellwether, 1971); <u>Negro Caravan</u>, Ed. by Sterling A. Brown, et al.
   (Arno Pr. & N.Y. Times, 1969); <u>Who's Who in Colored America</u>, Ed.
   by G. James Fleming & Christian E. Burckel & Assoc., 7th ed., 1950.

ROLLINS, CHARLEMAE HILL. 1897- . Librarian,
   Writer, Teacher
Biographical-Personal. Born June 20, 1897, in
   Yazoo City, Miss. D. of Allen G. and Birdie
   [Tucker] Hill. <u>Educ.</u>: Columbia U.; Grad.
   Lib. Sch., U. of Chgo. <u>Family</u>: m. Joseph
   Walter Rollins, April 8, 1918; son, Joseph W.
   Rollins, Jr. <u>Mailing address</u>: 500 E. 33rd
   St., Chgo., Ill. 60616.
Career-Professional. Chgo. Public Lib., 1927-
   1963, Children's Librn., George C. Hall
   Branch, 1932-63; Instr., Children's Lit.,
   Roosevelt U., Chgo., 1949-?; Summer Instr.,
   Fisk U., 1950; Morgan State Coll., 1953-54;
   Human Relat. Workshop, San Francisco State
   Coll.; Dept. of Lib. Sci., Rosary Coll., Riv-
er Forest, Ill.; Pres., Children's Div., ALA, 1957-58; Chmn.,
Children's Div., Ill. Lib. Assn., 1954-55; Chmn., Newbery Calde-
cott Awards Com., ALA, 1956-57; Chmn., Elementary Section, Ill.
Unit, Catholic Lib. Assn.

Rowan, Carl Thomas

WRITINGS: We Build Together (Nat'l. Counc. of Tchrs. of Eng.,
1941, 1951); The Magic World of Books (Science Res. Assoc., 1952);
Juveniles: Christmas Gift; an anthology of Christmas poems, songs
and stories (Follet, 1963); They Showed the Way (Crowell, 1964);
Famous American Negro Poets (Dodd, Mead, 1965); Famous Negro En-
tertainers of Stage, Screen and TV (Dodd, Mead, 1967); Great Negro
Poets for Children (Dodd, Mead, 1965); & Black Troubadour; Langston
Hughes (1970). Contrib.: American Childhood, Illinois Libraries,
Junior Libraries, ALA Bulletin, Elementary English.
HONORS AND AWARDS: Amer. Brotherhood Award of Nat'l. Counc. of
Christians and Jews, 1952; Lib. Letter Award of ALA, 1953; Grolier
Soc. Award of ALA, 1955; Good Amer. Award of Chgo., Com. of One
Hundred, 1962; Negro Centennial Awards (in 3 areas), 1963; Chil-
dren's Reading Round Table Award, 1963; Hon. mem., Phi Delta Kappa
Award; Woman of the Yr. Award (Zeta Phi Beta), 1956 Hon. Dr. of
Humane Letters, Columbia Coll, Chgo. Mem. Ed. Bd. of World Book
Encyclopedia & of American Educator.
SIDELIGHTS: One of the most noteworthy facets of the professional
career of the grand dame of children's librarianship was the publication of We Build Together, under the auspices of the National
Council of Teachers of English. "This was an annotated list of 18
books which were least offensive in their stories and illustrations. Publishers were roundly criticized, in the book's introduction, for the caricatures, plantation themes, and homemade
dialects directed toward impressionable young minds. This small,
potent paperback became the conscience and guidebook for the industry and professionals around the country" (Ebony).
Sources. Authors of Books for Young People, Ed. by Martha E. Ward &
Dorothy A. Marquardt (Scarecrow, 1964); Contemporary Authors,
Vols. 11-12, Ed. by James M. Ethridge and Barbara Kopala (Gale
Res., 1965); Famous American Negro Poets, Charlemae Rollins (Dodd,
Mead, 1955); "Goodbye Black Sambo," Carlo A. Parks (Ebony, Nov.
1972, Johnson Pub.); Something About the Author, Vol. 3, Ed. by
Anne Commire (Gale Res., 1965); Pub. inform.

ROWAN, CARL THOMAS. 1925- . Former USIA Director, Syndicated
Columnist, Journalist
Biographical-Personal. Born Aug. 11, 1925, in Ravenscroft, Tenn.
Son of Thomas David and Johnnie B. [Bradford] Rowan. Educ.: B.A.,
Oberlin Coll., 1947; M.A., (Journalism) U. of Minn., 1948; D.Litt.
(hon.), Simpson Coll., 1957, Hamline U., 1958; LHD (hon.) Washburn
U., 1964, Talladega Coll., 1965, St. Olaf Coll., 1966, Knoxville
Coll., 1966; LL.D. (hon.), Howard U., 1964, Alfred U., 1964,
Temple U., 1964, Atlanta U., 1965, Allegheny Coll., 1966; D. Pub.
Admin., Morgan State Coll., 1964. Family: m. Vivien Louise Mur-
phy (public health nurse), Aug. 2, 1950; d. Barbara, son, Carl,
Jr., son, Geoffrey. Mailing address: 3116 Fessenden St., N.W.,
Wash., D.C. 20008.

Russell, Charlie L.

Career-Professional. U.S. Navy, 1943, Ensign, Naval Reserve; Copywriter, 1948-50, Staff writer, 1950-61, Minneapolis Tribune;
Deputy Asst. to Secy. State for Public Affairs, Dept. of State,
1961-63; U.S. Ambassador to Finland, 1963-64; Dir., USIA, Wash.,
1964-65; Columnist, Chicago Daily News, 1965- ; Syndicated
columnist.
WRITINGS: South of Freedom (Knopf, 1952); The Pitiful and the
Proud (Random House, 1956); Go South to Sorrow (Random House,
1957); Wait Till Next Year (Random House, 1960); No Need for Hunger (1962); Just Between Us Blacks (Random House, 1974).
HONORS AND AWARDS: Include Sidney Hillman Award, Best newspaper
reporting, 1952; ALA annual list of best bks., South of Freedom,
1953; Amer. Teamwork Award, Nat'l. Urban League, 1955; Foreign
Corresp. Medallion for article on India, 1955, and on S.E. Asia,
coverage of Bandung Conf., 1956; ALA annual list of best bks., The
Pitiful and the Proud, 1956; Phila. Fellow. Com., 1961; Communications Award, Human Relat., Anti-Defamation League, B'nai Brith,
1964; Distinguished Serv. Award, Capital Pr. Club, 1964; Nat'l.
Brotherhood Award, Nat'l. Conf. of Christians and Jews, 1964;
Amer. S. Region, Pr. Inst. Award, 1965.
SIDELIGHTS: "For five consecutive years, beginning in 1952, Carl
T. Rowan, young Negro journalist, won national honors as a newsman
and author for reports which ranged from race relations in the
South and the plight of the American Indian to the political and
social turmoil in Asia. In 1956 he became the only newspaperman
ever to win three successive annual awards from Sigma Delta Chi,
journalism fraternity" (Current Biography).
"His articles for the (Minneapolis) Tribune 'How Far from
Slavery?' won the following recognition for him: 'Service to Humanity' award of Minneapolis Jr. Chamber of Commerce, and his
designation as Minneapolis's 'outstanding young man of 1951,' etc.
These articles were a starting point for his first book South of
Freedom."
"As Director of USIA, Carl Roman supervised 12,000 employees in
106 countries, was the highest ranking Negro in the federal gov-
ernment, and the first to sit in on meetings of the National Se-
curity Council" (Negroes in Public Affairs and Government).
Sources. Current Biography, 1958, Ed. by Margaret Dent Candee (H. W.
Wilson, 1958); Negro Handbook, Comp. by Eds. of Ebony (Johnson
Pub., 1966); South of Freedom, Carl T. Rowan (Knopf, 1953); Negroes
in Public Affairs and Government, Ed. by Walter Christmas (Educ.
Her., 1966).

RUSSELL, CHARLIE L. 1932- . Editor, Lecturer
Biographical-Personal. Born 1932, in Monroe, La. Educ.: B.A.
(Eng.), U. of San Francisco; M.S.W., N.Y.U.

Russwurm, John B.

Career-Professional. Counselor, City Coll. of
N.Y.; Lectr., Basic writing, Livingston Coll.,
Rutgers U.; Founder-ed., Onyx Public.
WRITINGS: A Birthday Present for Katheryn
Kenyatta, novella (McGraw-Hill, 1970); Five
on the Black Hand Side, play and film script;
"The Black Church," (Nat'l. ABC-TV script);
"A Man is Not Made of Steel," (for On Being
Black, WGBH-TV, Boston). Contrib. of short
stories to periodicals.
Source. "Nat'l. Conf. of Afro-Amer. Writers"
(Program), Howard U., Inst. for Arts & Hu-
manities, Nov. 1974.

RUSSWURM, JOHN B. 1799-1851. Editor, Poli-
tician, Statesman
Biographical-Personal. Born Oct. 1, 1799, in
Jamaica, Brit. W. Indies. Son of a White
Amer. father and a Jamaican mother. Sent to
Can. by father where he received early train-
ing; Grad., Bowdoin Coll., Maine, 1826, Master's degree, 1829. Died June 17, 1851.
Career-Professional. Established Freedom's
Journal, 1827 (with Samuel E. Cornish); Ed.,
The Rights of All (Newspaper), 1828. (Anti-
slavery societies used The Rights of All as a
forum, and the editor became a staunch advocate of immediate emancipation). In Liberia:
Supt. of Schools; Governor of Md. Province
(at Cape Palms) before it became part of Liberia; Founded Liberia Herald.
SIDELIGHTS: "John B. Russwurm, the founder of the first Negro
newspaper, Freedom's Journal, was also the first Negro to receive
a degree from a college in the United States...
For four years, Russwurm directed his paper toward a program of
abolition, of equal rights for the Negro in America and of opposi-
tion to the colonizationists. In 1830, The Rights of All published an article that praised the work of Paul Cuffee, the colo-
nizationist who had taken 30 Negroes to Sierra Leone. This article destroyed Russwurm's influence among the various groups of
free Negroes in the North. Furthermore, he himself finally believed that it was hopeless 'to talk of ever enjoying citizenship
in this country.' Subsequently joining the colonizationists, he
went to Liberia, where he served creditably as superintendent of
schools and as governor of the Maryland Province...." (Historical
Negro Biographies).
Sources. Historical Negro Biographies, Wilhelmena S. Robinson (ASNLH,
1967); Negro Handbook, Comp. by Eds. of Ebony (Johnson Pub., 1966).

SANCHEZ, SONIA. 1934- . Poet, Activist, Playwright

Biographical-Personal. Born Sept. 9, 1934, in Birmingham, Ala. D. of Wilson L. and Lena [Jones] Driver. Educ.: B.A., Hunter Coll., 1955; N.Y.U. Family: d. Anita, d. Morani, d. Mungu. Mailing address: 86 College St., Amherst, Mass. 01002.

Career-Professional. Instr., San Francisco State Coll., 1966-68; Asst. Prof., U. of Pittsburgh, 1969-70; Asst. Prof., Rutgers U., 1970-71; Asst. Prof. of Black Lit. & Creative writing, Manhattan Community Coll., 1971- ; Tchr. of writing, City Coll. of City U. of N.Y., 1972; Assoc. Prof., U. of Mass., Amherst, 1972-73.

WRITINGS: Poetry: Homecoming (Broadside Pr., 1969); We A BaddDDD People (Broadside Pr., 1970); It's A New Day: Poems for Young Brothers and Sisters (Broadside Pr., 1971); Three Hundred and Sixty Degrees of Blackness Comin' at You, Ed. (5x Pub. Co., 1971); We Be Word Sorcerers (Bantam, 1973). Plays: The Bronx is Next; Sister Son/ji; Dirty Hearts. In progress: Behind the Bamboo Curtain (Broadside Pr.). Anthol.: Potero Negro ["Black Power"]; Black Fire; For Malcolm; The Writing on the Wall; In a Time of Revolution; Soulscript; Broadside Treasury; Black Poets; We Speak As Liberators; Understanding the New Black Poetry. Period.: Black Collegian; Black Creation; Black Scholar; Black Theatre; Black World; Journal of Black Poetry; Liberator; Massachusetts Review; Minnesota Review; Muhammad Speaks; Negro Digest; New England Review; New York Quarterly; New York Times; Nommo; Soul Book; Transatlantic Review; Tulane Drama Review.

HONORS AND AWARDS: P.E.N. Writing Award, 1969; Acad. of Arts & Letters $1000 Award to continue writing; Hon. Ph.D. degree in Fine Arts, Wilberforce U.

SIDELIGHTS: Her plays: The Bronx is Next, 1st prod. in N.Y.C. at Theatre Black, Oct. 3, 1970; Sister Son/ji, 1st prod. (with Cop and Blow, Players Inn & Gettin' It Together) as Black Visions, Off-Broadway at N.Y. Shakespeare Festival Public Theatre, 1972 (included in New Plays from Black Theatre).

"In the introduction to We A BaddDDD People, Sonia Sanchez's second collection of poetry, Dudley Randall writes: 'This tiny woman with the infant's face attacks the demons of this world with the fury of a sparrow defending her fledglings in the nest. She hurls obscenities at things that are obscene. She writes directly, ignoring metaphors, similies, ambiguity, and other poetic devices. But her bare passionate speech can be very effective'" (New Black Voices).

Schuyler, George S.

Sources. Black Fire, Ed. by LeRoi Jones & Larry Neal (Morrow, 1968);
Broadside Authors and Artists, Comp. by Leaonead P. Bailey (Broad-
side Pr., 1974); Contemporary Authors, Vols. 33-36, Ed. by Clare
D. Kinsman & Mary A. Tennenhouse (Gale Res., 1973); Ebony (Johnson
Pub., Mar. 1974); For Malcolm, Ed. by Dudley Randall & Margaret
Burroughs (Broadside Pr., 1969); The New Black Poetry, Ed. by
Clarence Major (Internat., 1969); New Black Voices, Ed. by Abraham
Chapman (New Amer. Lib., 1972); Poetry of Black America, Ed. by
Arnold Adoff (Harper & Row, 1973); Soulscript, Ed. by June Jordan
(Doubleday, 1970); Books in Print, Supplement, 1975-76 (Bowker,
1976).

SCHUYLER, GEORGE S. 1895- . Editor, Journal-
ist, Writer
Biographical-Personal. Born Feb. 25, 1895, in
Providence, R.I. Son of George Schuyler.
Educ.: Public schs. of Syracuse, N.Y.; U.S.
Army (1st Lt.), 1912-1918. Family: m.
Josephine Schuyler Jan. 1928 (dec.); d.
Philippa Schuyler (celebrated pianist-com-
poser-dec.). Mailing address: 270 Convent
Ave., N.Y., N.Y. 10031.
Career-Professional. Asst. Ed. & Managing Ed.,
Messenger Magazine, 1923-28; Ed., Illustrated
Feature Section for Negro Pr., Chgo., 1928-
29; Publicity Dept., NAACP, 1933-35, N.Y.;
Bus. Mgr., Crisis mag., NAACP, 1937-44;
Assoc. Ed., The Pittsburgh Courier, N.Y. of-
fice, 1942-64. Ed. staff, Plain Talk, 1946- ; Columnist, Spadea
Syndicate, 1953-61; Contrib., N. Amer. Newspaper Alliance.
WRITINGS: Novels: Black No More (Macavlry, 1931); Slaves Today!
(Brewer, Warren & Putnam, 1931); Black and Conservative, autobiog.
(1966). Racial Intermarriage in the United States, monograph
(Little Blue Book No. 1387). Anthol.: Behold America (1930);
What the Negro Wants (1943); The Future of the American Negro, Ed.
(1965). Period.: American Mercury; World Tomorrow; New Masses;
Modern Quarterly; Opportunity; Nation; National Review; The Free-
man; Christian Herald; Crisis; Negro Digest; Plain Talk; & Annals
of the American Academy of Political Science.
HONORS AND AWARDS: Citation of merit, Outstanding Journalist,
Sch. of Journalism, Lincoln U., Jefferson City, Mo., 1954.
MEMBER: Bd. of Governors, Post War World Counc., 1947-49; V.
Pres., Amer. Writers Assn., 1946-60; Bd. Amer.-Asian-African Educ.
Exchange; Citizen Foreign Relat. Com.; Amer. Com. for Cultural
Freedom, 1950-56; Amer. Soc. of African Culture; Joint Com. Against
Communism in N.Y.; Com. for One Million Against the Admission of
China to the UN; Amer.-African Affairs Assn.

Schuyler, Philippa Duke

SIDELIGHTS: "Mr. Schuyler has lectured in all important cities of
the United States, and in Manchester, England; Bogota, Colombia;
Panama City, Panama; Berlin, Germany; and Brussels, Belgium" (Pub.
inform.). "During twenties was a regular columnist for the black
socialist monthly, The Messenger. But has since been conservative
columnist on Pittsburgh Courier" (Afro-Amer. Writing).
  "As a special correspondent for New York Evening Post investi-
gated charges of slavery in Liberia in 1931, labor conditions in
Mississippi Flood Control Project, 1932-33, labor unionism in 40
U.S. industrial centers in 1937, and civil rights compliance in
state capitals across the nation. Traveled in Latin America and
the Caribbean Islands, and toured the South, gathering material
for 'What's Good About the South?', a series of articles that
aroused much public discussion" (Blackamerican Literature).
Sources. Afro-American Writing, Ed. by Richard A. Long & Eugenia W.
  Collier (N.Y.U. Pr., 1972); Blackamerican Literature, Ed. by Ruth
  Miller (Glencoe Pr., 1971); Negro Caravan, Ed. by Sterling A.
  Brown (Arno Pr. & N.Y. Times, 1969); Pub. inform.

SCHUYLER, PHILIPPA DUKE. 1932-1967. Concert
Pianist, Composer, Writer
Biographical-Personal. Born Aug. 21, 1932, in
    N.Y.C. D. of George S. (ed., journalist,
    novelist) & Josephine [Duke] Schuyler (danc-
    er, painter, poet). Educ.: Manhattanville
    Convent of Sacred Heart; piano and composi-
    tion with Herman Wasserman, Otto Cesana,
    Gaston Dethier. Family: Single. Killed in
    crash of U.S. Army helicopter in Da Nang Bay,
    S. Vietnam, May 9, 1967, while on concert
    tour.
Career-Professional. Started touring as a child
    prodigy. First symphonic composition, Man-
    hattan Nocturne, was performed at Carnegie
    Hall (at age 12); her scherzo "Rumplestilts-
kin" performed by Dean Dixon Youth Orchestra, Boston Pops, New
Haven Symphony, N.Y. Philharmonic (at age 13); soloist, N.Y.
Philharmonic (at age 14); debuted in dual role of composer &
pianist with N.Y. Philharmonic playing Saint-Saëns's Concerto no. 2
in A minor & her own "Rumpelstiltskin," written as part of her
planned Fairy Tale Symphony. Concerts in over 80 countries, many
under auspices of U.S. State Dept. Formerly foreign correspondent for United Press Features, New York Daily Mirror, Manchester
Union Leader, & Spadea News Syndicate, Afro-Asian Educational Exchange, secretary.
WRITINGS: Adventures in Black and White, autobiog. (Speller,
1960); Who Killed the Congo? (Devin, 1962); Jungle Saints (Herder,

Scott, Cornelius A.

1963); <u>Kingdom of Dreams</u> (Speller, 1963). In preparation at her
death, <u>Good Men Die</u>.
HONORS AND AWARDS: Twenty-seven music awards, including two from
Wayne State U. for composition, and award for symphonic poem, <u>Man-
hattan Nocturne</u>, & for symphonic scherzo, "Rumpelstiltskin," &
three decorations from foreign governments.
SIDELIGHTS: "...The only child of an interracial marriage...who
at age four gained musical recognition in the annual competition
of the National Guild of Piano Teachers by playing ten compositions, over half of which were her own.... Philippa's early life
is heavily documented. Her progress was measured periodically by
the Clinic for Gifted Children at New York University.... (Her)
parents often credited her genius to a curious diet of raw vege-
tables and raw meat..." (<u>Biographic Encyclopedia of Women</u>).
Sources. <u>Biographic Encyclopedia of Women</u> (World Biography Pr.,
1975); <u>Contemporary Authors</u>, Vols. 5-8, Ed. by Barbara Harte &
Carolyn Riley (Gale Res., 1969); <u>Negro Almanac</u>, Comp. by Harry A.
Ploski & Roscoe C. Brown (Bellwether, 1967); <u>Negro Digest</u> (Sept.
1944).

SCOTT, CORNELIUS A. 1908- . Publisher
Biographical-Personal. Born Feb. 8, 1908, in Edwards, Miss. <u>Educ.</u>:
Morris Brown Coll., 1929; Morehouse Coll., 1930; U. of Kan., 1931.
<u>Family</u>: m. Ruth Perry, Jan. 27, 1940; d. Jocelyn, d. Portia.
<u>Mailing address</u>: (Office) 210 Auburn Ave., N.E., Atlanta, Ga.
Career-Professional. Publisher, <u>Atlanta Daily World</u>.
HONORS AND AWARDS: Recipient, Lincoln U.'s Sch. of Journalism
Award, 1957; Ga. State Chamber of Commerce Citizen Award, 1959;
Nat'l. 4-H Award, 1953.
MEMBER: NAACP, YMCA, Frontiers Internat. Club; Atlanta Chap.,
Newspaper Pub. Assn.; Dir., Mutual Fed. Savings & Loan, Atlanta.
Source. <u>Negro Handbook</u>, Comp. by Eds. of <u>Ebony</u> (Johnson Pub., 1966).

SCOTT, NATHAN A., JR. 1925- . Theologian,
Priest, Critic, Essayist
Biographical-Personal. Born April 24, 1925, in
Cleveland, Ohio. Son of Nathan A. and Maggie
[Martin] Scott. <u>Educ.</u>: B.A., U. of Mich.,
1944; B.D., Union Theol. Sem., 1946; Ph.D.,
Columbia U., 1949. <u>Family</u>: m. Charlotte
Hanley (Asst. V. Pres., Fed. Reserve Bank,
Chgo.); son, Nathan A. Scott, III, d. Leslie
Kristin Scott. <u>Mailing address</u>: The Divin-
ity Sch., The U. of Chgo., Chgo., Ill. 60637.
Career-Professional. Shailer Mathews Prof. of
Theol. & Lit., U. of Chgo., Divinity Sch. &
Dept. of Eng. (Chmn., Theol. & Lit. Field);
Priest of the Episcopal Church; Canon Theol.

Scott, Nathan A., Jr.

of the Cathedral of St. James, Chgo.; Co-ed. of The Journal of Religion. Fellow, Sch. of Letters, Ind. U., 1965-72; Adjunct Prof., Eng., U. of Mich., 1969; Walter & Mary Tuohy Vis. Prof., Relig. Stud., John Carroll U., 1970.
WRITINGS: Rehearsals of Discomposure: Alienation and Reconciliation in Modern Literature (King's Crown Pr., Columbia U., 1953; John Lehmann, 1952); The Tragic Vision and the Christian Faith (Assoc. Pr., 1957); Modern Literature and the Religious Frontier (Harper & Row, 1958); Albert Camus (Ser. "Studies in Modern Literature and Thought" Bowes, 1962; Hillary House, 1962); Reinhold Niebuhr (U. of Minn. Pr., 1963); The New Orpheus: Essays Toward a Christian Poetic (Sheed & Ward, 1964); The Climate of Faith in Modern Literature (Seabury, 1964); Samuel Beckett (Ser. "Stud. in Modern European Literature & Thought" Bowes, 1965; Hillary House, 1965); Four Ways of Modern Poetry (John Knox Pr., 1965); Man in the Modern Theatre (John Knox Pr., 1965); Forms of Extremity in the Modern Novel (John Knox Pr., 1965); The Broken Center: Studies in the Theological Horizon of Modern Literature (Yale U. Pr., 1966); Ernest Hemingway (Eerdmans, 1966); The Modern Vision of Death (John Knox Pr., 1967); Adversity and Grace: Studies in Recent American Literature (U. of Chgo. Pr., 1968); Craters of the Spirit: Studies in the Modern Novel (Corpus Bks., 1968; Sheed & Ward, 1969); Negative Capability: Studies in The New Literature and the Religious Situation (Yale U. Pr., 1969); The Unquiet Vision: Mirrors of Man in Existentialism (World, 1969); Nathanael West (Eerdmans, 1971); The Wild Prayer of Longing: Poetry and the Sacred (Yale U. Pr., 1971); Three American Moralists--Mailer, Bellow, Trilling (U. of Notre Dame Pr., 1973); Legacy of Reinhold Niebuhr (U. of Chgo. Pr., 1975). Essays in: Religious Symbolism; Symbolism in Religion and Literature; Society and Self; Christian Faith and the Contemporary Arts; Graham Greene: Some Critical Considerations; The Scope of Grace; The Search for Identity: Essays on the American Character; Literature and Belief; The Added Dimension: The Mind and Art of Flannery O'Connor; Conflicting Images of Man; Existentialism; Man and the Movies; The Shapeless God; Religion and Contemporary Western Culture; Dark Symphony: Negro Literature in America; Black Expression: Essays by and About Black Americans in the Creative Arts; Five Black Writers: Essays on Wright, Ellison, Baldwin, Hughes, and LeRoi Jones; Cavalcade: Negro American Writing from 1760 to the Present; The Black Novelist; The Shaken Realist: Essays in Modern Literature in Honor of Frederick J. Hoffman; Literature and Religion; Humanities, Religion, and the Arts Tomorrow; The Westminster Dictionary of Christian Education; Contemporary Literary Criticism, ol. I. Period.: Journal of the American Academy of Religion; The Journal of Religion; The Christian Scholar; Anglican Theological Review; Religion in Life; Cross Currents; Journal of Religious Thought;

245

Scott-Heron, Gil

> Motive; Christianity and Crisis; Union Seminary Quarterly Review; Christian Century; Review of Metaphysics; Centennial Review; Chicago Review; London Magazine; University of Kansas City Review; Kenyon Review; Denver Quarterly; Thought; New Scholasticism; Boundary 2; & others.
> HONORS AND AWARDS: Litt.D., Ripon Coll.; L.H.D., Wittenberg U., 1965; D.D., Phila. Divinity Sch., 1967; S.T.D., Gen. Theol. Sem., 1968; Litt.D., Saint Mary's Coll., Notre Dame, 1969.
> MEMBER: Kent Fellow, Soc. for Relig. in Higher Educ.; Amer. Philosophy Assn.; Mod. Lang. Assn.; Amer. Acad. of Relig.; Bd. of Trus.: Chgo. Hist. Soc.; Seabury-Western Theol. Sem.; Soc. for Art, Relig. & Contemporary Culture; & Episcopal Radio-TV Found.
> SIDELIGHTS: "Relatively unknown as a Negro, Nathan A. Scott, Jr. is a critic of modern literature who has written extensively on the relationships between the literary and religious imagination ...Scott's essays are noted for their length, diversity and equality" (AFRO USA).

Sources. AFRO USA, Comp. by Harry A. Ploski & Ernest Kaiser (Bellwether, 1971); Author inform.; Cavalcade, Ed. by Arthur P. Davis & Saunders Redding (Houghton Mifflin, 1971).

SCOTT-HERON, GIL. 1949– . Musician, Writer
Biographical-Personal. Born in Chgo., Ill. in 1949.
Career-Professional.
> WRITINGS: Small Talk at One Hundred Twenty Fifth & Lenox, poetry (World, 1970); Vulture, novel (World, 1970); The Nigger Factory (Dial, 1972).

Sources. Small Talk at One Hundred Twenty Fifth & Lenox, Gil Scott-Heron (World, 1970).

SEALE, BOBBY. 1936– . Activist
Career-Professional.
> WRITINGS: Seize the Time; The Story of the Black Panther Party and Huey P. Newton (Random House, 1970).

Source. Seize the Time, Bobby Seale (Random House, 1970).

SÉJOUR, VICTOR. 1817-1874. Dramatist, Poet
Biographical-Personal. Juan Victor Séjour Marcon et Ferrand. Son of François Marcon (Negro from Santo Domingo), & Eloisa Phillipe Ferrand (a quadroon). His father was a New Orleans dry cleaner owner. Educ.: Saint Barbe Acad., conducted by Michel Seligny. Séjour escaped local frustrations and went to France. Died in charity ward of a Paris hospital of tuberculosis in 1874.

Career-Professional. One of three New Orleans poets who produced a collection called Les Cenelles (1845), first anthology of American Negro poetry.
> "In France he was a very popular dramatist, twenty-one of his best plays being staged there, the first in 1844. In the 1850's

Sengstacke, John Herman Henry

at least three of his plays were produced in New Orleans" (<u>Early Black American Poets</u>).

WRITINGS: "...he was accepted in the literary circles of Paris, where he became acquainted with Alexandre Dumas and Emile Augier. Because of these friendships, he became intrigued with drama. His first stage play, <u>Diegarias</u>, was produced in 1844 at the Théâtre Français and was followed in 1849 by <u>La Chute de Sejan</u>. His greatest plays were <u>Richard III</u> (1852); <u>Les Noces Vénitiennes</u> (1855); <u>Le Fils de la nuit</u> (1856); <u>Les Grands Vassaux</u> (1859); <u>Les Fils de Charles Quint</u> (1864); and <u>Les Volontaires de 1814</u> (1862), which is his only work based on an American theme" (<u>Historical Negro Biographies</u>).

SIDELIGHTS: "His works were noted for the grandiose verse, the sumptuous costuming and spectacular settings--all of which were popular in Paris during the mid-19th century..." (<u>Historical Negro Biographies</u>).

Sources. <u>American Negro Reference Book</u>, Ed. by John P. Davis (Prentice-Hall, 1966); <u>Early Black American Poets</u>, Ed by William H. Robinson, Jr. (Wm. C. Brown, 1969); <u>Historical Negro Biographies</u>, Wilhelmena S. Robinson (ASNLH, 1967).

SENGSTACKE, JOHN HERMAN HENRY. 1912- . Newspaper Publisher

Biographical-Personal. Born Nov. 25, 1912, in Savannah, Ga. Son of Herman Alexander (minister) & Rose Mae [Davis] Sengstacke. Educ.: B.S. (Bus. Admin.) Hampton Inst., 1933; Mergenthaler Linotype Sch.; Chgo. Sch. of Printing; Northwestern U.; Ohio State U. Family: m. Myrtle Elizabeth Picou, July 9, 1939; son, John Herman, son, Robert Abbott, son, Lewis Willis. Mailing address: Office, 2400 S. Mich. Ave., Chgo., Ill. 60616.

Career-Professional. With Robert S. Abbott Pub. Co., pub. of <u>Chicago Defender</u> & <u>Tri-State Defender</u> since 1934, v. pres. & mgr., 1934-40; Pres. & Gen. Mgr., 1940- ; Chmn., Bd. of Dirs., <u>Michigan Chronicle</u> (Detroit), <u>Louisville Defender</u>; Pres., <u>Tri-State Defender</u>, Defender Public., Amalgamated Pubs., Inc.; Pub., <u>Daily Defender</u>.

MEMBER: Has been Dir., Ill. Fed. Savings & Loan Assn.; Dir., Golden State Mutual Life Ins. Co.; Bd. of Trus., Bethune-Cookman Coll., Fla.; Bd. of Trus., Hampton Inst.

SIDELIGHTS: The <u>Chicago Defender</u> was founded by the present publisher's uncle, Robert Sengstacke Abbott in 1905. Its affiliates are the <u>Michigan Chronicle</u> and the <u>Louisville Defender</u> in Kentucky. Sengstacke is the founder of the Negro Newspaper Publishers' Association.

Shangé, Ntozake

When Sengstacke joined the staff of the <u>Chicago Defender</u> in 1934, that paper had been in existence approximately twenty-nine years...with the slogan 'American race prejudice must be destroyed,' and with a goal of 'opening up of all trades and trade unions to black as well as white,' 'representation in the President's Cabinet,' 'Federal legislation to abolish lynching,' and 'full enfranchisement of all American citizens.'"

As president of the Negro Publishers Association, the <u>New York Times</u> stated, "...he was able to 'list among the accomplishments of the association the accrediting of Negro correspondents to the White House conferences and in war coverage, and the establishment of a Washington news bureau for newspapers represented by the association'" (<u>Current Biography, 1949</u>).

Sources. <u>Current Biography, 1949</u>, Ed. by Anna Roethe (H. W. Wilson, 1950); <u>Negro Handbook</u>, Comp. by Eds. of <u>Ebony</u> (Johnson Pub., 1966).

SHANGÉ, NTOZAKE [Williams, Paulette L.].
1948- . Writer, Dancer, Teacher
Biographical-Personal. Born Oct. 18, 1948, in Trenton, N.J. D. of P. T. (doctor) and Eloise [Owens] Williams. <u>Educ.</u>: B.A. (Amer. Stud.), Barnard Coll.; M.A., (Amer. Stud.), U. of S. Cal.; Studied Contemporary Afro-Amer. Dance, San Francisco. <u>Family</u>: Single. <u>Mailing address</u>: 280 States St., #1, San Francisco, Cal. 94114.

Career-Professional. "Readings of poetry throughout northern California (University Museum, Intersection, The Coffee Gallery, A Woman's Place) as well as readings organized by Poetry-In-the Schools and readings in prisons. Performing dancer with Raymond Sawyer & Halifu...I teach in Humanities & Womens Studies at Sonoma College, Cal." (Author).

WRITINGS: <u>For Colored Girls Who Have Considered Suicide When the Rainbow is Enuf</u>, a play; <u>Invisible City</u>; <u>Anon.</u>; <u>Third World Women</u>; <u>Time to Grease</u>; <u>Phat Mama</u>; <u>The Gallery</u>; <u>Sassafrass</u>, novel (Shameless Hussy Pr., 1975); <u>North Ridge 127</u> (Photography of Jules Allen & poem-montage of Hunter's Point, San Francisco.)

SIDELIGHTS: Studied Contemporary Afro-Amer. Dance with Raymond Sawyer, Halifu, Ed Mock, & Saundra McPherson in San Francisco. <u>Sassafrass</u> was presented by the Raymond Sawyer Afro-American Dance Company as a dance-drama in spring '75. "...I write in English, French, & Spanish cuz my conscious-nesses mingle all New World Afrikan experiences" (Author).

Source. Author inform.

248

SHINE, TED. Playwright, Teacher
Biographical-Personal. Born in Baton Rouge, La. Educ.: Public
   schs. of Dallas, Tex.; Howard U.; M.A., U. of Iowa; U. of Cal.
Career-Professional. Karamu Theatre, Cleveland, Ohio; Taught & lec-
   tured on drama at several coll., including Howard U. & Dillard U.
   Presently: Eng. Dept., Prairie View Coll., Prairie View, Tex.
   WRITINGS: One-act plays performed while student at Howard: Cold
   Day in August & Sho is Hot in the Cotton Patch. Others: Epitaph
   for a Bluebird; Contribution (1969). One-act plays: Shoes &
   Plantation. Other produced plays: Morning, Noon and Night; Miss
   Weaver; Comeback; After the Fire; Idabel's Fortune; & Flora's
   Kisses. Has also written all-black soap opera about urban prob-
   lems, prod. by The Md. Center for Public Broadcasting, Baltimore.
   SIDELIGHTS: Studied under Dr. William Reardon, U. of Iowa. Epitaph for a Bluebird (thesis play) was performed by Dept. of Drama
   at Iowa. Mr. Shine's Contribution was presented by Negro Ensemble
   Co. at St. Mark's Playhouse on Mar. 25, 1969 marking his N.Y. debut. Directed by Douglas Turner Ward, this play won special
   praise from Walter Kerr of New York Times. In March 1970, his
   three one-act plays, Shoes, Plantation, and Contribution were presented off-Broadway.
      Mr. Shine is establishing a major in drama at Prairie View Col-
   lege (Black Drama).
Sources. Black Drama, Ed. by William Brasmer & Dominick Consolo
   (Merrill, 1970); Black Scenes, Ed. by Alice Childress (Doubleday,
   1971).

SHOCKLEY, ANN ALLEN. Writer
Biographical-Personal. Born in Louisville, Ky.
Career-Professional.
   WRITINGS: Living Black American Authors, Ed. with Sue P. Chandler
   (Bowker, 1973); Loving Her, a novel (Bobbs-Merrill, 1974).
Source. Living Black American Authors, Comp. by Ann A. Shockley &
   Sue P. Chandler (Bowker, 1973).

SIMMONS, HERBERT A. 1930- . Novelist, Playwright
Biographical-Personal. Born 1930 in St. Louis, Mo. Educ.: B.A.,
   Wash. U., St. Louis, 1958; Writers Workshop, U. of Iowa.
Career-Professional.
   WRITINGS: The Stranger, a play. Novels: Corner Boy; Man Walking
   on Eggshells (1962).
   HONORS AND AWARDS: Writers Workshop Fellow, U. of Iowa; Sara B.
   Glasgow Award for The Stranger, 1956; Houghton Mifflin Lit. Award
   for Corner Boy.
   SIDELIGHTS: "He is presently involved in co-ordinating the
   Original Watts Writers Workshop and in the formation of an all-

Sinclair, John

black communications media industry called <u>Watts 13</u>, in L.A."
(<u>The New Black Poetry</u>).
Source. <u>The New Black Poetry</u>, Ed. by Clarence Major (Internat.,
1969).

SINCLAIR, JOHN. 1941- . Poet, Editor
Biographical-Personal. Born Oct. 2, 1941, in Flint, Mich. <u>Educ.</u>:
Albion Coll.; B.A., U. of Mich., 1964; Grad. work, Wayne State U.,
1964-65.
Career-Professional. Ed. & Pub., Artists' Workshop Pr.; Ed.: <u>Work</u>
(poetry); <u>Change</u> (new/jazz mag.); <u>Whe're</u> (literary mag.).
WRITINGS: Poetry: <u>This Is Our Music</u> (Artists' Workshop Pr.,
1965); <u>The Leni Poems</u> (Artists' Workshop Pr., 1966); <u>Fire Music</u>:
<u>A Record</u> (Artists' Workshop Pr., 1966); <u>Bridgework</u> (Fenian Head
Centre Pr., 1967). Contrib.: <u>el corno emplumado</u>, <u>Work</u>, <u>Poems</u>
<u>Now</u>, <u>Jazz</u>, <u>It</u>, <u>Out of Sight</u>, <u>Spero</u>, <u>Change</u> & <u>Arts and Artists</u>.
Period.: <u>Downbeat</u>, <u>Coda</u>, <u>Sounds and Fury</u>, <u>Kulchur</u>, <u>New University</u>
<u>Thought</u>.
Sources. <u>For Malcolm</u>, Ed. by Dudley Randall & Margaret G. Burroughs
(Broadside Pr., 1969); <u>The New Black Poetry</u>, Ed. by Clarence Major
(Internat., 1969).

SMITH, ARTHUR L. [Molefi Kete Asante]. 1942- .
Specialist: Interracial and Institutional Com-
munication; Communication Dynamics
Biographical-Personal. Born Aug. 14, 1942, in
Valdosta, Ga. Son of Arthur and Lillie
Smith. <u>Educ.</u>: Southwestern Christian Coll.;
B.A., Okla. Christian Coll., 1964; M.A.,
Pepperdine U., L.A., 1965; Ph.D., UCLA, 1968.
<u>Family</u>: m. Jean [Ngena] Smith; d. Kasina
Eka. <u>Mailing address</u>: 190 Chaumont Drive,
Williamsville, N.Y. 14221.
Career-Professional. Prof. & Chmn., Dept. of
Speech Communication, State U. of N.Y., Buf-
falo; Dir., Center for Afro-Amer. Stud.,
UCLA, 1970-73; Assoc. Prof., Speech, 1971-73,
Asst. Prof., 1969-71; Asst. Prof., Purdue U.,
Lafayette, Ind., 1968-69. Bd. of Eds., <u>Black Man in America</u>,
Repr. ser., N.Y., 1969-70; Ed. Assoc., <u>The Speech Teacher</u>, 1970-72,
72-74; Ed., <u>Journal of Black Studies</u>, 1969- ; Contrib. Ed.,
<u>Encore</u>, 1970-72; Book Reviewer, <u>Journal of Communication</u>, 1970-
present; Advis. Bd., <u>Black Law Journal</u>, 1971- . Bd. of Dir.,
Internat. Communication Assn., 1973-74; Item Writer, Speech Educ.
Test, Educ. Testing Serv., Princeton, 1969-70; Selection Com.,
Martin L. King Fellow., Woodrow Wilson Fellow., Princeton:
1970-1971, 1972; Cons. Ed., Books on Persuasion, Contemporary

Smith, Arthur L.

Rhetoric, Speech Communication, & Lang. Acquisition for following
pub.: Chandler; Prentice-Hall; Harper & Row; Scott, Foresman;
Addison-Wesley; Allyn & Bacon, McGraw-Hill; Sage.
WRITINGS: Break of Dawn, poetry (Dorrance, 1964); Rhetoric of
of Black Revolution (Allyn & Bacon, 1969); Toward Transracial
Communication (Center for Afro-Amer. Stud., 1970); Rhetoric of
Revolution, with Andrea Rich (Moore, 1970); The Voice of Black
Rhetoric, with Stephen Robb (Allyn & Bacon, 1971); How to Talk
With People of Other Races (Trans-Ethnic Found., 1971); Language,
Communication and Rhetoric in Black America (Harper & Row, 1972);
Transracial Communication (Prentice-Hall, 1973). "Interpersonal
Communication with transracial Contexts," in Speech Communication
Behavior, Ed. by Larry Barker & Robert Kebler & in Intercultural
Communications, Ed. by Larry Samovar & Richard Porter; "Black
Revolution--1954 to Present," in America in Controversy, Ed. by
Dewitte Holland. Articles: Journal of Black Studies; Eric Re-
search in Education; Encore; UCLA Center for Afro-American Stud-
ies, (Position pap. #2); Colorado Journal of Education Research;
Language Quarterly; Today's Speech; Quarterly Journal of Speech;
Speech Monographs; Pacific Speech Quarterly; Central States Speech
Journal; The Speech Teacher; Relevance; Speech Abstracts.
HONORS AND AWARDS: Internat. Men of Achievement, 1974; Christian
Guild Writer's Award, 1965; Outstanding Young Men of America,
1970.
MEMBER: Internat. Soc. for Gen. Semantics; Internat. Assn. for
Symbolic Analysis; Internat. Communication Assn., Bd., 1970-72;
W. Speech Assn.; Central States Speech Assn.; S. Speech Assn.;
Pacific Speech Assn.; Nat'l. Assn. for Dramatic & Speech Arts;
Amer. Acad. of Polit. & Soc. Sci. Educ. Resources Inform. Center;
Speech Communication Assn.; African Stud. Assn.; Eastern Communi-
cation Assn.; New York State Speech Assn.; Legislative Assembly
Speech Communication Assn., 1971-73.
SIDELIGHTS: Travel: Senegal, Ghana, Nigeria, Tanzania, Kenya,
Ethiopia, Mexico, Canada, Jamaica, Bahamas, England. Languages:
French, German, Spanish, Twi. Consultant: Center for Extending
American Hist., Textbook cons., 1971; Trans-Ethnic Educ./Communi-
cation Project Cons., Dir., 1969-72; Communication cons., Spec. in
Black Rhetoric, L.A. Co. Probation Dept., Rodeo Project, Fall 1969
to present. Grants: Prin. Investigator, M. L. King-Drew Medical
Complex, Curriculum Evaluative Model for Pre-Sch. Instr., $30,000;
Prin. Investigator, Black Coll. Commitment Prog., Model Cities,
HEW, $113,000, 1971-72, renewed for 1972-73, $145,000; Several
UCLA Acad. Senate Grants of less than $2,000, 1969-73; Purdue U.,
XL Grant 1968-69; SUNY-Buffalo, Institutional grant. On-Going
res.: Role of the Spoken Discourse in Development of Contemporary
Black Leadership; Nature of Black Communication Experience as Ex-
pressed in Language Styles; Taxonomic Aspects of Afro-American

Smith, Vern E.

Kinesics; Exploration of Principal Symbols & their Value for a
Multi-Ethnic Society; Transracial Communication & Higher Educa-
tion.
Source. Author inform.

SMITH, VERN E. Novelist, Correspondent
Biographical-Personal. Educ.: B.A., San Fran-
cisco State Coll., 1969; Grad. Sch. of Jour-
nalism, Columbia U.
Career-Professional. Gen. Assignment Reporter,
Long Beach Independent-Press Telegram;
Corresp., Newsweek, Detroit bureau; Corresp.
Newsweek, Atlanta bureau (currently).
WRITINGS: The Jones Men, novel (Regnery,
1974).
HONORS AND AWARDS: Ford Found. Fellow, Co-
lumbia U.; Detroit Pr. Club Found.'s annual
mag. writing award, Newsweek article enti-
tled "Detroit's Heroin Subculture."
Source. Pub. inform.

SMITH, WELTON. 1940- . Writer
Biographical-Personal. Born 1940 in Houston, Tex. Grew up in San
Francisco, Cal. Has lived in N.Y.C.
Career-Professional.
WRITINGS: Penetration, poetry (1972); The Roach Riders, play.
Anthol.: Black Fire (1968); The New Black Poetry (1969); The
Poetry of the Negro (1949, 1970); Black Spirits (1972); & The
Poetry of Black America (1973).
SIDELIGHTS: "...has written an unpublished volume entitled The
Art of Marihuana Ceremony As Performed on the Lower East Side of
Manhattan, A.D. 1950-1980: A Primary Account of Ritual Among In-
digenous and Emigre Potheads by a Black Nationalist of Leisure and
Genius" (Poetry of Black America).
Source. The Poetry of Black America, Ed. by Arnold Adoff (Harper &
Row, 1973).

SMITH, WILLIAM GARDNER. 1927-1974. Novelist, Reporter, Editor
Biographical-Personal. Born Feb. 6, 1927, in Phila, Pa. Educ.:
Temple U., Phila. Family: div.; d. Michele, son, Claude. Died
Nov. 5, 1974.
Career-Professional. Novelist; News Ed., Eng. Lang. Serv., Agence
France-Presse (French News Agency).
WRITINGS: Novels: Last of the Conquerors (Farrar, Straus, 1948);
Anger at Innocence (Farrar, Straus, 1950); South Street (Farrar,
Straus, 1954); The Stone Face (Farrar, Straus, 1963) & Return to
Black America (Prentice-Hall, 1970); L'Amerique Noire.

Southern, Eileen Jackson

SIDELIGHTS: "Published his first book, Last of the Conquerors at
the age of 20 and followed this three years later with Anger at
Innocence. He went to Paris in 1951 and wrote his third novel,
South Street. He subsequently married a French lycee teacher and
decided to stay in France. He has two children, one born in Paris
and the other in Africa. A fourth book, The Stone Face, was pub-
lished in 1963" (Black American Writer).
Sources. Black American Writer, Vol. I: Fiction, Ed. by C. W. E.
Bigsby (Penguin, 1969); Black World (Johnson Pub., Feb. 1975);
Pub. inform.

SOUTHERN, EILEEN JACKSON. 1920- . Music
Educator, Writer
Biographical-Personal. Born Feb. 19, 1920, in
Minneapolis, Minn. D. of Walter Wade Jackson
and Lilla [Gibson] Jackson Rose. Educ.:
B.A., M.A., U. of Chgo.; Ph.D., N.Y.U.;
(Piano) Chgo. Musical Coll.; Boston U.;
Juilliard. Family: m. Joseph Southern; d.
April. Mailing address: 115-05 179th St.,
St. Albans, N.Y. 11434.
Career-Professional. Prof. of Music, York
Coll., City U. of N.Y., 1968-present; Brook-
lyn Coll., 1960-68; Public Sch., City of
N.Y., 1954-60; Southern U., 1943-45, 1949-51;
Claflin U., 1946-48; Prairie View Coll.,
1941-42.
WRITINGS: The Buxheim Organ Book (Inst. of Medieval Music, 1963);
The Music of Black Americans: A History (Norton, 1971). Readings
in Black American Music, Ed. (Norton, 1971). In progress: Anony-
mous Chansons in a Manuscript at El Escorial (Amer. Inst. of Musi-
cology, Rome). Jl., Ed. & Pub.: The Black Perspective in Music,
vol. 1, no. 1, Mar. 1973; Black Perspective in Music, vols. 3 & 4
(Found. for Res. in the Afro-Amer. Creative Arts, Inc., Cambria
Heights, N.Y., 1975, 1976). Articles: Universal Encyclopedia and
Encyclopedia International (over 50 small articles on Renaissance
music); Music Lib. Assn. Notes (1963); Acta Musicologica (1963);
Aspects of Medieval and Renaissance Music; Amer. Musicological
Soc., Journal (1968); Coll. Music Soc., Symposium (1968, 1973);
Black Music in Our Culture (Kent State U. Pr.); Encyclopedia of
Black America (McGraw-Hill, forthcoming); The Black Scholar (June
1972); Grove's Dictionary of Music and Musicians, 25 biographies
(forthcoming 6th ed.); Dictionary of American Biography ("Harry T.
Burleigh," Supplemental vol., 1973); Black World (Nov. 1973).
Book Reviews: Notes (1972, 1973); Black Perspective in Music
(1973, 1974).

Spellman, A. B.

HONORS AND AWARDS: U. of Chgo. Alumni Assn., Achievement Award,
1971; Nat'l. Assn. of Negro Musicians, Achievement Award, 1971;
Voice of America, Citation, 1971; Appt., U.S. Bicentennial Com. of
Amer. Musicology Soc., 1971-76; Appt., Com. of Examiners, Advance
Music Test, Grad. Record Exams, Educ. Testing Serv., Princeton,
N.J., 1971-pres.; Distinguished Woman Award, Delta Alpha Hon. Soc.,
U. of Mo., Kan. City, 1972; Outstanding Educator in Music Award,
Chgo. Chapter, Phi Delta Kappa, 1973; ASCAP-Deems Taylor Award for
excellence in nonfict. writing about music, 1973; Election:
Counc., Amer. Musicological Soc., 1973; Bd. of Dir., Amer. Musi-
cological Soc., 1974-76.
SIDELIGHTS: "I have traveled all over the U.S. giving lectures
(since 1971); also to the University of Ghana" (Author).
Sources. Author inform.; Books in Print, Supplement, 1975-76 (Bow-
ker, 1976).

SPELLMAN, A. B. 1935- . Poet, Jazz Critic and Historian
Biographical-Personal. Born Aug. 7, 1935, in Elizabeth City, N.C.
Sch.-tchg. parents. Educ.: B.A., (Polit. Sci.), Howard U.;
Grad. work in Law & Eng. Lit. Lived in N.Y.C. since 1959.
Career-Professional. Ed., The Cricket (mag. of Black music); Writer-
in-Residence: Morehouse Coll. & Emory U. (Atlanta, Ga.).
WRITINGS: The Beautiful Days, poetry (1965); Four Lives in the
Bebop Business, essays (Schocken, 1966). Anthol.: Beyond the
Blues (1962); New Negro Poets: USA (1964); Black Fire (1968); The
New Black Poetry (1969) & Dices or Black Bones (1970). Period.:
Journal of Black Poetry, The Nation, The Republic, Metronome, The
Liberator, Black Dialogue & Umbra.
SIDELIGHTS: Four Lives in the Bebop Business, concerns the ca-
reers of musicians, Ornette Coleman, Herbie Nichols, Jackie
McLean, and Cecil Taylor (Poetry of Black America).
Sources. Black Fire, Ed. by LeRoi Jones & Larry Neal (Morrow, 1968);
The Poetry of Black America, Ed. by Arnold Adoff (Harper & Row,
1973).

SPENCER, ANNE SCALES. 1882-1976. Poet,
Librarian
Biographical-Personal. Annie Bethel Scales was
born Feb. 6, 1882, in Henry Co., Va. D. of
Joel Bannister and Sarah Scales; she was
reared in Bramwell, W. Va. Educ.: Virginia
Sem. & Coll., grad. 1899. Family: m. Edward
Alexander Spencer in 1901 (widowed May 1964);
son, Chauncey Edward Spencer, d. Bethel
Spencer Stevenson, d. Alroy Spencer Rivers.
Died 1976.
Career-Professional. Librn., Dunbar Lib.,
Lynchburg, Va., 1920-43; Readings at Randolph

Staples, Robert

Macon Coll. for Women, Lynchburg, c.1930; TV appearance, Lynch-
burg, c.1969.
WRITINGS: Poetry: "Before the Feast of Shushan," "At the Carni-
val," "The Wife-Woman," "Translation," and "Dunbar," in Book of
American Negro Poetry, Ed. by James Weldon Johnson. Die Woche
(Germany, c. 1929); Negro in Virginia, Robert Kerlin; Caroling
Dusk, Countee Cullen; Negro Caravan, Sterling Brown & Others;
Anthology of Verse, Alain Locke (Segur Pub. Co. book in France,
c. 1969, Anna Segur). Norton's Anthology of Modern Poetry; Dos
Siglos de Poesia Norteamericana, Poetas Blancos y Negros de los
EE. UU., Alfredo Casey, Claridad, Buenos Aires, c. 1950).
SIDELIGHTS: "None of her original poems has been published for
well over a quarter of a century, though she never has ceased
writing poems. In preparation at this time is the first collec-
tion of her poetry (edited by J. Lee Greene) which will include
previously published and unpublished poems.
  "...the most detailed and complete biographical-critical study
of Anne Spencer is my own: J. Lee Greene, 'Anne Spencer: A Study
of Her Life and Poetry'" (Ph.D. dissertation, U. of N.C. at Chapel
Hill, 1974)" (J. Lee Greene, biographer).
  (Card written by Langston Hughes, Jan. 4, 1950): "Dear Anne
Spencer: I thought it would interest you to know that your poems,
DUNBAR and TENGO UN AMIGO, are contained in an anthology of Ameri-
can poetry that I have just received from the Argentine: DOS
SIGLOS DE POESIA NORTEAMERICANA..." "Sincerely, (signed) Langston"
Sources. Mrs. Bethel Stevenson (daughter); J. Lee Greene (biographer).

STADLER, QUANDRA PRETTYMAN. Poet, Teacher
Biographical-Personal. Born in Baltimore, Md. Educ.: Antioch Coll.;
  U. of Mich. Family: husband and daughter.
Career-Professional. Instr.: New Sch.; N.Y. Coll. of Insurance;
  Summer Prog., Conn. Coll.; Tchr., Eng., Barnard Coll.
  WRITINGS: Ed.: The Open Boat and Other Stories by Stephen Crane
  (1968); Out of Our Lives (Howard U. Pr., 1975). Anthol.: I Am
  the Darker Brother (1968); Black Out Loud (1970); Poetry of Black
  America (1973). Period.: Negro Digest/Black World.
Sources. Out of Our Lives, Quandra P. Stadler (Howard U. Pr., 1975);
  Poetry of Black America, Ed. by Arnold Adoff (Harper & Row, 1973).

STAPLES, ROBERT. 1942- . Writer
Biographical-Personal. Born June 28, 1942, in
  Roanoke, Va.
Career-Professional.
  WRITINGS: The Black Family: Essays and
  Studies, Ed. (Wadsworth, 1971); The Black
  Woman in America (Nelson-Hall, 1973). In
  progress: Introduction to Black Sociology
  (McGraw-Hill).
Source. Books in Print, Supplement, 1975-76
  (Bowker, 1976).

255

Steptoe, John Lewis

STEPTOE, JOHN LEWIS. 1950- . Artist, Juvenile
Writer

Biographical-Personal. Born Sept. 14, 1950, in
Brooklyn, N.Y. Son of John Oliver and Ele-
steen L. Steptoe. Educ.: Grammar sch.--St.
Benedict's Our Lady of Good Couns.; High Sch.
of Art and Design (11th yr. completed).
Family: Single; d. Bweela, son, Javaka.
Mailing address: 66 Grove St., Peterboro,
N.H. 03458.

Career-Professional. Artist; Juvenile Writer.
WRITINGS: Juveniles: Stevie (Harper & Row,
1969); Uptown (Harper & Row, 1970); Train
Ride (Harper & Row, 1971). Birthday (Holt,
1972); My Special Best Words (Viking, 1974);
Marcia, short novel (Viking, 1976).

HONORS AND AWARDS: ALA Notable Children's Bk. Award for Stevie;
Soc. of Illustrator's Gold Medal for Stevie; Stevie illustrations
reproduced in their entirety in Life mag., Aug. 29, 1970; Brooklyn
Public Lib., Citation for children's bks.; Brooklyn Museum's show,
"Dreams and Delights at Christmas 1972."

SIDELIGHTS: "This letter is to inform you that I am now making
available for sale the original paintings from my first children's
book, 'Stevie.' ...It's very difficult for me to part with them
as they mean so much to me personally.... My primary interest is
to have these paintings hung in a place where they may be viewed
by children...The seven paintings were done in marker with pastel
overpainting. They are about 6" by 9"" (Letter from author).

Sources. Author inform.; Books in Print, Supplement, 1975-76 (Bowker, 1976); Pub. inform.

STILL, WILLIAM. 1821-1902. Abolitionist,
Historian

Biographical-Personal. Born free, 1821, in Bur-
lington Co., N.J. Son of parents who had
escaped slavery. Died 1902.

Career-Professional. Clerk, Phila. Anti-Slavery
Soc. (met and helped hundreds of Blacks who
were fleeing to N. via underground railroad;
Kept record of slaves' experiences, collected
between 1850-1860.

WRITINGS: The Underground Railroad. A Record of Facts, Authentic Narratives, Letters,
etc., Narrating the Hardships, Hairbreadth
Escapes and Death Struggles of the Slaves in
Their Efforts for Freedom as Related by Themselves, and Others, or Witnessed by the Au-

Still, William Grant

thor; Together with Sketches of Some of the Largest Stockholders, and Most Liberal Aiders and Advisers of the Road (1872).
SIDELIGHTS: "Still not only forwarded numberless Negro passengers on the Underground but also aided the escape of several of John Brown's men after Harpers Ferry. Nineteen out of twenty fugitives stopped at Still's house on their way through Philadelphia" (Negro Caravan).
    "In order to continue collecting and preserving data on the Negro, in 1861 William Still organized a 'social, civil, and statistical association,' which was an early forerunner of Carter G. Woodson's Association for the Study of Negro Life and History. In 1880 he established one of the earlier YMCA branches for Negroes" (Cavalcade).
Sources. Cavalcade, Ed. by Arthur P. Davis & Saunders Redding (Houghton Mifflin, 1971); Negro Caravan, Ed. by Sterling A. Brown & Others (Arno Pr., & N.Y. Times, 1969).

STILL, WILLIAM GRANT. 1895- . Composer
Biographical-Personal. Born May 11, 1895, in
    Woodville, Miss. Mother a sch. tchr. Educ.:
    Little Rock, Ark., Wilberforce U.; Oberlin
    Conservatory of Music; New Eng. Conservatory.
    Family: Married.
Career-Professional. Jazz arranger; composer.
    WRITINGS: William Grant Still and the Fusion
    of Cultures in American Music (Black Sparrow,
    1975). Symphonies: Afro-American Symphony;
    Africa; Symphony in G Minor. Operas: Blue
    Steel; Troubled Island. Musicals: Running
    Wild; Dixie to Broadway. (Symphonic Poem)
    Darker America.
    HONORS AND AWARDS: Received Harmon Award,
    1927, for Troubled Island; Cited by Nat'l.
Assn. for Amer. Composers & Conductors for distinguished contrib. to Amer. music; Commissions from Columbia Broadcasting Co. & N.Y. World's Fair (1935). Hon. degrees: Wilberforce U.; Oberlin U.
SIDELIGHTS: "In 1926, the International Guild of Composers presented four of his songs, one of which was sung by Florence Mills ...A year later, his Darker America...was performed by the Rochester Symphony. In 1935, his Afro-American Symphony was played by the New York Philharmonic at the International Music Festival in Frankfurt, Germany and, two years after that, his New Symphony in G Minor was featured by the Philadelphia Symphony Orchestra" (Negro Almanac).
    "In 1936, Still became the first Negro to conduct a major American orchestra when he gave a program of his own compositions at the Hollywood Bowl" (Negro Almanac). "Some of his better known

Tarry, Ellen

songs are 'Breath of a Rose,' 'Levee Land' and beautiful 'Kain-
tuck'" (Great Negroes Past and Present).
Sources. Great Negroes Past and Present, Russell L. Adams (Afro-
Amer. Pub., 1964); Negro Almanac, Ed. by Harry A. Ploski & Roscoe
C. Brown (Bellwether, 1967); Negro Handbook, Comp. by Eds. of
Ebony (Johnson Pub., 1966).

TARRY, ELLEN. 1906- . Juvenile Writer, Social
Worker
Biographical-Personal. Born 1906 in Birmingham,
Ala. Educ.: S. convent sch.
Career-Professional. Journalist; Assoc. with
Catherine De Hueck, founder of Friendship
House, Harlem, N.Y., 1929- ; Established
similar inst. in Chgo.; Staff, Nat'l. Catho-
lic Community Serv. (during World War II).
WRITINGS: Janie Bell (Garden City, 1940);
Hezekiah Horton (Viking, 1942); My Dog Rinty,
with Marie H. Ets (Viking, 1946); The Run-
away Elephant (1950); Katherine Drexel;
Friend of the Neglected (1958); The Third
Door, autobiog. (Negro U. Pr., 1955); Martin
de Porres, Saint of the New World (1963);
Young Jim: The Early Years of James Weldon Johnson (Dodd, Mead,
1967).
SIDELIGHTS: "Ellen Tarry's service as the 'Story Lady' of Friendship House, a Catholic community center in Harlem, brought her into close contact with the actual person who served as the model
for 'Hezekiah Horton,' the character she created in the book of
the same name. This same character appears in The Runaway Elephant which was enthusiastically received by both critics and the
public alike after its publication in 1950.
   The Runaway Elephant was illustrated by cartoonist Oliver Harrington whose 'Bootsie' is one of the best-known cartoon characters in the Negro press" (AFROUSA).
Sources. AFROUSA, Comp. by Harry A. Ploski & Ernest Kaiser (Bellwether, 1971); Young Jim, Ellen Tarry (Dodd, Mead, 1967).

TATE, MERZE. Professor of History, Historian, Lecturer
Biographical-Personal. Born in Blanchard, Mich. D. of Charles and
Myrtle Tate. Educ.: B.A., W. Mich. U.; M.A., Columbia U.;
B.Litt., Oxford U.; Ph.D., Radcliffe Coll. & Harvard U.; D.Litt.,
Western Mich. U.; D. Laws, Morgan State Coll.; Further study:
Geneva Sci. Internat.; Berlin U. Family: Single. Mailing ad-
dress: 1314 Perry St., N.E., Wash., D.C. 20017.
Career-Professional. Prof. of Hist., Howard U., 1942- ; Vis. Prof.,
Wayne State U., Summer 1953; Vis. Prof., W. Mich. U., Kalamazoo,

Taylor, Clyde R.

Summer 1955. Holder of GS-18 U.S. Civil Serv. rating as hist. in
3 areas of hist.
WRITINGS: The Disarmament Illusion--The Movement for a Limitation
of Armaments to 1907 (Macmillan, 1942; repr., Russell, 1970); The
United States and Armaments (Harvard U. Pr., 1948; repr., 1969);
The United States and the Hawaiian Kingdom (Yale U. Pr., 1965);
Hawaii: Reciprocity of Annexation (Mich. State U. Pr., 1968).
Diplomacy in the Pacific, collec. of 27 articles on diplomacy in
the Pacific and the influence of the Sandwich (Hawaiian) Islands
Missionaries (Hist. Dept., Howard U., Wash., D.C., 1973). "Australia from the Tropics to the Pole" (under revision).
HONORS AND AWARDS: Scholarship & honor student, W. Mich. U.,
elected to Pi Gamma Mu; Recipient of 3rd Alpha Kappa Alpha Sorority foreign fellow.; 1st Amer. woman of color to matriculate at
Oxford U. & 1st Amer. Negro--man or woman--to receive a higher
degree there; Julius Rosenwald Fellow, 1939 (yr.'s residence at
Radcliffe toward Ph.D.); Elected to Phi Beta Kappa; Rep. U.S.,
1948 UNESCO Seminar, Lake Success & Adelphi Coll., on teaching
about UN & related agencies; Nat'l. Urban League Achievement
Award, 1948; Fulbright Lectr. in India, 1950-51; W. Mich. U. Disting. Alumna Award, 1970; Named Mich.'s Isabella County's most
disting. citizen, 1969; Amer. Counc. of Learned Soc. res. grant,
1959; Washington Evening Star res. grant, 1961; Rockefeller Found.
res. grant, 1961; Several Howard U. sponsored res. grants; One
time mem., Nat'l. Bd. Radcliffe Coll.; Mem., 1960 Screening Com.
for United Kingdom of the Inst. of Internat. Educ.; Among "Two
Thousand Women of Achievement," London, 1972.
SIDELIGHTS: As Fulbright Lecturer in India, assigned to Rabin-
dranath Tagore's World U., lectured at 11 other Indian universities, in Burma for the USIS in Ceylon, Thailand, Singapore, Manila,
Tokyo, & Honolulu. The Disarmament Illusion..., The United States
and Armaments, & The United States and the Hawaiian Kingdom all
received a publication subvention from Bureau of International
Research, Harvard U. & Radcliffe Coll. (Travel) Twice around the
world, 8 times to or through Europe, including Scandinavia & USSR.
Pursued research in England, Hawaii, Fiji, New Zealand, Australia,
France & West Germany. Dec. 1973-Jan. 1974 visited 11 different
African countries. Research on African Mineral railways.
Source. Author inform.

TAYLOR, CLYDE R. 1931- . Teacher, Critic
Biographical-Personal. Born July 3, 1931, in Boston, Mass. Son of
Frank and E. Alice Taylor. Educ.: B.A. (Eng.), M.A. (Eng.),
Howard U.; Ph.D. (Eng.), Wayne State U. Family: div.; d. Shelley,
d. Randi. Mailing address: Afro-Amer. Stud., U. of Cal., Berke-
ley, Cal.
Career-Professional. Afro-Amer. Stud. Dept., U. of Cal., Berkeley;
Assoc. Ed., Black Folks.

Taylor, Mildred

WRITINGS: Vietnam and Black America, Ed. (Doubleday-Anchorbooks,
1973). Contrib.: "Iconographical Themes in William Blake,"
Blake Studies, I (Fall, 1968); "Black Folk Spirit and the Shape of
Black Literature," Black Folk (June 1972; repr. in Black World
Aug. 1972); "Baraka As Poet," in Donald Gibson, Ed., Modern Black
Poets: Twentieth Century Views (Prentice-Hall, 1973); "Black
Consciousness in the Vietnam Years," Black Scholar (Oct. 1973).
HONORS AND AWARDS: Fulbright Fellow. to U. of Manchester, Eng.,
1963; Richard Wright Award for Literary Criticism, 1973.
SIDELIGHTS: Lectures on Black Language; travel to Africa, the
Caribbean, Europe (Author).
Source. Author inform.

TAYLOR, MILDRED. Writer
Biographical-Personal. Born in Jackson, Miss.;
reared in Toledo, Ohio. Educ.: U. of Tole-
do; U. of Col. (Journalism).
Career-Professional. Peace Corps, Ethiopia;
Recruiter, Peace Corps, U.S.
WRITINGS: Song of the Trees (Dial).
Source. "Second Annual Authors Autograph Party"
(brochure), Cal. Librns. Black Caucus, July
1975.

Rockie D. Taylor. See Ologloni, Tejumola.

TEAGUE, BOB. 1929- . Television Newscaster
Biographical-Personal. Born 1929; grew up in Milwaukee, Wis. Educ.:
Journalism grad., U. of Wis. Family: m. Mrs. Teague (Martha
Graham dancer); son, Adam.
Career-Professional. Newscaster, NBC-TV, N.Y.C.; Reporter, New York
Times; Reporter, Milwaukee Journal.
WRITINGS: Letters to a Black Boy (Walker, 1968); Adam in Blunder-
land (Doubleday, 1971).
Source. Afro-American Literature--Non Fiction, Ed. by William Adams,
et al. (Houghton Mifflin, 1970).

TERRY, LUCY. Poet
Biographical-Personal. "Kidnapped as a child and brought to Rhode
Island, where she was bought as a servant to Ebenezer Wells, who
had her baptized in 1744 in his Deerfield, Massachusetts home.
[The semi-literate slave] married the very capable Abijah Prince
in 1756...six children later--their names were Cesar, Duroxa,
Drucilla, Festus, Tatnai and Abijah, Jr...." (Early Black American
Poets).

Thompson, Era Bell

Career-Professional. "Lucy Terry is generally considered to be the
first Negro poet in America. In a ballad which she called 'Bars
Fight,' she recreated an Indian Massacre which occurred in Deerfield, Massachusetts in 1746 during King George's War. (Although
of little poetic value, 'Bars Fight' has been hailed by some historians as the most authentic account of the massacre).
   "...The Prince house served as a center for young people who
gathered to listen to their hostess' story-telling" (Negro Almanac).
Sources. Early Black American Poets, Ed. by William H. Robinson,
   Jr. (Wm. C. Brown, 1969); Negro Almanac, Comp. by Harry A. Ploski
   & Ernest Kaiser (Bellwether, 1971).

THOMAS, LORENZO. 1944- . Poet, Editor
Biographical-Personal. Born Aug. 31, 1944, in
   Panama, Republic of Panama. Son of Herbert
   Hamilton and Luzmilda [Gilling] Thomas.
   Educ.: Public sch. Jamaica, N.Y.; Andrew
   Jackson High Sch., St. Albans, N.Y.; B.A.
   (Eng. Lit.), Queens Coll., Flushing, N.Y.
   Family: Single. Mailing address: 161-21
   119th Dr., Jamaica, N.Y. 11434.
Career-Professional. Ed., Roots mag., 1974- ;
   Advis. Ed., Black Box mag.; formerly Co-ed.,
   Omnivore. Writer-in-Residence: Tex. S. U.,
   1972-73; Black Arts Center, Houston, Tex.,
   1973-74.
   WRITINGS: Dracula (Angel Hair Bks., 1973);
   Fit Music (Angel Hair Bks., 1972). Anthol.:
Black Fire (1968); New Black Voices (1972); The Poetry of Black
America (1973). Period.: Art & Literature; CLA Journal of
Poetry; El Corno Emplumado; The Massachusetts Review; Umbra;
Liberator; & others.
HONORS AND AWARDS: Lucille Medwick Award, 1974; Poets Found.
Award, 1966, 1974.
MEMBER: Grants Com. of Coord. Counc. of Literary Mags., 1973.
SIDELIGHTS: Currently concerned with translations and transforma-
tions of ancient and Third World literature (Author).
Sources. Author inform.; New Black Voices, Ed. by Abraham Chapman
   (New Amer. Lib., 1972); The Poetry of Black America, Ed. by Ar-
   nold Adoff (Harper & Row, 1973).

THOMPSON, ERA BELL. Editor, Writer
Biographical-Personal. Born in Des Moines, Iowa. Educ.: U. of N.D.
(2 yrs.); B.A., Morningside Coll., Sioux City, Iowa, 1933; Grad.
study, Medill Sch. of Journalism, Chgo.; Hon. doctorates: Morningside Coll., 1965; U. of N.D., 1969. Family: Single. Mailing
address: c/o Johnson Pub. Co., 820 S. Mich. Ave., Chgo., Ill.
60605.

Thompson, James W.

Career-Professional. Interviewer, Ill. & U.S. Employment Services, Chgo. (5 yrs.); Assoc. Ed., Ebony (4 yrs.); Co-Managing Ed., Ebony, 1951-1964; Internat. Ed., Johnson Pub. Co., 1964- .
WRITINGS: American Daughter, autobiog. (U. of Chgo. Pr., 1946; reissued, Follett, 1967); Africa, Land of My Fathers (Doubleday, 1954); White on Black, Co-ed. (Johnson Pub., 1963). Bk. reviewer for Chgo. and N.Y. papers.
HONORS AND AWARDS: Wesleyan Serv. Guild scholarship; Won sweater in athletics & was secy. of Alpha Kappa Delta (honor soc.), Morningside Coll.; Won Patron Saints Award for American Daughter, 1968; Fellow. Bread-loaf Writer's Conf., 1949; Iota Phi Lambda's Outstanding Woman of the Year, 1965.
MEMBER: Bds. of Dir.: Chgo. Metropolitan YWCA, 1944-47; Friends of Chgo. Public Lib., 1959-60; Hull House, 1960-64; Soc. of Midland Authors, 1961- ; Mem.: Urban League; NAACP, Zonta Internat.; Chgo. Pr. Club; N. Central Region Manpower Advis. Com.; Chgo. Counc. on Foreign Relat.
SIDELIGHTS: Established 5 state & tied 2 national intercollegiate women's track records while in college. American Daughter was translated into Italian, published in England. Africa, Land of My Fathers was translated into German. Miss Thompson has traveled extensively in five continents as Internat. Editor (Author).
Sources. American Daughter, Era Bell Thompson (Follett, 1967); Author inform.

THOMPSON, JAMES W. 1935- . Dancer, Choreographer, Dance Editor
Biographical-Personal. Born in Detroit, Mich.
Career-Professional. Reviewer for The Feet, a dance mag.; Artist-in-Residence, Antioch Coll.
WRITINGS: First Fire: Poems 1957-1960 (London, Paul Bremen, 1970). Anthol.: Sixes and Sevens (1962); Beyond the Blues (1962); Black Spirits (1962); The Poetry of Black America (1973).
SIDELIGHTS: As Artist-in-Residence at Antioch College and together with Cecil Taylor, the jazz musician, "was involved in the creation of The Choir of the Spoken Word in celebration of the Aframerican oral tradition" (Poetry of Black America).
Source. Poetry of Black America, Ed. by Arnold Adoff (Harper & Row, 1973).

THORPE, EARLIE ENDRIS. 1924- . Professor of History, Historian
Biographical-Personal. Born Nov. 9, 1924, in Durham, N.C. Son of
   Eural Endris and Vina [Caloris] Thorpe. Educ.: U. of Florence,
   Italy (U.S. Army Extension Prog.--1 semester); B.A. (Soc.-Hist.),
   1948, M.A. (Hist.-Educ.), 1949, North Carolina Coll., Durham;
   Ph.D. (Hist.) Ohio State U., 1953. Family: m. Martha Vivian
   Branch; d. Rita Harrington, d. Gloria Earl. Mailing address:
   164 Oakmont Circle, Durham, N.C.
Career-Professional. Tchr.: Stowe Teachers Coll., St. Louis, Mo.,
   1951-52; Ala. A & M Coll., Normal, Ala., 1952-55; Southern U.,
   Baton Rouge, La., 1955-62. Prof. & Chmn., Dept. of Hist. & Soc.
   Sci., N.C. Central U. (formerly N.C. Coll.), 1962-present.
   WRITINGS: Negro Historians in the United States (1958), reissued
   under title, Black Historians: A Critique (Morrow, 1971); The
   Desertion of Man: A Critique of Philosophy of History (1958); The
   Mind of the Negro: An Intellectual History of Afro-Americans
   (1961, reissued by Greenwood Pub., 1970); Eros and Freedom in
   Southern Life and Thought (1967); The Central Theme of Black His-
   tory (1969); The Old South: A Psycho-history (1972). General Ed.
   of 10-booklet ser., "The Black Experience in America," pub. by
   Amer. Educ. Public., Middletown, Conn.
   HONORS AND AWARDS: Vis. Prof. of Hist., Duke U., 1969-70; Vis.
   Prof., Afro-Amer. Stud., Harvard U., 1971.
   MEMBER: Omega Psi Phi Fraternity; Phi Alpha Theta, Nat'l. Hon.
   Soc.; Pi Gamma Mu, Nat'l. Soc. Sci. Honor Soc.; Org. of Amer.
   Hist.; Soc. for Study of S. Lit.; Amer. Hist. Assn.; Assn. of Soc.
   & Behavioral Scientists; ASNLH.
   SIDELIGHTS: "A long-time member of Mt. Gilead Baptist Church,
   Durham, North Carolina, where he has served as member of the
   Trustee Board, and as Director and Class Leader of the Baptist
   Training Union" (Author).
Source. Author inform.

THURMAN, HOWARD. 1900- . Clergyman,
Theologian
Biographical-Personal. Born Nov. 18, 1900, in
   Daytona Beach, Fla. Son of Saul Solomon and
   Alice [Ambrose] Thurman. Educ.: B.A., More-
   house Coll., 1923, D.D. (hon.), 1935; B.D.,
   Rochester Theol. Sem., 1926; D.D. (hon.):
   Wesleyan Coll., Conn., 1946, Lincoln U.,
   Howard U., 1955; H.H.D. (hon.): Ohio Wes-
   leyan U., 1954; LL.D. (hon.): Wash. U., 1955,
   Allen U., 1954; Litt.D. (hon.), Tuskegee
   Inst., 1956; D.D., Oberlin Coll., 1958;
   H.H.D., Va. State U., 1959; L.H.D., Fla.
   Normal Coll., 1961; D.D. Boston U., 1967.

Thurman, Howard

Family: m. Sue E. Bailey, June 12, 1932; d. Anne Chiarenza, d. Olive Wong. Mailing address: 2020 Stockton St., San Francisco, Cal. 94133.

Career-Professional. Ordained in Bap. Church, 1925; Pastor, Mt. Zion Bap. Church, Oberlin, Ohio, 1926-28; Dir., Relig. Life & Prof., Relig., Morehouse Coll., Spelman Coll., 1928-31; Prof., Systematic Theol. & Dean, Rankin Chapel, Howard U., 1932-44; Pastor, Church for Fellow. of All Peoples, San Francisco, 1944-53 (1st completely integrated church in Amer. life); Dean, Marsh Chapel, Boston U., 1953-64, emeritus, 1964- ; Prof., Spiritual discipline & resources, Boston U., 1953-65; U. minister-at-large, 1964-65; Vist. Prof., Sch. Relig., Earlham Coll., 1966; Vis. Prof., Presby. Theol. Sem., Louisville, Ky., 1967; Apptd. Ingersol Lectr. on the Immortality of Man, Harvard U., 1947; Merrick Lectr., Ohio Wesleyan U., 1953; Ratcliff Lectr., Tufts U., 1957; Lectr., Beech Quiet Hour, Bangor Theol. Sem., 1958; Earl Lectr., Pacific Sch. Relig., 1959; Smith Wilson Lectr., Southwestern U., 1960; Mendenhall Lectr., De Pauw U., 1961; Wilson Lectures, Neb. Wesleyan U., 1961; Theme Lectr. gen. counc., United Church Can., 1962; Quaker Lectr., Earlham Coll., 1962; Vis. Prof., U. of Ibadan, Nigeria, 1963; Billings Lectr., U. Hawaii, 1964; Oswald McCall Memorial Lectr., Berkeley, Cal., 1964.

WRITINGS: The Greatest of These (1945); Meditations for Apostles of Sensitiveness (1947); The Search for Common Ground; Deep is the Hunger (Harper & Row, 1951); The Negro Spiritual Speaks of Life and Death (Harper & Row, 1947); Meditations of the Heart (Harper & Row, 1953); The Creative Encounter (Harper & Row, 1954); Deep River (Harper & Row, 1946; rev. 1955); The Growing Edge (Harper & Row, 1956); Footprints of A Dream (Harper & Row, 1959); The Inward Journey (Harper & Row, 1961); Disciplines of the Spirit (Harper & Row, 1963); The Luminous Darkness (Harper & Row, 1965); The Centering Moment (Harper & Row, 1969); Why I Believe There Is A God (Johnson Pub., 1965); Jesus and the Disinherited (Abingdon, 1948); Temptations of Jesus (L. Kennedy, 1962). Contrib. to Interpreter's Bible, Vol. 7.

HONORS AND AWARDS: Phi Beta Kappa; Gutenberg Award, Chgo. Bible Soc.

MEMBER: Bd., Meals for Millions, Inc.; Bd. Dir., Urban League Greater Boston, Inc.; Dir., Travelers Aid Soc., Hampton Inst.; Fellow, Nat'l. Counc. of Relig. in Higher Educ.; Amer. Acad. of Arts & Sci.; Fellow. of Reconciliation; Cal. Writers Club; Harold Brunn Soc. for Medical Res.; N. Cal. Serv. League; Martin L. King Memorial Center, Atlanta.

SIDELIGHTS: In 1935 he was the leader of a "pilgrimage of friendship" of students of religion to the colleges of Burma, India, and Ceylon.

"Dr. Thurman was photographed in Life (April 6, 1955) as one of twelve 'Great Preachers' of this century" (Current Biography, 1955).

Tolson, Melvin Beaunorus

Sources. Current Biography, 1955, Ed. by Margaret Dent Candee (H. W.
Wilson, 1955); Disciplines of the Spirit, Howard Thurman (Harper &
Row, 1963); Negro Caravan, Ed. by Sterling A. Brown & Others (Arno
Pr. & N.Y. Times, 1969); Who's Who in America, 37th ed., 1972-73
(Marquis, 1972).

THURMAN, WALLACE. 1902-1934. Novelist, Playwright
Biographical-Personal. Born 1902 in Salt Lake City, Utah. Educ.:
U. of S. Cal. Died in 1934.
Career-Professional. Served on ed. staffs of The Messenger & of the
Macaulay Pub. Co.; Helped found short-lived mags. Fire and Harlem.
WRITINGS: The Blacker the Berry, novel (1929); Harlem, play, with
W. J. Rapp (1929); Infants of the Spring, novel (1932).
SIDELIGHTS: "Wallace Thurman was a leader among the young black
intelligentsia who earned their literary reputations during the
Harlem Renaissance" (Black American Literature--Fiction).
    Best known for The Blacker the Berry. Died of tuberculosis at
age 32.
Sources. Black American Literature--Fiction, Ed. by Darwin T. Turner
(Merrill, 1969); The Negro Novel in America, Robert A. Bone (Yale
U. Pr., 1958); Negro Caravan, Ed. by Sterling A. Brown & Others
(Arno Pr. & N.Y. Times, 1969).

TOLSON, MELVIN BEAUNORUS. 1898-1966. Poet,
Educator, Playwright, Mayor, Poet Laureate of
Liberia
Biographical-Personal. Born 1898 in Moberly,
Mo. Educ.: Fisk U.; M.A., Columbia U.
Died 1966.
Career-Professional. Taught at various s. coll.
Became assoc. with Langston U., Okla., where
he was Prof. of Creative Lit. and directed
campus Dust Bowl Theater. Became Avalon
Prof. of Humanities at Tuskegee Inst.
WRITINGS: "Dark Symphony;" Rendezvous with
America (Dodd, Mead, 1944); Libretto for the
Republic of Liberia (Twayne, 1953); Harlem
Gallery (Twayne, 1965). Plays: The Moses of
Beale Street; Southern Front, dramatizations
of George Schuyler's novel Black No More & Walter White's Fire in
the Flint. Anthol.: Negro Caravan; Poetry of the Negro; Soon,
One Morning; American Negro Poetry; & Kaleidoscope. Period.:
Poetry; The Prairie Schooner.
HONORS AND AWARDS: Poem "Dark Symphony" won the Nat'l. Poetry
Contest conducted by Amer. Negro Exposition in Chgo. and was pub.
in The Atlantic Monthly; designated Poet Laureate of Liberia for
poem Libretto for Republic of Liberia, 1953; received Bess Hokin

Toomer, Jean

Award of Mod. Poetry Assn. in 1952; Received literary fellow. both
from Rockefeller Found. and Omega Psi Phi.
SIDELIGHTS: Elected Mayor of Langston, Okla. (all-Black town)
four times.
   "In an Introduction by Karl Shapiro, to <u>Harlem Gallery</u>, he said:
'A great poet has been living in our midst for decades and is al-
most totally unknown, even by the literati, even by poets. Can
this be possible in the age of criticism and publication unlimit-
ed? It is not only possible but highly probable'" (<u>Anger, and
Beyond</u>).
Sources. <u>Anger, and Beyond</u>, Herbert Hill (Harper & Row, 1966); <u>Black
American Literature--Poetry</u>, Ed. by Darwin T. Turner (Merrill,
1969); <u>Black Voices</u>, Ed. by Abraham Chapman (New Amer. Lib., 1968);
<u>Cavalcade</u>, Ed. by Arthur P. Davis & Saunders Redding (Houghton
Mifflin, 1971); <u>Dark Symphony</u>, Ed. by James A. Emanuel & Theodore
L. Gross (Free Pr., 1968); <u>Kaleidoscope</u>, Ed. by Robert Hayden
(Harcourt, 1967).

TOOMER, JEAN. 1894-1967. Poet, Novelist
Biographical-Personal. Nathan Eugene Toomer was
   born Dec. 26, 1894, in Wash., D.C. Son of
   Nathan and Nina E. [Pinchback] Toomer; grand-
   son of P. B. S. Pinchback (La. Reconstruction
   Lt. Governor). <u>Educ.</u>: U. of Wis.; City
   Coll. of N.Y. <u>Family</u>: 1st m. Margery Lati-
   mer (novelist), Oct. 30, 1931 (dec. 1932);
   2nd m. Marjorie Content (d. of prominent Wall
   St. broker). Died March 30, 1967.
Career-Professional. Beginning in 1918, contrib.
   poems, sketches and reviews to a variety of
   nat'l. mags. such as <u>Broom</u>, <u>Crisis</u>, <u>The Lib-
   erator</u>, <u>Little Review</u>, <u>Modern Review</u>, <u>Nomad</u>,
   <u>Prairie</u>, <u>Sun</u>, <u>Pagany</u>, <u>Bifur</u> (Paris), &
   <u>Adelphi</u> (London). Worked as sch. prin. in
   Ga. (1922).
WRITINGS: Only book was <u>Cane</u> (Boni & Liveright, 1923; rev. 1975)--
this classic in Black Amer. lit. was a mosaic of poems, short stories and intense sketches (which grew out of his S. sojourn).
SIDELIGHTS: One of the voices of the Negro Renaissance of the
1920's. Associated with such white intellectuals as Hart Crane,
Waldo Frank, Gorham Munson, and Kenneth Burke. Became a disciple
of the Russian mystic Gurdjieff. Lived in Carmel, Cal., Taos,
N. Mex., and finally in Bucks Co., Pa.
   "Professor Darwin T. Turner noted in a memorial tribute to
Toomer (that after <u>Cane</u>) 'He wrote, editors refused. Seeking an
excuse for failure, he blamed his identification as a Negro. He
denied that he came from Negro ancestry. Still the editors re-

Toure, Askia Muhammad

fused...He continued to write and rewrite; two novels, two books
of poems, a collection of stories, books of nonfiction, two books
of aphorisms. But editors never again accepted a book for publi-
cation'" (Black Voices).
Sources. Black American Literature--Poetry, Ed. by Darwin T. Turner
(Merrill, 1969); Black Voices, Ed. by Abraham Chapman (New Amer.
Lib., 1968); Cavalcade, Ed. by Arthur P. Davis & Saunders Redding
(Houghton Mifflin, 1971); The Negro Novel in America, Robert A.
Bone (Yale U. Pr., 1958).

TOPPIN, EDGAR ALLAN. 1928- . Professor of History, Historian
Biographical-Personal. Born Jan. 22, 1928, in N.Y.C. Son of Vivien
Leopold and Catherine Maud [Joell] Toppin. Educ.: B.A., 1949,
M.A., 1950, Howard U.; Ph.D., Northwestern U., 1955. Family:
m. Antoinette L. Lomaz (educ. instr., Va. State Coll.), April 2,
1953; son, Edgar Allan, Jr., d. Avis Ann Lillian, d. Antoinette
Louise. Mailing address: 20411 Williams St., Ettrick, Va. 23803.
Career-Professional. Instr., Hist., Ala. State Coll., Montgomery,
1954-55; Chmn., Soc. Sci., Fayetteville State Coll., N.C., 1955-59;
Asst. Prof., U. of Akron, Ohio, 1959-63; Assoc. Prof. of Hist.,
1963-64; Prof. of Hist., Va. State Coll., Petersburg, 1964- ; Vis.
summer prof.: N.C. Coll., 1959, 1963, Western Res. U., 1962, U.
of Cin., 1964, San Francisco State Coll., 1969; Lectr., CBS-TV
"Black Heritage" Ser.
WRITINGS: Pioneers and Patriots: The Lives of Six Negroes of the
Revolutionary Era, with Lavinia Dobler (Doubleday, 1965); A Mark
Well Made: The Negro Contribution to American Culture (Rand
McNally, 1967): The Unfinished March: The Negro in the United
States, Reconstruction to World War I, with Carol Drisko (Double-
day, 1967); Blacks in America: Then and Now (Christian Sci. Pub.
Soc., 1969); Biographical History of Blacks in America (David
McKay, 1971). Contrib. of articles & reviews to Phylon, African
Forum & to hist. jls.
MEMBER: Amer. Hist. Assn.; ASNLH (Executive counc., 1962-);
Assn. of Soc. Sci. Tchrs.; Org. of Amer. Hist.; S. Hist. Assn.;
Va. Hist. Assn.; Ohio Hist. Soc.
Source. Contemporary Authors, Vols. 21-22, Ed. by Barbara Harte &
Carolyn Riley (Gale Res., 1969).

TOURE, ASKIA MUHAMMAD. 1938- . Editor, Poet,
Teacher
Biographical-Personal. Born 1938 in N.C.
Career-Professional. Ed.-at-Large, Journal of
Black Poetry; Lectures widely around the
country; Tchr., Columbia U.; One of founders
of Black Arts Movement. Currently, Adjunct
Prof. of Creative writing, Manhattan Communi-
ty Coll., N.Y.C.

Trotter, William Monroe

WRITINGS: JuJu, poetry (1969) & Songhai!, poetry and sketches
from 1966 to 1971 (1972). Anthol.: Black Fire (1968); Black Arts
(1969); Natural Process (1970); The Poetry of the Negro (1949,
1970) & Poetry of Black America (1973). Period.: Umbra, Journal
of Black Poetry, Negro Digest/Black World, Freedomways, Liberator
& Soulbook.
Sources. "Nat'l. Conf. of Afro-Amer. Writing, (Program) Howard U.,
Inst. for Arts & Humanities, Nov. 1974; Poetry of Black America,
Ed. by Arnold Adoff (Harper & Row, 1973).

TROTTER, WILLIAM MONROE. 1872-1934. Publisher,
Civil Rights Activist
Biographical-Personal. Born April 17, 187, in
Springfield Township, Ohio. Son of James
Monroe (intellectual & politician) and Vir-
ginia [Isaacs] Trotter. Educ.: (Phi Beta
Kappa, magna cum laude), Harvard U., 1895,
M.A., 1896. Family: m. Geraldine Pindell.
Died April 7, 1934.
Career-Professional. Established Boston Guard-
ian newspaper (with George Washington Forbes),
1901; Real estate & insurance broker; Organ-
izer (with others): Niagara Movement; NAACP.
SIDELIGHTS: "...First Negro elected to Phi
Beta Kappa at Harvard.... Leader with W.E.B.
DuBois in the Niagara Movement, and later be-
came National Secretary of the National Equal Rights League, a
militant civil rights organization. As spokesman for this group
he took the case of the Negro to the League of Nations... He was
articulate, fearless and idealistic and under his editorship the
Guardian played an important role in reestablishing the Negro
press as a dominant force in the fight for Negro rights" (Negro
Handbook).
"He made five major contributions: 1. He startled the nation
by challenging Booker T. Washington at the outset of his career;
2. He defied President Woodrow Wilson when the latter instituted
segregation of Negroes employed in offices of the Federal Government in Washington; 3. He threw down the gauntlet against racial
discrimination on a world scale when he intervened at the Versailles Peace Conference in 1919; 4. He pioneered in the staging
of picket lines to protest plays derogatory to Negro people;
5. He was the first American Negro leader to organize mass struggle on issues with national and international significance since
the days of Frederick Douglass and the abolitionists" (Negro History Bulletin).
Sources. Afro-American Writing, Ed. by Richard A. Long & Eugenia W.
Collier (N.Y.U. Pr., 1972); Ebony (Johnson Pub., June 1968); His-

torical Negro Biographies, Wilhelmena S. Robinson (ASLNH, 1967); Negro Handbook, Comp. by Eds. of Ebony (Johnson Pub., 1966); Negro History Bulletin (ASLNH, Nov. 1947).

TROUPE, QUINCY. 1943- . Poet, Teacher, Editor

Biographical-Personal. Born 1943 in N.Y.C.
   Educ.: B.A., Grambling Coll., La.; UCLA.
Career-Professional. Tchr.: UCLA; U. of S. Cal.; Ohio U.; Ed. & founder, Confrontation: A Journal of Third World Literature, pub. by Black Stud. Inst., Ohio U., Athens; Ed., Mundus Artium (lit.). Currently: Faculty, Richmond Coll., Staten Island, N.Y.
WRITINGS: Embryo Poems 1967-1971 (Barlenmir House, 1972). Watts Poets: A Book of New Poetry and Essays, Ed., anthol. (House of Respect, 1968); Sun Sounds: An Anthology of Third World Writings, Ed. with Kaine Shutle; The Event (Crowell, 1975); Giant Talk: An Anthology of Third World Writings, with Rainer Schulte, Eds. (Random House, 1975). Anthol.: The New Black Poetry (1969); We Speak As Liberators (1970); New Black Voices (1972); Black Spirits (1972); Poetry of Black America. Period.: Negro Digest/Black World, Black Review #2, Umbra, Antioch Review, Mediterranean Review, Concerning Poetry, New York Quarterly, Black Creations, Sumac & New Directions 22.
SIDELIGHTS: Was an original member of the Watts Writers Workshop (Poetry of Black America).
Sources. "Nat'l. Conf. of Afro-Amer. Writers" (Program) Howard U., Inst. for Arts & Humanities, Nov. 1974; New Black Voices, Ed. by Abraham Chapman (New Amer. Lib., 1972); Poetry of Black America, Ed. by Arnold Adoff (Harper & Row, 1973); Watts Poets, Ed. by Quincy Troupe (House of Respect, 1968); Books in Print, Supplement, 1975-76 (Bowker, 1976).

TUCKER, STERLING.
Career-Professional.
   WRITINGS: Beyond the Burning; Life and Death of the Ghetto (Assoc. Pr., 1968); Black Reflections on White Power (Eerdmans, 1969); For Blacks Only (Eerdmans, 1971).
Source. Books in Print, 1976 (Bowker, 1976).

Turner, Darwin T.

TURNER, DARWIN T. 1931- . Professor of English, Literary Critic, Editor, Poet
Biographical-Personal. Born May 7, 1931, in Cin., Ohio. Son of Darwin Romanes and Laura [Knight] Turner. Educ.: B.A., (Eng., Phi Beta Kappa) 1947, M.A. (Eng.), 1949, U. of Cin.; Ph.D. (Eng. & Amer. Dramatic Lit.), U. of Chgo., 1956. Family: m. Maggie Jean Lewis; d. Pamela Welch, son, Darwin Keith, son, Rachon. Mailing address: Afro-Amer. Stud., 303 Eng.-Philosophy Bldg., U. of Iowa, Iowa City, Iowa 52240.
Career-Professional. Asst. Prof., Eng., Clark Coll., Atlanta, 1949-51; Asst. Prof., Eng., Morgan State Coll., Baltimore, 1952-57; Prof. & Chmn., Dept. of Eng., Fla. A.&M.U., Tallahassee, 1957-59; Prof. & Chmn., Dept. of Eng., N.C. Agricultural & Technical Coll., Greensboro, 1959-70, Prof. of Eng. & Dean, Grad. Sch., 1966-70; Vis. Prof., Eng., U. of Wis., Madison, 1969; Prof. of Eng., U. of Mich., Ann Arbor, 1970-71; Vis. Prof., Eng., U. of Hawaii, Summer 1971; Vis. Prof., Eng., U. of Iowa, Iowa City, 1971-72 & Prof., Eng. & Dir., Afro-Amer. Stud., 1972-present. Gen. Ed., Arno Pr. Afro-Amer. Culture Ser., 1969; Gen. Ed., Chas. E. Merrill Co.'s African/Afro-Amer. Ser., 1970- ; Advis. Ed., Bulletin of Black Books, 1971- .
WRITINGS: A Guide to Composition, Ed. (Office Serv. Co., 1960); Standards for Freshman Composition, Ed. (Deal Print. Co., 1961); Katharsis (Wellesley Pr., 1964); Images of the Negro in America, Co-ed. (D. C. Heath, 1965); Nathaniel Hawthorne's "The Scarlet Letter" (Dell, 1967); Black American Literature: Essays, Ed. (Merrill, 1969); Black American Literature: Fiction, Ed. (Merrill, 1969); Black American Literature: Poetry, Ed. (Merrill, 1969); Afro-American Writers, Comp. (Appleton, 1970); Black American Literature: Essays, Poetry, Fiction, Drama, Ed. (Merrill, 1970); Black Drama in America: An Anthology, Ed. with introduction (Fawcett, 1971); In a Minor Chord: Three Afro-American Writers and Their Search for Identity (S. Ill. U. Pr., 1971); Voices from the Black Experience: African and Afro-American Literature, Co-ed. (Ginn, 1972); The Teaching of Literature by Afro-American Writers: Theory and Practice, Co-auth. (Nat'l. Counc. of Tchrs. of Eng., 1972); Responding:Five, Co-ed. (Ginn, 1973); Frank Yerby: Golden Debunker (Third World Pr., 1974); Selected Writings of Jean Toomer, Ed. (Howard U. Pr., 1974). Original poetry: Circles, National Poetry Anthology, Journal of Human Relations, A Galaxy of Black Writing, Poetry of the Negro (rev. ed.), Black American Literature. Articles in bks.: Encyclopedia International, 1968 ed.; Encyclopaedia Britannica, 1968 ed.; The

Turner, Lorenzo Dow

Black Aesthetic; The Promise of English; The Black Novelist; What
Black Educators Are Saying; Black Studies Series; New Perspectives
on Black Studies; Backgrounds to Black American Literature; Con-
temporary Dramatists. Jls.: Journal of Human Relations, CLA
Journal, Alpha Kappa Mu Journal, Educational Theatre Journal,
Faculty Review; Negro Digest/Black World, College Composition &
Communication, Mississippi Quarterly, Southern Literary Journal,
North Carolina Agricultural & Technical Alumni Bulletin, College
English, CEA Critic, Journal of Negro Education, English Journal,
Bulletin of Black Books, Armchair Detective.
MEMBER: Grad. Record Exam., Bd., 1970-73; S. Assn. of Land-Grant
Coll. & State Supported U.; Coll. Lang. Assn., Pres., 1963-65 &
other offices; Nat'l. Counc. of Tchrs. of Eng., (Judge, State
Achievement Awards Prog., 1959, 1960, 1962, 1967; Nat'l. Counc.
Tchrs. Eng. Task Force for Studying Lang. Prog. for Disadvantaged,
1965; Com. on Dialect Recordings for Elem. Schs., 1966-67; Chmn.,
Nat'l. Counc. Tchrs. Eng. Study Group on Ethnic Lit., 1969; Chmn.,
Com. on Lit. of Minority Groups, 1970-), other offices; Conf. on
Coll. Composition & Communication; S. Atlantic Mod. Lang. Assn.;
Midwest Mod. Lang. Assn.; Piedmont Affiliate of Nat'l. Counc. of
Tchrs. of Eng.; N.C.-Va. Coll. Eng. Assn., Pres., 1964-65, other
offices; Mod. Lang. Assn.; Coll. Eng. Assn., Mem., Bd. of Dir.
1970- ; Assn. for Study of Afro-Amer. Life & Hist., Co-Dir. ASNLH
Branches for Iowa, 1973- ; Second World Festival of Black & Af-
rican Arts & Culture, Acting Chmn. for Iowa.
SIDELIGHTS: Entered U. of Cin. at age 13, elected to Phi Beta
Kappa at 15, received AB at 16, MA at 18. Dr. Turner has made
following tapes: "Invisible Man" (Ralph Ellison); "Native Son";
"The Outsider" (Richard Wright); "Cane" (Jean Toomer); "Original
Poetry" (Darwin T. Turner); "Langston Hughes" (criticism)--all
Everett/Edwards, Inc. (Author).
Sources. Author inform.; Black American Literature: Poetry, Ed. by
Darwin T. Turner (Merrill, 1969); Black Voices, Ed. by Abraham
Chapman (New Amer. Lib., 1968); Contemporary Authors, Vols. 21-22,
Ed. by Barbara Harte & Carolyn Riley (Gale Res., 1969); A Galaxy
of Black Writing, R. Baird Shuman (Moore, 1970).

TURNER, LORENZO DOW. English Professor, Linguist
Biographical-Personal. Educ.: B.A., 1914, M.A., 1917, Howard U.;
Ph.D., U. of Chgo., 1926.
Career-Professional. Prof. & Head, Eng. Dept., Howard U., 1917-29;
Prof. & Head, Eng. Dept., Fisk U., 1929-46; Prof., Eng., Roosevelt
U., Chgo., 1946- .
WRITINGS: Anti-Slavery Sentiment in American Literature Prior to
1865 (ASNLH, 1929); Collaborator, Readings from Negro Authors
(1931); Africanisms in the Gullah Dialect (1949). Essay: "Some
Contacts of Brazilian Ex-Slaves with Nigeria, West Africa," Jour-
nal of Negro History, Jan. 1942.

Turpin, Waters Edward

HONORS AND AWARDS: Charles H. Smiley Prize, U. of Chgo.
SIDELIGHTS: "Noted for study and recording of speech of groups of
people in both USA and Brazil, in search of African influences;
considered an authority in this field" (Who's Who in Colored
America).
"Lorenzo Turner has studied Gullah with scientific linguistic
techniques" (Negro in American Literature).
Sources. Negro in American Culture, Margaret Just Butcher (Knopf,
1956); Who's Who in Colored America, Supplement, 7th ed., Ed. by
G. James Fleming & Christian E. Burckel (Burckel & Assoc., 1950).

TURPIN, WATERS EDWARD. 1910-1968. Novelist, English Professor
Biographical-Personal. Born 1910 in Oxford, E. Shore of Md. Educ.:
B.A., Morgan Coll., Baltimore; M.A., Ph.D., Columbia U. Died
1968.
Career-Professional. Eng. Tchr., & Football coach, Storer Coll.,
Harper's Ferry; Eng. Tchr., Lincoln U.
WRITINGS: Novels: These Low Grounds (1937); O Canaan! (1939).
The Rootless, hist. of Md. slavery (1957). St. Michael's Dawn,
3-act drama of life of Frederick Douglass.
SIDELIGHTS: "He set the locale of his first novel, These Low
Grounds...on his native Eastern Shore of Maryland, where many Ne-
groes earn their livelihood by processing oysters for market.
O Canaan!...is the Story of Joe Benson's rise from a poor Mis-
sissippi field hand to a Chicago realtor and banker and his fall
back to poverty and to life as a Pullman porter.
The Rootless...is a historical treatment of black slavery as
practiced on a Maryland plantation in the late eighteenth century.
Born in Oxford, Maryland, near the birthplace of Frederick Doug-
lass, fifteen years after the death of the great anti-slavery
leader, Turpin felt a strong commitment to Douglass' ideals"
(Black Insights).
Sources. Black Insights, Ed. by Nick A. Ford (Ginn, 1971); Negro
Caravan, Ed. by Sterling A. Brown & Others (Arno Pr. & N.Y.
Times, 1969).

VAN DYKE, HENRY. 1928- . Novelist
Biographical-Personal. Born Oct. 3, 1928, in
Allegan, Mich. Son of H. L. (doctor) and
Bessie Van Dyke. Educ.: M.A., U. of Mich.
Family: Single. Mailing address: 64 St.
Mark's Pl., N.Y., N.Y. 10003.
Career-Professional. Writer-in-Residence, Kent
State U. (Fall Quarter, 1974); Coord., Cro-
well-Collier-Macmillan, 1959-67; Assoc. Ed.,
U. of Mich., engineering res., 1956-58.

Vann, Robert L.

WRITINGS: Novels: <u>Ladies of the Rachmaninoff Eyes</u> (Farrar, Straus, 1965); <u>Blood of Strawberries</u> (Farrar, Straus, 1969); <u>Dead Piano</u>.
HONORS AND AWARDS: Guggenheim Fellow., 1971; Amer. Acad. of Arts and Letters Award, 1974.
Source. Author inform.

VAN PEEBLES, MELVIN. 1932- . Actor, Composer, Playwright, Novelist, Film Maker
Career-Professional. Recording artist; Film maker; Novelist; Short story writer; Actor.
WRITINGS: <u>Sweet Sweetback's Baadasssss Song</u>, film (1971); <u>Aint Supposed to Die a Natural Death</u>, play; <u>Don't Play Us Cheap</u>, novel (Bantam, 1973); <u>Le Chinois du XIV</u> (J. Martineau, 1966); <u>La Fête à Harlem</u> (J. Martineau, 1967); <u>A Bear for the FBI</u> (Trident, 1968); <u>The True American</u>; <u>The Story of a Three-Day Pass</u>.
SIDELIGHTS: "Writer, composer, director, film maker, producer, promoter, actor, singer and one-man conglomerate, he's the first black man in show business to beat the white man at his own game" (<u>The New York Times</u>).
<u>Sweet Sweetback</u> grossed $12 million. Wrote 5 novels while in Paris; 4 in self-taught French. "Determined to do his next film (after <u>Watermelon Man</u>) without studio backing, he put up $70,000 and sweet-talked additional funds from others. With an amateur cast, a non-union crew and rented equipment, he filmed <u>Sweet Sweetback</u>" (<u>1000 Successful Blacks</u>).
Sources. <u>Afro-American Writers</u>, Darwin T. Turner (Appleton, 1970); <u>Don't Play Us Cheap</u>, Melvin Van Peebles (Bantam, 1973); <u>1000 Successful Blacks</u>, Vol. 1, Ebony Success Lib. (Johnson Pub., 1973).

VANN, ROBERT L. 1879-1940. Newspaper Publisher, Attorney
Biographical-Personal. Born Aug. 29, 1879, in Ahoskie, N.C. Son of ex-slave tenant farmer. Educ.: Va. Union U., Richmond; B.A., LL.B., U. of Pittsburgh. Family: m. Jessie Matthews of Gettysburg, Pa., 1910. Died 1940.
Career-Professional. Founder-Pub., <u>Pittsburgh Courier</u>, 1910; Lawyer; Asst. City Solicitor, Pittsburgh, 1918-22; Asst. U.S. Attorney Gen. HONORS AND AWARDS: Hon. degrees: Va. Union, Wilberforce. Memorial tower named for him at Va. Union U.; Liberty Ship named for him in Oct. 1943.

273

Vassa, Gustavus

MEMBER: Com. to Revise Constitution of State of Pa.; Virgin Islands Commission.
SIDELIGHTS: "...he published the first edition [of the Courier] on March 10, 1910. The venture was a success, and as a spokesman for the Republican Party, it became the news media for the Negro community in Pittsburgh. By the 1930's, its circulation reached from coast to coast, with branch offices and outlets throughout the United States.
    During the economic depression of the thirties, Vann saw fit to change the support of the Courier from the Republican Party to that of the New Deal Democrats. For his support of the Roosevelt program, he was appointed assistant U.S. attorney general in the late thirties" (Historical Negro Biographies).
Sources. Negroes Past and Present, Russell Adams (Afro-Amer. Pub., 1966); Historical Negro Biographies, Wilhelmena S. Robinson (ASNLH, 1967); Negroes in Public Affairs and Government, Ed. by Walter Christmas (Educ. Her., 1966).

VASSA, GUSTAVUS. 1745?-1801? Ship Steward
Biographical-Personal. Born c. 1745 in Benin, Nigeria, West Africa. Seized at age 11, thrust into slavery. First on a Virginia plantation; then in illegal service of a British naval officer (who gave him a fair education). Finally, slave on plantations and small trading vessels in West Indies as property of Philadelphia merchant (Negro Author).
Career-Professional. Bought freedom, his master becoming his adviser and protector. Traveled extensively as ship's steward. Converted to Methodism; settled down in England; engaged in anti-slavery work (Negro Author).
WRITINGS: The Interesting Narrative of the Life of Olaudah Equiano, or Gustavus Vassa, the African, autobiog. (1789, in 8th ed. by 1794).
SIDELIGHTS: The Narrative "regarded as highly informative account of the evils of slavery as it affected both master and slave" (Negro Almanac).
    "Not, strictly speaking, an American Negro; nevertheless he spent considerable time in bondage in this country and his book was so frequently reprinted in the United States that he might well be considered in this connection" (Early Negro American Writers).
Sources. Early Negro American Writers, Benjamin Brawley (U. of N.C. Pr., 1935); Negro Almanac, Comp. by Harry A. Ploski & Ernest Kaiser (Bellwether, 1971); Negro Author, Vernon Loggins (Kennikat, 1959).

Paul Vesey. See Allen, Samuel W.

VROMAN, MARY ELIZABETH. 1923– . Short Story Writer, Novelist
Biographical-Personal. Born 1923 in Buffalo, N.Y. Raised in Brit.
W. Indies. Educ.: Ala. State Coll.
Career-Professional.
    WRITINGS: Short stories: "See How They Run"; "And Have Not Char-
ity" (both pub. in Ladies Home Journal); Esther, novel (1963).
    HONORS AND AWARDS: First Negro woman to be granted membership in
Screen Writers Guild; Christopher Award for inspirational magazine
writing, 1952.
    SIDELIGHTS: "See How They Run" was purchased by Metro-Goldwyn-
Mayer & released in 1953 as the movie Bright Road.
Source. American Negro Short Stories, Ed. by John Henrik Clarke
    (Hill & Wang, 1966).

WADDY, WILLANNA RUTH. 1909– . Artist
Biographical-Personal. Born Jan. 7, 1909, in
Lincoln, Neb. D. of John Moses and Willie
Anna [Choran] Gilliam. Educ.: U. of Minn.,
1927-28, 1930-31. Family: m. William Henry
Waddy, Feb. 2, 1931 (div. June 1933); d.
Marianna. Mailing address: 1543 S. Western
Ave., L.A., Cal. 90006.
Career-Professional. Exhibited in one-man shows
at Jimmy Crawford's Frame Shop, L.A., 1963;
Safety Savings & Loan Assn., 1969; Independ-
ence Square, 1966; Contemporary Crafts Gal-
lery; Exhibited in group shows at Art W.
Assoc., Inc., 1963- ; Graphic aus fünf
Kontinenten, Leipzig, Germany, 1965; New
Perspectives, Oakland, Cal. Mus., 1968;
Permanent collec., include Oakland Mus., Golden State Mutual Life
Insurance Co., L.A. & Metropolitan Mus. of Art, N.Y.
    WRITINGS: Black Artists On Art, Vol. I, Ed. with Samella S. Lewis
(Ward Ritchie Pr., 1969); Black Artists On Art, Vol. II, Ed. with
Samella S. Lewis (Ward Ritchie Pr., 1971). Contrib., book of
prints.
    MEMBER: Art W. Assoc., Inc. (founder, 1962; pres., 1962, 1964).
Source. Who's Who in the West, 14th ed., 1974-75 (Marquis, 1974).

WALCOTT, RONALD. 1946– . English Teacher
Biographical-Personal. Born July 22, 1946, in N.Y.C. Son of Frank
and Ruth Walcott. Educ.: B.A., Hunter Coll.; M.A. & doctoral
candidate, Columbia U. Family: married; son, Christopher, son,
Quentin. Mailing address: 2400 Webb Ave., Bronx, N.Y. 10468.

Walker, Alice Malsenior

Career-Professional. Asst. Prof. of Eng.,
Kingsborough Community & Queens Colls. of
City U. of N.Y. (Afro-Amer. Thought & Lit.) &
other courses.
WRITINGS: Twenty-Eight Short Stories: An
Anthology, Tchr's. Manual, co-ed. with
Michael Timko (Random House, 1975). In
progress: a book of criticism assessing con-
temporary Black fiction. Contrib.: "The Man
Who Cried I Am: Crying in the Dark," Studies
in Black Literature (Spring, 1972); "Ellison,
Gordone and Tolson: Some Notes on the Blues,
Style and Space," Black World (Dec. 1972);
"The Early Fiction of John A. Williams," CLA
(Dec. 1972); "Chesnutt's 'The Sheriff's Chil-
dren' as Parable," Negro American Literature
Forum (Fall 1973); "The Novels of Hal Bennett, Part I: The Writer
as Satirist," Black World (June, 1974); "The Novels of Hal Ben-
nett, Part II: The Writer as Magician/Priest," Black World (July,
1974).
Source. Author inform.

WALKER, ALICE MALSENIOR. 1944- . Teacher,
Writer
Biographical-Personal. Born Feb. 9, 1944, in
Eatonton, Ga. D. of Willie Lee and Minnie
Tallulah [Grant] Walker (sharecroppers).
Educ.: Spelman Coll., 1961-63; B.A., Sarah
Lawrence Coll., 1965. Family: m. Melvyn R.
Leventhal (civil rights lawyer), Mar. 17,
1967; d. Rebecca Grant. Mailing address:
55 Midwood, Brooklyn, N.Y. 11225.
Career-Professional. Consultant, Black Stud.;
Friends of the Children of Miss., 1967-68;
Tchr., Writing & Black Lit., Jackson State
Coll. & Tougaloo Coll., Miss., 1968-70;
Wellesley Coll., Mass. (Lectr. in Writing &
Lit.), 1972- ; Lectr. in Lit., U. of Mass.,
Boston, 1972- . Contrib. ed.: Freedomways, Southern Voices, Ms.
WRITINGS: Once, poems (Harcourt, 1968); The Third Life of Grange
Copeland, novel (Harcourt, 1970); Revolutionary Petunias, poems
(Harcourt, 1973); Langston Hughes, juvenile biography (Crowell,
1973); In Love and Trouble: Stories of Black Women, short stories
(Harcourt, 1973); Meridian (Harcourt, 1976).
HONORS AND AWARDS: Breadloaf Writer's Conf., scholar, 1966; Mer-
rill Writing fellow, 1966-67; McDowell Colony Fellow, 1967; NEA
grant (for Third Life of Grange Copeland), 1969-70; Radcliffe

276

Inst. Fellow, 1971-73; Rosenthal Award, Nat'l. Inst. of Arts &
Letters, 1973 (for In Love and Trouble); Nomination for Nat'l.
Book Award, 1973 (for Revolutionary Petunias); Lillian Smith
Award (for Revolutionary Petunias), 1973.
MEMBER: Bd. of Trus., Sarah Lawrence Coll.
SIDELIGHTS: Active in welfare rights & voter registation activi-
ties in Ga. & New York, & has traveled in Kenya, Uganda, & the
Soviet Union (Poetry of Black America). Has lectured & read
poetry & prose at: Poetry Center, Tougaloo Coll., Harvard, Yale,
Sarah Lawrence, Jackson State, Brown, U. of Miami, U. of Wyo.,
Evergreen Coll., Conn. Coll., Wellesley, Acad. of Amer. Poets,
etc. (Author).
Sources. Author inform.; Best Short Stories by Negro Writers, Ed. by
Langston Hughes (Little, Brown, 1967); Contemporary Authors,
Vols. 37-40, Ed. by Clare D. Kinsman & Mary A. Tennenhouse (Gale
Res., 1973); Ebony (Johnson Pub., March 1974); Poetry of Black
America, Ed. by Arnold Adoff (Harper & Row, 1973); Books in Print,
Supplement, 1975-76 (Bowker, 1976).

WALKER, DAVID. 1785-1830. Abolitionist, Activist
Biographical-Personal. Born Sept. 28, 1785, in Wilmington, N.C. Son
of slave father & free mother. He felt such detestation for the
slave system that he resolved not to live in the South. Reaching
Boston after many trials, he learned to read & write. Joined a
Methodist church and married in 1828. Home became a shelter for
the poor.
Career-Professional. Opened a clothing store on Brattle St. and
prospered, 1827.
WRITINGS: In 1829 came, Walker's Appeal, in Four Articles; together with a Preamble to the Coloured Citizens of the World, but
in Particular and very Expressly to Those of the United States of
America. (In 3rd ed. in a year; Ed. by Henry H. Garnet with
sketch of author's life, in 1848).
SIDELIGHTS: "...in Savannah a copy of David Walker's Appeal was
found upon a luckless slave, and sixty copies were discovered in
the possession of a Negro preacher.... Two states promptly 'en-
acted laws forbidding the circulation of incendiary publications
and forbidding the teaching of slaves to read and write.' In
North Carolina a person found guilty of writing or circulating
publications which might 'excite insurrection, conspiracy, or resistance in the slaves or free Negroes' was to be 'imprisoned for
not less than a year and be put in the pillory and whipped at the
discretion of the court'.... A reward of $1000 was placed on
Walker dead, a reward of $10,000 on Walker alive" (Negro Caravan).
"After the consternation caused by the book in the South, his
wife and friends advised that he go to Canada, but he refused,
saying, 'I will stand my ground. Somebody must die in this cause.

Walker Alexander, Margaret Abigail

I may be doomed to the stake and the fire, or to the scaffold tree, but it is not in me to falter if I can promote the work of emancipation.' Before the close of 1830 he died, and the belief was persistent that he met with foul play" (Early Negro American Writers).
Sources. Early Negro American Writers, Benjamin Brawley (U. of N.C. Pr., 1935); Negro Caravan, Ed. by Sterling A. Brown et al. (Arno Pr. & N.Y. Times, 1969).

WALKER ALEXANDER, MARGARET ABIGAIL. 1915- .
Poet, Novelist, Professor of English
Biographical-Personal. Born July 27, 1915, in Birmingham, Ala. D. of Sigismund C. (minister) and Marion Dozier Walker (musician). Educ.: Gilbert Acad.; B.A., Northwestern U.; M.A., Ph.D., U. of Iowa; Hon. degrees: Fine Arts, Denison U., 1974; Dr. of Lit., Northwestern U., 1974. Family: m. Firnist James Alexander (interior decorator); d. Marion Elizabeth, d. Margaret Elvira, son, Atty. Firnist James, Jr., son, Sigismund Walker. Mailing address: P.O. Box 17315, Black Stud. Inst., Jackson State U., Jackson, Miss. 39217.
Career-Professional. Fed. Writers Project (during Depression); Livingstone Coll., Salisbury, N.C., 1941-42; W. Va. State Coll., Inst., W. Va., 1942-43; U. of Iowa Rhetoric Prog., 1962-64; Lecture Platform, Nat'l. Concert-Artists Corp., N.Y., 1943-48; Cape Cod Writers Conf., Craigville, Mass. (summer 1967 & 1969); Vis. Prof. in Creative Writing, Northwestern U. (Spring, 1969); At Jackson State Coll., Jackson, Miss. since 1949: Prof. of Eng. & Dir. of Inst. for the Study of Hist., Life, and Culture of Black People.
WRITINGS: For My People, poetry (Yale U. Pr., 1942); Jubilee, fiction (Houghton Mifflin, 1966; paper Bantam); Prophets for a New Day, poetry (Broadside Pr., 1970); October Journey, poetry (Broadside Pr., 1973); A Poetic Equation; Conversations Between Nikki Giovanni and Margaret Walker (Howard U. Pr., 1974). Period.: "Religion, Poetry, and History: Foundation for a New Education System," Vital Speeches of the Day (Oct. 1, 1968); "The Humanistic Tradition of Afro-American Literature," American Library Association Bulletin; "Black Studies: Some Personal Observations," Afro-American Studies Journal (1970); "A Brief Introduction to Southern Literature," Miss. Arts Festival Public., Bd. of Dir. (1971); "Richard Wright," U. of Mo. New Letters, vol. 38, no. 2 (Kansas City, 1971); "How I Wrote Jubilee" (Third World Pr., 1972).
HONORS AND AWARDS: Yale Award for Younger Poets, 1942; Rosenwald Fellow, 1944; Ford Fellow (Fund for Advancement of Educ.) Yale U., 1953-54; Houghton Mifflin Literary Fellow, 1966; Apptd. as Ful-

bright Prof. to Norway, 1971, appointment postponed; NEH Fellow,
1972; Alumni Merit Award, Northwestern U., 1974.
MEMBER: Nat'l. Com. of Tchrs. of Eng.; MLA; Poetry Soc. of Amer-
ica; Amer. Assn. of U. Prof.; Black Acad. of Arts & Letters; Mis-
sissippians for Educ. TV.
SIDELIGHTS: Jubilee was transl. into French, German, and Swedish.
Participated in Lib. of Congress Conf. on the Tchg. of Creative
Writing, Wash., D.C., 1973 (Author).
Sources. Author inform.; Black American Literature--Poetry, Ed. by
Darwin T. Turner (Merrill, 1969); Black Insights, Ed. by Nick A.
Ford (Ginn, 1971); Black Voices, Ed. by Abraham Chapman (New Amer.
Lib., 1968); Cavalcade, Ed. by Arthur P. Davis & Saunders Redding
(Houghton Mifflin, 1971); Dark Symphony, Ed. by James A. Emanuel &
Theodore L. Gross (Free Pr., 1968); Kaleidoscope, Ed. by Robert
Hayden (Harcourt, 1967); Pub. inform.

WALKER, WILLIAM O. 1896- . Publisher-Editor
Biographical-Personal. Born Sept. 18, 1896, in Selma, Ala. Educ.:
Grad.: Wilberforce U., 1916; Oberlin Bus. Coll., 1918.
Career-Professional. Secy. to Dir., Pittsburgh Urban League, 1918;
City Ed., Pittsburg Courier, 1919; City Ed., Norfolk Journal &
Guide, 1920; Co-found. & Managing Ed., Washington Tribune, 1921-30;
Advertising Mgr., then Asst. Mgr. Fair Dept. Store, downtown Wash.,
1930, Mgr., 1932; took over, revived Cleveland Call and Post, 1932.
HONORS AND AWARDS: Dir. campaign pub. for Senator Robert A. Taft
and Governor-Senator John W. Bricker. Elected to Republican State
Central and Executive Com. from 21st Dist., 1956, 1958; Dir., Dept.
of Indust. Relat. for State of Ohio, 1963- .
MEMBER: U.S. Delegate to inspect Armed Forces in Europe, 1946;
U.S. Delegate to Africa, 1960. Elected to Cleveland City Counc.,
1939, served 6 yrs.; Republican Ward Leader, Ward 17, 1946-56;
Mem. Cuyahoga Co. Republican Central Com.
Source. Negro Handbook, Comp. by Eds. of Ebony (Johnson Pub., 1966).

WALROND, ERIC. 1898-1966. Essayist, Short Story Writer
Biographical-Personal. Born 1898 in Georgetown, Brit. Guiana. Educ.:
Columbia U.; City Coll. of N.Y.
Career-Professional. Assoc. Ed., The Negro World, 1923.
WRITINGS: Tropic Death, short stories (1926). Period.: New
Republic.
SIDELIGHTS: "...he wrote an essay entitled "On Being Black" which
was published in The New Republic and brought him a measure of at-
tention from the literary world.
  "Tropic Death, his first and only book, was published in 1926.
It is a collection of stories depicting the contrast between the
natural beauty of the American tropics and the poverty, disease,
and death of its inhabitants" (AFROUSA).
Source. AFROUSA, Comp. by Harry A. Ploski & Ernest Kaiser (Bellwether, 1971).

Walton, Hanes, Jr.

WALTON, HANES, JR. 1942- . Political Scientist
Biographical-Personal. Born Sept. 25, 1942, in Augusta, Ga. Son of
  Thomas Hanes, Sr. and Estelle Walton. Educ.: B.A., Morehouse
  Coll., 1963; M.A., Atlanta U., 1964; Ph.D., Howard U., 1967.
  Family: m. Alice Walton. Mailing address: P.O. Box 20415, Sa-
  vannah State Coll., Savannah, Ga.
Career-Professional. Instr., Atlanta U., summer 1966; Assoc. Prof.,
  Savannah State Coll, 1967- .
  WRITINGS: The Negro in Third Party Politics (Dorrance, 1969); The
  Political Philosophy of Martin Luther King, Jr. (Greenwood, 1971);
  The Study and Analysis of Black Politics: A Bibliography (Scare-
  crow, 1973); Black Political Parties (Free Pr., 1972); Black Poli-
  tics: A Theoretical and Structural Analysis (Lippincott, 1972);
  Political Theory and Political Broadcasting (Wm. Frederick Pr.,
  1973); The Poetry of Black Politics (Regency Pr., 1972); Black
  Republicans: The Politics of the Black and Tans (Scarecrow, 1975).
  Period.: Quarterly Review of Higher Education Among Negroes; Ne-
  gro Education Review; Journal of Social and Behavioral Science;
  Faculty Research Bulletin; Journal of Human Relations; Journal of
  Black Studies; Negro History Bulletin; Ebony; The Black Politician
  and Economic Strategies for Black People in the Coming Decades;
  The Negro in Tennessee 1865-1965.
  HONORS AND AWARDS: Kappa Alpha Psi Scholarship and Achievement
  Award; Social Sci. Counc. Res. Fellow.
  MEMBER: Amer. Polit. Sci. Assn.; Nat'l. Conf. of Black Polit.
  Sci.; Acad. of Polit. & Social Sci.; Kappa Alpha Psi; Pi Sigma
  Alpha.
Source. Author inform.

WALTON, ORTIZ MONTAIGNE. 1933- . Teacher, Composer, Bassist
Biographical-Personal. Born Dec. 13, 1933, in Chgo., Ill. Son of
  Peter and Gladys Walton. Educ.: B.S., Roosevelt U.; M.A., Ph.D.,
  U. of Cal. at Berkeley. Family: m. Carol Walton; son, Omar
  Kwame. Mailing address: 1129 Bancroft Way, Berkeley, Cal. 94702.
Career-Professional. Tchr., Sociol. of Afro-Amer. music, Ethnic
  Stud., Lectr. & performer, Ellington Symposium, U. of Cal., Berke-
  ley; Tchr., Mission Sch. of Music, San Francisco; Tchr., E. Bay
  Music Center; Master Classes in art of double bass performance;
  Solo Bassist, Cairo, U.A.R. Symphony Orchestra; 1st Black and
  youngest, Boston Symphony Orchestra; Asst. prin., Buffalo Philharmonic; Mem., Hartford, Conn. and Springfield, Mass. symphony
  orchestras; Prin. bassist, Nat'l. Orchestra Assn., N.Y.C.
  WRITINGS: Music: Black, White and Blue (Morrow, 1972); Coronation of the King: Contributions by Duke Ellington to Black Culture (U. Cal., Berkeley Pr., 1969). Articles: "Rationalism and
  and Western Music," Black World (Nov. 1973); "Leadership with In-
  tegrity," The Yardbird Reader; "A Comparative Analysis of the
  Western Aesthetic," The Black Aesthetic.

Ward, Douglas Turner

HONORS AND AWARDS: Ford Found. Grant, 1972-73; Nat'l. Inst. of
Mental Health Grant, 1968-71.
MEMBER: Amer. Sociol. Assn.; Nat'l. Assn. of Afro-Amer. Musi-
cians.
SIDELIGHTS: Musical compositions: "Night Letter to Duke," (an
unaccompanied double bass sonata); Songs with lyrics by Ishmael
Reed, recorded by Black Box, 1972. Lectures: Black Music Conf.,
U. of Mass., 1973; UMUM: Black Music Seminar, Swarthmore Coll.,
1974; Paul Robeson Distinguished Lecture Ser., Temple U., 1974
(Author).
Source. Author inform.

WARD, DOUGLAS TURNER. Actor, Playwright, Producer
Biographical-Personal. Born near Burnside, La. Educ.: Wilberforce
U.; U. of Mich.; Paul Mann's Actors' Workshop, N.Y.C. Mailing ad-
dress: c/o Third Press, 444 Central Park W., Suite 1-B, N.Y.,
N.Y. 10025.
Career-Professional. Made debut as actor in The Iceman Cometh; next,
Lost in the Stars; Raisin in the Sun. Leading role: One Flew
Over the Cuckoo's Nest; Rich Little Rich Girl; The Blacks; Blood
Knot; Coriolanus. TV: East Side, West Side; The DuPont Show of
the Month; The Edge of Night and co-starred in CBS's special Look
Up and Live. Founder, Negro Ensemble Co., 1968; Productions:
Lonne Elder's Ceremonies in Dark Old Men, Wole Soyinka's Kongi's
Harvest, plays by other Black writers, and Peter Weiss's Song of
the Lusitania Bogey. Latest play: The River Niger (Ward took
lead).
WRITINGS: Two Plays (Third Press, 1972).
SIDELIGHTS: Served as understudy to Sidney Poitier in Raisin in
the Sun; Assumed leading role during 10-month road tour. His own
first two plays, Happy Ending and Day of Absence, were produced at
St. Mark's Playhouse on Nov. 15, 1965 and ran for 504 performances. They won both a Vernon Rice Drama Desk Award and an Obie
Award.
    "Douglas Turner Ward wrote an article for the New York Times in
August 1966, in which he called for the establishment of a Negro-
oriented theater in New York. He envisioned it as combining both
professional performances by a resident company, and an extensive
training program for promising actors, playwrights, directors, and
managerial and technical personnel. It is that vision which has
been realized in the establishment of the Negro Ensemble Company..." (New Black Playwrights).
Sources. Black Drama, Ed. by William Brasmer and Dominick Consolo
(Merrill, 1970); Black Scenes, Ed. by Alice Childress (Doubleday,
1971); New Black Playwrights, Ed. by William Couch, Jr. (Avon,
1970).

Ward, Samuel Ringgold

WARD, SAMUEL RINGGOLD. 1817-c.1864. Anti-slavery Agent
Biographical-Personal. Parents escaped from slavery and brought him to N.Y. at age 3. Received some education.
Career-Professional. Sch. tchr.; Minister; Anti-slavery agent (co-worker with Gerrit Smith).
WRITING: The Autobiography of a Fugitive Slave (1855).
SIDELIGHTS: "In 1851, because of his inflammatory speechmaking at the rescue of the fugitive Jerry McHenry in Syracuse...he was forced to follow Jerry into Canada. He... continued to lecture in Canada and England... Frederick Douglass was the only Negro orator who was considered to be his superior. Douglass said of him: 'In depth of thought, fluency of speech, readiness of wit, logical exactness, and general intelligence, Samuel R. Ward has left no successor among the colored men amongst us...'" He died in Jamaica (Negro Caravan).
Sources. Historical Negro Biographies, Wilhelmena S. Robinson (ASNLH, 1967); Negro Caravan, Ed. by Sterling A. Brown et al. (Arno Pr. & N.Y. Times, 1969).

WARD, THEODORE. 1908- . Playwright, Teacher, Actor
Biographical-Personal. Born 1908 in Thibodeaux, La. Educ.: U. of Utah; U. of Wis.
Career-Professional. "In 1940 he organized The Negro Playwrights Company in Harlem, in association with Langston Hughes, Paul Robeson and Richard Wright. He also aided in forming The Associated Playwrights, The Midwest People's Theatre, and The South Side Center of the Performing Arts, Inc." (Black Scenes).
WRITINGS: Plays: Big White Fog (1938); Our Lan' (1941); John Brown; Throwback; Whole Hog or Nothing; Even the Dead Arise & Shout Hallelujah.
HONORS AND AWARDS: Zona Gale Fellow, U. of Wis.; Guggenheim Fellow, 1948.
SIDELIGHTS: Studied the short story and poetry under D. Louis Zucker at U. of Utah. "His first major play, Big White Fog, was produced by the Federal Theatre (1938) in Chicago" (Black Scenes).
"One of the organizers of the Negro Playwrights Company, he is better known as the author of two powerful, enthusiastically acclaimed dramas--Big White Fog...which critic Sterling Brown described as the most artistic production of the Federal Theater during the 1930's, and Our Lan'.

Washington, Booker Taliaferro

After winning a Theatre Guild award, <u>Our Lan'</u> was first produced off Broadway in the Henry St. Playhouse in 1946. A modified version was produced on Broadway at the Royale Theatre in the fall of the same year" (<u>Black Drama in America</u>).
Sources. <u>Black Drama in America</u>, Ed. by Darwin T. Turner (Fawcett, 1971); <u>Black Scenes</u>, Ed. by Alice Childress (Doubleday, 1971).

WASHINGTON, BOOKER TALIAFERRO. 1856?-1915.
Educator, Statesman

Biographical-Personal. Born April 1856? in Hale's Ford, Va. Was 7 when slavery was abolished. <u>Educ</u>.: Entered Hampton Inst., Va. in 1872, grad. 1876; Wayland Sem.; Wash., D.C. "...The differences in the early experiences of (Frederick Douglass and Booker T. Washington) undoubtedly account for the differences in attitudes and approaches in their methods of attacking racial problems during their years of national leadership. While Douglass learned the hard way, through trial and error and bitter ideological battles with whites and blacks alike, Washington had the 'luxury' of a formal education in close association with white educators at Hampton Institute who considered themselves missionaries in the fullest sense of the word..." (<u>Black Insights</u>).
Career-Professional. Returned to Malden, W. Va. to become community leader (after grad. from Hampton). Became an orator; considered the law. Recalled to Hampton for further study. Dir. experimental prog. for Indians. Recommended to head new educ. project at Tuskegee, Ala. (became Tuskegee Inst.); Founded 1881 with $2,000. After 34 years, when he died Nov. 14, 1915, he left a coll. with 2500 students, 111 buildings, and 3500 acres of land. Considered the outstanding leader of his race; had written 10 bks., had delivered hundreds of speeches.
WRITINGS: <u>Up From Slavery</u>, autobiog. (Doubleday, 1901). <u>The Future of the American Negro</u> (1899); <u>Tuskegee and Its People</u> (1905); <u>Life of Frederick Douglass</u> (1907); <u>The Story of the Negro</u> (1909); <u>My Larger Education</u> (1911); <u>The Negro in the South</u>, co-authored with W. E. B. DuBois (1907). <u>Selected Speeches of Booker T. Washington</u>, Ed. by E. Davidson Washington (Kraus repr. of 1932 ed., 1976).
HONORS AND AWARDS: Apptd. advis. to two Pres.; first Black to receive hon. degree from Harvard U.; first to dine at White House with a Pres.
SIDELIGHTS: "...<u>Up From Slavery</u>...has probably been reprinted more frequently than any other book by a Negro author and ranks in popularity with Benjamin Franklin's <u>Autobiography</u>" (<u>Cavalcade</u>).

Washington, Joseph R., Jr.

"During the years following the Reconstruction period in the
South, Booker T. Washington became a proponent of the belief that
black people should help themselves through education rather than
political demands" (<u>Afro-American Literature--Non Fiction</u>).
"He was reviled by some Negroes who accused him of 'Uncle Tom-
ism,' but he was venerated by an overwhelming majority of blacks
as a modern savior. But even the black militants who denigrated
him most for his sanction in his Atlanta Exposition speech of social separation between blacks and whites are not only embracing
his basic concept, but are demanding separation in areas that
Washington would never have sanctioned" (<u>Black Insights</u>).
Washington insisted "no man, black or white, from North or South,
shall drag me down so low as to make me hate him" (<u>Afro-American
Literature--Non Fiction</u>).
Sources. <u>Afro-American Literature--Non Fiction</u>, Ed. by William Adams
et al. (Houghton Mifflin, 1970); <u>Black Insights</u>, Ed. by Nick A.
Ford (Ginn, 1971); <u>Cavalcade</u>, Ed. by Arthur P. Davis & Saunders
Redding (Houghton Mifflin, 1971); <u>Negro Almanac</u>, Comp. by Harry A.
Ploski & Ernest Kaiser (Bellwether, 1971); <u>Books in Print</u>, Supple-
ment, 1975-76 (Bowker, 1976).

WASHINGTON, JOSEPH R., JR. 1930- . Minister,
Chaplain, Professor of Religion
Biographical-Personal. Born Oct. 30, 1930, in
    Iowa City, Iowa. Son of Joseph R. (minister)
    and Susie [Duncan] Washington. <u>Educ.</u>: B.A.
    (Sociol.), U. of Wis., 1952; B.D. (Soc. Eth-
    ics), Andover Newton Theol. Sem., 1957, Ad-
    vanced Study, 1957-58; Th.D. (Soc. Ethics),
    Boston U. Sch. of Theol., 1961. <u>Family</u>: m.
    Sophia May Holland, Feb. 13, 1952; son, Bryan
    Reed, son, David Eugene. <u>Mailing address</u>:
    1430 Grove Road, Charlottesville, Va. 22901.
Career-Professional. Military Serv.: U.S.
    Army, Corps of Military Police (1st Lt.),
    1952-54. Ordained to Bap. Church, 1957; Be-
    came Methodist Asst. Minister, Bap. Church,
Woburn, Mass., 1954-56; Minister, Congregational Church, West New-
field, Maine, 1956-57; First Bap. Church, Brookline, Mass., Minis-
ter to students, 1957-58; Assoc. Protestant chaplain, Boston,
Mass., 1958-61; Dean of Chapel & Asst. Prof. of Relig. & Philoso-
phy, Dillard U., New Orleans; Chaplain & Asst. Prof. of Relig. &
Philosophy, Dickinson Coll., Carlisle, Pa., 1963-?; Chmn. Afro-
Amer. Stud., U. of Va. (presently).
WRITINGS: <u>Black Religion: The Negro and Christianity in the
United States</u> (Beacon Pr., 1964); <u>The Politics of God</u> (Beacon Pr.,
1967); <u>Black and White Power Subreption</u> (Beacon Pr., 1969); <u>Mar-</u>

Washington, Leon H., Jr.

riage in Black and White (Beacon Pr., 1970); Black Sects and Cults
(Doubleday, 1972). In progress: Englishmen's Blacks. Articles:
Christian Advocate (Jan. 1962); Motive (Jan. 1963); Theology Today
(Apr. 1963); Religious Education (Mar.-Apr. 1963); Foundations
(Jan. 1964); Religious Education (Mar.-Apr. 1964); The Upper Room
Disciplines (1965); Bronze (Dec. 1965); Cross Currents (Spring
1966); Christian Century (Nov. 1972); New York Times (Mar. 15,
1973); Black World (July 1973); Theology Today (July 1973).
HONORS AND AWARDS: Iron Cross, U. of Wis. (contrib. to the life
of the universe); D.D. degree, U. of Vt., 1969; Danforth Assoc.
MEMBER: Nat'l. Assn. of Coll. & U. Chaplains (treasurer, 1963-);
Nat'l. Assn. of Biblical Instr.; Soc. for Scientific Study of
Relig.
SIDELIGHTS: Guest lectures: Bennett Coll., Bucknell U., Colgate
U., Fla. A & M U., Fla. State U., Adrian Coll., Allegheny Coll.,
Arkansas Coll., Baldwin-Wallace Coll., Bates Coll., Berea Coll.,
Birmingham Southern Coll., Central State Coll., Clark Coll.,
Claremont Colleges, U. of Denver, DePauw U., Duke U., Franklin &
Marshall Coll., Grinnell Coll., Guilford Coll., Hollins Coll.,
Howard U., Kalamazoo Coll., Kan. State U., U. of Kan., U. of Mich.,
U. of Montana, Mt. Holyoke Coll., U. of Nebraska, U. of Pittsburgh,
U. of Ore. & Syracuse U. (Author).
Sources. Author inform.; Contemporary Authors, Vols. 11-12, Ed. by
James M. Ethridge & Barbara Kopala (Gale Res., 1965).

WASHINGTON, LEON H., JR. 1907-1974. Newspaper
Publisher
Biographical-Personal. Born April 15, 1907, in
Kan. City, Kan. Son of Leon and Blanche
Washington. Educ.: Sumner High Sch.; Wash-
burn Coll., Topeka, Kan. Family: m. Ruth
Washington. Died June 17, 1974.
Career-Professional. Moved to L.A. in 1930 and
worked with California News & California
Eagle. Started a throwaway weekly, Shoppers
News; later founded the Los Angeles Sentinel
(1934).
SIDELIGHTS: "Sentinel became known as the
'voice' of Black people west of the Rockies.
For the past forty-one years the Los Angeles
Sentinel has constantly and consistently ar-
ticulated the needs, hopes and aspirations of the Los Angeles
Black community...beginning in 1934 with the movement launched by
Colonel Washington with the slogan: 'Don't Spend Your Money Where
You Can't Work. That campaign, along with many similar activities,
put his paper in the forefront of the civil rights movement for

Weaver, Robert Clifton

equality in employment, education, housing and every phase of
American life for all minorities" (Obituary).
Source. Obituary, June 1974.

WEAVER, ROBERT CLIFTON. 1907- . Economist,
Former Secretary HUD, Professor of Urban Affairs
Biographical-Personal. Born Dec. 29, 1907, in
Wash., D.C. Son of Mortimer G. and Florence
E. [Freeman] Weaver. Educ.: B.S. (cum
laude), 1929, M.A., 1931, Ph.D., 1934, Har-
vard U. Family: m. Dr. Ella Haith, July 19,
1935; son, Robert. Mailing address: Dept.
of Urban Affairs, Hunter Coll., 790 Madison
Ave., N.Y., N.Y. 10021.
Career-Professional. Lectr., Tchrs. Coll., Co-
lumbia U., summer 1947; Vis. Prof., Sch. of
Educ., N.Y.U., 1947-51; Dir., Opportunity
Fellow., John Hay Whitney Found., 1949-54;
Deputy Commissioner of Housing, N.Y. State,
1954-55; State Rent Administrator, N.Y.
State, 1955-59; Cons., Ford Found., 1959-60; V. Chmn., N.Y.C.
Housing & Redevelopment Bd., 1960-61; Administrator, U.S. Housing
& Home Finance Agency, 1961-66; Secy., Dept. of Housing & Urban
Develop., 1966-68; Pres., Baruch Coll., City U. of N.Y., 1969-70;
Prof. of Econ., City U. of N.Y., 1970-71; Distinguished Prof. of
Urban Affairs, Hunter Coll., 1971- .
WRITINGS: Negro Labor: A National Problem (Harcourt, 1946; Ken-
nikat, 1969); The Negro Ghetto (Harcourt, 1948; Russell, 1967);
The Urban Complex (Doubleday, 1964; Anchor, 1966; Spanish:
Bibliografica Omeba, Buenos Aires, 1969); Dilemmas of Urban
America (Harvard U. Pr., 1965; Atheneum, 1967; Portuguese:
Distribuidora Record, Rio de Janeiro, 1967; Spanish: Pax-Mexico,
Mexico City, 1972). Male Negro Skilled Workers in the United
States, 1930-36, monograph (Govt. Print. Off., 1939). Pams.:
Race Relations in Chicago (Mayor's Com. on Race Relat., 1944);
Community Relations Manual (Amer. Counc. on Race Relat., 1945);
Manual for Official Committees (Amer. Counc. on Race Relat.,
1945); Hemmed In (Amer. Counc. on Race Relat., 1945); The Future
of the American City (Ohio State U., 1962); Cities in Crisis
(Urban Amer., 1966); The Urban University (State Coll., Buffalo,
1969) Commencement address. Articles: "Since 1933, I have pub-
lished over 130 articles" (Author). Articles included in: Annals
of American Academy of Political & Social Science; International
Labor Review; Journal of Land & Public Utility Economics; Journal
of Political Economy; Proceedings of Canadian Council on Urban &
Regional Research; Quarterly Journal of Economics; Social Forces;
Franklin Lectures; Opportunity; Journal of Negro Education;

Welburn, Ronald Garfield

Phylon; Journal of Housing; Discrimination & National Welfare;
Journal of Negro History; Journal of Educational Sociology; Les
Etudes Americaines; Inventory of Research in Racial & Cultural
Relations; Journal of Intergroup Relations; Construction Review;
Traffic Quarterly; Urban Condition; Vital Speeches of the Day;
Symposium on Housing & Home Finance, New York Law Forum; Annual
Proceedings of U.S. Conference of Mayors; UCLA Law Review; Poverty
in America; Town & County Planning; Essays in Urban Economics;
Urban Research & Policy Planning; Current History; Encyclopaedia
Britannica; Urbanization of Developing Countries.
HONORS AND AWARDS: Degrees: LL.D., Litt.D., D.H.L., D.S.S.,
D.P.A., Honorary degrees from 39 colleges and 7 universities, in-
cluding Amherst, Boston Coll, Columbia, Elmira Coll., Howard,
Harvard, Morehouse, Rutgers, U. of Ill., U. of Mich. & U. of Pa.
Awards: Spingarn Medal, 1962; Albert Einstein Commemorative Award,
1968; Russwurm Award, 1963.
MEMBER: Fellow, Amer. Acad. of Arts & Sci.; Advis. Bd., Cooper-
Hewitt Mus. of Decorative Arts & Design; Smithsonian Inst.; Comp-
troller General's Cons. Panel; Advis. Counc., Assn. for Integra-
tion of Management; Pres., Nat'l. Com. Against Discrimination in
Housing; Benjamin Franklin Fellow of Royal Soc. for Encouragement
of Arts, Manufacturing & Commerce; Bd. of Trus., Mt. Sinai Hos-
pital & Sch. of Medicine; Com. on Urban Affairs of Amer. Counc. on
Educ.; Bd. of Trus., Metropolitan Applied Res. Center; Nat'l. Acad.
of Public Admin.; Bd. of Dir., Nat'l. Housing Conf.; CUNY, Faculty
Senate Task Force on Educ. Mission of CUNY; Harvard Grad. Soc.
Counc.; Bd. of Dir., Com. for Econ. Develop. & mem. Res. Policy
Com.; Freedom House; Bowery Savings Bank; Metropolitan Life Ins.
Co.; Mutual Real Estate Investment Trust.
SIDELIGHTS: Dr. Weaver's wife, Dr. Ella Weaver, has been Asst.
Prof. of Speech, at Brooklyn Coll. He "served as member of the
'Black Cabinet' during Roosevelt's administration. It concerned
itself with recruiting Negro professionals for federal service and
was instrumental in breaking down long-established patterns of
segregation. The group, with Mary McLeod Bethune as titular head,
consisted of Ralph Bunche, William Hastie, James C. Evans and
others. Weaver was considered the architect of the group and the
most influential" (Negroes in Public Affairs and Government).
Sources. Author inform.; Negro Handbook, Comp by Eds. of Ebony
(Johnson Pub., 1966); Negroes in Public Affairs and Government,
Ed. by Walter Christmas (Educ. Her., 1966); Pub. inform.

WELBURN, RONALD GARFIELD. 1944- . Poet, Musician, Critic, Teacher,
Editor
Biographical-Personal. Born April 30, 1944, in Bryn Mawr, Pa. Son
of Howard (stepfather) and Jessie Watson. Educ.: B.A., Lincoln
U. (Pa.), 1968; M.A., U. of Ariz., 1970. Family: m. Eileen Wel-

Welburn, Ronald Garfield

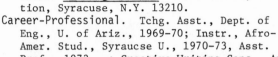

burn. <u>Mailing address</u>: P.O. Box 51, U. Station, Syracuse, N.Y. 13210.
Career-Professional. Tchg. Asst., Dept. of Eng., U. of Ariz., 1969-70; Instr., Afro-Amer. Stud., Syraucse U., 1970-73, Asst. Prof., 1973- ; Creative Writing Cons., Auburn Correctional Facility, Auburn, N.Y., 1972; Adjunct Faculty, Dept. of Eng., Onondaga Community Coll., Syracuse, 1972-73; Advis. Ed., <u>Open Workshop</u>, Ed. by Gil Scott-Heron, 1967-68; Assoc. Ed., <u>Obsidian: Black Literature in Review</u>, 1974; Ed.-in-Chief, <u>Dues: An Annual of New Earth Writing</u> (in progress).
WRITINGS: <u>Peripheries: Selected Poems, 1966-68</u>, Vol. I (Greenfield, 1972). Short stories: "The Prophet's Child," <u>Axiom</u> (1968); "Mythlost," <u>The Tongue</u> (1970); "The Nightsong of Dashieki Henry," <u>Intro</u>, no. 3 (1970); "The Green Lady," "And I'll Show You My Ring," & "The Crow's Nest," <u>Greenfield Review</u> (Jan. 1971); "Moon Woman," "Sunday's Child," <u>Essence</u> (Oct. 1971); "Off Cheyney Heights," <u>Hoodoo</u> (May 1973); "The Joy," <u>Greenfield Review</u> (Oct. 1973); "Albatross Anew," <u>Center</u> (Feb. 1974). In progress: <u>Along the Estabon Way: Poems</u> (Emerson Hall); <u>Moods, Bright and Indigo: Poems</u> (Carpet Bag); <u>Wordless</u>; <u>Selected Poems</u>; <u>Brownup, and Other Poems</u>; <u>Devon Hill: Tales of A Hoodoo-Gothic</u>; <u>New Spirituals: Collected Music Commentary, 1965-74</u>; <u>Thumbin' A Ride: Selected Poems, 1964-1967</u>; A study of jazz/black music in internat. perspective. Anthol.: <u>New Black Voices</u>; <u>Give Birth to Brightness</u>; <u>Bim</u>; <u>The Ash Tree</u>; <u>Works</u>; <u>You Better Believe It</u>; <u>Poetry of Black America</u>; etc. Essays: <u>Dining Out</u>, <u>Levels</u>, <u>Mankind</u>, <u>The Black Aesthetic</u>, <u>Liberator</u>, <u>Black Review</u>, <u>Syracuse New Times</u>.
HONORS AND AWARDS: Lincoln U.: Journalism Key, 1966-67; Edward S. Silvera Award for Poetry, 1967 & 1968; William Eichelberger Award for Prose, 1967; Amy T. Lockett Memorial Prize, Outstanding Serv. to Campus & Community, 1968; Class of 1899 Prize for Eng. Stud., 1968. S. Grad. Study Fellow, 1968-70.
MEMBER: Afro-Amer. Music Opportunities Assn., Inc.
SIDELIGHTS: Workshops in music journalism--Swarthmore Coll., Lincoln U.; Taped commentaries for radio WCOJ, Coatesville, Pa.: 2 prog. on jazz avant-garde, Spring 1966; Discussion co-ord.: "Student Action & Apathy" Sept. 1966; Jazz Concerts: Lincoln Contemporary unit (as musical dir.), 1966-68; Summer Literati, 1967, 1968 (for LIFT & Upward Bound Prog.); Ron Welburn Musical Ensemble (with Syracuse U. & local musicians), DuBois-Malcolm X Memorial Concert, Feb. 1971; A Symposium on Black Music, Syracuse U., 24-25 Mar., 1973. Has written "My foremost intentions in life are

1. explore the aesthetic value of human feelings; 2. advance the
stature of Afro-American culture through literature and music"
(New Black Voices).
Sources. Author inform.; New Black Voices, Ed. by Abraham Chapman
(New Amer. Lib., 1972); Poetry of Black America, Ed. by Arnold
Adoff (Harper & Row, 1973).

WELLS (BARNETT), IDA BELL. 1862-1931. Civil
Rights Activist, Editor, Teacher, Writer
Biographical-Personal. Born July 16, 1862, in
Holly Springs, Miss. D. of James and Eliza-
beth [Warrenton] Wells. Educ.: Rust Coll.,
Miss.; Fisk U. (Summer, 1884-1891). Family:
m. Ferdinand Lee Barnett (attorney), 1895;
son, Charles A., son, Herman K., d. Ida B.
Wells-Barnett, Jr., d. Alfreda M. Barnett
Duster. Died March 25, 1931.
Career-Professional. Writer, The Living War
(newspaper); Part-owner, ed., Memphis Free
Speech; Assoc. (to T. Thomas Fortune), New
York Age; Nat'l. Equal Rights League (with
William Monroe Trotter); Civic & polit. lead-
er, Chgo.
WRITINGS: Crusade for Justice: The Autobiography of Ida B. Wells,
Ed. Alfreda M. B. Duster (U. of Chgo. Pr., 1970); On Lynchings:
Southern Horrors (1892); A Red Record (1895); Mob Rule in New
Orleans (1900), preface by August Meier (Arno Pr. & N.Y. Times,
1969)--selected from The American Negro: His History and Litera-
ture, William Loren Katz, Gen. Ed. (Pam.) "Lynch Law in All Its
Phases," in Our Day (May 1893); The Reason Why the Colored American is not in the World's Columbian Exposition (printed & distributed by Ida B. Wells, Aug. 30, 1893, Chgo., Ill.). Articles:
"Lynch Law in America," Arena (Jan. 1900); "Lynching and the Excuse for It," Independent (May 16, 1901); "Our Country's Lynching
Record," Survey (Feb. 1, 1913); "How Enfranchisement Stops Lynching," Original Rights Magazine (June 1910).
HONORS AND AWARDS: "The first Federal Housing Project in Chicago
was named The Ida B. Wells Homes in 1940. There are several clubs
named for her throughout the country" (Alfreda B. Duster, daughter).
Ida B. Wells's home from 1918-1930, at 3624 S. Martin Luther King
Jr. Dr., Chgo., Ill. 60653 is soon to be named an historical site.
SIDELIGHTS: Miss Wells attended Rust Coll., a Freedmen school of
which her father (a literate carpenter) was a trustee. "In 1892,
three Negro businessmen were horribly lynched in Memphis and Ida B.
Wells charged, in the columns of Free Speech, that the murders had
been instigated and planned by the white business community. She
urged Blacks not to support these business establishments, but to

Wesley, Charles H.

migrate to new Oklahoma territory. Business suffered and they
migrated by the scores. Fortunately she had left town, but her
presses and equipment and building were destroyed by fire. She
was threatened with execution, so she could not return" (Negro
Handbook).
Sources. Inform. from author's daughter; Negro Handbook, Comp. by
Eds. of Ebony (Johnson Pub., 1966).

WESLEY, CHARLES H. 1891- . College President,
Historian
Biographical-Personal. Born Dec. 2, 1891, in
Louisville, Ky. Educ.: B.A., Fisk U., 1911;
M.A., Yale U., 1913; Guild Internationale,
Paris, France, 1914; Howard U. Law Sch.,
1915-16; Ph.D., Harvard U., 1925. Family:
m. Louise Johnson, Nov. 25, 1915; d. Louise
Johnson, d. Charlotte Harris. Mailing ad-
dress: c/o ASNLH, 1538 Ninth St., N.W.,
Wash., D.C. 20001.
Career-Professional. Instr., Howard U., 1914-18,
Asst. Prof., 1918-19, Assoc. Prof., 1919-20,
Prof. of Hist. & Head, Dept., 1921-42, Acting
Dean, Coll. of Liberal Arts, 1937-38, Dean of
Grad. Sch., 1938-42; Pres., Wilberforce U.,
1942-47 (became Central State U., Wilberforce, Ohio), 1942-?
Pastor & presiding elder, AME Church, 1918-37. Executive Dir.,
ASNLH, to present.
WRITINGS: Negro Labor in the United States, 1850-1925 (Russell &
Russell, 1927); The History of Alpha Phi Alpha: a Development in
Negro College Life (1929, rev. 1950); Richard Allen, Apostle of
Freedom (Assoc., 1935); The Collapse of the Confederacy (Russell,
1937, reissued, 1968); The Negro in the Americas (1940); A Manual
of Research and Thesis Writing for Graduate Students (1941); Ohio
Negroes in the Civil War (Ohio State U. Pr., 1962). Many articles
& monographs on phases of Black history.
HONORS AND AWARDS: Hon. degrees: Wilberforce U., D.D., 1928;
LL.D.: Allen U., 1932, Va. State Coll., 1943, Morris Brown U.,
1944, Paul Quin Coll., Campbell Coll., 1946; Western U., Litt.D.,
1946; Morgan State Coll., Ped.D., 1961. Scholarships: Yale U.,
1913, Harvard U., 1920-21. Guggenheim Fellow, 1930-31.
MEMBER: Army & Navy Dept. Com., Nat'l. Counc. of YMCA; Com. on
Negro-White Relat., YMCA, & mem. counc. of Ohio & W. Va.
Sources. Negro Almanac, Comp. by Harry A. Ploski & Roscoe C. Brown
(Bellwether, 1967); Negro Caravan, Ed. by Sterling Brown & Others
(Arno Pr., & N.Y. Times, 1969); Negro Handbook, Comp. by Eds. of
Ebony (Johnson Pub., 1966); Who's Who in Colored America, Ed. by
Christian E. Burckel Assoc., 7th ed., 1950.

WESLEY, RICHARD ERROL. 1945– . Playwright, Editor
Biographical-Personal. Born July 11, 1945, in Newark, N.J. Son of
George Richard and Gertrude Wesley. Educ.: B.F.A., Howard U.,
1967. Family: m. Valerie Wesley; d. Thembi Amala. Mailing ad-
dress: Nasaba Artists, Inc., Suite 910, 1860 Broadway, N.Y.,
N.Y. 10018.
Career-Professional. Passenger agent, United Air Lines, 1967–1969;
Managing ed., Black Theatre. Tchr., Wesleyan U., Conn. & Manhat-
tanville Coll., Purchase, N.Y.
WRITINGS: Plays: Put My Dignity on 307, presentation on WRC–TV's
"Operation Awareness" (May 1967); The Streetcorner, prod. at Black
Arts/W. Seattle, Wash. (1970); Headline News, Black Theatre Work-
shop, Harlem (1970); Knock, Knock, Who Dat, Theatre Black, U. of
the Streets, N.Y.C. (1970); Getting It Together, Theatre Black,
Bed-Sty Theatre, Brooklyn (1971); Black Terror, Howard U., Wash.
(1971); The Sirens; The Mighty Gents; The Past Is The Past; Goin'
Thru Changes. Movies: Uptown Saturday Night; The Ernie Davis
Story.
HONORS AND AWARDS: Spec. playwriting, Samuel French Pub. Co.,
1965; Drama Desk Award for Outstanding Playwriting, 1972.
MEMBER: New Lafayette Theatre in Harlem.
Source. Author inform.

WEST, DOROTHY. Editor, Writer
Biographical-Personal. Born in Boston, Mass. Educ.: Boston Latin
Sch.; Boston U. Lived for a time on Martha's Vineyard.
Career-Professional. In the 1930's, she was editor of Challenge and
New Challenge, two periodicals devoted to Black life and art. She
contributed short stories regularly to a news syndicate, while
completing her first full-length novel during the 1940's. During
Depression years in Harlem, she worked as relief investigator, and
for a time on the Federal Writers Project.
WRITINGS: The Living Is Easy, novel (Houghton Mifflin, 1948).
Contrib.: Boston Post, Opportunity & Saturday Evening Quill (in
1930's).
Sources. The Living Is Easy, Dorothy West (Houghton Mifflin, 1948);
Negro Novel in America, Robert A. Bone (Yale U. Pr., 1958); Soon,
One Morning, Ed. by Herbert Hill (Knopf, 1963).

WHARTON, CLIFTON REGINALD, JR. 1926– . University President,
Economist, Foreign Policy Specialist
Biographical-Personal. Born Sept. 13, 1926, in Boston, Mass. Son of
Clifton Reginald (America's 1st Black career diplomat & ambassa-
dor) and Harriette [Banks] Wharton. Educ.: Boston Latin Sch.;
B.A. (cum laude), Harvard U., 1947; M.A. (Internat. stud.), Johns
Hopkins Sch. of Advanced Internat. Stud., 1948; M.A. (Econ.),
1956, Ph.D. (Econ.), U. of Chgo., 1958. Family: m. Dolores Dun-

Wharton, Clifton Reginald, Jr.

can (writer); son, Clifton R. III, son, Bruce D. Mailing address: President's Office, Mich. State U., E. Lansing, Mich. 48823. Career-Professional. Amer. Internat. Assn. for Econ. & Soc. Develop., N.Y., Head of Reports & Analysis Dept., 1948-53; Vis. Prof., U. of Malaya, 1958-64, & Stanford U., 1964-65; Agricultural Develop. Counc., N.Y.; Counc. Assoc. for Malaysia, Thailand, Vietnam, & Cambodia, 1964-66, Act. Dir., 1966-67, V.-pres., 1967-70; Mich. State U., E. Lansing, Pres. & Prof. of Econ., 1970- . WRITINGS: Books and monographs: Subsistence Agriculture and Economic Development, Ed. (Aldine, 1969); Research on Agricultural Development in Southeast Asia (1965); U.S. Graduate Training of Asian Agricultural Economists (1959). Over 40 articles in professional journals.
HONORS AND AWARDS: Named Boston Latin Sch. "Man of the Year," 1970; Amistad Award from Amer. Missionary Assn. 1970; D. Laws: U. of Mich., Johns Hopkins U. & Wayne State U., 1970; Dr. of Pub. Serv., Central Mich. U., 1970; Alumni Prof. Achievement Award, U. of Chgo., 1971; D.H.L., Oakland U., 1971.
MEMBER: Trus. or Dir.: Asia Soc., 1967- ; Equitable Life Assurance Soc., 1969- ; Overseas Develop. counc., 1969- ; Carnegie Found. for Advancement of Tchg., 1970; Ford Motor Co., 1973- ; Burroughs Corp., 1973- ; Agricultural Develop. Counc., 1973- . (Former Dir. or Trus.) African-Amer. Inst., 1968-69; Amer. Agricultural Econ. Assn., 1968-70; Agri-bus. counc., 1967-69; Educ. Development Center, 1967-69; Franklin Bks. Prog., 1968-69; Mus. of Modern Art, 1970-74; Public Broadcasting Serv., 1970-73; Bd. on Sci. & Technology for Internat. Develop., Nat'l. Acad. of Sci., 1968-69; Res. Advis. Bd., Com for Econ. Develop., 1969. (Public Serv.) Pres. Mission to Latin America, 1969; UN Assn. Panel on World Population, 1968-69; Governor's Econ. Expansion Counc. (Mich.), 1972- ; Com. on U.S. Latin Amer. Relat., 1974- ; Food Panel, Office of Technological Assessment, U.S. Congress (Chmn.), 1974- .
SIDELIGHTS: The son of a career diplomat, Dr. Wharton spent six years of his childhood in the Canary Islands, Spain, where he learned fluent Spanish (Inform. Serv.).
Sources. Contemporary Authors, Vols. 41-44, Ed. by Clare D. Kinsman (Gale Res., 1974); Inform. Serv., Mich. State U., 1974.

WHEATLEY, PHILLIS. 1753-1784. Poet

Biographical-Personal. Born 1753 in Senegal, W. Africa. Kidnapped on slave ship to Boston, c.1761. Personal servant to wife of John Wheatley, who educated her liberally. Married John Peters (free Black), 1778; 3 children. Died 1784.

Career-Professional.

WRITINGS: First poem, "A Poem, by Phillis, A Negro Girl in Boston, on the Death of the Reverend George Whitefield, 1770;" only book, Poems on Various Subjects, Religious and Moral (1773); forty-six known poems left by Miss Wheatley; eighteen of which were elegies.

SIDELIGHTS: Exposed to typical New Eng. educ. after alertness noted; able to read most difficult parts of classics and Bible, within 16 months of being in the country. High point of life, in 1773 when she received freedom, and was sent to London for health. Met distinguished Londoners, had book published. Returned to Boston because of ill-health of Mrs. Wheatley. Fortunes declined, her mentors died, she married, bore children; reduced to common domestic work and early death at age 31, when frail health completely gave way (Early Negro American Writers).

Sources. Black American Literature--Poetry, Ed. by Darwin T. Turner (Merrill, 1969); Cavalcade, Ed. by Arthur P. Davis & Saunders Redding (Houghton Mifflin, 1971); Early Black American Poets, Ed. by William H. Robinson, Jr. (Wm. C. Brown, 1969); Early Negro American Writers, Benjamin Brawley (U. of N.C. Pr., 1935); Poetry of the Negro, 1746-1949, Ed. by Langston Hughes & Arna Bontemps (Doubleday, 1949); Who Was Who in America. Historical Vol., 1607-1896. Rev. ed. (Marquis, 1967).

WHITE, WALTER FRANCIS. 1893-1955. Novelist, Essayist, Secretary, NAACP

Biographical-Personal. Born July 1, 1893, in Atlanta, Ga. Son of George W. (postman) and Madeline [Harrison] White. Educ.: B.A., Atlanta U., 1916; Coll. of City of N.Y.; LL.D. (hon.), Howard U., 1939. Family: m. Leah Gladys Powell of Ithaca, N.Y.; d. Jane, son, Walter Carl Darrow. Died 1955.

Career-Professional. Atlanta Life Insurance Co.; Asst. Executive Secy., (to James Weldon Johnson), NAACP; Secy., NAACP, 1934-1955.

WRITINGS: Novels: Fire in the Flint (Knopf, 1924); Flight (1926). Essays: Rope and Faggot: A Biography of Judge Lynch (1929); A

Whitman, Albery Allison

Rising Wind (Doubleday, 1945); A Man Called White (Viking, 1948);
How Far the Promised Land? (Viking, 1955). Contrib. to: Bookman,
Century, Harper's, American Mercury, The Crisis, Forum, The Na-
tion, New Republic, & Survey Graphic.
HONORS AND AWARDS: Guggenheim Fellow, 1927, 1928; Spingarn Medal,
1937; Delegate, Second Pan-African Congress, 1921.
MEMBER: Apptd. Advis. Counc. for Gov't. of Virgin Islands, 1934.
Mem. P.E.N.; Bd., N.Y. State Training Sch. for Boys; Chmn., Harlem
low-cost housing project, 1935; Mem., Governor's Com. on the Con-
stitutional Convention of N.Y., 1938.
SIDELIGHTS: "The NAACP under White's direction fought diligently
and forcefully for equality in civil rights, focusing attention on
the evils and horrors of lynchings and pushing relentlessly for an
end to discrimination and segregation in travel and education....
   The famous 1954 decision of the Supreme Court against segregated
schools was one of the goals that Walter White set out to achieve"
(Historical Negro Biographies).
Sources. Current Biography, 1942, Ed. by Maxine Block (H. W. Wilson,
1942); Historical Negro Biographies, Ed. by Wilhelmena S. Robinson
(ASNLH, 1967); Negro Caravan, Ed. by Sterling A. Brown et al.(Arno
Pr. & N.Y. Times, 1969); The Negro Genius, Benjamin Brawley (Dodd,
Mead, 1937).

WHITMAN, ALBERY ALLISON. 1851-1901. Poet
Biographical-Personal. Born May 30, 1851, near Munfordsville, Hart
Co., Ky. Educ.: Intermittent; Wilberforce U., Ohio. Died 1902.
Career-Professional. Poet-Evangelist, AME circuit, Ohio and Kan.;
Sch. tchr.
WRITINGS: Poetry: Essays on the Ten Plaques and Other Miscel-
laneous Poems (before 1873); Leelah Misled (Elizabethtown, Ky.,
1873); Not a Man and Yet a Man, with Miscellaneous Poems (Eliza-
bethtown, 1877); Twasinta's Seminoles, or Rape of Florida (St.
Louis, 1885); Drifted Leaves (St. Louis); The World's Fair Poem:
The Freedmen's Triumphant Song; An Idyl of the South, An Epic Poem
in Two Parts (New York, 1901).
SIDELIGHTS: Whitman was one of the many beneficiaries of Bishop
Daniel Payne. Drifted Leaves was dedicated to Confederate veterans and "received wide circulation in the press throughout the
country" (Early Black American Poets).
Sources. Early Black American Poets, Ed. by William H. Robinson, Jr.
(Wm. C. Brown, 1969); Negro Caravan, Ed. by Sterling A. Brown et
al. (Arno Pr. & N.Y. Times, 1969).

WIDEMAN, JOHN E. 1941- . Novelist, Teacher
Biographical-Personal. Born in 1941. Educ.: B.Phil., New Coll.,
Oxford U., 1966.

Williams, Ethel Langley

Career-Professional. Assoc. Prof. in Eng. &
Dir. of Afro-Amer. Stud. Prog., U. of Pa.,
1967- .
WRITINGS: Novels: A Glance Away (Harcourt,
1967); Hurry Home (Harcourt, 1970); The
Lynchers (Harcourt, 1973). Contrib. to mags.
& jls.
HONORS AND AWARDS: Rhodes Scholar, New
Coll., Oxford, 1963-66.
Source. Interviews with Black Writers, Ed. by
John O'Brien (Liveright, 1973).

WILLIAMS, CHANCELLOR. Historian
Career-Professional. Tchr., Howard U.
WRITINGS: The Destruction of Black Civilization: Great Issues of
a Race from 4500 B.C. to 2000 A.D. (Third World Pr., rev. ed.,
Chicago, 1974); The Raven, novel (Third World Pr.).
Source. The Destruction of Black Civilization,...rev. ed., Chancel-
lor Williams (Third World Pr., 1974).

WILLIAMS, ETHEL LANGLEY. 1909- . Librarian
Biographical-Personal. Born July 13, 1909, in Baltimore, Md. Educ.:
B.A. (Hist.), Howard U., 1930; B.S., Columbia U., 1933; M.L.S.,
1950 (Lib. Sci.); Howard U., 1947-50. Family: m. Louis J. Wil-
liams; d. Carole Juanita Jones. Mailing address: 1925 Primrose
Rd., N.W., Wash., D.C. 20012.
Career-Professional. Process filer & order searcher, Lib. of Con-
gress, 1936-40; Supv., at Howard U: (WPA) Moorland-Spingarn
Collec., 1939, Ref. Librn., Cataloger, 1941-47, Sch. of Relig.
Lib., 1946 to present.
WRITINGS: Biographical Directory of Negro Ministers, Ed. (Scare-
crow, 1965; 1970; 1974); Afro-American Religious Studies. A Comprehensive Bibliography with Locations in American Libraries,
Co-ed. (Scarecrow, 1970; 1974); A Catalogue of Books in the Moor-
land Foundation, Co-comp., mimeographed (1939); Handbook of Instruction in the Use of the School of Religion Library, mimeo-
graphed (1955; 1968); "Current Literature on Negro Education,
Books, Pamphlets and Monographs, A Bibliography," Journal of Negro
Education, Comp. (1945-46); Biographical Directory of Negro Ministers, 3rd ed. (G. K. Hall, Ser. Seventy, 1975).
MEMBER: NAACP; Amer. Theol. Assn.; D.C. Lib. Assn.; Urban League.
Sources. Author inform.; Books in Print, Supplement, 1975-76 (Bowker,
1976).

Williams, George Washington

WILLIAMS, GEORGE WASHINGTON. 1849-1891.
Historian, Lawyer, Minister
Biographical-Personal. Born 1849 in Bedford
    Springs, Pa. Father was of Negro and Welsh
    descent and mother was of Negro and German
    descent. Enlisted in Union Army at age 14,
    serving through the War and becoming a lieu-
    tenant colonel in Mexican Army. Educ.: How-
    ard U., Newton Theol. Sem., grad. 1874; Cin.
    Law Sch. Died in Blackpool, Eng.
Career-Professional. Ed.: The Commoner (Wash.,
    D.C.) and Southwestern Review (Cin.); Passed
    Ohio bar; Practiced law; Admitted to practice
    before Ohio Supreme Court; Served in Ohio
    State Legis., 1879 Minister to Haiti, 1885;
    Pastor, Boston & Cin. Developed interest in
Congo & entered serv. of Belgian govt. there.
WRITINGS: The History of the Negro Race in America from 1619 to
1880 (1883); A History of the Negro Troops in the War of the Re-
bellion (Harper & Row, 1888).
SIDELIGHTS: "His histories were recognized in their day as the
most authoritative accounts of the Negro that had appeared" (Negro Caravan).
Sources. Cavalcade, Ed. by Arthur P. Davis & Saunders Redding
    (Houghton Mifflin, 1971); Historical Negro Biographies, Wilhelmena
    S. Robinson (ASNLH, 1967); Negro Caravan, Ed. by Sterling A. Brown
    et al. (Arno Pr. & N.Y. Times, 1969); Negro Genius, Benjamin
    Brawley (Dodd, Mead, 1937).

WILLIAMS, JOHN ALFRED. 1925- . Novelist,
    Essayist, Editor
Biographical-Personal. Born 1925 in Jackson,
    Miss. Son of John Henry Williams and Ola
    Williams Page. Educ.: Syracuse, N.Y. pub-
    lic schs.; B.A., Syracuse U., Grad. Sch.,
    1951. Family: m. Lorrain Isaac; son, Greg-
    ory, son, Dennis (1st m.), son, Adam. Mail-
    ing address: 35 W. 92nd St., N.Y., N.Y.
    10025.
Career-Professional. Ed. & Pub., Negro Market
    Newsletter, 1956-57; Asst. to pub., Abelard
    Schuman, 1957-58; Co-ed., Amistad (Vintage),
    1969-71; Ed. Bd., Audience Magazine, 1970-72;
    Contrib. Ed., American Journal, 1972-73.
    Lectr., Black Lit., Coll. of the Virgin Is-
lands, 1968; Lectr., Creative Writing, City Coll. of N.Y., 1968-
1969; Regents Lectr., U. of Cal., Santa Barbara, Nov. 1972; Guest

Williams, Lance A.

Tchr., Writing, Sarah Lawrence Coll., Bronxville, N.Y., 1972–73; Distinguished Prof. of Eng., CUNY, LaGuardia Coll., 1973–75.
WRITINGS: Novels: The Angry Ones (Ace, 1960; Pocket Bks., 1970); Night Song (Farrar, Straus, 1961; Pocket Bks., 1970); Sissie (Farrar, Straus, 1963; Doubleday, 1969); The Man Who Cried I Am (Little, Brown, 1967; New Amer. Lib., 1968); Sons of Darkness, Sons of Light (Little, Brown, 1969; Pocket Bks., 1970); Captain Blackman (Doubleday, 1972; Pocket Bks., 1974); Mothersill and the Foxes (Doubleday, 1975). Nonfiction: Africa, Her History, Lands and People (Cooper Sq., 1963); The Protectors (Farrar, Straus, 1964); This Is My Country Too (New Amer. Lib./World, 1965; New Amer. Lib., 1966); The Most Native of Sons (Doubleday, 1970); The King God Didn't Save (Coward-McCann, 1970; Pocket Bks., 1971); Flashbacks (Doubleday, 1973, Doubleday, Anchor, 1974). Anthol. ed.: The Angry Black (Lancer, 1962); Beyond the Angry Black (Cooper Sq., 1967; New Amer. Lib., 1970). Anthol. contrib.: Different Drummers; An Introduction to Poetry; Racisim; Cavalcade; The Immigrant Experience; Black Insights; 19 Necromancers from Now; Amistad I & II; Brothers and Sisters; The New Lively Rhetoric; A Native Sons Reader; Black Identity; The Black Novelist; Black Literature in America; New Black Poetry; Now Reader; Nat Turner: 10 Black Writers Respond; Dark Symphony; How We Live; 34 Schwartze Lieb; Black on Black. Period: Yardbird; Essence; Vista; Les Nouveaux; Cahiers; Negro Digest; Swank.
HONORS AND AWARDS: Nat'l. Inst. of Arts & Letters, 1962; Centennial Medal for Outstanding Achievement, Syracuse U., 1970.
MEMBER: Counc., Authors Guild; Black Acad. of Arts & Letters; Rabinowitz Found.; N.Y. State Counc. on the Arts.
SIDELIGHTS: Countries visited: Belgium, Cameroun, Canada, Caribbean, Congo Brazzaville, Cyprus, Denmark, Egypt, Ethiopia, France, Germany, Ghana, Great Brit., Greece, Israel, Italy, Mexico, Netherlands, Nigeria, Portugal, Senegal, Spain, Sudan, Sweden, Zaire. Has been Co-producer, Narrator & Writer for Nat'l. TV; Foreign Corresp. for Newsweek, WOV, New York; Ebony-Jet Corresp., Europe; Amer. Com. on Africa, Dir. of Inform. (Author).
Sources. Author inform.; Black Insights, Ed. by Nick A. Ford (Ginn, 1971); Cavalcade, Ed. by Arthur P. Davis & Saunders Redding (Houghton Mifflin, 1971); Dark Symphony, Ed. by James A. Emanuel & Theodore L. Gross (Free Pr., 1968); Negro Almanac, Comp. by Harry A. Ploski & Roscoe C. Brown (Bellwether, 1967).

WILLIAMS, LANCE A. Editor, Teacher
Biographical-Personal. Educ.: M.A. (Folklore); Ph.D. candidate (Anthropology), UCLA. Mailing address: 2214 S. Ridgeley Dr., L.A., Cal. 90016.
Career-Professional. Dir., Central City Community Serv. Center, L.A.; Tchr., Cal. State U., L.A.; Asst. Prof., Afro-Ethnic Studies, Cal. State U., Fullerton.

Williams, Ruby Ora

WRITINGS: Pub. as reviewer, essayist, and poet, with work appearing in little mags. as well as the Los Angeles Times. Ed., Blackfolk, Journal of Afro-American Expressive Culture, L.A.
Source. Blackfolk: Journal of Afro-American Expressive Culture, Ed. by Lance A. Williams (Fall-Winter 1973-4, Los Angeles).

Paulette L. Williams. See Shangé, Ntozake.

WILLIAMS, RUBY ORA. 1926- . Lyric Coloratura Soprano, English Teacher
Biographical-Personal. Born Feb. 18, 1926, in Lakewood, N.J. D. of Charles and Ida [Bowles] Williams. Educ.: B.A. (Eng.), Va. Union U.; M.A. (Eng.), Howard U.; Further study: Columbia U.; N.Y.U.; Ph.D., U. of Cal., Irvine. Family: Single. Mailing address: 362 Redondo Ave., Long Beach, Cal. 90814.
Career-Professional. Instr., Eng. Dept., Southern U., Baton Rouge, La., 1953-55; Instr., Eng. Dept., Tuskegee Inst., 1955-57; Instr., Eng. Dept., Morgan State Coll., Baltimore, 1957-65; Prog. Advis., Nat'l. Headquarters, Camp Fire Girls, Inc., N.Y.C., 1965-68; Assoc. Prof., Eng. Dept., Cal. State U., Long Beach, 1968- . Particip. in N.Y.U. "Joy of Singing" Ser., Town Hall, 1967; Occasional soloist, First Unitarian Church, Baltimore; Recitals: Glassboro State Coll., N.J.; Cochran Bap. Church, L.A.; Triangular Church of Religious Science, L.A.; Bethel AME Church, San Francisco. Reviewer, Bibliographic Survey: The Negro in Print, 1968.
WRITINGS: American Black Women in the Arts and Social Sciences: A Bibliographic Survey (Scarecrow, 1973). Articles: CLA Journal; The Camp Fire Girl; Journal of Negro Education. Reviews in: Bibliographic Survey: The Slave Stealers, by Upchurch Boyd; Black Abolitionists, by Benjamin Quarles; Crusade for Freedom, by Alma Lutz; Black Struggle, by Bryan Fulks; Ely: Too Black, Too White, by Ely Green.
HONORS AND AWARDS: Danforth Fellow. for Relig. Perspectives in Higher Educ.; The Vassie D. Wright Authors Award, Our Authors Study Club.
SIDELIGHTS: Miss Williams "has performed with a number of ensembles. For many years she was one of the Five Williams Sisters, an instrumental group. Later, she was vocalist with the Four Williams Sisters. She has also been a member of Voices Inc., N.Y.; and the Overtones, Washington, D.C., and the New Choral Ensemble, Teaneck, New Jersey.... She has appeared at the 1964 New York

Wilmore, Gayraud Stephen

World's Fair, on the WCAU Television Series, June 1965, and in
recital at the Camden Community College, Blackwoods, New Jersey,
June 1971" (Author).
Source. Author inform.

WILLIE, CHARLES V. 1927- . Social Scientist
Biographical-Personal. Born Oct. 8, 1927, in
Dallas, Tex. Son of Dr. Louis J. and Carrie
[Sykes] Willie. Educ.: B.A., Morehouse
Coll., 1948; M.A., Atlanta U., 1949; Ph.D.,
Syracuse U., 1957. Family: m. Mary Sue
Conklin; d. Sarah Susannah, son, Martin
Charles, son, James Theodore. Mailing ad-
dress: 41 Hillcrest Rd., Concord, Mass.
Career-Professional. Instr., Dept. of Preven-
tive Medicine, State U. of N.Y., 1955-60;
Vis. Lectr., Dept. of Psychiatry, Harvard
Medical Sch., 1966-67; Instr. to Prof., Dept.
of Sociol., Syracuse U., 1967-71; V. Pres.,
student affairs, Syracuse U., 1972-74; Prof.
of Educ. & Urban Studies, Grad. Sch. of Educ.,
Harvard U., 1974- . Res. Dir., Wash., D.C., 1962-64.
WRITINGS: Church Action in the World (1969); The Family Life of
Black People (1970); Black Students in White Colleges (1972);
Racism and Mental Health (1973); Oreo (Parameter Pr., 1975). In
progress: Ed., Black/Brown/White Relations (Transaction Bks.);
A New Look at Black Families. Contrib. to jls.
HONORS AND AWARDS: Phi Beta Kappa, Morehouse Coll., 1972; D.H.L.,
Berkeley Divinity Sch., Yale U.; D.D., Gen. Theol. Sem., N.Y.;
Distinguished Alumnus Award, Maxwell Sch., Syracuse U., 1974.
MEMBER: Pres., E. Sociol. Soc., 1974-75; V. Pres., House of Depu-
ties, Episcopal Church of the U.S.; Executive Com., Soc. Sci. Res.
Counc.
Source. Author inform.

WILMORE, GAYRAUD STEPHEN. 1921- . Theologian,
Editor
Biographical-Personal. Born Dec. 20, 1921, in
Phila., Pa. Son of Gayraud S. Sr. and Patri-
cia [Gardner] Wilmore. Educ.: U. of Flor-
ence, Italy; B.A., Lincoln U. (Pa.); M.Div.,
Lincoln U. Theol. Sem.; S.T.M., Temple U.;
Drew Theol. Sem. Family: m. Lee Wilson;
son, Stephen, son, Jacques, d. Roberta, son,
David. Mailing address: Colgate Rochester,
Bexley Hall, Crozer Theol. Sem., 1100 S.
Goodman St., Rochester, N.Y. 14620.

Woodson, Carter Godwin

Career-Professional. Ed.; Lectr.; Dir. Amer. Forum in Internat. Stud.
in Ghana, 1971.
WRITINGS: Ed. Westminster Pr. Ser., "Christian Perspectives on
Social Problems," 1962-64, 10 vols.; The Secular Relevance of the
Church (Westminster, 1962); Black Religion and Black Radicalism
(Doubleday, 1972); Asians and Blacks, with C. S. Song (East Asia
Christian Counc., 1973).
HONORS AND AWARDS: D.D., Lincoln Coll., Ill.; D.D., Tusculum
Coll., L.H.D., Lincoln U., Pa.
MEMBER: Founding mem. of Nat'l. Conf. on Black Churchmen; Amer.
Soc. of Christian Ethics; Amer. Theol. Soc.; Soc. for Study of
Black Relig.
SIDELIGHTS: Lectures in Amer. coll. & universities, travel in
Middle East, Europe & Africa. Cook lectures (1972), in India,
Thailand, Indonesia, Korea, Japan, Taiwan; Guyana, 1974 (Author).
Source. Author inform.

WOODSON, CARTER GODWIN. 1875-1950. Educator,
Historian
Biographical-Personal. Born in New Canton, Va.,
Dec. 19, 1875. Son of James Henry and Anne
Eliza [Riddle] Woodson. Educ.: Berea Coll.,
Litt.B., 1903; studied La Sorbonne, Paris;
U. of Chgo., B.A., 1907, M.A., 1908; Harvard
U., Ph.D., 1912; Va. State Coll., LL.D.,
1941. Died Apr. 3, 1950; buried Lincoln
Memorial Cemetery, Wash.
Career-Professional. Tchr. high schs., Wash.,
1908-18; prin., Armstrong Manual Training
High Sch., D.C., 1918-19; dean, Sch. of Lib-
eral Arts, Howard U., 1919-20; Dean, W. Va.
Collegiate Inst., Inst., W. Va., 1920-22;
Dir. (executive), ASNLH; Chmn. Bd., Assoc.
Pubs., Inc.; Founder/Ed., Journal of Negro History (quar.), 1916;
Founder/Ed., Negro History Bulletin, 1937.
WRITINGS: The Education of the Negro Prior to 1861 (Putnam,
1915); A Century of Negro Migration (ASNLH, 1918); History of the
Negro Church (Assoc. Pub., 1921); The Negro in Our History (Assoc.
Pub., 1922); Negro Orators and Their Orations (Assoc. Pub., 1925);
Free Negro Owners of Slaves in the United States in 1830 (ASNLH,
1925); Free Negro Heads of Families in the United States in 1830
(ASNLH, 1925); The Mind of the Negroes Reflected in Letters during
the Crisis (ASNLH, 1925); African Myths (1928); Negro Makers of
History (Assoc. Pub., 1928); The Rural Negro (1930); The Negro
Professional Man and the Community (ASNLH, 1934); The Story of the
Negro Retold (1935); The African Background Outlined (1936). Joint

Work, Monroe Nathan

Author: <u>The Negro Wage Earner</u>; <u>The Negro As a Business Man</u>; Ed.:
<u>The Works of Francis J. Grimke</u> (1942).
HONORS AND AWARDS: Recipient of Spingarn Medal, NAACP, 1926.
SIDELIGHTS: "The 'father of Negro history,' Carter G. Woodson was
for many years the lone voice of any consequence in American Negro
historiography" (<u>Black Historians</u>).
   The ASNLH published more than 30 volumes in the first 25 years
of its existence. A tremendous impetus to scholarship in history
was given by black scholars in <u>Journal of Negro History</u>. In 1926,
Negro history Week was taken over by the Association, and it became
a national success. He never married (<u>Current Biography</u>, 1944).
Sources. <u>Black Historians: a Critique</u>, Earl E. Thorpe (Morrow);
<u>Current Biography 1944</u>, Ed. by Anna Roethe (H. W. Wilson, 1945);
<u>The Negro Almanac</u>, Comp. & Ed. by Harry A. Ploski & Ernest Kaiser
(Bellwether, 1971); <u>Who Was Who in America</u>, Vol. III, 1951-60
(Marquis, 1960).

WORK, MONROE NATHAN. 1866-1945. Scholar,
Publisher
Biographical-Personal. Born 1866 in Iredell
   Co., N.C. <u>Educ.</u>: Chgo. Theol. Sem.; B.A.
   (Philos.), <u>M.A.</u>, U. of Chgo. Died 1945.
Career-Professional. Prof. of Pedagogy & Hist.,
   Ga. State Indust. Coll., 1903- ; Dir., Dept.
   of Records & Res., Tuskegee Inst., Ala.,
   1908-38 (collected pertinent data & statis-
   tics on the Negro).
WRITINGS: <u>Negro Yearbook</u>, biennial; <u>Bibliog-
   raphy of the Negro</u> (1928).
HONORS AND AWARDS: In 1928, received Harmon
   Award in Education for "scholarly research
   and educational publicity through periodic
   publication of the <u>Negro Yearbook</u> and the
compilation of a <u>Bibliography of the Negro</u>." U. of Chicago Alumni
Assn. presented him with the Alumni Citation, in 1942, in recognition of his 40 years of public service.
SIDELIGHTS: "Through his research in Europe and America, Dr. Work
obtained important data for his compilation of the <u>Bibliography of
the Negro</u>. This publication was a significant achievement because
it was the first effort of its kind. In one volume, he presented
the works or publications about Negroes in all parts of the world
from ancient times to 1928" (<u>Historical Negro Biographies</u>).
Source. <u>Historical Negro Biographies</u>, Wilhelmena S. Robinson
   (ASNLH, 1967).

Wright, Charles

WRIGHT, CHARLES. Novelist, Essayist
Career-Professional.
WRITINGS: Novels: The Messenger (Farrar,
Straus, 1963; Manor Bks., 1974); The Wig
(Farrar, Straus, 1966); Absolutely Nothing
to Get Alarmed About, nonfiction (Farrar,
Straus, 1973); Bloodlines, poetry (Wesleyan
U. Pr., 1975); Hard Freight (Wesleyan U. Pr.,
1973).
Sources. Interviews with Black Writers, Ed. by
John O'Brien (Liveright, 1973); Books in
Print, Supplement, 1975-76 (Bowker, 1976).

WRIGHT, JAY. 1935- . Poet, Playwright
Biographical-Personal. Born May 25, 1935, in Albuquerque, N. Mex.
Educ.: B.A., U. of Cal., Berkeley; M.A., Rutgers U., 1966.
Career-Professional. A playwright as well as a poet. His plays have
been produced in California and have been published.
WRITINGS: Death As History (Kriya Pr., 1967); The Homecoming
Singer, poetry (Corinth, 1971). Anthol.: New Negro Poetry: U.S.A.
(1964); For Malcolm (1967); 31 New American Poets (1969); Natural
Process (1970) & Poetry of Black America (1973); Dimensions of
History (Kayak, 1976). Period.: New American Review; Evergreen
Review; Hiram Poetry Review; The Nation; Yale Review; & Negro
Digest/Black World.
HONORS AND AWARDS: Has held several fellowships, including a
Rockefeller Brothers Theological Fellowship.
Sources. Black Fire, Ed. by LeRoi Jones & Larry Neal (Morrow, 1968);
For Malcolm, Ed. by Dudley Randall & Margaret G. Burroughs (Broad-
side Pr., 1969); New Black Voices, Ed. by Abraham Chapman (New
Amer. Lib., 1972); Poetry of Black America, Ed. by Arnold Adoff
(Harper & Row, 1973); Books in Print, Supplement, 1975-76 (Bowker,
1976).

WRIGHT, NATHAN, JR. 1923- . Educator, Civil
Rights Activist, Consultant, Priest
Biographical-Personal. Born Aug. 5, 1923, in
Shreveport, La. Son of Nathan (insurance
agent) and Parthenia [Hickman] Wright. Educ.:
B.A., U. of Cin., 1947; B.D., Episcopal
Theol. Sch., Cambridge, Mass., 1950; S.T.M.,
Harvard U., 1951; Ed.M., State Tchrs. Coll.,
Boston, 1962; Ed.D., Harvard U., 1964; LL.D.
(hon.) Upsala Coll., 1969. Family: m. Car-
olyn Elliott May, July 18, 1969; 2 sons, 3
daughters. Mailing address: Wright Rd.,
Box 157, Selkirk, N.Y. 12158.

Wright, Nathan, Jr.

Career-Professional. Prof. of Urban Affairs and Former Chmn., Dept.
of Afro-Amer. Stud., State U. of N.Y. at Albany, 1969 to present;
Assoc., Nat'l. Humanities Faculty, 1971-present; Vis. Prof. &
Cons., C. W. Post Coll., Brookville, Long Island, 1969-70; Cons.
to Supt., Minneapolis Public Schs., Minneapolis, 1968-69; Cons.,
Upsala Coll., E. Orange, N.J., 1967-present; Cons., Orange, N.J.,
1956-66; Educ. Cons., Self-employed, Newark, N.J., 1964-69; Cons.
and Staff Assoc., Mass. Educ. Com., Boston, 1963-64; Prog. & Staff
Orientation, Dept. of Educ., State of Minn., St. Paul, 1968-69;
Res., Newark Com. of Better Pub. Schs., Newark; Tchg., Colgate-
Rochester Divinity Sch., Rochester, N.Y.; Chmn., Nat'l. & Internat.
Conf. on Black Power, Newark and Phila., 1967-68; Executive Dir.,
Dept. of Urban Work, Diocese of Newark, N.J., 1964-69; Lectr.,
Wide World Lecture Bureau, N.Y.C.
WRITINGS: The Riddle of Life (Bruce-Humprhies, 1952); The Song of
Mary (Bruce-Humphries, 1952); One Bread, One Body (Seabury, 1962);
Black Power & Urban Unrest (Hawthorn, 1967); Ready to Riot (Holt,
1968); Let's Work Together (Hawthorn, 1968); Let's Face Racism
(T. Nelson, 1970); What Black Educators are Saying (Hawthorn,
1971); What Black Politicians are Saying (Hawthorn, 1972); Pros-
pects for World Peace (Counc. on Afro-Amer. Stud., 1974). Schol-
arly commentary & reviews: Christianity Today; The Living Church;
The Catholic Church; The American Journal of Economics and Sociology; Church in Metropolis; Freedomways; Black Scholar; Journal
of Afro-American Issues; "Some 370 published articles and scholarly commentary in magazines, books and newspapers" (Author).
HONORS AND AWARDS: Citation from U.S. Army for Promoting Military
Morale, 1944; 1st Prize (Internat.) for One Bread, One Body,
Christian Res. Found.; Media Workshop Award for Black Power and
Urban Unrest; Nomination for Pulitzer Prize for Let's Work Together, 1969.
SIDELIGHTS: "Dr. Wright is said to be 'perhaps the foremost living exponent of the point of view that 'cities are people'" (C. May
Associates). Research on Untouchables in India, 1971; Travel in
Africa, 1970; 220 coll. & university convocation lectures in
U.S.A.
    "A Publishers Weekly writer notes that Wright 'thinks the only
way for the Negro to achieve his rightful place in our society is
through self-direction, even if that means separation.' He be-
lieves that, with white financial and moral support, the black man
'has to overcome his monumental inferiority complex' and get 'into
the dynamics of American life'" (Contemporary Authors).
Sources. Author inform.; Contemporary Authors, Vols. 37-40, Ed. by
Clare D. Kinsman and Mary A. Tennenhouse (Gale Res., 1973).

Wright, Richard

WRIGHT, RICHARD. 1908–1960. Novelist, Essayist
Biographical-Personal. Born Sept. 4, 1908, on a
plantation near Natchez, Miss. Educ.: Seventh Day Adventist Sch.; Primarily self-educated. Family: married; two daughters.
Died in 1960.
Career-Professional. Began work in Memphis,
Tenn., at age 15, later in Chgo. worked on
odd jobs; On Fed. Writers Project, Chgo.,
1935; N.Y.C., 1937; Began writing for smaller
mags.; also contrib. to Daily Worker and New
Masses.
WRITINGS: Uncle Tom's Children (World, 1938);
Native Son (Harper & Row, 1940, 1957); 12 Million Black Voices (1941); Black Boy, autobiog. (Harper & Row, 1945); The Outsider
(1953); Black Power (Harper & Row, 1954);
Savage Holiday (1955); The Color Curtain (1956); Pagan Spain
(1957); White Man, Listen (1957); The Long Dream (Doubleday, 1959);
Eight Men (Avon, 1961); Lawd Today (Walker, 1963).
HONORS AND AWARDS: Won $500 prize for Uncle Tom's Children (Story
Mag.); Received Guggenheim fellow. for Native Son (1st Bk. by
Afro-Amer. to become Bk.-of-the-Month Club selection); also became
successful Broadway prod. & film in S. Amer.; Black Boy repeated
as Book-of-the Month selection; in decade and a half after Native
Son, nearly 50 translations and foreign eds. of his works were pub.
SIDELIGHTS: An expatriate for 15 years, he died Nov. 28, 1960;
buried Père Lanchaise, Paris, France. Agent: c/o Paul R. Reynolds.& Son, 599 Fifth Ave., New York, N.Y. 10017 (Who Was Who in
America).
Sources. Black American Literature—Fiction, Ed. by Darwin T. Turner
(Merrill, 1969); Black Voices, Ed. by Abraham Chapman (New Amer.
Lib., 1968); American Negro Reference Book, Ed. by John P. Davis
(Prentice-Hall, 1966); Cavalcade, Ed. by Arthur P. Davis & Saunders
Redding (Houghton Mifflin, 1971); Dark Symphony, Ed. by James A.
Emanuel & Theodore L. Gross (Free Pr., 1968); Who Was Who in America, Vol. IV, 1961–1968 (Marquis, 1968).

WRIGHT, SARAH ELIZABETH. Poet, Novelist
Biographical-Personal. Born in Wetipguin, Md. D. of Willis C. and
Amelia Wright. Educ.: Howard U.; U. of Pa.; New Sch. for Soc.
Res. Family: son, Michael, d. Shelley. Mailing address: 780
West End Ave., 1D, N.Y., N.Y. 10025.
Career-Professional. Fic. cons., Creative Artists Public Serv. Prog.,
N.Y. State Coun. on the Arts; Pres., Writers for Our Time (Intercommunity creative writers' workshop).

Yerby, Frank

WRITINGS: Give Me A Child, poetry (1955);
This Child's Gonna Live, novel (Delacorte,
1969; Calder & Boyars, 1970). Anthol.:
Poets of Today (1964); Poetry of the Negro;
Poetry of Black America (1973). Period.:
The American Pen & Freedomways.
HONORS AND AWARDS: This Child's Gonna Live
was selected by the New York Times as one of
the Outstanding Books of the Year, 1969;
Chosen by The Baltimore Sun for its 1969
Readability Award.
MEMBER: Pen-Amer. Center; Pen Internat.;
The Authors League of America, Inc.; Authors
Guild Inc.; McDowell Colony Fellow.
SIDELIGHTS: Lectures: Afro-Amer. Cultural
Found., White Plains, N.Y.; Langston Hughes

Lib. & Cultural Center, Corona, N.Y.; Strawberry Mansion Center,
Phila., Pa.; Stuyvesant High Sch., Mini-Course Lecture Ser. Poetry
recitations: WBAI & WEVD-FM, N.Y.C.; Syndicated radio prog., "The
Second Forty," prod. by Inform. Center for Mature Woemn. Talk
Shows: WABC TV; WNBC; WLIB; WNYC; WPEN; Frank Ford Show, Phila.;
WFIL TV (ABC) Phila.; WFLN.
"I am working on another novel and a collection of poems" (Au-
thor).
Sources. Author inform.; Poetry of Black America, Ed. by Arnold
Adoff (Harper & Row, 1973).

YERBY, FRANK. 1916- . Novelist
Biographical-Personal. Born Sept. 5, 1916,
Augusta, Ga. Son of Rufus Garvin and Willie
[Smythe] Yerby. Educ.: B.A., Paine Coll.,
Augusta, Ga., 1937; M.A., Fisk U., 1938;
Further study, U. of Chgo. Family: 1st m.
Flora H. Claire Williams, Mar. 1, 1941
(div.); son, Jacques Loring, d. Nikki
Ethlyn, d. Faune Ellena, son, Jan Keith;
2nd m. Blanquita Calle-Perez, 1956. Mailing
address: c/o William Morris Agency, 1350
Ave. of the Americas, N.Y., N.Y. 10019.
Career-Professional. Tchr., Fla. A. & M. Coll.,
Tallahassee, 1939-40; Southern U., Baton
Rouge, La., 1940-41; War work, Ford Motor Co.,
Dearborn, Mich., 1942-44; Ranger Aircraft,
Jamaica, N.Y., 1944-45.
WRITINGS: Novels: The Foxes of Harrow (Dial, 1946); The Vixens
(Dial, 1947); The Golden Hawk (Dial, 1948); Prides Castle (Dial,
1949); Floodtide (Dial, 1950); A Woman Called Fancy (Dial, 1952);
Saracen Blade (Dial, 1953); Devil's Laughter (Dial, 1954); Benton's

Yette, Samuel J.

Row (Dial, 1955); Treasure of Pleasant Valley (Dial, 1956); Captain Rebel (Dial, 1957); Fair Oaks (Dial, 1958); Bride of Liberty (Doubleday, 1958); The Serpent and the Staff (Dial, 1959); Jarrett's Jade (Dial, 1960); Gillian (Dial, 1961); The Garfield Honor (Dial, 1962); Griffin's Way (Dial, 1963); The Old Gods Laugh (Dial, 1964); An Odor of Sanctity (Dell, 1965); Goat Song (Dial, 1967); Judas, My Brother (Dial, 1968); Speak Now (Dial, 1969); The Dahomean (Dell, 1971); The Girl from Storyville; The Voyage Unplanned (Dial, 1974); Tobias and the Angel (Dial, 1975); A Rose for Ana Maria (Dial, 1975). Contrib. short stories to Harper's, Liberty & Colliers.
SIDELIGHTS: Received the O. Henry Memorial Award, 1944 for best first short story. His twenty-plus best-selling novels have sold more than 21,000,000 copies, and have been translated into nearly a dozen languages. A number have been made into movies. Yerby now lives in Madrid (Contemporary Authors).
Sources. American Negro Short Stories, Ed. by John H. Clarke (Hill & Wang, 1966); Best Short Stories by Negro Writers, Ed. by Langston Hughes (Little, Brown, 1967); Black American Literature--Fiction, Ed. by Darwin T. Turner (Merrill, 1969); Contemporary Authors, Vols. 11-12, Ed. by James M. Ethridge & Barbara Kopala (Gale Res., 1965); Who's Who in America, 37th ed., 1972-73 (Marquis, 1972); Books in Print, Supplement, 1975-76 (Bowker, 1976).

YETTE, SAMUEL J. 1929- . Journalist
Biographical-Personal. Born in 1929 in Harriman, Tenn. Educ.: B.A. in Eng. and Speech, Tenn. State U.; M.A. in Journalism & Gov't., Indiana U.; Doctor of Humanities (hon.), Prentice Inst., Miss.
Career-Professional. Wash. corresp., Newsweek; Prof., Journalism, Howard U.
WRITINGS: The Choice: The Issue of Black Survival in America (Putnam, 1971).
HONORS AND AWARDS: The Choice was selected by Black Academy of Arts & Letters as the Non-Fiction Work of Distinction, 1972.
SIDELIGHTS: "The extermination of the black man in America...emerges from Samuel J. Yette's startling research as a genuine possibility...
Drawing on a wealth of fact and documentation, Mr. Yette lets us see White America through the eyes of Black America, and we learn why Blacks feel that the issue facing them is one of survival" (Sen. Birch Bayh in The Choice).
Sources. The Choice, Samuel J. Yette (Putnam, 1971); "Nat'l. Conf. of Afro-Amer. Writers," Program (Howard U., Inst. for Arts and Humanities, Nov. 1974).

YOUNG, AL. 1939- . Poet, Novelist, Teacher, Musician

Biographical-Personal. Born May 31, 1939, in Ocean Springs, Miss. Son of Albert James (professional musician & auto worker) and Mary [Campbell] Young. Educ.: U. of Mich., 1957-61; Stanford U. (fellow in creative writing), 1966-67; B.A., U. of Cal., Berkeley, 1969. Family: m. Arlin Belch (free-lance artist), Oct. 8, 1963; son, Michael James. Mailing address: Creative Writing Center, Stanford U., 2455 Alpine Rd., Menlo Park, Cal. 94025.

Career-Professional. Free-lance musician, playing guitar & flute & singing professionally throughout U.S., 1957-64; Disc jockey, Radio Sta., KJAZ-FM, Alameda, Cal., 1964-65; Writing instr. & lang. cons., Berkeley Neighborhood Youth Corps, 1968-69; Jones Lectr. in Creative Writing, Stanford U., 1969- . Founder, ed., Loveletter (irregular review, late 1960's).

WRITINGS: Dancing, poetry (Corinth Bks., 1969); Snakes, novel (Holt, 1970); The Song Turning Back into Itself, poetry (Holt, 1971); Earth Air Fire and Water, poetry (Coward & Geoghegan, 1971); Who Is Angelina?, novel (1974); Geography of the Near Past (Holt, Rinehart & Winston, 1976); Sitting Pretty (Holt, Rinehart & Winston, 1976). In progress: A Pictorial History of White People in America. Anthol.: New Black Poetry; 19 Necromancers from Now; Dices; Natural Process; New Black Voices. Period.: Massachusetts Review; Evergreen Review; Rolling Stone; Journal of Black Poetry.

HONORS AND AWARDS: Wallace E. Stegner Fellow, Creative writing; Joseph Henry Jackson Award, San Francisco Found., 1969 for Dancing; NEA Grant (poetry), 1969-70; Nat'l. Arts Counc. Awards, 1968, 1969; Cal. Assn. of Tchrs. of Eng., Spec. Award, 1973.

MEMBER: Amer. Assn. of U. Prof.; Com. of Small Mag. Ed. & Pub.; Sigma Delta Pi; American Civil Liberties Union; Writers' Guild of America, W.; Authors Guild; Authors League.

SIDELIGHTS: Lectures include: MIT, R.I. Sch. of Design, U. of Cal., Berkeley, Mills Coll., U. of N. Mex., Acad. of Amer. Poets.

"Young's first novel [Snakes] has been acclaimed by several reviewers, including Martin Levin and L. E. Sissman, as an authentic exploration of the experiences of a jazz-oriented black youth growing up in a middle American city...."

Young has said: "'I write out of spiritual need. I consider it a religious experience. It has been an essential part of my life since I was nine years old. My influences stem from living rather than from literary traditions'" (Contemporary Authors).

Young, Bernice Elizabeth

Sources. <u>Contemporary Authors</u>, Vols. 29-32, Ed. by Clare D. Kinsman
& Mary A. Tennenhouse (Gale Res., 1972); <u>New Black Voices</u>, Ed. by
Abraham Chapman (New Amer. Lib., 1972); <u>Poetry of Black America</u>,
Ed. by Arnold Adoff (Harper & Row, 1973); <u>Books in Print</u>, Supple-
ment, 1975-76 (Bowker, 1976).

YOUNG, BERNICE ELIZABETH. 1931- . Non-Fiction Writer
Biographical-Personal. Born Oct. 7, 1931, in Cleveland, Ohio. D. of
James Anthony Young and Josephine Juanita Paige. <u>Educ.</u>: Vassar
Coll.; W. Reserve U. <u>Family</u>: Single. <u>Mailing address</u>: 333 E.
34th St., Apt. 17H, N.Y., N.Y. 10016.
Career-Professional. Author, 1970 to present; "You and Your Money,"
daily WLIB radio ser., consumer educ. (26 weeks), 1970; Account
Executive, Addison, Goldstein & Walsh, 1969-70; Protestant Advis./
Media Advis., Girl Scouts of U.S.A., 1968; Dir., BEATLES (U.S.A.)
LIMITED (America Rep. for The Beatles, Cilla Black, Gerry and the
Pacemakers & Others under management of the late Brian Epstein),
1964-67; Asst. to Dir., of Advertising, Charles of the Ritz,
1961-64.
WRITINGS: <u>Harlem, The Story of a Changing Community</u> (Julian Mes-
sner, 1972); <u>The Picture Story of Hank Aaron</u> (Julian Messner,
1974); <u>The Picture Story of Frank Robinson</u> (Julian Messner, 1975);
<u>The Story of Hank Aaron</u> (Prentice-Hall, 1976). In progress:
<u>Tribes of Africa</u> (Julian Messner, 1975).
MEMBER: Bd. of Dir., Sheltering Arms Children's Serv.; Altar
Guild, St. Thomas Church, N.Y.C.; Acolytes of St. Thomas Church,
N.Y.C.; Book Reviewer, <u>The Living Church</u>; Authors Guild/Authors
League; Internat. Platform Assn.; Friends of the Joffrey Ballet;
Young Friends of City Center.
SIDELIGHTS: Foreign Languages: French, Spanish (Author).
Sources. Author inform.; <u>Books in Print</u>, Supplement, 1975-76 (Bow-
ker, 1976).

YOUNG, MARGARET BUCKNER. 1922- . Children's Writer
Biographical-Personal. Born Mar. 20, 1922, in Campbellsville, Ky.
D. of Frank & Eva [Carter] Buckner. <u>Educ.</u>: B.A., Ky. State Coll.,
1942; M.A., U. of Minn., 1946; Further study, Atlanta U., 1958.
<u>Family</u>: m. Whitney Young, Jr. (Executive Dir., Nat'l. Urban
League), Jan. 2, 1944 (he died March 11, 1971); d. Marcia Elaine,
d. Lauren Lee. <u>Mailing address</u>: 330 Oxford Rd., New Rochelle,
N.Y. 10804.
Career-Professional. Instr. at Ky. State Coll., Frankfort, 1943 &
Atlanta U., 1958; Instr. in Educ. & Psychology, Spelman Coll.,
Atlanta, 1958-60.
WRITINGS: <u>The First Book of American Negroes</u> (Watts, 1966); <u>The
Picture Life of Martin Luther King</u> (Watts, 1968); <u>The Picture Life
of Ralph J. Bunche</u> (Watts, 1968); <u>Black American Leaders</u> (Watts,

Young, Whitney Moore, Jr.

1969); The Picture Life of Thurgood Marshall (Watts, 1970). "How
to Bring Up Your Child Without Prejudice," pam.
MEMBER: Nat'l. Com. for the Day Care of Children, 1963-66 and
New Rochelle Volunteer Bureau, 1963-67; Child Study Assn. of
America, Bd. of Dirs., 1962- .
Source. Something About the Author, Ed. by Anne Commire (Gale Res.,
1973).

YOUNG, THOMAS WHITE. 1908- . Lawyer, News-
paper Publisher
Biographical-Personal. Born Oct. 26, 1908, in
    Norfolk, Va. Educ.: B.S., LL.B., 1932, Ohio
    State U. Family: m. Marguerite J. Chisholm,
    March 2, 1943; d. Millicent Marguerite.
    Mailing address: 719 E. Olney Rd., Norfolk,
    Va.
Career-Professional. Admitted to Norfolk bar,
    1933, practiced in Norfolk, Va. 1933-36. War
    corresp., Journal and Guide (Norfolk), 1943-
    1945; Pres., The Guide Pub. Co., Inc., Nor-
    folk, 1947- .
    HONORS AND AWARDS: Wolfe Journalism Honor
    Medal, 1931.
    MEMBER: V. chmn., Citizen Democratic Govt.;
Va. Advis. Com., U.S. Com. Civil Rights, 1962- ; Executive Com.,
S. Regional Counc.; Dir., Hunton YMCA; Secy.-Dir., Amalgamated
Pubs., Inc.; Trus., Hampton Inst.; Nat'l. Newspaper Pub. Assn.
Source. Negro Handbook, Comp. by Eds. of Ebony (Johnson Pub., 1966).

YOUNG, WHITNEY MOORE, JR. 1921-1971. Executive
Director, National Urban League
Biographical-Personal. Born July 31, 1921, in
    Lincoln Ridge, Ky. Son of Whitney M. and
    Laura [Ray] Young. Educ.: B.S., Ky. State
    Coll., 1941; Mass. Inst. Technology, 1942-43;
    M.A., U. of Minn., 1947; Harvard U., 1960-61;
    LL.D. (hon.): N.C. Agricultural & Technical
    Coll., 1961; Tuskegee Inst., 1963. Family:
    m. Margaret Buckner, Jan. 2, 1944; d. Marcia
    Elaine, d. Lauren Lee. Drowned while swim-
    ming off W. Coast of Africa, March 1971.
Career-Professional. Indust. Relat. & Vocation-
    al Guidance Dir., St. Paul (Minn.) Urban
    League, 1947-50; Executive Secy., Omaha Urban
    League, 1950-53; Instr., Sch. of Soc. Work,
U. of Neb., 1950-58; Dean, Sch. of Soc. Work, Atlanta U., 1954-60;
Executive Dir., Nat'l. Urban League, N.Y.C., 1961-71. Frequent
lectr.

Young, Whitney Moore, Jr.

WRITINGS: <u>Intergroup Relations as a Challenge to Social Work Practice</u> (1960); <u>Integration: The Role of Labor Education</u> (1959); <u>Status of the Negro Community: Problems--Proposals--Projections</u> (1959); <u>A Second Look--The Negro Citizen in Atlanta</u>, Co-author (1958); <u>To Be Equal</u> (McGraw-Hill, 1963).
HONORS AND AWARDS: Florina Lasker Award ($1000 for outstanding achievement in field of soc. work), 1959; Outstanding Alumni Award, U. of Minn., 1960.
MEMBER: Pres. Com. on Youth Employment; Nat'l. Adv. Counc., AFL-CIO Community Serv. Com.; Advis. Bd., N.Y. Sch. Soc. Work, Columbia; Advis. Com. to Secy., HEW; Cons. U.S. Public Health Dept.; Executive Com., Nat'l. Soc. Welfare Assembly; V. Pres., Nat'l. Assn. Soc. Workers; Alpha Phi Alpha.
SIDELIGHTS: "In the Negro revolt of the 1960's, Whitney Young, as executive secretary of the National Urban League, accepted the challenge of directing the organization into a more dynamic role in the struggle for civil rights...

He attempted to restore the League to the front rank of leadership in the revolution of the 1960's" (<u>Historical Negro Biographies</u>).
Sources. <u>Contemporary Authors</u>, Vols. 13-14, Ed. by Clara D. Kinsman & Mary A. Tennenhouse (Gale Res., 1972); <u>Historical Negro Biographies</u>, Wilhelmena S. Robinson (ASNLH, 1967); <u>Negro Handbook</u>, Comp. by Eds. of <u>Ebony</u> (Johnson Pub., 1966).

Title Index

Titles listed are of plays, radio, television and motion picture scripts, as well as of books, and in some cases year of publication. Series are indicated. See the main author entry for full information.

American Black Women in the Arts
and Social Sciences: A Bibliographic Survey. Ruby Ora
Williams. Scarecrow, 1973

American Culture in Literature.
Nick Aaron Ford. Rand McNally, 1967

American Daughter. Era Bell
Thompson. U. of Chgo. Pr.,
1946; Follett Pub. Co., 1967

American Negro Folklore.
J. Mason Brewer. Quadrangle,
1968

The American Negro: Old World
Background and New World Experience. Rayford W. Logan
(with Irving S. Cohen).
Houghton Mifflin, 1967; 1970

American Negro Short Stories.
Ed., John H. Clarke. Hill &
Wang, 1966

The American Negro Writer and
His Roots. Loften Mitchell

The American Revolution. James
Boggs. Monthly Review Pr.,
1963

The American Revolution. Kenneth B. Clark. Enterprise,
1974

American Society and Black Revolution. Frank Hercules.
Harcourt, 1972

America's Color Caravan. Warren
J. Halliburton. Singer-
Graflex, n.d.

America's Majorities and Minorities. Warren J. Halliburton
(with William L. Katz). Arno
Pr., n.d.

L'Amérique Noire. William
Gardner Smith

Amongst Thistles and Thorns.
Austin C. Clarke. McClelland,
1965

Analytical Study of Afro-American
Culture. Larry P. Neal. Random House, 1972

Anchor Man. Jesse Jackson.
Harper & Row, 1947

And Bid Him Sing. David Graham
DuBois. Ramparts Pr., 1975

And Then We Heard the Thunder.
John O. Killens. Knopf, 1961;
1971

Angela Davis. Angela Davis.
Random House, 1974

Anger at Innocence. William
Gardner Smith. Farrar, Straus,
1950

Angle of Ascent. Robert E. Hayden. Liveright, 1975

Angles. Sam J. Cornish. Bean
Bag Pr., 1971

The Angry Black. Ed., John A.
Williams. Lancer Pr., 1962

The Angry Ones. John A. Williams.
Ace, 1960; Pocket Bks., 1970

Animals Made By Me. Margery
Brown. Putnam, 1970

Annie Allen. Gwendolyn Brooks.
Harper & Row, 1949

Anon. Ntozake Shangé

Another Country. James Baldwin.
Dial, 1962

Another Kind of Rain. Gerald W.
Barrax. Pittsburgh U. Pr.,
1970

Anthology of Magazine Verse.
Ed., William Stanley Braithwaite, 1913-1929

Anthology of Magazine Verse for
1958. Ed., William Stanley
Braithwaite. Pentelic Pr.,
1959

Anthology of the American Negro
in the Theatre: a Critical
Approach. Ed., Lindsay Patterson. Pub. Co., 1968

"Anti-Slavery Coins." Middleton
Harris, 1967

The Anti-Slavery Harp. Ed.,
William Wells Brown

Anti-Slavery Sentiment in American Literature Prior to 1865.
Lorenzo Dow Turner. ASNLH,
1929

Anyplace But Here. Arna Bontemps, 1967

An Apology to My African Brother.
Eugene Perkins

An Appeal to Conscience. Kelly
Miller, 1918

Beautiful Are the Souls of My People: Biography of Langston Hughes. James Haskins. Holt, Rinehart & Winston, n.d.

The Beautiful Days. A. B. Spellman, 1965

Beckonings. Gwendolyn Brooks. Broadside Pr., 1975

Beetlecreek. William Demby. Pantheon Bks., 1965

Before the Darkness Covers Us. Clyde O. Jackson. Exposition Pr., 1969

"Before the Feast of Shuskan." Anne Spencer

Before the Mayflower. Lerone Bennett, Jr. Johnson Pub., 1962; 1964

Belly Song and Other Poems. Etheridge Knight. Broadside Pr., 1972

The Bench and the Ballot, Southern Federal Judges and Black Voters. Charles V. Hamilton. Oxford U. Pr., 1974

"Benefit Performance." William B. Branch

A Bent House. Owen V. Dodson

Benton's Row. Frank Yerby. Dial, 1955

The Best of Simple. Langston Hughes. Hill & Wang, 1961

The Best Short Stories by Negro Writers. Ed., Langston Hughes. Little, Brown, 1967

The Betrayal of the Negro: From Rutherford B. Hayes to Woodrow Wilson. Rayford W. Logan. Collier-Macmillan, 1965

The Bewitched Parsonage. William S. Braithwaite, 1950

Beyond the Angry Black. John A. Williams. Cooper Square, 1967; New Amer. Lib., 1970

Beyond the Burning: Life and Death of the Ghetto. Sterling Tucker. Assoc. Pr., 1968

Bibliography of the Negro. Ed., Monroe N. Work, 1928

The Big Black Fire. Robert H. DeCoy, 1969

The Big Gold Dream. Chester Himes. New Amer. Lib., 1975

The Big Sea. Langston Hughes. Hill & Wang, 1940

The Big Walk. Willie Clay. Ebony, 1974

Big White Fog. Theodore Ward, 1938

Biographical Directory of Negro Ministers. Ed., Ethel L. Williams. Scarecrow Pr., 1965; 1970; 1974; G. K. Hall, 1975

Biographical History of Blacks in America. Edgar A. Toppin. McKay, 1971

The Biology of the Cell Surface. Ernest E. Just

Bird At My Window. Rosa G. Guy. Lippincott, 1965

Birthday. John L. Steptoe. Holt, Rinehart & Winston, 1972

A Birthday Present for Katheryn Kenyatta. Charlie L. Russell. McGraw-Hill, 1970

Black Abolitionists. Benjamin Quarles. Oxford U. Pr., 1969

The Black Aesthetic. Ed., Addison Gayle. Doubleday, 1971

Black Africa on the Move. Leslie A. Lacy. Watts, 1969

The Black American. Benjamin Quarles (with Leslie H. Fishel, Jr.). Morrow, 1970

Black American and the World Revolution. Claude M. Lightfoot. New Outlook, 1970

Black American Leaders. Margaret Young. Watts, 1969

Black American Literature: Essays. Ed., Darwin T. Turner. Merrill, 1969

Black American Literature: Essays, Poetry, Fiction, Drama. Ed., Darwin T. Turner. Merrill, 1970

Black American Literature: Fiction. Ed., Darwin T. Turner. Merrill, 1969

Black American Literature: Poetry. Ed., Darwin T. Turner. Merrill, 1969

Title Index

The Crisis of the Negro Intellectual. Harold Cruse. Morrow, 1967

Crispus Attucks: Boy of Valor. Dharathula Millender. Bobbs-Merrill, 1965

Crusade for Justice: the Autobiography of Ida B. Wells. Ed., Alfreda Duster. U. of Chgo. Pr., 1970

Cry Baby! Warren J. Halliburton. McGraw-Hill, 1968

Curtain Call, Mr. Aldridge, Sir. Ossie Davis. 1963

Daddy Was a Number Runner. Louise Meriwether. Prentice-Hall, 1970

The Dahomean. Frank Yerby. Dell, 1971

The Dancers. Walter Dean Myers. Parents Mag. Pr., 1972

Dancers on the Shore. William Melvin Kelley. Doubleday, 1964

Dances of Haiti. Katherine Dunham, 1946; 1948

Dancing. Al Young. Corinth Bks., 1969

The Dark. Clarence Major. 1974

Dark Ghetto: Dilemmas of Social Power. Kenneth B. Clark. Harper & Row, 1965

The Dark Messenger. Clarence Cooper. Regency, 1962

Dark Princess. W. E. B. DuBois. Harcourt, 1928

"Dark Symphony." M. B. Tolson

Dark Symphony. Eds., James A. Emanuel (with Theodore L. Gross). Free Pr., 1968

Dark Testament. Pauli Murray, 1969

Darkwater. W. E. B. DuBois. Harcourt, 1920

David He No Fear. Lorenz B./ Graham. Crowell, 1971

Davis-Eells Test of General Intelligence. Allison Davis (with Kenneth Eells). World Bks., 1953

The Dawn and Other Poems. Benjamin G. Brawley

The Day and the War. James Madison Bell

De-Mayor of Harlem. David Henderson. Dutton, 1971

The Dead Lecturer. Amiri Baraka, 1964

Dead Piano. Henry Van Dyke

Deadly Circle of Violence. Lonne Elder, III

Dear John, Dear Coltrane. Michael S. Harper. U. of Pittsburgh Pr., 1970

Death as History. Jay Wright. Kriya Pr., 1967

Debridement. Michael S. Harper. Doubleday, 1973

Deep is the Hunger. Howard Thurman. Harper & Row, 1951

Deep River. Howard Thurman. Harper & Row, 1946; 1955

Deep South. Allison Davis (with Others). U. of Chgo. Pr., 1941

The Degenerative. Joseph Seamon Cotter, Sr.

dem. William Melvin Kelley. Doubleday, 1967

"Denmark 43." James V. Hatch, 1972

Desegregation of Missouri Schools, 1954-1959. Lorenzo J. Greene. 1959; 1961

The Desertion of Man: A Critique of Philosophy of History. Earl E. Thorpe, 1958

The Desire of the Moth for the Star. Benjamin G. Brawley

Destination: Ashes. Norman Jordan. Vibration Pr., 1969

The Destruction of Black Civilization: Great Issues of a Race from 4500 B.C. to 2000 A.D. Chancellor Williams. Third World Pr., 1974

Detention Center. Lorenz B. Graham. Houghton Mifflin, 1972

The Devil Finds Work. James Baldwin. Dial, 1976

324

325

Title Index

TITLE INDEX

I Love You. June Jordan. Emerson Hall, 1974

I, Momolu. Lorenz B. Graham. Crowell, 1966

I Sing Because I'm Happy. Jesse Jackson. Rutledge Bks., 1970

I Want a Black Doll. Frank Hercules. Simon & Schuster, 1967

I Wonder As I Wander. Langston Hughes. Holt, Rinehart & Winston, 1956

Idabel's Fortune. Ted Shine

An Idyl of the South, an Epic Poem in Two Parts. Albery A. Whitman. N.Y., 1901

If Beale Street Could Talk. James Baldwin. Dial, n.d.; New Amer. Lib., 1975

If He Hollers Let Him Go. Chester B. Himes. New Amer. Lib., 1945

If They Come in the Morning. Ed., Angela Davis. Okpaku, 1971

If We Must Die. Junius Edwards

Illustrated History of Black Americans. John Hope Franklin (with Eds. of Time-Life Bks.). Time-Life Inc., 1970; 1973

I'm Sorry. Loften Mitchell

The Image Makers. Eugene Perkins

Images in Black. Johari M. Amini. Third World Pr., 1967

Images of the Negro in America. Darwin T. Turner. Heath, 1965

Imperium in Imperio. Sutton E. Griggs. Bks. for Lib. repr., 1899

Impressions in Asphalt: Images of Urban America. Eugenia W. Collier (with Ruthe T. Sheffey). Scribners, 1969

Impressions of African Art Forms. Margaret E. Danner. Broadside Pr., 1962

In a Minor Chord: Three Afro-American Writers and Their Search for Identity. Darwin Turner. S. Ill. U. Pr., 1971

In a Minor Key. Ira De A. Reid, 1940

In a Time of Rain and Desire. Eugene B. Redmond. Black River Writers, 1973

In Battle for Peace. W. E. B. DuBois. Masses & Mainstream, 1952

In Dark Confusion. Ann Petry

In Defense of the People's Black and White History and Culture. Ernest Kaiser, 1970

In His Own Write. Adrienne Kennedy

In Love. Gordon A. Parks. Lippincott, 1971

In Love and Trouble: Stories of Black Women. Alice Walker. Harcourt, 1973

In New England Winter. Ed Bullins

In Old Plantation Days. Paul L. Dunbar, 1903

In Our Terribleness. Amiri Baraka, 1971

In Search of Common Ground. E. Erickson. Dell, 1974

In Splendid Error. William B. Branch, 1954-55

In the Mecca. Gwendolyn E. Brooks. Harper & Row, 1968

In This Corner. Sam J. Cornish

Infants of the Spring. Wallace Thurman, 1932

The Inside Man. E. Richard Johnson, 1969

Insights and Poems. Huey P. Newton (with Ericka Huggins). City Lights, 1975

Instructor's Guide to Accompany Cavalcade: Negro American Writing. Charles H. Nichols. Houghton Mifflin, 1970

Integration. Loften Mitchell

Integration. The Role of Labor Education. Whitney M. Young, Jr., 1959

Intelligence and Cultural Differences. Allison Davis (with Kenneth Eells and Others). U. of Chgo. Pr., 1951

The Journal of Charlotte Forten.
Ed., Ray Allen Billington.
Dryden, 1953; Collier, 1961,
1967

Journey to Accompong. Katherine
Dunham, 1946

Journey to Africa. Hoyt W.
Fuller. Third World Pr., 1971

Journey to Shanara. Clifton E.
Marsh. Shanara Public.

Jubilee. Margaret Walker.
Houghton Mifflin, 1966;
Bantam

Judas, My Brother. Frank Yerby.
Dial, 1968

Juju. Askia Muhammad Toure, 1969

Jule. George W. Henderson, 1946

Julius K. Nyere: Teacher of
Africa. Shirley Graham.
Julian Messner, 1975

Jumbish. Elouise Loftin, 1972

Jump Bad. Ed., Gwendolyn E.
Brooks. Broadside Pr., 1971

Jungle Saints. Philippa D.
Schuyler. Herder, 1963

Junior Casebook on Racism. Toni
C. Bambara. Bantam, 1973

Just a Little Simple. Alice
Childress

Just around the Corner. Langston Hughes.

Just Between Us Blacks. Carl T.
Rowan. Random House, 1974

Just Give Me a Cool Drink of Water 'Fore I Diiie. Maya
Angelou. Random House, 1971

Justice in the Round; the Trial
of Angela Davis. Reginald W.
Major. Third World Pr., 1973

Kaleidoscope. Ed., Robert E.
Hayden. Harcourt, 1967

Katharsis. Darwin T. Turner.
Wellesley Pr., 1964

Kasamance: A Fantasy. Katherine Dunham. Third Pr., 1974

Katherine Drexel; Friend of the
Neglected. Ellen Tarry, 1958

Kawaida Studies. Amiri Baraka,
1972

The King God Didn't Save. John
A. Williams. Coward-McCann,
1970; Pocket Bks., 1971

Kingdom of Dreams. Philippa D.
Schuyler. Speller, 1963

The King's Dilemma. Willis
Richardson, 1955

The Knee-High Man and Other Tales.
Julius Lester. Dial, 1972

Knock, Knock, Who Dat. Richard
E. Wesley, 1970

Knock On Any Door. Willard Motley. Appleton, 1947

The Ku Klux Klan Spirit. J. A.
Rogers. Messenger, 1923

Labor, Free and Slave: Working-
Men and the Anti-Slavery Movement in the United States.
Bernard Mandel. Assoc. Authors, 1955

Ladies of the Rachmanioff Eyes.
Henry Van Dyke. Farrar,
Straus, 1965

Land Beyond the River. Loften
Mitchell

The Land of Cotton and Other
Plays. Randolph Edmonds

Land of the Free. John Hope
Franklin (with Others).
Franklin Pub., Benziger
Brothers, 1965

The Landlord. Kristin Hunter.
Scribners, 1966

Langston Hughes. Alice Walker.
Crowell, 1973

Langston Hughes. James A.
Emanuel. Twayne, 1967

Langston Hughes, Black Genius: A
Critical Evaluation. Ed.,
Therman B. O'Daniel. 1971

Langston Hughes's Don't You Turn
Back. Ed., Lee B. Hopkins.
Knopf, 1969

The Langston Hughes Reader.
Braziller, 1958

Language and Literature Series.
Warren J. Halliburton. Globe,
n.d.

Language, Communication and
Rhetoric in Black America.
Arthur L. Smith. Harper &
Row, 1972
Language in Uniform. Nick Aaron
Ford. Odyssey, 1967
Last Dance for Sybil. Ossie
Davis
The Last Days of Louisiana Red.
Ishmael Reed. Random House,
1974
Last of the Conquerors. William
Gardner Smith. Farrar,
Straus, 1948
The Last Ride of Wild Bill.
Sterling A. Brown. Broadside
Pr., 1974
Laughing to Keep from Crying.
Langston Hughes. Holt, Rine-
hart & Winston, 1952
Lawd Today. Richard Wright.
Walker, 1963
The Learning Tree. Gordon A.
Parks. Harper & Row, 1963
The Least of These. Maya
Angelou
Leelah Misled. Albery A. Whit-
man. Elizabethtown, Ky.,
1873
Legacy of Reinhold Niebuhr.
Nathan A. Scott, Jr. U. of
Chgo. Pr., 1975
Legends of the Saints. Ann
Petry. Crowell, 1970
The Legislation of Morality.
Troy Duster. Free Pr., 1969
The Leni Poems. John Sinclair.
Artists' Workshop Pr., 1966
Leopold Senghor's "Elegy for
Martin Luther King." Samuel
W. Allen. Benin Review, n.d.
A Lesson in Dead Language.
Adrienne Kennedy, 1964
Let Me Breathe Thunder. William
A. Attaway. Doubleday, 1939
Let No Man Write My Epitaph.
Willard Motley. Random House,
1958
Let Noon Be Fair. Willard Mot-
ley. Putnam, 1966

Let's Face Racism. Nathan Wright,
Jr. Nelson, 1970
Let's Go Somewhere. Johari M.
Amini. Third World Pr., 1970
Let's Work Together. Nathan
Wright, Jr. Hawthorn, 1968
Letters Found Near a Suicide.
Frank S. Horne
Letters to a Black Boy. Bob
Teague. Walker, 1968
Liar, Liar. James V. Hatch.
Gen. Music Corp., 1972
Liberation and Reconciliation:
A Black Theology. J. Deotis
Roberts, Sr. Westminster,
1971
Libretto for the Republic of Li-
beria. M. B. Tolson. Twayne,
1953
Libretto of Troubled Island.
Langston Hughes
The Life and Loves of Mr. Jiveass
Nigger. Cecil Brown. Farrar,
Straus, 1969
Life and Times of Frederick
Douglass. Frederick Douglas,
1881
Life Insurance Companies in the
Capital Markets. Andrew F.
Brimmer. Mich. State U. Pr.,
1962
The Life of Charles Sumner, the
Scholar in Politics. Archi-
bald H. Grimké, 1892
Life of Frederick Douglass.
Booker T. Washington, 1907
The Life of John Wesley Anderson.
J. Mason Brewer, 1938
Life Studies: The Need for
Afrikan Minds and Institu-
tions. Don L. Lee. Broad-
side Pr., n.d.
Lift Every Voice. Benjamin
Quarles (with Dorothy Ster-
ling), 1965
"Light in the Southern Sky."
William B. Branch, 1958
Like One of the Family: Conver-
sations from a Domestic's Life.
Alice Childress

The Magic World of Books.
Charlemae Rollins. Sci. Res.
Assoc., 1952
Majors and Minors. Paul Laurence
Dunbar, 1895
Make A Joyful Noise to the Lord:
The Life of Mahalia Jackson.
Jesse Jackson. Dell, 1975
Malcolm X Speaks. Malcolm Lit-
tle, 1966
Malcolm X The Man and His Times.
John H. Clarke. Macmillan,
1969
Male Negro Skilled Workers in the
United States, 1930-36. Rob-
ert C. Weaver. Govt. Printing
Office, 1939
Mamadou Dia's African Nations and
World Solidarity. Trans.,
Mercer Cook, 1961
A Man Ain't Nothing But a Man.
John O. Killens. Little,
Brown, 1975
A Man Called White. Walter
White. Viking, 1948
Man in the Modern Theatre.
Nathan A. Scott, Jr. John
Knox Pr., 1965
"A Man is not Made of Steel."
Charlie L. Russell
The Man: the Hero: the Chris-
tian! A Eulogy on the Life
and Character of Thomas
Clarkson. Alexander Crummell,
1847
Man Walking on Eggshells.
Herbert A. Simmons, 1962
The Man Who Cried I Am. John A.
Williams. Little, Brown,
1967; New Amer. Lib., 1968
Manchild in the Promised Land.
Claude Brown. Macmillan,
1965
Manifesto for a Black Revolu-
tionary Party and Race and
Class Struggle. James Boggs
(with Grace Lee Boggs).
Monthly Review Pr., 1974
Manual for Official Committees.
Robert C. Weaver. Amer.
Counc. on Race Relat., 1945

A Manual of Research and Thesis
Writing for Graduate Students.
Chalres W. Wesley, 1941
Many But One: The Ecumenic of
Charity. Joseph H. Jackson,
1964
Many-Colored Coat of Dreams: The
Poetry of Countee Cullen.
Houston A. Baker, Jr. Broad-
side Pr., 1974
Many Thousand Gone. Ronald Fair.
Harcourt, 1965
Many Thousand Gone, the Ex-Slaves
Account of Their Bondage and
Freedom. Charles H. Nichols.
E. J. Brill, 1963; Ind. U.,
1969.
Marching Blacks. Adam Clayton
Powell, Jr. Dial, 1945
Marcia. John L. Steptoe. Viking,
n.d.
Marcus Garvey and the Vision of
Africa. Eds., John H. Clarke
(with Amy Jacques Garvey).
Random House, 1974
A Mark Well Made: The Negro Con-
tribution to American Culture.
Edgar A. Toppin. Rand McNally,
1967
Maroons of the West Indies and
South America. J. A. Rogers,
1921
Marriage in Black and White.
Joseph R. Washington, Jr.
Beacon Pr., 1970
The Marrow of Tradition. Charles
W. Chesnutt, 1901
Martin de Porres, Saint of the
New World. Ellen Tarry, 1963
Martin Luther King, A Critical
Biography. David L. Lewis.
Praeger, 1971
Martin Luther King at Montgomery,
Alabama. Alice Childress
The Masquerade: An Historical
Novel. Oscar Micheaux. AMS
Pr., repr., 1947
Mastering American English. Rob-
ert E. Hayden. Prentice-Hall,
1956

Masterpieces of Negro Eloquence.
Ed., Alice Dunbar Nelson, 1913
*The Master's Slave--Elijah John
Fisher.* Miles M. Fisher, 1922
The Matrix: Poems 1960-1970.
Norman H. Pritchard, II.
Doubleday, 1970
Maud Martha. Gwnedolyn Brooks.
Harper & Row, 1953
Me and Nessie. Eloise Green-
field. Crowell, 1975
A Medal for Willie. William B.
Branch, 1951-52
Medea. Trans., Countee Cullen.
(Medea and Other Poems).
Harper & Row, 1935
*Meditations for Apostles of
Sensitiveness.* Howard Thur-
man, 1947
Meditations of the Heart. Howard
Thurman. Harper & Row, 1953
The Meeting Point. Austin C.
Clarke. Can., Macmillan, 1967
Memoirs of A Monticello Slave.
Rayford W. Logan. U. of Va.
Pr., 1951
The Memorial Discourse. Henry
Highland Garnet, 1865
Mercy Is King. James Mays
Meridian. Alice Walker. Har-
court, 1976
Message to the Black Man.
Elijah Muhammad. Muhammad's
Mosque #2, 1964
A Message to the World. Roland
Gordon
The Messenger. Charles Wright.
Farrar, Straus, 1963
The Mighty Gents. Richard E.
Wesley
*Militant Black Writer in Africa
and the United States.* Mer-
cer Cook (with Stephen E.
Henderson). U. of Wis. Pr.,
1969
The Militant South, 1800-1860.
John Hope Franklin. Belknap,
Harvard U. Pr., 1956

*The Mind of the Negro: An Intel-
lectual History of Afro-Ameri-
cans.* Earl E. Thorpe. 1961;
Greenwood, 1970
*The Mind of the Negroes Reflected
in Letters During the Crisis.*
Carter G. Woodson. ASNLH,
1925
Minds and Institutions. Don L.
Lee. Broadside Pr., 1973
"Minority of One." Kristin Hunt-
er, 1955
*A Minority of One: A Biography
of Lew Alcindor.* James Has-
kins. Lothrop, n.d.
A Mirror: A Soul. Sarah W.
Fabio, 1969
Miss Muriel and Other Stories.
Ann Petry. Houghton Mifflin,
1971
Miss Weaver. Ted Shine
Mr. Death: Four Stories. Anne
Moody. Harper & Row, 1975
Mob Rule in New Orleans. Ida B.
Wells, 1900
"Modern Arabic Women." James V.
Hatch, 1964
*Modern Literature and the Reli-
gious Frontier.* Nathan A.
Scott, Jr. Harper & Row, 1958
*The Modern Structural Theory of
Organic Chemistry.* Lloyd N.
Ferguson. Prentice-Hall,
1963; 1965; 1969
The Modern Version of Death.
Nathan A. Scott, Jr. John
Knox Pr., 1967
The Moderns. Amiri Baraka.
Corinth Bks., 1963
*Moja Means One: the Swahili
Counting Book.* Muriel Feel-
ings. Dial, 1971
Mongo's Back in Town. E. Richard
Johnson, 1969
The Monster. Ron Milner
Montage of a Dream Deferred.
Langston Hughes, 1951
*Morals and Manners Among Negro
Americans.* W. E. B. DuBois.
Atlanta U. Pr., 1914

No More Lies: The Myth and Reality of American History. Eds., James R. McGraw (with Dick Gregory). Harper & Row, 1971

No Name in the Street. James Baldwin. Dial, 1972

No Need for Hunger. Carl T. Rowan, 1962

No Place to be Somebody. Charles E. Gordon/e. Bobbs-Merrill, 1969

No Separation. Loften Mitchell

Nobody Knows My Name. James Baldwin. Dial, 1960

Les Noces Venitiennes. Victor Séjour, 1855

Le Noir. Mercer Cook. Amer. Bk., 1934

Nommo: A Modern Anthology of Black African and Black American Literature. William H. Robinson. Macmillan, 1971

North American Negro Poets: A Bibliographical Checklist of Their Writings, 1760-1944 Dorothy B. Porter. The Bk. Farm, 1945

North Carolina Negro Oral Narratives. J. Mason Brewer. N.C. Folklore Soc., 1961

North Ridge 127. Ntozake Shangé (with Jules Allen)

North Town. Lorenz B. Graham. Crowell, 1965

Not a Man and Yet a Man, with Miscellaneous Poems. Albery A. Whitman. Elizabethtown, Kentucky, 1877

Not Without Laughter. Langston Hughes. Knopf, 1930

Notes of a Native Son. James Baldwin. Beacon Pr., 1955

Nothing Personal. James Baldwin (with Richard Avedon). Atheneum, 1964

Nova. Samuel R. Delaney. Doubleday, 1968

O Canaan! Waters Turpin, 1939

Oak and Ivey. Paul Laurence Dunbar, 1893

Oak and Ivy: A Biography of Paul Laurence Dunbar. Addison Gayle. Doubleday, 1971

Objects. Russell Atkins. Hearse Pr., 1963

Objects 2. Russell Atkins. Renegade Pr., 1963

October Journey. Margaret Walker. Broadside Pr., 1973

Odds Against Tomorrow. John O. Killens, 1960

An Odor of Sanctity. Frank Yerby. Dell, 1965

Of Love and Dust. Ernest J. Gaines. Dial, 1967

Official Report of the Niger Valley Exploring Party. Martin R. Delany, 1861

O'Grady. Nolan Davis. Tarcher/Hawthorn, 1974

Ohio Negroes in the Civil War. Charles H. Wesley. Ohio State U. Pr., 1962

Old Fashioned Pilgrimage Poems. Austin C. Clarke. Dufour, 1967

The Old Gods Laugh. Frank Yerby. Dial, 1964

Old Greenbottom Inn. George M. McLlelan, 1896

The Old South: A Psycho-history. Earl E. Thorpe, 1972

Ollie Miss. George W. Henderson, 1935

The Omni-Americans. Albert L. Murray. Avon Bks., 1970

On Being Black: writings by Afro-Americans from Frederick Douglass to the Present. Eds., Charles T. Davis (with Daniel Walden). Fawcett, n.d.

On Black Education. Jim Haskins. Morrow, n.d.

On Lynchings: Southern Horrors. Ida B. Wells, 1892

On These I Stand. Countee Cullen. Harper & Row, 1947

The One. Oliver Pitcher

One and the Many. Naomi Madgett. Exposition Pr., 1956; U. Microfilms, 1970

Title Index

One Bread, One Body. Nathan
Wright, Jr. Seabury, 1962
100 Amazing Facts About the
Negro. J. A. Rogers, 1963
100 Years of Negro Freedom. Arna
Bontemps. Dodd, Mead, 1961
One Way Ticket. Langston Hughes,
1949
One Way to Heaven. Countee Cul-
len. Harper & Row, 1932
"One Woman's Opinion." Anna A.
Hedgeman.
Once. Alice Walker. Harcourt,
1968
Once Upon A Time. Ed., Augusta
Baker, 1964
The Open Boat and Other Stories
by Stephen Crane. Ed., Quan-
dra P. Stadler, 1968
An Ordinary Woman. Lucille T.
Clifton. Random House, 1974
Oreo. Charles V. Willie. Pa-
rameter, 1975
Organic Chemistry: A Science and
an Art. Lloyd N. Ferguson.
Willard Grant Pr., 1972
Origins of Afro-Americans. Vin-
cent Harding. Holt, n.d.
Ouanga: a Drama and a Libretto.
John F. Matheus
Our Essayists and Critics of To-
day. William Stanley Braith-
waite, 1920
Our Lan'. Theodore Ward, 1941
Out Jumped Abraham. Billie M.
Phillipa. McGraw-Hill, 1967
Out of Our Lives. Quandra P.
Stadler. Howard U. Pr., 1975
Out of the House of Bondage.
Kelly Miller. Neal, 1914
Outline for the Study of the
Poetry of American Negroes.
Sterling A. Brown. Assoc. in
Negro Folk Educ., 1931
An Outline of African Art. Rich-
ard A. Long, 1974
The Outsider. Richard Wright,
1953
Overshadowed. Sutton E. Griggs.
Bks. for Lib. repr., 1901

The Owl Answers. Adrienne Kennedy, 1963

P. K. Harris. Odie Hawkins
Pagan Spain. Richard Wright,
1957
Pan Africanism Reconsidered.
Samuel W. Allen, 1962
The Panther and the Lash.
Langston Hughes, 1967
A Panther Is a Black Cat. Regi-
nald W. Major. Morrow, 1971
Panther Man. James A. Emanuel.
Broadside Pr., 1970
"Paper Pulp from Sugar Cane."
James V. Hatch, 1965
Paper Soul. Carolyn Rodgers.
Third World Pr., 1968
The Parchments. Nanina Alba,
1963
The Parchments II. Nanina Alba
Passing. Nella Larsen. Knopf,
1929
Past and Present Condition, and
the Destiny of the Colored
Race. Henry Highland Garnet.
Bks. for Lib. repr., 1848
The Past Is the Past. Richard E.
Wesley
Patent Leather Sunday; and S'more
One Act Plays. W. F. Lucas.
Carpetbag Pr., 1975
Path of Dreams. George M.
McLelan. Louisville, 1916
Pathos of Power. Kenneth B.
Clark. Harper & Row, 1975
The Paul Laurence Dunbar Reader.
Eds., Jay Martin (with Gossie
Hudson). Dodd, Mead, 1975
Paul Robeson. Eloise Greenfield.
Crowell, 1975
Paul Robeson, Citizen of the
World. Shirley Graham. Julian
Messner, 1946
Paul Robeson, Negro. Eslanda
Robeson, 1930
Paul Robeson: The Life and Times
of a Free Black Man. Virginia
Hamilton. Harper & Row, 1974
Paul Vesey's Ledger. Samuel W.
Allen. Broadside Pr., 1975

Selected Poems. Langston Hughes. Knopf, 1959

Selected Poems. Robert E. Hayden. October House, 1960

Selected Poems. Ed., William Stanley Braithwaite, 1948

Selected Speeches of Booker T. Washington. Ed., Darwin T. Turner. Wash., 1976

Selected Writings of Jean Toomer. Ed., Darwin T. Turner. Howard U. Pr., 1974

Self Determining Haiti. James Weldon Johnson, 1920

The Semi-Centenary and the Retrospection of the African Methodist Episcopal Church. Daniel A. Payne, 1866

The Senate and the Versailles Mandate System. Rayford W. Logan. Greenwood repr., 1945

Senghor's African Socialism. Trans., Mercer Cook, 1959

Sentry of the Four Golden Pillars. Eugene B. Redmond. Black River Writers, 1970

Seraph on the Suwanee. Zora Neale Hurston, 1948

The Serpent and the Staff. Frank Yerby. Dial, 1959

Services of Colored Americans in the Wars of 1776 and 1812. William C. Nell, 1851

Seven Black American Scientists. Robert C. Hayden. Addison-Wesley, 1970

The Seven Sleepers of Ephesus. Benjamin G. Brawley

Seventh Son: The Thoughts and Writings of W. E. B. DuBois. 2 vols. Ed., Julius Lester. Random House, 1971

Sex and Race. J. A. Rogers. (3 vols., 1940-44).

Sex and Racism in America. Calvin C. Hernton. Doubleday, 1964

The Shabby Breath of Yellow Teeth. Sam J. Cornish

Shades and Shadows, Six Plays for a Negro Theater. Randolph Edmonds

Shadow and Act. Ralph Ellison. Random House, 1964

The Shadow of the Plantation. Charles S. Johnson, 1934

The Shadow That Scares Me. Dick Gregory. Doubleday, 1968

Shakespeare in Harlem. Langston Hughes

Shaping of Black America. Lerone Bennett, Jr. Johnson Pub., 1975

Share My World. Georgia D. Johnson, 1952

Sharecroppers All. Ira De A. Reid, 1941

Shaw's Universe. Wilmoth A. Carter. Nat'l., 1973

She Come Bringing Me That Little Baby Girl. Eloise Greenfield. Lippincott, 1974

She Walks in Beauty. J. A. Rogers. Western, 1963

Sho is Hot in the Cotton Patch. Ted Shine

Shoes. Ted Shine

A Short History of English Drama. Benjamin G. Brawley, 1921

A Short History of the American Negro. Benjamin G. Brawley, 1918

A Short History of the Baptist Denomination. Miles M. Fisher, 1933

Short Stories Anthology. Warren J. Halliburton. Globe, n.p.

Shout Hallelujah. Theodore Ward

The Sickest Don't Always Die the Quickest. Jesse Jackson. Doubleday, 1970

Sidewalk Story. Sharon Bell Mathis. Viking Pr., 1971

The Sign in Sidney Brustein's Window. Lorraine Hansberry. Random House, 1964

Silver Burdette Music. Albert J. McNeil (with Others). (Ser.: Silver Burdette, 1975-76)

*The Sparrow's Fall and Other
Poems.* Frances E. W. Harper

Speak Now. Frank Yerby. Dial,
1969

Spin A Soft Black Song. Nikki
Giovanni. Hill & Wang, 1971

Spirit Reach. Amiri Baraka, 1972

Spirits Unchained. Keoropetse
Kgositsile. Broadside Pr.,
1969

The Spirituals and the Blues.
James H. Cone. Seabury, 1972

The Spook Who Sat by the Door.
Sam Greenlee. Allison &
Bushy, 1969

The Sport of the Gods. Paul
Laurence Dunbar, 1902

Spring in New Hampshire. Claude
McKay, 1920

Stage Door Canteen. Adam Clayton
Powell, Jr., 1944

*Standards for Freshman Composi-
tion.* Ed., Darwin T. Turner.
Deal Print Co., 1961

Star by Star. Naomi Madgett.
Harlo, 1965; Evenill, 1970

Star of the Morning. Loften
Mitchell

Stars in the Night. Joseph H.
Jackson, 1950

States' Laws on Race and Color.
Comp. & ed., Pauli Murray

*Status of the Negro Community:
Problems--Proposals--Projec-
tions.* Whitney M. Young, Jr.,
1959

Steps to Break the Circle. Sterling D. Plumpp. Third World
Pr., 1974

Stevie. John L. Steptoe. Harper
& Row, 1969

*"Still A Brother: Inside the
Negro Middle Class."* William
B. Branch, 1968

The Still Voice of Harlem. Conrad K. Rivers

*Stokely Speaks: Black Power to
Pan-Africanism.* Stokely Carmichael. Random House, 1971

Stolen Car. Lorenz B. Graham.
Houghton Mifflin, 1972

The Stone Face. William Gardner
Smith. Farrar, Straus, 1963

*Stories from Black History: Nine
Stories.* 5 vols. John A.
McCluskey. New Day Pr., 1975

Storm of Fortune. Austin C.
Clarke. Little, Brown, 1973

The Story of a Three-Day Pass.
Melvin Van Peebles

Story of Dorothy Stanfield.
Oscar Micheaux, 1946

*The Story of George Washington
Carver.* Arna Bontemps. Grosset, 1954

The Story of Hank Aaron. B. E.
Young. Prentice-Hall, 1976

The Story of Jesus. Lorenz B.
Graham. Gilberton, 1955

The Story of Phillis Wheatley.
Shirley Graham. Julian Messner, 1949

The Story of Pocahontas. Shirley
Graham. Grosset & Dunlap,
1954

The Story of Stevie Wonder.
James Haskins. Lathrop, 1976

The Story of the Great War. William Stanley Braithwaite, 1919

Story of the Negro. Arna Bontemps. Knopf, 1948; 1958

The Story of the Negro. Booker
T. Washington, 1909

The Story of the Negro Retold.
Carter G. Woodson, 1935

"Storyline." Nolan Davis, 1971

The Stranger. Herbert A.
Simmons

Stranger and Alone. Saunders
Redding. Harcourt, 1950

*Strategy and Tactics of a Pan
African Nationalist Party.*
Amiri Baraka, 1972

The Street. Ann Petry. Houghton
Mifflin, 1946

*Street Gangs: Yesterday and To-
day.* Jim Haskins. Hastings,
1974

A Street in Bronzeville. Gwendolyn Brooks. Harper & Row,
1945

The Streetcorner. Richard E. Wesley, 1970

Street Scene. Langston Hughes, 1946

Strength of Gideon and Other Stories. Paul Laurence Dunbar. Bks. for Lib. repr., 1900

Strength to Love. Martin Luther King, Jr. Harper & Row, 1963

Stride Toward Freedom. Martin Luther King, Jr. Harper & Row, 1958

The Study and Analysis of Black Politics: A Bibliography. Hanes Walton, Jr. Scarecrow, 1973

Subsistence Agriculture and Economic Development. Ed., Clifton R. Wharton, Jr. Aldine, 1969

Success in Language and Literature. Naomi Madgett. Follett, 1967

Sudan Rajul Samia. El Muhajir. Al Kitab Sudan, 1967

Sula, a Novel. Toni Morrison. 1973; Bantam, 1975

Sun Sounds: An Anthology of Third World Writings. E , Quincy Troupe (with Kaine Shutte)

The Suppression of the African Slave Trade. W. E. B. DuBois. Harvard U. Pr., 1896

A Survey of Texas Southern University Library, Houston, Texas. E. J. Josey, 1967

The Survivors. Kristin Hunter. Scribners, 1975

The Survivors of the Crossing. Austin C. Clarke. McClelland & Stewart, 1964

Swallow the Lake. Clarence Major. Wesleyan U. Pr., 1970

Sweet Sweetback's Baadasssss Song. Melvin Van Peebles, 1971

Symptoms & Madness. Clarence Major. Corinth Bks., 1971

Syncopated Cakewalk. Clarence Major, 1973

Syphillis and Its Treatment. William A. Hinton, 1936

The System of Dante's Hell. Amiri Baraka. Grove Pr., 1965

T. W. Higginson's __Army Life in a__ __Black Regiment__. Ed., John Hope Franklin. Beacon Pr., 1962

Today's Negro Voices: an Anthology by Young Negro Poets. Beatrice Murphy. Julian Messner, 1970

A Tale of Time & Toilet Tissues. Eugene B. Redmond. Black River Writers, 1969

A Tale of Two Toms. Eugene B. Redmond. Black River Writers, 1968

Tales. Amiri Baraka. Grove Pr., 1967

Tales and Short Stories for Black Folks. Toni C. Bambara. Zenith, 1971

Tales of Darkest Africa. Fenton Johnson, 1920

Tales of Momolu. Lorenz B. Graham. Reynal, 1947

Talking to Myself. Pearl Bailey. Harcourt, 1971

Talking Tree. Ed., Augusta B Baker. Lippincott, 1955

Tambour. John F. Matheus, 1929

Tambourines to Glory. Langston Hughes. Day, 1959

The Teaching of Literature by Afro-American Writers: Theory and Practice. Darwin T. Turner. Nat'l. Counc. of Tchrs. of Eng., 1972

Teacup Full of Roses. Sharon Bell Mathis. Viking, 1972

Teen-age Alcoholism. James Haskins. Hawthorn, 1976

Tell Me How Long the Train's Been Gone. James Baldwin. Dial, 1968

The Urban Negro Worker in the United States: 1925-1936. Ira De A. Reid, 1938

Urban Reader. Warren J. Halliburton. D. C. Heath, n.d.

Utopian Literature. James W. Johnson. Random House, 1968

Vacuum Cantos and Other Poems. Lawrence McGaugh, Jr. Oyez, 1969

"Venetian Blinds." Rosa Guy, 1954

The Vengeance of the Gods and Three Other Stories of Real American Color Line Life. William Pickens, 1922

Vibration Cooking. Verta Mae Grosvenor. Doubleday, 1970

Victory! Celebrated by 38 American Poets. Ed., William Stanley Braithwaite

Vietnam and Black America. Ed., Clyde Taylor. Doubleday, 1973

Violets and Other Tales. Alice Dunbar Nelson, 1894

Virginia Union University and Some of Her Achievements. Miles M. Fisher, 1924

Visions of the Dusk. Fenton Johnson, 1915

The Vixens. Frank Yerby. Dial, 1947

Voice. John F. Matheus, 1934

The Voice of Black Rhetoric. Arthur L. Smith (with Stephen Robb). Allyn & Bacon, 1971

The Voice of the Children. June Jordan. Holt, Rinehart & Winston, 1971

The Voice of the Land. Zora Neale Hurston, 1945

Voices from the Black Experience: African and Afro-American Literature. Darwin T. Turner. Ginn, 1972

Voices of the Black Theatre. Loften Mitchell. J. W. White, 1975

Les Volontaires de 1814. Victor Séjour, 1862

The Voyage Unplanned. Frank Yerby. Dial, 1974

Vulture. Gil Scott-Heron. World, 1970

W. E. B. DuBois: A Biography. Virginia Hamilton. Crowell, 1972

W. E. B. DuBois's The Education of Black People: Ten Critiques, 1906-1960. Ed., Herbert Aptheker. Monthly Review Pr., 1975

W. E. B. DuBois's The Suppression of the African Slave Trade. Ed., John Hope Franklin. La. State U. Pr., 1969

WPA Poems. Fenton Johnson

Wait Till Next Year. Carl T. Rowan. Random House, 1960

Wait Until the Evening. Hal Bennett. Doubleday, 1974

Walker's Appeal, in Four Articles; together with a Preamble, to the Coloured Citizens of the World, but in Particular and very Expressly to Those of the United States of America. David Walker, 1829

The Walls of Jericho. Rudolph Fisher, 1928

Walt Whitman's Poems. Charles T. Davis (with Gay Wilson Allen)

The War and the Protest: Vietnam. James Haskins. Doubleday, 1971

War Within: Violence or Nonviolence in the Black Revolution. Eldridge Cleaver (with Others). Sheed & Ward, 1971

The Warning: A Theme for Linda. Ron Milner

Watch My Tracks. Bob Kaufman. Knopf, 1971

Watch Out for C. Billie M. Phillips. McGraw-Hill, 1965

Watts Poets: A Book of New Poetry and Essays. Ed., Quincy Troupe. House of Respect, 1968

TITLE INDEX

Subject Index

SUBJECT INDEX

DISCIPLINES AND OTHER CATEGORIES

Abolitionism

Bell, James Madison; Brown, William Wells; Cornish, Samuel E.; Douglass, Frederick; Garnet, Henry Highland; Harper, Frances E. W.; Langston, John Mercer; Payne, Daniel A.; Russwurm, John B.; Still, William; Walker, David; Ward, Samuel Ringgold

Activism

Baraka, Imamu Amiri; Carmichael, Stokely; Cleaver, Eldridge; Davis, Angela; DeCoy, Robert; DuBois, W. E. B.; Garnet, Henry Highland; Garvey, Marcus; Giovanni, Nikki; Gregory, Dick; Hare, Nathan; Jackson, George; Josey, E. J.; Lee, Don L.; Lester, Julius; Lightfoot, Claude M.; Little, Malcolm (X); Lomax, Louis E.; Lomax, Pearl C.; McKissick, Floyd B.; Muhammad, Elijah; Neal, Larry P.; Newton, Huey P.; Sanchez, Sonia; Seale, Bobby; Smith, Arthur L.; Smith, Welton; Trotter, William Monroe; Walker, David; Ward, Samuel Ringgold; Wells, Ida B.; Williams, Chancellor; Wright, Nathan, Jr.; Yette, Samuel J.

Anthropology and Sociology

Billingsley, Andrew; Carter, Wilmoth A.; Cayton, Horace R.; Davis, Allison; Drake, St. Clair; DuBois, W. E. B.; Dunham, Katherine; Edwards, Harry; Fauset, Arthur H.; Frazier, E. Franklin; Greene, Lorenzo J.; Gwaltney, John L.; Johnson, Charles S.; Lincoln, C. Eric; Quarles, Benjamin; Reid, Ira De A.;

Robeson, Eslanda C.; Staples, Robert; Washington, Joseph R.; Weaver, Robert C.; Willie, Charles V.; Woodson, Carter G.; Young, B. E.; Young, Whitney M., Jr.

Art

Brown, Margery; Burroughs, Margaret G.; Demby, William; Feelings, Tom; Joans, Ted; Johnson, Charles R.; LaGrone, Oliver; Lewis, Samella; Locke, Alain Leroy; Long, Richard A.; McGaugh, Lawrence; Phillips, Billie M.; Steptoe, John; Waddy, Ruth

Civil Rights

Abbott, Robert S.; Baldwin, James; Bond, Julian; Brooke, Edward; Bunche, Ralph J.; Chisholm, Shirley; Davis, Angela; Delany, Martin R.; Douglass, Frederick; DuBois, W. E. B.; Edwards, Harry; Garnet, Henry Highland; Garvey, Marcus; Gregory, Dick; Grimké, Archibald; Hamilton, Charles V.; Hedgeman, Anna A.; Johnson, James Weldon; Josey, E. J.; King, Coretta Scott; King, Martin Luther, Jr.; Lester, Julius; Lightfoot, Claude M.; Little, Malcolm (X); McKissick, Floyd B.; Major, Reginald; Moody, Anne; Pickens, William; Powell, Adam Clayton, Jr.; Randolph, A. Philip; Rollins, Charlemae; Schuyler, George S.; Trotter, William Monroe; Walker, Alice; Washington, Leon H.; Wells, Ida B.; White, Walter; Wright, Nathan, Jr.; Young, Whitney M., Jr.

hajir (Marvin X); Mathis, Sharon Bell; Mayfield, Julian; Mays, Benjamin E.; Meriwether, Louise; Millender, Dharathula; Miller, Adam David; Miller, Kelly; Miller, Loren; Mitchell, Loften; Molette, Carlton W.; Murphy, Beatrice; Neal, Larry P.; Nell, William C.; Nelson, Alice Dunbar; O'Daniel, Therman B.; Ottley, Roi; Parks, Gordon A.; Patterson, Raymond R.; Peters, G. Raymond; Petry, Ann; Phillips, Billie M.; Pitcher, Oliver; Plumpp, Sterling D.; Poinsett, Alex; Powell, Adam Clayton, Jr.; Reid, Ira De A.; Reynolds, Barbara A.; Rodgers, Carolyn M.; Rogers, J. A.; Rowan, Carl T.; Russell, Charlie L.; Russwurm, John B.; Schuyler, George S.; Scott, Nathan A., Jr.; Sinclair, John; Smith, Arthur L.; Smith, Vern E.; Smith, William Gardner; Spellman, A. B.; Taylor, Clyde; Teague, Bob; Thomas, Lorenzo; Thompson, Era Bell; Thurman, Wallace; Toure, Askia M.; Troupe, Quincy; Turner, Darwin T.; Walker, Alice; Walker, William O.; Welburn, Ron; Wesley, Richard E.; West, Dorothy; Williams, George Washington; Williams, John A.; Williams, Lance A.; Yette, Samuel J.

Juvenile Writing (Includes the Young Adult)

Baker, Augusta; Bambara, Toni Cade; Bontemps, Arna W.; Brooks, Gwendolyn E.; Brown, Margery; Burroughs, Margaret G.; Childress, Alice; Clifton, Lucille T.;

Cornish, Sam J.; Cullen, Countee; Evans, Mari; Feelings, Muriel; Feelings, Tom; Giovanni, Nikki; Graham, Lorenz; Graham, Shirley; Greenfield, Eloise; Hamilton, Virginia; Haskett, Edythe; Haskins, James; Hughes, Langston; Hunter, Kristin; Jackson, Jesse; Jordan, June; Killens, John Oliver; King, Helen H.; Lacy, Leslie A.; Lee, Don L.; Lester, Julius; Mathis, Sharon Bell; Meriwether, Louise; Millender, Dharathula; Myers, Walter D.; Newsome, Effie Lee; Petry, Ann; Phillips, Billie M.; Richardson, Willis; Rollins, Charlemae; Steptoe, John; Tarry, Ellen; Walker, Alice; Young, Margaret

The Novel

Attaway, William A.; Baldwin, James; Banks, Irma L.; Bennett, Hal; Brooks, Gwendolyn E.; Brown, Cecil; Brown, Frank London; Brown, William Wells; Cain, George; Chesnutt, Charles W.; Clarke, Austin C.; Cooper, Clarence; Cullen, Countee; Davis, Nolan; Delaney, Samuel R.; Delany, Martin R.; Demby, William; Dodson, Owen V.; DuBois, W. E. B.; Dunbar, Paul Laurence; Edwards, Junius; Ellison, Ralph; Fair, Ronald; Fauset, Arthur H.; Fauset, Jessie R.; Fisher, Rudolph; Gaines, Ernest J.; Graham, Shirley; Greenlee, Sam; Griggs, Sutton E.; Guy, Rosa; Harper, Frances E. W.; Heard, Nathan C.; Henderson, George W.; Hercules, Frank; Himes, Chester B.;

SUBJECT INDEX

(The Novel)
Hughes, Langston; Hurston,
Zora Neale; Johnson,
Charles R.; Johnson, E.
Richard; Johnson, James
Waldon; Jones, Gayl; Kel-
ley, William Melvin; Kil-
lens, John Oliver; Koiner,
Richard B.; Larsen, Nella;
Lucas, W. F.; McCluskey,
John A.; McKay, Claude;
Major, Clarence; Marshall,
Paule; Mayfield, Julian;
Mays, James; Meriwether,
Louise; Micheaux, Oscar;
Morrison, Toni; Motley,
Willard; Ottley, Roi; Per-
ry, Richard H.; Petry, Ann;
Pharr, Robert Deane; Po-
lite, Carlene; Pritchard,
Norman H.; Redding, J.
Saunders; Reed, Ishmael S.;
Schuyler, George S.; Scott-
Heron, Gil; Shangé, Nto-
zake; Shockley, Ann Allen;
Simmons, Herbert A.; Smith,
Vern E.; Smith, William
Gardner; Taylor, Mildred;
Thurman, Wallace; Turpin,
Waters E.; Van Dyke, Henry;
Van Peebles, Melvin; Vro-
man, Mary E.; Walker,
Alice; Walker, Margaret A.;
West, Dorothy; White, Wal-
ter; Wideman, John E.;
Williams, Chancellor; Wil-
liams, John A.; Wright,
Charles; Wright, Richard;
Wright, Sarah E.; Yerby,
Frank; Young, Al
Playwriting
Baldwin, James; Baraka,
Imamu Amiri; Bontemps,
Arna W.; Branch, William
B.; Brown, William Wells;
Bullins, Ed; Burrell, Wal-
ter P., Jr.; Childress,
Alice; Cullen, Countee;
Davis, Ossie; Dodson, Owen;
Edmonds, Randolph; Elder,

Lonne; Gordon/e, Charles
E.; Grimke, Angelina W.;
Guy, Rosa; Hansberry, Lor-
raine; Hatch, James V.;
Hill, Leslie P.; Hughes,
Langston; Jackmon, Marvin;
Jones, Gayl; Jordan, Nor-
man; Kennedy, Adrienne;
Killens, John Oliver;
Lomax, Pearl C.; Lucas,
W. F.; Martin, Herbert W.;
El Muhajir (Marvin X);
Matheus, John F.; Miller,
May; Milner, Ron; Mitchell,
Loften; Molette, Barbara
J.; Molette, Carlton W.;
Perkins, Eugene; Pitcher,
Oliver; Richardson, Willis;
Russell, Charlie L.; San-
chez, Sonia; Séjour, Vic-
tor; Shine, Ted; Simmons,
Herbert A.; Smith, Welton;
Thurman, Wallace; Tolson,
M. B.; Turpin, Waters E.;
Van Peebles, Melvin; Ward,
Douglas, Turner; Ward,
Theodore; Wesley, Richard
E.; Wright, Jay
Poetry
Alba, Nanina; Allen, Sam-
uel; Amini, Johari M.; At-
kins, Russell; Baraka,
Imamu Amiri; Barrax, Ger-
ald W.; Bell, James Madi-
son; Bontemps, Arna W.;
Braithwaite, William Stan-
ley; Brawley, Benjamin G.;
Brooks, Gwendolyn E.;
Brown, Sterling A.; Bryant,
F. J., Jr.; Burrell, Eve-
lyn P.; Campbell, James E.;
Clifton, Lucille T.; Cobb,
Charlie; Cornish, Sam J.;
Cortez, Jayne; Cotter,
Joseph S., Sr.; Crouch,
Stanley; Cruz, Victor H.;
Cullen, Countee; Danner,
Margaret E.; Davis, Frank
Marshall; Dodson, Owen V.;
Duckett, Alfred A.; Dumas,

380

Bibliography of Sources

Books

ADAMS, RUSSELL, ed. <u>Great Negroes Past and Present</u>. 3rd ed. Chicago: Afro-Amer. Pub. Co., 1969.

ADAMS, WILLIAM. <u>Afro-American Authors</u>. Boston: Houghton Mifflin, 1972.

ADAMS, WILLIAM, et al., eds. <u>Afro-American Literature: Drama</u>. New York: Houghton Mifflin, 1970.

_____. <u>Afro-American Literature: Fiction</u>. New York: Houghton Mifflin, 1970.

_____. <u>Afro-American Literature: Non-Fiction</u>. New York: Houghton Mifflin, 1970.

ADOFF, ARNOLD, ed. <u>The Poetry of Black America: Anthology of the Twentieth Century</u>. New York: Harper & Row, 1973.

ANGELOU, MAYA. <u>Gather Together in My Name</u>. New York: Random House, 1974.

_____. <u>Just Give Me a Cool Drink of Water 'Fore I Diiie</u>. New York: Random House, 1971.

BAILEY, LEAONEAD PACK, comp. & ed. <u>Broadside Authors and Artists: an Illustrated Biographical Directory</u>. Detroit: Broadside Pr., 1974.

BAKER, HOUSTON A. JR. <u>Singers of Daybreak; Studies in Black American Literature</u>. Washington, D.C.: Howard U. Pr., 1974.

BAKWELL, DENNIS C., comp. <u>The Black Experience in the United States: a Bibliography Based on Collections of the San Fernando Valley State College Library</u> (pamphlet). Northridge, Cal.: San Fernando Valley State Coll. Found., 1970.

BARBOUR, FLOYD B., ed. The Black Seventies. Boston: Porter Sargent, 1970.

BARDOLPH, RICHARD. The Negro Vanguard. New York: Random House, 1959.

BARKSDALE, RICHARD and KENETH KINNAMON, eds. Black Writers of America; a Comprehensive Anthology. New York: Macmillan, 1972.

BIGSLY, C. W. E., ed. The Black American Writers. Vol. II: Poetry and Drama. Baltimore, Md.: Penguin Bks., 1969.

Black List: The Concise Reference Guide to Publications and Broadcasting Media of Black America, Africa and the Carribean. New York: Panther House, 1971.

BONE, ROBERT A. The Negro Novel in America. New Haven, Conn.: Yale U. Pr., 1958.

BONTEMPS, ARNA. Famous Negro Athletes. New York: Dodd, Mead, 1964.

_____. 100 Years of Negro Freedom. New York: Dodd, Mead, 1961.

_____, ed. American Negro Poetry. New York: Hill and Wang, 1963.

Books in Print, Supplement, 1974-75. New York: Bowker, 1975.

Books in Print, 1976. New York: Bowker, 1976.

BRASMER, WILLIAM and DOMINICK CONSOLO, eds. Black Drama, an Anthology. Columbus, Ohio: Chas. E. Merrill, 1970.

BRAWLEY, BENJAMIN. Early Negro American Writers. Chapel Hill: U. of N.C. Pr., 1935.

_____. Negro Builders and Heroes. Chapel Hill: U. of N.C. Pr., 1937.

_____. The Negro Genius: a New Appraisal of the Achievement of the American Negro in Literature and the Fine Arts. New York: Dodd, Mead, 1937.

BROOKS, GWENDOLYN. Jump Bad, a New Chicago Anthology. Detroit: Broadside Pr., 1971.

BROWN, PATRICIA L., et al., eds. To Gwen with Love: an Anthology Dedicated to Gwendolyn Brooks. Chicago: Johnson Pub., 1971.

BROWN, STERLING A., et al., eds. The Negro Caravan: Writings by American Negroes. New York: Arno Pr. and N.Y. Times, 1969.

Bibliography of Sources

BRUNER, RICHARD. Black Politicians. New York: David McKay, 1971.

BULLINS, ED., et al., eds. A Black Quartet: Four New Black Plays by Ben Caldwell, Ronald Milner, Ed Bullins, and LeRoi Jones. New York: New Amer. Lib., 1970.

BURRELL, EVELYN P. Weep No More. Kansas City, Mo.: Burton-Johns, 1973.

BUTCHER, MARGARET JUST. The Negro in American Culture. New York: Knopf, 1956.

CAIN, GEORGE. Blueschild Baby. New York: Dell, 1970.

CALVERTON, V. F., ed. Anthology of American Negro Literature. New York: Mod. Lib., 1929.

CARMICHAEL, STOKELY and CHARLES V. HAMILTON. Black Power: the Politics of Liberation in America. New York: Random House, 1967.

CATTELL, JAQUES, ed. Directory of American Scholars; a Biographical Directory, Vol. I--History. 5th ed. New York: Bowker, 1969.

_____. Directory of American Scholars; a Biographical Directory. Vol. IV--English, Speech and Drama. 5th ed. New York: Bowker, 1969.

CHAMBERS, BRADFORD, ed. Right On. New York: New Amer. Lib., 1970.

CHAPMAN, ABRAHAM, ed. Black Voices: an Anthology of Afro-American Literature. New York: New Amer. Lib., 1968.

_____. New Black Voices: an Anthology of Contemporary Afro-American Literature. New York: New Amer. Lib., 1972.

CHAPMAN, DOROTHY H. Index to Black Poetry. Boston: G. K. Hall, 1974.

CHILDRESS, ALICE, ed. Black Scenes. Garden City, N.Y.: Doubleday, 1971.

CHRISTMAS, WALTER, ed. Negroes in Public Affairs and Government. Yonkers, N.Y.: Educ. Her., 1966.

CLARKE, JOHN HENRIK, ed. The American Negro Short Stories. New York: Hill and Wang, 1966.

COMMIRE, ANNE, ed. Something about the Author, Vols. 1-3. Detroit: Gale Res., 1973.

385

CONE, JAMES H. Black Theology and Black Power. New York: Seabury Pr., 1969.

Contemporary Authors; a Bio-bibliographical Guide to Current Writers and Their Works, Vols. 1-48. Detroit: Gale Res., 1963-74.

COOMBS, ORDE, ed. What We Must See; Young Black Storytellers. New York: Dodd, Mead, 1971.

COUCH, WILLIAM JR., ed. New Black Playwrights: Six Plays by Douglas Turner Ward, Ed Bullins, Paul Carter Harrison, Adrienne Kennedy, and William Wellington Mackey. New York: Avon, 1970.

CRONON, E. DAVID. Black Moses: the Story of Marcus Garvey. Madison: U. of Wis. Pr., 1969.

CULLEN, COUNTEE, ed. Caroling Dusk; an Anthology of Verse by Negro Poets. New York: Harper & Row, 1927.

Current Biography: Who's News and Why, 1941-73. New York: H. W. Wilson, 1941-73.

DANNETT, SYLVIA G. Profiles of Negro Womanhood. Yonkers, N.Y.: Educ. Her., 1964.

DAVID, JAY, ed. Black Joy. Chicago: Cowles Bk. Co., 1971.

DAVIS, ARTHUR P. From the Dark Tower: Afro-American Writers, 1900 to 1960. Washington, D.C.: Howard U. Pr., 1974.

DAVIS, ARTHUR P. and SAUNDERS REDDING, eds. Cavalcade: Negro American Writing from 1760 to the Present. Boston: Houghton Mifflin, 1971.

DAVIS, CHARLES and DANEIL WALDEN, eds. On Being Black: Writings by Afro-Americans from Frederick Douglas to the Present. Greenwich, Conn.: Fawcett, 1970.

DAVIS, JOHN P., ed. The American Negro Reference Book. Englewood Cliffs, N.J.: Prentice-Hall, 1966.

DAVIS, NOLAN. Six Black Horses. New York: Putnam, 1971.

The Destruction of Black Civilization: Great Issues of a Race from 4500 B.C. to 2000 A.D. Chicago: Third World Pr., 1974.

DREER, HERMAN, ed. American Literature by Negro Authors. New York: Macmillan, 1950.

DUCKETT, ALFRED A. Changing of the Guard. New York: Coward, McCann & Geoghegan, 1972.

_____. Raps. Chicago: Nelson-Hall, 1973.

EDWARDS, HARRY. Revolt of the Black Athlete. New York: Free Pr., 1975.

EMANNUEL, JAMES A. and THEODORE L. GROSS, eds. Dark Symphony: Negro Literature in America. New York: Free Pr., 1968.

EMBREE, ERWIN R. 13 against the Odds. New York: Viking Pr., 1944.

FEELINGS, MURIEL. Zamani Goes to Market. New York: Seabury, 1970.

FIDELL, ESTELLE A., ed. Public Library Catalog. 5th ed. New York: H. W. Wilson, 1969.

FIDELL, ESTELLE A. and ESTHER V. FLORY, eds. Fiction Catalog. 7th ed. New York: H. W. Wilson, 1961.

FINNEY, HILDA G. Black Writers in Los Angeles, California, (pamphlet). Los Angeles: Center for Extending Amer. Hist., n.d.

FLEMING, JAMES and CHRISTIAN E. BURCKEL, eds. Who's Who in Colored America. 7th ed. Yonkers-on-Hudson, N.Y.: Christian E. Burckel & Assoc., 1950.

FLEMING, KARL and ANNE T. The First Time. New York: Simon & Schuster, 1975.

FORD, NICK AARON, ed. Black Insights: Significant Literature by Black Americans--1760 to the Present. Waltham, Mass.: Ginn, 1971.

Forthcoming Books, Sept. 1975. New York: Bowker, 1975.

FRANKLIN, JOHN HOPE. From Slavery to Freedom: a History of American Negroes. 2nd rev. ed. New York: Knopf, 1956.

FRAZIER, E. FRANKLIN. The Negro Church in America. New York: Schocken Bks., 1963.

GAYLE, ADDISON JR., ed. Bondage, Freedom and Beyond, the Prose of Black Americans. Garden City, N.Y.: Doubleday, 1971.

GLOSTER, HUGH. Negro Voices in American Fiction. New York: Russell, 1965.

GRAHAM, SHIRLEY. Paul Robeson, Citizen of the World. New York: Messner, 1946.

GREENLEE, SAM. The Spook Who Sat by the Door. New York: Bantam, 1969.

GUY, ROSA. Bird at My Window. Philadelphia, Pa.: Lippincott, 1965.

HASLAM, GERALD W., ed. Forgotten Pages of American Literature. New York: Houghton Mifflin, 1970.

HATCH, JAMES V. Black Images on the American Stage: a Bibliography of Plays and Musicals, 1770-1970. New York: Drama Bk. Specialists, 1970.

HAYDEN, ROBERT C. Seven Black American Scientists. Reading, Mass.: Addison-Wesley, 1970.

HEARD, NATHAN C. A Cold Fire Burning. New York: Simon & Schuster, 1974.

HILL, HERBERT. Anger and Beyond, the Negro Writer in the United States. New York: Harper & Row, 1966.

_____. Soon, One Morning: New Writing by American Negroes. New York: Knopf, 1963.

HILL, ROY L. Who's Who in the American Negro Press. Dallas, Tex.: Royal Pub. Co., 1960.

HUGHES, LANGSTON. The Best Short Stories by Negro Writers: an Anthology from 1899 to the Present. Boston: Little, Brown, 1967.

_____. Famous American Negroes. New York: Dodd, Mead, 1954.

_____, ed. New Negro Poets, U.S.A. Bloomington, Ind.: Indiana U. Pr., 1964.

HUGHES, LANGSTON and ARNA BONTEMPS, eds. The Poetry of the Negroes, 1749-1949. Garden City, N.Y.: Doubleday, 1949.

JACKSON, GEORGE. Soledad Brother: the Prison Letters of George Jackson. New York: Bantam, 1970.

JOHNSON, JAMES WELDON, ed. The Book of American Negro Poetry. New York: Harcourt, Brace & World, 1959.

JONES, LE ROI and LARRY NEAL, eds. Black Fire: an Anthology of Afro-American Writing. New York: Morrow, 1968.

JORDAN, JUNE, ed. Soulscript: Afro-American Poetry. Garden City, N.Y.: Doubleday, 1970.

KENT, GEORGE E. Blackness and the Adventure of Western Culture. Chicago: Third World Pr., 1972.

KERLIN, ROBERT T., ed. Negro Poets and Their Poems. 3rd rev. ed.
Washington, D.C.: Assoc. Public., 1935.

Kirkus Reviews. Mar. 1, 1977.

KUNITZ, STANLEY J. and VINETA COLBY, eds. Twentieth Century Authors, First Supplement: a Biographical Dictionary of Modern
Literature. New York: H. W. Wilson, 1955.

KUNITZ, STANLEY J. and HOWARD HAYCRAFT, eds. Twentieth Century Authors, a Biographical Dictionary of Modern Literature. New York:
H. W. Wilson, 1942.

LA BRIE, HENRY G. III. The Black Newspaper in America: a Guide.
Iowa City, Ia.: Inst. for Communication Stud., Sch. of Journalism, U. of Iowa, 1970.

LACY, LESLIE A. Native Daughter. New York: Macmillan, 1974.

LACY, LESLIE A. and EDRIS MAKWARD. Contemporary African Literature.
New York: Random House, 1972.

LIGHTFOOT, CLAUDE M. Ghetto Rebellion to Black Liberation. New
York: Internat. Pub., 1968.

LOGGINS, VERNON. Negro Authors, His Development in America to 1900.
Port Washington, N.Y.: Kennikat Pr., 1959.

LOMAX, ALAN and RAOUL, ABDUL, eds. 3000 Years of Black Poetry: an
Anthology. Greenwich, Conn.: Fawcett, 1970.

LOMAX, LOUIS E. The Reluctant African. New York: Harper & Row,
1960.

LONG, RICHARD and EUGENIA COLLIER, eds. Afro-American Writing, an
Anthology of Prose and Poetry. Vol. 1. New York: N.Y.U., 1972.

LOUIS, RITA VOLMER, ed. Biography Index: a Cumulative Index to
Biographical Material in Books and Magazines, Sept. 1967-
Aug. 1970. New York: H. W. Wilson, 1971.

McCLUSKEY, JOHN A. Look What They Done to My Song. New York: Random House, 1974.

McKAY, CLAUDE. Harlem: Negro Metropolis. New York: Dutton, 1940.

McNEIL, ALBERT J., et al. Silver Burdette Music. Morristown, N.J.:
Silver Burdette, 1975-76.

MAJOR, CLARENCE, ed. The New Black Poetry. New York: Internat.
Pub., 1969.

Bibliography of Sources

MAJOR, REGINALD W. <u>Justice in the Round; the Trial of Angela Davis</u>. New York: Third World Pr., 1973.

MARGOLIES, EDWARD, ed. <u>A Native Son's Reader</u>. Phila.: Lippincott, 1970.

MILLER, RUTH. <u>Black American Literature, 1760-Present</u>. Beverley Hills, Cal.: Glencoe Pr., 1971.

MITCHELL, LOFTEN. <u>Black Drama, the Story of the American Negro in the Theater</u>. New York: Hawthorn Bks., 1967.

MORRIS, HERBERT. <u>History of the Negro in Medicine</u>. 3rd ed. New York: N.Y. Pub. Co., 1969.

MURPHY, BEATRICE M., ed. <u>Today's Negro Voices; an Anthology by Young Negro Poets</u>. New York: Messner, 1970.

MURRAY, ALBERT L. <u>The Omni-Americans</u>. New York: Avon, 1970.

<u>National Conference of Afro-American Writers</u>, (program). Washington, D.C.: Inst. for Arts & Humanities, Nov. 1974.

<u>The Negro Handbook</u>. Chicago: Johnson Pub., 1966.

O'BRIEN, JOHN, ed. <u>Interviews with Black Writers</u>. New York: Liveright, 1973.

<u>1000 Successful Blacks</u>, Vol. 1. Chicago: Johnson Pub., 1973.

PATTERSON, LINDSAY, comp. & ed. <u>An Introduction to Black Literature in America; from 1746 to the Present</u>. New York: N.Y. Pub. Co., 1968.

PEEBLES, MELVIN VAN. <u>Don't Play Us Cheap</u>. New York: Bantam, 1973.

PLOSKI, HARRY A. and ROSCOE C. BROWN, JR., comp. & eds. <u>The Negro Almanac</u>. New York: Bellwether, 1967.

_____. <u>The Negro Almanac</u>. New York: Bellwether, 1971.

PLOSKI, HARRY A. and ERNEST KAISER, eds. <u>AFROUSA; a Reference Work on the Black Experience</u>. New York: Bellwether, 1971.

RANDALL, DUDLEY and MARGARET G. BURROUGHS, eds. <u>For Malcolm: Poems on the Life and the Death of Malcolm X</u>. Detroit: Broadside Pr., 1969.

REDDING, SAUNDERS. <u>The Lonesome Road; the Story of the Negro's Past in America</u>. Garden City, N.Y.: Doubleday, 1958.

REED, ISHMAEL S. Flight to Canada. New York: Random House, 1976.

REYNOLDS, BARBARA A. Jesse Jackson: the Man, the Movement, the Myth. Chicago: Nelson-Hall, 1975.

ROBINSON, WILHELMENA S. Historical Negro Biographies. New York: ASNLH, 1967.

ROBINSON, WILLIAM H., et al., eds. Early Black American Poets. New York: Brown, 1969.

ROGERS, J. A. World's Great Men of Color. Edited by John H. Clarke. New York: Macmillan, 1972.

ROLLINS, CHARLEMAE. Famous American Negro Poets. New York: Dodd, Mead, 1955.

_____. They Showed the Way: Forty American Negro Leaders. New York: Crowell, 1964.

RUSH, THERESSA, et al., eds. Black American Writers Past and Present. New York: Scarecrow, 1975.

SANDERS, CHARLES L. and LINDA McLEAN, comps. Directory of National Black Organizations. Chicago: Afram Assoc., Inc., 1972.

SCHULBERG, BUDD, ed. From the Ashes: Voices of Watts. New York: New Amer. Lib., 1967.

SCOTT-HERON, GIL. Small Talk at One Hundred Twenty-Fifth & Lenox. New York: World, 1970.

Second Annual Authors Autograph Party (brochure). Los Angeles: Cal. Librns. Black Caucus, July 1975.

SHERMAN, JOAN R. Invisible Poets: Afro-Americans of the Nineteenth Century. Urbana, Ill.: U. of Ill. Pr., 1974.

SHOCKLEY, ANN A. and SUE P. CHANDLER. Living Black American Authors: a Biographical Directory. New York: Bowker, 1973.

SHUMAN, BAIRD. A Galaxy of Black Writing. Durham, N.C.: Moore Pub. Co., 1970.

_____, ed. Nine Black Poets. Durham, N.C.: Moore Pub. Co., 1968.

SIMMONS, WILLIAM. Men of Mark. Chicago: Johnson Pub., 1970.

Some Ground to Fall On. Vermont Square Writers Workshop, Los Angeles Public Lib., 1971.

Bibliography of Sources

SPAULDING, MARY MACE. In Black and White: Afro-Americans in Print:
a Guide to Afro-Americans Who Have Made Contributions to the United States of America from 1916 to 1969, (pamphlet). Kalamazoo,
Mich.: Kalamazoo Lib. System, 1971.

STADLER, QUANDRA P. Out of Our Lives. Washington, D.C.: Howard U.
Pr., 1975.

TARRY, ELLEN. Young Jim: the Early Years of James Weldon Johnson.
New York: Dodd, Mead, 1967.

THOMPSON, ERA BELL. American Daughter. Chicago: Follett, 1967.

THORPE, EARL E. Black Historians: a Critique. New York: Morrow,
1969.

THURMAN, HOWARD. Disciplines of the Spirit. New York: Harper &
Row, 1963.

TOPPIN, EDGAR A. A Biographical History of Blacks in America since
1528. New York: David McKay, 1969.

TROUPE, QUINCY, ed. Watts Poets: a Book of New Poetry and Essays.
Los Angeles: House of Respect, 1968.

TURNER, DARWIN T., ed. Afro-American Writers. New York: Appleton,
1970.

_____. Black American Literature--Essay. Columbus, Ohio: Chas. E.
Merrill, 1969.

_____. Black American Literature--Fiction. Columbus, Ohio: Chas.
E. Merrill, 1969.

_____. Black American Literature--Poetry. Columbus, Ohio: Chas. E.
Merrill, 1969.

_____. Black Drama in America: an Anthology. Greenwich, Conn.:
Fawcett, 1971.

WAGNER, JEAN. Black Poets of the U.S. from Paul Lawrence Dunbar to
Langston Hughes. Urbana, Ill.: U. of Ill. Pr., 1973.

WARD, MARTHA E. and DOROTHY A. MARQUARDT. Authors of Books for Young
People. New York: Scarecrow, 1964.

WEST, DOROTHY. The Living Is Easy. Boston: Houghton Mifflin, 1948.

WHITE, NEWMAN I. An Anthology of Verses by American Negroes. Durham,
N.C.: Moore Pub. Co., 1924.

Bibliography of Sources

Who Was Who in America, Historical Vol., 1607-1896, rev. ed. Chicago: Marquis Who's Who, 1967.

Who Was Who in America, Vol. III, 1951-1960. Chicago: Marquis Who's Who, 1960.

Who Was Who in America, Vol. IV, 1961-1968. Chicago: Marquis Who's Who, 1968.

Who's Who in America, Vol. 2, 37th ed., 1972-73. Chicago: Marquis Who's Who, 1972.

_____, 39th ed., 1976-77. Chicago: Marquis Who's Who, 1976.

Who's Who in the West. 14th ed., 1974-75. Chicago: Marquis Who's Who, 1974.

WILLIAMS, JOHN A. and CHARLES HARRIS. Amistad I. New York: Random House, 1970.

YETTE, SAMUEL F. The Choice: the Issue of Black Survival in America. New York: Putnam, 1971.

Newspapers & Periodicals

Black Enterprise, Sept. 1973.

Black World, Apr. 1972; Dec. 1974; Jan. 1975; June 1975. Chicago: Johnson Pub.

Ebony, Feb. 1957; June 1968; Nov. 1972; Mar. 1974. Chicago: Johnson Pub.

Jet, July 9, 1970. Chicago: Johnson Pub.

Los Angeles Herald Examiner, Dec. 9, 1971.

Los Angeles Sentinel, Dec. 16, 1971

Los Angeles Times, Feb. 16, 1971.

National Guardian, Dec. 18, 1965.

Negro Digest, Sept. 1944; Aug. 1945.

Negro History Bulletin. Washington, D.C.: ASNLH. (Various issues)

New York Amsterdam News, Jan. 15, 1928.

Bibliography of Sources

New York Herald Tribune, Dec. 14, 1965.

New York Times, Feb. 16, 1960; Dec. 14, 1965.

Pittsburgh Courier, Dec. 7, 1974.

The Worker, Dec. 19, 1965.

Photograph Credits

	Author	Credit
1	Abdul, Raoul	Lida Moser
2	Amini, Johari	Personal collection
3	Angelou, Maya	Nat'l. Conf. of Afro-Amer. Writers, Brochure
4	Atkins, Russell	Personal collection
5	Baker, Houston	Charlotte P. Baker
6	Baldwin, James	Jill Krementz
7	Baraka, Imamu Amiri	Leroy McLucas
8	Bennett, Hal	Alex Gotfryd
9	Billingsley, Andrew	Personal collection
10	Bogle, Donald	Daniel Dawson
11	Bontemps, Arna	Frank O. Roberts Studio
12	Branch, William B.	Personal collection
13	Brewer, John M.	Personal collection
14	Brooke, Edward	T. Polumbaum
15	Burroughs, Margaret	Personal collection
16	Carter, Wilmoth A.	Personal collection
17	Childress, Alice	Willard Moore
18	Chisholm, Shirley	Houghton Mifflin
19	Clarke, Austin	Graeme Gibson
20	Clifton, Lucille	Rollie McKenna
21	Collier, Eugenia	Personal collection
22	Cone, James	John H. Popper
23	Davis, Nolan	Calif. Librarians' Black Caucus, Brochure
24	Douglass, Frederick	Urban League, Brochure
25	Elder, Lonne	Nat'l. Conf. of Afro-Amer. Writers, Brochure
26	Fair, Ronald	Mike Mole
27	Ferguson, Lloyd	Personal collection
28	Fisher, Miles M.	Obsequies brochure

Photograph Credits

Author	Credit
29 Ford, Nick A.	Rettberg Bros., Baltimore
30 Franklin, John H.	U. of Chgo., Hist. Dept.
31 Fuller, Hoyt W.	Personal collection
32 Gaines, Ernest	Edward Spring
33 Giovanni, Nikki	Betsy Nolan Public Relations
34 Graham, Lorenz	Personal collection
35 Greene, Lorenzo	Personal collection
36 Gregory, Dick	Personal collection
37 Halliburton, Warren	New York Times Studio
38 Hamilton, Virginia	Audree Distad
39 Harper, Michael S.	Personal collection
40 Haskett, Edythe R.	Personal collection
41 Hedgeman, Anna	Personal collection
42 Hughes, Langston	Dodd, Mead
43 Hunter, Kristin	Margery Smith
44 Jackson, Clyde O.	Joseph's Studio, Houston
45 Jackson, Mae	Charles McClary
46 James, Charles	Personal collection
47 Johnson, Charles	Jill Krementz
48 Johnson, John H.	L.A. Public Library, Photo collection
49 Jones, Aurilda	Calif. Librarians' Black Caucus, Brochure
50 Jordan, June	Chester Higgins, Jr.
51 Josey, E. J.	Personal collection
52 Kelley, William M.	Adger Cowans
53 Kelsey, George	Drew U., Office of Public Relations
54 Killens, John O.	Willard Moore
55 King, Martin L., Jr.	L.A. Public Library, Photo collection
56 King, Woodie	Personal brochure
57 Lane, Pinkie G.	Personal collection
58 Lee, Don L.	Nat'l. Conf. of Afro-Amer. Writers, Brochure
59 Lester, Julius	David Gahr
60 Lewis, Samella	Personal collection
61 Little, Malcolm	Grove Press
62 Long, Richard A.	Personal collection
63 McGaugh, Lawrence	Personal collection
64 McPherson, James	Bill Trayer
65 Madgett, Naomi	Perry's Studio, Detroit
66 Major, Clarence	S. J. Skeeter
67 Major, Reginald	Third Press
68 Mapp, Edward C.	Personal collection
69 Marsh, Clifton	Personal collection
70 Mathis, Sharon B.	Dexter Oliver
71 Mays, James	Calif. Librarians' Black Caucus, Brochure

Photograph Credits

	Author	Credit
72	Murphy, Beatrice C.	Personal collection
73	Murray, Albert	Hugh Bell
74	Myers, Walter D.	Ann Gonfalconi
75	Nichols, Charles H.	Personal collection
76	Oden, Gloria	Personal collection
77	Owens, Jesse	Personal collection
78	Parks, Gordon	David Parks
79	Patterson, Lindsay	Karen Tweedy Holmes
80	Perkins, Eugene	Nat'l. Conf. of Afro-Amer. Writers, Brochure
81	Petry, Ann	Personal collection
82	Pharr, Robert	J. R. Humphreys
83	Phillips, Billie M.	Personal collection
84	Poinsett, Alex	Personal collection
85	Polite, Carlene	Jerry Bauer
86	Powell, Adam C.	James J. Kriegsmann
87	Pritchard, Norman	David Perry Jenks
88	Quarles, Benjamin	Little, Brown, Publicity Dept.
89	Redmond, Eugene	Personal collection
90	Richardson, Nola	Personal collection
91	Robinson, Florine	Personal collection
92	Rollins, Charlemae	Personal collection
93	Rowan, Carl	L.A. Public Library, Photo collection
94	Russell, Charlie	Nat'l. Conf. of Afro-Amer. Writers, Brochure
95	Schuyler, Philippa	World Biography, Publishers' brochure
96	Scott, Nathan A.	Daniel J. Davis
97	Smith, Arthur L.	Personal collection
98	Smith, Vern E.	Ron Sherman
99	Southern, Eileen	Gill, St. Albans, N.Y.
100	Steptoe, John	Nat'l. Conf. of Afro-Amer. Writers, Brochure
101	Still, William G.	Personal collection
102	Taylor, Mildred	Calif. Librarians' Black Caucus, Brochure
103	Thompson, Era B.	Personal collection
104	Toure, Askia	Nat'l. Conf. of Afro-Amer. Writers, Brochure
105	Troupe, Quincy	Nat'l. Conf. of Afro-Amer. Writers, Brochure
106	Turner, Darwin	Personal collection
107	Van Dyke, Henry	Don Lynn
108	Waddy, Ruth	Calif. Librarians' Black Caucus, Brochure
109	Walker, Alice	Personal collection

Photograph Credits

All photographs listed above were rephotographed
by the author to meet the specifications of this
volume. The author claims credit for all other
photographs.